Handbook of Learning Disabilities
Volume I: Dimensions and Diagnosis

Handbook of Learning Disabilities
Volume I: Dimensions and Diagnosis

Kenneth A. Kavale, Ph.D.
Professor and Chair
Division of Special Education
The University of Iowa
Iowa City, Iowa

Steven R. Forness, Ed.D.
Director of Mental Retardation and
Developmental Disabilities Program
Principal, Neuropsychiatric Hospital School
Professor of Psychiatry and Biobehavioral Sciences
UCLA School of Medicine
Los Angeles, California

Michael Bender, Ed.D.
Vice President of Educational Programs
The Kennedy Institute
Professor of Education
The Johns Hopkins University
Joint Appointment, Department of Pediatrics
The Johns Hopkins School of Medicine
Baltimore, Maryland

A College-Hill Publication
Little, Brown and Company
Boston/Toronto/San Diego

College-Hill Press
A Division of
Little, Brown and Company (Inc.)
34 Beacon Street
Boston, Massachusetts 02108

Library of Congress Cataloging in Publication Data
Main entry under title:

Handbook of learning disabilities.

  Includes index.
  1. Learning disabilities — Handbooks, manuals, etc.
I. Kavale, Kenneth A., 1946–   . II. Forness,
Steven R., 1939–   . III. Bender, Michael, 1943–   .
[DNLM: 1. Learning Disorders — handbooks, WS 39 H236]
LC4704.H365   1987   371.9   86-26396

ISBN 0-316-48368-0 (v. 1)

Printed in the United States of America

Contents

Preface

Over the past twenty five years, the field of learning disabilities (LD) has witnessed amazing growth. From modest beginnings, it has become the special education category serving by far the most individuals. Accompanying this unprecedented growth has been a significant increase in the literature available about all aspects of LD. Consequently, it has become a challenge for even the most dedicated professional to keep abreast of the latest information. The many books now available tend to be either texts, providing basic information but little critical evaluation, or highly technical publications focusing on specific topics.

The *Handbook of Learning Disabilities* volumes are intended to occupy a place between these two extremes. The comprehensive coverage of these two books will provide the basic information, as well as a more in-depth critical evaluation. Our main goal is to provide students and practitioners with ready access to the essentials for understanding and treating LD.

Our thesis is that, although an individual with learning disabilities may have an underlying neurologic processing difficulty that may indeed have had something to do with the development of the learning disability, the documentation of such problems is only necessary to the extent that federally or locally mandated procedures now call for such evidence in determination of eligibility for services. Such information has not proven critical in determining which approaches need to be used or in planning remedial programs. Therefore, there are no chapters on visual processing or sensory–motor integration, since these areas have not been shown to be areas of prime importance to remediation; nor are there separate chapters on attention and memory or on information processing, since these areas are still inchoate and have not yet led to specific remedial strategies. Each of these areas is discussed, however; and possible principles or guidelines that can be gleaned from existing evidence are suggested. There is a focus on direct instruction of academic skills, on language strategies to the extent that these are integrated into the reading lesson or taught as skills valuable unto themselves, on increasing the time the child actually spends in reading instruction or in the experience of reading, and on related matters such as social functioning, family issues, and maturational outcomes.

It is clear that learning disabilities is a field fraught with controversy, even in terms of its most basic diagnostic criteria and remedial methods. The focus of these *Handbooks* is on a balanced evaluation of these issues and on what can reasonably be deduced, from existing knowledge, about the nature of LD, the diagnostic process, and the basic strategies of remediation. Our purpose is not an extensive review of controversial ideas, although these will be presented periodically throughout, as preambles to specific procedures or approaches.

These volumes stand somewhere between "edited" and "authored" texts most contributed chapters were first published as papers in *Learning Disabilities: An Interdisciplinary Journal,* but they have been substantially updated and adapted in collaboration with the original authors. In these chapters, we have credited the original author(s) on the first page of the chapter. However, it should be understood that we made editorial changes and additions to the original material in every case. Other chapters were written by us expressly for these volumes. Our primary goal throughout has been to provide the best and most recent information possible for understanding, assessing, and treating individuals with learning disabilities.

Introduction to Volume I

It is true that the field of learning disabilities is controversial, but equally true is the fact that it is interesting. The first volume of the *Handbook of Learning Disabilities* deals with two interesting but controversial issues. The first, *What is a learning disability?*, is a particularly vexing question that is not easily answered. While we are not seeking to avoid answering this question, we believe that a more productive stance is to survey the current primary issues and major characteristics of learning disabilities. No one area is singled out as more important, but rather the most often cited characteristics of LD are summarized and placed in perspective.

The remainder of Volume I deals with a closely related issue: *How do we determine that an individual should be classified as learning disabled?* Perceptions about what constitutes a learning disability certainly exert a strong influence on how LD is diagnosed. Our focus is on assessment as a multidisciplinary process and how the components interrelate to reach a final decision about an individual's LD status.

The first volume of the *Handbook* takes us up to the point of intervention. In *Volume II*, our focus will shift to the nature of the treatment process of LD — the procedures by which we treat learning disabilities are closely linked to how we conceptualize, assess, and diagnose them.

Handbook of Learning Disabilities, Volume I: Dimensions and Diagnosis provides a comprehensive overview of the problems inherent in the field, the primary characteristics associated with learning disabilities, and the means by which we determine the presence or absence of learning disabilities in a child.

Contributors

Marguerite C. Radencich, Ph.D.
Supervisor of Reading
Dade County Public Schools
Miami, Florida

Shelley D. Smith, Ph.D.
Boys Town National Institute for
  Communication Disorders in
  Children
Associate Professor of
  Otolaryngology and Human
  Communication
Omaha, Nebraska

Bruce F. Pennington, Ph.D.
Associate Professor of Psychiatry
Department of Psychiatry
University of Colorado Health
  Sciences Center
Denver, Colorado

Brad W. Friedrich, Ph.D.
Former Chief of Audiology
The Kennedy Institute for
  Handicapped Children
Baltimore, Maryland

Willie P. Cupples, Ph.D.
Coordinator, Speech and Hearing
  Center
George Washington University
Washington, DC

M. E. B. Lewis, Ed.D.
Principal, Kennedy School
The Kennedy Institute for
  Handicapped Children
Baltimore, Maryland

Nancy J. Spekman, Ph.D.
Director of Training and Research
  Projects
Marianne Frostig Center of
  Educational Therapy
Pasadena, California

Paul R. Daniels, Ed.D.
Professor of Education
The Johns Hopkins University
Baltimore, Maryland

Leo E. Otterbein, Ed.D.
Psychologist in Private Practice
Lutherville, Maryland

Jeannette E. Fleischner, Ed.D.
Associate Professor
Department of Special Education
Teachers' College
Columbia University
New York, New York

Katherine Garnett, Ed.D.
Associate Professor
Department of Special Education
Hunter College
City University of New York

Peter J. Valletutti, Ed.D.
Professor and Dean of Graduate
  Studies
Coppin State College
Baltimore, Maryland

Patricia M. Bricklin, Ph.D.
Professor, Division of Psychology
Hahnemann University
Philadelphia, Pennsylvania

Robin Gallico, Ed.D.
Director of Special Education
The Kennedy Institute for
  Handicapped Children
Baltimore, Maryland

Lynn Fox, Ph.D.
Former Professor of Education
The Johns Hopkins University
Baltimore, Maryland

Chad Nye, Ph.D.
Department Chair, Speech
  Pathology and Audiology
Associate Professor
Northern Arizona University
Flagstaff, Arizona

Robert Johnston, M.D.
Assistant Professor of Pediatrics
The Johns Hopkins University and
  School of Medicine
Baltimore, Maryland

Kevin Dwyer, M.A.
School Psychologist
Montgomery County Public School
Rockville, Maryland

Darlene Gould Davies, M.A.
Assistant Professor
Department of Communicative
 Disorders
San Diego State University
San Diego, California

Stanley L. Rosner, Ph.D.
Professor
School Psychology Department
Temple University
Philadelphia, Pennsylvania

Richard Selznick, Ph.D.
Psychologist, Eye Institute
Pennsylvania College of Optometry
Philadelphia, Pennsylvania

Eleanor W. Lynch, Ph.D.
Professor of Special Education
San Diego State University
San Diego, California

Rena B. Lewis, Ph.D.
Professor of Special Education
San Diego State University
San Diego, California

PART I

The Phenomenon of LD

The chapters in Part I provide perspectives about learning disorders (LD) by summarizing the many problems and issues that have become almost standard features. The introductory chapter explores a variety of topics with the goal of providing the reader with some insight into the current status of the LD field. What issues pervade the field? The analyses focus on conceptualization, definition, and associated topics (i.e., prevalence, policy). These very basic concerns are then placed in a broader context addressing LD as a science and LD as a category of special education with a multitude of social and political forces exerting influence on it. The first chapter provides few answers but does crystallize the many questions associated with LD into a general statement about why LD is such a diverse field and fraught with so many difficulties.

The second chapter represents an attempt to provide an answer to the question: Why does the LD field experience so many difficulties? As is pointed out in Chapter 1, the issues and concerns in LD are many and varied. Why have they occurred? Perhaps even more importantly, why has it been so difficult to do anything about them?

These two chapters lay the foundation for the remainder of the *Handbook of Learning Disabilities.* Hopefully, the reader will not come away with a sense of pessimism that leads to a jaundiced cynicism about LD. While these chapters do not "sugar coat" the problems, they do articulate clearly the major concerns of the field and place these concerns in perspective. Understanding a problem is a first step towards its resolution. These chapters are designed to provide that understanding and, in that sense, should be viewed with a sense of optimism.

CHAPTER 1

The Learning Disability Phenomenon

Bertrand Russell's definition of mathematics as "the subject in which we never know what we are talking about, nor whether what we are saying is true" is perhaps even more applicable and appropriate to the field of learning disabilities (LD). The contention and controversy that has been an integral part of LD since its inception now places the field at a critical juncture historically. A diagnostic entity that emerged not much over two decades ago has now become the category containing by far the most children receiving special education. More than two in five handicapped children are considered LD, according to the latest figures from the U.S. Department of Education. This is more than four percent of all school-aged children. The number of LD children has increased more than 100 percent in the past few years since federal legislation mandating special education first took effect. This rapid growth has alarmed those in government who see LD as the diagnostic category most open to vague interpretation and thus most likely to contain children who were never intended to receive special education funds. This is witnessed by the fact that the initial drafts of federal legislation on the handicapped contained a provision, later eliminated, that no more than two percent of all schoolchildren could be considered eligible for these funds under the LD category.

At the same time, professionals in the LD field have tended to factionalize into groups that represent polar opposites with respect to substantive methodological and ideological issues. This polarization was most clearly articulated in the recent reorganization of the principal LD professional organizations. The Council for Learning Disabilities (CLD) recently seceded from its parent special education association, the Council for Exceptional Children (CEC) and was reformed as an entirely separate professional organization. It was subsequently replaced by a new Division of Learning Disabilities (DLD) within CEC.

The field of learning disabilities can be likened to a Hydra, a many-headed serpent of Greek mythology. When one head was cut off, two grew in its place. Its middle head could not die. Finally, Hercules killed the monster by burning off all but one of its heads. He then cut off the immortal head and buried it under a rock.

The field of learning disabilities appears to share this ability to regenerate parts of its body, never growing old, but continually developing in different directions. These small appendages develop tentacles and eventually break off and live as independent Hydras to become the answer to the problem of all children who cannot learn.

As we view this Hydra-like phenomenon that serves children who cannot learn, it is interesting to speculate on its component parts. The immortal head is represented by the regular classroom teacher. No matter how many other appendages may sprout to serve the child with learning disabilities, no other profession seems about to take the place of the regular classroom teacher in serving these children. However, depending on the hypothesized cause of an individual child's problem, a whole host of other professionals stand ready to step in with their unique approaches to his or her problem.

- If the cause of the learning problem is thought to be mental retardation, the child may be served by a teacher certified to teach the mentally retarded in an EMR classroom.
- If the cause of the learning problem is thought to be poor teaching, or lack of opportunity to learn, or lack of motivation to learn, or a slightly reduced rate of learning, the child may be served by a remedial education teacher.
- If the child happens to be in an innovative program, it could have been funded under Chapter IV or with Right-to-Read funds.
- If the cause of the problem is thought to be a bilingual-bicultural background, the Chapter I bilingual teacher may teach the child to read.
- If the cause of the learning problem is thought to be economic deprivation, a Chapter I program of compensatory education may be provided.

- If the child happens to be a migrant child, yet another special program may be provided.
- If the cause is connected to a speech problem, the child may be served by the speech clinician.
- If the child is identified by educational and/or psychological and/or medical diagnosis as having a learning disability, he or she may be taught by a teacher certified in learning disabilities.
- If the child has been diagnosed as having specific developmental dyslexia, the parents are probably wealthy enough to send him or her to a private school where someone else will try to teach the child to read.

In addition to those delivery systems that exist within the public schools, parents are being bombarded with a plethora of panaceas or potential answers from outside the school system.

- Eye training exercises may be touted as the treatment of choice by some practitioners.
- Amphetamines and anti-convulsants seem to be continuing in popularity — if a recent meeting on Attentional Deficit Disorders is any criterion.
- Vitamins, massive doses of them, are being fed to children as an answer to their hyperactivity and learning problems.
- Diet control — specifically the elimination of food additives and dyes — continues to enjoy much popularity in the United States and abroad.
- At a conference several years ago, convincing evidence was presented that fluorescent lights in classrooms may be causing hyperactivity in students.
- There are some who tout the virtues of yoga to reduce hyperactivity and increase the ability to concentrate.
- Biofeedback is also available to increase attending behavior and reduce hyperactivity.
- A proposal sent to the U.S. Office of Special Education proposed to address learning and behavioral problems in young handicapped children by multi-sensory cutaneous stimulation, translated as using a hair dryer to blow warm and cool air on their bodies as part of the adaptive physical education program.

As rapidly as one bud of our Hydra breaks off and fades into oblivion, we seem to be able to come up with two or three more — both within the school system and within delivery systems ancillary to education.

DEFINITION

A major detour in LD continues to be definitions. The field seems no closer to resolution of this problem than in 1968 when a Federal definition was first proposed. The most recent effort, ongoing since 1981, has involved the National Joint Committee for Learning Disabilities (NJCLD), composed of official representatives of the Association for Children and Adults with Learning Disabilities; American Speech-Language-Hearing Association; Division for Children with Communication Disorders, Council for Exceptional Children; Division for Children with Learning Disabilities, Council for Exceptional Children; International Reading Association; and the Orton Society. The NJCLD definition is an effort to resolve some of the problems of misinterpretation of the learning diabled as a homogeneous group, of failure to include adults and preschool children, of vagueness in regard to etiology, and of the relationship between the learning disabled and cultural or linguistic differences, or other handicapping conditions. The following definition has been approved by the boards of the participating organizations:

> Learning disabilities is a generic term that refers to a heterogeneous group of disorders manifested by significant difficulties in the acquisition and use of listening, speaking, reading, writing, reasoning or mathematical abilities. These disorders are intrinsic to the individual and presumed to be due to central nervous system dysfunction.
>
> Even though a learning disability may occur concomitantly with other handicapping conditions (e.g., sensory impairment, mental retardation, social and emotional disturbance), or environmental influences (e.g., cultural differences, insufficient/inappropriate instruction, psychogenic factors), it is not the direct result of those conditions and influences. (Hammill, Leigh, McNutt, & Larsen, 1981)

In order to fully understand the concepts in this definition it is necessary to review the concept paper in which this definition is imbedded. Among the important clarifying concepts are these:

1. Learning disabled is a general term referring to a heterogeneous group of disorders, which includes different subgroups.
2. Learning disabilities must be viewed as a problem not only of the school years, but also of early childhood and adult life.
3. Learning disability is intrinsic to the individual, with the basis of the disorder presumed to be due to central nervous system dysfunction.
4. Learning disabilities may occur together with other handicapping conditions, as well as within different cultural and linguistic groups.

Can we resolve the definitional problem? Probably not if we persist in the same manner as we have been going. Most definitions, either implicitly or explicitly, include a number of components that possess little validity and only confound the problem. Kavale and Forness (1985a) identified five such components and found each to be problematic. These postulates emanate from the seminal work of Alfred Strauss, Heinz Werner, and their colleagues at the Wayne County Training School.

Through experimental investigations and conceptual exposition (Strauss & Kephart, 1955; Strauss & Lehtinen, 1947), the Strauss and Werner "paradigm" includes (in varying degrees) the following postulates:

1. LD fits a medical model (implying something wrong with the child);
2. LD is associated with (or caused by) neurological dysfunction;
3. LD academic problems are related to process disturbance, most notably in perceptual-motor functioning;
4. LD is associated with adacemic failure as defined by discrepancy notions; and
5. LD cannot be due primarily to other handicapping conditions.

Thus, the Strauss and Werner paradigm provided the foundation for LD, and the resulting fundamental postulates regarding the nature of LD were incorporated into LD definitions. The question arises: How valid are these postulates?

Validity of LD Definition Components

Locus of the Problem

The Strauss and Werner paradigm suggests that the locus of the problem is within the affected individual. The medical (disease) model assumes that the disorder emanates from some underlying physical cause. Consequently, symptom alleviation is not appropriate because it does not treat the difficulty (i.e., the underlying cause). The medical model perspective in the Strauss and Werner paradigm has proved problematic for the LD field because:

1. It places too much emphasis on etiology (Ullman & Krasner, 1965).
2. There is no evidence that treatment of symptoms will lead to symptom substitution (i.e., the appearance of new symptoms because the underlying cause was not removed).
3. Data collected from a medical model perspective are of little value to education (MacMillan, 1973).
4. Grouping on the basis of etiology does not produce educationally homogeneous groups (MacMillan, 1973).
5. There is an increased probability of a "self-fulfilling prophecy" because medical model categories are basically deficit oriented (MacMillan, 1973).

6. Scant evidence suggests that LD emanates solely from a biophysical basis (Owen, Adams, Forrest, Stolz, & Fisher, 1971).
7. The medical model does not consider the role of psychosocial forces in producing LD (Forness, 1982; Mayron, 1978).

Physiological Correlates

The most prominent physiological correlate of LD is central nervous system (CNS) dysfunction. Strauss and Lehtinen's (1947) brain damage syndrome was extended to include children with relatively borderline disturbance only suggestive of a brain damage syndrome. The organicity was reduced to a subclinical level with fewer overt manifestations, which resulted in the diagnostic category of minimal brain dysfunction (MBD) (Clements, 1966; Wender, 1971).

The MBD concept that has evolved from Strauss and Werner's description of brain damage is controverisal for the LD field because:

1. Diagnosis on the basis of purely behavioral signs is a product of tautological reasoning (Sarason, 1949).
2. The fact of brain damage (i.e., an anatomic or physiological alteration of the brain) must be differentiated from the concept of brain damage (i.e., a pattern of behavioral disturbance not necessarily applicable to all brain damaged children) (Benton, 1973; Birch, 1964; Gallagher, 1966).
3. The adjective *minimal* in MBD is problematic since minimal manifestations may stem from maximal damage or vice versa (Bax & MacKeith, 1963; Koupernik, MacKeith, & Francis-Williams, 1975).
4. Researchers have failed to find evidence for a homogeneous MBD syndrome (Crinella, 1973; Paine, Werry, & Quay, 1968; Routh & Roberts, 1972; Schulman, Kaspar, & Throne, 1965).
5. Most MBD children fail to reveal "hard signs" (i.e., unequivocal evidence of underlying central nervous system impairment) (Cohn, 1964; Kenny & Clemmens, 1971; Schain, 1970).
6. "Soft signs" (i.e., minimal, borderline, or equivocal indices of central nervous system impairment) are only presumptive of neurological dysfunction (Ingram, 1973; Touwen & Sporrel, 1979).
7. Assessments of "brain damaged" children find an excess of soft signs but no major hard signs (Hertzig, Bortner, & Birch, 1969; Nichols & Chen, 1981; Owen et al., 1971).
8. There has been a failure to differentiate LD and normal children on the basis of soft signs (Adams, Kocsis, & Estes, 1974; Copple & Isom, 1968; Hart, Rennick, Klinge, & Schwartz, 1974).
9. Problems have been associated with diagnosing MBD on the basis of electroencephalographic abnormalities (Freeman, 1967; Hughes, 1978; Satterfield, 1973).

10. Psychological tests used to diagnose MBD have failed to meet acceptable psychometric standards (Coles, 1978; Herbert, 1964; Yates, 1954).
11. The MBD diagnosis has been of limited usefulness for educational purposes (Barnes & Forness, 1982; Bateman, 1974; Birch & Bortner, 1968; Cohen, 1973).

Psychological Process Deficiency

Most definitions of LD posit deficits in basic psychological processes. These process deficits are assumed to be primary manifestations of MBD and to underlie LD academic difficulties. Strauss and Werner (Strauss & Kephart, 1955; Strauss & Lehtinen, 1947; Werner, 1948) laid the foundation for process concepts in LD, which were later refined and extended (e.g., Barsch, 1967; Chalfant & Scheffelin, 1969; Frostig & Horne, 1964; Getman, 1965; Kephart, 1964, Wepman, 1964) and incorporated into definitional proposals (e.g., Cruickshank, 1981; Wepman, Cruickshank, Deutsch, Morency, & Strother, 1975). As a matter of fact, the current definition of LD in federal law begins with the phrase, "specific learning disability means a *disorder in one or more of the basic psychological processes...*" (italics added, *Federal Register,* 1977, p. 65083).

The assumptions of psychological process deficiencies underlying LD have been subject to debate because:

1. Measures of psychological processes assess hypothetical constructs and generally fail to demonstrate satisfactory construct validity (Cronbach & Meehl, 1955).
2. The limited empirical support for the constructs (abilities) makes it difficult to determine whether performance differences are the result of real ability differences or the method of measurement (Mann, 1971; Mann & Phillips, 1967).
3. It has been found that the relationship of perceptual abilities (visual and auditory) to academic achievement is of insufficient magnitude to validate the assumption that perceptual skills underlie academic learning (Hammill & Larsen, 1974b; Kavale, 1981b, 1982; Larsen & Hammill, 1975).
4. LD children do not exhibit greater difficulty than normal children in their ability to integrate one modality function with another modality function (intersensory integration, cross modal perception, intermodal transfer) (Freides, 1974; Kavale, 1980a).
5. Evidence suggests that, although LD children may exhibit perceptual deficiencies, reading ability is not related to the degree of perceptual deficiency (Bibace & Hancock, 1969; Black, 1974; Camp, 1973; Fisher & Frankfurter, 1977; Hare, 1977; Stanley, Kaplan, & Poole, 1975; Vellutino, 1979; Zach & Kaufman, 1972).

6. Among subgroups of LD children, only a very small percentage exhibit perceptual difficulties as the major performance deficit (Boder, 1973; Denckla, 1972; Lyon & Watson, 1981; Mattis, 1978; Satz & Morris, 1981; Vellutino, Steger, Moyer, Harding, & Niles, 1977).
7. Perceptual-motor deficiencies may be present in LD children, but it has been found that perceptual-motor skills are often minor contributors to the learning process (Bateman, 1969; Cohen, 1969).

Academic Failure

Strauss and Lehtinen (1947) implied the presence of academic difficulties when they stated, "the response of the brain-injured child to the school situation is frequently inadequate, conspicuously disturbing, and persistently troublesome" (p. 27). Academic failure in the form of a discrepancy has become the most commonly accepted characteristic of LD. Definitions suggest a discrepancy between expected and actual achievement. Definitions of discrepancy appear straightforward, but are fraught with complex issues and problems, among which are the following:

1. There have been difficulties in measuring *actual* achievement based on standardized achievement measures. Tests with the same labels may not measure similar functions; scores have been found to be partially dependent on the test series used; and problems in norming and scoring (especially grade equivalents) have been found (Goolsby, 1971; Jenkins & Pany, 1978; Kelley, 1927; Lennon, 1951; Salvia & Ysseldyke, 1985; Stanley & Hopkins, 1981).
2. *Expected* achievement is usually measured on the basis of intelligence tests, which include a variety of definitions of intelligence and which reveal a high correlation with achievement measures (Boring, 1923; Coleman & Cureton, 1954; Gallager & Moss, 1963; McCall, Appelbaum, & Hogarty, 1973; McNemar, 1964; Sarason, 1949).
3. Underachievement has been confused with low achievement; the content is further complicated by the less-than-perfect correlation between aptitude and achievement (Lavin, 1965; Thorndike, 1963).
4. Unreliability in discrepancy formulations has been caused by the phenomenon of regression (Crane, 1959; McLeod, 1979; Yule, Rutter, Berger, & Thompson, 1974).
5. Some difficulties are inherent in the procedures for determining discrepancy, including mental age methods, discrepancy quotient methods, transformed score discrepancy methods, and regression discrepancy methods (Algozzine, Forgnone, Mercer, & Trifiletti, 1979; Cronbach, Gleser, Nanda, & Rajoratnam, 1972; Macy, Baker, & Kosinski, 1979; Shepard, 1980; Shepard & Smith, 1983; Spache, 1969; Ullman, 1969).

6. All methods do not yield identical levels of expected achievement and reveal large standard errors of estimate (Bruininks, Glaman, & Clark, 1973; Dore-Boyce, Misner, & McGuire, 1975; Forness, Sinclair, & Guthrie, 1983; Simmons & Shapiro, 1968).

Exclusion Component

Most LD definitions state that LD must not be primarily the result of other handicapping conditions. The origins of this tradition are found in Strauss and Lehtinen's (1947) diagnostic criteria for minor brain injury, wherein endogenous mental retardation was excluded by the criterion that "the immediate family history indicates that the child comes from a normal family stock and that he is, in general, the only one of the sibship so affected" (p. 12).

The exclusion component has not isolated a unique and distinct LD category because:

1. When considered within a behavioral rather than a categorical framework, LD reveals more similarities than differences when compared to mental retardation (MR) and behavioral disorders (BD). (For a complete discussion of these issues, see Dickie, 1982; Hallahan & Kauffman, 1977; Hewett & Forness, 1984; Lilly, 1977.)
2. Diagnostic test data have not reliably differentiated LD from MR and BD (Gajar, 1980; Webster & Schenck, 1978).
3. Although average intelligence (IQ = 100) is a requisite for inclusion in the LD category, findings have shown that anywhere from 25 to 40 percent of children labeled LD are depressed in intellectual functioning (Ames, 1968b; Belmont & Belmont, 1980; Kirk & Elkins, 1975b; Koppitz, 1971; Norman & Zigmond, 1980; Smith, Coleman, Dokeck, & Davis, 1977a). Even though this is a systemic problem, it nonetheless illustrates the problematic nature of exclusionary criteria.
4. Although social-emotional problems represent the primary defining characteristics of BD, the LD groups has been shown to manifest significant social-emotional difficulties that cannot be reliably distinguished from the behavioral profiles of BD children (Barr & McDowell, 1974; Bryan & Bryan, 1977; Coleman & Sandhu, 1967; Hartlage, 1970; Kronmick, 1981; McCarthy & Paraskevopoulos, 1969).
5. Although academic underachievement is considered the primary criterion for LD, it is equally applicable to both MR and BD (Forness, Bennett, & Tose, 1983; Kavale, Alper, & Purcell, 1981; Meyen & Hieronymous, 1970; Morse, Cutler, & Fink, 1964; Schwarz, 1969; Schwarz & Cook, 1971; Wagonseller, 1973).
6. Although problems resulting primarily from environmental, cultural, or economic disadvantages (CD) are eliminated from LD considerations,

conditions in CD environments place a child at high risk for academic failure and can result in learning impairments that are indistinguishable from the cognitive, perceptual, linguistic, and informative processing behavior considered primary characteristics of LD (Hallahan & Cruickshank, 1973; Herrick, 1973; Kavale, 1980b). As a result, any exclusionary criteria are determined by an arbitrary cut-off point within a continuum of causality.

7. Because approximately 75 percent of LD children exhibit reading problems as a primary deficit and approximately 87 percent of LD children receive remedial reading instruction, there is difficulty in reliably differentiating LD and reading disability (RD) with respect to etiology, identification procedures, or intervention techniques (Artley & Hardin, 1976; Gaskins, 1982; Hartman & Hartman, 1973; Jakupcak, 1975; Kirk, 1975; Lerner, 1975).

Evaluation of the primary definitional components of LD derived from the paradigm developed by Strauss and Werner finds that each is problematic and cannot be accepted unequivocally. Subsequent research has failed to demonstrate the manifest validity of the paradigmatic assumptions found in LD definitions. Consequently, the Strauss and Werner paradigm cannot be viewed as a framework for problem-solving in LD, since there is still argument over fundamental issues like "What is the nature of LD?" and "What should research in LD entail?"

The problem of definition is not simply an academic one. Although the LD field has functioned without a definition reaching broad consensus, there have been some serious consequences. These consequences include widely variant estimates of prevalence, an inability to unequivocally delineate LD from low achievement, undifferentiated disciplinary boundaries, and policy constraints.

PREVALENCE OF LD

Under federal guidelines developed to implement Public Law 94-142, it was estimated that approximately 2% of the school-age population would be learning disabled. At that time (1975-77) 2% represented 17% of the population of handicapped children. According to the report from the Government Accounting Office (1981), in 1980 12 states reported that LD represented 40% of their total population of handicapped children; 6 other states reported a 50% figure. Figures contained in the 1984 *Sixth Annual Report to Congress* on the implementation of Public Law 94-142 confirm the high number of children identified as LD. Table 1-1, taken in part from the *Annual Report* (1984), lists number and percent of identified LD and mentally retarded individuals (ages 3-21) by state and by category. In 1982-83

TABLE 1-1.

Number and Percent of Identified LD and MR Individuals (ages 3-21) According to State or Territory.

State	Total No. Handicapped	LD N	%	MR N	%
Alabama	81,609	20,899	26%	34,986	43%
Alaska	12,017	6,826	57%	665	6%
Arizona	51,862	25,710	50%	6,002	12%
Arkansas	49,004	19,436	40%	16,013	33%
California	364,318	198,696	55%	28,580	8%
Colorado	45,126	19,654	44%	5,795	13%
Connecticut	66,010	29,352	44%	6,208	9%
Delaware	14,405	6,670	46%	2,115	15%
Florida	155,609	58,105	37%	27,537	18%
Georgia	112,555	35,722	32%	28,214	25%
Hawaii	12,876	8,189	64%	1,514	12%
Idaho	17,673	8,233	47%	2,948	17%
Illinois	261,769	96,805	37%	44,546	17%
Indiana	100,228	27,434	27%	24,189	24%
Iowa	56,109	21,340	38%	12,228	22%
Kansas	44,159	16,190	37%	6,779	15%
Kentucky	73,170	20,064	27%	21,741	30%
Louisiana	86,009	39,707	46%	15,742	18%
Maine	26,485	8,974	34%	5,167	20%
Maryland	90,879	48,366	53%	7,943	9%
Massachusetts	138,480	48,884	35%	29,357	21%
Michigan	155,771	55,467	36%	26,971	17%
Minnesota	77,658	34,748	45%	13,789	18%
Mississippi	50,883	16,788	33%	15,381	30%
Missouri	99,984	36,224	36%	19,530	20%
Montana	15,215	7,208	47%	1,515	10%
Nebraska	30,448	12,227	40%	5,669	19%
Nevada	13,326	7,041	53%	1,047	8%
New Hampshire	14,143	8,220	58%	1,419	10%
New Jersey	161,481	62,736	39%	12,463	8%
New Mexico	26,334	12,237	46%	2,782	11%
New York	264,835	116,753	44%	37,810	14%
North Carolina	120,586	49,019	41%	33,240	28%
North Dakota	10,802	4,340	40%	1,920	8%
Ohio	202,234	72,031	36%	56,802	28%
Oklahoma	65,819	28,625	43%	12,582	19%
Oregon	46,201	23,459	51%	4,781	10%
Pennsylvania	196,277	63,413	32%	46,402	24%
Rhode Island	18,589	11,729	63%	1,498	8%
South Carolina	71,705	20,830	29%	22,404	31%
South Dakota	11,841	3,563	30%	1,481	13%

continued

TABLE 1-1 (continued)

State	Total No. Handicapped	LD N	%	MR N	%
Tennessee	106,091	42,804	40%	20,245	19%
Texas	289,343	150,768	52%	30,769	11%
Utah	38,968	13,611	35%	3,159	8%
Vermont	9,309	2,973	32%	2,563	28%
Virginia	100,713	38,614	38%	16,878	17%
Washington	64,295	31,286	49%	9,400	15%
West Virginia	42,418	14,719	35%	11,066	26
Wisconsin	72,219	27,224	38%	13,234	18%
Wyoming	11,144	5,095	46%	943	8%
Territories					
Washington, D.C.	5,809	1,629	28%	1,237	21%
Puerto Rico	35,173	1,852	5%	21,159	60%
American Samoa	244	1	.4%	161	66%
Guam	2,031	530	26%	913	45%
Virgin Islands	1,237	220	18%	626	51%
Bur. of Indian Aff.	4,849	2,531	52%	723	15%

Modified from the *Sixth Annual Report to Congress* prepared by the Division of Educational Services, Special Education Programs, 1984.

the total number of handicapped individuals ages 3 to 21 (aggregated across states and territories) was 4,298,237; of that number 1,745,871 or 40.6% were classified as LD. This is in contrast to 1976-77 when 757,213 individuals were identified as LD. The 1983 figure represented over 3% of all school children nationally, but now it is over 4%.

Two points about prevalence deserve attention. The first has to do with the variation in prevalence by states, the second with the dramatic change in prevalence rates over time. Referring to Table 1-1, it may be seen that for the 1982-83 year Hawaii (64%) and Rhode Island (63%) had the highest percentage of identified LD children; Alabama (26%), Indiana (27%), and Kentucky (27%) had lowest. Among the territories prevalence ranged from a high of 26% in Guam to a low of 4% in American Samoa. The District of Columbia identified 28% of all handicapped children as LD; the Bureau of Indian Affairs so identified 52%. Looking at the states reporting high numbers of handicapped children, it is clear that variation is still the rule. On average, the five states with over 200,000 identified handicapped children classified 46% of them as LD. The percentages by states were: California, 55%; Illinois, 37%; New York, 44%; Ohio, 36%; and Texas, 52%. Comparable LD figures for the 21 states with fewer than 50,000 identified handicapped children varied from 58% (New Hampshire) to 30% (South Dakota). On average, these 21 states identified 42% of all handicapped children as LD. Since the average percentage of LD pupils was similar for the states with over 200,000 and the states with under 50,000 handicapped children (46% and 42%, respectively), it appears that identification as LD is not a function of total number of children identified. Given the disparities in the percentages of LD individuals identified by states, it does seem fair to conclude that identification as LD is strongly influenced by local policies and procedures.

The second point relates to changes in prevalence figures. Citing figures from the *Liaison Bulletin*, Edgar and Hayden (1984-85) noted that the numbers of individuals in all handicapping conditions has increased 16% since 1976-77, but LD has increased 119%. Figures from the *Annual Report* reflect the pattern of change. In 1976-77, the four major categories of handicapping conditions (in rank order of numbers served) were speech impaired (1,302,066), mentally retarded (969,547), LD (757,213), and emotionally disturbed (283,072). In 1982-83, by contrast, rank order and numbers were LD (1,745,871), speech impaired (1,134,197), mentally retarded (780,831), and ED (353,431). Both speech impaired and mentally retarded categories dropped in number while there was a modest increase in the number of individuals identified as emotionally disturbed. The major increase was in the LD category, where the number of pupils more than doubled (797,213 to 1,745,871).

According to the *Eighth Annual Report to Congress* (1986), the dramatic rate of increase during the first years of the LD category has slowed. Ten states reported that numbers of LD students decreased, nine reported moderate increases. Analyzing an earlier *Annual Report*, Gerber (1984) suggested that these figures were misleading, since only four states reported lower percentages of children served. One of these states was New Mexico, which does not provide services under PL 94-142. Gerber estimated that 16 states had no change or less than 1% change in service rates and concluded that "... most of the decrease in number of students identified as learning disabled is simply an artifact of overall enrollment declines. Actually, most states are continuing to identify the same or an increasing percentage of students as learning disabled despite declining enrollment" (p. 214).

LD and Low Achievement

The disparities in prevalence by state or geographic area suggest differences in the characteristics of individuals served. The heterogeneity of subjects subsumed by the LD classification has been well documented (see Kavale & Nye, 1981; Keogh, Major-Kingsley, Omori-Gordon, & Reid, 1982; Kirk & Elkins, 1975b; Norman & Zigmond, 1980; Torgeson & Dice, 1980). In a series of studies Ysseldyke and colleagues (Algozzine & Ysseldyke, 1983; Ysseldyke, Algozzine, Shinn, & McGue, 1982; Ysseldyke, Algozzine,

Richey, & Graden, 1982) have questioned the validity of many classification decisions, finding that school district classified LD and nonclassified children were virtually indistinguishable. Support for their work has been provided by Shepard and colleagues (Shepard & Smith, 1981; Smith, 1982) in a detailed study of LD in the State of Colorado. In a quantitative analysis of 1,000 "representative" LD cases (school district identified), Shepard and Smith (1983) found that 28% met strict LD criteria and that an additional 15% showed "weak signs of the handicap." Fifty-seven percent of the 1,000 did not meet Colorado LD criteria: 10.6% were normal; 11.4% were slow learners; and 6.6% had some specific language interference problems. A qualitative analysis of an additional 200 cases yielded similar, if anything, more powerful results, leading the authors to conclude that while 60% of the cases needed special educational help, 22% needed other than "LD-type" interventions, for example, psychotherapy or intensive English training.

The confounding of LD and other achievement-related problems is also found in the work of the Kansas group (Schumaker, Deshler, Alley, & Warner, 1980; Warner, Schumaker, Alley, & Deshler, 1980). These investigators studied 246 school-identified LD students in grades 7 through 12 and a comparison group of 229 low achieving (LA) students of comparable grades. The Kansas group found that the major difference between the LD and LA groups was degree of disability. The LD students' performance in reading, math, and written language was significantly below that of the LA students at both junior and senior high school levels; and the groups also differed on estimated ability at the senior high school level. The average intellectual ability score for the LD groups, however, was "substantially below" the norm of 100. Based on their sample, the Kansas investigators suggest that "... for many of the LD students, the traditional label of 'slow learner' would be more appropriate" (Warner et al., 1980, p. 31). Further, there were significant school district effects such that mean IQs for LA and LD students differed in some districts but not in others. Apparently, in some districts the defining criterion for selection as LD was low achievement, rather than a significant discrepancy between ability and achievement. Thus, district selection criteria may confound the problematic LD-LA question. The Kansas researchers documented considerable overlap between school-identified LD and LA pupils, finding that many students identified as LD were characterized by "generalized rather than specific learning deficits," which made it difficult to separate them from other low-achieving students. In essence, the LD students represented a more extreme position on the achievement deficiency continuum. Often "LD-ness" was a matter of degree, not of kind or pattern of deficits. Following this notion, Zigmond (1983) suggested a definition of LD based on an "easy-to-teach" to "very-hard-to-teach" continuum. In this view LDs are those who, despite aptitude, are nonresponders to educational treatments. In contrast, the underachievers are more responsive to instruction.

Taken as a whole, it appears that it is difficult to distinguish between individuals with learning disabilities and those who are more properly viewed as low achievers. Edgar and Hayden (1984-85) suggested that "the early quantifiable aspect of the LD definition is low achievement" (p. 533). As noted by Turner and Wade (1982), issues of definition and identification of LD are "even more acute in the birth to 3-year-old range" (p. 83). Given the escalating numbers of individuals identified as eligible for LD services, and given the overlap of identified LDs with normally developing and underachieving groups, it is clear that, to date at least, there is no agreed upon conceptual or operational criteria for classification. It is not surprising that the prevalence figures vary dramatically from state to state, from school district to school district, and from clinician to clinician.

Professional and Disciplinary Perspectives

In contrast to some problem areas in which disciplinary or professional lines and responsibilities are clearly drawn (e.g., physical illness), LD is viewed as a legitimate problem for professionals from many different disciplinary backgrounds. Learning disabilities are discussed in diverse literatures (e.g., neurology, psychiatry, ophthamology, optometry, psychology, education, occupational therapy, physical therapy, speech and language, social work, and the like). Professionals in these fields have different views of what consitutes LD, how it should be assessed and diagnosed, and what should be done about it (Keogh et al., 1982). To illustrate these differences, four somewhat different perspectives are summarized in Table 1-2. Particular techniques or approaches that characterize particular disciplines are provided as examples, not as comprehensive descriptions.

These approaches are not mutually exclusive, and there is overlap across perspectives. Yet, it is apparent that there are differences on a number of dimensions: focus and etiology, time of identification, symptoms, identification techniques, treatment, and professional responsibility. Although some children will likely be identified as LD by all approaches, particular perspectives and practices will lead to differences in numbers identified and the manner in which individuals are identified. The diversity of perspectives and techniques was well illustrated in the UCLA Marker Variable Project (Keogh et al., 1982), which included a detailed review of 408 published research articles focused on LD. Disciplines represented included medicine, education/psychology, and related fields (e.g., speech and hearing, optometry, and the like). More than 1,400 techniques and tests, including 38 different ability tests and 78 achievement measures, were reported to have been used in diagnosis and identification of LD. The array of symptoms reported was also diverse (e.g., hyperactivity, hypotonia,

TABLE 1-2.
Disciplinary Perspectives on Learning Disabilities.

Aspects of LD	Medical/Neurological	Process	Behavioral	Educational
Focus and etiology	Organic, in child	Psychological, in child	Setting/child interaction	Child/instructional program interaction
When identifiable	Infancy, preschool	Preschool	Preschool, school	School
Symptoms	Physical, neurological anomalies, soft signs	Visual, auditory, motoric, processing problems	Disturbed behavior and achievement problems	Low achievement, behavioral problems
How identifiable	Neurological examination, EEG, psychoneurological tests	Process measures: ITPA, Bender, Gestalt, psychoneurological tests	Behavior observation, task analysis	Educational and ability tests
Treatment emphasis	Medication, diet	Process training	Behavior modification, situational change	Pedagogy, remedial intervention
Major professional	M.D.	Psychologist	Psychologist/teacher	Teacher

sleep problems, vision inefficiencies, as well as general school failure and specific and limited disabilities). The range of attributes thought to characterize LD is probably related, in part, to differences in professional or disciplinary training and perspective (i.e, the eye of the beholder), as well as reflective of the complexity of the condition itself.

Policy Constraints

A number of recent analyses of special education programs (Chalfant, 1984, Christianson, Ysseldyke, & Algozzine, 1982; Mehan, Meihls, Hertweck, & Crowdes, 1981; Shephard & Smith, 1981b) have suggested that referral, identification, and placement of pupils was influenced, even determined in part, by "institutional constraints," that is, by federal and state legislation, by school district policy, and by organizational arrangements within school districts. Mehan and associates (1981) based their argument on theories of organizational behavior that consider the school districts, like other public organizations, as facing competing demands or imperatives in the conduct of their business. For special education, personnel may be faced with performance demands that may or may not be consistent with administrative requirements based on extra-district legislation or policy (e.g., legal limits on numbers of pupils identified or assessment procedures and time-lines). Within the U.S., states use different guidelines for identifying mildly impaired pupils (Frankenberger, 1984; Norman & Zigmond, 1980). Further, changes in definition, legislation, and availablility of resources lead to selection of different individuals as representatives of a given special education category or classification (Keogh & MacMillan, 1983; MacMillan, Meyers, & Morrison, 1980). The case is well illustrated by changes in the population served as mentally retarded (Algozzine & Korinek, 1985; Polloway & Smith, 1983).

Based on a microethnographic study of one public school district in California, Mehan and colleagues (1981) identified powerful institutional constraints that affected the referral and placement process and, thus, the nature of educational decisions about individual pupils. These institutional constraints also determined, in part, the number of pupils identified as LD. In the district studied, 141 new referrals (5% of the total 2,781 pupils enrolled) were processed in a given calendar year. Thirty-six (25.7%) of those referred were placed in LD programs; 28 pupils (20%) were reviewed by the school appraisal team but were retained in regular classes; another 29 pupils (20%) remained in regular classes because of interruptions in the review process — in a sense, a placement by default. As Mehan and colleagues pointed out, progress through the system was not primarily a function of pupil characteristics but rather was based on a number of decisions related directly to institutional constraints.

Differences in definitions of LD and in formal and informal screening practices across schools lead to differences in formal referral rates. Mercer, Forgonne, and Wolking (1976) found 75 different educational components represented in the formal definitions of LD in 42 different states. Robbins, Mercer, and Meyers (1967) noted that there was variability in referral rates according to schools within one school district, with some principals encouraging referrals while others discouraged them. In the school district studied by Mehan and colleagues (1981), formal referral rates varied because some building principals were actively involved in school-level informal screening and review. In such cases, students were expedited through the system, which led to faster placement decisions and higher placement rates. Time of year was also found to influence referral rates, with few referrals occurring in the last months of the school year (May and June) and the highest referral rates occurring in mid-fall (October) and mid-winter (February and March). These peaks and valleys in referrals reflected, in part, teachers' awareness of children's problems and their feelings that referral would lead to services. They also may have reflected the school psychologists' case loads, the backlog of accumulated cases in the spring, or the availability of space in particular programs. This interpretation was supported by the findings of Robbins and associates (1967) who found that referral rates were related to psychologists' time allocations.

The effect of policy on prevalence may also be seen in the adoption of a 50% discrepancy formula as a criterion for identification as LD in New York. As noted by Stark (1982), in the 12 months following adoption of the 50% discrepancy criterion, the number of pupils identified as LD dropped from 28,000 to 12,167. In essence, the 50% discrepancy criterion made the LD category available primarily to severely impaired pupils. This policy was challenged by 18 LD pupils and their parents on the basis that it exclusively affected one disability group (LD) and that it disfavored children with mild handicaps. The court ruled in their favor. By this decision the "unclassified" pupils were still LD and eligible for services. The decision by the U.S. District Court, however, was reversed by the U.S. Court of Appeals. In arriving at this decision, the Court acknowledged that the 50% discrepancy rule might deny special education opportunities to children but noted that, according to the Compliance Officer for PL 94-142 from the U.S. Office of Special Education, the federal regulations did not prohibit such a formula. Apparently, the number of children identified as LD in New York may vary as a function of particular court decisions.

Finally, Christianson and colleagues (1982) studied the influences on teachers' decisions to refer children for evaluation and possible placement. These investigators suggested that factors influencing referral could be grouped into two general categories. The first, institutional constraints, included three factors: organizational factors (e.g., district procedures), availability of services, and "hassle" (e.g., amount of paperwork, scheduling of meetings). The second, external pressures, included: external agencies (advocacy groups), federal and state guidelines and regulations, parents, and the sociopolitical climate. The institutional and external pressures as perceived by teachers were consistent with the findings of other investigators, thus, lending support to the importance of system variables in decision making. It is likely that a range of system-related variables also influences decisions of placement teams, as it has been shown that team decisions are often not data based (Ysseldyke, Algozzine, Richey, & Graden, 1982).

The evidence, then, supports Mehan and associates (1981) contention that most special education decisions are "rarely developed in the manner implied by law" (p. 147), as the force of the many institutional constraints practically negates this possibility. This is not to imply anything negative about school district personnel but rather to emphasize that classifications are not only functions of child characteristics but also involve powerful organizational influences. Number of programs, availability of space, incentives for identification, range and kind of competing programs and services, number of professionals, and federal, state, and community pressures all affect classification decisions. Given the many influences and the lack of a clear consensus on what constitutes and characterizes LD, it should not surprise us that we face a serious and continuing definitional program.

THE DEFINITIONAL PROBLEM

To this point, no attempt has been made to define LD. This has not been an oversight but rather was a purposeful omission. The history of the LD field has been characterized by controversy about "the definition." It seems unlikely, however, that a single theoretically sound and empirically verifiable definition is possible, at least at this time in our history. Rather, it seems more reasonable and more productive to direct our efforts toward a comprehensive description that can encompass many notions about LD. The search for a single definition has proven fruitless in the past; somewhat pessimistically, it will probably continue to be so in the future.

While acceptance of a single definition of LD is improbable, it is instructive to consider some of the reasons for the continuing definitional arguments. Most fundamental, however, is the point that definitions serve different purposes, have meaning for different constituencies, and provide diverse operational and conceptual implications. The researcher who attempts, for example, to test particular components of memory must define LD in certain conceptually and operationally concise ways; only a few individuals from a large LD pool may meet these specific definitional criteria. In contrast, a school district arguing for more support of LD programs may apply a broader definition. Such a definition would likely subsume a number of researcher-defined groups and would ensure services to the largest possible number of pupils. Definitions are linked to purposes, and thus, the reasons for definition require specification and clarity. Recognition of the multiple purposes for defining LD is a first and necessary step in reducing the present confusion and controversy.

Another step toward resolving the definitional problem is to acknowledge that there are few, if any, specific criteria for definition of LD. Within the school context, at least, there are a number of individuals whose low performance, relative to their presumed aptitude, makes them eligible for further consideration as possible LD. In addition, there are also a number of attributes or symptoms that appear in varying combinations and in different degrees of severity, intensity, and chronicity. Thus, one pupil identified as LD may, for example, have mild signs of impulsivity, inattention, social withdrawal, poor fine motor coordination, and clumsiness in addition to a performance-aptitude difference. The combination of these problems may be enough to lead to his identification as LD. In contrast, a second LD pupil in the same group may have excellent fine and gross motor coordination and be socially adequate but be extremely hyperactive and inattentive. Although few in number, the severity of symptoms or attributes may also lead to identification as LD. In short, LD definitions must necessarily take into account both number and severity of attributes.

LIMITATIONS ON RESEARCH AND PRACTICE

The need for a closer liaison between research and practice has been a continuing call in special education. The notion has intuitive appeal, but the state of the art in both research and practice suggests that the combined efforts to date have not worked well. It might be argued that the research process is weakened by efforts to be relevant, while practice is too often carried out in ignorance of — or in actual rejection of — research findings. The LD literature is replete with examples (e.g., the issues surrounding process training). In the face of this conflict, it is not possible to say whether the clinician or the researcher is correct, because they ask different questions: What do we know about the nature of this condition? What services should be provided? The first is a scientific question, the second is a systems or organizational question. Unfortunately, by trying to respond to each question the answers tend to confound rather than clarify.

The problematic nature of LD research is easily demonstrated by providing an example of the difficulties inherent in making a policy decision based upon *what the research says.*

The Illinois Test of Psycholinguistic Abilities (ITPA) has served as the clinical model for a variety of remedial and developmental language programs (Kirk, 1968). These programs are based upon the assumption that language is comprised of discrete components and that these components can be trained. It is this last assumption that has precipitated debate over the efficacy of psycholinguistic training. Further examination of the literature would identify reviews summarizing available primary research. At this point, however, scientific knowledge becomes obscured because of different interpretations of this literature. To illustrate, Hammill and Larsen (1974a) constructed a table of "+" and "0" which paralleled statistical significance (.05 level) or nonsignificance and summarized the findings from 39 studies for either total ITPA score, ITPA subtests, or both. Hammill and Larsen (1974a) concluded that "researchers have been unsuccessful in developing those skills that would enable their subjects to do well on the ITPA... [and]... the idea that psycholinguistic constructs, as measured by the ITPA, can be trained by existing techniques remains nonvalidated" (pp. 10–11).

Minskoff (1975) offered a critique of Hammill and Larsen's (1974a) review, which suggested:

> Because of Hammill and Larsen's oversimplified approach, 39 studies with noncomparable subjects and treatments were grouped together. Moreover, for the most part, they reviewed methodologically inadequate studies in which there was short-term training using general approaches to treatment primarily with mentally retarded or disadvantaged students having no diagnosed learning disabilities. (p. 137)

In effect, Minskoff (1975) suggested that Hammill and Larsen had compared "apples and oranges" and then provided guidelines for research on psycholinguistic training; specifically, 15 criteria were established for evaluating psycholinguistic remediation. It was suggested that psycholinguistic disabilities can be trained, and a major criterion for evaluating effectiveness should be its relationship to various academic and social demands made upon a child at a particular age. Minskoff (1975) concluded by decrying the skepticism surrounding psycholinguistic training since "it can be dangerous if it leads to the abolition of training methods that may be beneficial to some children with psycholinguistic disabilities" (p. 143).

Immediately following was a response by Newcomer, Larsen, and Hammill (1975) that contested the major points made by Minskoff (1975). Suffice it to say that the rhetoric became increasingly confusing and enmeshed in trivial controversy. Nevertheless, Newcomer and colleagues (1975) contended that "the reported literature raises doubts regarding the efficacy of presently available Kirk-Osgood psycholinguistic training programs" (p. 147).

The debate lay dormant for some three years when Lund, Foster, and McCall-Perez (1978) offered a reevaluation of the 39 studies reviewed by Hammill and Larsen (1974a). The studies were reexamined individually to determine the validity of negative conclusions regarding the effectiveness of psycholinguistic training. Six of the 24 studies clearly showed positive results for psycholinguistic training and "contraindicate the conclusions that such training is nonvalidated" (p. 317). Of 10 studies showing negative results, only two were reported accurately. The remaining eight were either equivocal or showed positive results. Lund and colleagues (1978) reached conclusions markedly at variance with the statement that psycholinguistic training is nonvalidated.

> Our analysis indicates that some studies show significant positive results as measured by the ITPA, some studies show positive results in the areas remediated, and some do not show results from which any conclusions can be drawn. It is, therefore, not logical to conclude either that all studies in psycholinguistic training are effective or that all studies on psycholinguistic training are not effective. (p. 317)

The LD community did not wait long for the debate to continue. Hammill and Larsen (1978) reaffirmed their original position. The point-by-point rebuttal of the Lund and colleagues (1978) reevaluation was presumed to show that, in fact, their original report did not either inaccurately report, inappropriately categorize, or misinterpret any of the original 39 studies. The rebuttal concluded with the statement that

> the cumulative results of the pertinent research have failed to demonstrate that psycholinguistic training has value, at least with the ITPA as the criterion for successful training. It is important to note that, regardless of the reevaluations by pro-psycholinguistic educators, the current state of research strongly questions the efficacy of psycholinguistic training and suggests that programs designed to improve psycholinguistic functioning need to be viewed cautiously and monitored with great care. (p. 413)

Thus, after some five years of feckless debate, polemics abounded but a nagging question remained: What is really known about the efficacy of psycholinguistic training? Increasingly, the principal issue had become entangled in a maze of extraneous detail only tangentially related to the major question. This is not the stuff of scientific knowledge nor the foundation for sound practice. Research should be more than semantic arguments and statistical nitpicking; but, unfortunately, most issues in LD resist resolution because efforts to design a single study to extend and improve existing basic research generally fail. This is due partially to the difficulties in controlling the many sources of variability that impinge upon research in LD. Many of these sources of variation are noted in Table 1-3.

TABLE 1-3.
Sources of Variability in Learning Disabilities Research.

- Differences in the theoretical frameworks (paradigms) underlying research in special education (e.g., behavioral, biophysical, cognitive, process, psychodynamic, psychoeducational)
- Differences in research design (e.g., subject sampling, subject assignment, data collection, measurement scale, experimental control)
- Differences in data analysis methods (e.g., unit of analysis)
- Differences in procedural rigor (i.e., degree of imprecision in the experimental protocol)
- Differences in LD samples (i.e., heterogeneity resulting from the lack of precise identification criteria)
- Differences in similarly labeled treatments or programs (i.e., important and subtle diversity among, for example, psycholinguistic or perceptual-motor models)
- Differences in setting-by-treatment interactions (i.e., program effectiveness as a function of who participates, where they participate, and other situational factors)
- Differences in outcome assessments (e.g., reliability, validity, norm interpretation, reactivity)
- Differences in scope of LD research (i.e., alternative theoretical foundations and research designs favored by psychology, medicine, sociology, and child development)

The example provided by psycholinguistic training demonstrates the fragility of many findings in LD. Too often, findings from individual studies have proved to be conflicting, variable, and sometimes paradoxical. Although a dozen studies may resolve a matter in the physical sciences, a dozen studies investigating something like the efficacy of psycholinguistic training yield inconsistent findings. Such conditions led Andreski (1972) to argue that what passes as scientific study of human behavior (e.g., learning disabilities) is little more than sorcery. Consequently, an analogy for LD may be drawn from Frazer's (1963) account of early man's development from magic to science. The comparison may seem otiose but consider the following: because of an inability to explain phenomenon in terms of natural and predictable laws, man reverted to a primitive cause and effect termed *sympathetic magic,* wherein events may exert influence on other events although separated by distance, time, or relevance. Sympathetic magic may be further divided into homeopathic magic based upon the principle of similarity (i.e., like produces like) and contagious magic based upon the principle of contiguity (i.e., once in contact, two things influence each other even when separated).

These principles formed the basic approach to reality but were applied in the wrong places to the wrong events. Thus, magical thinking possessed the irreparable flaw of unreliability (i.e., the magic neither produced nor explained the phenomenon). Unfortunately, some current conceptions in LD evidence such magical thinking. For example, the assertion that perceptual-motor training improves academic functioning represents a form of homeopathic magic while conceptions about "minimal brain dysfunction" and its influences are akin to contagious magic. These types of magical thinking have led LD professionals to neglect fundamental principles of logic and scientific method in favor of mystical notions that ignore reason, disregard rationality, and assume truth can be discovered without disciplined inquiry. Under these circumstances, the study of LD is likely to be irrational, illogical, and without scientific merit.

SUMMARY

It is clear that we know more about LD than we did 10 years ago. Equally clear, however, is the fact that we are still far from understanding LD. This chapter has pointed out the directions in which the field is moving but also the many detours encountered in seeking the goal: a unified and comprehensive perspective about LD. The LD field is marked by ambiguities, inconsistencies, and controversies that defy resolution because, while we possess much knowledge, we lack a coherent and organized conceptualization that can order our knowledge of LD. Consequently, this chapter has highlighted several problems (i.e., variant prevalence estimates, difficulties in separating LD and low achievement, overlapping professional boundaries, and the lack of congruence between policy and practice). Because the LD field is characterized by empricism (i.e., emphasis on data collection and analysis), Kavale (in press) has suggested that more emphasis be placed on generalized theory development in order to provide a context for facts. In this way, facts become more than data and will possess a scientific merit that may be useful for resolving the many dilemmas currently facing the LD field. This effort may remove the detours and allow us to proceed in the most straightforward direction.

CHAPTER 2

The Learning Disability Paradigm

Marguerite C. Radencich

The definition of learning disability remains a contentious issue facing the field. Decisions about such an issue should be grounded in a comprehensive theoretical framework which is accepted by the profession at large (see Kavale, in press, for a decision on the need for macro-level theory in LD). Does the LD field possess such a theoretical basis? If not, is one emerging? Without a comprehensive and unified theoretical framework, the existence of learning disabilities cannot be justified as an entity separate from, say, reading or math disabilities.

As discussed in Chapter 1, controversy can be said to be the most salient characteristic of the field today. Children labeled as learning disabled are found to be indistinguishable from other low achievers with disquieting consistency. Prevalence figures vary widely. Intense disagreement among the "experts" has led to the establishment of separate professional groups. Is this controversy based on sound theoretical debate or is it indicative of the chaotic state of an atheoretical field?

One way of addressing these questions is to borrow the conceptual framework provided by Thomas Kuhn in *The Structure of Scientific Revolutions* (1970). Examining one's field of study from the perspective of

This chapter originally appeared as an article by **Marguerite Radencich** in *Learning Disabilities: An Interdisciplinary Journal* (Vol. III, 1984) and was subsequently updated and adapted by permission of Grune & Stratton for inclusion in this *Handbook*.

another field can provide surprising insights and creative solutions to problems that have appeared to be insoluble from within. Kavale and Forness (1985b) suggested that Kuhn's work can in fact provide a cogent framework with which to analyze the history and current status of learning disabilities as a discipline. It is the purpose of this chapter to undertake such an analysis.

Kuhn prefaces *The Structure of Scientific Revolutions* by speaking of the differences between social and natural scientists in terms of the number and extent of overt disagreements between them about the nature of scientific problems and methods. Attempting to discover the source of this difference led him to formulate a theoretical base that is common to both types of scientific endeavors.

Kuhn refers to the usual state of a discipline as normal science. Normal science is research firmly based upon a paradigm, a constellation of beliefs, values, norms, techniques, and methods shared by the members of a scientific community. Paradigms are acknowledged for a time by some particular scientific group as the foundation for its further practice. However, normal science typically undergoes periods of revolution during which anomalies (i.e., exceptions to paradigm-based expectations) arise and paradigms change.

According to Kuhn, there can be certain types of scientific research without binding paradigms. Acquisition of a paradigm and of the more esoteric type of research it permits is a sign of maturity in the development of a scientific field.

In the absence of some candidate for a paradigm, all of the facts that could possibly pertain to the development of a given science are likely to seem equally relevant. As a result, early fact-gathering is a nearly random activity. In the early stages of the development of any science, different persons confronting the same range of phenomena interpret them in different ways. The disappearance of such divergences is usually caused by the triumph of one of the pre-paradigm schools, which emphasized only some part of a too sizable and inchoate pool of information.

Once a paradigm is selected, there is a basis for the solution of the remaining puzzles of normal science. Investigations into the puzzles of normal science proceed according to the dictates of the accepted paradigm until anomalies emerge. Anomalies may be ignored at first or put aside while scientists work on more immediate problems. After a time, however, the anomalies can no longer be ignored, and there begins a series of debates and extraordinary investigations that lead the profession to a new set of commitments. This period of uncertainty may last so long and be so pervasive that the field goes into a period of extraordinary science during which the field is in a state of crisis. During such a period, the resolution of the conflict may become the subject matter of the discipline.

Early attacks upon a resistant problem will have followed the paradigm rules quite closely. But with continuing resistance, more and more of the attacks will involve new articulations of the paradigm. Through this proliferation of divergent interpretations, the rules of normal science become increasingly blurred. Although there is still a paradigm, few practitioners completely agree about what it is.

Crisis may end in one of three ways. Normal science may ultimately prove able to handle the situation. The problem may have to be set aside for a new and better-equipped generation of scientists. Or a new potential paradigm may emerge and come to be accepted.

The transition process is not cumulative. Rather, it is a reconstruction of the field from new foundations. Proponents and supporters of competing paradigms will often disagree about the list of problems that any potential paradigm must resolve. There may be a large overlap between the problems that can be solved by the old and the new paradigm. But there will also be a decisive difference in the modes of solution. The new paradigm may display a quantitative precision that is strikingly better than its competitor. When the transition to the new paradigm is complete, the views and goals of the profession will have changed.

Proponents and supporters of competing paradigms practice their trades in different worlds. Before they can hope to communicate fully, one group or the other must experience a conversion similar to that which may occur with the perception of a second visual gestalt from a single stimulus.

The extraordinary episodes in which such shifts occur are referred to as scientific revolutions. The persons who develop a paradigm have almost always been either very young or very new to the field. They are little committed to the traditional rules. When, in the development of a natural science, an individual or group first produces a synthesis able to attract most of the next generation's practitioners, the older schools gradually disappear. The new paradigm implies a more rigid definition of the field. Those unwilling or unable to accommodate their work to it must proceed in isolation. It is often the acceptance of a paradigm that transforms a group into a profession or discipline.

ROOTS OF THE FIELD

In order to understand the relationship between Kuhn's framework and the status of the LD field, it would be helpful to review the field's history, despite the familiarity of many readers with this topic. It can be said that the field began when Kirk (1962) proposed the term "learning disabilities," leading to its adoption by the newly formed ACLD (then Association of Children with Learing Disabilities) in 1963. But the field's

origins certainly predate 1963. Determining when the field began — as is
the case with any paradigm — is a difficult undertaking. There are always
those researchers whose work, often ignored, foreshadows the birth of a
paradigm. Thus, it can be said that the LD field began with any of the
theorists listed in the three strands of Figure 2-1, as described by
Weiderholt (1974).

The first label attached to what would later be called learning disabilities was Strauss and Lehtinen's (1947) brain-injured child. Their
criteria included perceptual and conceptual disorders, perseveration, soft
neurological signs, history of neurological impairment, and a lack of history of mental retardation.

Although the concept of the exogenous (brain injured) mentally retarded
child evolved into the notion of learning disabilities, Kavale and Forness
(1984b) found little empirical support for the perceived behavioral differences between exogenous (brain injured) and endogenous (familial or
cultural) forms of mental retardation.

These findings are significant because the present-day LD field owes
much of its theoretical orientation to the presumed differences found by
Strauss and Werner (1943) in their study of exogenous and endogenous MR
children. On the basis of their findings, Strauss and Werner concluded that
the effects of brain injury were manifested in a definite set of behavioral

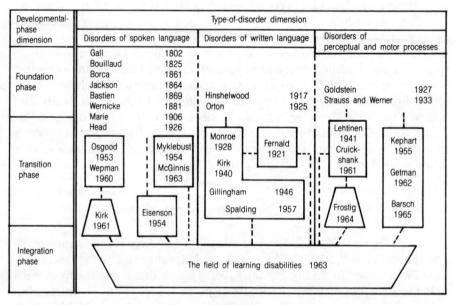

FIGURE 2-1
A two-dimensional framework in the study and remediation of learning disabilities.
(From Wiederholt, 1974, p. 105)

characteristics across a broad range of functioning. From these assumptions and a series of modifications (e.g., the equivalent characteristics in children with brain injury but normal intelligence, and the specification of the parameters of the Strauss syndrome), the concepts surrounding exogenous MR evolved into the present day conceptualization of LD. But the present findings call into question Strauss and Werner's notions regarding the supposed behavioral consequences of brain injury because of the failure to uncover useful distinctions between exogenous and endogenous groups. The comparisons failed to produce differences of a magnitude that would unequivocally separate exogenous and endogenous functioning and that might provide a prototype for LD.

The approach exemplified by Strauss and Werner was perpetuated by their colleagues at Wayne County Training School. Kavale and Forness (1985b) traced the profound influence of Strauss and Werner in a genealogical diagram of the LD field (see Figure 2-2). The linkages are irrefutable in some instances, more tenous in others, but everywhere suggestive of the profound influence of Strauss and Werner in people and events in the evolution of learning disabilities. Consequently, there exists a bias toward the ideas of Strauss and Werner; and, since paradigms are always relative to the assumptions, preconceptions, and models existing at the time of conception, the Strauss and Werner paradigm, while appropriate for the early state of LD development, no longer possesses the relevance

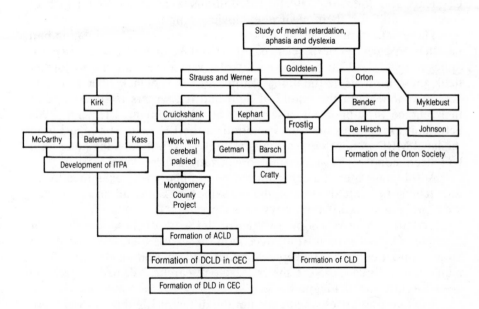

FIGURE 2-2

The "family tree" outlining the genealogical development of the LD field.

necessary for advancing learning disabilities towards a more comprehensive and unified theoretical perspective.

The prolific work of these men provided the foundation for much subsequent research. Their achievement was also sufficiently open-ended to leave many problems for their followers to resolve. Such a foundation is necessary in realizing paradigm status and in establishing a period of normal science. Also necessary is that such work be sufficiently unprecedented to attract an enduring group of adherents. Among the most notable adherents of the perceptual-motor school were Getman, Barsch, and Frostig, to name but a few.

Eventually, the Strauss and Lehtinen definition was judged to be too broad; behavioral aspects of the condition needed to be defined; teaching approaches had to be outlined. In 1966, Clements as director of Task Force I presented the first formal definition proposed at a national level.

Clements' label was "minimal brain dysfunction" or MBD. His definition differed from that of Strauss and Lehtinen in two ways: it excluded children with low IQs, and it was expanded to include motor and language disorders. In 1967, Johnson and Myklebust introduced a definition with a focus similar to that of Clements. They referred to children as having a psychoneurological learning disability, meaning that behavior has been disturbed as a result of a dysfunction of the brain and that the problem is one of altered processes, not of a generalized incapacity to learn. Both the Clements and Johnson-Myklebust definitions were criticized for lack of specificity and for their medical-etiological emphasis.

These definitions established no decisive paradigm. This situation had parallels in early modern science; jfor example, in the field of physical optics prior to the 17th century, each writer was forced to build his or her field anew from its foundations (Kuhn, 1970). The lack of a generally accepted view about the nature of light had left writers relatively free in their choice of supporting observation and experiment. Clements' 1966 definition exemplifies the same situation in the LD field. His report used the label MBD rather than learning disabilities even though the latter term had been adopted by a national organization three years earlier.

At this stage there was no standard set of phenomena examined by all researchers. Individuals confronting the same types of children interpreted their problems in different ways (see Appendix A).

Certainly there was some overlap in the work of these theorists. For example, Osgood's path from reception to expression was related to Strauss and Lehtinen's perceptual deficit and to Gillingham and Stillman's faulty linkages. Nevertheless, each researcher seemed to feel the need to start the field anew.

The question arises whether or not the different LD theories were representative of different paradigms. Or were there no pararadigms? There is no real basis for arguing that each of the LD theories constituted separate paradigms. However, each may have contributed toward a process or modality paradigm. This paradigm explained performance in terms of strengths and weaknesses in the sensory systems of receiving, processing, and responding to information. As a corollary, students would benefit if taught through their stronger modality.

The field did not possess shared rules at this stage, but operated from the borrowed rules of the established fields of psychology and medicine. According to Kuhn, scientists work from models, often without understanding them fully. In the LD field, Osgood's (1957) model would be the classic example. The model served as the basis for the Illinois Test of Psycholinguistic Abilities (ITPA) (Kirk, McCarthy, & Kirk, 1968), which became widely used in instructional decision-making. Yet the model was based on nothing more than a series of constructs. These was no "proof" that processes, channels, and levels really existed as entities. If they did, there was no guarantee that they were measurable, much less that they were measurable by the ITPA.

During this stage it was difficult to sort out relevant from irrelevant facts. How important to academic achievement was the ability to stay within the lines on the Frostig materials? or the ability to do well in visual reception on the ITPA? or the ability to crawl with correct cross dominant patterns?

This lack of shared rules and this difficulty of sorting out relevant from irrelevant facts are characteristic of Kuhn's preparadigm period. And yet, as was pointed out earlier, the LD field did have some characteristics of established paradigms. (The dominant model, which had a large group of adherents, had formed a foundation for research.) The preparadigm stage is very similar to a period of changing paradigms; the difference lies in the fact that in the latter case the focus is both smaller and more clearly defined. But the focus in the LD field has been steadily growing less well defined. Criteria for MBD and LD syndromes had progressively become more ambiguous.

Nevertheless, the modality model did constitute a paradigm of sorts. To achieve the status of paradigm, a theory must merely seem better than its competitors. A sizable percentage of the LD field's theorists and practitioners did subscribe to some form of the modality model. There was no serious competition. The process model was eagerly embraced as *the* explanation underlying the difficulties of so many bright children. Parents were relieved that the problem wasn't their fault; teachers were relieved that it wasn't their fault; and, of course, children were relieved that they weren't at fault either.

Normal science is a devoted attempt to force nature into the conceptual boxes of a paradigm. Anomalies subversive of a paradigm's basic commitments are often supressed. Certainly, the modality theorists have done their utmost to fit data into the process "paradigm." The fact that research has not supported this hypothesis has not deterred its proponents (e.g., Arter & Jenkins, 1977; Kavale & Forness, in press). The assumption seems to have been that the discrepancies in the research would resolve themselves in time. Rationales given for the lack of empirical support are many: inadequate instrumentation, methodological problems, other stronger and uncontrolled factors concealing the effects of modality preferences, and the use of instructional procedures that are not modality-pure (Arter & Jenkins, 1977). Recent meta-analyses (Kavale, 1981, 1982) seem to show that visual and auditory perception do account for a moderate proportion of the total variance in reading ability. However, with intelligence controlled for, this relationship virtually disappears.

Kuhn posits that, with a paradigm, a community acquires a criterion for choosing problems that have solutions. It is mostly these problems which a community will encourage its members to undertake. This insulates a community from important problems that cannot be stated in terms of its paradigm. The process model also fits this criterion for paradigm status in that it opened a vast territory for potential research. Yet this territory was bordered by "No trespassing" signs into competing areas such as behaviorism.

FEDERAL RECOGNITION

In 1968, the term learning disabilities was selected from a long list of competing terms (Clements, 1966) for inclusion in the 1969 Elementary and Secondary Act amendments (PL 91-230). This legislation established the term for common use in education and research. Under Kirk's leadership, the USOE National Advisory Committee on Handicapped Children (NACHC) presented the following definition:

> Children with special learning disabilities exhibit a disorder in one or more of the basic psychological processes involved in understanding or in using spoken or written languages. These may be manifested in disorders of thinking, reading, writing, spelling, or arithmetic. They include conditions which have been referred to as perceptual handicaps, brain injury, minimal brain dysfunction, dyslexia, developmental aphasia, etc. They do not include learning problems which are due primarily to visual, hearing or motor handicaps, to mental retardation, emotional disturbance or to environmental disadvantage. (NACHC, 1968)

This definition was more widely accepted than its predecessors had been. Nonetheless, criticisms have been numerous: the definition does not include Bateman's (1965a) discrepancy clause; it depends too heavily on exclusion to define its target population; it is general and ambiguous and has not generated consistent incidence figures (Mercer, 1983).

Public Law 94-142, The Education for All Handicapped Children Act (1975), defined learning disabilities in almost the same way as the earlier NACHC definition. No substantive differences had emerged, but some progress appeared to have been made with the definition proposed by the National Joint Committee for Learning Disabilities (see Chapter 1).

Early attacks on the problem of definition had followed the rules of the process paradigm quite closely. But with continued resistance, divergent articulations of this paradigm had begun to proliferate, leaving the rules of normal science increasingly blurred. Furthermore, a paradigm that had been developed for one set of phenomena was ambiguous in its application to other closely related ones (e.g., brain injury to minimal brain dysfunction to LD). The extent to which models developed at each of these stages were generalizable to those of later stages was left unclear.

The definition gradually became more educationally oriented. The presumed etiology, however, is central nervous system dysfunction. McLeod (1983) argues in favor of an eduational definition, "In the vast majority of cases, treatment of learning disabled children is still and educatiónal responsibility. It is therefore not unreasonable to insist that learning disability be defined in educational terms." The opposite point of view is voiced by Cruickshank (1983), "A definition of learning disabilities is based upon certain 'givens'... all learning is neurological. It can be nothing else...."

Even though the definition has become more educationally oriented, the field is experiencing a strong pull back to the medical model. One of the highlights of a recent ACLD International Conference was a neurobiological workshop. Research in the neurotransmitter area is examining various treatment theories of LD such as those pertaining to diet, neurotoxicity, and drugs. Definitiveness in diagnosis may soon be achievable with the PET scan (positron-emission tomography), with the CAT scan (computerized axial tomography), and with NMR (nuclear-magnetic resonance) (Cruickshank, 1983). Neurometrics provides for computerized analysis of measured response time (Wacker, 1982).

There has also been an upsurge of interest in right-brain/left-brain specialization (e.g., Galaburda, 1980; Witelson, 1976) and interhemispheric transfer (Gross, Rothenberg, & Schottenfeld, 1978). Another area that is stirring interest is the genetic differentiation of some disabled readers from the general population.

OPERATIONALIZATION OF THE CONSTRUCT

The field has gotten no closer to reaching agreement on placement decisions than it has on the definitional issue. Whether or not the 1981 definition can be operationalized any more consistently than has been the case with previous definitions remains to be seen. In defining what an LD student is, we must be able to determine *some* attributes that *some* LD students have in common but which are not shared by other students. Ysseldyke (1983) found over 40 ways of operationalizing the LD definition reported in the literature. The findings of his extensive research on this issue are far from reassuring, regardless of whether decisions are based on strict criteria or on clinical judgments. LD professionals contend that an LD child is distinct from a slow learner. However, in comparing 18 LD definitions, Ysseldyke (1983) found that 99% of diagnosed LD students and of other low achievers could be identified as LD by at least one of these sets of criteria. Ysseldyke, Algozzine, and Epps (1982) also found that over 75% of normal (nonidentified) students could be labeled LD, and about 25% of school-identified LD students could not be classified as such. The federal standard score formula identified only 2 of 50 students in LD classrooms (Warner, Schumaker, Alley, & Deshler, 1980). These findings are in line with the report by Mann, Davis, Boyer, Metz, and Wolford (1983) on the lack of compliance with the federal definition by the Child Service Demonstration Centers.

Vinsonhaler, Weinshank, Wagner, and Polin (1983) offer quite interesting findings regarding the diagnostic and remedial performance of reading and LD specialists and classroom teachers. Mean diagnostic agreement between two clinicians across six studies remained close to 0.10. Even more interesting is the fact that mean diagnostic agreement for a single clinician diagnosing the same case twice was no higher than around 0.20 across the six studies.

Epps, Ysseldyke, and Algozzine (1984) found that, given scores on psychometric measures, psychologists and resource teachers are able to differentiate between low achievers and students labeled LD with only 50% accuracy. But, lo and behold, the hit rate of "naive" engineers was a whopping 75%. It seems that the engineers followed criteria strictly, whereas the psychologists and teachers were influenced by subjective judgments. The use of subjective criteria by educators is questioned by further data (Ysseldyke, 1983) that shows the influence of factors such as the child's physical attractiveness on placement decisions.

These unwelcome findings and awkward facts lend some support to Coles' (1978) scathing attack on the field in terms of its use of unscientific diagnostic judgments, its indefensible claim to any special knowledge, and its inability to differentiate LD students from the general population.

The poorly understood construct of learning disabilities has sometimes been paired with the even more poorly understood concept of dyslexia. Researchers have gathered data that support the association of various deficits with dyslexia. These include problems with temporal order perception (Bakker, 1972), phonetic synthesis and analysis (Shankweiler & Liberman, 1972), verbal labeling (Vellutino, 1977), short-term memory

(Morrison, Giordani, & Nagy, 1977), eye-movement control (Leisman, 1975; Pavlidis, 1982), visual-spatial order perception (Mason, 1975), selective attention (Ross, 1976), and visual information processing (Senf & Freundl, 1971; O'Neill & Stanley, 1976).

The research of Pavlidis (1982) is particularly intersting in that he not only differentiates dyslexia from normals but, more importantly, dyslexics from other low achievers. He found erratic eye movements for dyslexics, both when they were following a print and when they were following a beam of light. This was not the case for normal or nondyslexic low achievers. (His definition of dyslexia was an exclusionary one similar to the 1981 LD definition.) The cause behind these erratic eye movements remains undetermined.

Harris (1982) examined current theories of reading disability. He found that most deal with disabilities that are of constitutional origin even though the theorists recognize that these cases probably constitute a minority of the reading disabled population. He divided existing theories into single factor and multiple factor theories and concluded that each of the single cause proponents were probably dealing with only one part of a complex situation.

In analyzing the multiple-causation views, Harris adopted the framework of Satz and Morris (1980). This framework identified subtypes of reading disability under two categories: clinical-inferential and statistical. Notable studies under the first category include those of Johnson and Myklebust (1967), Boder (1973), and Das, Leong, and Williams (1978). Leaders in the movement to apply advanced statistical techniques to the identifcation of subgroups of learning disability include, for example, Doehring, Hoshko, and Bryans (1979); Lyon and Watson (1981), and McKinney, Short, and Feagans (1985). (see Rourke, 1985, and Satz and Morris, 1981, for reviews.) Studies under both categories tended to identify a language deficit group, a perceptual deficit group, and, possibly, a verbally nonfluent group. But all of the studies reported sizable numbers of children who did not fit neatly into any of the subgroups. These cases are probably not of consitutional origin. And, of course, the more common pattern is probably that which involves both constitutional and environmental factors.

The LD field seems to be left with the unsettling situation it's been in all along. According to a recent survey (Tucker, Stevens, & Ysseldyke, 1983), the "experts" generally continue to see learning disabilities as a viable classification, even though they perceive its limitations. A majority of the respondents to this survey estimated the LD incidence to be 3% or less of the general population. When Hammill (1980) stated that in a room of 100 kids he would probably single out the same ones as being LD as would Kirk, Frostig, and Cruickshank, he was probably referring to this hard core group of children. The real problems begin when placement decisions must be made on children outside of this group. McGrady's (1980) way of putting it was that "the definition of learning disabilities is like the definition of pornography: 'No one seems to be able to agree on a definition, but everyone knows it when they see it' " (p. 510).

The problem of definition is, of course, somewhat contingent upon the purposes for which the definition will be used. Keogh (1983) sees three primary purposes for LD classification: as a focal point for private and government advocacy, as a mechanism for providing services, and as a system for organizing research. For research purposes, Keogh (1978) proposed a system of marker variables: learning disabilities with behavior disorders, learning disabilities with neurological problems, and so forth. Thus, markers define the LD groups such that we have LD with variables I, X, Y for *this* study; LD with variables M, W, Y for *that* study, and so on. Lilly (see Tucker et al., 1983) sees LD as a category of services rather than a category of children. Ysseldyke (1983) concludes that LD is whatever society wants it to be, needs it to be, or will let it be.

Kuhn posits that evolution of a science calls for the development of an esoteric vocabulary and skills and a refinement of concepts that increasingly lessens their resemblance to their usual common-sense prototypes. The LD field has certainly outdone itself in the establishment of an esoteric jargon. With phrases like "visual perceptual hypothesis of deplexia [sic], motor/kinesthetic/praxic/visuospatial output," or "dichotomous tactual stimulation in spatial processing," the field has nothing to envy in the jargons of more established fields such as medicine and law.

According to Kuhn, this professionalism leads to an immense restriction of the scientist's vision and to the establishment of competing camps. Scientists who began in closely related fields, studying many of the same books and achievements, have acquired different paradigms in the course of professional specialization. The prolonged discussion and compromise that preceded the adoption of the NJCLD theoretical definition are an indication of the difficulty that fields related to learning disabilities have in agreement on terms. Even after such prolonged discussion it seems that agreement on an operationalized definition was still not possible. McLeod (1983) refers to the NJCLD definition as "a form of words designed to appease every pressure group and offend none." This disagreement among the experts in the related fields is, of course, mirrored in the field's practitioners. At one ACLD conference, Lieberman (1982) stated that he works with people every day who have masters and doctorates in fields such as psychology and special education but who haven't the faintest idea of what learning disabilities are all about.

ANOMALY

Normal science possesses a built-in mechanism that ensures the relaxation of restrictions that bind research whenever the paradigm ceases to function effectively. One of the indices of the lack of effectiveness of the process paradigm is the wide discrepancy in prevalence figures. Estimates have varied from 2% (USOE, 1976) to 50% (Ensminger in Tucker et al., 1983) as a result of the lack of a standard definition. Ensminger's 50% figure is, of course, tongue-in-cheek: "if you assume, as some educators do, that anyone who is achieving below the mean is having trouble in school."

When anomalies occur, such as those in Ysseldyke's (1983) data and in the disparate prevalence figures cited above, anomaly can no longer be ignored. Yet Kavale and Forness (1985b) have shown how anomalous postulates have been either implicitly or explicitly incorporated in LD definitions. The assumptions that LD fits a medical model, is associated with neurological dysfunction, is related to process deficiencies, is marked by an academic discrepancy, and cannot be due primarily to other handicapping conditions are all problematic and cannot be accepted unequivocally. The preservice of anomalies should lead to a period of extraordinary science that results in a paradigm shift. This also marks the beginning of a period of scientific revolution. The community no longer accepts without question the particular problem solutions already achieved.

The LD field, however, has not experienced a paradigm shift. The Strauss and Werner paradigm has biased the research process in LD from initial problem formulation to final data interpretation. There is more often an attempt to prove rather than to modify a paradigm, which results in an unconscious focus on supportive data and a neglect of data not in harmony with the paradigm. Consequently, anomalies become accepted and, in a field like LD, persist for so long that the resolution of the definitional problem becomes the subject matter of the discipline. Thus, for example, the January 1983 issue of the *Journal of Learning Disabilities* included a symposium of 11 articles on this subject.

PARADIGM STATUS

The LD field, which began with great promise, has not always been able to live up to expectations. Haight (1979) speaks of the development of the LD field in terms of stages. She posits that any new branch of knowledge goes through stages of infancy, childhood, adolescence, and adulthood.

The infancy stage is typified by a direct search to identify interindividual differences through one syndrome of related behaviors; thus, there is much agreement that the category exists as a distinct entity. With time, subgroups become evident when analyzing the intraindividual differences in the new category, and the period of childhood begins. During the rapid growth of this period, there are a plethora of perspectives with which to view the child; assessment systems are intensified to provide more magnified views of the individual. Next, the field enters adolescence where the search for scientific identity reaches a climax. Research presenting microscopic and highly diverse cross-sections of the individual accumulates, resulting in concern as to whether there are *any* unifying commonalities in the heterogeneous group of individuals. In the adult stage, the field is either absorbed into another schema or solidified into a category that has a set of universally accepted subdivisions.

Haight posits that the LD field is in its adolescence; perspectives, labels, descriptors, assessment techniques, etiologies, terminology, and research data are colliding in a seemingly irrational pattern. The search for scientific identity has definitely reached a climax.

To be accepted as a paradigm, a theory must seem better than its competitors even though it never explains all the facts with which it can be confronted. Has the LD field achieved this criterion with regard to a single paradigm? The authors of the 1981 definition recognize that it is not perfect — yet there is certainly no better one. The definition is certainly open ended enough to allow for much related research. However, does agreement on a definition constitute the birth of a new paradigm?

Does the field have appropriate instrumentation to allow it to match fact with theory? The reliability and validity problems that have plagued test instruments used in evaluating LD candidates are notorious (e.g., Arter & Jenkins, 1977; Kavale, 1981b, 1982; Larsen & Hammill, 1975). Ysseldyke and Algozzine (1979) claim that there *are* technically adequate norm-referenced tests that can be used to make decisions about students — in the domains of intelligence and academic achievement. However, he makes no such claims for measures of specific processes or of personality. (He defines adequate tests as those having reliabilities above .90 and as those which are valid for the purposes used.)

Etiology behind learning disabilities has not been established. Methods of identifying the LD population have not been reliable. Remediation leaves much to be desired. In Haight's terms, the stage of adulthood has not been reached. In Kuhn's framework, we are still searching for a common paradigm.

Despite discontent with the process paradigm, the field has not yet agreed on the paradigm that will take its place. Ysseldyke and Algozzine (1983) mention several alternatives that are available when any system addresses the need for change. First, criticism can be ignored; this is often accompanied by heightened attempts to reaffirm the appropriateness of current practice. This may be the case with the renewed interest in the NJCLD definition. The second alternative would be to disband the system. The third would be to start to "start playing hard ball." Ysseldyke and Algonzzine conclude that we must take this third alternative in order to develop a new philosophy of education, a new perspective on assessment, and a new perspective on intervention. This advice is timely.

To "start playing hard ball," several suggestions are offered to assist in breaking the bonds of the past. A major first step would be to realize that

LD is really in a preparadigmatic period. This would allow for the admission that any and all data are appropriate and justified for delineating the LD phenomenon. Under such a framework, the initial empirical efforts are likely to be based on an unclear conceptual understanding of the observed phenomena. But as the subject matter is systematically studied, it will eventually coalesce into a more structured conceptual system. This process will make for distinct similarities and differences in preparadigmatic theories; and, although the various schools would be in competition, a more important outcome will be the realization that they also have much in common. Commonality is important because, once recognized, it can serve to disprove invalid hypotheses. Although there may be several rival preparadigms, the constructive, cumulative, and cooperative endeavors within each preparadigm will provde a broad empirical foundation for LD.

A next step would be to question whether the natural sciences provide the most appropriate model for understanding the LD phenomenon. The field has yearned after such a paradigm as the only one that would assure respectability. However, the natural science paradigm ignores the fact that a field like LD is composed of two parts: the science and the art, that is, LD can be divided into a part that can be attacked scientifically (within strict boundaries) and a part that cannot. This recognition that LD possesses aspects of art would not prevent the development of a scientific paradigm. Kuhn (1970) suggested that paradigms could be conceived of in a sociological sense. A paradigm in this sense might encompass the entire constellation of values and beliefs shared by a given community. LD might be viewed within a sociological perspective that considers the structural relationships within the LD system as well as within the wider social structure of which LD is a part. Further, scientific development involves nonrational elements such as imagination and intuitive processes. Advances in science involve creative problem solving and are inherently unpredictable. Polanyi (1958) termed this aspect of scientific development "tacit knowing;" he argued against strict rules for establishing knowledge and emphasized the indeterminacy of science with respect to its content. Similarly, Feyerabend (1975) suggested an "anarchistic epistemology" wherein "anything goes." There are neither absolute judgments nor fixed conceptions of rationality. Scientific development is viewed as complex, unpredictable, and requiring anarchy for the growth of knowledge. Three recommendations are offered:

1. A *counter-inductive procedure:* Evidence relevant for theory testing can often be discovered only with the aid of an incompatible theory.
2. The *principle of proliferation:* The invention and elaboration of theories that are inconsistent with the accepted point of view will foster advances in knowledge.

3. A *pluralistic methodology:* A variety of approaches is preferable to a
   single approach.

An LD field developed along these lines would still be marked by dis-
unity because of inter-theory competition. A general, unified theory of LD
would have to be approached not through a reductionist methodology but
through a type of bridging methodology that attempts to abstract principles and concepts from a number of disparate theories. This abstraction
would not involve a precise and formal mathematical structure but a
rational explication of the interrelations between theories. Darden and
Maull (1977) termed such an approach "interfield theory" and suggested
that theories of the same phenomenon (e.g., LD) are better designated as
"fields." Within interfield theory, the various fields are positionally
established in a multilevel, hierarchically arranged type of structure that
represents a unified framework. At this point, the LD field would be able
to move towards a paradigmatic stance. Such a paradigm may induce major
shifts in a science and does not arise solely from the paradigm clashes
described by Kuhn (1970); it arises through contact with a field, its past, its
present, and a grasp of its future.

CONCLUSIONS AND RECOMMENDATIONS

The development of the LD field may be likened to that of the computer industry. Had a standard operating system been utilized for all computers from the beginning, all programs would be compatible. As this was
not the case, we struggle with ever-increasing incompatibility. Some of this
variation has grown from dissatisfaction with existing operating systems;
some has simply grown from the greed of companies that wish to insure
consumer dependence in the marketplace. The LD field has similarly
become increasingly varied, partly because of dissatisfaction with the
status quo but, perhaps also because of the need of professionals to come
up with novel ideas simply to survive in the publish-or-perish market of
academia. As consumers are now demanding that the computer industry
start to move toward compatibility, so too should LD professionals be
asked to synthesize existing knowledge before advocating new perspectives.

It is as crucial for professionals to keep up with developments in the
LD field as it is for computer specialists to keep up in their field. Computer specialists simply cannot fail to do so and expect to survive. Staying
current is more a matter of individual choice for professionals involved
with the learning disabled. Perhaps state legislatures and school systems
should see to it that there is no failure in this regard through certification
and inservice requirements.

With such an educated cadre of professionals, the field would be in a
stronger position to integrate theory and practice in the solution of its prob-

lems. Ideally, education of professionals would culminate in their having an empirically based philosophy of identifying and educating learning disabled youngsters. Moreover, their instructional methods and materials would follow this philosophy, and the instruments they would use for identification and evaluation would be only the more valid and reliable ones.

Professionals in the field should be honest about their uncertainties in dealing with lay people such as parents. Such a position may be uncomfortable for professionals and lay people alike. However, this is better than having people receive conflicting information from every authority they consult.

While we search for a paradigm, we are still faced with daily decisions of identification, instruction, and evaluation. These procedures are bound by local, state, and federal guidelines. It is hoped that the authorities responsible for these guidelines will become leaders in making use of research findings to steadily improve their procedures. Meanwhile, school-level personnel are charged with the onerous task of staying current with the field, of educating their colleagues, and of making defensible decisions for the children whose education they are entrusted with.

PART II

The Nature and Characteristics of LD

Heterogeneity is an often-cited problem in the LD field. Individuals classified as LD are likely to reveal a wide variety of characteristics. It is reasonable, therefore, to ask: What is a learning disability? The answer, unfortunately, is neither simple nor straightforward. A learning disability is not one thing (i.e., homogeneous), and hence any description must take into account the heterogeneity associated with LD. If a learning disability were a homogeneous phenomenon, then this section might possibly consist of a single chapter. Instead, this section assembles chapters on a variety of topics that are all associated with the nature and characteristics of LD.

Chapter 3 reviews the genetic influences on learning disabilities. The causes of LD are just as heterogeneous as its characteristics. Therefore, instead of listing the myriad causes of LD, which would not be a productive exercise since the cause is unknown in a large majority of cases, we have focused on genetics as a more fruitful approach to understanding the varied etiology of LD.

With this foray into etiology, attention is then focused on the nature and characteristics of LD. The analysis proceeds from process skills to academic skills, to correlative behavior problems, and finally, LD in a special group. The goal is to provide a broad based view of LD that, while not exhaustive, is, at least, comprehensive with respect to the major areas of deficiency commonly associated with LD.

Chapter 4 begins the description of process skills with a review of auditory dysfunction and its negative impact on communicative abilities. The analysis not only assesses the consequences of central auditory system dysfunction (e.g., auditory discrimination) but also the role of peripheral auditory system dysfunction in relation to LD. Chapter 5 provides analysis of dysfunction in the linguistic processes, including a comprehensive description of language-learning disabilities and the consequences of linguistic dysfunction through several case studies. Chapter 6 focuses on the pragmatic language deficiencies in LD children. In this analysis focusing on language use, there is a review of difficulties associated with both discourse (i.e., interactive conversation) and narrative (e.g., extended verbal explanations) skill deficiency of the LD child.

The next chapters deal with the academic characteristics of LD individuals. A large majority of LD children reveal reading to be their primary problem area. What do we know about the relationship between reading and learning disabilities? Chapter 7 traces the historical legacy of reading disabilities with its emphasis on neurological concepts and then reviews the current concepts related to reading deficiency. In this analysis, the influences of attention, memory, and linguistic functioning, as well as ecological factors (e.g., classroom and instructional factors), are discussed in relation to reading difficulties. The next chapter on academic difficulties deals with comprehension problems, defining comprehension in its broadcast sense involving physical, psychological, and sociological phenomena. The necessary prerequisite skills are reviewed, and instructional procedures are discussed in relation to enhancing "understanding." Chapter 9 reviews the problems associated with LD in the area of written language, specifically spelling and writing. Viewed as part of language processing, spelling and writing errors are categorized and explained. These errors are placed in a context involving phonological, orthographic. lexical, syntactic, and semantic levels of linguistic functioning. Only slightly less prominent but often neglected are arithmetic difficulties. Chapter 10 provides an analysis of the factors involved in arithmetic difficulties (e.g., intelligence, verbal ability, and visual-spatial ability). Then reviewed are the roles of neurological factors and cognitive abilities in producing arithmetic deficits. Finally, instructional processes are analyzed with respect to making arithmetic instruction more effective.

There are many correlative problems associated with LD, but perhaps the most prominent are behavior problems — particularly social and emotional difficulties. Chapter 11 reviews the social and emotional difficulties associated with LD, including poor self-concept, rejection by others, impulsivity, negative mood, and physiological concomitants. This chapter concludes with dimension of direct teaching of social skills as an important part of the total programming for the LD individual. Chapter 12 then delineates the relationship between learning disabilities and behavior disorders. This relationship is viewed within a dynamic ecological perspective and provides guidelines for classification and service delivery. Chapter 13 discusses the learning-disabled gifted child. By providing empirical data and clinical impressions, this chapter provides guidelines for identification and intervention, especially model programs and counseling for parents.

This section concludes with two summary pieces. Chapter 14 reports the findings of a research synthesis investigating the question: What is the basic nature of LD? The data from some thousand studies covering four primary areas were integrated in an effort to determine where the greatest differentiation between LD and normal groups might be. The results only affirm the complex and multivariate nature of LD. Given the heterogeneity of LD, any theoretical statement must take that heterogeneity into account. Most LD "theories," however, emphasize a single dimension and hence lack explanatory power. The last chapter in this section presents a conceptual model (i.e., archetype) that incorporates many notions about LD. The framework provided includes components of the teaching-learning process (e.g., student, environment, instruction), as well as ideas about the nature of LD, to demonstrate how some children disassociate themselves from academic learning and come to be termed learning-disabled.

We hope the reader comes away with a sense of what factors are involved in learning disabilities. Although not a full and complete rendering of the characteristics of LD, this section aims at providing insight into the nature of LD. One obvious conclusion is that learning disabilities are complex and not easily described along any single dimension.

CHAPTER 3

Genetic Influences

Shelley D. Smith
Bruce F. Pennington

T he purpose of this chapter is to demonstrate the influences of genes on learning disabilities and to provide practical guidelines for teachers, clinicians, and researchers working with learning-disabled children. The contributions of clinical and behavioral genetics research will be reviewed, with particular emphasis upon the methodologies used in behavioral genetics studies. Basic principles of genetics will be presented first, followed by a description of various genetic syndromes that possess a high frequency of learning disabilities. Next, behavioral genetics methodologies will be analyzed critically. Genetic studies of cognition will then be reviewed with reference to normal variation in intelligence and the genetic contribution to specific disabilities. These specific disabilities are best seen in studies of specific learning disability.

These studies have also produced recommendations for diagnosis and therapy. Professionals involved with LD children may find themselves working closely with a family for whom genetic evaluation should be considered. Understanding the procedures for genetic evaluation and counseling aids the professional in deciding when a referral is appropriate, in preparing the family for such an evaluation, in determining if an appropriate evaluation was done, and in interpreting the results to the family.

This chapter originally appeared as an article by **Shelley Smith and Bruce Pennington** in *Learning Disabilities: An Interdisciplinary Journal* (Vol. II (3), 31–42, 1983) and was adapted by permission of Grune & Stratton for inclusion in this *Handbook*.

BASIC PRINCIPLES OF GENETICS

Although the idea that characteristics are transmitted from parent to child has existed for centuries, it is only since the turn of the century that the rules for this transmission have been known (Mendel, 1866, rediscovered by DeVries, 1900, 1966); and only since 1953 has the basic mechanism for this transmission been recognized (Watson & Crick, 1953). In 1952 we did not know how many human chromosomes there were, and we did not learn how to tell them apart until 15 years ago. The last few years have brought new discoveries regarding the organization of genes on the DNA molecule, and the next 10 years will surely bring other major advances in reading the genetic code.

As a basis for the following discussion, a brief review of genetic principles and terminology is in order. The reader will recall that the genes, which direct the development and metabolism of our bodies, are encoded on the molecules of DNA that comprise the chromosomes. Chromosomes come in pairs called homologs. One member of the pair comes from the mother and the other from the father. In turn, one member from each pair is chosen at random for transmission to a given child. Humans normally have 23 pairs of chromosomes, 22 autosomal pairs and one pair of sex chromosomes. Chromosomes can be visualized under the microscope, photographed, and arranged in pairs in a karyotype, as shown in Figure 3-1. Individual genes, however, cannot be directly visualized. Both members of a homolog pair carry the codes for the same traits in exactly the same linear order. Thus, each trait is determined by a pair of genes, which may or may not carry the same code.

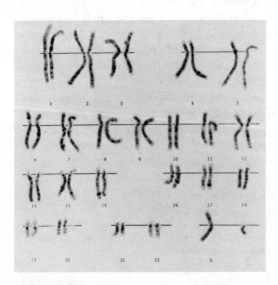

FIGURE 3-1.
Normal male chromosomes
arranged in a karyotype.

The different codes for a given genetic trait are called alleles. If both of the alleles of the pair are the same, the person is said to be homozygous for that gene; if the alleles differ, the person is heterozygous for that gene. The genes for the *ABO* blood group types, for example, will always be in the same position (or locus) on the ninth pair of chromosomes; but a given homolog may carry the *A* allele derived from one parent whereas the other homolog may carry the *O* allele from the other parent. Such an individual would be heterozygous at that locus. The two alleles constitute the person's genotype for that trait. In the example above, the person's genotype at the *ABO* locus is *AO*. The interaction of the two alleles determines the phenotype, that is, the physical expression that can be observed. In the case of the *AO* genotype, the resulting phenotype is *A* blood type.

The relative influence of one allele compared to another is represented by the terms *dominant* and *recessive.* An allele is said to be dominant when it can determine the phenotype in both the homozygous and heterozygous states. For example, the *AA* and *AO* genotypes produce essentially the same phenotype, so the *A* allele is said to be dominant. The recessive *O* allele is recognized phenotypically only in the homozygous genotype *OO*. The *B* allele, however, is codominant with *A*, in that the heterozygote *AB* genotype expresses the *AB* phenotype.

Autosomal dominant inheritance is probably the easiest to recognize in a family. Since the dominant allele is manifested in all who carry it, the trait can be seen from generation to generation (see Fig. 3-2). Heterozygotic individuals will randomly pass the dominant or recessive allele to their children so that on the average 50% of their offspring will show the dominant trait. There are, however, some exceptions to this. Some genes show incomplete penetrance, meaning that they are not always manifested in the

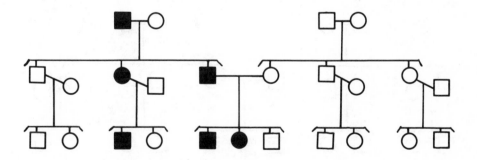

FIGURE 3-2. Sample pedigree of autosomal dominant inheritance.

heterozygote. Expressivity may also vary, in that the heterozygotes can show a wide range in phenotype. Thus, the terms *dominance* and *recessiveness* do not refer to a strict dichotomy but rather to a continuum of expressiveness. Sometimes *carriers* (individuals with one recessive allele for an abnormal trait) are not completely normal phenotypically. An example of this state of affairs will be presented in the discussion of phenylketonuria (PKU). In addition, a dominant gene with reduced penetrance is not totally dominant. As we come to recognize the full range of expression of a given gene, it may be detected in supposedly nonpenetrant individuals.

Autosomal dominant genes can also appear in an individual with a negative family history (i.e., no other family members have the gene) through the process of new mutation. While it is very rare for a gene to mutate (approximately 1 in 10^6), a significant number of individuals with a rare dominant disorder, particularly one that limits reproduction, will be the result of a new mutation.

In autosomal recessive inheritance the allele must be present in the homozygous state to be expressed. Since a child with a recessive trait had to receive one recessive allele from each parent, the unaffected parents must both be heterozygous carriers. Such parents would have a 25% chance of having an affected child. Typically, a rare autosomal recessive disorder occurs among children of one set of parents (a sibship) but nowhere else in the families of either parent (see Fig. 3-3). The exception to this is inbred, interrelated populations in which the chances that carriers will marry other carriers increase. In the same way, the affected individual with an unrelated, unaffected spouse would have a very low risk of having an affected child. In general, autosomal dominant disorders involve developmental or structural abnormalities, whereas the biochemical

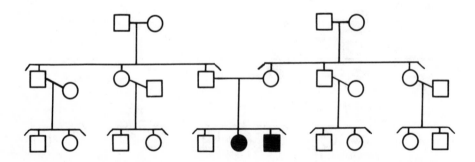

FIGURE 3–3. Sample pedigree of autosomal recessive inheritance.

defects tend to be recessive. In cases where there are dominant and recessive forms of the same clinical syndrome, the recessive form is the more severe, presumably because there are two defective alleles rather than just one.

A third mode of inheritance is termed sex-linked. Recall that the 23rd pair of chromosomes, the sex chromosomes, determine the sex of the individual. A person with two X chromosomes is a female, while one with an X and a smaller Y chromosome is male. The X chromosome contains a considerable number of genes that have nothing to do with sexual development, but the only trait assigned with confidence to the Y chromosome is maleness. In females, the alleles on the two X chromosomes interact in the same ways described for homologous autosomes. The male, however, having nothing on the Y to counteract the alleles on the X, expresses all of the alleles as if they were dominant. Thus, a female with a recessive allele for a disorder such as hemophilia on one X chromosome will at most only mildly manifest the disorder, but a son who receives that allele (and any son is at 50% risk) will have the full disease.

As in recessive disorders, X-linked traits are often biochemical in nature. The typical family history will show only affected males, related to each other through unaffected females (see Fig. 3-4). It is important to note that an X-linked trait will not show male-to-male transmission since an affected father cannot pass the gene on to a son. This is quite obvious when one realizes that for a son to *be* a son he had to receive the Y chromosome from his father and not the affected X chromosome. Thus, a disorder that shows a preponderance of males is not necessarily sex-linked.

Many disorders cluster in families but do not show the Mendelian (single-gene patterns) of inheritance described above. The recurrence risks

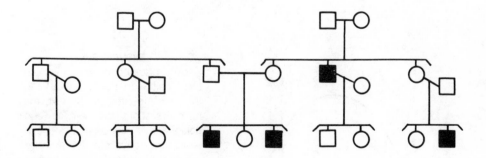

FIGURE 3-4. Sample pedigree of X-linked recessive inheritance.

for relatives of affected individuals are higher than those of the general population but are still considerably less than the 25% to 50% recurrence risks observed for single-gene traits. Exact recurrence risks depend upon the frequence of the particular disorder but are generally under 10%.

The model of multifactorial inheritance has been developed to explain these disorders (Carter, 1969; Falconer, 1960). *Multifactorial* refers to the interaction of many genes (polygenes) and unspecified environmental influences. These factors are presumed to be distributed normally in the population. They may interact to produce a phenotype with continuous variation, such as height, or the phenotype may be dichotomous, as in cleft lip and palate. The latter is explained as the effect of a threshold superimposed on the liability distribution. Anyone with an accumulated liability below the threshold level will have a cleft lip and palate (see Fig. 3-5). Furthermore, in the case of cleft lip and palate, it appears that males have a lower threshold than females, with the result that more males are affected. However, since affected females must have a comparatively higher proportion of deleterious genes, their relatives are at greater risk.

Thus, the family patterns seen in the multifactorial case are quite irregular and the phenotypes can be variable (Fig. 3-6). In a population study, however, multifactorial threshold traits will follow certain rules, and these can be used as criteria to test whether a trait might be transmitted in this manner. These primarily involve the expected frequency of the trait among relatives of a proband.

1. If one sex is affected less frequently, then the relatives of a proband of that sex will be affected more often than relatives of the affected sex. This has been discussed above with regard to cleft lip and palate.

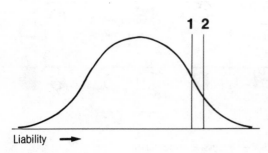

Liability ➡

FIGURE 3–5.

Liability distribution for a multifactorial trait with two thresholds. In the example cited in the text, the male threshold for cleft lip and palate would be indicated by line 1, while the threshold for females would be at line 2. Thus, fewer deleterious factors are required for expression of cleft lip and palate in males.

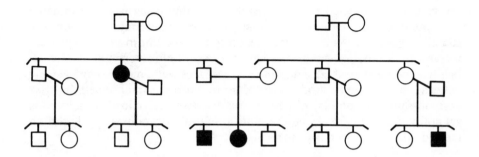

FIGURE 3-6. Sample pedigree of multifactorial inheritance.

2. More severely affected individuals will be found to have more affected relatives than less severely affected individuals.
3. Overall, the risk to relatives will be proportional to the frequency of the disorder; the more common the disorder, the higher the incidence among relatives which, of course, does not hold true for single gene disorders.
4. The risk to first-degree relatives (siblings, offspring, parents) will be approximated by the square root of the population frequency.
5. Finally, the risk to relatives will drop rapidly as the degree of relationship decreases. The recurrence risk for an autosomal dominant trait will drop by 50% with each degree of relationship, for example, 50% risk for first-degree relatives, 25% for second-degree, and so on; multifactorial traits do not show this regularity.

While this can be the most confusing mode of inheritance to study, it is suspected that most of the common structural birth defects (e.g., club foot, pyloric stenosis, spina bifida) are inherited in this fashion. Furthermore, the autosomal dominant trait is probably the most relevant to learning disabilities, since it would be expected that complex cognitive abilities will be influenced by many genes and environmental factors and may also show different thresholds for each sex.

Chromosomal disorders are quite different from those discussed above in that they concern visible variations in the amount of chromosomal material. Extra or missing chromosomal material (aneuploidy), whether it involves part or all of a chromosome, is generally deleterious since thousands of genes are involved. As a result, multiple systems are usually affected with defects arising very early in embryological development. Down's syndrome, caused by extra chromosome material from the 21st pair, is the most commonly seen autosomal chromosomal abnormality. Others exist but are rarer, primarily because their effects are so severe that the affected pregnancies do not come to term. It is estimated that one-third to one-half of all first trimester miscarriages are chromosomally abnormal. As cytogenetic techniques have improved, however, an increasing number of syndromes with very small chromosomal abnormalities are being described, and some syndromes with inconsistent genetic patterns have been found to be due to chromosomal deletions. Sex chromosome aneuploidy, which will be discussed later in this chapter, is generally not as severe as the autosomal abnormalities; and certain individuals are essentially normal.

GENETIC SYNDROMES ASSOCIATED WITH LEARNING DISABILITIES

The influence of certain major genes on learning abilities can be seen in particular genetic syndromes with a high frequency of learning disabilities (see Table 3-1). In Table 3-1 we are attempting to go from a known genotype to an appreciation of the phenotype, that is, the degree and type of associated learning disability. In some cases listed, the genetic deficit is known — a given enzyme defect, for example. In none of these cases is the actual mechanism through which the defect influences brain development to produce a learning disability known. The understanding of this mechanism in any one of the disorders discussed in this section would be a major breakthrough and would provide valuable insight into the pathways affecting learning. The following compilation is not presented as being exhaustive. Other such syndromes may well exist but not be easily recognized, particularly since most clinical studies have reported only a general statement of intelligence level. It should be noted in this discussion of syndromes that a learning disability is considered to be a deviation in specific cognitive abilities below that which would be expected given the individual's apparent IQ. Thus, a specific disability may be superimposed over a more general mental retardation. Recognition of discrepancies in abilities can be more important in the remediation of these children than it is in children with normal IQs since their strengths may be hidden by the label of the syndrome.

BEHAVIORAL GENETICS METHODOLOGY

Research in the genetics of behavioral traits is complicated by the very basic problem of establishing whether or not the trait in question is influenced by genes at all and then, even more difficult, discovering what

TABLE 3-1.

Genetic Syndromes with Associated Learning Disabilities.

Syndrome	Transmission	Characteristics
Noonan	autosomal dominant	verbal disability performance apraxia
Neurofibromatosis	autosomal dominant	learning disabilities
Dysmorphic facies, laryngeal and pharyngeal hypoplasia, spinal abnormalities, learning disabilities	autosomal dominant	verbal disabilities
Velo-cardial-facial	autosomal dominant	abstraction visual motor deficits
Tourette	possible autosomal dominant	reading disability learning disabilities
Phenylketonuria (treated)	autosomal recessive	learning disabilities, neuropsychological deficits
Aarskog	X-linked recessive	learning disabilities and dyslexia
Lesch-Nyhan	X-linked recessive	expressive language deficits, dysarthria
Cleft lip and palate	multifactorial	sensory-integration deficits
Fragile X, X-linked mental retardation	X-linked recessive	verbal apraxia in some
45 X (Turner syndrome)	chromosomal	spatial, numerical, subtle language and attention deficits
47,XYY	chromosomal	slight depression of verbal IQ
47,XXY	chromosomal	language delay, depressed verbal IQ, dysphasia, dyslexia
Trisomy 9p	chromosomal	disproportionate language delays
18p-	chromosomal	disproportionate expressive language delays

the mode of that action might be. Several strategies have been developed in attempts to identify genetic effects and to estimate their relative importance. These fall into three primary categories: family studies, twin studies, and adoption studies; each has advantages and limitations.

Family Studies

In family studies, the trait in question is evaluated in family members, and the results are compared with the expectations of a genetic model. In the case of dichotomous variables, simple segregation analysis can be used to see if the transmission of the trait in families is consistent with the requirements of Mendelian inheritance. For example, if a trait occurs in several siblings in unrelated families, and the researcher wishes to determine if it could be due to an autosomal recessive gene, the number of affected sibs in each family would be tabulated and compared to the number of unaffected sibs with appropriate adjustment for ascertainment biases. If the proportion of affected sibs is not significantly different from 25%, the hypothesis of recessive inheritance cannot be rejected. Dominant inheritance would be tested similarly, with 50% of at-risk individuals expected to be affected. Segregation analysis, then, can identify the most likely mode of inheritance of a dichotomous trait.

Most behavioral traits, however, are not dichotomous but are measured quantitatively. If segregation analysis is to be used, the variable may be dichotomized artificially with cut-off points established to define affected and unaffected individuals. For some continuous variables, such as test scores, this would be inappropriate; and the correlations between various family members are examined instead. The correlations between family members should be proportional to their degree of realtionship, which reflects the average proportion of genes they have in common. The correlation between siblings or between parents and children should average 0.50, whereas the correlation between grandparents and grandchildren, or aunts/uncles and nieces/nephews, should be approximately 0.25; and correlations between cousins should be around 0.125. Environmental influences may alter the exact correlations, but they should remain in those proportions. Although such results would not prove a genetic influence, and cannot identify a mode of inheritance, the precision of these relationships would be unusual in strictly environmentally influenced traits.

Family studies, then, can give supportive evidence for genetic influences; but since environmental influences are also present, they cannot constitute proof of gene action. (The exception to this, linkage analysis, which can identify major gene effects, will be discussed later in this chapter. Its application in behavior genetics research thus far has been limited.) Two other types of studies attempt to control for environmental influences: twin studies attempt to hold between-twin family environment constant and look for genetically produced variation, and adoption studies remove common environment and look for the persistence of genetic effects.

Twin Studies

Identical, monozygotic (MZ), twins are unique in that they share both genes and family environment. Fraternal, dizygotic (DZ), twins share a common environment but are no more alike genetically than siblings. Thus, by comparing MZ and like-sexed DZ twins, the researcher is theoretically assessing genetic effects. (This assumes that the researcher actually knows the zygosity of the twins. This must be confirmed and is usually done by examination of fetal membranes and/or blood typing.)

In the case of dichotomous variables, the concordance rates are compared. Monozygotic twins would be expected to be 100% concordant for a genetically determined trait, that is, either both twins would mainfest the trait or neither would have it. DZ twins would be expected to be alike only 50% of the time for a dominant trait, 25% of the time for a recessive trait, and around 5% of the time for a multifactorial trait (depending upon its particular recurrence risk). For a continuous quantitative trait, correlations between twins can be used. Monozygotic twins would be expected to have a correlation of 1.0, while the DZ correlation should be 0.50. In practice, however, these absolute expectations are not reached, indicating that environmental effects still exist. The relative proportions should still be maintained since these environmental effects should be independent of zygosity. Thus, if MZ twins have significantly higher concordances or correlations than DZ twins, genetic influence is supported.

Twin studies have been criticized primarily on two points. Some studies have suffered from ascertainment biases in which concordant, affected monozygotic twins are more likely to be ascertained. The analysis must also take into account whether the twin pair was ascertained because one twin was affected by the trait being tested or if they were ascertained because they were twins, and then evaluated for the trait. Unfortunately, many studies appear to be combinations of the two. The other criticism, which has impact upon the methodology itself, is that the environments of MZ twins may not be the same as those of DZ twins. Recent studies, however, have not supported the contention that differential treatment of MZ twins contributes to any significant extent to overall MZ-DZ differences in cognitive traits (Vandenberg & Wilson, 1979). (See also DeFries & Plomin, 1978, or Fuller & Thompson, 1978, for reviews of this issue.)

Adoption Studies

Adoption studies offer the greatest potential for determining whether a behavioral trait has a significant genetic influence. With such studies one has the opportunity to separate genetic influences from the environment that the family provides. These studies have been most helpful in determining that schizophrenia involves genetic susceptibility and is not just produced by being around a schizophrenic parent. Similar studies have been done with intelligence test scores, as will be discussed; and the methodology promises to be very useful in the study of learning disabilities.

Adoption studies *ideally* involve children adopted in infancy, and information should be available on both of the biological parents and both of the adoptive parents as well as on the adoptive and natural children in the family. There should also be a well-matched control group of nonadoptive families to get an idea of the expected family patterns. Other variables that need to be considered include selective placement of children, particularly if attempts are made to match biological and adoptive parents or if adoptive parents are screened so that they are more similar than nonadoptive families. DeFries and Plomin (1978) have outlined these requirements in greater detail.

Families may be ascertained either through the biological parent or through the adopted child. In the former case, individuals are sought who have relinquished a child for adoption, and the trait in question is evaluated. The adopted child and its adoptive family are then sought, and these individuals are similarly evaluated. In the latter case, adopted probands are ascertained, and the trait is evaluated in their biological and adoptive families. In both cases it is useful to have unaffected control adoptive families, ascertained in the same manner, as well as the nonadaptive control families mentioned above. If a trait is genetically influenced, one would expect significantly more resemblance between individuals who are biologically related than between those who share only common environments.

Often, of course, the ideal criteria are not met. The biological father has rarely been included in a study; data from the mother alone have been used. As DeFries and Plomin (1978) have pointed out, this can lead to overestimation of genetic influences if there is assortative mating (nonrandom mating with respect to the variable in question); and this has been detected in the studies of cognitive ability in which it has been assessed. Other studies have only had information on the adoptive or the biological parents, with comparisons to control families or natural siblings. These shortcomings do not negate the significance of such studies as long as the limitations are taken into account. A study may, for example, indicate that a given trait is frequently seen in the natural parents of affected children in nonadoptive homes but that the adoptive parents of affected children are themselves affected no more frequently than the natural parents of unaffected children. Although supportive of a genetic influence, the study is not complete since the incidence of the trait in the biological parents of the affected adoptees is not known. The results would demonstrate, however, that environment alone is not sufficient to produce the trait and that a genetic hypothesis could explain the results.

When properly designed, adoption studies can effectively separate genetic from environmental influences; and for many behavioral traits, adoption studies may be the only way to resolve the nature-nurture argument.

Heritability and Other Statistical Analyses

Family and twin studies can be used to get an estimate of a parameter termed heritability, designated h^2. Heritability refers, broadly, to the proportion of the variance in a trait that is due to genetic influences. Heritability, in the narrower sense, in which it is more commonly used, however, refers only to the contribution of additive (polygenic) effects to the variance. The derivations of these statistics are beyond the scope of this chapter and may be found in any behavior genetics text. The important point to be made is that heritability is a statistic that describes only the population being studied. It is not an estimate of some universal genetic influence; that is, it cannot be generalized to any other population; and increasing the sample size of a study does not produce a more "accurate" parameter. As such, it would be incorrect to interpret an h^2 of 0.80 as meaning that 80% of a trait is determined genetically. Rather, it would mean that in that study 80% of the observed variance could be attributed to additive genetic effects. If many studies obtain similarly high estimates of h^2, the presence of genetic influences could be suspected, and other studies could be designed to test for them.

Such hypothesis testing often involves sophisticated statistical analyses, including path analysis, that have the ability to take many different genetic and environmental influences into account. In any study evaluating such interactive models, the results are only as good as the model; and the possibility that another model could also explain the data must be considered. Again, consistent refusal by researchers to reject genetic hypotheses while rejecting strictly environmental models indicates the need for further research into possible genetic mechanisms.

GENETIC INFLUENCES ON COGNITIVE ABILITIES

Research regarding the genetic influences on cognitive ability has been in existence since the turn of the century and has consistently demonstrated a genetic component. This research was primarily concerned with determining how much of the variability in cognitive ability was contributed by genetic factors. With the statistical and technical methods currently being developed, we can anticipate the discovery of what these genetic influences are and how they interact with surrounding factors to produce their effects.

Normal Variation in Cognitive Abilities

Certainly the most studied behavioral variable is the IQ score, and as such it can provide a model for the study of other cognitive variables. Family studies have produced correlations close to what would be expected for degree of relationship, and twin studies have consistently produced higher correlations between MZ twins than for DZ twins. (See Fuller & Thompson, 1978 for a review of both types of studies.) In the compilation of twin studies by Fuller and Thompson, for example, the correlations in IQ scores between MZ twins have ranged from 0.75 to 0.92, whereas the correlations between DZ twins were between 0.39 to 0.73. The mean difference in the correlations was 0.25, with a range of 0.15 to 0.36. Heritability estimates for IQ have ranged from 0.49 to 0.80, with figures between 0.50 to 0.70 more common in recent studies.

Adoption studies are probably the most informative in the study of intelligence, and the studies that come closest to the ideal design have demonstrated patterns of correlations supporting a genetic influence. As summarized by Loehlin (1980), the correlations between an adopted child and his biological parents in three such studies averaged 0.36 (range 0.23 to 0.42), whereas the mean correlation between the adopted child and his adopted parents was 0.16 (range 0.09 to 0.23). The mean difference in the correlation between biological and adoptive parents was 0.20 (range 0.04 to 0.32). Loehlin also noted that seven adoption studies, all indicating genetic influences, had been published after the well-known paper by Kamin (1974), which had argued that there was no evidence for genetic influence on intelligence.

The effects of environment on IQ cannot be ignored and, in fact, can be measured very nicely using genetic paradigms. The adoptive studies suggest that adoptive siblings (unrelated children in the same family environment) have higher correlations at a young age than they do when ascertained at an older age. Path analysis is also able to estimate environmental influences. For example, although studies by Rao and Morton (1978) indicated that the relative variance due to inherited factors is greater than that due to family environment (0.689 as compared to 0.157), another study including the same authors demonstrated that an IQ difference of 15 points between black and white students could be reduced to a nonsignificant 3 points when the effect of social class was controlled (Rao, Morton, Elston, & Yee, 1977).

Specific cognitive abilities including verbal, spatial, perceptual, and memory measures have also been studied. Such abilities are particularly relevant to the present discussion since they are often measured in learning disability evaluations, with the assumption that they contribute to learning ability. DeFries and colleagues (1979) and Parks and colleagues (1978) have demonstrated significant parent-offspring and sib-sib resemblances, presumably mediated by genetic and environmental factors in these specific cognitive abilities. In the DeFries and colleagues study, regression coefficients averaged 0.50 for residents of Hawaii who were of European descent and 0.35 for those of Japanese descent. The regression coefficient of midchild on midparent (i.e., the mean value for children in the family regressed upon the mean of their parents) is usually taken as an estimate of heritability. However, in this study, because of the presence of between-family environmental influences, this was taken to be a measure of familiality only. The Korean study by Park and colleagues found somewhat higher regression coefficients due, perhaps, to greater assortative mating, Interestingly, twin studies have produced comparable heritabilities. Using path analysis techniques, Salzano and Rao (1976) found that of eight apti-tude tests (e.g., verbal reasoning, abstract reasoning, spatial relationships, etc.), heritability values were greater than 0.50 for five of the tests. Similarly, a twin and half-sib study of perceptual speed produced a heritability of 0.76 (Rose, Miller, & Fulker, 1981).

Cognitive abilities in general, including IQ, are presumed to be inherited in a multifactorial manner, with many genes interacting with environment to produce the normal distribution of performance. If some specific cognitive abilities are determined independently, it is possible that an individual could have a deficit in one such skill, that is, perform at the low end of that particular distribution, which would be at variance with his abilities in other cognitive skills. If the specific skill is necessary for learn-ing, that deficit could show up as a learning disability. Further, if that skill is geneticallly influenced such a deficit could be inherited. Skills deter-mined by a multifactorial threshold mechanism may be especially involved in learning disabilities because they would tend to be present in an all-or-none fashion. In addition, it is quite possible that some of the genes influencing a cognitive trait have greater effects than others, so that single gene effects might be detectable in an overall background of mul-tifactorial influences.

The variation in the ability to perceive spatial relationships is a good example of a cognitive trait that has been thought to involve a single gene. Numerous studies have reported that females performed more poorly than males on tests of spatial relationships, and it has been suggested that this is due to an X-linked recessive gene with a positive influence on spatial abilities (Bock & Kolakowski, 1973; Stafford, 1961). Although the presence of a single X-linked gene has not been supported (DeFries et al., 1979; Loehlin, Sharan, & Jacoby, 1978), there is support for an autosomal domi-nant gene with decreased penetrance in females (Fain, 1976). Presumably, environmental factors could influence penetrance. The more general consideration of male-female differences in spatial and temporal abilities, and their contribution to learning disabilities, is still a controversial topic.

In further consideration of the possibility of influence by major genes, Childs (1972) suggested that learning disabilities should be viewed in the same way that mental retardation is seen with respect to overall distribution of intelligence; that is, IQ scores at the lower end of the distribution can be attributed to multiple genetic and environmental factors, but there will also be a contribution from single major genes defining specific syndromes such as tuberous sclerosis or phenylketonuria. The presence of these genes produces the often observed "bump" at the tail end of the distribution of intelligence. In the same way, a single deleterious gene affecting a given cognitive ability may produce a specific syndrome of learning disability.

Specific Learning Disabilities

Most genetic studies of learning disabilities have dealt with specific reading disability (dyslexia). Both family studies and twin studies have been done and have supported a genetic component. Family studies have shown an increasing frequency of reading disability in the families of reading disabled children, and several modes of inheritance have been proposed. However, just as no *one*, unitary etiology has been identified for reading disability, no one mode of inheritance explains all cases, no one mode of inheritance explains all cases. Twin studies have consistently indicated greater concordance between MZ than DZ twins. Since complete reviews of this literature have been reported elsewhere (Finucci, 1978; Herschel, 1978), only the more recent developments will be discussed here.

The most important conclusion to come out of the genetic studies is that reading disability itself is a heterogeneous classification, not surprisingly, with heterogeneous genetic influences. The heterogeneity is important in considering comparative studies of small samples of good and poor readers. If the poor readers have different etiologies for their disabilities, efforts to find common deficits are certainly hampered, are perhaps futile, and may even be misleading. The significance of the genetic influences is that they may give us clues to the underlying biologic causes of reading disability.

The Colorado Family Reading Study is the largest project to date designed to investigate the genetics of reading disability. One hundred twenty-five disabled readers and their families were matched with 125 control families, and all were given an extensive battery of achievement and aptitude tests. By showing an increased incidence of similar cognitive deficits in families of disabled readers, these studies have clearly demonstrated the familial nature of specific reading disability with particular support for a deficit in verbal processing (Decker & DeFries, 1980; DeFries et al., 1979). The data as a whole support the multifactorial mode of inheritance; but because their population was a random sample of disabled readers, it is most likely heterogeneous, which could mask a single-gene effect. There may even be several modes of inheritance. As previously alluded to, heterogeneity would not be surprising in a process as complicated as reading. In recognition of this probability, Lewitter, DeFries, and Elston, 1980) analyzed this data in subsets determined by sex of the proband and severity of the disorder. The data from families with a female proband were compatible with autosomal recessive inheritance, whereas the other groups apparently were still heterogeneous. Further studies were designed to separate these groups by cognitive profiles (Decker & DeFries, 1981). Using factor analysis of the total battery, three "ability dimensions" were identified, and four subgroups of disabled readers were defined according to their abilities in the three areas. The hope was that the subgroups would reveal distinct modes of inheritance. Unfortunately, there was no consistency in subgroup classification between parents and their children, and only one subtype showed consistency among siblings. This particular subtype showed the least deficit in the nonreading ability factors.

Finucci (1978), Childs and Finucci (1979), and Omenn and Weber (1978) have utilized spelling error types as a basis for subclassification of dyslexics. This may be a more direct measure of disability than other achievement and aptitude tests. All roughly followed the method of Boder (1973) in classifying errors as dysphonetic (auditory) or phonetic (visual). Childs and Finucci found that the proportion of dysphonetic errors tended to be consistent within families; and Omenn and Weber, who classified subjects as auditory, visual, or mixed, also found intrafamilial consistency of classification. Pedigree inspection in both studies, regardless of subtype, suggested genetic heterogeneity. Childs and Finucci made the interesting observation that reading scores of siblings and probands with severe reading disability tended to show wide variation, whereas the scores of siblings of mildly affected probands show less variability. This would be expected if single gene effects are segregating in the sibships of some of the severely affected probands.

Our own studies have been directed at the identification of a single major gene influencing dyslexia. The studies cited above, and others (Brewer, 1963; Hallgren, 1950; Zahalkova, Vrzal, & Kloboukova, 1972), have suggested that an autosomal dominant gene may exist but without a biological or behavioral marker. This cannot, however, be proven in population studies. Our approach has been to specifically ascertain families consistent with autosomal dominant transmission of dyslexia (e.g., a three generation history on one side of the family) and to use linkage analysis to detect a single gene.

Two genes are said to be linked when they are located close together on the same chromosome and, consequently, tend to be inherited together. Recall that, otherwise, genes sort independently as in the traits in Mendel's peas. The deviation of linked genes from random assortment can be detected by statistical analysis of family pedigree. The significance of such deviation is measured by the *lod* score, which is the *lo*g of the *od*ds of likelihood of linkage. The lod score from individual families can be summed, and linkage is accepted if two genes give a total lod score greater than 3. This is roughly equivalent to a significance level of 0.001.

If a trait can be shown to be linked to a known gene, it is assumed that the unknown trait is influenced by a major gene on the same chromosome as the known gene (Haseman & Elston, 1972). In other words, if the transmission of dyslexia was found to be linked to the transmission of a known genetic trait, it could be concluded that a single gene influencing dyslexia does exist.

We have ascertained and tested 13 families (104 individuals) with pedigrees compatible with dominant inheritance. Initial studies included analysis of over 20 blood group and red cell enzyme genes, as well as chromosomal staining variants. These staining variants (heteromorphisms), seen with quinacrine or centromeric banding techniques, are inherited and are not clinically significant. They are useful genetic markers, however, and linkage studies in 9 of the families have given us a lod score of 3.241 between dyslexia and heteromorphisms of chromosome 15 (Smith, Kimberling, Pennington, & Lubs, 1983). This implies that a gene influencing dyslexia is on chromosome 15. It must be noted that different families had different heteromorphisms of the 15s, so that the variations themselves were in no way causally related to the dyslexia.

This finding, if confirmed, could have specific clinical and research applications. In suitably large families, the particular chromosome 15 segregating with the dyslexia could be identified, and any young prereading children inheriting that chromosome would be known to be at high risk of developing reading disability. Appropriate remediation could be initiated without delay. From a research standpoint, families showing linkage of dyslexia to chromosome 15 would represent a homogeneous subgroup ideal for research into both the biological mechanism and the specific cognitive deficit underlying their disability. Our own research using neuropsychological testing has not revealed any striking deficits in our population of dyslexics but does suggest a mild problem with word retrieval and/or auditory verbal short-term memory.

These genetic studies have been similar to practically every other study of reading disability in that they show a preponderance of males. Our own studies, and those of Childs and Finucci (1979), have indicated that males are more severely affected, so ascertainment bias may be partially responsible. The multifactorial model with lower thresholds for males does not appear to be appropriate, because neither study fulfilled the other predictions of this model.

Although the terms "minimal brain dysfunction," "hyperactivity," "learning disabled," and "dyslexia" have at times been used interchangeably, a family study by Singer, Stewart, and Pulaski (1981) has demonstrated that hyperactivity and specific reading disability are distinct in their cognitive profiles and family characteristics. Reading disability was found more frequently in the families of reading disabled probands, whereas hyperactivity was found more frequently in families of hyperactive probands. Additionally, higher rates of psychopathology were reported in the relatives of hyperactive children. This is somewhat similar to the findings in adoption studies by Morrison and Stewart (1973), Cantwell (1975), and Cadoret and Gath (1978). These studies demonstrated greater concordance for hyperactivity between adoptees and their biological families than their foster families, suggesting a genetic component. These studies also found an association with alcoholism. While this may suggest a pleiotropic genetic effect, a further study by Stewart, deBlois, and Cummings (1980) was not able to confirm association between specific psychiatric disorders or alcoholism in the families of hyperactive children. They point out the necessity of using families of children with other psychiatric diagnoses as controls and the need for a standard definition of hyperactivity. Further, an additional adoption study by Bohman and Sigvardsson (1980) did not support the findings of the earlier studies. Thus, the difficulties in defining and isolating hyperactivity makes elucidation of the genetic influences, if any, even more difficult than it has been for reading disability. Similarly, genetic studies of other types of learning disabilities will depend upon the development of reliable diagnostic methods and, hopefully, of some physiologic markers to define specific etiologic subgroups.

No discussion of reading disability would be complete without at least some mention of cerebral lateralization, particularly since lateralization would be expected to be subject to genetic influences. Orton, in 1925, observed a higher frequency of left-handedness and mixed dominance in dyslexics. He proposed that this reflected a lack of dominance of one cerebral hemisphere over the other, so that the two halves of the brain presented conflicting mirror-images of letters and words. Further studies have shown that visual-perceptual problems are not a significant cause of reading disability (Benton, 1975; Vellutino, 1979), and left-handedness or mixed dominance is not sufficient to cause dyslexia. Still, attempts to relate specific disabilities in dyslexics to alterations in hemispheric specialization for language have persisted. Although the earlier literature is quite confusing due to differences in tasks and measures of lateralization, some interesting concepts are emerging. Several studies have suggested that dyslexics show deficits in particular "left hemisphere" temporal processing abilities with comparative strengths in "right hemispheric" spatial strategies (Witelson, 1977). Gordon (1980) found that dyslexics and their nondyslexic relatives showed a predominantly "right hemispheric" cognitive style and suggested that this might represent a genetic predisposition for dyslexia. Galaburda and Kemper (1979) demonstrated microscopic anatomic abnormalities of the brain localized to a specific portion of the left hemisphere in the brain of an adult dyslexic with dyslexic relatives. Geschwind and Behan (1982) have combined these observations with their own regarding association of dyslexia with left-handedness, autoimmune disorders, and the prevalence of male dyslexics to develop an elaborate hypothesis. According to their formulation, development of laterality is influenced by testosterone, a male sex hormone. Inappropriate levels could result in left-handedness or even abnormal cerebral organization. Additionally, testosterone influences the developing thymus and thus, the immune system. The B_2 microglobulin gene is thought to influence both the immune system and male sexual development, so it and neighboring genes are likely candidates for genetic mediators. Interestingly, the B_2 microglobulin gene is on chromosome 15 (Goodfellow, Jones, Van Heyningen, Solomon, & Bobrow, 1975).

The above hypothesis is one example of how a genetic influence on reading disability could be mediated. There are many approaches to the study of cerebral organization, including refinement of tasks designed to tap specific processes and new techniques for examining anatomic or physiologic differences. In addition to the histologic work of Galaburda and Kemper, cited above, other studies have utilized CT scanning, mapping of electrical activity through EEG or magnetic methods, or observation of metabolic activity through positron emission tomography. These methods can all be effective probes for genetically influenced alterations in development.

Genetic influences may also be basically biochemical in nature. In an intriguing preliminary study, Kripke, Lynn, Madsen, and Gay (1982) described an apparent autosomal dominant syndrome of learning disability, fatigue (particularly when reading), and clumsiness, which showed improvement with small doses of MSG. The study was carefully designed but, unfortunately, the number of subjects was small and further family studies were not reported. The authors were careful to point out that this appears to be a specific disorder that would affect only a small proportion of the learning-disabled population. Other research advances include epidemiologic studies, such as those being conducted by Finucci and Childs, that will be valuable in formulating a practical definition for specific reading disability in children and adults and in describing the natural history of these disorders.

Recognition of the long-term effects is important in designing appropriate remediation and in the understanding of the underlying processes that are affected. As the means for determining the phenotypes are perfected, so are our abilities to analyze the genotypes. Statistical methods of analysis, including complex segregation analysis and path analysis, are being used to detect different genetic effects within a hetergeneous population. Linkage analysis will be used more often with the development of new restriction enzyme length polymorphisms. These provide many easily detectable landmarks to be traced, along with a given cognitive variable, through a family. If the variable is influenced by a single major gene, the chances are great that linkage with one of these landmarks will be detected. Finally, the process of gene isolation and sequencing will ultimately permit geneticists to actually "read" the genes they are studying.

CLINICAL IMPLICATIONS

With the multitude of new genetic syndromes being described, it is difficult to list every feature indicative of a genetic problem, but certain characteristics that should raise suspicion can be covered. Any child with unexplained mental retardation or major birth defect merits a genetic evaluation, but such children comprise a small part of all those with genetic syndromes. In a child with learning disabilities, findings that would suggest a genetic syndrome would include problems such as congenital heart or kidney disease, short stature or skeletal problems, neuromuscular problems, hand abnormalities, or distinctive facial features that do not resemble those of other family members. The presence of several defects in different systems is particularly suggestive. Additionally, a positive family history showing segregation of a unique constellation of findings may represent a syndrome. Knowledge that the parents are related would raise the possibility of a recessive disorder. Any sign of neurological deterioration should be followed up immediately since a biochemical defect may be responsible.

Chromosomal analysis has generally been thought to be indicated in any child with two or more major defects in early embryogenesis, but more recent studies of sex-chromosome abnormalities or very small chromosomal aberrations have indicated that these criteria are overly restrictive. It may be that the true contribution of genetic and particularly of chromosomal abnormalities to learning disabilities will be found only by screening this population, which may not routinely come to the attention of a geneticist. Indeed, Friedrich, Dalby, Stachelin-Jensen, and Bruun-Peterson (1982) propose that chromosomal studies be done on any child with unexplained language problems. It should also be noted that babies with certain genetic problems are particularly susceptible to neonatal difficulties, so the often-cited "birth trauma" may actually be a symptom of a genetic problem rather than a nongenetic etiology for a learning disability.

Certainly not all children fitting the above criteria will have genetic syndromes, and many will remain unexplained after a thorough genetic evaluation. There are, however, several advantages to detection of a genetic syndrome. As mentioned above, recognition that a child is at risk for learning disabilities can facilitate early detection and appropriate remediation. It can also call a halt to unnecessary medical evaluations and may stimulate diagnosis and treatment for medical problems known to be associated with the syndrome. In the same manner, searches for underlying emotional problems, with concomitant blame on parental inadequacy, can be terminated and redirected towards helping families cope with the frustrations of a learning-disabled child. And finally, the identification of a genetic syndrome and delineation of the particular problems that accompany it can lead to development of specific methods of remediation based on the pathogenesis of the syndrome itself.

In what follows we will attempt to sketch out the various levels of evaluation that could occur in the work-up of a child suspected of a learning disability and how information relevant to possible genetic factors can be utilized by professionals at various levels. At the outset, it is important to emphasize that *clinical* use of genetic information in learning disability is in its infancy and that in most cases of learning disability a conclusive etiology, whether genetic or otherwise, will not be found. Nonetheless, we have enough information from research at this point to be helpful in the case of *some* learning disabilities. If utilized appropriately, this information can aid in the diagnosis and treatment of learning-disabled children.

Most children with a learning disability are initially identified by a classroom teacher or a parent. Such children are usually referred to the school's special education team, which in many schools includes a school psychologist, a school nurse practitioner, a speech and language pathologist, and, frequently, an occupational or physical therapist. An evaluation by such a team can usually determine whether a learning disability is present; such an evaluation can also provide fairly detailed information about a child's ability strengths and weaknesses and about his or her social and emotional adjustment at school.

At this primary level of evaluation, we would recommend that a preliminary genetic history, especially for learning problems in other family members, be taken. If such a history is found, a referral to a genetics clinic, a developmental evaluation clinic, or a pediatrician (depending on what services are available) would be appropriate. A second recommendation that grows out of our research on genetically-influenced learning disabilities is that the school be sensitive to the possibility of fairly *subtle* learning disabilities, especially in bright children. In our studies of families with three generations of affected relatives who showed evidence of genetic linkage, some of the dyslexic children were not identified by their schools because they did not meet the school's criteria for a learning disability (e.g., they were not two years behind grade level). Yet these children certainly had a deficit in reading and spelling skills that was affecting their overall academic progress. In such subtle cases, the presence of a positive family history provides additional evidence that the child does have a learning disability and needs professional intervention. A third point, perhaps too obvious to mention, is that the presence of socioemotional or behavioral problems in the child being evaluated does *not* rule out a primary learning disability. Many learning-disabled children have secondary emotional or behavioral problems *because* they have learning difficulties. Making a differential diagnosis between these possibilities frequently requires consultation with mental health professionals who have specific training in sorting out the relative contribution of ability versus emotional factors to a child's school adjustment.

Once a child with a learning disability is referred outside the school, a work-up of possible genetic factors requires the interaction of a team of professionals, including a pediatrician, a medical geneticist, and a child psychologist with training in child development or a child neuropsychologist. This core team may later decide referrals to other specialists are needed.

This team strives to answer two questions: What is the diagnosis? Is it inherited? The diagnostic process begins with the medical history, including the pregnancy history, and the physical examination. The historical information should include notation of any complications or implications or exposures to harmful drugs or viruses in pregnancy, difficulties at the time of birth, age of attainment of developmental milestones, and any serious illness, fever, or trauma in childhood, in addition to a complete account of the presenting complaint.

For the team to understand the presenting complaint, it is first important to get a clear picture of which academic skills the child finds difficult. In the area of reading, comprehension should be treated separately from decoding skills because, in some learning-disabled children (e.g., specific dyslexia), there can be a significant disparity between these two aspects of reading. It is also important to ask about the child's handwriting, as well as his or her skill at written language in general. Finally, it is also important to inquire about a child's planning and organizational skills because some children with good basic academic skills nonetheless do poorly at school because they are deficient in the conceptual skills necessary for planning and organizing more complex assignments.

A second crucial step in understanding the presenting complaint is getting an accurate school history beginning with preschool or kindergarten. Both parental reports and school records need to be utilized in reconstructing *when* the child's problems first appeared and in *what* ability areas. Most children with specific learning disabilities have fairly distinctive school histories. For instance, the specific dyslexic child almost always has trouble with early reading instruction, especially phonics; and such problems are nearly always evident in first grade or even in kindergarten. In contrast, children with deficits in conceptual and organizational skills may have problems noted in the preschool period, such as delays in language development. In some learning-disabled children, however, there are no obvious precursors in the preschool period.

In summary, to properly understand the presenting complaint, the diagnostician should obtain a clear and coherent picture of both its current and its earlier manifestations.

As part of the genetic evaluation, a thorough family history is taken, with construction of a pedigree including at least third-degree relatives (grandparents, aunts, uncles, cousins). Each person is discussed separately and pertinent medical or historical information is noted. In the case of learning disabilities, questions about school progress, reading and letter-writing habits, and occupation may help reveal problems in the older generations, where actual diagnosis of learning disabilities would be rare. With at least some types of reading disability, spelling problems persist into adulthood even when reading has improved. In practice, it is rarely possible to obtain reliable information beyond the generation of the grandparents. As in any genetic evaluation, secondhand information that appears to be relevant must be further examined either by personal evaluation or requests for records.

A careful physical examination will sometimes reveal a pattern of findings consistent with a genetic syndrome. These findings may be quite subtle, as is evident in some of the descriptions of syndromes. The combination of historical information and the physical evaluation may suggest further studies, either evaluations by other professionals (neurologists, cardiologists, audiologists) or laboratory tests such as chromosome or biochemical studies. Records of previous psychological evaluations should be studied and further testing ordered if needed. A literature search may be required. All of the information is then put together to see if a diagnosis can be made.

The diagnosis will often carry with it the knowledge of the mode of inheritance. In some syndromes, however, the mode of inheritance is unclear or it may be different in different families, so inspection of the pedigree is necessary. Particularly in dominant traits with wide variation, seemingly unrelated signs may be seen in relatives. Occasionally, the findings of the team may not fit into a known diagnostic category but the family history may demonstrate a pattern of inheritance, such as when siblings are affected, parental consanguinity suggests a recessive trait, or several generations are affected in a dominant fashion. Counseling is given cautiously, and the case is reported to colleagues to see if similar families have been found. All too often, however, the physical findings do not fit a recognized pattern or are completely normal, and the family history is irregular or negative.

The genetic counseling process goes beyond these questions of diagnosis and recurrence risk. A trained genetic counselor, preferably certified by the American Board of Medical Genetics, sees genetics counseling as follows:

> a communication process which deals with the human problems associated with the occurrence, or risk of occurrence, of a genetic disorder in a family. This process involves an attempt by one or more trained persons to help the individual or family to (1) comprehend the medical facts, including the diagnosis, probable course of the disorder, and the available management; (2) appreciate the way heredity contributes to the disorder, and the risk of recurrence in specified relatives; (3) understand the alternatives for dealing with the risk of recurrence; (4) choose the course of action which seems appropriate in view of their risk, their family goals, and their ethical and religious standards, and to act in accordance with that decision; and (5) to make the best possible adjustment to the disorder in an affected family member and/or to the risk of recurrence of that disorder. (Ad Hoc Committee on Genetic Counseling, 1975, pp. 240–241)

This is a nondirective interaction and a conscientious counselor will strive to offer information and support to help families to make their own decisions rather than advising them on such matters as whether or not they should have children. The counselor must also be sensitive to the emotional and ego-threatening aspects of being told that "defective genes" are in one's family and work to defuse feelings of inadequacy or guilt. It may be necessary to have second sessions with a family to work through the parents' reaction to the diagnostic information and to make sure their emotional reactions haven't distorted the diagnostic information or its implications.

The above process of diagnosis illustrates the problems inherent in the genetic evaluation of children with a specific learning disability, especially when there is no recognizable genetic syndrome or environmental cause. A positive family history for similar problems can suggest a genetic contribution, but at this point it would be premature to assign it a particular mode of inheritance to a given family based on a few affected individuals. An affected father and son could represent multifactorial inheritance just as easily as dominant, but there would be great differences in the recurrence risks between these two possibilities. In the same way, several children in a family with unaffected parents could represent recessive or multifactorial inheritance. On the other hand, a large pedigree with many affected individuals in several generations should suggest that the children of an affected individual from that family may run a risk as high as 50%.

The inability to designate an exact mode of inheritance does not detract from the value of recognizing a genetic contribution to a learning disability in a family. The presence of a positive family history in a child with unexplained difficulties in school should prompt an immediate evaluation for learning disabilities. If a learning disability is diagnosed, this diagnosis can help the parents and educators realize that the child is not lazy, immature, retarded, or "brain damaged" so that the child is not stigmatized by a misleading label. Parents can be alerted to watch for signs in a younger child who may be at an increased risk for learning disabilities, so that proper remediation can be instituted. We have sometimes found that the recognition of a genetic factor can help the child cope with his problems because he is not unique in his family. In our clinical work with learning-disabled children, we have sometimes found that parents have not shared with the child the fact that they themselves had similar problems. We strongly encourage the parent to share this information in a supportive way. The diagnosis may also relieve the bewilderment of an affected parent who always wondered why he or she had difficulty with seemingly simple tasks.

Most importantly, finding that a specific learning disability is, or may be, genetic does not imply that it is hopeless. This is an especially important point for teachers who sometimes feel that the presence of an identified medical condition in a child makes him or her qualitatively different from other children who have, in fact, quite similar problems. So it is important for the diagnostic team to complete the evaluation process by providing adequate feedback to the child's teachers so that they will not adopt a hands-off approach once a diagnosis is made. Instead, the results of the evaluation should make the teachers' work easier since the diagnosis will, hopefully, relieve the vague anxiety that surrounds an undiagnosed learning problem and will also provide a more specific focus for information. Individuals with genetically influenced learning disabilities, like most learning-disabled individuals, benefit from specialized instruction and may learn by adulthood to compensate quite well.

Finally, in terms of the future, it would seem that the genetically influenced learning disabilities are ideally suited to research into causes and mechanisms and show great promise for more sophisticated clinical interventions ranging from early diagnosis to the use of microcomputers in remediation. The potential for defining homogeneous subgroups has been discussed above. A better understanding of the cognitive pheontype in a given subgroup would greatly assist in both differential diagnosis and individual remedial instruction. More significantly, just as the genetically produced errors of metabolism are invaluable clues to the elucidation of the biochemical pathways, the unraveling of the genetic influence on reading and their mechanisms will lead to the understanding of the biological bases of the reading process itself.

SUMMARY

The influences of genes on learning disabilities can be seen at several levels. Genes appear to influence the normal variation in cognitive abilities that, if deficient, could result in learning disabilities. In addition, certain genes may have more direct effects in producing a specific disability. Reading disability, in particular, has shown evidence of single gene influences. Families with reading disability have demonstrated similarities in other cognitive characteristics as well. Some genetic syndromes and chromosomal abnormalities also tend to produce characteristic patterns of ability and disability. The complexity of the cognitive processes underlying learning and the resulting heterogeneity among children with learning disabilities is reflected in the many different ways genes can interact with nongenetic factors to influence these processes. Thus, there is evidence for single-gene and multiple-gene effects, and these may be specific to learning or produce other related or unrelated findings.

The identification of these genetic influences can have clinical importance in individual cases, and certainly has significant implications for research. In individual cases, recognition of a genetic susceptibility, even if undefined, can facilitate early diagnosis and identification of at-risk children. As the genetic mechanisms are elucidated, the development of more effective means of remediation can be anticipated. In research, studies proposing to define underlying causes or subtypes of learning disability will be influenced by genetic variables that must be controlled or acknowledged in the research design. Consideration of these variables has heuristic value as well. Hypotheses can be generated around expected differences between groups with different genetic patterns, or they may test genetically mediated factors that may have effects on learning. Study of a genetically homogeneous population would have great potential for identifying the salient characteristics of various learning disabilities and, eventually, their biological bases.

CHAPTER 4

Auditory Dysfunction

Brad W. Friedrich

T he purpose of this chapter is to review the origins and nature of auditory dysfunction in school-age children. Auditory dysfunction may
interfere with the normal process of communication and compromise a
young child's acquisition of speech and language skills. Consequently,
language and communication deficits may influence a child's learning and
educational achievement (Silva, Chalmers, & Stewart, 1986). The sources of
communicative difficulty associated with pathology of the human auditory
system will receive particular emphasis in this chapter. An understanding
of the communicative impact of auditory dysfunction is central to the
development and implementation of programs to optimize the educational
achievement of youngsters with auditory problems.

The framework for this discussion will be provided by a consideration
of the communication channel that exists between a sound source and a
listener. Attention will be centered on the transmission of spoken messages
between a speaker and those structures in the auditory system that are
responsible for the reception and perception of auditory signals. Initially,
the anatomical and physiological bases of auditory dysfunction will be
reviewed. An overview of the structures and functions of both the peripheral and central auditory systems will be provided. Specific sources of
communicative difficulty in auditory dysfunction will be identified. In addi-

This chapter originally appeared as an article by **Brad W. Friedrich** in *Learning Disabilities: An
Interdisciplinary Journal* (Vol. I (6), 63–78, 1982) and was adapted by permission of Grune &
Stratton for inclusion in this *Handbook*.

tion, special emphasis will be placed upon a consideration of the auditory environment and the manner in which it may facilitate or compromise the performance of auditorily-disordered students in the classroom. Both hearing loss and disorders of central auditory processing, which are frequently associated with learning disabilities, will be addressed in this discussion. In addition, specific principles and procedures underlying the audiologist's evaluation of auditory function will be reviewed as appropriate.

THE COMMUNICATION CHANNEL

Figure 4-1 provides a model depicting the communication channel between a speaker or other sound source and those structures in the auditory system that mediate the reception and perception of auditory signals. The model of the communication channel accounts for only the transmission of auditory information *from* a speaker *to* a listener. Thus, the model does not represent a complete system of communication. Such a system would need to take into account the responses of a listener, self-monitoring of spoken messages, the ongoing interchange of auditory information between speaker and listener, and the utilization of additional modes of communication through other sensory channels, among other factors.

THE PERIPHERAL AUDITORY SYSTEM

In order to achieve an understanding of auditory dysfunction and the manner in which it may impact communicatively upon a student, a review of the structure and function of the auditory system is necessary. While a detailed discussion of the anatomy and physiology of the system is impossible in this chapter, an overview designed to provide a basic understanding will

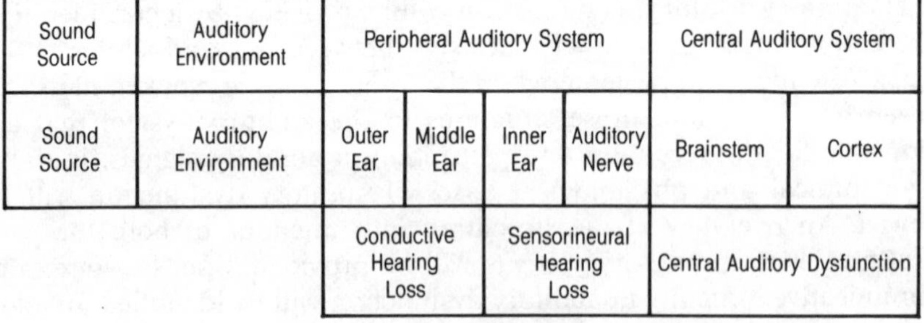

Sound Source	Auditory Environment	Peripheral Auditory System				Central Auditory System	
Sound Source	Auditory Environment	Outer Ear	Middle Ear	Inner Ear	Auditory Nerve	Brainstem	Cortex
		Conductive Hearing Loss		Sensorineural Hearing Loss		Central Auditory Dysfunction	

Figure 4-1.

The communication channel from a sound source through the anatomical structures responsible for the reception and perception of auditory signals.

be provided. (Comprehensive reviews of the auditory system have been provided by Zemlin, 1968; and Durant and Lovrinc, 1977, among others.)

The auditory system is described most easily in terms of its major subdivisions and structures. The ear is a highly specialized mechanism responsible for converting acoustical energy into electrical energy. When sounds are emitted by a speaker or other sound source, they travel through air as acoustical energy. Acoustical energy must be converted ultimately into electrical energy. The electrical form of energy is represented by neural impulses that code an auditory message into a form suitable for the processing and perceptual activities attributed to the central nervous system. In essence, the neural impulses constitute the language of the central nervous system. Effecting this transformation in energy constitutes the basic task of the human ear. The transformation takes place in a series of steps mediated by three major parts of the ear: the outer ear, middle ear, and inner ear.

At the outset, a distinction must be made between the peripheral and central auditory systems. For purposes of this discussion, the peripheral auditory system will be defined as consisting of the outer ear, middle ear, inner ear, and auditory (or VIIIth cranial) nerve. The demarcation of the peripheral and central auditory system is at the synapse in the lower brain stem. As neural impulses travel above the ventral and dorsal cochlear nuclei, they do so within the central auditory nervous system. Figures 4-2

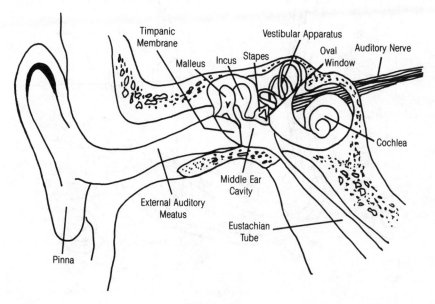

Figure 4-2.

Schematic diagram of the basic subdivisions and structures of the peripheral auditory system.

and 4-3 present schematic diagrams of the peripheral and central auditory systems.

The outer ear is composed of the pinna, or auricle, and the external auditory meatus (canal). The outer ear in man serves primarily as a mechanism for channeling and directing sound to the tympanic membrane, or eardrum.

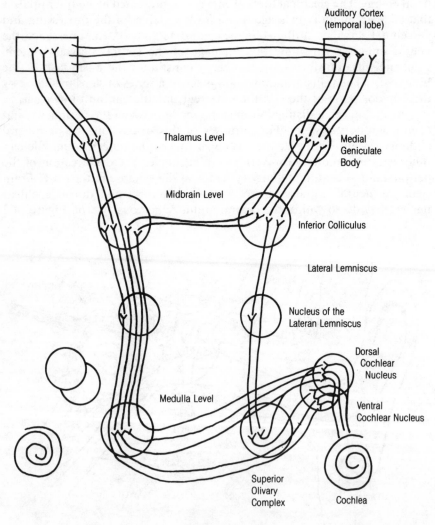

Figure 4-3.
Schematic diagram of the central auditory system, depicting afferent pathways and major way stations.

The tympanic membrane forms the barrier between the outer ear and the middle ear. It is a conically-shaped, translucent structure that is set into complex patterns of vibration when acoustical energy impinges upon it. The tympanic membrane is extraordinarily sensitive to the pressure changes associated with airborne sound waves. As a result, the tympanic membrane converts acoustical energy to mechanical motion. Thus, the first major energy transformation accomplished by the human ear occurs at this point.

The middle ear is an air-filled cavity composed of a number of major landmarks. The most widely known among them are the auditory ossicles. The ossicles are the three smallest bones in the human body. They are known as the malleus, incus, and stapes. The ossicles are the major structures responsible for the transmission of sound energy through the middle ear cavity. The ossicles are suspended within the middle ear space by a rather complex system of ligaments and muscles. The long process of the malleus, known as the manubrium, or handle, is imbedded in the tympanic membrane. The malleus, in turn, articulates directly with the incus, and the incus is attached directly to the stapes. Thus, when the tympanic membrane is set into motion in response to sound, the auditory ossicles are also set into patterns of motion, which are transmitted across the middle ear space to the oval window, which separates the middle and inner ear.

The inner ear, in contrast to the middle ear, is fluid-filled. The middle ear assists in matching the transmission characteristics of air to those of fluid. This is accomplished by two mechanisms. The area of the tympanic membrane is considerably larger than that of the oval window. This difference results in a considerable increase in the effectiveness of sound transmission to the inner ear since the sound energy is concentrated upon the smaller surface area of the oval window. In addition, the ossicles function, in part, as a lever and restore some of the sound energy that would be lost were sound to impinge directly upon the inner ear fluid. These factors constitute the middle ear transformer action.

The inner ear is composed of the vestibular apparatus and the auditory apparatus known as the cochlea. Only the latter concern us in this discussion. The cochlea is the sensory receptor for hearing. It is responsible for the conversion of sound delivered from the middle ear into a series of electrical discharges that can be transmitted via the neural pathways. Thus, it is responsible for the final conversion of sound to electrical energy. The cochlea is located in the temporal bone of the cranium. It is an elogated structure which is coiled into a spiral. As noted above, the cochlea is fluid-filled. Thus, the mechanical movement of the stapes is delivered to the fluids of the cochlea by way of the oval window. A hydromechanical disturbance results in the fluid. In essence, waves which travel through the membranous structure of the inner ear are set up within the fluid. These waves serve to displace cilia, which project from the cochlea's highly structured hair cells.

The hair cells, which number in the thousands, are the sensory cells of audition. An electrochemical process occurs within the hair cells in response to mechanical deformation of the cilia. This activity results in a transmission of chemicals across the synapse between the hair cells and the neurons of the auditory nerve. Thus, in turn, may lead to the firing of neural impulses. Hence, the final conversion of sound to electrical energy is complete. Obviously, the cochlea is a highly specialized and intricate structure. This discussion has been no more than a brief summary of the basic process which takes place in the inner ear. No attempt has been made to address the detailed anatomy or intricate physiological processes of this structure.

The Central Auditory System

The central auditory nervous system begins at the root of the auditory nerve at the level of the cochlear nuclei in the brainstem. Figure 4-3 schematically depicts the afferent pathways and major way stations of the central auditory system. The auditory nerve divides as it enters the brainstem. The two branches terminate in the ventral and dorsal cochlear nuclei. A recording of auditory stimuli from each ear occurs in the cochlear nuclei. In fact, recoding of signals probably occurs throughout the central auditory system from the lower brainstem through the auditory cortex. Furthermore, a particularly significant function occurs at the level of the superior olivary complexes where stimuli from both ears for the first time have the opportunity to be integrated within the central auditory system. The integration and correlation of information from the two ears underlies many important binaural listening functions.

Neural impulses ascend from the superior olives via tracts known as the lateral lemnisci. The lateral lemnisci terminate at the level of the midbrain in structures known as the inferior colliculi. The auditory pathways radiate from the medial geniculate bodies to the temporal lobes of the two cerebal hemispheres. A number of intrahemispheric areas are then responsible for the reception, asssociation, and perception of auditory information. In addition, the auditory areas of the two cerebral hemispheres are connected by way of interhemispheric auditory tracts. The left cerebral hemisphere is dominant for speech and language function. Indeed, speech information received by the right hemisphere eventually crosses to the appropriate association area of the left hemisphere for final processing.

COMMUNICATION AND AUDITORY DYSFUNCTION

Since speech is the primary tool by which man is able to communicate complex thoughts and messages, few people would disagree that it is the most significant of the auditory signals with which humans deal. Normal hearing is clearly a prerequisite for the use of speech for communicative purposes and for the acquisition of speech and language skills in infancy and childhood. Dysfunction at any point within the peripheral or central auditory system may interfere with the reception and processing of speech signals. Thus, in the child with auditory dysfunction that is congenital or of very early onset, development of speech and language skills may be affected. The impaired infant is unable to learn and benefit fully from the normal speech and language models to which he would otherwise be exposed. He is also unable to monitor his own vocalizations. In essence, the child has a disrupted feedback system. Auditory problems acquired after some level of linguistic competence has been achieved may result in a reduction in communicative efficiency, introduce a delay in the acquisition of new speech and language skills, or lead to a deterioration in skills. Obviously, a child's educational achievement and performance may suffer as a consequence.

As noted previously, Figure 4-1 provides a model that highlights the communication channel between a speaker or other sound source and those anatomical structures and physiological processes that mediate the reception and perception of auditory signals. The anatomical and physiological bases of the model have already been introduced. The model serves chiefly as a framework for identifying specific factors that contribute to the communicative difficulty associated with auditory dysfunction. Attention will be directed initially toward peripheral hearing impairment.

Peripheral Hearing Impairment

Peripheral hearing impairments are classified into three types: conductive, sensorineural, and mixed. Conductive hearing losses result from lesions or disease processes affecting either the outer or middle ear. Sensorineural hearing losses result from lesions involving either the cochlea (cochlear losses) or the auditory nerve (retrocochlear losses). Mixed hearing losses reflect both conductive and sensorineural components. As this description readily indicates, the three types of hearing loss all relate to dysfunction in the peripheral auditory system. The vast majority of hearing losses in man are indeed a product of peripheral problems. Nonetheless, lesions in the central auditory nervous system can also result in auditory dysfunction. Dysfunction at this level does not typically result in hearing impairment as we commonly think of it, that is, the need for sounds to be made more intense to be detected. However, dysfunction at lower brainstem levels may result in hearing impairment in this sense. Central auditory system dysfunction will be addressed in greater detail later in this chapter.

The etiologies underlying both conductive and sensorineural hearing impairments are many. Commmon etiologies, particularly those observed more frequently in children, are identified in Table 4-1. Conductive hearing

TABLE 4-1.
Some Etiologies and Conditions Associated with Peripheral Hearing Impairment in School-aged Children.

Conductive Hearing Impairment

otitis media (including middle ear fluid)

otitis externa

discontinuity of the ossicles

congenital malformation of the outer ear

congential malformation of the middle ear

genetic syndromes (e.g., Downs syndrome, Hunter's syndrome)

perforation of the tympanic membrane

impacted cerumen (wax)

blockage of the external auditory meatus by foreign object

cholesteatoma

cleft palate

traumatic head injury

eustachian tube dysfunction

Sensorineural Hearing Impairment

congenital viral infections
  maternal rubella
  cytomegalovirus

prematurity and low birth weight

perinatal anoxia or hypoxia

hyperbilirubinemia

Rh-factor incompatibility

maldevelopment of inner ear

hereditary familial hearing impairment (congenital or acquired)

noise-induced hearing loss

genetic syndromes (e.g., Waardenburg's syndrome, Hunter's syndrome)

meningitis

encephalitis

scarlet fever

measles

mumps

influenza

other viral infections

cerebrovascular disorders

drug ototoxicity

congenital syphilis

unexplained high fever

traumatic head injury

auditory nerve tumors (e.g., neurofibromatosis)

impairment should be viewed as often reversible and amenable to medical intervention. Regimens of medication and/or surgical intervention often successfully remediate the underlying medical problem and restore hearing to normal. On the other hand, the large majority of sensorineural impairment are irreversible. Thus, sensorineural hearing losses usually require aggressive long-term communicative and educational intervention and follow-up in children.

Three principles source of communicative difficulty in peripheral hearing impairment merit our attention:

1. loss in auditory sensitivity
2. auditory discrimination deficits
3. auditory environment

Additional factors that may contribute to the communication problems encountered by a peripherally impaired child exist. However, the scope of this discussion will be limited to the above factors.

Loss in Auditory Sensitivity

A loss in auditory sensitivity means that a child's threshold for detecting the presence of sound is abnormal. Threshold is defined as the intensity at which sound is just detectable. This aspect of hearing loss is the easiest to understand. Assessment of auditory sensitivity constitutes the cornerstone of any audiological evaluation. This assessment is accomplished through measurement of a child's responses to carefully controlled and calibrated stimuli. Measurements are completed using a battery of behavioral and electrophysiological, or objective, procedures.

Auditory thresholds are typically noted on an audiogram (see Fig. 4-4). The audiogram is a graph that plots the intensity level corresponding to

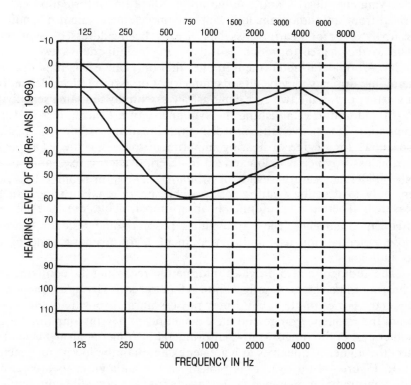

Figure 4-4.
The audiogram. Overlay represents the average speech spectrum.

auditory threshold as a function of stimulus frequency. Consequently, any deviation from 0 dB HL line represents a loss in auditory sensitivity. However, thresholds within the 0–20 dB HL range are generally viewed as constituting hearing within normal limits. Thresholds within that range typically do not present an individual with communicative problems. Nonetheless, recent concerns have been raised regarding the possible effects of very mild losses in sensitivity upon speech and language development in children who experience transient, fluctuating hearing impairments related to middle ear dysfunction.

Several investigators have suggested that children with histories of recurrent middle ear problems may evidence delays in the acquisition of specific speech and language skills or exhibit auditory learning problems (Holm & Kunze, 1969; Kaplan, Fleshman, Bender, Baum, & Clark, 1973; Needleman, 1977). Additional research is necessary, however, if this question is to be answered definitively and our understanding of the nature of the problems these children encounter is to be expanded.

A peripheral hearing impairment is typically described in terms of its type, symmetry, degree, and configuration. All of this information can be derived from an audiogram following a complete assessment of auditory sensitivity. Type of hearing loss has already been addressed. Symmetry refers to the degree to which sensitivity in an individual's two ears is similar. A unilateral impairment implies that only one ear is impaired. Bilateral impairments may be either symmetrical or asymmetrical, depending on whether or not the two ears demonstrate essentially the same sensitivity.

In addition to establishing the symmnetry of a hearing loss and differentiating conductive and sensorineural impairments, the audiogram also allows the degree of hearing impariment to be specified. Degree of hearing loss is typically characterized in descriptive terms (e.g., mild, moderate, moderately severe, severe, or profound). The term profound is used here only to describe hearing losses where no residual hearing can be measured. Therefore, profound hearing impairments are a relatively infrequent occurrence. Most individuals possess some residual hearing, whose potential for use and development is of primary concern to the audiologist.

The audiogram also provides information regarding the configuration of hearing impairment. Configuration refers to sensitivity as a function of frequency. For example, a child may possess normal sensitivity for a portion of the frequency range and have a significant hearing impairment for another part of the range. Many sensorinueral hearing impairments tend to affect the higher frequencies to a greater extent than the lower frequencies.

In Figure 4-4 an overlay is plotted on the audiogram to provide an additional frame of reference for understanding the potential communicative significance of peripheral hearing impairment. The overlay represents the range of intensities of the various frequency components of normal conversational speech. This is known as the average speech spectrum. The overlay shown in Figure 4-4 is a modification of that presented by Fletcher (1970). The overlay reveals that the entire frequency range represented on the audiogram contributes to the perception of speech.

Different phonemes, or speech sounds, have their principle spectral energy located at different frequencies and intensities. The differences in these acoustic features are responsible, to a major extent, for our ability to distinguish between individual speech sounds. For example, among consonants, sibilant sounds (s, th, f, ch, etc.) are thought of as a group of high frequency phonemes. All consonants and vowel sounds also vary in terms of their relative intensities. While the vowels tend to have their energy concentrated in the low and middle frequencies, they are in general more intense than the consonants. It is noteworthy that repetitions of the same sound by a single speaker will vary in their frequency and intensity characteristics. The utterances can also be expected to vary in their temporal charactertistics. The differences between speakers in the production of the same phonemes is even greater for these parameters. In addition, speech sounds can be expected to vary depending upon the phonemes that precede or follow them and upon the context in which they are spoken.

Obviously, an elaborate description of the acoustic features that distinguish speech sounds in isolation and in combination is possible. However, this brief discussion should suffice to introduce the reader to the manner in which losses in auditory sensitivity may influence a hearing impaired student's understanding of speech. Depending on the degree and configuration of a hearing loss, the acoustic features that contribute to successful identification of certain speech sounds may be rendered inaudible. Thus, a student whose loss in sensitivity is limited to frequencies above 1000 Hz may be expected to encounter difficulty in the perception of high frequency consonants. Impaired reception of these sounds may result in the student's impaired production of the same sounds. A student whose auditory thresholds fall at intensity levels of 60 dB HL or greater can be expected to find normal conversational speech virtually inaudible. A plot of these thresholds on the audiogram would clearly fall outside the average speech spectrum. Essentially no acoustic cues for distinguishing the fine acoustic features of speech sounds would be audible to this student.

Hearing aids, of course, will amplify speech and provide for improved auditory thresholds. Thus, amplification will assist the hearing impaired student by providing increased access to the average speech spectrum, improving ability to understand speech messages. While the scope of this discussion precludes a detailed consideration of the intricacies of amplification devices and their use, it is important to note that hearing aids are able to selectively amplify sounds as a function of frequency. Thus, the audiologist is able to meet the specific needs of individual hearing impaired listeners based upon such factors as degree and configuration of hearing loss in addition to a variety of other factors.

Auditory Discrimination Deficits

Deficits in auditory discrimination ability constitute the second major factor contributing to the communicative handicap associated with peripheral hearing impairment. Even when auditory signals, particularly speech, are presented to a hearing impaired individual at an intensity level well above threshold and comfortable for listening, difficulty understanding or discriminating the stimuli presented may be encountered. In essence, an internal distortion of incoming speech may be produced by the underlying pathology. The overlay on the audiogram in Figure 4-4 does not reflect speech discrimination deficits associated with this internal distortion.

Discrimination deficits are generally associated with sensorineural rather than conductive hearing impairments. In such instances, the lesion or pathology results in neural coding that is a distorted representation of the input signal. Thus, the individual's discrimination and perception of speech signals may be significantly compromised. Generally speaking, the degree of auditory discrimination deficit is directly related to the degree of sensitivity loss, although exceptions to this rule are frequent. Loss in discrimination ability is often the factor that most adversely influences communication abilities in a hearing impaired student. This factor clearly contributes to delay and disorder in the acquisition of speech and language skills in students whose hearing impairments date to birth or early infancy.

A variety of standardized procedures exist for the assessment of auditory speech discrimination abilities. The procedures most widely used in audiological facilities utilize monosyllabic words as test stimuli. The test items have been chosen to represent the relative frequency of speech sounds (phonemes) in the English language. The tests are, therefore, said to be phonemically-balanced. In addition, the individual tests have been developed utilizing words that are judged to be familiar to the average English-speaking child or adult.

The Auditory Environment

Deficits in auditory sensitivity and auditory discrimination obviously relate in a very specific manner to the point in the peripheral auditory system where the pathology underlying an individual's hearing impairment is located. However, the model presented in Figure 4-1 also introduces the auditory environment as a significant factor in the communication channel. The potential communicative impact of a hearing impairment on a child cannot be assessed thoroughly without a recognition of the potential detrimental effects posed by the auditory environment. This factor is of particular importance when dealing with a student in a classroom setting.

The auditory environment is complex. It should be viewed as capable of both facilitating and compromising communication. It varies from moment to moment as a function of such factors as noise and reverberation. We live in a world that is essentially noisy. At any point in time, noise can mask, or render inaudible, other sounds. Masking effects are often frequency-specific, depending upon the predominant frequency components of the noise. The task of any listener is to separate primary signals from the variety of competing signals that characterize the auditory environment. The very young child must acquire the experience and attentional skills necessary for accomplishing this basic figure-ground task.

While the absolute intensity level of noise is of concern in understanding the effects of noise on listening and understanding of speech, the intensity relationship between speech and noise is of critical importance. This relationship typically is specified in terms of a signal-to-noise (S/N) ratio, or a speech-to-competition (S/C) ratio. These ratios express the difference in the intensity of a primary auditory signal and that of background or competing stimuli. Thus, for example, a higher speech-to-competition ratio in a classroom will usually create a more optimal listening situation, facilitating a student's ability to distinguish primary from secondary auditory signals.

The auditory environment is also influenced by the effects of sound striking surfaces. When sound strikes a surface, it may be absorbed by that surface, transmitted through it, or reflected by it. Reflected sounds are responsible for reverberation. Reverberation is the persistence of sound over time in an enclosed space and results from the reflections of sounds by surfaces within that space. Thus, a message delivered by a teacher in a classroom can be expected to travel by way of a number of pathways to any given student. This is depicted in Figure 4-5. If no physical barrier exists between the teacher and student, the sound will be received by the student directly with no interruption. Yet, since sound emanates from the teacher in all directions, sound will also reach the student's ears by way of indirect routes resulting from the reflection of sound waves off of the various surfaces in the classroom. These indirect pathways actually constitute "delay lines" since the sound waves will travel greater distances and reach the student's ears at varying times.

Most normal listeners are well aware of the potential problems in communication that can result from excessive noise levels and reduced signal-to-noise ratios. Normal listeners have also encountered the unpleasant effects of highly reverberant environments. In such instances, the intelligibility of speech messages may be reduced. Several studies have investigated the effects of reverberation and noise, both alone and in com-

Figure 4-5.
Reverberation in an enclosed space. Lines represent direct and reflected sound pathways to a listener's ears.

bination, on speech intelligibility in a systematic manner (Crum, 1974; Gelfand & Hochberg, 1976; Moncur & Dirks, 1967; Nabelek & Pickett, 1974; Nabelek & Robinette, 1978).

Results obtained by these investigators have suggested that speech intelligibility is actually improved for normal listeners under certain conditions of reverberation. For example, speech intelligibility has been shown by Nabelek and Robinette to be optimal for normal listeners in the presence of sound waves that persist over periods of .02 to .03 seconds. Lochner and Burger (1964) suggested that repetition of sound waves over a period of .08 sec may enhance intelligibility. Interestingly, the effect has not been observed for hearing impaired listeners. Results obtained by the investigators cited above have collectively demonstrated that speech intelligibility can be expected to deteriorate for normal listeners with more prolonged periods of reverberation. The effects have been shown to be compounded for peripherally hearing impaired listeners.

Finitzo-Hieber and Tillman (1978) documented the interactive effects of noise and reverberation on normal-hearing and hearing impaired listeners by studying school-age youngsters under a number of conditions of noise and reverberation in classroom-size environments. Reverberation periods of .04 sec were shown to diminish the performance of their normal-hearing subjects when compared to their performance in an environment free of reverberation. All subjects were tested utilizing a standardized word identification test used in the audiological evaluation of preschool and school-age children. The performance of the hearing impaired youngsters deteriorated to an even greater degree. Additional increases in reverberation caused further decreases in the average word identification performance of both groups. Again, the hearing impaired youngsters showed a significantly greater decrease in performance.

Increasing the complexity of the listening situation by introducing competing speech stimuli (recorded multiple talkers reading prose) at a speech-to-competition ratio of +6 dB created additional problems for both groups of subjects in the Finitzo-Hieber and Tillman study. In the reverberation free condition, the addition of competition produced poorer performances than those observed for groups in quiet. Not surprisingly, the hearing impaired youngsters were placed at a particular disadvantage. Both groups revealed similar breakdowns in performance as reverberation increased; however, the hearing impaired group performed markedly poorer than their normal-hearing peers in all test conditions.

The purpose of the preceding discussion is obvious when recognition is given to the fact that many newer classrooms, designed and engineered with acoustical characteristics in mind, yield reverberation periods of 0.6 sec (Olsen, 1981). Many older classroom environments have been shown to have even less desirable reverberation characteristics. Sanders (1965) has reported that signal-to-noise ratios of +5 dB are not uncommon in classrooms. Thus, the concern of educators and other professionals as well as audiologists for the auditory environment should be heightened. These are the environments in which we expect children with auditory dysfunction to comprehend spoken messages and acquire the language skills and information necessary to ensure their academic progress.

As a significant component of the communication channel for any listener, irrespective of age or auditory status, the auditory environment should be viewed as a particularly critical variable in the habilitation and education of students with auditory dysfunction. Historically, too little emphasis has been placed on the highly variable environments in which these students find themselves. Negative aspects of the auditory environment must be recognized as contributing to the communication deficits associated with hearing problems.

A classroom can be treated acoustically to optimize signal-to-noise ratios and reverberation characteristics. Increased or improved patterns of sound absorption and reflection through the use of acoustical ceiling or wall tiles, rugs or carpets, and draperies have all proven beneficial. Rearrangement of barriers, which are reflective surfaces, in a classroom may also assist in appropriately modifying the auditory environment. In addition, preferential seating of a student in group learning and listening situations to maximize use of both auditory and visual cues for communication is important. This position may not always be toward the front and center of a classroom directly by the teacher. The most beneficial seating position will depend upon the specific acoustical characteristics of the classroom. The student is also likely to benefit from adopting strategies such as repeating instructions and statements, gaining the student's attention before speaking, and requesting feedback from the student to indicate his understanding of a speech message.

Central Auditory Dysfunction

The audiologist's role in the evaluation of disorders of the central auditory nervous system has been both increasing and changing in recent years. Traditional audiological procedures used in the identification and evaluation of peripheral auditory dysfunction have proven far less useful in the evaluation of the central auditory system. Central auditory problems typically do not produce abnormal results on measurements of auditory sensitivity. In addition, deficits are not usually observed on standardized tests of word identification or discrimination administered with conventional protocols in quiet listening environments.

Test batteries designed to assess peripheral auditory function attempt to establish both the origin, or site, of a hearing impairment and the communicative problems it may present to the individual listener. Tests developed for purposes of assessing the integrity of the central auditory system have been used largely to assist in establishing the site of a lesion in adults. They have also been used to shed light on brain mechanisms and processes underlying audition, particulary the perception of speech. These tests have proven useful in these respects.

These procedures are being administered in audiological facilities with increasing frequency to children who are identified as language or learning disabled. Many of these children are referred for evaluation because they are felt to have auditory perceptual problems, central auditory processing disorders, and so forth. The utilization of these tests for this purpose is not surprising in view of the frequent statements in professional literature citing disorders of auditory processing as a major contributing factor to language and learning problems in school-age children. Before considering the actual value of the audiological tests, the nature of the procedures and the rationale underlying their development will be addressed.

The evaluation of central auditory system function by the audiologist takes into account the dual principles of intrinsic and extrinsic redundancy

(Bocca & Calearo, 1963). Our prior review of the pathways and major way stations of the central auditory system revealed that recoding, duplication, and integration of auditory information occurs at various levels in the system from the low brainstem through the cortex. Due to contralateralization of many nerve fibers, information from each cochlea is represented bilaterally in the central pathways at points above the cochlear nuclei. Crossover connections have been noted to exist at several levels within the system. As a result, the central auditory nervous system may be viewed as intrinsically redundant.

Extrinsic redundancy refers to the extensive amount of information and wealth of cues inherent in almost any speech message which contribute to the identification and understanding of that message. Extrinsic redundancy is perhaps most easily understood if one recognizes that a listener, in many instances, need not hear the entirety of a spoken message to understand it. A variety of cues and features that allow a listener to receive and understand speech are available. For example, a variety of acoustic cues exist that distinguish individual speech sounds or phonemes. Characteristics of speech such as rhythm, intonation, and duration also assist in conveying the meaning of a spoken message. In addition, experienced listeners know that any given verbal message is likely to follow certain phonologic and syntactic rules; and, of course, most speech occurs in a context, which allows listeners to predict the content of messages. Thus, speech, in and of itself, is highly redundant.

A student with a central auditory system problem may be viewed as having a reduction in intrinsic redundancy. The student might not be expected to encounter a great deal of difficulty understanding a spoken message as long as the extrinsic redundancy of the message is high. In essence, the reduction in intrinsic redundancy may be compensated for by the redundant nature of speech. Conversely, within limits, reduction of the extrinsic redundancy of a message will not pose problems to a student if sufficient intrinsic redundancy is provided by intact peripheral and central auditory systems. However, the student with a reduction in intrinsic redundancy can be expected to encounter increased difficulty if the extrinsic redundancy of speech is diminished. The purposeful reduction of extrinsic redundancy constitutes the basis for central auditory tests utilizing speech stimuli. In other words, the disordered central auditory system must be taxed with more complex and challenging listening tasks if it is to be successfully identified with auditory tests. Thus, in theory, such tests will distinguish normal and disordered groups.

A variety of procedures have been developed to degrade speech stimuli for purposes of reducing extrinsic redundancy. This has been accomplished through the filtering, interruption, time-compression, and alternation between ears of speech stimuli. Speech stimuli are also degraded through presentation in a background of noise and simultaneous stimulation of both ears with different messages. Central lesions have been demonstrated to produce fairly predictable effects on standardized word identification or discrimination tasks, similar to those used in assessment of the peripheral system, when the test stimuli are so degraded. Certain central tests are felt to be sensitive to cortical lesions while others are felt to be sensitive to brainstem lesions.

Many students enrolled in educational programs for students with learning disabilities are judged to have difficulties in the processing of auditory information. They have been characterized as possessing auditory perceptual deficits, auditory language learning disorders, and central auditory processing disorders. Additional terms have been used to describe these students as well. Consequently, the application of central auditory test batteries to children with learning problems has seemed a sensible extension of the more traditional application. Several of the tests used for site-of-lesion testing in adults with suspected or confirmed central auditory system lesions have been applied directly or modified for use with children. Even as site-of-lesion tests, these procedures have offered no concrete information regarding the locus of central auditory nervous system breakdown in learning disabled children. Careful research designed to further examine the possible utility of these tests with these students has been limited, and the results have been equivocal at best .

Willeford (1976) and Willeford and Billger (1978) have reported an experimental battery for assessment of central auditory function in learning disabled children. Their battery incorporates two tests that purportedly examine cortical integrity and two additional tests that examine integrity at the level of the brainstem. All four tests parallel procedures that have been utilized in the assessment of adults with suspected or confirmed lesions of the central auditory nervous system. For example, one of the cortical tests involves the simultaneous delivery of a different sentence to each of a student's two ears. The student under test is charged with attending to and repeating only the sentence delivered to a specified ear. Tests incorporating competing speech stimuli have been useful in identifying cortical lesions in adults. Recognition of the sentences delivered to the ear contralateral to the involved cerebral hemisphere is often disturbed.

One of the brainstem tests used by Willeford and Billger involves the delivery of a spondaic word (e.g., baseball) to both ears simultaneously. However, the word is filtered in such a manner that one ear receives a band of low frequency energy and the other ear a high frequency band. This test is patterned after earlier procedures used with adults (Matzker, 1962). The filtered stimulus delivered to either ear alone is insufficient for correct word identification. However, the simultaneous presentation of the two filtered words to the two ears allows for correct identification of the word. Correct identification presumably is mediated in the lower brainstem where the stimuli from the two ears are fused, or integrated.

Willeford and Billger report that over 90 percent of the learning disabled students referred for suspected central auditory problems performed abnormally on at least one of the tests in their battery. However, they also report that their subjects exhibit considerable variability on any single test. Willeford and Billger also report considerable variability in their normative population of young children. The variability and overlap in the performance of their normal and learning disabled groups highlight the problems associated with the use of such tests with students who have learning problems.

Other investigators (Martin & Clark, 1977; Stubblefield & Young 1975) have utilized other audiological procedures to assess learning disabled students. When reviewed together, their results are clearly equivocal. They reveal no clear pattern to suggest that existing central auditory tests can be relied upon to definitively identify children with learning disabilities.

In view of the historic basis for these tests, they ultimately might be imagined to provide some information regarding the site of organic dysfunction in central auditory problems. However, at this time, they do not appear to provide information useful in specifying the source or nature of the problems. In addition, these tests are not generally appropriate for use with younger children (below 6 years of age). Thus, they do not contribute significantly to the earlier identification of children with central auditory processing deficits or learning problems. To be exact, most children are referred for these tests only after learning, language, or behavorial problems have already surfaced at home or school. A poor performance on these tests may well suggest or confirm the presence of an already suspected problem, but the tests do little to better define or increase understanding of the problem. Using the results of these tests to plan or develop new and innovative strategies for instruction and intervention seems extremely tenuous. Indeed, Rees (1973), in a careful review of a number of investigations, challenged the presumed relationship between auditory processing disorders and language or learning disorders. She questioned whether any single auditory skill or set of auditory skills could be found to be impaired in students with language or learning problems. Rees proposed instead that such problems may, in fact, be attributable to specific cognitive or linguistic defects rather than to problems of auditory processing.

Rees' statement of almost 15 years ago remains a powerful word of caution today. Considerable caution needs to be exercised in the administration of central auditory test procedures to school-age populations for purposes of either identifying or proposing management strategies for learning disabled youngsters.

If auditory processing problems are to be identified and evaluated successfully, irrespective of the relationship between these problems and learning disabilities, audiologists are likely to require tests that reflect a greater understanding of the functions mediated at different points within the central auditory system. This author obviously questions the benefit to be derived from the administration of extensive central auditory test batteries, particularly those in current use with speech stimuli. A rather dramatic change in the audiologist's approach to the question of central auditory system assessment may be necessary. The development of new procedures using alternative stimuli, including nonspeech stimuli, that are able to tap these mechanisms and functions in a more controlled and precise manner appears necessary.

In spite of the questions and concerns raised in the preceding discussion, the audiologist has an important role to play in the management of students with central auditory deficits. A return to a consideration of the communication channel and the principles of extrinsic and intrinsic redundancy will clarify this role. Like any other student the student with central auditory system dysfunction receives auditory input through an auditory environment. The auditory environment is a medium capable of reducing the extrinsic redundancy associated with a spoken message. Thus, undesirable effects associated with reduced speech-to-competition ratios and increased reverberation may well compromise the listening skills of a student with centrally-based auditory deficits. In addition, any auditory environment can be expected to change and fluctuate widely and frequently over time. Thus, active classrooms may present students with inconsistent listening situations for learning.

As noted previously, such detrimental effects can create problems for even the normal hearing student with no central or peripheral auditory system pathology. However, the redundancy intrinsic to an intact auditory system usually assists in compensating for the problems. The student with a central problem is faced, as we know, with a system with reduced intrinsic redundancy. He is placed at an added disadvantage in a classroom environment that does not optimize the transmission of auditory signals.

Unfortunately, careful research in this area is virtually absent, and no definitive conclusions can be drawn regarding the interaction of environment and central auditory problems. However, it does seem reasonable to conjecture that assessing and controlling the auditory environment is necessary for effective educational management of learning disabled youngsters. Thus, irrespective of central auditory testing, the audiologist appears to have an immediate role to fulfill with this student population. Some audiologists may argue that central auditory test batteries are necessary prior to intervention in this manner. However, the lack of specificity in the information provided by these tests suggests they are not likely to be useful in planning specific modifications of the environment. At this time, appropriate modifications can be based most solidly upon an understanding of the potentially deleterious effects of various listening conditions and recognized procedures for manipulating the environment and a student's interactions with it. In large part, these modifications currently parallel those for peripherally hearing impaired youngsters. As previously described, these modifications may involve manipulation of the acoustical characteristics of the classroom or the adoption of specific strategies for interacting with the student. In large part, these strategies result in an increase in extrinsic redundancy for the student.

SUMMARY

The expressed purpose of this chapter was to review the origins and nature of auditory dysfuntion in school-age children. Initially, the components of the communication channel between a speaker and a listener were identified. An understanding of the communication channel is integral to recognizing the implications of auditory dysfunction for communicative behavior in school-age children. The audiologist is the principal professional responsible for the identification and evaluation of auditory dysfunction and associated communicative disabilities. Any problem that inteferes with the development of speech and language skills or the ability to communicate may potentially compromise a student's classroom performance and educational achievement. Thus, educators and other professionals involved in the education and care of children with auditory impairments should be aware of the origins and implications of auditory dysfunction.

Basic features of the anatomy and physiology of both the peripheral and central auditory system were reviewed. The manner in which the auditory system changes the acoustical energy of airborne sound waves to neural impulses meaningful to the central nervous system was described. Specific structures and mechanims responsible for the reception and perception of auditory signals were identified.

Three specific sources of communicative difficulty in the presence of peripheral hearing impariment were discussed. They included loss in auditory sensitivity, auditory discrimination deficits, and the auditory environment. Special attention was focused on the auditory environment and the manner in which such factors as reverberation, noise, and competing stimuli may interact with hearing impairment and influence classroom performance. Principles underlying the audiologist's clinical evaluation of peripheral auditory function were also introduced.

The role of the audiologist in the evaluation of children with learning disabilities and presumed central auditory dysfunction was also reviewed. While audiologists are evaluating these students with increasing frequency, the tests used for this purpose have yielded equivocal results. The rationale underlying these procedures and the information available on their application were reviewed. In general, the procedures appear limited in their ability to identify these students or contribute to our understanding of the nature of the problems they encounter. Their usefulness in the development of specific programs of intervention is considered tenuous.

CHAPTER 5

Language Processes

Willie P. Cupples
M. E. B. Lewis

T he chapter discusses Bloom and Lahey's model for treating oral
language deficits. The model includes therapeutic classroom treatment in three areas: *language form,* addressing structural aspects of language; *language content,* stressing vocabulary and comprehension in
language development; and *language use,* centering on application of language in functional, vocational, and social situations.

Supplementary language processing models are also discussed as they
relate to the Bloom and Lahey model. Three case studies are presented to
describe strategies used in the classroom. A summary with the prognosis
for each case follows.

LANGUAGE KNOWLEDGE

A model that has been particularly beneficial in the differential
diagnosis of language disorders is that of Bloom and Lahey (1978); they

This chapter originally appeared as an article by **Willie P. Cupples** and **M. E. B. Lewis** in
Learning Disabilities: An Interdisciplinary Journal (Vol. III, 1984) and was adapted by permission
of Grune & Stratton for inclusion in this *Handbook.*

propose a model of oral language containing three major components; language form, language content, and language use.

Language form can be described as the component that defines and dictates the structure of language. Language form includes a child's knowledge of grammar, syntax, and morphology, as well as the sound patterns of English, often referred to as phonology. This chapter does not discuss phonological disorders in learning-disabled children as the focus is on language disorders and not speech disorders. In assessing and remediating language form, it is important to determine the range of sentence structures available to a child in order for him or her to communicate adequately (e.g., passive voice, active voice, and auxiliary inversion to ask questions). In addition, it is important to consider the prefixes and suffixes a given child has available to communicate distinctions in meaning (e.g., the /s/ morpheme to distinguish plurals, /ed/ to mark regular past tense, and auxiliary verb forms such as *do, can,* and *have* to modulate verb meanings).

Language content attempts to describe the word meanings, concepts, and lexical entries available to a child. This language element is particularly important for the learning-disabled child since academic progress is partially dependent upon the ability to grasp new concepts and to symbolize these concepts with new vocabulary items. Included in language content is a child's knowledge of vocabulary, which includes the dictionary entries of words and their definitions, often referred to as the lexicon. Language content consists of much more, however. Not only must a child have a vocabulary consisting of single words and their definitions, but the relationships between words must also be understood. Thus, a child must be facile with homonyms, antonyms, and synonyms. An understanding of antonyms entails knowing what a word means, as well as what it does not mean. A broad use of synonyms adds depth to a child's language experience, for he or she then can use and understand words of similar meanings that signal subtle distinctions.

Another important aspect of language content is an understanding of the hierarchical structure of word meanings. There are superordinate terms that circumscribe a certain lexical field (e.g., animal, plant, or mineral). Within these linguistic categories defined by the superordinate term are subordinate terms that, in turn, circumscribe another lexical field (e.g., within the animal category are birds, fish, and mammals), which further defines other hierarchical relationships.

It is also important for children to understand that there are instances in which words are chosen intentionally in violation of their conventional meanings. These instances are exemplified by figures of speech and idiomatic expressions. Learning-disabled children sometimes miss the meanings conveyed in these expressions because they attempt to define them literally (Wiig & Semel, 1980).

Finally, is it important that the child have the conceptual base in order to acquire and use words appropriately. The exact relationship between cognition and language has been debated for ages. (It is not within the scope of this chapter to explore this relationship). Rice (1980) provides a thorough discussion of the major theories relating language and cognition. It is important to realize that concepts can exist apart from language and that all the major theories of cognition propose a level where language and cognition interact to a greater or lesser extent (Bates, 1976a; Piaget, 1977). Because of this interaction, it is important to assess various aspects of cognitive functioning in learning disabled children.

Perhaps the most powerful component of Bloom and Lahey's (1978) model of language is that of *language use.* This component attempts to specify how children use language form and content in order to communicate effectively. Included in language use are such things as a child's ability to alter vocabulary and sentence structure and to use polite forms depending upon the communicative context (e.g., communicating with peers on the playground versus communicating with the classroom teacher). In addition, language use attempts to describe how a child can assume another speaker's perspective in a communicative situation, providing the appropriate background information and referents so that the speaker is able to understand the message. This ability has been described by Bates (1976a, 1979) as the ability to provide adequate presuppositions. As she states, the child must be taught *not to presuppose* (i.e., not to assume that adults automatically know what went on before a communicative event or that adults automatically know the referents when a child initiates communication). Thus presuppositions include the knowledge shared or assumed when two people begin to communicate. Bates (1976a, 1979) also describes the performative, which specifies the purpose for the communication. Young children often communicate to request, refuse, and inform. Older children and adults have a broader range of communicative intents or performatives, which include denying, lying, imploring, and flattering.

An important use of language that develops in the elementary school years is the ability to hold a conversation or to engage in discourse. Among the abilities necessary for conversation are the ability to take turns and maintain fairly equal talking time, to initiate and maintain a topic of conversation, to terminate a conversation appropriately, and to repair a conversation when there is miscommunication (Spekman, 1983).

There is overwhelming evidence that learning-disabled children experience difficulties in one, two, or all three areas of this model. Johnson and Myklebust (1967), Wiig and Semel (1980), and Wren (1983) present clinical case studies and research that documents the difficulties encountered by learning-disabled children in acquiring and using language form.

Some children have difficulty with oral instructions in the classroom because they do not understand the syntax and morphology used by the teacher. These deficits also may be observed in reading, since oral language is considered to be the foundation on which reading skills develop (Johnson & Myklebust, 1967; Mattingly, 1972). Other learning-disabled children may experience expressive language problems in addition to or separate from receptive problems in syntax and morphology. Their expressive language may be devoid of auxiliary verbs, plural markers, and other morphologic forms that modulate the meaning conveyed in a sentence (Brown, 1973). Johnson and Myklebust (1967), Wiig and Semel (1980), Hoskins (1983), and Harris-Schmidt (1983) describe clear examples of learning-disabled children who exhibit deficiencies in language content. These are children who lack adequate concepts and vocabulary in order to comprehend basic academic information. Spekman (1983) and Bryan, Donahue, Pearl, and Sturm (1981) describe learning-disabled children who lack the appropriate social abilities and knowledge of language use to communicate effectively. These children withdraw, have poor peer relationships, and may rebel because they lack the basic abilities to establish effective and rewarding contact with others.

LANGUAGE PROCESSING

While the model of Bloom and Lahey (1978) describes the multidimensional nature of linguistic knowledge (e.g., *what* a child needs to know about language in order to communicate effectively), it does not describe *how* this information is processed.

A complete differential diagnosis of language-based learning disabilities needs to include some description of how a given child processes language.

At the present time there are numerous models that attempt to describe how language is processed. While there is general agreement that the processing is hierarchical, beyond this, there is much debate concerning what the levels are, how many levels exist, and what the relationships are between the levels (Carrow-Woolfolk & Lynch, 1982; Gerber & Bryen, 1981; Johnson & Myklebust, 1967; Wiig & Semel, 1980).

For the current discussion, the processing model formulated by Wren (1983) is presented. It has been chosen because Wren integrates traditional processing models (e.g., Johnson & Myklebust, 1967) with models based on current information processing research (Johnson, 1981, 1982). The model she presents includes the following levels:

1. metacognition
2. conceptualization
3. symbolization
4. short-term memory
5. perception
6. attention
7. sensation

Briefly, in order for a stimulus to be processed it must first register with the peripheral senses *(sensation)*. Once a stimulus is registered the *attentional* mechanisms are alerted and decide whether the stimulus will be transmitted to higher neurological levels. When the stimulus is *perceived* (e.g., as being the same or different from prior stimuli, and then differentiated into kinds of stimuli), according to Wren, it is registered in *short-term memory*. Once short-term memory has stored the stimulus, meaning can be attached to it *(symbolization)*. At a higher level, *conceptualization,* the stimulus is broken into its component parts and compared with prior knowledge or concepts in order to establish abstract relationships. Conceptualization may lead to the formation of generalizations, rule-governed behavior, and hypothesis formulation. The highest level discussed by Wren (1983) is *metacognition*. At this level, a child is able to adopt an objective stance and look at what a concept, knowledge, or language is. In other words, a child uses concepts to analyze concepts and language to analyze and talk about language. At this level there is a conscious manipulation of knowledge in order to reveal further knowledge.

Learning-disabled children manifest difficulties in attention and all of the levels above attention. While these levels of processing are not totally independent, specific deficits in processing can sometimes by isolated (Johnson & Myklebust, 1967; Wiig & Semel, 1976, 1980). A differential diagnosis should include an attempt to isolate deficits in language processing as well as deficits in the components of language knowledge.

METHODS OF ASSESSMENT AND DIAGNOSIS

In this era of IEPs and accountability, teachers and clinicians must provide objective, quantifiable data in support of a diagnosis. While there are standards that define what behaviors constitute a learning disability (National Joint Committee on Learning Disabilities, 1981) and a wide range of standardized tests are available for assessment purposes, the diagnosis of language-based learning disability is not always clear-cut. Thus, teachers and clinicians must rely on clinicial judgment. There are a number of reasons for this, some of which relate to language acquisition and intervention models, while others relate to shortcomings in the standardized tests currently available.

The models of language presented were discussed in terms of multidimensional components. While each of the components can be described independently, it is not always possible to assess them in an independent fashion. For example, children with selective attention deficits may manifest difficulties in symbolization and conceptualization. Further, it is not clear whether general conceptualization deficits lead to attention deficits or vice versa (Johnson, 1982). Similarly, children exhibiting deficits in language form may be deficient in language use because certain syntactic patterns are necessary for good social interaction (Bloom & Lahey, 1978; Roth & Spekman, 1984a).

The nature of the standardized tests currently available forces the clinician and teacher to use clinical judgment in the diagnostic process. The broad range of tests do not adhere to one particular psycholinguistic model. In fact, few of them present a clear theoretical rationale or construct validity. Many of them are ill-conceived and poorly constructed when evaluated with acceptable psychometric criteria (McCauley & Swisher, 1984; Muma, 1978, 1981, 1983; Weiner & Hoock, 1973).

There is currently no test that assesses all aspects of language knowledge or processing. The clinician must rely on a battery of tests that have been standardized on different normative populations and which yield different kinds of scores (e.g., mental ages, percentiles, standard scores, or grade levels). Clinical judgment is necessary in interpreting these sometimes disparate test scores.

The following section describes some of the standardized tests and informal assessment procedures currently available for assessing the various aspects of language. As stated previously, none of the components of the model are completely independent; therefore, the tests listed under each component do not simply assess that component. The division has been made on the basis of the primary area of assessment as stated in test manuals and, in some instances, based on the authors' clinical experience with a given test. Since this article focuses primarily on school-age children, the tests discussed are appropriate for that age group.

Assessing Language Form: Syntax and Morphology

Perhaps the greatest number of tests are available for assessing syntax and morphology. In the interest of differential diagnosis, it is important to assess reception versus expression of language, although they are not always assessed separately in a given test.

The following list includes tests that may be used to assess receptive syntax and morphology. This first set simply requires pointing to a picture that best represents a given stimulus sentence.

1. Clinical Evaluation of Language Functions
   a. word and sentence construction
   b. linguistic concepts
2. Northwestern Syntax Screening Test: receptive subtest
3. Test for Auditory Comprehension of Language
4. Test of Language Development-Primary: grammatic understanding

Some tests are a combination of receptive and expressive language. They require listening to a stimulus and making a verbal response; for example, sentence completion, sentence imitation, or sentence construction when presented with a one-word stimulus.

1. Illinois Test of Psycholinguistic Abilities: grammatic closure subtest
2. Northwestern Syntax Screening Test: expressive subtest
3. Test of Language Development-Primary
   a. sentence imitation
   b. grammatic completion
4. Test of Language Development-intermediate
   a. sentence combining
   b. word ordering
5. Carrow Elicited Language Inventory

The procedure that represents the best measure of expressive syntax and morphology at the present time is the analysis of a language sample collected in a situation of spontaneous interaction (Miller, 1981). Some of the procedures recommended for analyzing the sample are:

1. Developmental Sentence Scoring (Lee, 1974)
2. Language Assessment, Remediation and Screening Procedure (Crystal, Fletcher, & Graham 1976)
3. Teaching the American Language to Kids (Dever, 1978)
4. Assigning Structural Stage (Miller, 1981).

Assessing Language Content: Semantics

The first task in assessing language content is to assess receptive vocabulary. Tests that require pointing to or selecting a picture which best represents a stimulus word include:

1. Peabody Picture Vocabulary Test-revised
2. Test for Auditory Comprehension of Language
3. Test of Language Development-Primary: picture vocabulary
4. Test of Adolescent Language: listening vocabulary

Other vocabulary tests require naming a picture. These tests may also reveal word retrieval difficulties if a child's responses are analyzed informally. Two vocabulary tests are the Expressive One-Word Picture Vocabulary Test and the picture vocabulary subtest of the Woodcock Language Proficiency Battery.

Another aspect of assessing language content is presenting a stimulus word that a child must define. This task combines receptive and expressive content in that the child has to comprehend the word and formulate an appropriate definition. Assessing language content is included in the following tests:

1. Stanford-Binet: vocabulary
2. Wechsler Intelligence Scale for Children-Revised: vocabulary
3. Test of Language Development-primary: oral vocabulary
4. Test of Adolescent Language: speaking vocabulary
5. Detroit Test of Learning Aptitude: social adjustment-B

A final aspect of the model of language content discussed previously is the knowledge of lexical relationships and hierarchical word meanings. These skills are also referred to as verbal reasoning. Some of the tests that assess these aspects are:

1. Wechsler Intelligence Scale for Children-Revised: similarities
2. Detroit Tests of Learning Aptitude:
   a. likenesses and differences
   b. verbal opposites
3. Clinical Evaluation of Language Functions:
   a. processing word classes
   b. processing relationships and ambiguities
   c. producing word associations
4. Test of Language Development-intermediate:
   a. characteristics
   b. generals
5. Woodcock Language Proficiency Battery:
   a. antonyms-synonyms
   b. analogies

Some tests assess a combination of form and content in the receptive and expressive modalities. A child has to process the semantic and syntactic content of the stimulus and then formulate an appropriate response. Two such tests are the Wechsler Intelligence Scale for Children-Revised: (a) information and (b) comprehension and the Detroit Tests of Learning Aptitude: (a) verbal absurdities and (b) social adjustment-A.

Assessing Language Usage: Pragmatics

Because of the recent evolution of pragmatics as a part of language acquisition and language disorders, there are no standardized tests available for assessing language usage. However, a number of informal observation and assessment techniques are available. The reader is referred to Lund and Duchan (1983), Prutting (1979), Roth and Speckman (1984a), Simon (1979), and Spekman (1983) for a variety of methods to assess language usage.

ASSESSING LANGUAGE PROCESSING

Since the level of sensation is not considered to be the level at which a learning disability occurs (since deficits in sensation include peripheral hearing loss and blindness; Wren, 1983), a discussion of processing deficits in learning-disabled children begins at the level of attention. Assessing attention requires a qualitative analysis of a child's response patterns and behavior. Deficits in attention may be revealed by the following behaviors:

1. A child may have difficulty comprehending directions and instructions even though the content and form of the signal are within the understanding of the child.
2. Inconsistent and sporadic error patterns may emerge in testing situations when it is clear the stimulus items are simple enough for the child to understand.
3. A child may have difficulty completing work in the allotted time.
4. A child may work more accurately in an environment in which visual and auditory distractions are minimized.

It is important to emphasize that deficits in attention may resonate through all areas of processing. Thus, children with attentional problems may manifest difficulties in memory, perception, symbolization, conceptualization, and/or metacognition.

When assessing memory it is important for the teacher and clinician to determine how a child functions in different kinds of memory. Lezak (1976) discusses the difference between registration, two kinds of immediate memory, and long-term memory. Registration is the process whereby information is initially received. If the stimulus is not immediately transferred to short-term memory it decays. If Lezak's concepts are placed into the present processing model, it would appear that registration is the link between perception and short-term memory. The first component of short-term memory, immediate memory, involves the recording of information that will be used in some fashion within a short time. Auditory memory tasks that require digit or sentence repetition or that require comprehension of a set of facts or instructions fall in this category of memory. A second subset of short-term memory involves memory for information that is held in storage for more than an hour or two but less than one or two days. Some diagnosticians refer to this as recent memory. This seems to be the link between immediate memory and long-term memory. The information has been rehearsed enough to be retained but, apparently, is not a part of learned material. Long-term memory refers to information that is clearly learned and appears to be organized on the basis of meaning.

The majority of memory tests assess immediate memory. Thus, it is important to devise informal tasks that assess recent and long-term memory. A measure of recent memory might be how well a child remembers a homework assignment when he or she gets home from school. Long-term memory abilities seem to be related to the processes of symbolization and conceptualization.

Digit-span tests are found as part of the WISC-R, Stanford-Binet, and Illinois Test of Psycholinguistic Abilities, to name a few. Lezak (1976) indicates that digit span has little to do with verbal ability; thus, other tests of memory for linguistic material are needed. The following are some suggested tests:

1. the Token Test for Children
2. Rey Auditory-Verbal Learning Test
3. Detroit Tests of Learning Aptitude
   a. auditory attention span for unrelated words and
   b. auditory attention span for related syllables.

The processes of symbolization and conceptualization are tested directly by all the instruments listed in the assessment of form and content since language is a way of representing concepts and symbols. What is important at this level of processing is an assessment of visual problem-solving skills and visual concepts. If the strict definition of learning disabilities is adhered to, then the child with language-based disabilities should perform in the normal range on visual processing tests. The following are commonly used instruments to assess visual conceptual abilities:

1. Wechsler Intelligence Scale for Children-Revised
2. Stanford-Binet Intelligence Scale
3. Kaufman Assessment Battery for Children
4. Columbia Mental Maturity Scale
5. Raven's Standardized Progressive Matrices.

The final and highest level of processing, metacognition, has no standardized assessment instruments devised specifically to assess this area. However, any task that requires a child to analyze language as rule-governed behavior, for example, breaking language into its component parts, analyzing and reintegrating, is a test of metacognition (Wren, 1983). Bloom and Lahey (1978) describe this ability as metalinguistic. This level of cognitive functioning is particularly important in remediation programs with older learning-disabled children and adolescents. For instance, if the improvement of memory deficits is a remediation goal, then certain strategies are taught to facilitate retention of information. Adolescents with word-retrieval difficulties are taught strategies such as phonemic and semantic cuing to help them retrieve the word (Wiig & Semel, 1980). If deficits in socialization are apparent, role-playing is a technique by which appropriate communication skills can be taught. All of these techniques require the ability to analyze language units and communication and thus are metacogitive skills.

Once a learning-disabled child's abilities and deficiencies are delineated using this model of differential diagnosis, the task is to formulate appropriate strategies for remediating deficits. Strategies should be realistic, and a prognosis concerning improvement should be made. The next sections discuss factors that should be considered in making a prognosis and formulating appropriate intervention strategies.

A PERSPECTIVE ON INTERVENTION

Boyce and Larsen (1983) provide an overview of intervention for language-learning disabled adolescent students that is adaptable to elementary as well as secondary classrooms. This model, based upon the analysis of need within the student, his or her instructional setting, and his or her home and social environment, directs that intetrvention strategies be prioritized and organized into objective statements of purpose. Such a goal-attainment model makes the process of intervention more comprehensible to the student, the parent, and the professional.

Intervention strategies discussed in this article are for use in the classroom by the classroom teacher or special educator and *not* for use in clinical intervention by the speech–language professional. A pragmatic model of intervention is promoted with the clinician's role being that of facilitator or consultant to the teacher, as proposed by Bloom and Lahey.

By the intermediate grades, severely learning-disabled students have often been channeled into resource classes if not self-contained classes for the purpose of remediation. Although such placements are worthwhile, they place students in isolation from nondisabled students and, consequently, reduce their contact with those whose conversational skills and thinking processes may be age- and grade-appropriate. The intervention strategies mentioned are still applicable in these classes, however.

Craig (1983) outlines the distinct theoretical interpretations of pragmatics as narrowly defined sets of structural rules for conversational contents in contrast to globally applied integral rules for maintenance of clarity. In the classroom setting, the more global interpretation seems applicable, since rigid structure setting can serve to unnecessarily complicate curriculum by being misinterpreted by teachers as an additional set of activities rather than as a framework for overall language development and instruction. The natural interactions and sequences of communication that the classroom's socialized setting affords must be monitored, however, for their potential for distraction.

Any treatment of language problems in students must reflect an adequate system of scheduling. Traditional language arts block scheduling, which emphasizes basic reading and writing skills, may not serve well in pragmatic remediation. Speaking and listening skills, removed and closely planned for the daily curriculum, are essential. As students approach the late intermediate and secondary levels of content-based curricula, a thematic approach to intervention, such as that outlined by Lewis (Kavale, in press) can serve to connect what may seem disjointed subjects to the learning-disabled student.

Thematic units of study, in which all content is connected to an underlying conceptual framework such as *travel* or *politics,* allows all levels of skill to be addressed in the student's day-to-day programming. Since all instructional activities are related to concepts of travel, for example, the student can use his or her experience of travel in order to perceive the content stimuli and organize it for storage (short-term memory), later retrieval, and usage (symbolization, conceptualization and metacognition).

The case studies that follow illustrate students with various degrees and types of language difficulties and the measures that were taken in their instructional treatment. Each student's needs are different, and prognoses range from good to poor. The strategies described are not exclusively clinical and can be used successfully in a regular classroom.

A word about the term *prognosis*. Since the school setting described is a clinical one, certain medical terminology is appropriate. The medically oriented *diagnostic/prescriptive* to describe a type of teaching has long been used in the education field. If there is indeed a "treatment" protocol in education, then the establishment of a prognosis is a logical step. Educational prognosis thus may be defined as the "prediction of an individual's probable upper level of general or specific learning and his or her probable quality of achievement; usually based on objective tests . . ." (Good, 1973). Prognoses are usually described as good, guarded, or poor. The cases included here represent each level.

EXAMPLES OF LANGUAGE-LEARNING DISABLED CHILDREN

The Case of Aurora

Aurora is a twelve-and-a-half year old girl who was placed in special education after a bout with viral encephalitis five years previously. Prior to this illness, Aurora was a bright and well adjusted child who was active in sports and a good student. The effects of her illness are uncontrolled seizures, language delays, poor memory, severe word retrieval difficulties, and oppositional behavior that make therapy and instruction difficult at times. Aurora's memory problems vary, depending upon how recently she has had a seizure. If it is within three hours, it usually means that she will not perform well.

Aurora's treatment involves implementation strategies used in therapy, twice a week for half an hour each time, and therapeutic techniques employed by her teachers in the classroom. (These techniques are tried after weekly consultations with the therapist.)

The thrust of therapy is compensation for auditory memory deficits and compensatory strategies for word retrieval. These activities are both structured and spontaneous. The structured activities represent a hierarchy of prompts; phonetic cuing, syllabic cuing, semantic class cuing, associational cuing, salient feature cuing, sentence completion, and multiple choice formatting. Word-naming in the therapy session is then extended to such spontaneous activities as taking a break for a soda or light snack and making Aurora use language in order to accomplish a functional goal (e.g., using vending machines). For her word retrieval skill development, repetition of auditory stimuli is tried first, followed by the use of visual clues. Generalization to a main idea for long pieces of information is a future goal.

Aurora has two other opportunities in her academic programming for the reinforcement of the skills isolated for treatment in therapy. These are the daily speaking and listening class (30 minutes) and the weekly oral language class (30 minutes) offered to students with language difficulties. The speaking and listening class centers on development of discourse skills within an identified thematic area, stressing turn taking and topic maintenance, termination, and organization within a given topic and time frame. In this class, Aurora has difficulty, and her oppositional behaviors often emerge. For example, Aurora's classmates were discussing a recent trip to the aquarium, and she was asked to talk about her favorite animal.

Teacher: Aurora, did you like going to the aquarium?
Aurora: Yes.
   T: What did you see at the aquarium?
   A: Some ... some ... some ... (puts head down).
   T: Did you see some fish?
   A: (head comes up) ... Yes ... fish.
   T: Which one did you like best?
   A: I liked the ... the ... water ... the water .... and the ... the ... water.
   T: (pointing to a poster with several types of animals found at the aquarium). Do you see your favorite fish here? Point to it.
   A: (becoming angry) ... You don't like me! I don't like you!

At this point she left and the discussion continued for the other students. Two hours later, during mathematics, Aurora left her class to find her speaking and listening teacher. When she did find her, she burst into the teacher's room, interrupting the lesson in progress to say, "The shark! I liked the shark! It has big teeth!"

Aurora's teachers report that she has become more compliant of late but still insists on following through on her delays in retrieval, often making nontopical comments in class as she attempts to catch up.

In oral language class, conducted by an LD specialist and a speech–language pathologist, assisted by the team teachers of Aurora's homeroom, Aurora is relaxed and able to participate in a compliant manner. This class has only nine students and four special educators present to work with students. The thrust of this class for Aurora is to manage to get herself through a variety of role-play situations involving making her feelings, needs, and opinions known to one or more persons. Early in the year, she practiced these skills by pretending to go to the bank to open an imaginary bank account. Throughout the year's sessions, relevant to bank transactions, she has had to demonstrate skills in greeting and leave taking, announcing her purpose, correcting the errors of others in conducting transactions, using ritualistic phrases, gaining attention, and, making a protest. Later on, Aurora expanded her skills by taking out a loan (skills of sequencing information, responding to contingent inquires, justifying need and purpose, and making choices). The final stage of activities in this class for Aurora was using and demonstrating the use of an automatic bank machine, which she is still unable to do completely.

This functional approach to Aurora's instruction is related to her academic placement. At this time, (five years post-trauma), seizures are still not controlled with medication and her emotional control is still precarious. She demonstrates lability of affect and has attempted suicide twice. Her depressions result in extreme noncompliance and running away. Her ability to function effectively in a regular middle or junior high school, even in a special class, is questionable. At this time, another school for students with language-learning disabilities that can provide ancillary services for behavior and emotional support is being sought.

The Case of Bronson

Bronson is a nine year old boy whose special education needs have been identified from early childhood. His medical diagnosis includes hydrocephalus (corrected with a shunt), cerebral palsy (mild), and a specific learning disability. As a young child, Bronson was originally diagnosed as being mentally retarded. He has had occupational therapy since preschool for assistance with fine motor problems; his production of written material is adequate, however, for his classwork.

Recent psychological testing reveals a 32 point discrepancy between performance and verbal potential, with verbal abilities in the high average range. Because of this, it is difficult to assess Bronson's potential as indicated by a full scale score on the Wechsler Intelligence Scale for Children-Revised (WISC-R).

Speech–language assessment reveals that his receptive language abilities range from four to nine years. His strengths are in understanding syntatics and morphological forms, grammatic closure, and understanding grammatic incongruities. His weaknesses are in the pragmatic area of discourse, involving topic maintenance, making appropriate comments, and the introduction of appropriate topics into conversation. Teachers describe talking to Bronson as" . . . like talking to a 50 year old in a child's body." When Bronson was asked what you call your father's father, his response was, "My ancestor."

Working Bronson into any discussion in speaking and listening class can be a trying task for his teachers. No matter what the topic is, if Bronson is interested in something else, *that* interest will be manifested in his answers. For example, the following exchange is typical:

Teacher: (holding up a model dinosaur). Who can tell me what this is?
Bronson: A truck.
   T: Look at it again, Bronson, and think about your answer.
   B: It's a truck that takes them.
   T: Listen to someone else's answer, Bronson.

The other children name different dinosaurs and discuss the aspects of these beasts and their environment millions of years ago. Bronson explains that what he meant was that, when he saw the dinosaur exhibit at the museum, he found out that the various bones were packaged and delivered to the museum in a specific type of truck.

This is typical of Bronson's inability to introduce topics appropriately. Although his information was noteworthy, it was not a direct response to the question asked. He is often noncompliant in class when he is not interested in the topic of discussion. He'll raise his hand and blurt out, "Let's talk about baseball! My dad took me to the baseball game last Sunday!"

Therapeutic intervention for Bronson (twice a week for half an hour each time) centers on his attentional deficits, which lead to memory difficulties and poor comprehension for connected language. Activities for verbal organization and sequencing include using picture stories, following recipes, assembling toys from instructions on cassette (reinforced with written instructions), anticipating outcomes with open-ended stories and tasks, sequencing school and home routines, and spontaneously describing events in progress using an "Eyewitness News" format.

Bronson is in an oral language class, which offers him the opportunity to interact verbally with others in a structured setting while individualized goals are pursued. Instructional strategies include an exercise in which Bronson and another student use the telephone to play a game. The game is played with a game board that contains steps up to a goal sticker. Each child spins a spinner, moves the appropriate number of steps, and then selects a task card requiring him or her to make a telephone call for a defined purpose. The student must then locate the phone number, make the call, and, when the call is answered, carry out the task. On the other end of the line is the blindfolded teacher, indicating that Bronson must make his needs known in a purely oral fashion (no gesturing or facial expressions to convey meaning) and do it with dispatch. A timer is used for the tasks so that students understand that they must organize their messages and deliver them in as timely a manner as possible. Samples of the situations that Bronson might have to role play in the telephone exercise include:

1. Order a pizza with half mushrooms and half pepperoni
2. Call the fire department and give them directions to his house which is on fire
3. Call the police to come because the house across the street is being robbed
4. Order an item from a catalog
5. Call the mayor's office to complain of glass in the street
6. Call the mayor's office again to complain that the previous calls have not gotten action
7. Call a restaurant and make reservations for a party
8. Call a travel agent to arrange a vacation.

Bronson has done well in both his therapy sessions and in his language class. Performance in the speaking and listening class remains inadequate, but that is probably related more to Bronson's attention-seeking behaviors than to real processing difficulties. Most recently, Bronson achieved the privilege of being given a job as a tutor to a preschool student. Bronson's job includes eating lunch with the preschooler, giving her directions about how to use utensils appropriately, telling her what to do in mealtime routine, and taking her for a walk each day, during which he elicits appropriate responses about items and events seen. Each day, Bronson dictates into a tape recorder a journal of what he did on his preschool job. This task requires him to sequence events and describe them fully, and his grade depends upon how well he conveys his message to his unseen audience. Bronson has progressed so well that he is preparing to enter a regular elementary school next year.

The Case of Courtney

Courtney is an eight year old boy whose learning disabilities essentially are related to his limited use of vocabulary and, hence, his limited ability to convey information. His psychological testing reveals a 27 point discrepancy between performance and verbal abilities, with performance (the higher score) in the average range. Courtney draws well and illustrates many of his classmates' stories as his contribution to reading class. He is virtually a nonreader, with only *a* and *I* in his sight vocabulary. His ability to name common objects is severely limited, and responses to inquiries are single word answers. When forced into language situations in which yes or no answers are not sufficient, he shrugs and stops before getting through an answer. Although his receptive language is age appropriate according to language testing, his expressive abilities are in the range of a three or four year old. When presented with a visual stimulus, Courtney can sequence materials appropriately and with speed. His affect is sad, but assessment by a mental health counselor reveals no depression or other emotional problems. He is an exceptionally good math student.

Therapeutic intervention with Courtney has centered on the oral language class given once a week for 30 minutes. In this class, Courtney excels in Language Baseball, a game in which he scores by giving antonyms, synonyms, and attributes for given words and phrases. For example, in order to get a triple, Courtney must answer the following inquiry: "Can you tell me three things about *summer*? If he can, he gets his triple. If he can name only two things, he gets a double, and so forth.

In speaking and listening class, Courtney is expected to meet a given objective of contributions to be made in the course of the class. The objective for a given week may be: "Courtney will describe two events in which he was involved this week in school," or "Courtney will contribute to the class's Family Feud team twice this week."

The use of feely bags with Courtney is more successful now than it was early in the year. In the fall, he refused to participate in the class activity. When that behavior began to cost him points in the class behavior management system (which stresses participation), he began to make tentative, single word contributions. Courtney is basically a well-behaved, compliant child, who wants to do well and is extremely proud when he succeeds. Motivating him to participate and, therefore, achieve is still the goal. With small, repetitive steps, Courtney has improved significantly in his language skills, and he now can use a more inclusive vocabulary with his peers. He wants to be assigned a job with the preschool class, eating lunch with a student. This assignment, he knows, will require him to use his vocabulary and give directions to his preschool charge. His teachers feel that this desire is a very positive sign, and they hope that he will eventually be a tutor in the preschool art class. With continued improvement his chances for success are good. For the present, his prognosis is guarded, as his teachers wait to see if his level of enthusiasm and his degree of improvement are maintained.

SUMMARY

These cases illustrate treatment in the instructional/therapeutic setting for children with severe language-learning disabilities. Some of these students have a more optimistic prognosis than others. Aurora's prognosis is poor at present because of post-encephalitic language delays and concomitant limits in her social and educational functioning. For her, the emphasis on the functional skills of communication seems appropriate. Bronson is an interesting child with a good prognosis. He can use the strategies he has learned in the intense clinical setting and perform with limited assistance in the mainsteam. The prognosis for a student like Courtney remains guarded as the development of basic language skills and vocabulary is the crucial factor in his progress. For him, intense treatment may eventually result in the emergence of his latent language skills. The absence of the confounding factors of an emotional or medical etiology offers encouragement.

APPENDIX A: LIST OF TESTS AND ASSESSMENT INSTRUMENTS

Carrow Elicited Language Inventory-
  Teaching Resources
30 Pond Park Road
Hingham, MA

Clinical Evaluation of Language
  Functions
Charles C. Merrill Publishing Co.
Columbus, OH

Columbia Mental Maturity Scale
Harcourt Brace Jovanovich
New York, N.Y.

Detroit Tests of Learning Aptitude
PRO-ED Inc.
Austin, TX

Expressive One-Word Picture Vocabulary
  Test
Academic Therapy Publications
Novato, CA

Illinois Test of Psycholinguistic Abilities
University of Illinois Press
Urbana, IL

Kaufman Assessment Battery for
  Children
American Guidance Service
Circle Pines, MN

Northwestern Syntax Screening Test
Northwestern University Press
Evanston, IL

Peabody Picture Vocabulary Test
American Guidance Service
Circle Pines, MN

Raven's Standardized Progressive
  Matrices
The Psychological Corp.
New York, N.Y.

Rey Auditory-Verbal Learning Test,
  in C.M. Taylor:
Psychological Appraisal of Children with
  Cerebral Defects.
Cambridge, MA
Harvard University Press, 1959

Stanford-Binet Intelligence Scale-Form
  L-M
Houghton-Mifflin Co.
Boston, MA

Test for Auditory Comprehension of
  Language
Teaching Resources
Hingham, MA

CHAPTER 6

Communication Skills

Nancy J. Spekman

Many learning-disabled (LD) students have been described as experiencing a variety of interpersonal problems. For example, they have been reported to be less well accepted and more socially rejected by their peers and teachers, to have a variety of social perception problems, to say the wrong thing at the wrong time, and to experience considerable difficulty conveying their ideas, both orally and in writing (Bryan, 1974, 1976; Chapman, Larsen, & Parker, 1979; Garrett & Crump, 1980; Johnson & Myklebust, 1967). While certainly not typical of all LD students, reports such as these have been common enough to stimulate research in a variety of areas that might help to explain the presence of social deficits and rejection. One line of investigation has involved the in-depth examination of the interpersonal communication skills of LD students.

The study of communication skills represents a major shift in focus for language researchers studing both normal and disordered populations. This shift, from a focus on language structure (phonology, morphology, and syntax) and content (semantics) to language use in natural interactions, has developed out of a re-emerging interest in pragmatics. As defined by Bates (1976), pragmatics refers to the rules governing the use of language in a social context. In other words, emphasis is on the use of language to accomplish a variety of purpose within different contexts, for example to communicate.

This chapter originally appeared as an article by **Nancy J. Spekman** in *Learning Disabilities: An Interdisciplinary Journal* (Vol. III, 1984) and was adapted by permission of Grune & Stratton for inclusion in this *Handbook*.

Communicative competence is dependent upon the complex integration of linguistic, cognitive, and social skills. Thus, at least some individuals with identified deficits in one or more of these three areas might be predicted to demonstrate concomitant problems in the area of communication. Indeed, there is a growing body of literature that focuses on pragmatic skills of children with specific language impairments, (see Fey & Leonard, 1983, for a review), mental retardation (Guralnick, 1978), or social differences or deviance (Schumaker, Hazel, Sherman, & Sheldon, 1982). However, linguistic, cognitive, and social competence demonstrated separately are not sufficient to guarantee that an individual will demonstrate appropriate language use. Numerous clinical reports and empirical analyses indicate that there are also children who demonstrate major communication deficits that transcend linguistic or cognitive limitations and that exist even in the presence of normal language and cognitive skills (Blank, Gessner, & Esposito, 1979; Byron & Pflaum, 1978; Spekman, 1981). Many LD students could be included in this latter group. The reports of communication differences between LD and normally achieving peers typically cannot be explained as being due to linguistic and cognitive deficits.

The primary purpose of this chapter is to present a framework for understanding and studying the development of language use and to review the extant literature related to the pragmatic skills of LD students. Selected research focusing on young language-impaired children is also included because many of these children, upon entry into school and exposure to academic demands, will be considered learning disabled. Two major components within the broad area of language use will be considered. The first, discourse skills, involves the use of language during ongoing conversations and interactions between two or more individuals. The second, narrative skills, involves the use of language during storytelling and other extended verbal elaborations or explanations. To conclude, a brief discussion of assessment and intervention is presented.

DISCOURSE SKILLS

Although taken for granted by most of us, the development of discourse or conversational skills requires the integration of a complex set of behaviors. Conversations are seen as dynamic interchanges between a minimum of two communication partners. Successful conversation requires that the speaker knows what to talk about, under what circumstances, and how to say it. It also requires that the listener attend to the speaker and provide appropriate feedback and that both partners know and follow the rules regarding cooperation, turn-taking, sequencing, violations and repairs, and other responsibilities (Grice, 1975; Hymes, 1971; Schegloff,

1972). Performance must be monitored and adapted continuously and should reflect the ability to utilize these complex and diverse factors in the generation of messages.

Clearly, children are not born with the ability to participate successfully in conversations; even as adults, individuals continue to err with respect to what they say, to whom they say it, and how they say it. Like most forms of human knowledge, receptive and expressive communication skills develop gradually throughout childhood (Prutting, 1979).

Organizational Framework

To insure a mutual understanding of terminology and a shared frame of reference, it is helpful to begin with the presentation of an organizational framework for approaching the study of discourse (see also Roth & Speckman, 1984a, 1984b; Spekman, 1983; Spekman & Roth, 1982, 1984). The following is a brief summary of each component within this framework.

Communicative Intentions

The notion of communicative intentions refers to the purpose, function, or intended meaning of a message and to the form those intentions can take. Looking first at function, we see that messages can be used to serve a wide variety of intentions. For example, a message can be used to comment, gain attention, request information, direct the behavior of others, persuade, greet, protect, promise, or respond to questions and comments of another (Austin, 1962; Dore, 1977; Searle, 1969). Competent communicators understand and produce a full range of such intentions.

In addition, competent communicators utilize different forms, both verbal and nonverbal, to convey their intentions. Communicative intentions can be conveyed *gesturally,* through any number of body movements and facial expressions; *paralinguistically,* through changes in stress patterns, duration, intonation, pitch, and intensity levels; and/or *linguistically,* through words, phrases, and sentences. Any particular intention can be conveyed in different ways. For example, someone desiring a piece of pie might merely point at the pie or to her empty dessert plate. She might also say "Give me a piece of pie (please)," "I want some pie," "Would you mind if I had a piece?" or "Ah...pecan pie...my favorite!" Further, any particular gesture or utterance can be used to convey more than one communicative intention. For example, the statement, "I wish I had a watch," could be used as a hint to solicit the current time from someone or as a request for an upcoming birthday present.

It is evident from the above examples that communicative intentions can be conveyed very explicitly in forms in which the intent is easily recognized (e.g., "Give me a piece of pie") or more implicitly in forms requiring some degree of inference to ascertain the intended meaning (e.g.,"Ah ... pecan pie ... my favorite"). Also, a variety of different forms are frequently used simultaneously, and the messages conveyed may or may not be congruent. In instances of sarcasm, for example, the message conveyed by the tone of voice may be at odds with the verbal message. The recipients of such messages must determine the real meaning intended by the speaker and, thus, decide to which message attention should be directed.

In summary, individual speakers and listeners must develop both receptive and productive mastery of the possible range of communicative intentions and of the forms available for coding such intentions. Selection of the most appropriate form to use, given a particular listener or social situation, or of the most likely meaning intended by a speaker is related, in part, to the next component, presuppositional abilities.

Presupposition

The notion of presupposition has to do with the ability to take the perspective of one's conversational partner. As noted, listeners often must infer the speaker's intent rather than rely exclusively on a literal interpretation of what is said. Speakers also must infer information about their partners and the context to determine the appropriate content and form of a message. Presupposition, then, has to do with that information that is not necessarily explicit in a message but which must be shared by the communication partners if a message is to be properly understood (Bates, 1976b).

Information or knowledge that is shared by communication partners is considered to be old information and may thus be assumed and need not be explicitly stated. For example, when speaking about a sculpture that is currently being viewed by two interlocutors, it is acceptable for one to say "I wonder what *he* was trying to say" and not have to specify the meaning of "he" as being the sculptor. Such shared knowledge can be established in several ways: (a) by mutually monitoring some shared aspect of the physical setting (as in the preceding example); (b) by sharing some general knowledge of the speech situation itself or of the partner (e.g., age, cognitive level, status); and (c) by mutually monitoring the preceding discourse (Fillmore, 1975; Spekman 1983).

In contrast to old information, information that is new (i.e., *not* shared by the conversational partners), must be clearly and explicitly expressed. Using the preceding example, the statement would not be understandable and would create confusion if one art gallery visitor expressed it to a friend without first establishing that she was speaking about a particular sculpture by Brancusi. However, once an entity being referred to has been clearly established (i.e., is now considered shared knowledge), it can then be referred to either more specifically (a dog → the dog) or less specifically by using personal and demonstrative pronouns (Mary → she, the doll → that) and terms of location (the park → there) or time (May 13 → then) (Speckman & Roth, 1982). Speakers and listeners both must accurately differentiate between that which can be presupposed (old information) and that which must be asserted (new information).

There are many factors that need to be considered when determining what can or cannot be presupposed and which thus influence the form and content of messages. First, a variety of listener characteristics, such as listener age, social status, verbal ability, cognitive level, degree of familiarity to speaker, current state of knowledge, or shared past experiences, are important. We tend to talk differently to different communication partners. For example, "Shut the door" might be an acceptable form to use with a child or a friend, but "Would you please close the door?" would probably be a more acceptable form when addressing one's boss. We also talk differently in different situations. "What's that?" might be appropriate when accompainied by pointing to the object in question but would be inappropriate if the listener were in another room. Social context (e.g., place of employment, school, formal dance, informal get-together) and the avaibility of feedback (e.g., phone conversations versus face-to-face interactions) are other important factors.

Social Organization of Discourse

The third component, the social organization of discourse, involves a level of analysis that focuses more on the dynamic, reciprocal, and ongoing nature of dialogue. A dialogue can be considered as a series of conversational turns that focus on a particular topic. Participants are expected to demonstrate a wide variety of appropriate conversational behaviors.

New topics must be initiated clearly and at appropriate times (e.g., not before another topic has been terminated). Ensuing utterances should be on topic and relevant and should serve to maintain the topic (e.g., answer a specific question) or to maintain the topic and add new information, and then to transfer the conversational floor. Turn-taking should be shared, and partners should be able to successfully assume the responsibilities of both the speaker and listener roles. Messages should be intelligible, unambiguous, and appropriate to one's partner and the situation and should be issued once a partner's attention has been secured.

Partners should provide feedback to each other indicating their receipt of the message and any possible confusion regarding the message. Feedback indicating successful exchange of information may take the form of head nods, a variety of vocalizations (e.g., "yeah," "uh-huh," "I see"), facial expressions and body posture. Similarly, indications of communicative breakdown may take the form of quizzical facial expressions, shrugged shoulders, or a variety of questions and statements such as "Huh?" "I don't understand," and "What time did you say?" that indicate the need for information to be elaborated, clarified, or repeated (Garvey, 1977a).

In instances of communicative breakdown, partners must first recognize that a breakdown exists; second, determine the cause (e.g., poor intelligibility, low volume, failure to establish mutual attention, failure to clearly establish a referent [Garvey, 1975; Mueller, 1972]); and third, select and implement an appropriate strategy to repair the breakdown (e.g., repeat the message, enunciate more clearly, reword the message).

Finally, once both partners have made their contributions, topics need to be terminated either with successful shifts to new topics or cessation of dialogue.

In sum, social interactions require the utilization or the potential to utilize all of the above skills on a continuing basis. Ongoing monitoring of dialogue by both partners and the ability to respond flexibly to the changing demands of the situations are obvious needs.

Context

The final element of the framework involves the context in which an interaction occurs. Each of the preceding three components really can be evaluated only when context is considered (Bloom, 1970; Keller-Cohen, 1978). The nature of the interaction and the formulation and comprehension of messages are influenced, for example, by the channels available for communication, the availability of feedback, and the physical environment itself.

Discourse Skills of Learning-Disabled Students

Given the relative recency of interest in the general area of language use, it is not surprising that there is limited body of literature that has focused on students experiencing a variety of learning difficulties. Utilizing the above framework, the following sections review the current literature that examines the discourse skills of young language-impaired and school-aged LD students. Children with language impairments have typically been identified as having deficits in the comprehension and/or production of language in the absence of significant cognitive, emotional, and sensory impairment. Samples of LD children are typically even more heterogeneous and are selected on the basis of a significant discrepancy between intelligence and language skills and/or one or more academic skill areas. Frequently, these samples have been poorly described in the literature, making it somewhat difficult to compare the results of different research studies. Thus, the findings of the reports reviewed here should be considered suggestive, not definitive, and, hopefully, will serve as the foundation for future research efforts.

Communicative Intentions

There are numerous clinical reports that suggest that language-impaired and LD students demonstrate the use of language without communicative intent, the use of a limited range of intentions, or the use of limited coding mechanisms (Blank et al., 1979; Geller & Wollner, 1976). However, empirical research on the range and form of communicative intentions understood and expressed by these children is at a preliminary stage and is limited, typically by small sample sizes, restricted age ranges, and a restricted focus on the intentions investigated.

Three studies compared the communicative intentions of language-impaired children at the one-word stage of development with those of normal children matched for mean length of utterance (MLU). Snyder (1978) and Rowan and Leonard (1981) both successfully elicited declarative (informing) and imperative (directing) utterances from their subjects using structured tasks. Snyder (1978), however, reported that the language-delayed children were less likely to code their intentions linguistically despite the presence of an adequate vocabulary and tended to rely more on relatively primitive gestures. In direct contrast, Rowan and Leonard (1981) reported that both groups primarily used verbal means to code the two intentions. Leonard, Camarata, Rowan, and Chapman (1982) investigated a broader range of intentions and reported that the language-impaired and normal children produced a similar range with nearly equivalent frequency and coded those intentions in a very similar manner.

Rom and Bliss (1981) and Fey, Leonard, Fey, and O'Connor (1978) all investigated the range of communicative intentions produced by more linguistically advanced language-impaired children when compared to age-matched and/or linguistic-level-matched normal peers. Despite the use of different coding systems, all three investigations found no differences in the range of intentions expressed by their subjects. Unfortunately, none of these studies looked at differences in the coding mechanisms used.

Others have investigated comprehension skills when the communicative intent (usually request or directive forms) is expressed in direct versus indirect ways. Conti and Friel-Patti (1982) found differences in the ability of language-impaired and normal peers, matched on a variety of language measures, to comprehend direct and indirect directives presented by an experimenter but found no group differences when the same directives were presented by each child's mother. Results were explained by the fact that the experimenter was limited to producing each directive only once, whereas the mothers were allowed to repeat directives and to make frequent reference to the background scenario and objects to be manipulated. Prinz and Ferrier (1983) also reported that most of their language-impaired subjects (ages 3½ to 9 years) comprehended both direct and indirect forms.

Only one study that focused specifically on students identified as learning disabled was found in this area. In a study of responses to requests, Pearl, Donahue, and Bryan (1981b) found that their LD subjects in grades three through eight were as likely as their normal peers to respond appropriately to both direct and indirect requests for more information.

In summary, little is known about LD students and how they perform in this area. However, the research on young language-impaired children suggests that they comprehend and produce a full range of communicative intentions, but that they may be somewhat deficient or delayed in the forms they use to express their intentions. It might be suggested that more advanced syntactic forms require increased levels of attention during production. This absence of automaticity requires that attention be directed toward linguistic demands rather than toward disclosure demands (Snyder & Downey, 1983). Children with language impairments might thus elect to use simpler, more automatic forms so that their attention can be directed more appropriately to accomplishing their communicative intent within the constraints of a discourse situation.

Presupposition

The presuppositional abilities of students with language and learning problems have been investigated from several perspectives. The intent has been to find evidence within discourse of their perspective-taking abilities and their use of coding mechanisms appropriate to particular audiences and situations. Some of the studies reported have looked at language use within relatively naturalistic free-play sessions; most studies, however, have utilized structured experimental tasks that place the child within a contrived context.

One line of investigation has examined how children code information that is new or changing and, therefore, cannot be presupposed but must be explicitly coded. Snyder (1978) reported that the verbal utterances of her language-delayed subjects at the one-word stage were less likely to convey the most informative element than those of the chronologically younger children.

Referential communication tasks were used by Noel (1980) and Spekman (1978, 1981), both of whom compared and found significant differences between 9- and 11-year-old LD and normally achieving boys in their abilities to convey essential information. Referential communication tasks typically require that two subjects, a speaker and a listener, speak together to accomplish a joint goal; the communication partners are usually separated by an opaque barrier. Noel's (1980) subjects were asked to describe novel/ambiguous figures so that listeners could select the correct one from among several choices. Listener identification errors were greater for messages from LD speakers than for those from normal speakers. Spekman's (1978, 1981) subjects had to describe a pattern of blocks so that the listener could produce the same pattern with the correct blocks in the correct locations. The LD children provided significantly less information needed for successful task completion. Further analysis of the language used to complete the task revealed that both LD and normally achieving children demonstrated some difficulty in being able to consistently differentiate appropriately between old and new information and to maintain their listener's perspective on a continuing basis (Spekman, 1978). Typical errors were total failure to establish a referent, ambiguous reference, too great a time lapse between initial identification of a referent and subsequent reference to it, and failure to consider that one's listener was not sharing the same visual environment. Interestingly, the LD children made significantly more errors than the normally achieving children in their use of terms of spatial reference.

Similarly, Caro and Schneider (1982) reported that LD adolescents were more likely than normal students to use the definite article inappropriately with the first mention of a referent; for example, they tended to use the definite article (e.g., "the boy") for first mention, before which boy had been established. Feagans, Fisher, and Short (1982) also reported that their LD students used pronouns whose referents had not been specified.

Donahue (1981a) reported the results of a study that compared LD and nondisabled children in grades one to six on the comprehension and production of syntactic devices for marking given (old) versus new information. The children were first shown pairs of pictures in which two elements differed and one was constant (a boy riding a bike and a girl riding a horse). A sentence (representing one of five sentence types) was presented and the children were asked to select the correct picture. Because neither picture was accurately described by the sentence (e.g., The boy is riding the horse), it was presumed that the child's choice indicated which component of the sentence was considered given or presupposed. For the production task, the children were asked to correct each sentence by saying what should have been said to describe the picture. This required that the children specifically note the mismatched element. Group differences for comprehension were found only for LD girls due to their lower comprehension of cleft sentences (e.g., It is the boy who is riding the horse). Productively, the LD students relied on less complex sentence types, but they were equally clear in marking old versus new information as were their nondisabled peers.

A second stream of research in the area of presupposition has to do with the ability of children to make certain linguistic changes as a function of listener or partner characteristics. Fey, Leonard, and Wilcox (1981) reported that a group of preschool language-impaired children, like normal preschool children, made lingusitic adjustments such as using simpler language when interacting with younger children. This provided some evidence for their sensitivity to listener age.

Bryan and Pflaum (1978) and Donahue (1981b) investigated the ability of LD students to modify syntactic complexity and the degree of politeness and persuasiveness of messages according to attributes of the listener. The results of both studies suggested there are potentially important gender differences within sample of LD children with only the boys in these studies being less sensitive than the nondisabled children to their audiences. To date, however, no satisfactory explanation for this difference has been offered. Pearl, Donahue, and Bryan (1981a) also reported that their LD subjects were less tactful.

Bryan and his colleagues (Bryan & Perlmutter, 1979; Bryan & Sherman, 1980) have conducted a series of experiments that focus on the ingratiation tactics of LD students. These investigations developed out of the consistent finding that LD students engaged in a dyadic interactions could be differentiated from nondisabled students by groups of naive adults. Bryan, Sonnefeld, and Greenberg (1981) found that LD children were more likely than nondisabled children to endorse ingratiation tactics that were judged by college students to be relatively undesirable, despite the finding by Bryan and Sonnefeld (1981) that LD and nondisabled children and adults tend to agree on the desirability of particular tactics directed towards particular targets. More recently, however, Perlmutter and Bryan (1984) found that when LD students were told to "act naturally" in an interview situation, they were judged more negatively than their nondisabled peers; but when the LD students were directed to ingratiate the interviewer, they were judged equally as positively.

While replication is certainly needed in other areas, this latter finding may have considerable import. It may indicate that previously identified differences might not be present in situations in which LD students have been explicitly directed to behave in a certain way (e.g., be polite, be tactful). In other words, reported differences might not be due to certain skill area deficits but due more to an inability to utilize consistently or know when to utilize skills that they already possess.

Social Organization of Discourse

Early work on the social skills of LD students interacting with normal peers characterized their interactions as more hostile and less cooperative than those of normal peers (Bryan & Bryan, 1978). Recent work which has focused more on the reciprocal relations established during interactions, suggests that LD and language-impaired children are somewhat less successful in assuming role responsibility in both speaker and listener positions. Spekman (1981) suggested, for example, that the fourth- and fifth-grade LD boys in her study performed like their normally achieving peers when primary responsibility for structuring the task rested with the nondisabled student, whereas significant differences were found when the LD boys were expected to provide the structure and control. Sadler (1982) found that language-impaired preschoolers demonstrated greater conversational skill and success when interacting with language-normal than with language-impaired peers, in part, because of the skill of the normal peers.

The results of several studies have suggested that LD and language-impaired children assume less assertive roles during interactions with their normally achieving peers. Watson's (1977) 5-year-old, language-impaired children used more "back channel" responses (e.g., "yeah," "oh," "okay"), which do not result in their user's assumption of the conversational floor or transference of control.

Bryan, Donahue, Pearl, and Strum (1981) investigated the conversational control demonstrated by second- and fourth-grade LD and nondisabled children within a setting in which both groups of children were given explicit responsibility for controlling the interaction. Subjects were asked to be the hosts on a videotaped TV talk show and were to interview a nondisabled peer about movies and TV shows. The LD children were found to be less skilled in initiating and maintaining the interaction and in maintaining the dominant speaker's role. They were less likely to ask questions and, of those questions used, asked a smaller proportion of open-ended questions (i.e., those questions most apt to elicit extended responses). Further, eight of nine instances in which a guest took over or assumed the host role involved LD hosts.

Bryan, Donahue, and Pearl (1981) and Bryan, Donahue, Pearl, and Herzog (1984) also found differences in the manner in which the LD children participated in small-group problem-solving tasks. The LD subjects were less persuasive and more submissive to both their peers and their mothers. However, Markoski (1983), utilizing a similar group-decision activity, found that the LD and nondisabled students were equally persuasive in getting their own choices to be group choices.

When information is not successfully conveyed, for whatever reason, a communicative breakdown occurs. Responsibility for recognizing and repairing the breakdown lies with one or both partners. Spekman (1981) found that her LD subjects asked fewer questions that requested new information needed for task success. Donahue, Pearl, and Bryan (1980) reported that their subjects were less likely to initiate repair by requesting clarification when presented with messages which were either partially informative or uninformative. Spekman (1978), although not testing for group differences, reported that both normally achieving and LD listeners were able to tolerate high levels of confusion or ambiguity without requesting clarification. Finally, Pearl and colleagues (1981b) directed explicit and implicit requests for clarification to LD and nondisabled children and reported that the groups behaved very similarly in their recognition of the need to provide more information.

In summary, the above results certainly suggest that students exhibiting different learning problems also demonstrate some areas of difficulty with respect to their interaction skills. Obviously, more research is needed, some of which needs to occur within more naturalistic settings. Further, while numerous hypotheses have been generated to attempt to explain these difficulties (e.g., production deficit, different perceptions of communicative roles, learned helplessness), all remain to be further tested.

NARRATIVE SKILLS

Narratives involve the expression of more extended or elaborated units of text. As used in the literature today, the term narrative can refer to storytelling (either of fairy and folktales or familiar or original stories), retelling of movie sequences or the like, and relating of personal experiences. Narrative may be oral or written.

Narratives involve many of the same requirements as discourse. For example, a topic or purpose must be clearly established, referents and new information must be clearly identified, and the content and language structure should be geared appropriately to the audience. However, in contrast to dialogue in which shared interaction is expected, narratives carry the expectaion that the speaker maintains an oral monologue and that the listener(s) listen. Although it is possible for a listener to interrupt an oral narrative to request clarification (and such is obviously the case, especially when listening to the narratives of young children), such action would appear to violate the expectation for mature, well-developed narratives. Thus, it is up to the speaker to present the information in an organized, coherent, and interesting manner and to be responsible for the continuity and completeness of the information.

Written narratives place even greater demands on the narrator. Without an immediate audience, there are no possibilities for receiving external feedback regarding confusing messages. The writer must assume sole responsibility for monitoring message effectiveness through rereadings and revisions. Further, the audience for one's written work is frequently unknown, thereby further increasing the demands for specificity and clarity of presentation. Finally, written narratives require the complex integration of all of these organizational, language, and perspective-taking skills with the other demands of writing such as handwriting, spelling, and punctuation.

Framework For Analysis

Johnston (1982) has suggested that there are at least four levels of analysis that may be useful when examining narratives: narrative structure, scripts, cohesion within the text, and adaptation to one's audience. Each is discussed in turn, and then the relevant research on LD subjects is reviewed.

Narrative Structure

Regardless of the type of narrative, some type of structure or organizational rule system exists. Although it might vary somewhat from genre to genre, there appears to be considerable overlap in terms of some shared essential components. Narrative structure has been examined primarily from two perspectives.

The first, or story grammar, approach has attempted to analyze the internal structure of stories and thereby has identified the various components of stories and the rules governing their sequence and combination. Despite differences in terminology and some proposed rules, such investigators as Stein and Glenn (1979) and Mandler and Johnson (1977) are in general agreement with respect to major constituents and their typical sequence.

According to Stein and Glenn (1979), for example, a story is viewed as a hierarchical network of categories and logical relations connecting them. The basic categories include a *setting,* which introduces the main character(s) and describes the physical, social, and temporal context, and a series of one or more *episodes,* each of which describes a behavorial sequence. It is proposed that each episode consists of (a) an initiating event; (b) an internal response — the feelings, thoughts, and goals of a character in response to an initiating event; (c) a plan — the intended action of the character; (d) an attempt — overt action(s) of the character; (e) a consequence — the successful or unsuccessful results of the attempt in terms of goal attainment; and (f) a reaction — an emotional or evaluative response to the behavorial sequence by the character. Episodes are logically connected by casual, temporal, or additive relations. Further, episodes may be embedded within other episodes.

It has also been proposed that this organizational structure corresponds in some way to the manner in which hearers and producers of stories organize story information. In other words, we are thought to have an internalized story schemata resembling this framework that is utilized in our comprehension and formulation of stories. The psychological validity of story grammar schema and episode structure has been demonstrated across diverse age groups in a variety of experiments utilizing story retelling tasks (e.g., Bower, 1978; Mandler & Goodman, 1982; Mandler & Johnson, 1977; Stein & Glenn, 1979).

A second way of examining story structure has developed out of the research on "sharing time" narratives produced by young children (Michaels, 1981). Sharing time, according to Michaels (1981), is a "recurring classroom activity where children are called upon to describe an object or give a narrative account about some past [or future] event to the entire class" (p. 423). Topics are usually personal, out-of-school experiences. Narratives produced during sharing time tend to begin with temporal and spatial information, introduce a key agent, and then get right into the action (Michaels, 1981). Michaels identified two narrative styles. *Topic-centered* narratives tend to be highly organized and focused on a single, clearly identifiable event. In contrast, *topic-associating* narratives consist of a series of implicitly associated personal anecdotes. Listeners unaccustomed to such narratives report that it is difficult to determine the overall theme and to follow the chain of events because of the absence of explicit, logical connectors. Michaels (1981) stresses that such narratives are *not* random sequences but that the relationships must be inferred. Topic-centered narratives tend to fulfill the expectations held by most teachers regarding narrative structure and are typically well accepted. Topic-associating narratives, however, violate many of these expectations, frequently create confusion in listeners, and thus tend to be less well accepted.

Regardless of one's framework for studying narrative structure, it is clear that a sense of narrative grows and matures with continuing development of children. According to Applebee (1978), for example, children's stories progress from "heaps" (diffuse and undirected texts in which unrelated objects or events seem to be related only by chance) through a series of stages culminating in mature "narratives," characterized by events tied to a concrete or abstract core, a beginning and conclusion, and a theme or moral. Others, using a story grammar scheme, have also demonstrated developmental differences (Mandler & Johnson, 1977; Stein & Glenn, 1979).

Scripts

The notion of scripts relates to the content of certain narratives. *Scripts* are predictable mental representations of the chain of events involved in everyday life situations (e.g., taking a bath, going to

McDonald's, doing laundry) that develop through the child's participation in and observation of others in specific, recurring daily routines (Schank & Abelson, 1977). Individuals utilize their knowledge of scripts (i.e., their knowledge about their world) in comprehending narratives, in generating expectations regarding what is likely to occur, and in making inferences regarding information that is not explicitly coded. As with story grammar schemas, research involving the notion of scripts (Gibbs & Tenney, 1980; Wimmer 1979) provides useful information regarding children's underlying knowledge of narratves.

Text Cohesion

The third level of analysis involves the study of specific cohesive devices that tie the text together into a coherent whole. Coherence is the quality that makes the text stand as a unit and that relates messages within the text in some salient way. Halliday and Hasan (1976) present one system for looking at cohesion. They have identified the following five types of cohesive relations:

1. *Reference* involves the use of personal pronouns (e.g., he, him, she, it, they), demonstratives (e.g., this, that, these, those), and comparatives (e.g., same, different). Such terms are themselves empty of meaning and serve to point to or refer to something else; they can be interpreted only by something else being clearly established within the text. For example, Mother went to the store. *She* bought a coat *there.*
2. *Substitution* can be either nominal (e.g., one, ones), verbal (e.g., do, be, do so, have), or clausal (so, not). These items function in a similar manner to reference items but must be of the same grammatical category as the item substituted. For example, I like to play tennis. So *do* my sisters.
3. *Ellipsis* is actually cohesion by omission and occurs when an already established unit of information is omitted. For example, I debated over which sweater to take. I decided to take the red *(sweater).*
4. *Conjunction* involves the use of ties that presuppose the presence of other components in the discourse. Such ties can be additive (and), adversative (but, although, yet), causal (because, therefore), and temporal (then, next, soon). For example, Mary was feeling very ill. *Therefore,* she decided to miss the party.
5. *Lexical* cohesion refers to the repetitive use of the same word, or the use of synonyms, superordinates, and general words (e.g., thing) that serve to establish a continuity of meaning across a unit of discourse. For example, The first graders went to the zoo and saw elephants, giraffes, and lions. It was late afternoon and the *animals* were being fed by the keeper.

In each of the above examples, interpretation of the italicized words in the second sentence is dependent upon information contained in the first sentence. In this manner, the two sentences are tied to each other.

Audience Adaptation

The final level of analysis is not as formalized as the preceding areas. It concerns the degree of sensitivity of narratives to the particular needs of different audiences. Information gathered utilizing the preceding three variables can provide information regarding listener sensitivity. First, the structure of any narrative may serve either to facilitate or inhibit listener comprehension. Narratives in which the setting is not found at the beginning, events are out of sequence, or episodic structure is incomplete may create considerable listener confusion. Second, it is the responsibility of the narrator to clearly establish knowledge that must be shared by partners for comprehension to occur. It might be assumed, thus, that narratives about highly personal or idiosyncratic events place greater demands on the narrator than those that focus on highly familiar scripts. Cohesive ties (their appropriate or inappropriate use) will also provide information regarding the narrator's proper manipulation of old versus new information; that is, the use of cohesive ties presumes that certain information is already established within the text and may, therefore, now be presupposed.

Finally, the spontaneous repairs made by narrators provide evidence of attempts to clarify information for a listener (Cazden, Michaels, & Tabors, in press; Clark & Anderson, 1979). Repairs may take the form of modifications in linguistic structure (word or syntactic changes, reformulations), content (clarification or elaboration of information; addition of new, needed information; recognization of thematic content), or extralinguistic form (use of variable pitch or stress, or the addition of nonverbal gestures). Repairs would appear to indicate that users are monitoring listener needs and thinking ahead about whether their message will be successfully conveyed.

Narrative Skills of Learning-Disabled Students

There is currently a paucity of empirical data on the narrative skills of language-impaired and LD students. For years there have been clinical reports that the extended explanations and narratives of some LD students could be characterized by poor organization, improper sequencing, and failure to clearly introduce or establish and maintain a topic, (Johnson & Myklebust, 1967). Blalock (1982) reported that similar problems continued to exist in 21% of a group of LD adults studied. Few people, however, have utilized more formal analytic procedures to evaluate the narratives of these individuals.

In the area of story grammars, Graybeal (1981), Weaver and Dickinson (1979), and Worden, Malmgren, and Gabourie (1982) investigated the story recall abilities of groups of LD children or adults. Their results seem to suggest that the amount of information recalled by the exceptional students was lower than that recalled by the nondisabled individuals, but that the stories of exceptional students retained many of the essential components of a story grammar schemata and maintained the same relative saliency of categories. In many ways, their stories resembled those of younger individuals. McNamee and Harris-Schmidt (1984) reported that very few of the narratives of their LD subjects (ages 6 to 11 years) were classified at either of Applebee's (1978) two highest levels. Roth and Spekman are currently involved in analyzing the story grammars found in original stories produced by LD and nondisabled students, but data are not yet available.

Liles (1982) and Feagans and colleagues (1982) have examined cohesive devices in verbal narratives of language-disordered and LD students. Feagans and colleagues (1982) reported that the story retellings of LD individuals were characterized by the frequent use of pronouns whose referents had not been specified. Liles' (1982) language-disordered and normal subjects (ages 7 years, 5 months to 10 years, 8 months) were shown a movie and asked to recall it once to a listener who had also seen the movie and once to a naive listener. In both conditions, the language-disordered children made significantly more errors in their use of cohesive terms, resulting in erroneous or ambiguous information. As Liles notes, however, the results of studies involving recall may be confounded by some aspects of story comprehension. The language-disordered children who made the most errors in their use of cohesive ties also answered 65% or less of questions regarding the *relationships* between characters and events in the movie; these same children, however, answered factual questions accurately.

ASSESSMENT AND INTERVENTION

Because there is a need for increaed research describing the use of language by language-impaired and LD students, there is also a need for increased attention to be directed towards diagnostic techniques and procedures and toward the development and validation of various intervention strategies. Roth and Spekman (1984a, 1984b) and Spekman and Roth (1982, 1984) have proposed some general guidelines and considerations as well as specific strategies for both assessment and intervention in the area of discourse. However, these areas are ripe for research.

Donahue and Bryan (1983) utilized modeling as an intervention strategy with LD boys in grades two to eight. The intent was to test the effects of modeling on the conversation skills of students playing the role of host on a TV talk show. Experimental subjects listened either to a tape of a dialogue involving a child interviewer modeling open-ended questions, conversational devices, and contingent comments and questions or to a monologue of only the interviewee's responses. LD subjects in the dialogue condition increased their use of process questions and contingent comments to the level of their nondisabled peers and increased their overall contributions to the interaction. Donahue and Bryan suggest that success with such a brief exposure to modeling and no direct instruction probably indicates that the skills were already within the children's repertoire but needed to be stimulated or tapped.

Finally, the work of McNamee (1985) and McNamee and Harris-Schmidt (1984) appears to offer considerable promise with respect to intervention aimed at the development of narrative skills. Utilizing the theoretical perspective of Vygotsky, McNamee (1985) has proposed that the origin of narratives is social and interactive in nature. She describes the narratives of preschool children as consisting of a series of exchanges between a child and an adult. The adult who becomes an active participant provides comments and questions that serve to help the child focus and structure the narrative and provide clarifying or additional information when needed. Peer listeners may also serve the same function. According to McNamee, it is this input by adults and peers that aids the development of the child's thinking and independent functioning and fosters the eventual internalization of the essential components and structure of a narrative. In other words, guidance that is initially provided externally becomes internalized and is used by the child as a means of self-guidance.

McNamee (1985) and McNamee and Harris-Schmidt (1984) utilized this theoretical background in their intervention studies with normal and LD students. As part of the daily school routine, students were given the opportunity to tell stories. An adult transcribed what was said and asked the sort of guiding and structuring questions described above. Students were also given the opportunity to dramatize their stories. The dramatization proved to be an additional compelling stimulus for storytelling, ideas were shared and the narrator received additional feedback from peers. Their results suggest that the combined use of adult cueing and dramatization served to improve the narratives produced by normal preschool children and by school-aged LD students over relatively short periods of time (6 to 10 weeks). Such instructional strategy avoids direct instruction regarding the structure of stories but permits the adult to play a critical role of guiding while allowing the children to play with the various forms of language about which they are learning.

SUMMARY

The focus of this chapter has been on language use. In particular, discourse and narrative skills, two areas assumed under the broad scope of language use, have been examined. Within each area an organizational framework has been presented, and the relevant research focusing on language-impaired and learning-disabled individuals has been reviewed. It has been the intent to provide the reader with a foundation and to stimulate interest in this area of pragmatics.

CHAPTER 7

Reading Disabilities

H istorically, remediation of reading disabilities has tended to focus on treatment of perceptual-motor problems. Although specific neurological or perceptual deficits continue to be an issue, more recent thinking has largely shifted towards a variety of other areas thought to be important for understanding disabilities in reading.

Reading disabilities, let alone their remediation, remains a controversial area. We will be using a definition of the term, discussed in more detail elsewhere (Kavale & Forness, 1985a), which implies a significant discrepancy between reading performance and intelligence, as measured by careful individual assessment, in the absence of serious physical or sensory handicaps, emotional disorder, mental retardation or inadequate previous instruction. This is an operational definition in which neurological etiology is neither implied nor ruled out. Historically, however, neurological concepts have greatly influenced the field; this legacy will be discussed first.

HISTORICAL LEGACY OF READING DISABILITIES

Since its initial clinical description of the turn of the century (Hinshelwood, 1900; Morgan, 1896), the syndrome of specific reading disabilities has generated controversy regarding both cause and treatment.

Hinshelwood (1917) described "visual word blindness" as an inability to recognize words resulting from damage to the visual memory center in the left hemisphere. Subsequently, Orton (1925) advanced the idea that specific reading disorders resulted from a lag in the development of left-hemisphere dominance leading to strephosymobolia ("twisted symbols"). From these foundation statements, refined conceptualizations interpreting the role of visual perceptual deficits continued to promote the concept of specific deficits or lags in neurological or perceptual development as primary causes of reading disorders (Bender, 1975; Benton, 1962; Birch, 1962; Fernald, 1943; Hermann, 1959; Monroe, 1932).

The assumption of a single type of disability underlying the reading problem led to a variety of programs developed primarily in the 1960s that purported to "treat" perceptual problems as a means of remediating reading disabilities. Typical of these programs was Kephart's (1960) approach, which focused on motor activities as a basis for developing perceptual skills. In the same vein, but perhaps less theoretically accepted, were programs developed by Barsch (1965) and Delacato (1966) in which the evolutionary progression of physical movement patterns was seen as basic to complete perpectual development. Exercises for remediation of visual-motor deficits were the focus of approaches devised by Frostig (Frostig & Horne, 1964; Frostig, Maslow, Lefever, & Whittlesey, 1964) and by Getman (1965). Cruickshank (1967, 1977) developed a structured classroom enviroment devoted to helping the learning-disabled disabled child compensate for certain visual-perceptual deficiencies.

Developing simultaneously, but with somewhat less impact, were programs based on the assumption that language processing disabilities were at the root of reading problems. Kirk (1966) developed a widely used instrument for assessing underlying psycholinguistic abilities that revealed differences between good and poor readers (Bateman, 1965b, Kass, 1966). Language problems were also considered fundamental deficits in other formulations regarding the nature of specific reading disabilty (de Hirsch, 1963; Ingram, Mason, & Blackburn, 1970; Johnson & Myklebust, 1967; Lyle, 1970; Myklebust, 1968a; Rabinovitch, 1962). Related to linguistic deficits were suggestions that basic auditory perceptual problems were fundamental to reading disorders (Dykstra, 1966; Kavale, 1981b; Poling, 1953; Silver & Hagin, 1960; Tallal, 1976, 1980; Wepman 1961); but disagreement exists over whether the impaired auditory processes represent a language disorder (Liberman & Shankweiler, 1979) or a nonverbal perceptual deficit (Wepman, 1975b). Besides deficits in either visual or auditory perception, suggestions were offered stressing the relationship of the visual and auditory systems and a reading-disabled child's problems in transforming equivalent information from one system to the other (Ayres, 1973; Berry, 1967; Birch & Belmont, 1964, 1965; Kahn & Birch, 1968; Muehl & Kremenak, 1966; Vandervoort & Senf, 1973). It was also postulated that specific read-

ing disability was associated with dysfunction in temporal-order perception, that is, related to the ability to serialize a sequence of events (Bakker,
1970, 1972; Bakker, & Schroots, 1981; Corkin, 1974; Doehring, 1968; Zurif
& Carson, 1970).

Finally there were suggestions that structural abnormalities in the
brain could interfere with reading by producing reading difficulties
analogous to acquired alexia (Benson, 1976; Hecaen & Kremin, 1976;
Marshall & Newcombe, 1977). Attention was directed to *deep* alexia,
wherein phonemic recoding skills are lost as a result of left-hemisphere
damage and reading is largely a process of visual access through the right
hemisphere (Coltheart, Patterson, & Marshall, 1980). These observations
led to the suggestion that all reading disabilities are the result of a
genetically based left-hemisphere dysfunction analogues to deep alexia
(Jorm, 1979); others have suggested that reading disability may be more
analogous to *surface* alexias that involve only partial failure to convert
grapheme-phoneme correspondences (Ellis, 1979; Patterson, 1979; Saffran,
1980). The assumption of some genetic basis for dyslexia has been a consistent theme in theorizing about dyslexia (Childs, Finucci, & Preston,
1978; Finucci, 1978; Foch, DeFries McLearn, & Singer, 1977; Hallgren,
1950; Hinshelwood, 1917; Marshall & Ferguson, 1939; Vandenberg, 1967;
Zahalkova, Vrzal, & Kloboukova, 1972).

It is important to note that the validity of many of the above theories
has been seriously challenged and that virtually none have resulted in
cohesive remedial approaches that have proved consistently effective in
well-controlled studies (Mann, 1979). The assumption that letter or word
reversals are necessarily evidence of a significant perceptual deficit, and
should thus be a primary focus of remediation, has been widely questioned
(Black, 1974; Camp, 1973; Fisher & Frankfurter, 1977; Zach & Kaufman,
1972). Studies have shown that such reversals are often due to a child's
lack of awareness that directionality of a letter (e.g., *b* versus *d*) is important (Moyer & Newcomer, 1977); that such reversals are rarely in a consistent direction as theory might predict Corkin (1974); that type of reversal
errors are similar for both good and poor readers (Holmes & Peper, 1977);
and that reversals are more apt to result from linguistic rather than perceptual problems (Gupta, Ceci, & Slater, 1978; Vellutino, Smith, Steger, &
Kaman, 1975). Additionally, research on eye movements in good and poor
readers has failed to present convincing evidence that abnormal eye movements contribute to reading disability (Fisher, 1979; McConkie, 1979;
Pirozzolo & Rayner 1978).

Though visual-perceptual skills appear to be related to reading
achievement (Kavale, 1982), remedial programs based on visual-motor perceptual approaches, such as those of Kephart, Getman, and Frostig,
generally have not been shown to result in significant reading improvement when subjected to well-controlled study (Goodman & Hammill,

1973; Hammill, 1972; Kavale & Mattson, 1983; Keogh, 1974; Larsen & Hammill, 1975), even though teachers continue to believe in the efficacy of training deficits in visual perception to improve reading ability (Allington, 1982). Delacato's patterning and laterality approaches have been singled out for especially damaging criticism (Cohen, Birch, & Taft, 1970; Robbins & Glass, 1968; Zigler & Seitz, 1975). Psycholinguistic training programs, while improving functions assessed by the Illinois Test of Psycholinguistic Abilities (ITPA), do little to ameliorate reading problems (Kavale, 1981a). Reviews of programs focusing on specific linguistic or auditory perceptual deficits as a basis for reading also show little promise, in terms of their effectiveness in remediation (Hammill & Larsen, 1974b, 1978; Vellutino, 1979; Wilson, Harris, & Harris, 1976). The intersensory integration approach has also been questioned, since research has failed to demonstrate that poor readers do poorly on such tasks when intellectual, memory, and linguistic factors are ruled out (Bryant, 1975; Friedes, 1974; Kavale, 1980a; Vellutino, 1979). Thus, despite disclaimers to the contrary (Cruickshank, 1977; Dalby, 1979; Fletcher & Satz, 1979; Gross & Rothenberg, 1979; Lund, Foster, & McCall-Perez, 1978), unitary deficit theories developed in the 1960s or before have largely failed either to adequately explain the development of reading disabilities or to provide proven remedial approaches. Indeed, such approaches have been dismissed as "irrational" (Kinsbourne & Caplan, 1979) or "pseudomedical" (Cambourne & Rousch, 1982).

CURRENT CONCEPTS IN READING DISABILITIES

More recent thinking has focused on the interaction of attention, memory, and linguistic functions, as well as on ecological factors inherent in classroom instruction, as the basis for remediation of reading disabilities. Each area can only be summarized here, but interested readers are referred to two excellent reviews by Benton and Pearl (1978) and Wong (1979a, 1979b).

Attention and Memory

A number of authors (Hallahan & Kauffman, 1976; Samuels & Edwall, 1981; Senf & Freundl, 1971) have suggested that attention deficits should be a primary focus in remediation. In fact, LaBerge and Samuels (1974) developed a theory of automaticity of information processing in which the primary component is attention that is assumed to be both selective (Ross, 1976) and of limited capacity (Massaro, 1977). For the disabled reader, information at the visual and phonological levels is not processed automatically, thereby taking a major portion of attention and leaving little to focus at the semantics level and, thus, reducing understanding. Because of limited processing space, when more space is consumed by decoding, less is available for comprehension. Inefficient decoding thus creates a bottleneck with the available space engaged in word recognition rather than in acquiring meaning through comprehension activities (Perfetti & Lesgold, 1979). One implication for remediation is a divide-and-conquer strategy wherein reading is divided into smaller subunits so that attention costs do not exceed capacity. In practice, this is illustrated by the repeated/assisted reading method (Hoskisson & Krohn, 1974; Samuels, 1979), which has proved useful (Carbo, 1978; Chomsky, 1976; Dahl, 1979), and the neurological impress method (Heckelman, 1969), which has also been found efficacious (Hollingsworth, 1970, 1978; Kann, 1983; Langford, Slade, & Barnett, 1974; Moyer, 1982).

Keogh and Margolis (1976) have proposed a three-dimensional model of attention problems. Their model implies that the choice of a particular approach for a child might be based on whether his or her problems occur in (a) coming to attention, (b) decision-making based on attentional input, or (c) maintaining attention. Problems in coming to attention not only have to do with hyperactivity but also with focusing on relevant aspects of the task (Willows, 1974), which would seem to call for behavioral programs in which reinforcers are contingent on successive approximations of correct attending behavior. Decision making may be impaired because of impulsive or rapid responses based on limited or fragmentary information, which would call for cognitive behavioral programs to modify impulsivity (Blackman & Goldstein, 1982; Hresko & Reid, 1981). Maintaining attention refers to problems in sustained attention or vigilance during prolonged tasks that are often deficient in poor readers (Noland & Schuldt, 1971). Such problems suggest a call for more careful selection of materials related to either the child's individual interests and/or his or her cognitive schema (Krupski, 1981).

Keogh and Margolis' formulations are thus quite useful for helping teachers choose programs that are more likely to be effective for a particular type of attention problem. Koppell (1979) likewise notes that a learning-disabled child might attend intermittently to irrelevant aspects of a task or with intermittent intensity to relevant aspects. At the same time, the child's inattention may be classified as general and pervasive (task independent) or linked only to the demands of certain tasks (task dependent). Multiple aspects of attending behavior are apparent in studies that suggest that poor readers have very heterogeneous performance on various attention tasks and that the tasks themselves appear to often measure very different constructs (Pelham, 1979). Koppell further questions whether attending problems are due to specific deficits or to a generally diminished processing capacity and suggests that attentional deficits may not necessarily be causes of reading disability but may result from a poor reader's previous failure experiences or anxiety about task performance. Not only does this suggest that approaches to attention problems, per se, must be chosen carefully but also that memory- and information-processing strategies are likely to be just as essential as strategies to improve attention.

Like Koppell, Senf (1976) suggests that attention deficits may not be primary disorders but may be secondary to previous problems in organizing and processing information. Some support for this thinking comes from Morrison, Giordani, and Nagi (1977), who showed that poor readers do as well as normal readers in the initial phase of processing when information is first perceived (zero to 300 milliseconds) but do not do as well in the memory or encoding stage (300 to 2000 milliseconds) when information has more time to be assimilated (i.e., when their poor memory strategies are more apparent). Senf (1976) posits an information-processing system in which reading deficits are caused either by a child's failing to receive adequate stimuli presented in one or more sensory modalities, or failing to relate it to his or her existing information array, which might itself be diminished because of previous faulty information. His system stresses the notion of a feedback loop in which the reader acts on incoming information by relating it to previously stored information as well to sounds, sights, and other sensations occurring at the same time. This implies that the teacher's role in remediation is to assist poor readers, as much as possible, to relate incoming stimuli (e.g., letters, sounds, and words) to material already learned and/or to contextual cues in the learning situation. These strategies are frequently dependent on the child's language functioning.

Memory is also considered important for reading (Just & Carpenter, 1980), but there is little evidence to suggest that memory deficits operate as casual factors in reading disability (Torgeson, 1978, 1979). Because memory involves a number of processes (e.g., encoding, retention, retrieval among others), it is difficult to determine which process is responsible for the perceived memory problems. For example, the recall of visual and auditory materials may be deficient because of phonological coding problems (Shankweiler, Liberman, Mark, Fowler, & Fisher, 1979), but no apparent memory difficulties were demonstrated by poor readers when phonological recoding was prevented (Cermak, Goldberg, Cermak, & Drake, 1980). Nevertheless, memory deficits may interfere with, for example, the acquisition of grapheme-phoneme correspondences (Bryden, 1972) because of problems with both short-term memory (Spring, 1976) and long-term memory (Corkin, 1974) in general, rather than specific, processes.

Difficulty in serial order recall, or the ability to remember letters or other items in sequence, has been suggested as a primary aspect of memory that is related to reading disability (Bannatyne, 1971; Kirk & Kirk, 1971). Bakker (1972) has studied poor readers using a variety of temporal-order tasks in visual, auditory, and tactile modalities and has concluded that deficits in both perceiving and recalling a sequence of events are directly related to reading disability. His idea received partial support in studies by Senf (1972) and Senf and Freundl, (1971) on bisensory memory, recalling a series of digits presented simultaneously in both visual and auditory modes. Poor readers were not only deficient on these tasks compared to normal readers, particularly when there was a half second or longer interval between digits, but also recalled fewer visual items when material was presented in both senses. Subsequent studies, however, by Davis and Bray (1975) and Vellutino, Smith, Steger, and Kaman (1975) that deemphasized the memory skill involved (for example, by having children recall the temporal order of only two digits in the series rather than the entire series) may suggest that perhaps gross memory and not temporal sequencing is involved.

Language

The thesis that various language problems are of central importance in remediation of reading disability receives support in several studies reviewed by Benton (1975, 1978) and from the fact that nearly half of the children referred to reading clinics have a history of speech and language difficulties (de Hirsh, Jansky, & Langford, 1966; Ingram, Mason, & Blackburn, 1970; Lyle, 1970). Liberman (1971) and Liberman, Shankweiler, Orlando, Harris, and Berti, (1971) have shown, moreover, that orienting and sequencing difficulties account for only one-fourth of the total reading errors and that the majority of errors seem to be due to linguistic intrusion problems. Indeed, several studies on subclassifications of reading disorders suggest that children with phonetic problems make up two-thirds or more of all reading-disabled subjects. Children with visual perceptual problems made up only a very small percentage. Other recent studies profiling test results of poor readers also demonstrate that their verbal skills tend to be quite low (Cullen, Boersma, & Chapman, 1981; Gottesman, Croen, & Rotkin, 1982; Hessler & Kitchen, 1980; Rudel, Denckla, & Bromen, 1981).

Linguistic deficits have long been posited as underlying reading disability (Kirk & Kirk, 1971; Myklebust, 1968a), but relatively less attention has been paid to this area until recently. Vellutino (1978, 1979; Vellutino, Steger, Moyer, Harding, & Niles, 1977) is among the foremost proponents of this position in recent years. He suggests that subtle disorders in language may be primarily responsible for reading disability, and that the validity of previous research on perceptual deficits should be questioned because of failure to take language factors into account on tasks that supposedly measure perception. In support of his hypothesis, Vellutino has conducted a number of studies. He has shown that poor readers could both perceive and reproduce potentially confusing words (e.g., was/saw, calm/clam), but could not name such words as well as normal readers (Vellutino, Smith, Steger, & Kaman, 1975). Using recall of unfamiliar symbols to reduce the effects of verbal deficits, he demonstrated that reading-disabled children made no more orienting or sequencing errors than normal children (Vellutino, Steger, Kaman & DeSetto, 1975). In another study (Vellutino, Harding, Phillips, & Steger, 1975), poor readers made more mistakes in visual-verbal associations but were similar to normal readers in nonverbal learning. Vellutino and colleagues (1975) have also shown that, even though reading-disabled children mispronounced a word, they could still name its letters in sequence.

Vellutino suggests that language deficits underlying reading disabilities may take the form of subtle disorders in semantic processing, syntactic difficulties, and phonological problems. In addition to his own studies, he cites as evidence the work of several authors. For example, Waller (1976) showed that poor readers could remember the basic meanings of sentences but made more errors than normal readers on recalling exact sentence order, tense markers, and plurality indicators. Perfetti, Finger, & Hogaboam (1978) presented disabled readers with colors, digits, pictures, and words and discovered that they did not do as well as normal readers in naming words but did as well in naming nonverbal stimuli. Denckla and Rudel (1976) described reading-disabled children as "subtly dysphasic," since they were slower than both normal and generally underachieving children in rapidly naming pictures of common objects, numbers, letters, and colors. Vogel (1974), and Clay and Imlach (1971) found that young children with reading disorders were markedly inferior on a variety of measures of grammatic competence. Liberman, Shankweiler, Fischer, and Carter (1974), Fox and Routh (1980), Helgott (1976), and Perfetti and Hogaboam (1975) demonstrated that poor readers have great difficulty in segmenting words into individual phonemes, and that ease in sound-symbol association, or sounding out words, predicts which children will be better readers. More recently Kagan and Moore (1981), Shankweiler, and associates (1979), and Swanson (1982) have shown that poor readers' memory ability tends to be further impaired by their poorer access to language skills. The consequences are found in poorer text organization skills in disabled readers, manifested by slower decoding speed (Perfetti & Lesgold, 1977, 1979; Spring & Capps, 1974), less accuracy in decoding (Golinkoff & Rosinski, 1976; Perfetti & Hogaboam, 1975), limited application of syntactic knowledge (Isakson & Miller, 1976), limited sematic knowledge (Belmont & Birch, 1966; Satz & Sparrow, 1970), and limited memory for discourse (Daneman & Carpenter, 1980; Perfetti & Goldman, 1976).

Vellutino further suggests that the fluent reader is a "verbal gymnast" who is able to readily cross reference visual information and has a variety of ways of identifying and extracting meaning from words in context. The reading-disabled child, on the other hand, is not only less flexible and adept but also seems unaware of the importance of many of these aspects of language. These difficulties are most clearly reflected in an inability to extract meaning from the printed page. Long ago, Thorndike (1917) drew an analogy between the reading comprehension process and problem-solving activities. In a test of this hypothesis, Kavale (1980c) found that learning-disabled readers less often applied identifiable sequences of steps representing reasoning strategies and were less often successful than normal readers in responding to comprehension questions. In fact, disabled readers most often applied either no line of reasoning to produce a response or applied less efficient strategies than normal readers to produce more incorrect responses. These performance differences were found to be related to disabled readers' difficulties in decoding and vocabulary and affirm the idea of an "idosyncratic response pattern" for poor readers (Cromer & Weiner, 1966). Such comprehension differences may, in turn, result in differential oral reading strategies, with disabled readers less efficient than normal readers (Pflaum & Bryan, 1982)

Although the seeming overreliance on linguistic deficits has been questioned (Fletcher, 1981; Fletcher & Satz, 1979), Vellutino's approach holds considerable heuristic promise. The teacher's role in remediation, under such an approach, is to facilitate the child's access to all of the various aspects of language during reading instruction and, thereby, help the child cross reference or anchor incoming sounds and words to as much phonetic, syntatic, and semantic information as possible (Bransford, Stein, & Vye, 1982; Glaser, Pelagrino, & Lesgold 1978).

Classroom Interaction and Instructional Factors

Lack of truly individualized instruction in school classrooms has been blamed, at the least, for the exacerbation of reading disabilities and, in some cases, has even been considered the cause of some reading disorders. Part of this thesis has to do with differential rates in development of certain children who are not ready to begin reading at the usual ages. Another has to do with the learning styles of children whose approach to tasks may not mesh with the style of instruction in the particular classroom to which they are assigned. The notion that certain skills may develop more slowly in reading disabled children has been suggested by Satz and his colleagues (Satz & Fletcher, 1980; Satz, Taylor, Friel, & Fletcher, 1978; Satz & Van Nostrand, 1973).

Satz contends that sensory perceptual skills, which are in their ascendancy in primary school years, are likely to be delayed in younger reading-disabled children and that conceptual linguistic skills, which develop in later elementary school years, mature more slowly in older children with reading disorders. According to this view, younger children may eventually mature in perceptual skills related to beginning reading but will consequently lag in conceptual and linguistic skills needed for later reading competence. Should such skills not develop by adolescence, a permanent deficit in reading might occur. It should be noted that the contentions of Satz and his colleagues derive from a single longitudinal study of over 400 male children who began kindergarten in 1970 (Satz & Fletcher, 1980; Satz & Friel, 1978; Satz, Taylor, Friel, & Fletcher, 1978). In regard to the above discussion on linguistic factors in reading disorders, it is of interest to note that a test of alphabet recitation was among the most consistent predictors of reading disorder, while a subsequent study of language measures by Satz, Taylor, Friel, & Fletcher (1978) showed grammatic closure and receptive vocabulary as highly predictive.

Torgesen (1977, 1979) extends the concept of maturational lag to the reading-disabled child's *approach* to tasks that are critical to reading. Noting that some learning-disability theorists stress underlying deficits within the child, he views the child's learning strategies as equally important. Torgesen sees the child with a reading disorder as a less "active agent" in his or her own learning. In the preschool years, learning proceeds through interaction with the environment, but school tasks require that the child more actively generate his or her own cognitive associations. The reading-disabled child, Torgesen contends, may enter school with less developed abilities to structure his or her own learning, (i.e., less ability to attend selectively or less awareness of and skill in memory strategies). He also notes that the cumulative effects of such difficulties lead to reduced self-confidence and reluctance to approach new tasks. Torgesen has demonstrated that poor readers can be trained to improve their orientation to tasks and thus "catch up" with normal readers (Torgesen, Murphy, & Ivey, 1979). As implied by Torgesen, a mismatch between the reading-disabled child's specific pattern of strengths and weaknesses and the type of instruction he or she receives could contribute to the development of a reading disability.

A similar idea has been advanced by Adelman (1971, 1972) who proposed that the discrepancy between child characteristics and the classroom environment may even be a primary reason for some learning problems. Adelman rejects the notion of the "disabled" child. He suggests that the greater the teacher's ability to individualize instruction, the less likely it is that reading failure will occur. Less effective teachers, on the other hand, might unwittingly contribute to reading disorders because of their failure to take into account individual differences in sensory, perceptual, linguistic, cognitive, or motivational variables.

A corollary hypothesis is that matching kindergarten children who have certain learning patterns to teachers whose instructional style represents the "best fit" may even prevent some cases of reading disability (Adelman, 1972). This would presumably involve careful assessment of children in the kindergarten and primary years and placement of certain children only with teachers whose teaching style complemented the child's particular learning needs (Holland, 1982). Others have advanced similar ideas. For example, Baron's (1979) work suggests that failure to develop skill in phonetic or whole-word approaches to reading may be a function of the type of instruction the child receives. Thomas and Chess (1977) have even proposed that a child's temperament could be inadequately matched with that of his or her teacher's, thereby leading to reduced opportunity for effective reading instructions. The implications are that certain changes in classroom instruction or environment might be expected to result in significant improvement in a child's reading disorder (Lindsay & Wedell, 1982)

Although these approaches seem logically compelling, there is only limited empirical support for such contentions. Although Feshbach, Adelman, and Fuller (1977) have shown that reading failure does appear to vary with first grade classroom experience, a specific cause-and-effect relationship has not yet been demonstrated. Indeed, a large body of research exists in which poor readers have been matched to instructional programs based on their presumed deficits in either auditory or visual processing (Arter & Jenkins, 1977; Bateman, 1967; Larivee, 1981; Robinson, 1972; Tarver & Dawson 1978), but the results have been singularly disappointing. One should note that despite the lack of empirical support for this practice in the literature, large numbers of teachers report that they not only continue to use such an approach but also believe that it is effective (Allington, 1982; Arter & Jenkins, 1977).

Kavale and Forness (1986) have extended these notions into a more comprehensive interactive LD model that emphasizes elements of the normal teaching-learning process and LD correlates to produce the "disassociated" learner (see Chapter 2).

SUMMARY

Some general conclusions can be derived from the above discussion. A common theme is the complexity of the reading disability syndrome. Most authors would admit that both sensory, perceptual, and conceptual linguistic deficits are implicated as underlying factors, but several seem to conclude that the perceptual impairments should no longer comprise the major focus of remediation, as they often have in the past. Use of pre-remedial motor or perceptual exercises in particular do not seem to be widely supported. Developmental lag is postulated as significant in several instances. Regardless of the particular deficits described, some authors seem to insist that observed process deficits do not necssarily differentiate between good and poor readers but rather that the difference is in the *rate* at which these critical skills mature. Finally, there are several cautions against imputing one specific cause to failure on a school task, since several other factors could be operating.

CHAPTER 8

Comprehension Problems

Paul R. Daniels

When dealing with the problems of living that impinge on the learning disabled student it is necessary to recognize that problems do not exist alone or in a vacuum (Abrams, 1973). This is especially true of problems in comprehension whether with objects or people, or language processes. A learner exists in at least three realms: physical, psychological, and sociological. Experience shows that treating any problem as if it exists alone in the totality of a person's life promotes strong probability of failure (Natchez, 1968).

All learners must have the necessary sensory apparatus; the mental capabilities, drive and needs to approach a task, and a setting in society that rewards and commends the effort put forth (Pearson, 1972). If all of these do not exist, the task of acquiring the necessary skills and abilities will not be faced; and unless the learner addresses the tasks of life, learning can not be anticipated; and comprehension, especially in written language, is not learned.

Comprehension difficulties caused by physical factors such as brain damage or insult are usually classified as some type of aphasia and should

This chapter originally appeared as an article by **Paul R. Daniels** in *Learning Disabilities: An Interdisciplinary Journal* (Vol. I, 1982) and was adapted by permission of Grune & Stratton for inclusion in this *Handbook*.

be documented medically. Treatment for these problems usually requires a medical base to the educational process (see Chalfant & Scheffelin, 1969).

If physical factors are indeed present, in most cases, their effects will be much more evident in other areas of life than comprehension deficits. Factors of vision, hearing, and neurological integration need to be ruled out as basic factors in the disability before a program of intervention is planned. Remedial and adaptive procedures would, of course, be of primary importance. Once again, in such a situation the interaction of the three realms of a child is clear (Stanovich, 1982).

Psychologically a number of factors must be noted about learning disabled students. One of the most important and probably basic to their failure is the problem of attention and concentration. This inability to focus their psychological energies on a task may account for the larger number of unsuccessful exposures for acquiring skills and information that usually characterizes learning disabled students (Rapaport, Gill, & Schafer, 1968).

Cause for this problem may be inherent in the students. They may be emotionally disturbed or anxiety ridden to such a degree that they cannot muster the psychological energy to concentrate, or other psychological needs may make learning academic skills insignificant or unimportant. In this case, it is obvious that treatment of the emotional disturbance must take precedence over the immediate attempt to solve the learning problem. Unfortunately, there are a number of such children in our schools for whom academic intervention is the only help provided, and failure is again thrust on the children.

If the appropriate counseling or therapy is lacking, even though remedial or adaptive procedures are tried for academic factors, the basic problem remains. It becomes increasingly evident to the children, teachers, and parents that these children are "hopeless" since the best services have not produced change. Change could not have been anticipated since only a symptom was being treated. The sociological factors begin to impact and exacerbate the already damaging emotional problem. Once again, the negative interaction simply fosters more difficulty (Rosner, Abrams & Daniels, 1981b).

It appears that we have a large number of learning disabled students with concentration problems. The general approach to reading instruction advocated by many basic reading programs does not address the learner's needs for direction — that conscious effort to recognize and organize data (Rapaport et al., 1968). One should not assume that children recognize the need to concentrate. They must be provided with techniques that foster concentration. If left to their approaches, children will usually attend. They will deal with those elements of an experience that require little effort and produce personal good feelings. This is an attitude that is truly childlike since the pleasure-pain principle is seldom adopted by a child at an early age. Unfortunately, school work, especially in our modern skill-oriented classrooms, seldom supports private joy or delight. Knowing a short vowel sound hardly compares with the satisfaction of saying a poem, telling a story, or stating a startling fact.

A second factor in the failure of many learning disabled students is their lack of organization. It may appear as disorganization. They may have a number of steps in a procedure yet seem unable to organize them in an appropriate sequence. It may appear as unorganization. The children will be apt to use both appropriate and inappropriate procedures in dealing with a situation. This dichotomy is often treated as if it represented the same problem. Both do involve the organization of behavior, but they require different approaches for their alleviation.

However, disorganization and unorganization may have their roots in concentration problems or in pedogogical techniques. The interaction of life's realms must be ascertained, and priorities for meeting the most appropriate and pressing needs must be developed.

A third crucial element in the psychological realm is the place of meaning in the lives of students with learning problems (Rapaport et al., 1968). If language is not recognized as a means of communication, then much of what goes on in a classroom is a meaningless mime show. The attribution of sounds to letters, meaning to noises, noises to print, and so on, might be absorbed as rote learnings; but understanding, concept development, and problem solving would not emerge. The dreadful interaction in that respect often involves the deprecation of ability and the lowering of self-worth which, in turn, interacts to produce even poorer concentration and effort. This interaction may have its beginning in the sociology of the children's lives, but it can not be denied that many of today's pedagogical procedures almost appear to accomplish this deliberately (Adamson & Adamson, 1979).

Sociologically a number of factors must be appreciated if one is to help students with learning problems learn to comprehend (Eisenberg, 1966). As noted above, the fundamental problem is often the failure of the family to use language as a communication tool. In many families of learning disabled students, language is used as a manipulative device. Intonation, stress, accent, and volume alone serve to move the children. They really do not need to comprehend more than those elements.

Secondly, in the sociology of many of these homes, there is no deliberate attempt to foster vocabulary, language sensitivity, or factual information. Whatever is enough to get by on in these areas is what is supplied.

On many standardized reading readiness tests or tests of early identification used in many states, children handicapped in the sociological realm often appear dull and uninterested (Filmer & Kohn 1967). The so-called remedial or compensatory programs then offered are based on this perception of dullness and real stimulation is not forthcoming. The perception then becomes a self-fulfilling prophecy.

When dealing with the learning disabled student, one must make a real effort to interrelate the realms of the child, to see the whole child. The whole child is a term now laughed at, a cliche, yet it is the concept around which every educational program should and must be built.

PROGRAMMING

Relevancy

Before any comprehension can occur, the learner must be willing to deal with the external environment. This statement may appear to be totally self-evident yet it is often ignored or not perceived in educational practices. Children can retreat into their own world of personal fantasy and almost totally ignore the world outside of themselves.

Many learning disabled students use, and must use, this retreat tactic for their own self-preservation. They have been repeatedly required to attempt tasks that are beyond their present capabilities or are meaningless in their views of the world they inhabit. In their views, school, home, and life do not appear relevant to their world.

Relevancy was a major term bandied about in the 1960s and 1970s. It was frequently derided, and deserved to be, as a technique for lessening standards and diluting conventional and accepted goals. However, relevancy is a very meaningful term when dealing with learning disabled students.

The initial approach to all students who have failed must be through a program in which they can see value. They must see its relevancy. This is not to imply that this must be the case throughout the program. An important element of any good instructional program must be the acceptance by the learners of tasks that have to be faced because of an overriding future goal. One must do some things in life whether one wishes or not. That is an important element in maturing. However, one must help learners begin to address reality as they perceive it before they can be expected to address the reality of others. For example, if a teacher wanted to develop a fundamental concept of physics, starting with an intense interest in cars could lead to that goal. Starting with principles of physics often will avail nothing.

Concentration

How does one get students to focus on an aspect of the external environment? One must create a need in them to do so. This need, in and of itself, creates a mild anxiety. The art of teaching these students becomes evident when a teacher can create this mild anxiety in a nonthreatening way while providing the students with the opportunity to dissipate the anxiety with sources from the environment. This source can be spoken language, a concrete object, a picture or a printed word; but through its use, the anxiety is being dissipated, and learning has occurred. This anxiety-arousing, anxiety-dissipating procedure is probably an excellent definition of good teaching.

Understood in such a procedure is sensitivity to the needs of the learners, confidence of the teacher, and clearly defined goals in both parties. The teacher must know which concepts need to be learned and to which percepts the students must be exposed. As always, at the end of the activity students will have felt satisfaction in accomplishing a task — diminishing of anxiety. They must recognize that they have learned something.

To initiate development in the area of comprehension, one fundamental attitude must be established. Learners must keep in mind (concentrate) what they are seeking while engaging in the seeking activity. Learners must be able to use and understand language purposefully. In the beginning a simple, directed listening-viewing activity can be employed.

Tell the group that they are going to see a picture of something. This could be a hand-held picture, a slide, or an overhead projection. Show it to them quickly and take it away. Begin to ask questions about what was seen. Have the learners note the answers they could not provide and the different answers that different students recalled. Probe for the reason behind this behavior.

Use the same approach for another viewing, but this time give the students one or two purposes for viewing. Show the picture and remove it as before, but before eliciting answers, ask the students how many of them can recall the questions they were supposed to use for guiding their viewing. Note the students who were unable to retain a purpose while engaging in the activity. These students may need more intensive work. Once this has been accomplished, ascertain how many students were able to provide the answer or answers required.

This type of activity should be complemented by oral language activities. Inform the learners that they will periodically hear something that does not make sense. Let them know when they hear nonsense they are to raise their hands. Be sure that the meaningless material sounds like running discourse not gibberish. Note the children who cannot handle this task. Try to discover if the cause is a fundamental language-processing problem or a problem of lack of concentration on spoken language.

If it appears to be a language-processing problem, a language specialist should be consulted for verfication of the problem and suggestions for diagnostic-prescriptive techniques to alleviate or compensate for the problem. If the problem appears to be a concentration problem, the procedures described above must be continued. However, these procedures are still best done with concrete and semi-concrete materials augmented by listening activities.

Meaning

As listed in the preceding section, the first crucial goal in a comprehension development program is to get a learner to recognize meaningful from meaningless language. Students should react to a statement such as, "Please stand with the line."

This recognition of meaningful material should be transferred as quickly as possible to print matter. Provide the learners with a simple declarative sentence. Ask then to decide if the sentence is meaningful. If not, why is it meaningless? The presentation of these materials should always contain both types of sentences and should not be viewed initially as proofreading materials. Once the concept of listening and reading for meaning has been established, proofreading should then be introduced. When an attitude of seeking meaning has been established, the introduction of short paragraphs should occur. Be sure that some element in one sentence of the paragraph has a direct influence that makes an element in another sentence meaningless. For example, when discussing a bitterly cold environment state that footwear was obviously not needed. Check whether or not incongruities within a body of information are noted.

At this stage of development, a combination of pictures and print can be used. It is helpful to present the meaningless material in both media. In fostering comprehension it is also important that a meaningless picture be accurately described by the print. In this way, the learners can begin to recognize that, even though print may be true to an idea, the idea might be false. This attitude eventually becomes one of the bases for critical comprehension.

If the program to foster concentration while structuring a program in comprehension is to be successful, it is crucial that the material used and the ideas being manipulated are a part of the learner's background. Teachers of learning disabled students with pronounced comprehension problems may need to develop their own materials. It is almost a given fact that no commercially prepared remedial or adaptive program will meet the varied needs of these students.

From the standpoint of the organization of this chapter, a rigid interpretation would mean that a discussion of other psychological factors should follow. This rigid adherence would be in direct conflict with the overridding concept to be presented. It is appropriate at this point to move to a sociological concept. Psychology and sociology can and do impinge on each other.

The previous discussion was based on some very important assumptions. First of all, the learner had appropriate or adequate language. Secondly, the learner used language to communicate. Thirdly, the background of experience and concepts was coordinated with the language demands. Unfortunately, for many learning disabled students with comprehension problems, these assumptions are false. To foster comprehension they must be addressed.

Vocabulary

It is interesting to note the number of learning disabled children who lack the vocabulary of everyday life as well as more specific vocabulary. Many of these children reflect homes and, unfortunately, schools where little attention is paid to vocabulary.

In many cases, these lapses result from well-meaning attitudes. The problems known as learning disabilities are evidenced, and everyone tries to make adjustments. Attempts are made to simplify concepts — which cannot be done. Vocabulary is kept simple and limited to prevent the child from being overly burdened. Classrooms are tailored to a slower pace, and very rigid structures are developed. Size, shape, color and so forth are highlighted, although the object to which these attributes are applied may be totally unlabelled. Children will be asked to note specific details but not to know the function of the object or, in some cases, its name.

However, vocabulary development starts with labeling. It might help children to note that an animal looks like a goat or antelope, is brown, is of comparative height and so forth. Nevertheless, someone must tell them that the animal is a chamois. Knowing these attributes will not help students juxtapose the word to the experience. This problem is especially acute with learning disabled children whose problems are primarily in reading. Shapes and configurations are considered so important to letter recognition that comprehension skills are totally ignored. The inability to comprehend is one important and prevalent type of learning disability (Rosner et al., 1981b).

The implications are rather evident. Teachers must be sure to help learning disabled children acquire labels. First of all, children must be able to use the terms for everything in the classroom and know the specific and functional relationship between the word and the object. Children also need to know the names for the facts and experiences of life. Body parts, clothing, foods, tools, utensils, furniture, and so on should be known and, if not known, taught.

This concept is vital to developing comprehension abilities. Discussing the listening-viewing activities described earlier, it is obvious that if the experiences were unknown and the words simply noises, the entire suggested procedure would be a farce. Since vocabulary arises basically out of sociological conventions, interaction with the psychological must be accepted.

How many children labelled learning disabled are really deprived in fundamental comprehension abilities that originate in sociological deprivation? Technically, these students should not be termed learning disabled; yet when this psychosocial interaction is prolonged and is profound, it would become almost impossible to decide if there is or is not a true learning disability. Human processes and systems intertwine so exquisitely that one could probably never delineate a single strand. In human beings all things human interact with all things human.

Word Recognition

If the need for meaning has been developed and if appropriate vocabulary has been developed, teachers can begin to initiate a program with problem readers to develop word recognition ability. This basic reading ability is the alpha and omega of the word-attack process, yet it is totally dependent on the learner's desire to comprehend. Too frequently, these word recognition skills are introduced as if they required no readiness. There must be the readiness in attitude and vocabulary.

Word recognition skills must be the alpha and the omega in word attack, since the reader should use them first when approaching an unknown word and employ them again to validate the sounds developed through a word analysis as meaningful.

The most important and fundamental word recognition skill is the use of context. This is the application of meaning to any language situation. Returning to an earlier point, the child who cannot comprehend the fundamental meaning of a sentence cannot use context. In many instances, if the learner uses the sentence as a psycholinguistic resource, the unknown word is narrowed to a few choices; and the overall meaning will produce a recognition of the word (the hypothesis-testing or top-down approach).

Another aspect of word recognition ability is the use of language rhythm skills. These are the elements that one normally calls word order. In any language there are patterns for subjects, predicate, object, noun, verb and so forth. Our language has these patterns and nearly all children know them. However, if a child has not been encouraged to comprehend a sentence but rather instructed to look and sound out individual words, this understood concept is not brought into play and, oftentimes, meaningless pronunciations are produced and accepted by the learner. Why would a learner not do so if there were no demand either internally or externally for meaning? Language rhythm in effect narrows down considerably the number of possible responses available when an unknown word is faced.

Finally, in the word recognition area, there are the typographical clues. These are the visualization-type materials supplied in most printed matter. There are pictures, graphs, charts, diagrams, headings, and so forth. These may actually provide problem-solving materials for words or contexts, or they may effectively supplement other word recognition skills. As was noted earlier, if comprehension of these materials is not developed, they become useless to a learner in the overall task of trying to comprehend a body of information presented in print.

These skills are, of course, important elements in listening activities. Through the application of these skills, words that are unknown are often given meaning by a listener.

Context and language rhythm clues are crucial to problem readers. Their alpha roles have already been mentioned. The omega role makes it possible for word-analysis skills to be effective.

If context has not provided a solution for the problem word, then it must be attacked by structural or phonic analysis. At best, these skills provide approximate pronunciation. Through context and language rhythm clues, the pronunciation obtained is adjusted to become a word in the learner's vocabulary and is placed in the content for meaning verification.

This procedure can be helpful for severe problem readers (Rosner et al., 1981b). For example, using word recognition skills and initial consonant substitution, an unknown word can be recognized quickly without the need for time consuming and less stable word-analysis skills. For children with reversals, these skills provide an opportunity to monitor the influence of a word on a given meaning. "Find the compass no the map" does not make sense contextually or linguistically, but the learner who is alert to the problem can be helped to compensate for it. The use of these procedures will provide compensatory or adaptive techniques that will be useful for the rest of the person's life.

Since all of these skills are totally dependent on the attitude of striving for comprehension, they simply cannot be approached in isolation (Bettleheim & Zelan, 1982). In and of themselves they are skills in comprehension for which the appropriate readiness must be developed. In practice these skills may be developed in tandem with the basic comprehension understandings stessed initially. However, it is probably better to develop one skill at a time and be sure that it is used effectively. Once a consistent demand for meaning has become a part of the instruction, most problem readers react easily and well to the demand. However, some children who have had intensive phonic instruction will find it difficult to strive for meaning and may even resist it. Psychologically, it is probably easier to react to a stimulus-response situation in reading than a gestalt approach, which says that reading is meaning or it is not reading. Comprehension is the emergence of meaning.

Organization

Comprehension must, of course, lead to understanding of the message being sent by the sender in the communication process. In listening, the sender is another person. In reading, this same concept is true except that the sender is not present. The responsibility to send the message falls on the receiver also. Word-attack skills are used in this process. However, what is sent and received must become a message or there is no communication. This knowledge of the message, comprehension, is based fundamentally on the organizational skills. This is an area in which nearly all learning disabled students evidence difficulty. An excellent elaboration of the need, value, and disturbances in organization has been developed by Pearson (1972).

In many diagnostic procedures, little effort is given to evaluating a student's organizational skills; yet such an evaluation might provide an important insight into why learning has not occurred or has been difficult. Many learning disabled children have trouble developing concepts. Some authorities (Rosner et al, 1981b) consider such a problem as a specific type of learning disability, yet is not the ability to organize discrete or unrelated data the primary requisite for concept formation?

Organizational disability seems to appear in two guises. Some children are disorganized; that is, they often have the appropriate steps or procedures but fail to apply them appropriately or systematically. The unorganized student often will attack a problem with inappropriate, irrelevant, or missing data and be unaware of the chaos engendered.

Disorganized children often profit from a deliberate step-by-step process in organizing data. Structure will often be required. If the following of a recipe is the goal, the teacher will need to dichotomize utensils and ingredients and actually discuss why this procedure is necessary. Students should be required to evaluate whether or not the proper and necessary utensils and ingredients are present in light of the demands of the recipe. At times items should be missing, and at other times superfluous items should be present. Disorganized students need to approach tasks in this manner. Appropriate sequential steps should be evaluated and categorized so that the steps no longer represent one long sequence but a series of smaller sequences organized by an overriding internal sequence, for example, pan dressing, batter preparation, batter placement, range procedures, baking regulations, cake removal, and so forth. Encourage these students to see how the large sequence is, in effect, a number of steps in smaller sequences that constitute the entire process. Children with learning problems whose approach is disorganized will profit from and need much work of this type before they integrate it systematically as a behavior.

Unorganized students will eventually profit from the procedure suggested for disorganized students. However, they seem to have some fundamental problems that must be addressed as readiness.

Many unorganized children have difficulty in appreciating the parts of the whole. They tend to see the chairness of a chair but not the components that constitute chairness. They tend to react to the gesalt. Whether this tendency is a cause or a result of the unorganization will probably be beyond determination. Consistent effort must be directed toward meeting this need. For example, the students might be asked to name the parts of a chair, bench, or stool. When pressed they often find a span of two. Most people cannot recall 10 digits yet can do so if they are presented as three groups of three numbers and a fourth digit. People seldom can recall 10 unrelated words but can recall a 10-word sentence exactly. Again, however, if the materials are not or cannot be made meaningful, these successful adaptive procedures are useless.

If short term memory problems are extremely pervasive, a multisensory approach using kinesthetic and tactile learning should be employed. These procedures can be used for words, number facts, or pieces of information (Johnson & Kress, 1966).

Retention and Recall

Many learning disabled children demonstrate problems in comprehension because of long-term memory or recall difficulties. In most cases, the problem may be based on retention or recall difficulties. The decision about which of these is operative must be made. Of course, without retention there is no recall; the converse is not true, however.

Retention is based on repetition. Each person seems to have a different need for the number of repetitions required for retention for different stimuli. Many learning disabled students seem to fail to comprehend on a day-to-day basis. Some of these students simply do not recall previous learnings. Many of them need to have more repetition or practice than other children. This is the classic case of slow learners. In programming for this group, it is clear that the amount of data presented must be limited to allow the students to repeat the materials often enough. Given time to do this, many of them will demonstrate comprehension abilities beyond expectations.

The other problem in long-term memory is that recall is based on the degree and appropriateness of the background of past experience. We relate new learnings to old learning to facilitate recall. Therefore, discrete learnings that cannot be superimposed on past learning are often poorly recalled (forgotten) over time. When programming for learning disabled students who demonstrate comprehension difficulties, it must be determined whether there is a comprehension problem or a problem in recall of past learnings. The only effective way to make this determination is through diagnostic observation and teaching using appropriately relevant materials. At this point, the teacher may have to take an active role for some learners, actually showing the students how information can be related to past learnings.

The problems with recall for learning disabled students must be investigated intensely, no matter what the specific disability appears to be. In a final analysis, data recorded and stored in the brain is virtually useless if it cannot be brought to bear on the learner's problems.

Literalness

Few human processes exist as either/or. At this time, even being dead or not dead appears to be debatable. One exception, of course, is pregnancy. A woman cannot be slightly pregnant. However, in the realm of learning disabilities, specifically in comprehension and all of its previously discussed ramifications, there may be an either-or proposition.

There may be a disability that cannot be remediated and is only slightly open to adaptation. The disability is literalness. For children who use language in such a way the need for very special concern is vital.

Some learning disabled children seem unable to appreciate connotation. They seem bound by denotation. Words mean what they mean. The disability is most pronounced in figurative language, nuance, sarcasm, double entendre, and so forth. These children are truly literal. Many aspects of humor depend on appreciating the connotation of words, and this area is often the best vehicle for diagnosis. If the children seem unable to appreciate verbal humor yet enjoy visual humor, then concern about this problem must be shown.

However, humor is not the only place where literalness affects comprehension. Many content disciplines use connotation for elaboration and example. Students who are unable to use connotation are apt to have a more difficult time comprehending than students who are less literal minded.

This problem is not demonstrated as a difficulty with semantic variation. These children usually do know that the same word in different contexts conveys different ideas. One group of children could deal with the word *run* in three different situations; however, when they saw mountain climbers dangling on ropes and the text said that they were going "to make a run at the summit," the children were totally confused.

If the literalness is a product of less-than-adequate aural stimulation, then work with figures of speech, nuances, and so forth, may be beneficial. If there is no basic disability in this respect, progress can be anticipated. However, if progress is not forthcoming, the disability might have to be accepted and programming to meet this need initiated.

Literalness in some children may not be refractory. They may even have to be given instructions on sensing the mood of a social group to permit a nonembarassing response: Learn to laugh when others laugh. Vocational counseling may be paramount so that these students devote their energies to careers in which literalness can be an asset, not an impediment. Most importantly, when these children are mainstreamed, teachers must be made aware of their problem and recognize certain reactions, or lack thereof, as being products of this particular type of disability. The impact on certain types of comprehension cannot be overemphasized. There is probably no aspect of living in which this disability does not have a pronounced influence.

This disability is often clearly evidenced in the students' inability to deal with propaganda devices. They tend to be susceptible to verbal manipulation, either orally or in print. Often they behave in a socially unacceptable manner, because they have been manipulated and have not recognized it.

Intervention in this area can be helpful if approached from a rather mechanical point of view. Even if they really do not comprehend the manipulation, they can recognize some of the indicators and become alert. Simple discussions of word values, amount of information carried, and overuse of certain words can be helpful in alerting those children with literalness that they must be careful.

Instructional Grouping

The responsibility for addressing the needs of students with comprehension difficulties falls on the teacher, sometimes a resource teacher but more and more often the classroom teacher, since these children are often mainstreamed. The bulk of instruction for areas in which the handicap plays a minor role is carried on by a generally certified classroom teacher. The handicapping condition is dealt with by a special education teacher or a specialist.

It is often beneficial to group these children for instruction. The basis for grouping should not be achievement or lack thereof, rather groupings should be made on the basis of a discerned common need. In this way, clearly defined goals are available to guide the teacher and, most importantly, involve the students. The children must be informed of the reason for their grouping and be given the opportunity to evaluate their progress at the end of the instructional period. The children must be given short-range attainable goals and must be allowed to evaluate their progress. This procedure, of course, feeds into one of the fundamental demands for comprehension.

There are advantages, socially and psychologically as well as educationally, in this grouping procedure. Children have a chance to interact about a common problem and, in many instances, support each other. A type of peer tutoring can emerge. Children can begin to recognize that others have the same problems and that they are really not that different or odd. For children who are genuinely disabled in comprehension this may be the most comforting thing ever to happen to them.

SUMMARY OF PROGRAMMING

In summary, the preceding, necessarily compact synopsis of programming for learning disabled students with comprehension problems emphasized the interaction of physical, psychological, and social elements in the children's lives.

It would probably be of little value to list the demands of comprehension that students must meet in order of priority. Children vary so much. However, a cluster of demands can be listed.

- ability to concentrate — need to know
- adequate and appropriate background of experience
- adequate and appropriate vocabulary commensurate with the experiential background
- adequate short-term and long-term recall
- inferential thinking
- organized, systematic behavior
- recognition of connotative and denotative aspects of language

It is possible that the above list might be considered a tabulation of readiness for comprehension. Few, if any of these skills are found exclusively in one realm of a child's life; that concept is nearly untenable. All of them impinge to some degree on any behavior that is not purely automatic. However, they are often accepted by parents and teachers as if they were parts of the autonomic nervous system. At best, these skills need to be learned, spontaneously and independently. If for some reason they are not learned, an effort must be made to teach them. This last statement presupposes that diagnostic teaching will be used to assess whether or not the need exists, and, if it exists, its degree. The gamut of these demands necessary for comprehension should be evaluated and, depending on the specific needs of a child, an attempt should be made to rank them in importance for teacher attention. When such a ranking is carried out for a number of children, it is nearly always possible to develop an instructional group based on a shared, common need. Usually, this is the most efficient means of addressing the problem.

INSTRUCTIONAL MATERIALS

It is important to understand that printed materials in themselves will do little to help the learning disabled student comprehend better. They are, after all, only vehicles in which comprehension can occur. Materials that require children to perform a comprehension task will not develop comprehension; since, implicitly and explicitly, the appropriate comprehension skills must be available to the student. Such materials might provide practice and an opportunity, but they will not teach comprehension. Programmed materials fall into the same vein; the child must be able to comprehend them to use them.

Initial Materials

Teachers need to begin comprehension development with concrete objects, models, pictures, or drawings. This concept is vital since it is so often attempted through oral language alone. It is important to associate oral language with something tangible that can be looked at repeatedly. Oral language is so transitory that it is gone as soon as it is heard.

As was suggested earlier, the classroom, the children, their clothes, and so forth are worthy instructional materials; and as oral language comprehension is enhanced, the same basic activities can be used with written language.

Language Experience

When progress in comprehension, which includes attitudes as well as skills, is enhanced, the need to progress to more realistic materials arises. Children must begin to be able to manipulate the mechanics of paragraphs.

The best way to begin paragraph analysis is with a language experience approach. A number of positive factors are involved in this pedagogy (Hammond, 1972). The background experiences are the students; the vocabulary comes from their vocabularies; interests are usually present. If the teacher incorporates the material and language of earlier comprehension activities, the experience background will facilitate recall.

Using their materials, children can deal with abstracting; classifying, inferential questions can be asked; and levels of abstraction can be developed. By rewriting the children's material, the teacher can introduce synonyms and antonyms, semantic variation, and topic sentences.

Rewritten Materials

Rewriting also permits the introduction of connotation and denotation as well as propaganda techniques. There has not been enough encouragement of teachers to use rewriting. In nearly all cases, teachers can adapt children's materials to introduce new concepts, skills, and vocabulary while still maintaining the students' fundamental control of the experiential background and basic vocabulary.

Commercially prepared materials often require so much pre-reading readiness instruction that the stated goal of the teacher and students gets buried in instructional procedures. There is no doubt that eventually children, even those with comprehension difficulties, will have to deal with conventionally prepared materials. That is what the comprehension program is designed to accomplish. It is doubtful, however, that these materials offer the best opportunity to inaugurate instruction and development of comprehension.

ASSISTANCE TO PARENTS

Students with learning disabilities almost always present problems for their parents. It is almost characteristic. However, those children whose difficulties are based on factors in comprehension usually present even greater problems. Many parents eventually accept the idea that their children have difficulty learning things. It is much more difficult to accept a child who cannot understand. The reactions are compounded because this problem influences life at home as well as in school. To many parents this inability to comprehend is the most difficult problem.

Effects On The Child

The problem at home often exacerbates the problems in school, once again, the negative interaction of the child's realms. Home problems in this area can develop in the preschool years and predispose the child to failure. The idea of being less competent than others, especially siblings, fosters negative behavior. The child may use the concept of incompetence to remain immature and not aspire to pleasure-pain growth. Parents and siblings often use this type of disability in the child to overprotect or pamper the child. Normal demands for socially acceptable behavior may not be placed on the child. The child, in effect, gets away with murder. For the immature child these attitudes provide overall delight; yet, because of the demands of society, the child must one day go to school, conform to regulations, and try to learn. Attitudinally, the pampered, spoiled child will be unable to deal with these societal demands, and reactions will inevitably occur.

A nearly converse set of circumstances may develop for the learning disabled child with comprehension difficulties. Attitudes and behaviors in the family rather than being overly supportive can be denigrating. The child can be regarded as unworthy of effort. These normal developmental procedures that parents use to foster growth in their children may be regarded as useless with this child. Siblings may look upon the child as a sign of shame for them, someone with whom and in whom they feel no pride or delight. Other children will not be able to accept the child, since they cannot understand anyone unable to function well in comprehending play or games. The child who cannot adjust activities inferentially is usually a poor partner or game participant, as in the example below.

Recently, five boys were playing baseball. The teams were three and two. Of course, a situation arose in which the bases were loaded and there was no batter. The children, except one, agreed that there was an "imaginary man" (their term) on third base. The concept made good sense to all the children except one. This boy could not comprehend the idea, and the fact that an imaginary man could score a run was mind-boggling. His comment about how a run could score if no one was on third base frustrated the others. Their response, understandably from their point of view, was "Never mind! Just do what we tell you to do, and we'll keep score." The game continued, but for one player it must have been less pleasant because of the obvious condescending attitude of the other children. He may not have appreciated the sarcasm, but he understood that his standing in their eyes had been diminished.

Children who are overly protected or denigrated eventually must face the problems of being educated. They must learn to listen, talk, read, write, and compute. The psychological attitudes that they bring, of course, influence their performances. Children with severe comprehension problems appear to have only two reactions to these demands. They can either retreat into fantasy or act out. Using either behavior they accomplish what they want. The too-demanding, unattainable activity is halted. In effect, they have to some degree made sure that they will not have to face the frustration.

It does not appear that the spoiled child uses one of these, and the denigrated child the other; rather it appears that each child chooses the most effective one for him.

Parental Education

Parents must be educated to these points. In many instances parents are not informed in these matters. The most effective point to begin enlightening parents is in pre-school or nursery school. Parents need to know what their responsibilities are to their children, especially in language development. Those with infants at risk should know that verbal stimulation is vital to child development. They should also be made aware of their role in vocabulary development and fostering experimental background. The first emphasis should always be on normal development. Critical milestones in development could even be printed so that parents might check the sequential development of the child.

Only when a standard has been established and the normal understood should an effort be made to note deviations. The role of parents in the early recognition of this type of learning disability cannot be overemphasized. The recognition of this problem cannot be placed on the school. If it is, it will probably be too late. Problems in comprehension surface early in a child's life, and parents must be alert to the symptoms.

Early recognition could in many ways mitigate the harmful, negative attitudes and behaviors that so often occur in these children. Parents could be helped with the sequelae of the problem to minimize their influences, but parents must be informed. They must know how to evaluate growth, and they must be helped to acquire techniques to deal with the child's needs. The family will need to be involved. Siblings and grandparents must be made to understand and accept the child's disability. Because this problem is developmental in nature, the burden falls on the parents and the family.

If detected early, a decision can be made about the etiology of the problem. If the problem is due to nurturing, adjustment can be made and normal development anticipated. If the problem is in the nature of the child, remedial, compensatory, or adaptive strategies can be put into place. However, if the problem goes undetected, stress can be expected in the family, school, and the individual. Such stress seldom promises happiness.

The School's Role

The school has a valid role in the parents' growth. In many states parents may seek assistance from the public schools for at-risk children at any age. For the health and success of the school, it cannot sit back and wait. Its stance cannot be reactive. Child study groups should be inaugurated, especially for parents of infants and preschoolers. Meetings, such as Parent-Teacher Associations, should be developed on a regular basis as informational in nature. A pediatrician, psychologist, language therapist, or social worker can be brought in to upgrade the overall knowledge of the lay public. School newsletters that are *educationally* oriented can provide knowledge and open up to the public the skill and knowledge of staff members. Principals should be able to adjust schedules to free staff members to participate in an "Open House on Language Development," for example.

If a school feels a genuine commitment to learning disabled students with comprehension problems, informing parents, soliciting their help and providing guidance is essential. Once again, it must be reiterated that if the bulk of the harm done to family, school, and the child is to be foreclosed, it must be done before the child reaches formal schooling. If it is not done, the negative elements noted earlier in this section will be inevitable.

SUMMARY

It is unfortunate that the role of comprehension in students' learning disabilities appears to be ignored or unappreciated. The emphasis is too frequently placed on rote, mechanical programs that seldom include problem appreciation and problem solving. Both of these represent an aspect of comprehension (Stanovich, 1982).

The interaction of the factors that make up human existence is unaddressed in diagnosing and planning an instructional program. Those non-school related components of learning, early experiences, early language, and curiosity must be an integral component for a diagnostic/prescriptive program to be effective. It seems to be a common understanding throughout the country that a good teacher is the only component necessary for learning. When learning does not occur, obviously, there has not been good teaching. If the interactions involved in failure or achievement in learning were accepted, this simplistic attitude could not be accepted.

Adjustment in programs must be encouraged. Teachers should feel free to use other approaches to instruction and learning that are commensurate with the needs of the children. Rigidity of approach is of little avail when the fundamental difficulty is comprehension. The concept of comprehension readiness and comprehension instruction must be understood by all teachers. Administrators at all levels should provide the instructional staff with this type of information.

Administrators must assume the responsibilities for educating parents. They are not required to know everything about everything, but they should be able to develop a framework for these activities to be presented and obtain the best possible professionals to make presentations. An entire community does not need to be instructed, since worthwhile materials are usually disseminated through adult community contacts. There is a pronounced spread of effect if worthwhile concepts are put forth.

Varied instructional materials as well as practice must be encouraged at all levels by the school administration. With the current emphasis on regular-education initiatives, now is a prime time to break instructional lock-step. The drastic changes in education which seem to be imminent make this flexibility urgent.

CHAPTER 9

Written Language Problems

Leo E. Otterbein

T he learning-disabled individual often experiences communicative disorders in processing the printed symbol as produced by others. The errors that plague someone with a reading disorder often occur simultaneously with disorders of outputs, more specifically, writing. Writing errors are peculiar; one can make errors in math, judgment, or taste, but none seem to have such potentially devastating consequences as errors in writing. We know that there is little correlation between the mechanical aspect of writing and verbal intelligence; we know it but don't necessarily show a belief in it. That's why work is edited, proofed, word processed; that's why some "writers" resort to dictation machines. That is also why many potentially fine writers never take the chance; they fear their fraility and ignorance will show, indelibly fixed in ink.

Learning-disabled students, specifically those with a writing disorder, make many errors in the course of their school day. As students, they cannot easily avoid writing lest they incur the wrath of their teachers or parents. Because the primary, if not exclusive, medium for communication in school is writing, students who cannot write, and who err wildly at times, all too frequently must publicize their confusion and their shame in naked black on white. For these writing-disabled students there is simply no place to hide and, unfortunately for them, the solutions to their painful dilemma do not exist.

This chapter originally appeared as an article by **Leo E. Otterbein** in *Learning Disabilities: An Interdisciplinary Journal* (Vol. III, 1984) and was adapted by permission of Grune & Stratton for inclusion in this *Handbook*.

This chapter will attempt to explain this peculiarity of writing errors. Such errors do, indeed, tell us a great deal about the souls — or more scientifically, the minds — of those who execute them.

Freud, of course, had much to say about slips of the tongue but considerably less about slips of the pen (Freud, 1901). He attributed the cause for such slips to unconscious motivation, essentially expressions of drives or desires that were, for one reason or another, unacceptable, inappropriate, or in conflict with the speaker's conscious communicative intentions.

The intent in this chapter is not to ignore Freud's enormous contributions to the study of errors; rather it is to take another perspective on it, one adopted by many investigators in cognitive psychology and in linguistics and psycholinguistics. That perspective is best expressed in a passage by one such investigator (Laver, 1969):

> To all intents and purposes, the healthy adult brain is not itself accessible to neurolinguistic experiment. This restricts us to a (widely accepted) research strategy which makes use of the fact that functional properties of unobservable control systems can be inferred from an examination of the output of those systems. This strategy can be applied to the error-free output and...to the output when malfunctions occur in the control-system. (p. 2)

The critical word in Laver's explanation is "malfunction," at least in terms of the goals of this chapter. In studying errors in writing (the output) I will infer properties of the human language processing system when malfunctions occur. Laver is not at all alone with Freud in his interest in errors. A considerable body of research, most completely represented in two recent volumes (Fromkin, 1973, 1980), has been developed on errors in speech, in signing, and, to some very modest degree, in writing. Unfortunately, investigations into writing errors almost inevitably devolve into investigations of spelling errors. These investigations have been, more unfortunately, limited in scope and value because they have labored under the misleading and nonproductive assumptions that spelling and writing are distinct activities and that both are no more than "speech written down." The mistakes in these assumptions are explained below. But even before those explanations are offered, the inadequacies of those assumptions can be sensed as one reads the paragraph developed by a 21-year-old student in a college level remedial writing class:

> The day I had an inprment to ment Mrs. Kovin. When I frist walked in to her office she ast me to have a set. She ast me watt I wored and sow told her my pralm that I have. And should her some of my wighing from school. She think my biges prolom is speeling she think that

something go's rogue in my brane it doset come out right. She is going to make two imprment for to see two dorters to thay can analyze my pralam that I have. I should be get a call from her in day or two.

While Mrs. Kovin may not win any awards for her identification of this writer's "biges prolom" as "speeling," she certainly cannot be chided for not being more perspicuous in her assessment of his "prolom." Indeed, anyone with even minimal experience in teaching or evaluating an individual's written language performance knows the overwhelming sense of frustration that arises when writers make mistakes like these. This frustration arises from the lack of any adequate set of criteria for making *sense* of those mistakes.

True enough, the errors can be evaluated in terms of their correspondence to rules of spelling and punctuation, but these rules help very little in *understanding* the errors and, therefore, in designing corrective strategies (Ruit & McKenzie, 1985). What can be said about the spelling of the word "appointment" as "imprment" except that it is wrong? Appeals to explanatory hypotheses like "poor phonics knowledge" or "inadequate phonetic analysis ability" are maddeningly inadequate, since one senses far, far more is wrong than these guesses suggest.

In the following pages, a model of spelling and written language is developed that enables one to begin to make sense of writing errors. But, as was indicated above, certain incorrect assumptions about, and perceptions of, written language and spelling must be explicated.

TRADITIONAL VIEWS OF SPELLING AND WRITTEN LANGUAGE

At its simplest, the most widely held view of spelling/writing is that it is "speech written down," a supremely tautological and vacuous definition. A more sophisticated version might be, "the recording of speech into visual symbols called letters."

Essentially, then, writing/spelling has been seen traditionally as the simple end product of the far more complex speech production process; one generates all linguistic matter in the "speech" mode and then finally encodes the sounds in letter shapes. Perhaps all of this arises from the feeling that our writing system is alphabetic and nothing more (Bloomfield, 1933).

Despite this rather common-sense view of what writing/spelling involves, attempts to explain spelling errors have been surprisingly unsuccessful. In fact, a recent effort (Moats, 1983) to explain the spelling errors of dyslexic students on the basis of phonetic accuracy led the author to conclude:

> The outcome of this study offers no support for prevailing diagnostic and classification approaches to dyslexia that characterize the majority of children as phonetically inadequate spellers. (p. 130)

In this same vein, a massive effort (Hanna, Hodges, & Rudorf, 1966) to develop a computerized algorithm for predicting sound-spelling corres-pondences was less accurate in its predictions of the spellings of unknown words than a fourth grader's efforts to predict spelling (Simon & Simon, 1973). It seems to have occurred to only a few (notably Hildun & Brown, 1956; Hodges & Rudorf, 1965; Plessas, 1963) that perhaps more than just letter-sound criteria should be considered in explaining spelling errors, but these few limited themselves to perhaps one other possible variable — morphemic structure, phonetic context, or meaning. But none considered a possible range of linguistic variables which could contribute to spelling errors.

Before phenomena can be explained, they must somehow be de-scribed and categorized. In efforts to describe and categorize spelling and writing errors, enormous problems have arisen, making those efforts frus-tratingly inconsistent. These problems again arise from the inadequate assumption that writing/spelling is phonetically based. A closer analysis of this erroneous assumption follows.

Conceptual Inadequacies

Spelling in the traditional sense of the term is regularly divorced from writing. Children are taught how to spell and how to write; their "writing" may be deemed "good" while their "spelling" may be seen as "poor." To be sure, some distinction between the two is valid. In oral language, for instance, a speaker may articulate words poorly, but the content of his speech may be superior. But this type of speaker's problem is minor; he may regularly pronounce /l/ as /w/ or /th/ as /f/. Even the initiate in speech pathology knows, however, that a speaker who makes multiple, seemingly random errors in articulation is likely to have a more profound "oral language disorder" that includes higher-order levels of linguistic ability. Similarly, the writer who regularly (and predictably) misspells a certain limited set of words may be a poorer speller than writer, but if errors are multiple and seemingly random, it is safe to conclude that a more pro-found writing problem exists. Fortunately for the language pathologist, as even a cursory review of titles in a library attests, a great deal of research has helped evolve models and tests of speech perception-production that permit the description of various pathological states and a more or less integrated understanding of those states. As a result, speech problems can be categorized at various levels of organization — phonetic, phonemic, phonological, morphemic, syntactic, lexical, and semantic. Speech disorders can be described at more than one level, and an understanding of the interaction of levels can be gained. An error can be seen to arise from one or more levels, and examinations of such errors lead to remarkable insights into the workings of the human mind as it processes language and to the development of more useful and effective treatment methods (Fromkin, 1980; Laver, 1980; MacKay, 1970).

To this writer's knowledge, such an integrated approach to the study of written language does not exist. Even the discussion of what does or does not constitute an error becomes quickly muddled because written errors are seen either as failures in coding sounds or in failures to conform to accepted usage. The phonetic correspondent of a written word is one criteria by which a written form is judged. Thus, in the sample quoted earlier, "speeling" is wrong because it does not contain the correct sequence of letters that represent the /e/ sound in /spĕlin/. The spelling of "shoud" is wrong because it is not, quite simply, in the dictionary; that is, it does not conform to accepted usage.

Practical Inadequacies

On the basis of these criteria — conformity to sound/symbol constraints or to accepted usage — investigators have developed hopelessly inadequate error categories. Generally, errors are categorized as errors of *omission, substitution,* or *addition* (Nelson & Warrington, 1974); but one can sense a difficulty with these categories immediately. In which category, for instance, would "speeling" fall? A first guess would be substitution (*e* for *l*) but *addition* and *omission* would serve just as well; that is, an *e* was *added* while an *l* was *omitted.* A complex error such as "imprment" defies categorization altogether.

Worse than the categorization dilemma, however, is the decision of what to identify as an error in the first place. While "imprment" and "speeling" are easily discerned errors, others are not, if one uses the two criteria for error definition discussed above. For instance, the word "watt" in the second sentence is correct according to both criteria; it is in the dictionary, and it does have a letter sequence that corresponds to its phonetic correlate. From the traditional point of view, this form could be at least an omission error (*h*) and an addition error (extra *t*); but it is surely not the same kind of error as his "shoud" or "prolom." The latter seem somehow more profound.

Similar error identification problems arise in the following illustrations:

- *there* house burned
- time to change his *flee* collar
- how a person dresses *reveal's* many things
- for *instants,* he wants to be a barber

None of the above violate phonetic or dictionary standards; that is, they are legitimate, dictionary-sanctioned letter sequences. Clearly, more than the word itself must be considered; the context of the form must be included as the following suggests.

What is even more perplexing, however, than categorization is the problem of identifying errors in a sentence context. In the paragraph, for instance, the writer states "I shoud be get a call from her in day or two." While "shoud" is clearly a traditional error, how shall we categorize the omitted *a* before "day"? Obviously, an omission error, a reader might say. Yet, enormous problems arise when one begins to universally assign the absence of letters to omission categories. One could not say then whether the error in the sentence, "The announcer say, 'Go home!' " is the omission of an *s* on "say" or on "announcer." Indeed, if one extends addition errors to this same degree, one could say the "be" in "I shoud be get a call . . ." is an addition error, the correct sentence being "I should get a call from her in a day or two."

While we may feel intuitively that these sentence errors are with "get" rather than "be," there is *no* way available by which one could prove it — short of asking the writer. And in fact, if one *asked* the writer, he or she may well provide us with the correction, or may just as well say, "Oh, I guess it could be either way" ("I should get a call"; "I should be getting a call").

Of literally thousands of errors collected, hundreds fall into several categories or into no category. The following typify these errors.

- *Each coaches spoke about their team.* Should *each* be *the* or *all the* or is the *s* on *coaches* wrong?
- *We had to worked around the house.* Is *had to* an addition error, or should *worked* be *work*?
- *My classmate is very attracted.* Is an *ive* missing from attract or has *to me* been deleted: My classmate is very attracted to me?
- *Flowers are very colored in many difference shades.* In this sentence, rearranging words would correct it; the problem is, what exactly is incorrect and what is correct: very, colored, or difference?

Clearly, clarification of the above issues is needed. Not surprisingly, the way to such clarification lies in the direction of a more highly integrated understanding of spelling/writing, of the relationship of spelling/writing to language, and of written error. Indeed, as will be seen, errors themselves permit one to evolve a model of written language production that is enormously helpful in making sense of the errors themselves. The description of such a model follows.

A MODEL OF WRITTEN LANGUAGE PRODUCTION

A recent burgeoning of interest in language errors (Fromkin, 1973, 1980) has resulted in the development of a complex speech-production model, the essential components and functions of which are discussed here. The model is a composite of several hypothesized models (Dell & Reich, 1980, Fromkin, 1973; Laver, 1980), and certain features pertinent to writing have been emphasized.

In describing the model, one must first appreciate the fact that the generation of a written message occurs over time, that it is a process that begins with an idea and ends not as one would suppose with the actual writing but with a "post-executive monitoring" phase that "edits" the writing and permits "error-pickup" (Gentry, 1984).

Since this process occurs over time, it is amenable to stage analysis, points in the generation process at which hypothesized linguistic activities occur (Bookmen, 1984). The following outline summarizes those stages:

Stage 1 Idea generation
Stage 2 Specification of syntactic and semantic features consistent with ideational content
Stage 3 Lexical search; formative selection
Stage 4 Organization of graphemes
Stage 5 Neuromuscular commands to articulators (fingers and hands)
Stage 6 Monitoring-editing (feedback evaluation)

Stage 1 can be construed as the prelinguistic or conceptual stage, the point at which an idea is generated, this idea being nonverbal.

In Stage 2, the features of that idea are given form by the selection of appropriate syntactic and semantic features. Thus, the syntactic features for "dog" might be noun, singular and so forth while the semantic features may be 4-legged, animate, household pet, and so forth. At the end of Stage 2 processing, a fully specific structure, including semantic and syntactic features most appropriate to the capturing of the idea, is completed.

In Stage 3, the Lexical Search Phase, the structural features are given verbal form by a search of the mental dictionary. An optimal match between the features of the concept and the word(s) available in the lexicon is sought. The lexicon contains not only words, but affixes, not only phonological information, but othrographic. Indeed, evidence suggests that the lexicon is a multitiered thesaurus in which many features —

morphemic, phonemic, orthographic — of a single word are housed (Fromkin, 1973).

Once the appropriate words are selected, general orthographic (or phonological) rules are applied, thus restructuring the Stage 3 output. Perhaps, ordering of elements occurs here, from letter to syllable to morpheme to phrase sequencing. One can assume that elements are unordered prior to Stage 4; that is, they have not been linearized. For instance, though *s* may be chosen, its orthographic features specified in the lexicon, it may not be *placed* accurately until Stage 4 is reached.

Assuming all elements are in order, the string of orthographic features is converted to a sequence of neuromuscular commands which are then executed. This Stage 5 process for writing is bound by exacting temporal and spatial constraints. The execution of a writing program is much slower than that of a speech program; thus, the intended or constructed program — including the ordering of neural impulses — must be held for relatively long periods in a short-term or buffer memory until the fully executed program can be compared to the intended program for editing purposes.

Stage 6 is the monitoring or editing phase, one in which the actual writing is compared to the intended one. Note how such a monitoring system works. It compares actual to intended utterance across semantic, lexical, syntactic, orthographic, and perhaps phonological criteria. Should errors — mismatches really — between intent and act be detected, appropriate corrective actions such as, erasures, strike-overs, and additions are taken.

Most obviously, this model suggests that orthographic rules are independent of phonological rules; that is, in the lexical search stage, the grapheme sequence of a given formative can be chosen without necessarily choosing its phonological correspondents. Thus, for the concept "dog," the sequence of graphemes *d, o, g,* can be selected while the phonemic sequence /d/, /ɔ/, /g/ can be ignored. Such, for instance, could be the case for some deaf writers.

The model also suggests that semantic/syntactic features can be assigned graphemic shapes that are traditionally considered punctuation marks, for example, the apostrophe indicating possession in "The dogs' collars." Note that this apostrophe is meaningful and is graphemically representable; it is not representable phonetically.

Perhaps the most useful feature of the model is its capacity to help develop more accurate and explicit descriptions of writing errors, to aid in developing reasonable categories of error types, and to point the way toward more productive explanatory statements of error. The section that follows represents an attempt to exploit the features of the model in order to build a taxonomy of writing errors and to begin an explanation of them.

SPELLING/WRITING ERRORS:
AN ATTEMPT AT CATEGORIZATION AND EXPLANATION

The categories and subtypes of errors discussed below are based on an analysis of a corpus of several thousand writing errors gleaned from the writings of hundreds of students in the author's undergraduate writing classes and graduate psychology/education classes. While some of this analysis is subjective, to be sure, every effort will be made to eliminate alternative category assignments and to relate errors to the appropriate linguistic processing levels in the model described earlier.

An error will be defined as a "mismatch" between the (admittedly hypothesized) intended program, errors that can occur at any of the stages between 2 and 5, and the actual written message.

Neuromuscular

These errors appear to occur at Stage 4 at the moment just prior to execution of Stage 5. Errors in this category often involve the addition, deletion, or mixing of letters or letter parts. They must really be seen as neuromuscular *command* errors in which discrete muscle movements are somehow out of phase with the overall program. Several illustrations and their explanations follow.

1. *Omissions or blends of letter parts* (features). These errors involve an extremely superficial kind of motor "lapse," a kind of short circuiting of the motor command sequence.
   - My friend wore a *rourd* button.
   Here, the second arc of the *n* may well have been blended with the initial arc of the *d,* this perhaps "read" by the monitor system as satisfying the muscle commands for the *n* and *d* sequence.

   Occasionally, one suspects, the similarity of motor movements can lead to such deletion errors.
   - I don't give my kid *canay* (candy).
   Here, the execution of the lower segment of the *d* may have arisen only from the fact that that segment and a cursive *a* are identical motorically. Again, the short-circuiting, that is, failure to complete the *d* arose from the fact that the incomplete motor movement was "read" as sufficient by the monitor system.

   A more interesting example is the following:
   - Many buttons were missing of it. (off of it)
   In this error, the repetition of motor movements in "off" and "of" were cancelled, perhaps because such motor repetition is rare in spelling — at least in immediately succeeding words.

2. *Duplication.* The repetition of a given command when it is not appropriate leads to a different type of error. These errors suggest that a kind
of graphic stuttering occurs in which letters or letter groups are simply
executed twice.

- He likes to *reaad* long stories
- Punishment can have a desirous or undesir*oro*us effect.
- Raising a child requires patien*en*ce.
- They *were were* their to help out.
- Many histor*ist* site to visit.

While the first four examples are relatively self-explanatory, the last is
interesting in that the *ist* segment may well be a kind of anticipatory
execution of the two *sit* segments in *si*te and vi*sit*. A similar anticipatory
motor execution is seen in the following:

- So *I* one day *I* say a bird.

These errors suggest that the spelling "program" is aligned with an
independent set of neuromuscular commands and that these commands can occasionally become "detached" from the program,
reiterated, deleted, or duplicated.

Some other illustrations of various neuromuscular errors follow.

- Several spaceships *containg* monsters.
- John is my *neighor*.
- *I'am* a student.
- I was saying to *myselp* please be a boy.

The first illustrates a deletion of the segment -*in* because it is a duplicate (contai*nin*g). In the next, the *h* is read as fulfilling the requirements of
a *b* and so the *b* is deleted. In the third example, the apostrophe *and* the *a*
of am are included. And in the last example, the final *f* is produced as a *p*
in anticipation of the *p* in "please."

All of these errors strongly suggest that the operation of motor command functions is independent or semi-independent of the input from
higher programming levels and that they are or can be fluid in their
positions in a chain of commands.

Further, there is the suggestion that the "intent" of the program is
stored in pre-execution buffer memory as a series of specified motor
features (rather than, say, visual features). Thus the post-executive monitoring system compares actual kinesthetic/tactile features of writing to the
planned features. Such a system of feedback analysis would explain nicely
how touch-typists and, indeed, all accurate writers know they've made an
error before they look at the product. In essence, their monitoring system
alerts them to a mismatch between the intended muscle movement and the
actual movements.

Several final illustrations follow:

- It was an embbrassing moment (duplication of *b* perhaps influenced by duplication of *s* later in program).
- On a two week vocation (duplication of "bridge" segment of *v*).
- He enjoys playing checkers, spades, and Ominoes (deletion of initial *d*; note capitalization of *O* occurs, thus suggesting a *capitalization feature* exists independently of individual letters).

Phonographic Errors

Errors in this category are commonly discussed in the literature on spelling-error types. Essentially, they are seen as mismatches between a sound and a letter or letters, a kind of "phonics" mistake. At an elementary level, the following illustrates this type of error:

- The old man was exstreamly seedy.
- The edges of the opennig were jagged.
- The room had a thick dengy wite paint on it.

Various phonic rules are broken here — or misapplied as in *exstreamly*. More interesting errors occur ironically when a speaker does try to follow the definition of spelling as "speech written down." These errors arise from a too literal or misdirected effort to encode speech into letter shapes.

The /N/ Errors

This group of errors illustrates a writer's inability to access the correct representation of syllabic *N* which in spelling can be represented by the following:

-en (dead*en*)	/dĕdn/
-ing (see*ing*)	/sēin/
-and	/n̩/
in	/n̩/
-ion (fashion)	/fašin̩/

Writers err in applying the correct segment or series of letters as the following indicate:

- There are four steps *and* giv*en* a child a bath.
- He was soak *and* wet.
- He had started tak*en* drugs.
- I create things *and* my mind and I show them.
- The reason why she's confused *in* depressed.

- hang my sto*kens.*
- all *and* all, it was good.
- bow *in* arrow.
- I had*en* been clean in two weeks.
- I read Robbins *and* Crusoe.
- everyone giv*en* and receiving gifts.

"I read Robbins *and* Crusoe" is a fascinating error in that it suggests that the writer inferred that not two but three characters appeared in the novel, vis. Robbins, Crusoe, and Friday. The final example above is as interesting because it almost "sounds" right — everyone can be "given" gifts. Only a grammatical analysis reveals the error; if one is "given" gifts, one is by definition "receiving" them.

Assimilated Errors

Assimilation of sounds occurs when phonemes with similar features occur in close proximity. In the following examples, more obvious assimilated sounds are encoded directly by the writer.

- We had cra*m*berry sauce.
- to the u*p*most.
- you hal*f* to stop that.
- bad a*d*ittudes.
- four shiny new hu*p*caps.

Some writers are aware of the assimilative penchants in speech and try vigorously to correct for them. In English, for instance, the sounds /t,d/ between /n/ and /s/ often disappear. (Compare: wind — wi*n*ds, wins; print — pri*n*ts, prince). Indeed, we acknowledge that *patients* and *patience* are homophones.

In the following errors, writers are trying to manage this exigency, occasionally overcorrecting:

- I see no differe*n*ts.
- He lives at a great dista*n*ts.

In other errors, the writer simply does not code the sound because it is fully or at least partially asssimilated.

- I love the atm*o*phere.
- I us*e* to go there.
- I have no money to spe*n* today.
- The day began to brighe*n*.
- He has few sy*m*toms.

In the last example, the writer deletes a suppressed /p/ sound. But in some cases, a sophisticated writer will predict the existence of a sound that does not exist.

- He ran *saftly* home.
- The new *inter* harbor.

In the first example, the writer may recognize that /t/ regularly disappears when endings are added to words ending in -ft such as sof*t*ly, of*t*en, lif*t*s and so forth. He may assume "safely" belongs to this group and so "creates" a *t* slot. In the last example a similar phenomenon occurs: a /t/ or /d/ after /n/ is often assimilated, for example, twenny (twenty), canny (candy), and so on. This writer, at some level aware of this, assumes the "real" word is *inter* (certainly sensible in the context of harbor since there are forms like interstate and intercity). This error becomes a very intelligent one.

A number of other errors of this type can be provided. A most interesting type, rare though it is, illustrates the hypothesis of many linguists that a single "deep" form is modified in language production to conform to various phonological rules. For instance, the /n/ of the prefix /in-/ is changed to /im-/ before roots beginning with /p/, /b/, or /m/ (cf. i*m*possible, i*m*balance, i*m*modest). In the following errors, it appears this and similar modification rules were bypassed.

- I got the i*n*pression.
- He is i*n*polite.
- I like to feel co*n*fertible.
- of great i*n*portance.
- he gave me great su*b*port.
- Su*b*pose he is wrong.

Final examples of general assimilation errors follow.

- She decid*e* to go.
- Putting away food is a *j*ore.
- He has not *j*et won.
- The person was *s*killed instantly.
- His lates*s* destruction.

As was mentioned earlier, these errors are ironic in that they arise because the writers are trying to get their *speech* written down. If they had ignored their speech, they would have been more accurate spellers.

Morpheme/Word Level Errors

These types of errors are perhaps the most frequent. They provide very convincing evidence that spelling programs are generated well before and, therefore, independently of phonological input. This is not to suggest that phonological information cannot be accessed at some level. It is merely to emphasize the fact that spelling/writing accesses linguistic information at multiple levels.

Errors of this type are manifested in the misapplication or misanalysis of morphemic rules, grammatical, inflectional, and lexical. If it is recalled that lexical information is derived from a matching of desired semantic/syntactic features with available forms from the lexicon, then errors in feature specification (Stage 2) or selection of lexemes during lexical search (Stage 3) can occur. Further, if it is also recalled that lexical units are unordered prior to Stage 5, then misordered, deleted, duplicated, and blended forms can appear as errors.

Deletions

This type of error seems to occur because the semantic or syntactic "message" conveyed by the deleted item is found elsewhere in the sentence.

- The three receptionis*t* left.
- Several student were there.
- Some of my interes*t* were swimming, basketball, and tennis.
- Two m*a*n up the street began to fight.
- He has many disappoin*t*ment in life.

In these examples, the plural morpheme has been deleted because the notion of plurality is carried by other sentence elements. This redundancy-deletion is common in English. For instance, one says, "I went but didn't want to." and omits "go" because it is implied by the other sentence elements and by convention.

Other deletion errors arise from more subtle determinants.

- He won a ward for best poem.

This error reflects the writer's misanalysis of "award'" as being article + noun.

- And then get a nother mop.

Above, the spacing suggests the writer has segmented "another" into article + adjective; this segmentation is very common even in educated speech in the context "a whole nother ballgame, story," and so on.

Duplication

Again, a common error, this type includes morphemes that are repeated, sometimes using allomorphic forms. The following illustrate a very interesting subtype.

- but know I realize.
- it would be know problem to have people believe it.
- I don't have know idea.

In all of these, the meaning "be aware" is contained, viz., realize, believe, idea. The spellings of *no* or *now* as *know* are seen as instances of a semantically motivated unit superseding an apparently more elementary one, this promoted by the phonological (know, no = /no/) or orthographic (know = now) resemblance between the units.

Other duplication errors, usually involving inflectional morphemes are included below.

- The black window*s* shades (plural).
- How in the world coul*d* she foun*d* her money (past tense).
- That's one kitchen I never *won't* to see again (negative).
- They couldn*'t not* have possibly learned to spell because they were too young (negative).
- I just*ed* want*ed* to be alone (past tense).
- None one but me (negative).
- A one parent cannot raise children (determiner).
- I had art for two periods last*s* year (plural).
- It doe*s*n't make*s* a city bad (present tense).
- It has always been *saided* (past tense).

Misanalysis

This category of errors probably teaches us more about the way in which the writer understands language than any other type. They suggest ways in which the writer interprets what he experiences in linguistic situations and develops rules from that interpretation.

- For *instants,* he likes to play baseball.

Above, the writer apparently interpreted *instance* as a base (instant) plus plural (s), a motivated mistake since the term does suggest more than one in many cases, such as, "For instance, he likes candy and gum, but not cigars." An alternative to this interpretation is captured in the next illustration.

- For *instant,* he played football.

The writer here has but one example, so he uses the singular form. Note that there is no way in English to express the difference between one and several illustrations of a generalization. That is, forms like "for *an* instant" or "For instances" are wrong. These writers solved the problem in reasonably intelligent, if incorrect, ways.

Another interesting set of errors arises from the incorrect use of the articles *a* and *an*. Evidence from the errors below suggests that the article — head noun dyad are closely bound, with interposed adjectives occurring later in sentence development. Note how the article agrees with the head noun.

- *a* innocent *b*ystander.
- *a* old *l*ady.
- *a* outgoing *p*ersonality.
- *an* computer *e*xpert.
- keep *an* close *e*ye on him.

A third group of errors points to the writer's confusion in the interpretation of mass/count nouns. For instance, one says, "The boys are here" but "The milk is here" because boys is a count noun, milk is mass. But there are instances when this distinction is not clear to some.

- The *glass were* broken (here glass seen as pieces by the writer).
- The mashed *potatoes* was lumpy (potatoes *seen* as mass noun).
- *Dust were* on the mirror (i.e., specks of dust).

Yet another category of misanalysis errors involves the failure on the part of the writer to recognize a specific grammatical rule. In the following, the writers fail to delete the plural marker before nouns of measurement (and similar quantifying substantives) when such nouns are used adjectivally. That is, they do not make the change from "He is seven inch*es* tall " to "He is a seven-inch-tall baby."

- A seven pounds, ten ounc*es* boy.
- The four year*s* college.
- A three *feet* trophy.
- She can lift a 200 lb*s*. box.

Similar errors without quantifying nouns follow:

- Table and chair*s* set.
- The glasse*s* case I have.
- Go to the home of the elderlie*s*.
- His eye*s*balls nearly fell out.
- He drinks tomato*es* juice.

In these, a plural rule fails to be deleted, suggesting it may be present generally in a writer's program but deleted if the noun to be pluralized is to be used adjectivally.

A final set of errors in this *misanalysis* category follows:

- friendly attatu*ed* (noun interpreted as verb)
- if a person dress is neat.

The latter is a complex error; a "competing program" (see below) may have caused this one. In other words, two forms "If a person's dress is neat" and "If a person dresses neat" could have been simultaneously developed; in any case, the term *dresses* seems to have been misanalyzed here as *dress is*.

Competing Morphemic Program Errors

In this category of errors, a context is developed in which two or more equally legitimate and synonymous strings are satisfactory, the selection of one over the other being based on stylistic or subtle semantic considerations. The point here is that two or more lexical strings are selected during lexical search perhaps because the preceding syntactic/semantic feature specifications are vague or equivocal.

- They feel inse*s*ure.

In this error, the notion of negative can be expressed by *in* or *un*, though *in* is selected. The base unit of *meaning* seems to be certainty, this meaning expressible in terms like secure or sure. This writer chose both.

- After washing dishes, I *got* to bed.

Here, since *tense* is not assigned in the initial phrase, either go or went is acceptable. The writer seems to have chosen the present base (go) with a past tense allomorph (t) as in spe*nt* or ke*pt*. Similar errors can be seen in the following:

- This ke*pts* happening (past and present).
- The most mem*ber*able thing about it (remember vs. memorable).
- After you have regis*trate* (register vs. registration).
- The glass case is *feels* pliable (copula + linking verb of sensation, both able to "take" a predicate adjective).
- A copper ½ half inch coin (selection of two representations of the meaning *half* similar to legal or formal convention of redundancy in number expression as in "We must receive payment in thirty days".
- As well as *visually discrimination* skills (adjective vs. adverb or noun vs. verb indecision).
- To last as long as possible as I can (indecision over "to last as long as I can" and "to last as long as possible." Note the *and* used in attempt to combine these strings grammatically).
- The patient is very discomfortable (noun vs. adjective).
- The table had crumbs on some part of the it (noun vs. pronoun).
- Several retardated children (participle vs. substantive-retarded, retardate, retard; note the pejorative connotation of "retardate" here obscured by the participle form).

- I'm going to keep my room clean for now on (from now on vs. for now).
- Everybodies friendly (plural vs. contracted copulative *is*).
- He served for three consequentive years (sequence vs. consecutive).

All of these errors suggest that at a very early level of programming, decisions are *not* made about the most desirable form in which to capture the idea. For instance, the grammatical features of "As well as visually discrimination skills" may not have been fully specified as noun or verb, adjective or adverb, that is, discriminate verb, discrimination noun, visual adjective, visually adverb. Thus, *all* available grammatical features were selected from the lexicon and "passed through" to executive stages without decision-making being completed. In "To last as long and as possible as I can," two entire strings expressing perseverance were selected from the lexicon, here the indecision being a function of uncertainty in semantic feature specification. The writer seemed unsure of exactly how long e intended to "last" — "as long as possible" or "as long as I can." Similar semantic indecision seems to govern "several retardated children" and "I am going to keep my room clean for now on."

A final set of such errors follows:

- My *see* almost dropped out of its socket.
- John spoke until he got a stand of applause (round of applause vs. standing ovation).
- An event that was taking right in place of your own presence.
- I *contacted* strep throat.
- The *up-routeing* of streets.
- And *mostly the time*.

SUMMARY

The notion that spelling, writing, and language are inextricably related one to the other has hopefully been adequately demonstrated. The writer who sincerely spells sickle-cell anemia as "sick as hell anemia" has *not* made a simple encoding error. Instead, he has generated a complex linguistic form that is itself the product of the interaction of multiple language and ideational components. In his comical error, he has drawn on information at phonological, orthographic, lexical, syntactic, semantic levels, producing in written form a "meaning" for a dreaded disease. He has communicated to his reader a message that goes far beyond what he could ever communicate in the spoken correlate of this term. And in his unwitting error, he has let us in on the workings of his own perceptions and feelings.

But the writers who make less spectacular errors — the ones who spell input as *imput* or the one who spells Woolworth's as Wool-Ward's — are also letting us in on some secrets that linguistics and psychologists and teachers have been trying to unlock for so long. Their errors reveal, piece by piece, not only the structure and content of the individual's linguistic competence but also allow us to construct a model of the process by which that competence is expressed in writing. We also learn what can go wrong in that generative activity, where it goes wrong, and from these findings, what, if anything, can be done to reduce such errors.

The paragraph at the beginning of this chapter represents a kind of condensation, a distillation, of the many things that can go wrong in writing. Hopefully, with the observations and inferences developed in this chapter, more meaningful conclusions about his language problems can be drawn. Clearly, for example, he has difficulty "processing" phonological data, transforming then to written form. In a sense, however, he is *too* facile at writing speech down. His *prolom* or *ast* or *biges* is certainly a function of the way he says these words — or hears himself say them. But what can we say of his spelling of appointment as *inprment*? Perhaps we could say that both *ap* and *in* are semantically related (both suggesting to or near); his error arose from an inadequate specification of semantic features so that he drew *in* from the lexicon instead of *ap*. Perhaps the glaringly inappropriate *r* arose from some confusion of *interview* with *appointment*? Perhaps the decision of *oint* arose from faulty phonological processing, this a consequence of slurred pronunciation?

A duplication rule seems to affect the writer's efforts. Note the repetition of the *ment* (for meet) after *inprment*; note the duplicate *e* in *speeling* (instead of a duplicate *l* as if the command to duplicate were independent of the letters themselves). Even the phrase "analyze my prolam that I have" is a duplication of sorts, this at a phase level.

But a pervasive kind of phonetic hypersensitivity seems also to course through the writing. Note his spelling of so as *sow*. The next word is *I*, and in English phonetics, a sequence of two vowels "raises" a glide between them, thus, /sowī/. The writer may have heard this, coded the /w/ and deleted the /ī/, giving the right number of letters totally but the wrong one finally. And the large number of omitted words suggests that his ability to store his intended message in some pre-executive buffer memory may be inefficient, data being deleted from it before it can be executed.

The impression one gets as one examines such writing is that of disarray, parts and features disorganized and disordered. But the important point is that this disorder seems to range along all linguistic fronts; and, as in the writer who wrote "sick as hell anemia," that far more can be learned about a writer's language than merely how well he remembers his spelling words or how good his phonics ability is.

For the reseacher, the taxonomy and language-processing model described in this chapter can provide a useful, if still vastly incomplete, paradigm for the investigation not only of spelling errors but also of language errors and of language itself, both pathological and normal. Are errors in listening and reading comprehension related; or are they of a different sort, this latter alternative suggesting that "reception" functions are absolutely distinct from "expressive?" Are written errors a result of — or even related to — short-term memory functions as they are now construed? Or are there two STMs — one receptive, the other expressive (pre-executive buffer memory)? How does the monitoring system work? Are some writers more dependent upon motor feedback while others have to "see" their work to assess accuracy? And is this "visual" speller also one who has motor-related disorders, for example, dysgraphia?

For the linguist, writing errors help to refine notions of deep structure and transformations. The spelling of *subport* for support is tantalizingly consistent with the linguist's hypothesis of deeper levels of organization. And in terms of syntactic and semantic theories, do errors like "an close eye" suggest something about the relations of articles to nouns and the timing of adjective interpositions in the sentence generation sequence? Are lexical units really stored as bundles of features, even derivational and inflectional (as the writer who wrote *intelligentical* for intelligent presumably combining intelligent and intellectual). And do these kinds of errors tell the linguist anything about word formation or derivation rules? Why, for instance, is the *i* inserted in *intelligentical* when it appears neither in intelligent nor intellectual?

For the teacher, errors can help in developing more appropriate instructional goals. Obviously, many spelling errors are context-dependent; thus, teaching students to memorize lists of words may be only very marginally helpful in improving their "in-context" spelling. Should phonics be taught at all or, if so (more likely), to whom? Certainly, to students who are virtual phoneticists, a less-direct sound/spelling system should be taught. Meaning too must clearly be included in spelling instruction since letter sequences clearly carry semantically and syntactically relevant information. Finally, and obviously, spelling cannot be divorced from writing and neither can be separated from language. Spelling and writing, like pronunciation and comprehension, are activities of an integrated intelligence, one that is not compartmentalized into autonomous functions in any absolute sense. Errors in spelling and writing really let us know that integration has failed at some point. Instead of fostering the continuation of that failure of integration by splitting off spelling from writing from language, it would behoove us to emphasize the remarkable and awesome interplay and interdependence of linguistic capacities.

CHAPTER 10

Arithmetic Difficulties

Jeannette E. Fleischner
Katherine Garnett

T he purpose of this chapter is to provide a framework within which to consider the arithmetic achievement deficits of learning-disabled students. Although achievement deficits in arithmetic appear to be as prevalent as deficits in reading, until recently relatively less attention has been paid to the sources and treatment of math disorders. In the sections that follow, factors involved in arithmetic difficulties are reviewed, important features of effective instruction are determined, and general findings of relevant research efforts at Teachers College of Columbia University are described.

ARITHMETIC DISABILITY: A NEGLECTED AREA

The current federal definition of children with specific learning disabilities includes disorders of mathematical calculations (*Federal Register*, 1977). While children manifesting deficits in mathematics are specifically included under this definition, arithmetic learning difficulties rarely precipitate referrals for evaluation. In many school systems, special education services are provided almost exclusively on the basis of children's difficulties in acquiring reading skills, thus excluding a potentially sizable number of youngsters with arithmetic disability (Badian, 1983). Even after children have been identified as learning disabled, substantive assessment

This chapter originally appeared as an article by **Jeannette E. Fleischner** and **Katherine Garnett** in *Learning Disabilities: An Interdisciplinary Journal* (Vol. II, 1983) and was adapted by permission of Grune & Stratton for inclusion in this *Handbook*.

and remediation of arithmetic difficulties are rarely provided (Goodstein & Kahn, 1974). Empirical investigations in this area have been few in number and narrow in focus, resulting in a limited knowledge base concerning the nature of children's arithmetic learning disabilities, effective procedures for diagnosing arithmetic disabilities, and the relationship between teaching approaches and diverse manifestations of arithmetic disablilities (Cawley, 1981a, 1981b; Wallace & Larsen, 1978). Clearly, learning disabilities in arithmetic have been substantially neglected — a thoroughly unwarranted situation since they are apparently as common and widespread as disabilities in other academic areas (McKinney & Feagans, 1980). While evidence is sparse, current findings consistently indicate that approximately 6% of school-aged children may have serious arithmetic difficulties (Badian & Ghublikian, 1983; Kosc, 1974; Weinstein, 1980). Neglect of these widespread difficulties may reflect cultural values that have accorded preeminent status to reading achievement and literacy with a consequent lack of importance accorded mathematical development. Poor functioning in math may be quite socially acceptable, particularly when not accompanied by similar poor performance in reading and writing (Denckla, 1975). Whatever the reasons for this neglect, an upsurge of interest is evident in the professional literature, suggesting that proper systematic attention finally may begin to be paid to a serious educational handicap (see, for instance, Cawley, 1981b).

WHAT'S INVOLVED IN ARITHMETIC-COMPETENCE DEFICIT?

Difficulties in acquiring arithmetic competence have been attributed to various influences, both internal and external to the learner. Mathematics educators often stress factors that interact with the learner's cognitive abilities, in particular, the complexity of the subject matter, insufficient mastery of prerequisite skills, motivational factors, and adequate instruction (Cawley, 1978). Russell and Ginsburg (1982) assert that the most significant contribution to arithmetic difficulties is the low quality of schooling: confusing textbooks, and woefully inadequate teaching. Arithmetic achievement apparently does correlate with a number of such "nonintellective" variables, including attitude, anxiety, interest, personality, and teacher factors (Aiken, 1970). At the same time, these variables themselves necessarily interact with intellective factors such as intelligence and verbal and spatial abilities.

Specialists in learning disabilities, while not altogether ignoring teacher, motivational, and other nonintellective variables, have tended to focus on cognitive factors. In general, factor analytic studies have distinguished four such cognitive factors: (a) a general factor, presumed to coincide with general intelligence, (b) a verbal factor, (c) a visual-spatial factor, and (d) a numeric factor specific to numerical test performance (Barakat, 1951: Wrigley, 1958).

Intelligence

Although normal intelligence is considered basic to success in mathematics in general and also to the elementary branch of mathematics, arithmetic, its relative contribution to arithmetic performance appears to vary considerably depending upon the population investigated and the arithmetic criterion measures employed. For example, in a study of learning-disabled and normal boys, Fleischner and Frank (1979) found that IQ accounted for the 18% of the variance in the performance of normal students on the Wide Range Achievement Test but for only 2.6% of the learning-disabled students' variance on that measure. Using the arithmetic subtest of the Peabody Individual Achievement Test, they found an opposite pattern: IQ accounted for only 3.1% of the normal students' variance but for 37% of the learning-disabled students' variance.

Goodstein and Kahn (1974) also found arithmetic ability to be independent of intelligence within a group of learning-disabled youngsters; neither IQ nor reading ability reliably predicted arithmetic performance. The independence of these factors within a learning-disabled population stands in marked contrast to findings of a close relationship among arithmetic disability, reading disability, and mental age within populations of educable mentally retarded children (Cawley & Goodman, 1968). Recent work suggests that the cognitive factors underlying mathematical performance also may differ for other distinguishable groups, for instance, males and females (Wormack, 1980). Thus, the relative contribution provided by general intelligence and also by other, more specific, cognitive factors to arithmetic achievement will vary as different populations are studied using different measures. The significance of this variability should serve as a caution in generalizing findings from one group to another and, as always, should prompt researchers to specify clearly the characteristics of groups investigated (Keogh, Major, Reid, Gandara, & Omori, 1978).

Verbal Ability

Verbal ability has been found to be important to mathematical achievement. Some have contended that the high positive correlations found between verbal and mathematical measures can be explained by their common correlation with overall intelligence (Wrigley, 1958). Others have argued that when linguistic abilities are partialed out the high correlation between mathematics performance and intelligence is appreciably reduced (Aiken, 1972). Thus, Aiken considered language factors, as distinct from general intelligence, to be important in mathematics, emphasizing their role in retention as well as in organization of mathematical learning. Additionally, Aiken proposed that mathematics itself is a specialized language. Others who share this view have noted the considerable degree to which arithmetical language differs from *ordinary* language, thereby posing a veritable second-language learning dilemma for children (Nesher, 1982).

Conn (1968) considered arithmetic ability to be part of our system of symbolic operations and thus an aspect of language. From his longitudinal study of learning-disabled children, he concluded that ability in arithmetic is neither better developed nor easier to achieve than other aspects of language learning (Cohn, 1971). Ansara (1973) has suggested that the same language difficulties that interfere with developing skill in reading also affect arithmetic performance: difficulties with arithmetic symbols or vocabulary and with language to organize and guide computational steps.

Language competence, or verbal ability, seems to represent a significant infuence on the overall arithmetic achievement of learning-disabled and nondisabled children. While it has been suggested that language deficiencies that impede reading may also hinder arithmetic, the influence of particular language deficits on arithmetic performance has yet to be explored.

Visual-Spatial Ability

Visual-perceptual and visual-spatial abilities have also been cited as significant to mathematical ability (Barakat, 1951). Because of the high incidence of visual-perceptual deficits among learning-disabled children and because of the importance accorded to reading difficulties, investigators have attempted to predict reading achievement from visual-perceptual performance. While concluding in their review that the evidence does not support a predictive relationship between visual perception and reading. Larsen and Hammill (1975) noted empirical evidence that visual perception may be significant in the arithmetic achievement of learning-disabled youngsters.

Strauss and Lehtinen (1947) considered arithmetic deficits to result from lack of visual-spatial organization, and although they did not view this as the sole component of arithmetic learning difficulties, they believed it to be the most problematic. Kalinski (1962) also described children with arithmetic difficulty as displaying fundamental disturbance of spatial relationships. Of related interest is the case provided by Turner's syndrome. In this chromosomal disorder the most striking combination of cognitive symptoms are visual-spatial deficit and numerical disability (Money, 1973). Fleischner and Frank (1979) found visual-perceptual ability and arithmetic achievement to be significantly related when they studied the performance of learning-disabled and nonhandicapped boys in grades four through six.

VIEWS FROM NEUROLOGY

In addition to the accumulated correlational and factor-analysis data that have established the influence of different cognitive variables in arithmetic-competence deficit, there is also a rich history of neurological evidence that has provided useful background for understanding the problems of youngsters disabled in arithmetic learning. Case studies and taxonomies from neurological perspectives may offer insights, provide directions, or serve as organizing frameworks for much-needed direct and systematic investigation of arithmetic difficulties among the learning disabled. Although caution is required in drawing analogies between acquired disorders of adults and developmental arithmetic learning difficulties, practitioners may find useful parallels and distinctions in the literature of acalculia, while those concerned with filling the empirical void may find bases for generating hypotheses to guide research.

ACQUIRED CALCULATION DISTURBANCES IN ADULTS: ACALCULIA

Acalculia is a descriptive term that refers to an acquired disorder in calculation ability. From an extensive survey of medical case reports of adults who displayed computational disorders following cerebral trauma, Henschen (1925) concluded that (a) the integrity of several cortical areas is necessary for calculation and (b) a distinct cortical network for arithmetic functioning probably exists.

Investigators since Henschen have focused, as he did, on describing and categorizing diverse manifestations of acalculia and designating the sites of cortical pathology. Although the accumulated literature yields considerable disagreement concerning both functional and anatomical groupings, there is reasonable consensus regarding three broad categorizations (Hacaen, 1962):

1. Number alexia or agraphia (also viewed as aphasic acalculia) — error related to reading numbers, writing numbers, or handling numbers as words
2. Visual-spatial acalculia — errors related to inability to align problems or to sustain place holding values
3. Anarithmetia — primary loss of calculation ability, errors in carrying out arithmetic operations

This classification of mathematical disorders displayed by adults with cortical pathology suggests that various cognitive factors exert influence on mathematical functioning; two of those significant influences clearly are language (or symbolic) functions and visual-spatial factors.

Cohn (1961), on the other hand, postulated disturbance in serial ordering and disturbance in memory processes as the two major underlying influences in adult acalculia. In those cases in which he viewed the ordering deficit as primary, Cohn noted misalignment of vertical and horizontal number sequences, accompainied by impaired time sense and impaired production of geometric forms, human figure drawings, and maps. When disturbance in memory processes was primary, Cohn noted prominent difficulty with number carrying, failure to follow operational signs, and lack of memory for the multiplication tables.

Right and Left Hemispheres

Issues concerning the role of right and left hemisphere functions in calculation disturbances have been discussed in the literature of acalculia. Verbal functions are generally mediated in the left hemisphere and nonverbal functions in the right hemisphere, but there is strong evidence that verbal ability facilitates nonverbal functioning to a considerable extent (Curry, 1966). In most individuals, the right hemisphere predominates for spatial and holistic processing, while the left hemisphere is specialized for analytic and logical aspects of both verbal and numerical functions (Battista, 1980). At the same time, problem-solving and other complex forms of thought are believed to require fluency and integration of hemispheric functions (Wheatley, Franklin, Mitchell, & Kraft, 1978). Denckla (1975) has characterized the roles of right and left hemispheres in arithmetic performance as involving an intricate *duet*. Their respective roles are viewed by Denckla as far more interdependent than might be expressed by the simplistic option that one or the other side of the brain is most influential during performance of arithmetic tasks.

Gerstmann Syndrome

In the 1930s it was proposed that a particular cluster of neurological symptoms constituted a specific syndrome (Gerstmann, 1940). This cluster, eventually called the Gerstmann syndrome, associated acalculia, right-left directional confusion, a disorder of finger recognition termed finger agnosia, and a handwriting disorder termed agraphia. Benton (1961) raised serious challenges to the validity of this syndrome in the early 1960s. By that time, however, the Gerstmann syndrome had already been extended to children's difficulties with arithmetic. The intriguing notion that finger differentiation might be intimately linked to competence in arithmetic gained currency among psychologists and anthropologists as well as among neurologists and neuropsychologists. While there is substantial reason to question the usefulness or even the existence of the Gerstmann syndrome (Spellacy & Peter, 1978), the framework provided by Gerstmann continues to influence investigations of acalculia. Even investigations of developmental arithmetic difficulties reflect this continuing influence (Kosc, 1974).

The study of adult acalculia is made both complex and problematic by the diversity of calculating deficiencies and the fact that they are so often accompained by or combined with language disorders, graphomotor disturbances, and other neurologically based dysfunctions. Acalculia, in any of its forms, apparently is not often found in isolation from other manifestations of neurological disturbance (Cohn, 1961). Loss of calculating ability, while frequently observed in the course of routine neurological assessment of adult patients, is rarely the major presenting symptom (Benson & Denckla, 1969). The issues, classifications, and concerns found in the literature on acalculia provided the starting point and framework for some of the early empirical investigations that focused directly on the nature of children's arithmetic learning disorders. Studies of adult acalculics offer an interesting, although insufficient, basis for understanding developmental difficulties in acquiring arithmetic competence.

Developmental Dyscalculia

A number of investigations of children who exhibit developmental arithmetic difficulties have drawn extensively on data available from the study of adult acalculia. Accordingly, these investigations have used the term developmental dyscalculia to designate disorders that some children exhibit in acquiring arithmetic competence. Dyscalculia denotes difficulty with calculating, rather than calculating inability per se.

Cohn (1968) considers that developmental dyscalculia represents one manifestation of a neurological disorganization syndrome. On the basis of a longitudinal study of children identified as developmentally dyscalculic, he suggests that "the underlying pathological process of delayed acquisition of language, of which arithmetic is one element, is a disturbance of organizational capacity (Cohn, 1971 p. 389). Cohn offers the following as manifestations of developmental dyscalculia:

1. Malformation or enlargement in the writing of number symbols
2. Strephosymbolia or twisted perception of images
3. Inability in the summing of single integers
4. Inability in the reorganization of operator signs and in the use of lines to separate parts of a problem
5. Failure in the discrimination of specific order characteristics of multi-digit numbers
6. Inability in remembering and using multiplication tables
7. Inability in the "carrying" of numbers
8. Inappropriate sequencing of numbers in multiplication and division

Cohn (1971), who views arithmetic ability as a component of symbol operations, considers dyscalculic performance to be intimately connected to difficulties with other symbolic operations such as reading and writing. In contrast, Kosc's (1974, 1981) definition of developmental dyscalculia places considerable emphasis on the relative isolation of mathematical abilities from other mental functions. Surprisingly, Kosc's empirical studies found that the children who were the lowest achievers in mathematics were also the lowest on measures aimed at identifying dyslexia and dysgraphia. Recently, McKinney and Feagans (1980) found poor arithmetic performance to be as common among learning-disabled children as poor performance in reading. On the other hand, in a study of 50 learning-disabled children, Goodstein and Kahn (1974) found isolated disability in quantitative performance as well as combined reading, language, and quantitative disabilities. Of particular interest in considering the relationship of arithmetic disability to deficits in other academic areas is the work of Rourke and his associates (Rourke & Finlayson, 1978; Rourke & Strang, 1978). These investigators partitioned learning-disabled students into three groups according to their reading, spelling, and arithmetic achievement:

1. Deficient in all three areas
2. Relatively adept at arithmetic as compared with reading and spelling
3. Relatively deficient at arithmetic while average or above at reading and spelling

The performances of these three groups were then compared on a large number of neuropsychological measures, and it was found that groups 1 and 2 were superior at visual-perceptual and visual-spatial tasks, while group 3 was superior on measures of verbal and auditory-perceptual abilities. Rourke argues convincingly that these differential academic patterns represent very different sorts of disabilities, with very different implications for treatment.

Thus, it may be important to distinguish arithmetic learning disabilities in relation to other areas of deficient performance — both academic and social. Badian (1983) made a strong case for the intimate relationship of some arithmetic disabilities to disorders of social perception. Myklebust and Johnson (1967) have long contended that such a link exists. While clarifying data on the significance of differential patterns of academic, social, and neuropsychological performance remains limited, it does appear that the only disability of some dyscalculic youngsters is in arithmetic, while others show concomitant disabilities in other spheres of learning and that the nature of arithmetic difficulty may vary in relation to these other deficiencies.

As in the study of adult acalculia, taxonomies of developmental dyscalculia have been proposed. Kosc (1974) has offered such a preliminary taxonomy:

1. Verbal dyscalculia is a disability in designating mathematical terms verbally and/or difficulty under the condition of oral presentation.
2. Lexical dyscalculia is a disability in reading mathematical symbols (digits, numbers, operational signs, etc.).
3. Graphical dyscalculia is a disability in writing mathematical symbols.
4. Pragnostic dyscalculia is a disability in the mathematical manipulation of real or pictured objects.
5. Ideognostical dyscalculia is a disability in the understanding of mathematical concepts and relationships and in performing mental calculations.
6. Operational dyscalculia is a disability in the carrying out of operations or in applying appropriate algorithms.

Verbal, lexical, and graphical (numbers 1, 2, and 3 above) dyscalculia seem to coincide substantially with one of the three major classifications of adult acalculia — alexic/agraphic. Pragnostic dyscalculia appears, at least in part, to be related to the adult category of visual-spatial acalculia. The ideognostic disability and operational dyscalculia might relate to the adult anarithmetia.

Unfortunately, Kosc's (1974) large-scale investigation does not support his diagnostic categories. While Kosc's categories may provide some useful distinctions, they do not represent an adequate or widely accepted taxonomy. Validated subtyping of developmental arithmetic disability remains an important goal for future research. Badian (1983) offered a model for classifying subtypes of dyscalculia based on Hacaen's (1962) categories. In addition to the three subtypes of number alexia/agraphia, spatial dyscalculia, and anarithmetia, Badian added a fourth — attentional-sequential dyscalculia.

Among 50 dyscalculic children studied by Badian, 42% were classified as attentional-sequential cases, 24% as spatial, 14% as anarithmetic, and 20% as a mixed disorder. (None were clearly alexic/agraphic.) Badian's largest subgroup — those viewed as manifesting attentional-sequential dyscalculia — was described as rarely making spatial errors and generally knowing how to perform processes. Children in this subgroup frequently added and subtracted inaccurately, omitting one of the figures in a column, forgetting to combine a carried figure just marked down, neglecting to include decimal points and dollar signs, and perseverating from one problem to the next by performing the operation of the previous problem. In addition to these deficits, and most prominent among the deficits of this attention-sequential subgroup, was difficulty in remembering basic number facts and multiplication tables. In the most severe cases, students who reportedly had had long-term remedial work still showed major difficulty with these basic arithmetic facts.

COGNITIVE PSYCHOLOGY AND ARITHMETIC LEARNING

While Cohn, Kosc, Badian, and others have offered clinical insights and carried out empirical investigations from a largely neurological perspective, others have criticized this orientation as overestimating the impact of *soft* neurological factors on arithmetic performance and as taking too little account of the specific details of children's mathematical thinking (Allardice & Ginsburg, 1983). Cognitive psycology of late has focused attention on the detailed analysis of children's mathematical thinking (Resnick, 1983; Resnick & Ford, 1981).

Within a broad framework of *cognitive science,* efforts have been aimed at constructing models of cognitive processes or strategies used during the performance of arithmetic tasks and at describing developmental changes in those processes. The methods used include diagnostic interviews with children engaged in arithmetic tasks, analysis of error profiles, reaction-time experiments, and computer simulations. A number of valuable generalizations and insights have emerged: learners are seen as *constructing* their understanding by spontaneously seeking regularity, order, and meaning; coming to *know* something is seen as a matter of drawing relationships, since knowledge is stored in organized clusters of relationships; new learning rests on prior knowledge; and the construction of understanding is constrained by a limited capacity to deal with several things simultaneously.

There are several significant instructional implications that derive from those cognitively oriented constructions of the learner's interchanges with events. One implication is that much time needs to be provided for active construction of relationships among elements of arithmetic learning. This extended activity time, according to Resnick and Ford (1981), needs to provide multiple examples, to include concrete representations, and to relentlessly offer feedback from the physical world, from adults, and from task-related social interaction with peers. Another implication is that we need to pay closer attention to the kinds of prior knowledge, or informed understanding, that children bring with them to the classroom learning environment. Such attention will make it possible to bridge the gap that exists for all children between a vast experiential understanding of collecting, distributing, and removing quantities of things and the *codified* arithmetic taught in schools (Ginsburg, 1977). Only certain aspects of school-taught arithmetic are new to children (e.g., vocabulary, symbols); to learn these, they need to draw linkages with what they already know (e.g., *to add* means to put things together).

Another educational implication is that we need to structure for, or to highlight, the links between related arithmetical concepts and procedures. Teaching and practice time spent making connections between old understandings may be more critical to learning than the introduction of new knowledge. Still other instructional implications relate to the limited human capacity to hold several things in the mind simultaneously. Children invent computational routines that are different and more efficient than those which are taught to them (Groen & Resnick, 1977). These more efficient inventions serve to reduce the processing load in working memory, making more complex performance possible. Youngsters with incomplete or incorrect understanding will also invent routines, resulting in systematic errors, which they will then practice and make more efficient. In teaching, it seems important that we analyze the faulty systematic inventions of our students and refocus our efforts based on a more complete underlying understanding. Additionally, we need to be more careful to ensure that sufficient speed is attained on the simple components of well understood arithmetic operations, so that these do not unduly burden a limited mental scratch pad.

ARITHMETIC LEARNING AND THE INSTRUCTIONAL CONTEXT

Tension between instruction that stresses conceptual understanding and approaches that emphasize efficiency has characterized the development of instructional practice since the turn of the century. The legacy of this instructional struggle remains evident in the varying emphases of current arithmetic teaching practice and, thus, is valuable to explore. Nowhere is this difference more pronounced than in instructional approaches to teaching basic facts.

The basic facts within each of the four whole number operations are considered to be all those numbers relations that result in sums from 0 to 18, differences from 0 to 18, products from 0 to 81 and quotients from 0 to 9. They include approximately 100 separate facts for each of the four arithmetic operations. Efficiency with the basic facts of addition and subtraction is a fundamental goal of teaching in first and second grade; mastery of the basic facts of multiplication and division is a major instructional goal for grades three, four, and five.

Basic facts, or basic number combinations, have assumed an important position in elementary arithmetic teaching, because proficiency at this early level has been consistently viewed as fundamental to developing overall computational competence. Additionally, basic number facts are deemed important because "they provide simple, 'small number' contexts for the development of mathematical ideas pertaining to an operation" (Suydam & Weaver, 1975, p. 57). Despite the diverse instructional approaches that have been taken to teach elementary level arithmetic, there has been consistent unanimity regarding the central importance of an adequate mastery of these elementary number combinations.

Although the ultimate concern in mathematics instruction should always be to produce conceptual understanding as well as efficiency in basic operations, the interaction between the two should not be forgotten. Inadequately automatized operations at one level will take up more processing capacity than is necessary and thus make the mastery of the next higher level concepts or algorithms more difficult. (Case, 1982. p. 169)

Methods of instruction in basic facts have reflected various theories of learning.

Drill Theory

During the first half of the century, this country saw the rise of Drill Theory, propelled by Thorndike's (1922) notions regarding associative bonding. The approximately 100 basic facts within each of the four whole number operations were parsed into small, discrete, and unrelated units. Teachers were admonished to drill each combination to proficiency and to avoid contamination of one combination by another related one (Morton, 1927). This discreteness was seen as paramount, since, otherwise, each bond would be weakened and would not be available to be called on automatically and without confusion. Arguments favoring this independence of each basic fact were many and even included strong statements denying the existence of interrelationships between facts (Knight & Behrens, 1928).

Incidental Learning Theory

In sharp contrast to this drill-connectionist orientation, which dominated arithmetic teaching well into the 1930s, two alternative theoretical perspectives found their way into the mainstream of teaching practice. The first, known as Incidental Learning Theory, was concerned with two major aspects of the learning situation: a child's motivation and the social usefulness of what was being taught (Washburne, 1930). Children were delayed in their introduction to number operations, and the study of arithmetic was included only incidentally as an outgrowth of particular activities or projects. In the early grades a specific fact or arithmetic process was to be taught only as the need for it arose. Though residual effects continue, school programs operating within the Incidental Learning Theory framework received serious criticism for their disregard of the necessarily sequential nature of arithmetic learning. While critics generally eschewed incidental learning practice, they praised its awakening of concern for social utility and the child's need for purpose.

Meaning Theory

William Brownell, considered the father of modern mathematics teaching, was the first to elaborate what he termed "Meaning Theory." Brownell's (1935) theory conceived of arithmetic "as a closely knit system of understandable ideas, principles, and processes." In his early work, he focused on the development of children's number ideas, noting a correspondence between the ease with which a dot configuration was apprehended and the number of dots shown. This correspondence faded as children became older, and children came to rely on more mature forms of number grouping. Interviewing students regarding the various methods they used, Brownell discerned a developmental sequence consisting of four stages. He described the first level as the counting stage. The second stage was seen to be partial counting, wherein the child takes one group as a whole, adding the remaining units to this base group. The third level was distinguished by subgrouping as when, for example, given the configuration ::: : : the child subgrouped 6 + 2 + 2 in order to arrive at an answer. Thinking in multiples characterized the fourth stage: given :: :. the child conceived of two 4s less 1. Brownell pointed out that, in most cases, the method a child employed remained consistent, irrespective of whether objects, dots, or numerals were used. It was striking that the children in Brownell's study were being taught number facts by stringent drill methods but, in actuality, were not learning in the associative manner expected. Instead, they were discovering and employing systems that made use of meanings and relationships. Apparently, as more recent cognitive studies have emphasized, coming to *know* a number fact involves a period of development, discovery of the relationships, and organization of those relationships into networks of related meanings.

A further extension of the basic notions found in Meaning Theory are evidenced in the work by Thiele (1938), who noted considerable agreement between his conceptions and those of Brownell, the major difference being a much greater emphasis on developing larger generalizations in Thiele's Generalization Theory.

Programs from Meaning Theory did not organize number learning experiences around these generalizations. In contrast, instruction following Thiele's theory made full use of generalizations, or reasoning schemes that apply across groups of combinations — schemes such as using 10, employing the commutative property, and making use of doubles and neighboring combinations.

The basic tenets of Meaning Theory have clearly exerted the most dominant influence on current teaching practice in elementary level arithmetic. As has been noted, the contribution of Drill Theory continues to find a place in present day programs, although its assertion that repetitive practice *alone* results in optimum learning has long been discarded (at least one hopes that this is actually so in practice). The praiseworthy strengths of Incidental Learning Theory have found their way into strands of modern mathematics, while its disregard for arithmetic's inherently systematic nature has been abandoned. It can be said that, starting with Meaning Theory, a major emphasis in all modern teaching of elementary arithmetic has been on the development of understanding. Many unresolved issues concerning how to best facilitate the development of understanding are expressed in programs with greatly divergent orientations: counting approaches (Nuffield Project, 1967); sets approaches (Suppes, 1965); and structural approaches (Cusinaire, 1972; Stern & Stern, 1971).

A survey of major arithmetic series currently in common use revealed that Generalization Theory has exerted only a minimal effect: the commutative property $(5 + 3 = 3 + 5)$, the distributive property $4 \times (5 + 7) = (4 \times 5) + (4 \times 7)$, and the law of adding 10 are the only generalizations that receive consistent attention in these series. The basic notion put forth and tested by Thiele (1938) regarding the benefits of grouping facts to be taught according to the generalizations that apply to them has not guided major arithmetic curriculum writers of our day.

There also has been renewed interest in organizing arithmetic instructions to give greater prominence to the generalizations that link number facts (Rathmell, 1978). Using regular class second and fourth graders, Thornton (1978) studied the effectiveness of resequencing the instruction of basic facts according to these generalizations or strategies. Results markedly favored the strategy groups for all four operations. Interviews conducted by Meyers and Thornton (1977) suggest that learning-disabled youngsters, unlike their normal peers, tend not to discover these generalizations on their own or to make consistent use of them. Some investigations have demonstrated that learning-disabled students frequently have persistent difficulty with basic facts (Badian, 1983; Fleischner, Garnett, & Shepard, 1982; Meyers & Thornton, 1977; Russell & Ginsburg, 1981). For example, Russell and Ginsburg (1981) found that students in their "math difficulties" group displayed considerable conceptual strength but were strikingly discrepant from younger, normally achieving schoolmates when calculating simple number facts. On the basis of these findings, it has been suggested that learning-disabled children might benefit from generalization-based instruction — from direct teaching of thinking strategies focused on the relationships among basic facts.

RECENT RESEARCH IN ARITHMETIC

A large-scale research effort was recently directed toward the arithmetic achievement deficits of learning-disabled students for the purpose of (a) describing the arithmetic computation and story-problems solving performance of learning-disabled students in the elementary grades, (b) studying selected cognitive correlates of arithmetic achievement in learning-disabled students, and (c) investigating the efficacy of teaching methods designed to improve computational and problem-solving performance of learning-disabled students.

As Connor (1983) put it, this work has been "guided by the hypothesis that learning problems exhibited by children described as learning disabled occur because the children have difficulty processing information." Information-processing difficulties of learning-disabled students must be considered from two perspectives: from the perspective of individual cognitive delays or differences and from the perspective of the processing demands imposed by the task at hand. The achievement deficits of learning-disabled students seem likely to result from an interaction between their own difficulties (in processing information in the way in which their peers are able to), and the imposed difficulties of complexity of subject matter, unclear presentation of material, or insufficient practice with material to be learned.

In the work reported here, an effort has been made to identify the nature and scope of the achievement deficits exhibited by learning-disabled students and, especially, to specify the characteristics of instruction that is beneficial in overcoming these deficits. Because this chapter reviews and synthesizes more than five years of research, findings will be reported generally. The reader will be directed to primary sources for full reports of research methods, data analyses, and findings.

Numerous subjects were used in the course of these investigations. Subject selection criteria remained constant across the studies. Learning-disabled students were selected for inclusion in the studies if they met the criteria for classification as learning disabled (neurologically or perceptually impaired in New Jersey) of the state in which they resided. In all, more than 275 learning-disabled students participated in the various studies. Learning-disabled students had IQ scores within the normal range and showed major discrepancies between expected and actual achievement. Most learning-disabled students had been referred for evaluation because of extreme difficulty in mastering reading and related subjects.

Interestingly, none had been referred or classified solely on the basis of arithmetic difficulties. While none of the learning-disabled students had primary emotional handicaps, a wide variety of behavioral disorders was reported in cumulative records; distractibility, hyperactivity, and attentional deficits were frequently mentioned.

Subjects represented the range of socioeconomic strata common in the greater New York metropolitan area. Both nonhandicapped and learning-disabled subjects were drawn from schools in New York City (urban), suburban, and rural areas. Some learning-disabled students were in private special day schools, although the majority of these students had tuition paid by their local school districts. Some learning-disabled subjects were in self-contained classes in public schools; the rest were served in resource room or supplementary instructional programs. Nonhandicapped students were those who never received special education services. In all, more than 1,000 nonhandicapped students participated in various studies. In several studies, groups of students were identified who were receiving compensatory services. About 125 students eligible for compensatory education served as subjects in these studies; comparisons of performance were then made for learning-disabled, compensatory education, and nonhandicapped students.

Computational Performance

A primary goal of the arithmetic curriculum in the elementary grades is to develop students' computational proficiency. In judging the relative proficiency of learning-disabled and nonhandicapped students, two types of measures were taken. Overall computational ability was measured by performance on the computation subtest of the Metropolitan Achievement Test. The forms used cover topics usually taught in grades 3 through 4 and 5 through 6. Standard directions were followed for administration of these tests to students in appropriate grades.

In order to evaluate students' proficiency in computing basic facts (which represents a frequently reported area of deficiency in students with math difficulties), timed tests were devised. Subjects were permitted three minutes for each test of 98 problems in addition, subtraction, and multiplication. In order to determine whether learning-disabled students were more likely than nonhandicapped students to disregard the sign of operation in basic fact problems or to perseverate, a mixed-sign (addition and subtraction) test of 98 problems also was administered.

When the performance scores of the 183 learning-disabled and 852 nonhandicapped students were compared, the achievement deficits of the learning-disabled subjects were strikingly apparent. For instance, it was found that the learning-disabled students attempted only about half as many problems in the three minutes allotted as did the nonhandicapped students (Fleischner, Garnett, and Shepard 1982). Two scores were obtained: number attempted and percent correct of number attempted (an index of accuracy). While the learning-disabled subjects showed clear-cut differences in the number attempted, their accuracy was comparable to that of the nonhandicapped subjects, although there was greater variability in learning-disabled subjects' performance.

In an effort to understand the source of the slow speed of computation and the unexpectedly high rate of accuracy in the learning-disabled students' performance, protocols were examined. It was found that learning-disabled students' protocols were much more apt to be covered with evidence of counting than were the protocols of the nonhandicapped students. Learning-disabled students frequently drew number lines or used hatch marks next to individual problems.

Groen and Parkman (1972) suggest that either *reproductive* or *reconstructive* strategies may be used successfully in computing basic facts. Reproductive strategies reflect habituated responses — answers automatically retrieved from memory. Use of a reproductive strategy is signaled by short response latency and self-report of no intervening cognitive manipulation of information. On interview, subjects using reproductive strategies are likely to proclaim "I memorized it" or "My teacher said so" when asked how they knew the answer. Responses such as these suggest that the answer indeed is retrieved directly from memory.

Reconstructive strategies are used in the variety of ways detailed earlier in this chapter. For example, subjects may count or may make use of well-known combinations as links or bridges to those that are less well-known. Signals of reliance on reconstructive strategies are relatively long response latency coupled with overt signs of such a strategy.

In the 99 learning-disabled and 67 nonhandicapped subjects in the study of computational strategies (Fleischner, Garnett, & Preddy, 1982), reproductive strategies were significantly more evident in the nonhandicapped than in the learning-disabled students. Moreover, when the types of reconstructive strategies used in the two groups were evaluated, learning-disabled students were found to rely on more primitive strategies, such as counting all, and to rely more on overt counting than on mental counting when compared to the nonhandicapped students.

Findings in this study support the fact that learning-disabled students do not develop or do not apply cognitive strategies to particular tasks in the same manner as their nonhandicapped peers do. Futher support for this notion is provided by the analysis of the two groups' performance on the Metropolitan Achievement Test (MAT). Whereas only simple operations were required in basic facts tests, the ability to perform both simple and complex operations was measured on the MAT.

When the protocols of the 177 learning-disabled and 853 nonhandicapped subjects had been scored and analyzed, it was found that the learning-disabled students' performances were significantly poorer than those of the nonhandicapped students. In an attempt to discover the source of this difference, a comparative analysis of errors made by learning-disabled and nonhandicapped students in grades 3 through 4 and 5 through 6 was undertaken (Fleischner, Garnett, & Shepard, 1982).

The first, and most obvious, difference in performance between learning-disabled and nonhandicapped subjects was in the number of problems attempted. Here, as was true in basic fact computation, the non-handicapped students' scores were significantly better because they attempted more problems. *Omission,* then, accounted for the largest number of errors by the learning-disabled subjects. Subsequent error analysis revealed that the types of errors made by younger nonhandicapped students (grade 3 to 4) were typically made by same-age or older learning-disabled subjects. No distinctive pattern was found to characterize the performance of the learning-disabled group, although the learning-disabled subjects had a higher rate of errors overall than did the nonhandicapped subjects.

As a follow-up to this study, clinical interviews were conducted with groups of learning-disabled, compensatory education (CE), and nonhandicapped students in grades 3 through 6. In all, there were 101 subjects equally distributed across grades (Frank, 1982). The purpose was to investigate the whole-number computational processes used by these subjects in order to determine whether the different groups used distinctive solution processes, or algorithms, in arriving at their answers. Frank found that nonhandicapped subjects correctly completed a higher percentage of problems than did subjects in the other two groups; learning-disabled subjects did less well than did CE subjects. No differences were found in the algorithms used by subjects in the three groups, although again there was a *rank-order* effect of group, with nonhandicapped students showing familiarity with and computational proficiency in harder problems than either CE or learning-disabled subjects.

Overall, the pattern of these findings supports the contention that learning-disabled students as a group do not use remarkably different, or idiosyncratic, processes in computing answers to arithmetic problems. As has been well documented, errors tend to be rule-governed; this seems equally as true of the errors of learning-disabled students as of the errors of nonhandicapped students. However, there does seem to be a definite difference in the rate of learning, reflected both in total performance scores and in the errors made by subject groups at different ages. Errors made by older learning-disabled subjects are similar to those made by younger nonhandicapped subjects.

Instructional Studies in Computation

Two studies were undertaken to investigate the efficacy of instruction in facilitating recall of basic facts; the second was a replication of the first. Both used similar materials and methodology (Fleischner, Garnett, & Preddy, 1982). They were designed to test the assumption that instruction based on the relationships among basic facts will differentially affect rate of mastery and retention of those facts, in contrast to instruction based on the traditional, fixed order of presentation (e.g., Meyers & Thornton, 1977).

In all, 177 learning-disabled students and their 18 classroom teachers participated in this study. Intact classes were randomly assigned to either the *traditional sequence* condition or to the nontraditional sequence condition for an 8-week period during which three 20-minute long instructional sessions were held each week. Careful attention was paid to control of length of instructional time and to the nature and amount of practice provided. The lessons were based on the principles of direct instruction with mastery learning theories providing guidelines for determining the pace of instruction. Students practiced facts through a variety of games and activities deemed to have high motivational properties, and they charted their own progress.

Tests administered immediately after the end of the experimental period and tests administered 6 weeks after instruction ended both showed marked improvement in the number of basic facts computed in three minutes, with no decrease in accuracy. No differences in gains were attributable to the ways in which facts were sequenced. Thus, it seems that the characteristics frequently associated with direct instructional techniques were equally effective in improving basic fact computational proficiency, regardless of the manner in which facts were sequenced.

These findings corroborate assertions and empirical evidence regarding the usefulness of direct instruction with learning-disabled students. Preliminary evidence from a series of studies employing direct instructional techniques to teach complex operations to learning-disabled students are equally encouraging.

Problem Solving

One of the primary ways of encouraging the application of computational skills to everyday situations is to provide elementary school pupils with story problems to solve. These problems generally simulate a real-life situation and should vary in complexity, subject matter, and operations required for solution with the child's age, interests, and computational ability if they are to be useful. While many factors affect ease of solution of problems, learning-disabled students have been found to have unusual difficulty in this sphere.

Achievement surveys revealed a subset of learning-disabled students who were able to do computations as well as their nonhandicapped classmates and whose reading skills enable them to read story problems but who, nonetheless, had high error rates on such problems. An instructional sequence for teaching problem-solving skills was designed and tested (Nuzum, 1982).

The literature on instruction in problem solving and clinical practice both supported the necessity of a comprehensive instructional unit. Description in the information-processing literature and the kind of task analysis suggested by Resnick and Ford (1981) led to the formulation of a sequence of instructional units designed to teach students that three levels of operations are necessary to solve problems. These were deemed to be three categories of knowledge.

The first has been called procedural knowledge, and involves awareness of the problem state and ability in devising, executing, and monitoring a cognitive plan that will facilitate solution of the problem. This level of operation may be considered metacognitive. Second, the student must be able to derive information from the problem itself — for instance, be able to identify what is wanted and what is given. Finally, task-specific knowledge is important in solving story problems. Task-specific knowledge in this case might involve selection of the correct computational operation (e.g., knowing when a two-step procedure must be employed).

This study relied on direct instruction and on certain tenets of cognitive behavior modification (Meichenbaum & Goodman, 1971). Students were taught that they should have a plan and what the steps in a good plan were. They were taught to clearly state the information provided in the problem and to reiterate the question posed in the problem. Finally, students were taught task-specific information, such as how to identify and solve problems requiring two steps.

Nuzum (1982) used a single-subject design with four replications to test the effectiveness of the instructional sequence. A replication of Nuzum's study using group instruction rather than tutorial has been conducted. There is significant post-treatment improvement in problem-solving performance in students who have mastered the material presented. This serves as additional confirmation of the notion that learning-disabled students can and do learn arithmetic, if instruction is appropriate, precise, and sufficient.

SUMMARY

Several points can be made regarding effective arithmetic instruction for learning-disabled students. Computational facility is based on understanding of concepts of quantitative representation and on mastery of instructed algorithms. It would seem that all students invent procedures for doing calculations and that the errors of learning-disabled students are as likely to be rule-governed as those of nonhandicapped students. Therefore, it seems to be important to analyze the error patterns of individual students in order to ascertain the nature of their misunderstanding, which is the probable source of their errors.

Direct instruction seems to be effective in teaching computational skills and problem-solving skills, if sufficient practice is provided to permit mastery of learned material. Among the encouraging findings reported are those that suggest a high rate of retention of mastered computational skills.

If they are to achieve, learning-disabled students can be expected to require the same level of intensity of instruction in arithmetic as in reading. It is important that we pay equal attention to difficulties in arithmetic and higher mathematics as to difficulties in reading if learning-disabled students are to compete in a society that places increasing demands for technological skills on its citizens.

CHAPTER 11

Social Problems

Peter J. Valletutti

S pecial educators of children with learning disabilities have concentrated on the remediation of learning discrepancies in the academic
realm, even when they recognize that many of these children manifest
substantial and debilitating social and emotional problems. This unidimensional focus has frequently resulted in socially maladjusted and
lonely adolescents and adults who, despite the acquisition of academic
skills, lead nonproductive, unsatisfying, and unhappy lives. In addition,
children "cured" of their academic learning difficulties yet remaining
socially maladjusted, often are no longer protected by Public Law 94–142
and its regulations.

Several reasons apparently exist for this unfortunate predicament.
Primary among them is the typical teacher preparation program model, in
which teachers of the learning disabled are trained as academic remediation specialists and are operating under a disease paradigm. A second
reason undoubtedly, is a function of the relative ease of programming in
the academic area, e.g., working on blending sounds or the recognition of
phonogram patterns. Academic programming is less demanding (or
perhaps more familiar) than working on the acquisition of self-control or
the perception of body language cues. Programming in the largely unchar-
ted waters of the affective domain requires creative risk-taking and insight,
traits that are rarely valued or rewarded. A third reason relates to the false

This chapter originally appeared as an article by **Peter J. Valletutti** in *Learning Disabilities: An
Interdisciplinary Journal* (Vol. II, 1983) and was adapted by permission of Grune & Stratton for
inclusion in this *Handbook*.

assumption held by so many educators of learning-disabled children that is epitomized by comments such as: "If we remediate his reading and other academic learning problems, his social/emotional problems will automatically improve." While it is recognized that improvement in academics often leads to emotional and/or social growth, it does not always have such positive results (Sheare, 1978). Manifested social and emotional problems of learning-disabled children are not always caused by lowered self-concept due to academic failure. Academic success has never been *that* highly valued in our culture. Indeed, academic failure may result from rather than be the cause of social and emotional learning disabilities.

Because it is so often impossible to distinguish which is the cause and which is the effect, it becomes necessary to teach directly to both problems. It is a useless exercise to engage in a chicken-or-egg debate; it *is* useful to teach directly to both areas of disability.

DIRECT TEACHING OF SOCIAL SKILLS

The maxim to teach "the whole child," often voiced but seldom honored, is especially applicable when addressing the total educational needs of children with learning disabilities (Schumaker & Hazel, 1984a, 1984b). The development of social competencies must assume its rightful place, if not a position of primacy, as one of the basics along with the revered three Rs (Ladd, 1981; Zigmond & Browniee, 1980). Gresham (1982) and Vaughn (1985) presented a powerful case for social skills training, asserting that mainstreaming has failed because handicapped children have not been previously provided with the social skills crucial to peer acceptance. Moreover, once they have been placed in mainstreamed classes, the curriculum invariably excludes experiences and activities designed to facilitate social competency (Cartledge & Milburn, 1978).

Minskoff (1982) has decried the fact that something is missing in the education of the learning disabled, namely, a program that prepares them to function in the everyday world as competent individuals. She has recommended training in functional academics, social information, verbal social skills, and nonverbal social skills. She pointed out that knowledge about oneself is especially important so that one can learn to solve social problems. In order to do so, learning-disabled individuals must become aware of their behavior, its effect on others, and vice versa. In commenting on language instruction, she wrote of the need to emphasize sociolinguistics, which is the appropriate use of language in different situations: "Students with problems in verbal social skills must be taught to analyze communications on the basis of four factors: participants, setting, topic, and objective" (pp. 314–315).

Communication problems cannot be discussed without considering the total communication act, including both verbal and nonverbal components. The purportedly high degree of gullibility of the learning disabled (Siegel & Gold, 1982) and the inability to distinguish between fact and fiction (Johnson & Myklebust, 1967) and between honesty and duplicity may result from failure to read nonverbal cues as well as failure to understand the meaning of the words spoken. A Machiavellian character, however, may not emit any nonverbal cues to his or her deception, and a judgement of the deceit may have to be based solely on cognitive processing of the words expressed, the credentials of the speaker, and an analysis of available supportive data. In fact, the skilled perceiver often must disregard nonverbal cues, which the crafty speaker has learned to manipulate to his or her advantage.

Social problems evidenced by learning-disabled children may frequently be attributed to difficulty in interpreting idiomatic and figurative speech. Imagine how the literally oriented child deals with the information that a friend has lost his or her head over someone, is up in arms about something, or is now footloose and fancy free somewhere (especially if this child has a body image problem!)

There may not only be a problem with the perception of oral language but also with its expression in social settings (Bryan, 1979; Cicourel, 1981). Learning-disabled children may not appreciate, for example, the need to display positive social behaviors, including the expression of concern and of verbal affection (Miller, 1984); Kronick (1976) has observed that the poorly organized communication skills of learning-disabled children cause others to be uncomfortable and fearful about engaging in genuine or in-depth interaction. This uneasy communication is then modeled by the learning-disabled child, which further contributes to his or her oral communication deficit. This lack of snychrony in interpersonal, face-to-face exchanges invariably leads to rejection, isolation, and a feeling of being different. Bryan, Wheeler, Felcan, and Henek (1976) noted that learning-disabled children emit more competitive statements than other children. In a study by Bryan and Pflaum (1978), learning-disabled and regular fourth and fifth graders were asked to explain a game to same-age peers and to a younger group. While the nonhandicapped students simplified their language when speaking to the younger pupils, learning-disabled children actually used more complex language. Also, many learning-disabled children fail to assume conversational responsibility, a likely cause of social rejection. Donahue (1981b) pointed out that learning-disabled children produce fewer appropriate requesting strategies even though no psycholinguistic problem exists, that is, even when they have in their repertoire the linguistic forms to convey the request. Thus both psycholinguistic and sociolinguistic factors may be part of the social problem that causes many learning-disabled individuals to lead unsatisfying, unhappy, and unfulfilled lives.

Ledebur (1977) has regretted the lack of affective educational goals, including decreased self-understanding and self-acceptance, increased social understanding and social relatedness, the development of personal values, and the understanding of the values of others. Is sufficient time being devoted to developing skills of cooperating, sharing, greeting others, asking for and giving information, holding conversations, and behaving in ways that will develop and maintain positive relationships with peers, relatives, and significant adults (Valletutti & Bender, 1982)? La Greca and Mesibov (1982) wrote of the need to train joining skills (i.e., initiating social interactions) and conversational skills. In an earlier article (1979), they spoke of nine areas of required social skills development: smiling and laughing with peers, greeting others, joining ongoing activities with peers, extending invitations to peers, conversational skills, sharing and cooperating skills, verbal affection and complimenting skills, playing skills, and physical appearance and grooming skills. Scott and Edelstein (1981) discussed the importance of developing competency in positive self-presentation; and Speer and Douglas (1981) offered the following suggestions for developing socialization skills: teach eye contact while talking, explain implications of voice qualities, role-play to examine emotions, and provide direct instruction regarding appropriate responses in specific social situations. Strain and Shores (1977) stressed the importance of developing social reciprocity through educational strategies designed to increase positive social interactions based upon a reciprocal conceptualization of social behavior, namely, teaching persons to reinforce each other at an equitable rate. Cooke and Apolloni (1976) taught four learning-disabled children, 6 to 9 years of age, the following positive social-emotional behaviors: smiling, sharing, positive physical contacting, verbal complimenting, and improved the quality of peer interaction. They suggested the use of live or filmed peer models. Bandura (1977) has asserted that peers with higher status are emulated more. Because of the relative frequency of situational rules (Argyle, Graham, Campbell, & White, 1979), it might prove beneficial to teach learning-disabled individuals the most commonly occurring rules based upon their situational contexts. Madden and Slavin (1982) cited the potential benefits that might accrue relevant to the social acceptance of mainstreamed, mildly handicapped students through a social skills training program designed to assist them in making friendships. As a result of their review of relevant literature on social skills training, they concluded that children who are poorly accepted by peers can be taught appropriate social skills through modeling, coaching, or reinforcing appropriate social behaviors and friendly initiations.

Verbal communication disorders and disabilities of a psycholinguistic nature and their fundamental auditory and visual processes have long received the attention and remedial fervor of teachers of the learning disabled. Particular obeisance has been given by teachers to reading, in disregard of the primacy of oral language. For example, children are frequently remediated for reading comprehensive problems even when the basic problem is failure to understand spoken language. While insufficient attention has been directed toward developing oral language skills, even less attention has been paid to the perception and expression of nonverbal communications, despite the fact that a substantial amount of beginning communication is nonverbal. The ability to read and use facial expressions, gestures, and other body language or kinesic cues is vital to interpersonal communication. The ability to read the paralinguistic elements, the nonword elements of the vocalization process, is also central to the communication process. Nonverbal communication includes distance between speaker and listener, how they look at each other, clothes and makeup worn, and physical attributes (Weiss & Lillywhite 1981). It has been suggested that up to 93% of the message's content is communicated nonverbally (Egolf & Chester, 1973). Krauss, Apple, Morency, Wenzel, and Winton (1981) disagree, since their study of judgments of affect found no support for the assumption that nonverbal channels from the primary basis for the communication of affect. This controversy may be a function of the relative explicitness of the verbal message (i.e., the more explicit the verbal message, the less attention is given to the nonverbal elements).

The impact of nonverbal factors can be best appreciated when the oral message lacks congruity with the nonverbal. "You're a little angel" can either mean what it says or its opposite, depending on vocal tone, posture, facial expression, and situational context. The child who has failed to read the situation (e.g., the broken knick-knack and the hostile facial expression and vocal tone of his or her mother) may wish to be hugged, while the skilled perceiver of nonverbal communications will beat a hasty retreat because he or she knows praise is not intended.

Like verbal communication, nonverbal communication exists in a situational context (Spignesi & Shor, 1981). Social kinesis refers to the role and meaning of different bodily movements within a social context (Devito, 1978). Ekman and Friesen (1969) have distinguished five classes of nonverbal movements based on the origins, functions, and coding of the behavior: emblems, illustrators, affect displays, regulators, and adaptors. Emblems are nonverbal behaviors that directly translate words or meaning units (e.g., the "come here" gesture). Illustrators accompany and clarify the verbal message, while affective displays are the facial movements that express emotional content. Regulators control the speech of another.

Adaptors are nonverbal actions that serve some kind of communicative need. The field of proxemics explores how people structure microspace (e.g., the space immediately surrounding one's body), primarily in face-to-face interactions. The ability to receive and process relevant interpersonal stimuli, along with the ability to read social situations (Johnson & Myklebust, 1967), is essential to effective social performance (Morrison & Bellack, 1981).

Children with learning disabilities have been described in a large body of professional literature as being deficient in social perception (Bryan, 1978; Bryan & Bryan, 1978b; Gearheart, 1983; Johnson & Myklebust, 1967; Lerner, 1981; Minskoff, 1980a, 1980b, 1982; Siegel & Gold, 1982; Wiig & Harris, 1974; Wiig & Semel, 1976). Social perception deficits mainfest themselves in problems with interpreting kinetic, paralanguage (vocalic), proxemic (space language), and artifactual clues (use of clothing and cosmetics as a means of communication), resulting in misunderstanding the attitudes, feelings, and intentions of others. Consequently, social imperceptions lead to difficulty in making appropriate social judgments and in adapting to social situations. Wallbrown, Fremont, Nelson, Wilson, and Fischer (1979) have observed that there is a growing evidence that many children who have been diagnosed as having behavior problems are, in fact, children with social imperceptions. Lerner (1981) pointed out that the learning-disabled child is different from the antisocial individual, who is deliberate in intentions and behavior.

Minskoff (1982) has admonished that social perception disabilities are the most serious of all types of learning disabilites and yet scant attention has been paid to their remediation. She has developed instructional programs for teaching children to discriminate, understand, and meaningfully use facial expressions and other kinetic clues (1980a), as well as programs designed to develop proxemics, vocalic, and artifactual clues (1980b).

Siegel, Siegel, and Siegel (1978) emphasized the importance of nonverbal communication, suggesting a variety of teaching techniques such as using filmstrips, silent movies, and pantomines to improve body language. Their approach is supported by Wiig and Semel (1976), who stressed the importance of using peer models. Siegel and colleagues (1978) also placed emphasis upon the importance of improving the nonverbal aspects of conversational speech. Johnson and Myklebust (1967) suggested that learning disabled children require initial practice in observing and interpreting the facial expressions of a single person. They also recommended the use of self-developing camera to record the student's facial expressions. In the later stages of the program they advocated the use of situational pictures in which body language clues are viewed as part of the contextual gestalt. It seems clear that understanding of nonverbal communication requires the same basic processes as understanding spoken language. If a child is unable to comprehend a spoken word, one might teach such a word by providing experience with its reality referent while drawing attention to its distinctive acoustic and visual features. Similarly, if a child is unable to understand a gestural cue, it is taught directly by providing experience with its communicative context while drawing attention to its distinctive visual features and other kinesic and sociolinguistic clues.

REJECTION AND LOW SELF-CONCEPT

Learning-disabled children consistently have been found to be less popular and more frequently rejected than normals by their regular class peers (Bruininks, 1978; Bryan, 1974b, 1976; Drabman & Patterson, 1981; Gable, Strain, & Hendrickson, 1979; Garrett & Crump, 1980; Pelhem & Milsch, 1984; Riddle & Rapoport, 1976; Silverman & Zigmond, 1983; Siperstein, Bopp, & Bak, 1978). In the Scranton and Ryckman (1979) study involving a sociometric questionnaire, learning-disabled girls were less likely to be positively chosen and more likely to be rejected than learning-disabled boys. Lower social expectations for boys may allow a socially disabled boy to blend more easily with age peers.

Rejection by regular class peers represents a significant problem when one considers that a major rationale for mainstreaming is the presumed benefit of enhanced self-esteem (Coleman, 1983a, 1983b). Clearly, peers significantly influence and shape the attitudes and behavior of group members (Bronfenbrenner, 1970); therefore, peer rejection is a particularly damaging phenomenon.

Peer rejection may be ascribed to a number of factors, including poor academic performance, social imperception, deficient social skills, the damaging effects of labels, and the segregating stigma of special class and special service programs. In a study of the affects of a drug treatment program on hyperkinetic boys (Riddle & Rapport, 1976), it was found that, while impulsive and hyperactive behavior was suppressed, there was no improvement in peer status. Drabman and Patterson (1981) identified several factors that are associated with social acceptance: attractiveness, sociability, cooperativeness, and conformity.

Bryan (1978) has pointed out that not only are learning-disabled children evaluated negatively by peers, they are also viewed in nonpositive ways by teachers and even strangers. Teachers typically rate learning-disabled children as being less cooperative, less socially acceptable, and less tactful than nondisabled children (Bryan & Bryan, 1978b). Keogh, Tchir, and Windeguth-Behn (1974) reported that teachers associated aggressiveness, hyperactivity, lack of discipline, poor interpersonal relationships, hostility, heightened field dependence (the reliance on other people and environmental clues), and isolation with children who are at risk for educational problems. Lerner (1981) observed that learning-disabled children received more negative and less positive reinforcement from teachers than their nonhandicapped peers. Meisgeier (1981), in his description of sociobehavioral program for the adolescent student with serious learning problems, discussed the finding that teachers and other school personnel reject learning-disabled students. Foster, Schmidt, and Sabatino (1976) have suggested that the label of *learning disabilities* generates negative expectancies in teachers. Even when teachers attempt to mask their negative feelings about students, they must be wary of the fact that their facial expressions, body movements, and vocalic elements have a strong impact upon students' self-esteem. Students may be getting the subtle message all too loudly and clearly that they are disliked (Brophy & Good, 1974).

Parents of learning-disabled children, as most parents of handicapped children, are frustrated because of their child's failures and lack of success in school and because of their own problems in communicating with their child (Kronick, 1975). "Children who perceive that significant others see them as being adequate physically, socially, and cognitively see themselves the same way, and tend to behave in ways consistent with this view." (Samuels, 1981, p. 26) Negative parental attitudes, on the other hand, can generate attentional, academic, and perceptual deficits (Klein, Altman, Dreizen, Friedman, & Powers, 1981). Parents of learning-disabled children describe them as "obstinate, sassy, bossy, stubborn, negativistic, disobedient, difficult to discipline, resistant to adult domination, and yet attempting to dominate peers." (Bryan & Bryan, 1978, p. 119). Parents cannot normally respond with pride to children who manifest these behaviors; and this results in anxiety, frustration, rejection, and overprotection (Lerner, 1981). In addition, permissiveness, inconsistency, and overprotection may affect the child's work habits and interfere with learning (Hawke & Lesser, 1977). Anderson (1980), in his characterization of learning-disabled children as tyrants, discussed the fact that having a tyrant in the house leads parents to give in to all their demands, creating children who are anxious, fearful, immature, and dependent outside the family, thus inhibiting the development of both cognitive and emotional skills.

Given the fact that learning-disabled children are invariably rejected by parents, peers, teachers and other school personnel, and even strangers, it is not surprising that they have a poor self-concept (Battle & Blowers, 1982; Bingham, 1980; Bruininks, 1978; Bryan & Pearl, 1979; Siegel & Gold, 1982). Low self-esteem feeds upon itself and exacerbates the social and learning problems of learning-disabled children (Epstein, Cullinan & Lloyd, 1986; McConaugh & Ritter, 1986). Helplessness, resulting from failure and the attribution of that failure to external, uncontrollable, and capricious circumstances (Grimes, 1981; Thomas, 1979), is a frequent way of displaying low self-esteem. Rist and Herrell (1982) have expressed the concern that the learning-disabled label results in learned helplessness from the self-attribution of such a label. Interestingly, in a study of the self-esteem of boys with low-average IQs, Opie and Lemasters (1975) cautioned against equating low IQ with low self-esteem, suggesting that low self-esteem may result from asynchronous affective states rather than from deviations in academic competency.

IMPULSIVITY

Learning styles and interpersonal behavioral styles may be a reflection of basic personality patterns (Thomas & Chess, 1977; Thomas, Chess & Birch, 1968). Two response styles that both characterize and influence learning and interpersonal behaviors are impulsivity and reflection. Impulsivity refers to a pattern of rapid responses to stimuli. On the other end of the response continuum is reflection, which involves the application of cognitive processes to mediate the solution of an academic task or the appropriateness or sensibility of a proposed action. According to Gelfand, Jenson, and Drew (1982), "The word 'impulsivity' suggests poor self-control, excitability, and the inability to inhibit urges ... [Impulsivity includes] the characteristic of acting before considering alternate responses" (p. 252).

In the enumeration of the behavioral attributes of learning disabilities, impulsivity is invariably listed as a frequently observed component (Bryan & Bryan, 1978b; Douglas, 1972; Lerner, 1981; Nagle & Thwaite, 1979; Ross, 1976; Siegel & Gold, 1982). The American Psychiatric Association (1987), in the *Diagnostic and Statistical Manual, DSM-III-R*, lists impulsivity as one of the diagnostic criteria of attentional deficit disorder with hyperactivity. In the area of interpersonal and other social skills, impulsivity is viewed as a significant factor in contributing to poor interpersonal relations and to the rejection of learning-disabled children who impulsively express thoughts and engage in actions without considering, appreciating, or caring about the consequences of their behavior. Who among us has not suppressed impulses to say shocking, unconventional, and even cruel comments and witticisms. We have kept these wayward thoughts to ourselves because we know the rules of the interpersonal game and/or because we respect or fear adverse consequences. On these occasions when discretion saved the day, we have exercised the self-control that comes from a reflective cognitive style and have inhibited such honest cruelties as, "Boy, that baby's really ugly!" upon viewing the heavenly bundle of a proud new mother. Many learning-disabled children, however, do not exercise such restraint and blurt out destructive remarks with no apparent concern for their probable impact on others or on the likely eventual effect on their own popularity.

The failure to judge the wisdom of an intended behavior is sometimes seen as a problem in social cognition. "It is how he thinks it through, rather than what he might think at any given instant, that becomes the important issue in understanding the likelihood of long-range social success or failure" (Spivack, Platt, & Shure, 1976, p. 1). Spivack and colleagues have proposed a theory of cognitive problem-solving that suggests a group of interpersonal cognitive problem-solving skills that mediate social adjustment. These skills include an awareness of the variety of problems that occasion human interactions, a sensitivity to the problems or awareness of the potential problems whenever people interact, an ability to generate alternative solutions to problems, the capacity to articulate the sequence of steps required to achieve desired ends, the skill of consequential thinking, and, lastly, the realization that interpersonal events have a continuity with past events and that social and personal motivation in oneself and others are part of the reality context. These are viewed as learned skills resulting from social experiences. Failure to acquire these skills can be either a function of social deprivation or a specific learning dysfunction related to a developmental delay or a restriction in social intelligence. The inappropriate, maladaptive performance and behavior of learning-disabled children may be a function of their poorly organized thought processes, (i.e., subvocal speech, thoughts, and images) (Meichenbaum, 1977). Luria (1961) pioneered the use of verbally mediated self-control bypostulating that internalized verbal commands are the principal means by which a child develops control over his or her behavior. According to Abikoff (1979), "Cognitive training implements a task-analysis approach whereby the child is taught appropriate task-relevant cognitions, or 'cognitive strategies,' which interrupt and inhibit maladaptive stimulus-response associations" (p. 124).

This self-instructional and self-monitoring approach involves the following steps. In the first stage, the teacher models the desired behavior; in the second stage, the student performs the task under the verbal direction of the teacher; in the third stage, the student instructs him or herself aloud and then whispers the instructions; in the fourth and final stage, the student directly practices internalized cognitions in direct performance (Meichenbaum & Goodman, 1971).

Cognitive training also involves problem-solving training (Wanant, 1983). In this sequential training model, the student is taught to recognize and define the problem, generate alternate solutions, consider and evaluate the consequences of the alternate solutions, and follow through on the chosen optimal solution. Whereas Spivack and colleagues (1976) have found great success, Abikoff (1979) cautioned that cognitive training has shown limited effectiveness in reducing inappropriate classroom behavior.

Blackman and Goldstein (1982) advocated the modification of the learner's cognitive style and matching the learning environment to the learner's cognitive style. They also concluded that, in general, field independence and a reflective cognitive style are associated with better academic performance, while field dependence and impulsivity are related to hyperactivity and underachievement. In their assessment of a cognitive training program, Douglas, Parry, Marton, and Garson (1976) emphasized self-reinforcement, the development of self-control, modeling, and self-verbalization. Finch and Spirito (1980) discussed the use of self-instruction training in learning-disabled children to modify impulsive thinking, in the belief that changing cognitive tempo might lead to improvements in the social-emotional sphere as well as in the academic domain. Camp and Bash (1981) provided 23 lesson plans in the use of verbal mediation, including cognitive modeling, self-instruction, and problem-solving. Training in metacognition (knowledge of one's own cognitive system) offers a future programming direction in the education of individuals with learning disabilities, especially in the area of judgment about competence, degree of self-control, and the reasons for success or failure (Hagen, Barclay, & Newman, 1982).

Impulsivity, however, may also be conceived of as an expression of hostility in which the individual has examined the consequences and has nevertheless consciously voiced a negative remark or engaged in destructive behavior. The author, in discussing the development of self-control in a student celebrated for his tactlessness, noted that the student responded to instruction in verbal mediation with the insightful, "But I'm not impulsive: I'm repulsive." In this case, the student welcomed peer attention (regardless of the cost) and welcomed the negative consequences as further evidence of his low status and as justification for his omnipresent anger and frustration. He did this while enjoying the disruption and albeit temporary mastery of his "Damn the torpedoes: full steam ahead!" approach to human interactions. Certainly, impulsivity as an aggressive act is not etiologically remote, since children with learning disabilities live in a frequently rejecting, hostile, pressurized, fathomless, and asynchronous world. The central idea of the frustration-aggression hypothesis is that aggression is the inevitable or, at least, the most common result of frustration (Hornstein, 1976).

Nagle and Thwaite (1979) have concluded that learning-disabled children are not really more impulsive than others but rather are deficient in processing information. What appears on the surface to be impulsivity may reflect a social naivete' that comes from being unable to comprehend verbal and nonverbal messages, so that the individual is unable to benefit from the information received from the obvious effects that his or her behavior has on others. Self-monitoring is not possible without the mediating effects of viewer and listener responses.

Douglas (1974) hypothesized that the fundamental cause of the maladaptive behavior of learning-disabled children is their inability to sustain attention and to inhibit impulsive responding. Ross (1976) suggested the possibility that the performance deficit of an impulsive child is really an attention deficit, and that impulsive responding is a learned response style resulting from frequent failure and therefore is the result, not the cause, of the learning problem.

Are impulsive children and youth high-stimulus seekers who require the attention of others even though their impulsive behaviors lead to aversive responses and sustained rejection (Wasson, 1980)?

NEGATIVE MOOD

Given the facts of low esteem, isolation, loneliness, and self-consciousness that often characterize learning-disabled children, it seems reasonable to assume that many of these children would not be cheerful, optimistic, or ebullient. On the contrary, depression would be a more expected sequela of inferior status, low self-esteem, and pervasive anxiety.

Mood is readily communicated through both verbal and nonverbal language, and depressed individuals arouse dysphoric feelings in others, who then reject the depressed individual (Winer, Bonner, Blancy, & Murray, 1981). Schumaker, Wildgen, and Sherman (1982), in their analysis of student-initiated instructional interactions, observed that learning-disabled junior high school students lacked pleasant facial expressions. On the other hand, the presence of a good mood enhances a listener's receptivity to a speaker's message (Dribben & Brabender, 1979), and humor leads to greater receptivity and compliance (O'Quin & Aronoff, 1981). Perhaps, the unnerving effects of immature social behaviors, including impulsivity and hyperactivity, are compounded by the unsettling projection of a depressed aura. This multiplying effect no doubt interferes with social interactions, reducing the opportunities for positive and comfortable contacts and the social learning that comes from these contacts. The presence of depression is even viewed by Colbert, Newman, Ney, and Young (1982) as the *cause* of learning problems, accounting for the misdiagnosis of learning disabilites in the presence of depression. As has been previously noted, the chicken-or-egg debate about academic and social learning disabilities is nonproductive. Both aspects must be addressed in educational programming.

PHYSIOLOGICAL DISABILITIES

Teachers, in their daily observations and in more structured evaluations, should be aware of the possibility that discrepancies in academic performance and behavior may result from underlying physical pathologies. Typically, teachers are assigned students who are free of physiologically disabling conditions. Teachers have been conditioned, because of the usual behaviorist emphasis of teacher preparation programs, to overlook physiological factors as etiologically insignificant in behavioral disorders. Invariably, teachers search for causative elements in the cognitive, motivational, and affective systems or in the sociocultural status and history of students experiencing behavioral difficulty. Increasing attention is now being directed toward the role of nutrition, metabolism, and other biological and dietary considerations in interpersonal relationships (Brenner, 1979; Cook & Woodhill, 1976; Crook, 1980). Many view food allergies as a significant etiologic agent in interpersonal relationship problems (Havard, 1973; Mayron, 1979; Rapp, 1978). The hazards of illicit drug use (Krippner, 1972) and the detrimental effects of high dosages of legal behavior-modifying stimulants (Brown, 1980; Brown & Sleator, 1979) are also discussed in the literature. Certainly, modifications in diet, the use of nutritional supplements, and reduced ingestion of foods containing sugar and caffeine should be actively pursued as possible strategies for improving social and/or emotional behaviors.

DISABILITIES ENDEMIC TO THE CULTURE

Role-Taking Disabilities

Role-taking refers to the ability to take the position of another person and thereby infer his or her feeling and perceptions. Cognitive skills are necessary in order for a child to understand the perspectives of others and him- or herself (Forman & Sigel, 1979; Schantz, 1975; Weiss, 1984). Dickstein and Warren (1980) reported role-taking deficits in learning-disabled individuals of all ages. Kornick (1978), in her analysis of the psychosocial aspects of learning-disabled adolescents, cited affective processing deficits that make learning-disabled individuals more egocentric and less able to empathize. Horowitz (1981) indicated that the learning-disabled performed less well on an interpersonal decentering task than their normal peers. No relationship between decentering ability and popularity was observed. Perhaps the inability to decenter is enedemic in contemporary society. Reports on the effects of violence, especially on television, suggest that feelings for others are ignored by most children and adults. This factor may indicate a society-wide social disability, which educators must address. Fincham (1979), in study of cognitive role-taking ability in learning-disabled boys, concluded that they did not significantly differ from normal peers and that inappropriate social behavior is probably not a result of deficiencies in cognitive role-taking. Rubin and Schneider (1973) found moderate correlations between role-taking and measures of altruism. Chandler (1973) has shown that a training program to enhance the ability to take different perspectives decreased the frequency of subsequent delinquent behavior.

One of the most useful instructional strategies for social skill development is role-playing. Role-playing has many useful applications for classroom practice, including the rehearsal and practice of social skills that, hopefully, will transfer later to functional contexts and scenarios (Bender & Valletutti, 1982; Vallettuti & Bender, 1982). Certainly, it provides a valuable means of fostering empathy for others. A further benefit of role-playing is that it allows for the training of the rules of different situations. Watching others role-play familiar but yet-to-be-encountered social situations may present models of interaction for future behavior. Watching others who are more skilled in interpersonal interaction may prove beneficial to children with learning disabilities, especially when follow-up discussions help to illuminate the dynamics of the simulated scenarios.

Children's Games and Social Skill Development

Piaget (1962) has discussed in detail the role of play in the transmission of social realities and social rules and in the reduction of egocentrism and the faciliation of social interaction and cooperation. The interrelatedness of socialization and cognition is also explored. The role of play in the development of social reciprocity is documented as well (Piaget, 1965). Garvey (1977b) pointed out that play allows children to explore objects, social roles, language, and feelings without serious risk. Becker (1977) reported that infants and toddlers learn to expand their social skills in the presence of peers, in their imitation of play activities, and in their mutual excitement about play.

If childhood play is critical to the development of social skills, then it is apparent that societal factors that endanger childhood play are likely to result in a diminution of social skills. Lovinger (1974) maintained that there has been a serious decline in the popularity of children's games and held that the subsequent deterioration in games parallels the increase in learning disabilities. The decline in childhood games can, in no small part, be blamed on the increase in television watching (Postman, 1982; Winn, 1977). Recently, the strong impact of television violence has been compounded by the ubiquitous single-mindedness and violence of video games. This human–machine interaction deprives the manipulator of opportunities for cooperative play with peers. Mesmerized interactors, bombarded with flashing lights and cacophonous sounds, are unlikely to reap the aforementioned benefits of childhood games. Will the increasing use of computers in education cause further problems in social competency in the coming years? Will the cooperative use of computers facilitate peer interdependence?

Disabilities Related to Classroom Factors

The sociology of the classroom also deserves the attention of those interested in understanding the remediating social and emotional disabilities. For example, a low-intensity student may be frightened or overwhelmed by a high-intensity teacher; a high-intensity student may view a low-intensity teacher as disinterested or boring. The search for causative factors, when restricted to the student, serves to divert attention from other relevant factors including deleterious physical and social environments, inappropriate teaching methods and materials, illogical instructional programming, and asynchronous teacher–student interactions.

An evaluation of a student's programming requirements and the design of individualized educational programs are insufficient unless attention is directed toward the student's learning style and classroom interactions. Teachers, however, do not always have the capacity to modify their teaching styles to match student needs. A teacher's personality attributes and flexibility in adjusting their expression should be identified and respected. Whenever feasible, however, the wisest approach is to match teacher traits and teaching style with student traits and learning style in a nonjudgmental way. In light of ecological theory, which suggests that disturbance may result from an interaction between a child's behavior and the reaction to that behavior within an ecosystem, Algozzine (1979) recommended that the Disturbing Behavior Checklist (DBC) be used as a method of matching teachers and students.

Teachers, however, should not overestimate the effect of their personality and behavior on their students since it is unlikely that students model their teachers to the same extent that they model peers (Bandura, 1969). Nevertheless, teachers hoping to influence the development of social competencies need to model interpersonal skills in their daily interactions. Teachers who foster a classroom that facilitates peer friendships, a sense of belonging, and group cohesiveness will aid those learning-disabled students who are egocentric, lack empathy or concern, and adopt a world view of "them" versus "me" (Anderson, 1980; Heath, 1917; Walberg, 1971; Walberg & Anderson, 1972).

As part of the socialization process, it is necessary for teachers to help students become skillful in reflecting about themselves and their world (Heath, 1971). Social maturation requires looking at oneself and at others from the perspective of others.

CONCLUSION

In conclusion, significant process in the total education of the learning disabled might be better realized if teachers trained in this area were provided with learning activities and experiences designed to acquaint them with the nature and remediation of social and emotional disabilities (Burns, 1976). If one examines the texts dealing with teaching the emotionally disturbed (see Hewett & Taylor, 1980, for a notable exception), scant attention is paid to academic remediation while learning-disability texts typically contain minimal information about dealing with social and emotional programming. Teacher preparation programs must work toward a more rational and realistic training model that deals with the learning disabled in a more logical and holistic manner. Social skill development must assume its rightful place, if not hegemony, and teachers of the learning disabled must shun educational models that myopically focus on academic remediation while neglecting the total functioning of learning-disabled students who are often lonely, bewildered, and frustrated.

CHAPTER 12

Emotional Disturbance

Patricia M. Bricklin
Robin Gallico

Professionals in the fields of learning disabilities and emotional disturbance are continually faced with the need to make decisions concerning a series of critical questions: Who is learning disabled? Who is
emotionally disturbed? What is the relationship between the two? Can they
co-exist? Which is the primary handicapping condition? To what extent do
the learning disabled have emotional problems? To what extent do the
emotionally disturbed have learning difficulties? Are service delivery needs
different for each group? Are there possibilities for an integrated model?
There is often much uncertainty, disorganization, and confusion among
professionals when attempting to find answers to these questions through
research and practice. The difficulties and confusions are particularly apparent when examining the definitions of learning disabilities and emotional disturbance that form the bases for decisions about who is eligible for services
under Public Law 94-142, the Education For All Handicapped Act.

Before considering specific definitions, a basic framework for understanding how a definition is generated can be helpful in developing a perspective from which to view the critical issues facing professionals dealing
with the concepts of learning disability and emotional disturbance. The
dilemma that decision-makers face must be eventually translated into the
delivery of services to handicapped children. Since definitions often determine
service delivery, it is important to understand the perspective of the
"definitions makers."

This chapter appeared as an article by **Pamela M. Bricklin and Robin Gallico** in *Learning Disabilities: An Interdisciplinary Journal* (Volume III, 1984) and was adapted by permission of
Grune & Stratton for inclusion in this *Handbook*.

It might be helpful to our discussion to consider the differences between the three types of definitions commonly used in special education: the research definition, the administrative definition, and the authoritative definition. The researcher defines parameters individually and thus determines not only whom the study will address but also the applicability of the results to the general population. The administrative definition is intended to guide the delivery of services and thus describes characteristics of those who will be eligible for these services.

Authoritative definitions are most often the consensus of a group of individuals representing a field who have agreed upon certain parameters. When the definition reflects one conceptual model and all members of the group espouse that model, the definition will be reasonably clear. When the definition, however, is constructed by theorists embracing varying conceptual models, however, it represents agreement and compromise among the individuals about the set of variables or parameters within which to view the concept. After consensus is reached and the definition promulgated, it often seems to take on a life of its own, becoming a "real thing" rather than an agreed upon concept. People tend to forget that they created the definition and act as if it cannot be changed. This is one major problem in creating definitions.

A second problem emerges in the potential manipulability of the definition. Regardless of the type of definition used, the degree to which it is operationalized will determine the degree to which it can be manipulated by the user. The definitions contained in PL 94-142 are both administrative and authoritative but are not well operationalized, thereby allowing opportunity for a great deal of manipulation by professionals to achieve certain goals. This is certainly true in the area of learning disabilities (LD), which represents a compromise definition. The definition of emotional disturbance (ED), modeled after one developed by Bower and Lambert (1965), was constructed to incorporate a variety of conceptual frameworks from which to view disturbance and also presents opportunities for manipulation. Problems associated with the implementation of both these definitions highlight the two major problems we have raised.

In addition, several other issues related to the implementation of definitions for assessment and service delivery must be considered. These include the potential fallout from labeling children and the need for a developmental perspective. When assigning children to diagnostic categories, one cannot avoid considering the issue of stigmatization. In order to get services for a troubled child, professionals may manipulate a definition to include a given student. One must carefully weigh the advantages of providing services against the possible disadvantages of self-fulfilling prophecy. When considering labels like learning disabilities or emotional disturbance, we are concerned with a set of characteristics agreed upon to describe children. However, these labels are only one perspective from which to view the child — the learning or emotional problem. In our zeal to provide intervention, we treat the identified problem as if it represented all of the child. Donnellan (1984) in an editorial entitled, "The Criterion of the Least Dangerous Assumption," accurately described the situation:

> Currently, educators lack longitudinal data measuring both the qualititative and quantitative outcomes at various educational interventions used with handicapped students . . . The criterion of the least dangerous assumption is presented as an interim standard to use until such data are available. The criteria of the least dangerous assumption holds that in the absence of conclusive data, educational decisions ought to be based on assumptions which, if incorrect, will have the least dangerous effect on the likelihood that students will be able to function independently as adults (p. 142).

A final construct necessary to developing a sound definitional framework is that of the developmental perspective. Research definitions do not take developmental considerations into account. When looking at specific behaviors, it is sensible to consider them within the developmental level of the child. Behaviors are not in and of themselves disordered. Behaviors that may be developmentally appropriate at one age may be considered disturbed at another. Ames (1983) cautions us to make absolutely certain that we do not label any child who is immature or young for grade and is thus failing to meet an arbitary expectation that is above his or her developmental level as learning disabled. The same can be said for labeling a child emotionally disturbed.

We have raised certain issues in definition-making and service delivery. We turn now to the literature on learning disabilities and emotional disturbance for an in-depth consideration of specific issues related to these general definitional problems.

LEARNING DISABILITIES AND EMOTIONAL DISTURBANCE

The relationship between learning disabilities and serious emotional and behavioral difficulties has received much attention in research and discussions that have either attempted to

1. describe academic deficits of children with emotional problems (Calhoun & Elliott, 1977; Forness, Bennett, & Tose, 1983; Galvin, Quay, & Werry, 1971; Stone & Rowley, 1964; Tamkin, 1960; Vance, Singer, Kitson, & Brenner, 1983);

2. document behavorial difficulties of students with learning disabilities (Epstein, Cullinan, & Rosemier, 1983; Friedrich, Fuller, & Davis, 1884; Neisworth & Greer, 1975); or
3. attempt to differentiate the categories of learning disability from emotional disturbance (Chandler & Jones, 1983a, 1983b; Hallahan & Kauffman, 1977; McCarthy & Paraskevopoulous, 1970; Webster & Schenck, 1982; Wright, 1974).

Review of this literature fails to reveal any unilateral evidence that can help to more clearly define the nature of either type of disability. The research has not provided convincing evidence that supports or rejects the distinctness of these categories. The problem of operationally defining these conditions remains a major obstacle in both diagnosis and research; and as a result, special education classes are more heterogeneous than homogeneous.

PL 94-142, however, forces educational teams to clearly distinguish between the categories of learning disability and emotional disturbance. In fact, the PL 94-142 definitions of both categories contain exclusionary factors that must be ruled out before group inclusion can be determined. Inherent in this is the assumption that these groups of children are so different that such distinction is possible and that cognitive, perceptual, psycholinguistic, and social behaviors vary significantly among these groups.

Before examining in depth the research that has attempted to study this, let us turn to the category definitions themselves and a discussion of related issues.

Federal and state mandates have established "distinct" categories into which handicapped children must fall before they can be provided with special education and related supportive services. Although many states provide for noncategorical placement of children, it must first be determined that a child meets one of the 12 handicapping conditions and is in need of special education. Of these categories, two of the most problematical from a definitional perspective are specific learning disability and serious emotional disturbance. Certain handicapping conditions, such as blindness or orthopedic impairment, are observable and can be objectively measured. Learning disability cannot be seen, and its measurement has been an ongoing controversy in the field. The raging debate over how to operationally define learning disability has been the topic of countless articles, books, symposiums, and federally sponsored task forces. Although it has not received the same attention, similar difficulty exists in the area of serious emotional disturbance. Definitions of both specific learning disabilities (SLD) and seriously emotionally disturbed (SED) categories contain exclusionary factors (etiological factors that must be ruled out as causing the problem) and a basic underlying component of failure to learn. The legal mandate established by The Education For All Handicapped Children's Act of 1975 is the structure within which educators must operate. It defines these categories as follows:

Specific Learning Disability
Means a disorder in one or more of the basic psychological processes involved in understanding or in using language, spoken or written, which may manifest itself in an imperfect ability to listen, think, read, write, spell, or to do mathematical calculations. The term includes such conditions as perceptual handicaps, brain injury, minimal brain dysfunction, dyslexia, and developmental aphasia. The term does not apply to children who have learning problems which are primarily the result of visual, hearing, or motor handicaps, of mental retardation, of emotional disturbance, or of environmental, cultural or economic disadvantage. (34C.F.R.300.5 (b) (9))

Seriously Emotionally Disturbed
The term means a condition exhibiting one or more of the following characteristics over a long period of time and to a marked degree, which adversely affects educational performance: (a) an inability to learn which cannot be explained by intellectual, sensory, or health factors; (b) an inability to build or maintain satisfactory interpersonal relationships with peers and teachers; (c) inappropriate types of behavior or feelings under normal circumstances; (d) a general pervasive mood of unhappiness or depression; or (e) a tendency to develop physical symptoms or fear associated with personal or school problems. The term includes children who are schizophrenic. The term does not include children who are socially maladjusted, unless it is determined that they are seriously emotionally disturbed. (34C. F.R. 300.5 (b) (8))

Basic to both categories is an inability to learn. In fact, Bower and Lambert (1965) felt that an inability to learn was the single most significant characteristic of the emotionally handicapped student. It should be possible, then, to accurately determine the difference between a disorder in a basic psychological processs and an inability to learn due to emotional disturbance. One must be cautious here not to assume that an inability to learn is synonymous with academic deficits. Any child who is unable to function in a traditional classroom because she or he is acting out or whose attention diverted away from learning because of anxiety is clearly not learning up to his or her ability. To rely on test scores alone results in a narrow interpetation of this aspect of the definition and does a disservice to both the definition and the child.

We can again turn to PL 94-142, or rather its implementing regulations and procedures for evaluating specific learning disabilities, for guidance here, but we are left with only vague references to team decisions and the existence of a severe discrepancy between achievement and intellectual ability. Educators have relied on qualified examiners, most often psychologists, to sort out the answers and to verify the existence of a severe discrepancy.

Methods used to do this can be categorized in four ways: number of years below grade level, ability-achievement discrepancy source, WISC-R verbal performance discrepancy, and WISC-R profile analysis (Berk, 1984b). Recent work has seriously questioned the reliability of these methods (Berk, 1982; Kaufman, 1982; Kavale & Forness, 1984a; Vance, Kitson, Singer, & Brenner, 1983; Ysseldyke, Algozzine, & Epps, 1983) and suggested that further refinement of our diagnostic skill is needed. A complete analysis of definitional problems in the field of learning disability has been done and will not be repeated in depth here. A summary of major concerns, however, is relevant to the discussion at hand. Ysseldyke and Algozzine (1983) point out that we have failed to identify the characteristics that are universal and specific to learning disabilities. Certainly, underachievement is universal but it is not specific only to the learning-disabled. After conducting many investigations, they concluded that:

1. the most important decision is made by the regular classroom teacher to refer the student for assesssment;
2. many nonhandicapped students are being declared eligible for services;
3. identification as handicapped varies and depends upon the criteria used;
4. advocates of clinical judgment are unable to differentiate learning disabled students from underachievers based on test data;
5. placement decisions by teams have little to do with data collected.

McLeod (1983) summarizes the problems: "Attempts to define learning disability have been bedeviled by confusing definition with diagnosis, by trying to reconcile disparate views from different vested interest groups, and by reacting irrationally to the concept of discrepancy between actual and expected achievement." (For a detailed analysis of definitional issues, the reader is referred to Berk, 1984b.)

Berk (1984b) has outlined recommended procedures for diagnosing learning disabilities, which take full advantage of available testing technology from test selection to team decision-making. No such recommended procedure exists for the diagnosis of serious emotional disturbance. The medical profession, so often relied on for its diagnostic expertise, does not use the PL 94-142 definition, rather, it has developed its own diagnostic manual which provides for a multiaxial diagnostic criteria utilized by the major mental health professionals (Williams, 1980). There have been few attempts in the literature to match the psychiatric DSM-III manuals with educational language and definitions (Forness & Cantwell, 1982).

Cooperation between special education and other mental health professionals can only be achieved through a systematic effort to understand each other's professional frame of reference (Forness & Cantwell, 1982). Understanding the DSM-III may make it easier for school personnel to relate psychiatric reports and mental health consultations to education team decision-making. More often than not, school teams misunderstand psychiatric reports using a DSM-III multiaxial diagnosis because they omit the specific term "serious emotional disturbance." In a broad sense, DSM-III defines mental disorder excluding social deviancy.

A definition of mental disorder was, after several attempts, adopted by the Task Force and various components of the American Psychiatric Association. Every word and comma was carefully examined, resulting in the following definition:

In DSM-III each of the mental disorders is conceptualized as a clinically significant behavior or psychological syndrome or pattern that occurs in an individual and that is typically associated with either a painful symptom (distress) or impairment in one or more important area of functioning (disability). In addition, there is an inference that there is a behavioral, psychological, or biological dysfunction, and that the disturbance is not only in the relationship between the individual and society. (When the disturbance is limited to a conflict between an individual and society, this may represent social deviance which may or may not be commendable, but is not by itself a mental disorder. (Williams, 1980, p. 6)

The difficulties in making this differentiation still leave open to interpretation questions such as whether a child is disturbed or socially maladjusted. This most difficult distinction is best made by qualified psychiatric or psychological personnel and not by educational teams. Both professions have a responsibility to aid the other in understanding their frame of reference. Forness and Cantwell (1982) have attempted to mesh DSM-III classifications with special education categories.

The educational definition of serious emotional disturbance contains specific references to behaviors manifested, poor interpersonal relationships, immaturity, inappropriate behavior, unhappiness, and physical symptoms associated with personal or school problems. The definition does not define social maladjustment but makes ruling it out primary to the classification of SED. DSM-III, on the other hand, contains four categories of conduct disorder: 312:00 — Conduct disorder, undersocialized, aggressive; 312:10 — Conduct disorder, undersocialized, nonaggressive; 312:23 — Conduct disorder, socialized, aggressive; and 312:21 — Conduct disorder, socialized, nonaggressive. In the DSM-III all conduct disorders are behavior disturbances, and not social deviance, which is excluded. School teams often exclude certain students from being emotionally disturbed because of a general misunderstanding of the categories of conduct disorders as social maladjustment, Kauffman (1980) comments that the stipulation of noninclusion of youngsters who are socially maladjusted but not emotionally disturbed to the original definition "makes the definition nonsensical by any conventional logic ."

The fact that emotional disturbance has no objective reality — like mental retardation, it is whatever we choose to make it — makes a social policy that mandates special services for all disturbed children and exacts penalties for noncompliance a tragic mockery. This would not necessarily be the case if there were highly reliable means of measuring the extent to which children meet an arbitrary behavior standard: the problem is not inherent only in the arbitrariness of the the the definition, but also in the difficulty in determining whether a given individual meets the standard set by the definition (Kauffman, 1982).

Adding to this already confused state of affairs is the discrepancy in terminology used by the different states. PL 94-142 uses the term serious emotional disturbance, but terms used by the states range from behavior disordered to emotionally disturbed to educationally handicapped to behavior and learning problems. Table 12-1 provides a profile of terminology usage by the states as of the fall of 1983.

Understanding and interpeting research studies in the area of emotional disturbance is made difficult by the ambiguity of the terms currently used (Kavale, Forness & Alper 1986). It cannot be assumed that a seriously emotionally disturbed youngster from Arkansas is similar to a behavior-disordered student from Maine. Studies that state that all subjects met state and federal guidelines for inclusion in the category are inadequate if they fail to operationally define what those guidelines for inclusion were. Keogh, Major-Kingsley, Omori-Gordon, & Reid, (1982) describe a system of marker variables that would facilitate description and reduce the considerable confusion in the research "due to sample variability; few synthesizing generalizations have emerged to guide research or practice; the lack of definitive findings relates more to sample variability than to faulty research methods." Markers are the variables used to describe subjects. Keogh and colleagues maintain that, if such a consistent system were adopted and used to define subjects from one study to another, "a step would be taken toward reducing the ambiguity that currently characterizes the field" (p. 15).

In 1980, an analysis of state definitions was prepared by the Council of Administrators of Special Education (CASE). The analysis (Table 12-2) demonstrates how state definitions may vary from the federal definition. Comparisons of definitions as of 1984 are currently being prepared (Cullinan, Epstein, & McLinden, in press).

Nowhere in the Federal law or its implementing regulations is the term *socially maladjusted* defined, and the fact that some states exclude socially maladjusted youngsters while others do not has caused services to be denied to some behavorially disordered students. PL 94-142 qualifies

TABLE 12-1.
1983 State Classifications.

State	Classification	State	Classification
Alabama	Emotionally conflicted	Montana	Emotionally disturbed
Alaska	Emotionally handicapped	Nebraska	Behaviorally impaired
Arizona	Seriously emotionally handicapped	Nevada	Emotionally handicapped
Arkansas	Seriously emotionally disturbed	New Hampshire	Seriously emotionally disturbed
California	Educationally handicapped	New Jersey	Emotinally disturbed
Colorado	Emotional or behavioral disorder	New Mexico	Behaviorally disordered
Connecticut	Socially and emotionally maladjusted	New York	Emotionally disturbed
Delaware	Social or emotional maladjustment	North Carolina	Seriously emotionally handicapped
D.C.	Emotionally disturbed	North Dakota	Emotionally disturbed
Florida	Emotionally handicapped	Ohio	Severe behavior handicap
Georgia	Emotional and behavior disorder	Oklahoma	Seriously emotionally disturbed
Hawaii	Emotionally handicapped	Oregon	Seriously emotionally disturbed
Idaho	Emotionally impaired	Pennsylvania	Socially and emotionally disturbed
Illinois	Behavior disorder	Rhode Island	Behaviorally disordered
Indiana	Emotionally handicapped	South Carolina	Emotionally handicapped
Iowa	Behavioral disorder	South Dakota	Noncategorical
Kansas	Personal and social adjustment problem	Tennessee	Seriously emotionally disturbed
Kentucky	Emotionally disturbed	Texas	Emotionally disturbed
Louisiana	Behavior disordered	Utah	Behavior disordered
Maine	Behavior disordered	Vermont	Serious emotional disturbance
Maryland	Seriously emotionally disturbed	Virginia	Seriously emotionally disturbed
Massachusetts	Noncategorical (behavior)	Washington	Seriously behaviorally disabled
Michigan	Emotionally impaired	West Virginia	Behavior impairments
Minnesota	Emotional/behavior disorders	Wisconsin	Emotional disturbance
Mississippi	Emotionally handicapped	Wyoming	Social/emotional handicap
Missouri	Behavior disorder/emotional disturbance		

From National Association of State Directors of Special Education, Inc., Washington, D.C.

TABLE 12-2.
State Policy Definitions of the Seriously Emotionally Disturbed in Relation to PL 94-142.

State	1	2	3	4	5	6	Other Criteria
Alabama	+	+	−		−		Deficiencies in group participation in awareness and/or understanding of self and environment
Alaska	+	+	−		−		Social or behavioral problems
Arizona	+	+	−		−		
Arkansas	+	+	−		−		Severe disturbance in thought processes
California	+	+	+		−		Dangerous behavior; behavior interferes with learning of classmates; limited self-control; withdrawal
Colorado	+	+	−		−		Disruption of educational development for child or other students
Connecticut	+	+	−	+	+		Acting-out behavior; withdrawing; defensive, disorganized behavior
Delaware	+	+	−	+	×		
Florida	+	+	−		−	+	Destructive to self or others
Georgia	+	+	−		−		Destructive to self or others
Hawaii	+	+		+	+		
Idaho	+	+	−		+		
Illinois	+	+	+		+		
Indiana	+	+	−		−		
Iowa	+	−	−		×		Disregard for consequences of actions
Kansas	+	+	−		−	+	Dangerous to health or safety; disruptive to program for others
Kentucky	+	+	−		−		
Louisiana	+	+	−	+	+		
Maine	+	+	−		−		
Maryland	+	+	+		+		
Massachusetts	+	+	+		+		
Michigan	+	+	+		+		
Minnesota							
Mississippi	+	+	−		−		Ineffective coping behavior
Missouri	+	+	−		−		
Montana	+	+	−		+		Inhibits educational rights of others

Column headings:

- Neurotic, psychotic, or character disordered
- Those with sufficient intellectual and emotional capacity to become responsible and self-supporting
- Failure to adapt and function at grade level
- Can profit from instruction
- Adequate intellectual potential demonstrated
- Cannot be adequately or safely educated in regular class
- Acting out, withdrawing, defensive, and/or disorganized behavior
- Limited ability of individual to govern own behavior

States:

Nebraska, Nevada, New Hampshire, New Jersey, New Mexico, New York, North Carolina, North Dakota, Ohio, Oklahoma, Oregon, Pennsylvania, Rhode Island, South Carolina, South Dakota, Tennessee, Texas, Utah, Vermont, Virginia, Washington, West Virginia, Wisconsin, Wyoming, D.C.

Key: +, required by PL 94-142 and similar language is found in state policy; −, required by PL 94-142 but similar language is not found in state policy; X, present in state policy but not required by PL 94-142; 1, duration/degree; 2, adverse effect on educational performance of child; 3, includes autistic and schizophrenic; 4, defines autistic separately; 5, excludes socially maladjusted; 6, defines socially maladjusted separately.

From an unpublished report of the Council of Administrators in Special Education of the Council for Exceptional Children, Reston, VA (1980).

the category of emotional disturbance with the word "seriously," imply-ing no responsibility for mildly or moderately impaired youngsters (Raiser & Van Nagel, 1980).

Given the limitations imposed by these definitional problems, an examination of what the research to date has shown regarding similarities and differences between students with learning disabilities and emotional disturbance is presented. The studies have been organized into three broad categories:

1. The existence of academic deficits in emotionally disturbed students
2. The extent of behavioral problems in learning-disabled students
3. The differentiation of learning disabilities from serious emotional disturbance

ACADEMIC DEFICITS OF EMOTIONALLY DISTURBED STUDENTS

Tamkin (1960) surveyed the educational achievement of emotionally disturbed children in a residential psychiatric facility to determine the relationship between arithmetic and reading skills. Using the Wide Range Achievement Test (WRAT), it was found that the achievement of the group as a whole was commensurate with their chronological age (CA), although individually about one-third demonstrated some degree of educational dis-ability where disability is defined as below-grade expectancy.

Stone and Rowley (1964) examined youngsters with average intelli-gence who were referred to diagnostic clinics. Findings indicated, that, whether using CA or mental age (MA) as the basis for comparison, over half of those referred were disabled achievers.

Based on earlier works (Glavin et al, 1971), Glavin and Annesley challenged two commonly held assumptions regarding emotionally dis-turbed students: (a) that it is necessary to change bad behavior before emphasizing academics, and (b) that academic pressure will stress students with behavior problems and cause aggressive outbursts. These data suggest that learning problems do not disappear after treatment of emotional prob-lems, and that, when greater emphasis was placed on academic achieve-ment, the students' academic and behavorial gains were greater.

Psychotherapeutic and educational approaches commonly used with disturbed youngsters have sometimes emphasized classroom deportment and peer relationships over academic programs (Forness et al., 1983). The incidence of serious academic deficiencies has been reported to be any-where from 50 to 80% among disturbed children. In an attempt to reevalu-ate the question of underachievement, Forness, and colleagues examined children admitted to a latency-aged inpatient ward. An analysis of sex and age variables indicated that there were no statistically significant sex dif-

ferences but that age differences and age and sex interaction were significant. When expected achievement was adjusted for mental age, one-third
of the sample had deficits of one year or more in reading and math with
spelling deficits somewhat more common than math deficits. Forness and
colleagues note that most of the children tended to display a homogeneous pattern of underachievement across subject areas.

Given the available research, it can be concluded that in the greater
proportion of cases there is a relationship between academic deficits and
emotional disturbance but that, even when age and IQ are contolled variables, and stable, individual measures of achievement are used, the extent of
those deficits in children with emotional disturbance remains unclear.

BEHAVIOR PROBLEMS OF LEARNING-DISABLED STUDENTS

While the field of learning disabilities was concerned with theoretical
issues and developing remedial techniques, the affective domain did not
receive as much attention. As the availability of remedial techniques
became more widespread, attention was focused on other related areas.
Learning-disabled youngsters have been described as impulsive, disractible,
experiencing personal difficulties, and having emotionally unsatisfying,
stressful relationships with peers and adults because they lack basic interpersonal skills (Bryan, 1982; Bryan & Bryan, 1978a; Bryan, Werner & Pearl,
1982). Prior to the implementation of PL 94-142, children with suspected
learning difficulties and behavorial disturbances were most often referred
to mental health centers and private psychiatrists. Nichol (1974) completed
a follow-up study on original data collected on children who received first-
time psychiatric care in metropolitan Vancouver in 1960. Presenting problems fell under the following headings: somatic, psychological, behavioral,
academic difficulty, delinquent behavior, suspicion of low intelligence,
other, and unknown. The most common problem secondary to academic
difficulty was delinquency or behavorial disturbance. Of the students
followed for 5 years, 90% received remedial education but only 25%
received any further psychiatric treatment. Nichol's data indicated that the
schools were carrying the bulk of the burden for treatment, both academic
and behavioral.

Although recent research has focused on the social skills of the learning disabled, few studies have attempted to categorize and describe the
behavior problems of these students. Analysis of behavior problems is
most often done by factor-analysis techniques. Epstein, and colleagues
(1983) factor-analyzed the behavior of 559 LD and 218 normal boys based
on the Behavior Problem Checklist (Quay & Peterson, 1967). Four basic
factors for LD appeared: conduct problem, attention deficit, social incom-

petence, and anxiety. For the normal group, the factors were conduct problem, anxiety-withdrawal, attention deficit, and social maladjustment. These emergent factors were similar to previously factor-analyzed data (McCarthy & Paraskevopoulos, 1970). Conduct problems accounted for the greatest amount of variance in both normals and the learning disabled. Results raised a question regarding the status of hyperactivity as a pattern separate from aggressive conduct problems.

Harris, King, Reifler, and Rosenberg (in press) also used factor analysis to compare behavior patterns of elementary-age learning-disabled and emotionally disturbed students in special schools. Results indicated that these children were similar in their overall profiles but that, while the ED group had more severe and frequent problems, the LD group's behavior problems were well above the expected level for normal youngsters.

Research indicates, therefore, that learning disabilities and emotional disturbance as defined in PL 94-142 are related to some degree. What is not clear, however, is the extent to which these two special education categories overlap or are distinct from each other. The data suggests that differentiation is often made on the basis of severity and frequency of the emotional/behavorial disturbance.

DIFFERENTIATING LEARNING DISABILITIES
FROM EMOTIONAL DISTURBANCE

The diagnostic label given to an individual student often dictates the type of intervention the student will receive. Often, mildly handicapped students are grouped together for instructional purposes while moderately and severely handicapped students are not as likely to be mainstreamed. It remains an unresolved question as to what the best practice is regarding categorical versus noncategorical grouping in special class placement. One reason for the varying opinions may be the lack of conclusive evidence provided from research.

McCarthy and Paraskevopoulos (1970) examined behavior patterns of 36 learning-disabled, 100 emotionally disturbed, and 41 average children to determine whether it was possible to distinguish among them. They looked at these students in terms of observable social behaviors utilizing The Behavior Problem Checklist (Quay & Peterson, 1967).

Three behavior dimensions, termed *unsocialized aggression, immaturity,* and *personality problem,* were analyzed. Results indicated that the ED students were rated significantly differently on all possible combinations of factors. This suggests that ED students are rated differently by their teachers on all three factors, while LD students differed on the first factor only. Teachers of ED students perceived their pupils as having more problem behaviors of greater severity than did teachers of LD and normal students. Although teachers of LD children perceived their students' problems as less severe than the ED group, their problems were more numerous and severe than the normal students. This study suggests that both ED and LD students exhibit all three types of behavior. By far, both ED and LD groups exhibited greater conduct problems (unsocialized aggression) than immaturity or personality problems. Conduct problems were characterized by restlessness, irresponsibility, tension, hyperactivity, distractibility, and jealousy. One problem raised but not answered is the role of teacher bias or teacher expectation in rating student behavior.

The McCarthy-Paraskevopoulos study was one of the first to address the relationship of conduct disorder to learning disability. Wright (1974) contended that there was considerable overlap between learning disabilities and emotional disturbances. He examined boys of normal IQ identified by their teachers as moderately to severely disruptive in class. Results indicated that 50% were underachievers in reading and 97% had processing dysfunction. Based on identification practices at that time, 51% of the boys referred for conduct problems could have been categorized as learning disabled.

In 1977, Hallahan and Kauffman reexamined labels, categories, and behaviors of emotionally disturbed, learning-disabled, and educable mentally retarded students and found no rational basis or instructional efficacy for grouping by label. They recommended class groupings by behavioral profile rather than by category. Hallahan and Kauffman point out that a student is disturbed when an adult says that the student's behavior is seriously discrepant from the expectations of the adult caretakers. This concept of a discrepancy between expected behavior and actual behavior is reminiscent of the ability-achievement discrepancy issue in the learning disability field.

Reported incidence rates for learning disabilities and emotional disturbance vary from 2 to 30%. Hallahan and Kauffman point out that, when incidence varies greatly depending on definition and arbitrary cutoff scores, it cannot be very stable. When the American Association on Mental Deficiency changed its criterion from one standard deviation below the norm, to two standard deviations, in many states, those students were excluded from the category of mental retardation and included in learning disabilities.

Historical analysis leaves little doubt that learning disabilities, emotional disturbance, and mild retardation have a great deal in common and that it is often impossible to differentiate among them (Hallahan & Kauffman, 1977).

Authorities (Hallahan & Kauffman, 1977; Hewett & Forness, 1974) have indicated that there are probably few relevant differences among pupils identified as EMR, LD, and ED with respect to etiology of handicap, learning and behavioral characteristics, or educative practices. Actually, there is relatively little research evidence for or against the cross-categorical arguments, but their apparent acceptance is reflected in, for instance, training programs for special education teachers, local programmatic offerings for handicapped pupils, and state special education policies.

Webster and Schenck (1982) looked at diagnostic test patterns of 1,524 learning-disabled, emotionally disturbed, and educably mentally retarded students. Results of discriminant analysis consistently failed to discriminate among these students. In reviewing research examining the discriminative efficacy of widely used diagnostic tests, results indicated that these tests have little utility in discriminating learning disabilities from nonlearning-disabled; and, in fact, the authors concluded that, if a child was of average ability and functioning below grade level on reading achievement measures, the tendency was to label the child learning-disabled. If the child's overall intelligence fell at the borderline or dull normal level and word analysis skills were at a level commensurate with borderline ability, the child would most likely be labeled mildly retarded. If the student was of average ability and was performing close to grade level in reading yet was still having problems learning, the child was classified emotionally disturbed.

McKinney and Forman (1982) investigated whether classroom teachers could differentiate among educably handicapped (EH), learning-disabled, and emotionally handicapped (EMH) in mainstreamed settings, based on their perceptions of classroom behavior patterns. Results indicated that LD students were perceived as more independent and task oriented than EMH or EH students, whereas EH students were perceived as more hostile and less considerate. These results must be cautiously considered, as the authors themselves noted, due to limitations by the identification procedures and population characteristics. This study differs from previous research reviewed in that it focused on mainstreamed students and not students in separate classes or special schools.

Chandler and Jones (1983) in a two-part editorial point out that:

> Emotionally disturbed children are being routinely diagnosed as learning disabled and are being placed into resource rooms under that label ... The term emotionally handicapped is as difficult to pin down as the term learning disabilities.

The reasons for this, according to Chandler and Jones, are that (a) the definitions are vague; and (b) fewer program exist that are geared specifically to the needs of ED students. They conclude, however, that it does everyone a disservice to call an ED child LD because of dislike for the label or because of a lack of programs.

The difficulty in discriminating ED children from LD children based on test patterns was examined again by Vance and colleagues (1983). They looked at WISC-R profile analysis in differentiating ED from LD. They concluded that there is little evidence to support the use of WISC-R subject scatter and profile analysis alone to make a differential diagnosis. Their results, and results of previous work, seem to indicate that with careful and conscientious usage of behavioral observation checklists and sound individually administered tests it should be possible to increase both the reliability and validity of the diagnosis.

In 1984, Freidrich, Fuller, and Davis reported on a Michigan task force that attempted to operationally define learning disabilities and to establish criteria for differentiating LD from ED. Using the criteria established by the task force on 1,600 students (433 LD, 229 EMR, 140 ED, 142 other, 435 normal, 217 no diagnosis), the "hit rate" was only 0.35 for grades 10 through 12 and 0.60 for grades 7 through 9. No diagnostic pattern that could adequately differentiate LD from ED emerged. They concluded that: (a) the WISC-R alone should not be a primary evaluation instrument for assessing LD students unless it is used in conjunction with a procedure for determining a valid severe discrepancy and (b) without assessment of behavior patterns, differentiation of LD from ED is not consistently reliable.

CONCLUSIONS DRAWN FROM RESEARCH

There is an Association Between Academic Deficiency and Emotional/Behavioral Problems

Research has suggested that parents and teachers view learning-disabled students differently than normal students (Bryan & Bryan, 1978), but there have not been many in-depth studies of adjustment factors that describe the extent of emotional and behavioral problems in these students. What has been done suggests that there are two broad dimensions of behavorial difficulty: conduct problems (acting out, aggressive) and personality problems (anxious, withdrawn, social deficiency). These problems are also in the emotionally disturbed population, and what seems to distinguish the emotionally disturbed group from the learning-disabled group is the frequency and severity of these problems.

Results Have Been Inconclusive Regarding the Extent of Academic Deficiency in Emotionally Disturbed/Behaviorally Disordered Students

An inability to learn is not necessarily synonymous with academic deficit. Research studies have reported conflicting conclusions regarding the extent of academic deficit in ED students. There has not been an attempt to apply a severe discrepancy model, common in learning disabilities diagnosis, to evaluate the "inability to learn" aspect of the PL 94-142 definition of serious emotional disturbance. As previously discussed, an ED student may not demonstrate a valid discrepancy between ability and achievement but may be unable to learn on a daily basis in the classroom. Previous studies have compared ability and achievement and have attempted to document academic deficits in a broad range of students who have emotional and behavorial disorders. These studies, however, have not addressed the question of whether the discrepancy is valid and reliable. Diagnostic and evaluative studies have not taken full advantage of currently available testing technology (Berk, 1984).

Differentiating Between the Special Education Categories of Learning Disabilities and Emotional/Behavioral Disorders is Difficult

Studies that have attempted to differentiate learning disabilities from emotionally/behavioral disorders have been fraught with problems. Often, the description of the population under study is vague and nonspecific. States vary in the terminology used, and therefore, assumptions regarding the applicability of the results are not possible.

Technically inadequate measures have been used inappropriately to draw conclusions about the achievement levels of LD and ED students. Comparisons of grade equivalent scores to age-based deviation IQs have been used to determine ability-achievement discrepancy, and few studies have used a standard score conversion approach or a regression model Variables such as age, sex, mental age, and race have not always been accounted for. Often comparability of the test norm sample with the subjects of a given study has not been identified. Most studies have not accounted for the differences in the norm samples of the achievement measures used from the ability measure used (Berk, 1984). These inadequacies in the data analyses have rendered inconclusive and/or erroneous results.

TOWARD AN INTEGRATED CONCEPTUAL MODEL

It seems clear from our review of the relevant issues and literature concerning learning disabilities and emotional disturbance that our current definitions are not working. We have not made sensible definitional agreements if we persist in defining learning disabilities and emotional disturbance in such a way that it is impossible to distinguish them not only from each other but also from other entities like underachievement. Our definitional agreements need to make sense and facilitate communication among professionals.

The National Joint Committee on Learning Disabilities, in its 1981 definition of learning disabilities, attempts to facilitate such communication:

> Learning disabilities is a generic term that refers to a heterogeneous group of disorders manifested by significant difficulties in the acquisition and use of listening, speaking, reading, writing, reasoning or mathematical abilities. These disorders are intrinsic to the individual and presumed to be due to central nervous system dysfunction.
>
> Even though a learning disability may occur concomitantly with other handicapping conditions (e.g., sensory impairment, mental retardation, social and emotional disturbance) or environmental influences (e.g., cultural differences, insufficient or inappropriate instruction, psychogenic factors), it is not the direct result of those conditions or influences.

This definition recognizes the *heterogeneity* of the disorders and includes an *intrinsic* component. It acknowledges the possible coexistence of learning disabilities and other handicapping conditions.

While there is still some disagreement, this definition represents the best agreement negotiated among professionals from a variety of disciplines involved with learning disabilities. However, operationalizing such a definition is still difficult. Despite the fact that learning disabilities and emotional disturbance may coexist, decisions as to primary handicapping condition — an endless chicken-egg question — must still be made. It is not clear that this definition would make the task of determining what was cause, and what was result, any easier.

The difficulties in comparing research information, the failure of efforts to identify characteristics that clearly identify and differentiate learning disabilities from emotional disturbance, and the inadequacies of even our best efforts at definition suggest that another approach is indicated. It is possible that a conceptual model, which might create a frame or context for considering both learning disabilities and emotional disturbance, would provide that needed approach.

Traditionally, conceptual models provide information about the nature, assessment, and treatment of problems. They are useful guides to predict and test the accuracy of the model. They are problematic only when the conceptual model itself is too narrow.

Historically, both learning disabilities and emotional disturbance have evolved from a variety of conceptual models. Prior to the late nineteenth century the primary conceptual differentiations were between "insanity" and "feeblemindedness." Beginning in the twentieth century, the evolution of various theories of personality and the manner in which each accounted for the psychopathology gave rise to a number of conceptual models for emotional disturbance. Biological, psychoanalytic, humanistic, behavioral, and sociological theories all provided a framework within which to consider various aspects of emotional disturbance.

Each model, as it considered learning and/or emotional disorders, has provided a particular point of view with respect to assessment and intervention. A brief summary would include psychodynamic theories, which have provided us with a variety of psychoeducational or learning therapeutic strategies. Behavioral technology has provided behavioral observation, task analysis, and management techniques. Cognitive theories have emphasized thinking and memory strategies as well as learning styles, while language theories have provided the impetus for various oral and written language remediation techniques. Sociological theories have begun to view the systems (home, school, and community) in which people operate as important sources of information as well as a focus of intervention. Each model has emphasized a particular point of view with respect to the child and the problem and thus has presented too narrow a focus to account for all contributing factors.

Within a variety of conceptual models, a number of professionals have attempted to understand and explain the interrelationship of learning disabilities and emotional disturbance through the concept of primary and secondary disorders. An early pioneer in this effort, Rabinovitch (1972) distinguished between primary and secondary reading retardation on the basis of differentating between children with a basic defect in the capacity to associate concepts with symbols (primary) from children with a normal potential to read that has not been utilized because of exogenous factors among which are anxiety, negativism, and emotion blocking (secondary). More recently, Adelman (1979) and others have looked at learning disabilities and emotional disorders from a similar perspective.

There is certainly enough evidence to support the conclusions that undetected learning disorders may result in behavioral/emotional difficulties, and that early behavioral/emotional difficulties that are untreated or poorly managed may contribute to a child falling further and further behind academically. Both conditions can have a severe negative impact on the child's concept of self as a learner such that at any given time it might be very difficult to differentiate the two.

The issues of primary and secondary disability appear to become less important than identifying the appropriate points of intervention from the standpoint of prevention in its broadest sense (i.e., interventions to prevent problems from developing in the first place), interventions to reduce the seriousness, duration, or complications of a disorder in already vulnerable persons, or interventions to educate and rehabilitate persons in order to minimize more serious disabilities and reduce residual effects. A conceptual model that is broad enough to encompass a wide spectrum of intervention possibilities is needed.

More recently, in our consideration of learning disabled and emotionally disturbed children, we have begun to shift from a narrowly focused model to a service delivery model that focuses on reciprocal person-environment interactions. In this model a child's development and education are viewed from a dynamic ecological perspective that acknowledges the mutual interdependence between an individual's behavior and the environment in which it occurs and offers interventions at the points of discord in the system.

In brief, the child is viewed as a developing organism with needs, drives, temperament, physiological conditions, and so forth, who interacts with external forces, important others' physical environments, rules, educational systems, and so forth, is changed by them and, in turn, changes them in a continuous reciprocal interaction. In such a reciprocal interaction, what is the cause and what is the effect is an irrelevant question. Cause and effect issues are answerable only in terms of the point at which one looks at the interaction. Every effect becomes the cause of a subsequent effect that, in turn, is the cause of a subsequent effect.

These continous reciprocal interactions are particularly significant in the young person with learning disabilities and/or emotional disturbance because they influence not only the nature and severity of the disability or disturbance itself and the way in which it manifests itself, but also the perceptions and expectations of the child or adolescent about her or himself as well as the perceptions and expectations of important others about her or him. The perceptions of others are a critical component since it is that first important decision to refer that begins the labelling process.

While lip service is given to interaction effects in many theoretical systems, assessment and intervention in these systems are usually focused almost exclusively on the child or adolescent with the problem. On the other hand, Apter (1982) suggests that, in an ecological model, assessment is directed as locating the points of interactive discord between the young person and the various settings in which she or he finds her or himself (schools, home, etc.). These settings comprise the child's ecosystem. When the points of discord have been located, appropriate interventions can be planned with awareness that any single intervention changes the entire system.

An intervention may be aimed at one or more of the following:

1. changing the child
2. changing the environment
3. changing the perceptions, attitudes, and expectations of important others toward the child
4. changing the child's perceptions, attitudes, and expectations towards her or himself and the situation

Thus, the goal of ecological intervention is to restore the child's ecosystem to its own productive equilibrium.

In a dynamic ecological approach, the professional tries to understand the network of interrelationships among individuals and settings in the child or adolescent's total ecosystem. When all of the data has been gathered, the focus of treatment may be on the individual, or it may be on other interactive elements, but it always emphasizes the individual as part of a system. The goal is not just to change the child or adolescent but to make the system function in a way that enhances the development and well-being of all its members. This approach looks not only for weaknesses but also for the strengths of an ecosystem, because the system's strengths represent its most valuable resource for solving problems.

Information is gathered from which all of the environments in which the child or adolescent spends time. This information is used to develop a picture of the entire system defined by the existence of the child or adolescent. Efforts are made to locate the points of discord as well as the points of accord in the system. Data is gathered from settings in which the problem is noticeable, from settings where it is not noticeable, as well as data on the perception of the problem by the child or adolescent and others. For example, the child or adolescent's perception of his or her learning disability may be "I'm dumb and that's why I don't understand what I read." A parent or teacher's perception may be "If she would try harder she could do it." The differing perceptions create a possible point of interactive discord.

Even if the learning disabiliity or emotional disturbance itself is intrinsic to the child or adolescent, we make every effort from an ecological perspective to locate the patterns of interaction that may be seriously exacerbating it. These usually center around those interactive points which, unintentionally, are maintaining the child or adolescent's view of himself in negative ways. In this connection, the unique learning style of the child or adolescent as it interacts with unique teaching and parenting styles must be considered. It is important to assess school–classroom climate, pupil–teacher interaction, peer relationships, pupil–curricular match, and family climate and interactions. Within this model, the phrase "inability to learn" takes on new meaning as the specific points of interactive discord are located.

SUMMARY

A dynamic ecological perspective is useful as an overall contextual frame when assessing and planning for the child or adolescent with learning disabilities or emotional disturbance. Such an approach helps us to maintain the overall interactive system perspective and direct our attention to the possibilities for intervention at the key points of interactive discord, which may involve a change in the child or adolescent, a change in the setting, or a change in the perception of those in the system. Ecological assessment and intervention allows us to locate and utilize the natural strengths of the child or adolescent's ecosystem as major problem-solving resources to restore the system to its own equilibrum. Within such a model, labels of learning disability or emotional disturbance and issues of primary and secondary or cause and effect, although they may exist, are less important than the appropriate systems intervention.

In the interim, however, as long as professionals are forced by law to make decisions as to primary handicapping condition, the assessment of emotional/behavioral components should be routinely included in diagnostic batteries for identification of LD as well as ED, which may be an additional, although sometimes arbitrary, criterion to be considered in determining whether a student's primary handicap is learning disability or emotional disturbance. The more behavioral problems present, and/or the greater the degree of severity, the more likely it is that the child could be identified as emotionally disturbed. Since research has consistently shown that the most common behavior problems in both groups are conduct disorders, provisions should be made for additional training in dealing with acting out, overly aggressive, hostile, and negative behavior within a systems perspective. In addition, more staff, such as crisis teachers, counselors, aides, and especially resource teachers who could begin to approach intervention from a dynamic, ecological perspective, should be assigned to programs dealing with learning-disabled and emotionally disturbed students. When viewed from an ecological perspective, as suggested by Apter (1982), the role of resource teacher carries great potential for delivering appropriate direct services to children and for effecting necessary system changes through a variety of more indirect service functions (consultation, in-service education, etc.). If children are to be truly served, however, unworkable definitions and their implementing policies, which create untenable dilemmas and ineffective intervention, must be changed.

CHAPTER 13

The Learning-Disabled Gifted Child

Lynn H. Fox

I n the book *Cradles of Eminence*, Goertzel and Goertzel (1962) contend that about a fourth of the 400 eminent men and women whose biographies they studied had overcome some sort of handicap. Although it is not possible to document the incidence of learning disabilities among the eminent solely on the basis of biographical or autobiographical data, many educators have speculated that scientific luminaries such as Albert Einstein and Thomas Edison suffered to some degree from learning disabilities (Elkind, 1973; Patten, 1972; Thompson, 1971). Certainly both are purported to have been poor students in their early years and to have had difficulties with reading or with writing and spelling tasks. In the areas of public and military leadership, persons such as Woodrow Wilson, Nelson Rockefeller, and George Patton have been cited as examples of successful adults who were probably learning-disabled.

Until very recently, the posibility that a child could be gifted and disabled at the same time has been ignored or disbelieved. While it is true that some definitions of giftedness specify high levels of academic performance in the classroom or on standardized tests and thus would seem to exclude the learning-disabled student, there are some definitions of giftedness in which the potential for creative or scholarly work is emphasized rather than the manifestation of special abilities in specific ways such as achievement test performance (Fox, 1981). Thus, the terms

This chapter originally appeared as an article by **Lynn H. Fox** in *Learning Disabilities: An Interdisciplinary Journal* (Vol. III, 1984) and was adapted by permission of Grune & Stratton for inclusion in this *Handbook*.

learning disability and *gifted* are viewed as contradictory by some educators but not by others.

The contention of this chapter is that learning-disabled gifted children are not paradoxical phenomena and that it is possible to develop methods and precedures to identify at least some of them.

DEFINING GIFTEDNESS

Early definitions of giftedness tended to focus on global intellectual ability as measured by intelligence tests. Today, most definitions are much broader and include mention of specific academic abilities as well as creativity and talents in some nonacademic areas. Renzulli (1978) noted that most conceptual definitions of giftedness are very similar and differ only in terms of specifics such as the exact level of scores to be considered as evidence of giftedness or the variety of categories of giftedness that are specified. Definitions, however, vary as to whether they stress manifest achievement (either in terms of performance in class or on a test) or potential for achievement (such as high scores on aptitude measures). Definitions in which achievement is not required and in which many independent areas of talent are specified are compatible with the concept of underachieving or learning-disabled yet gifted students (Fox & Brody, 1983; Whitmore, 1980).

Certainly the concept of the learning-disabled gifted child is compatible with the federal definition of giftedness as proposed in the Marland Report to Congress (1972):

> Gifted and talented children are those identified by professionally qualified persons (and) who by virtue of outstanding abilities are capable of high performance. These are children who require differentiated educational programs and services beyond those normally provided by the regular school program in order to realize their contribution to self and society. Children capable of high performance include those with demonstrated achievement and/or potential ability in any of the following areas: general intellectual ability, specific academic aptitude, creative or productive thinking, leadership ability, and visual and performing arts.

Prior to 1971 only four states (California, Illinois, Nebraska, and Pennsylvania) had formally defined giftedness. By 1978, 42 states had formal or informal definitions of giftedness, most of which closely resemble the above-mentioned federal definition (Karnes & Collins, 1978).

Even though most conceptual and legal definitions of giftedness do not automatically exclude the learning-disabled or underachieving student, in practice the operational definitions used by most school systems do exclude many if not all of them. Why is this so? Although most experts in the field of gifted education recommend the use of individual measures of intelligence such as the Wechsler Intelligence Scale for Children-Revised, schools tend to screen for gifted students on the basis of group measures of intelligence or achievement tests, often in conjunction with teacher nomination or recommendation. In some programs self, peer, or parent nominations are also considered. Thus, many learning-disabled gifted students will be overlooked because their performance on standardized group tests of achievement are not two or three years above their grade level placement.

Research on teacher nomination of students as gifted has found that teachers typically nominate dutiful students more often than those students who score well on individual intelligence tests (Gear, 1976). Teachers appear to do somewhat better with well-developed checklists and after receiving instruction (Gear, 1978), but few teachers are knowledgeable about the learning-disabled gifted child; and the behavior checklist developed by Tannenbaum and Baldwin (1983) is not widely known and used. Typically, children known to have a learning disability will not be considered by teachers for gifted programs, even sometimes when their gifts lie in nonacademic areas.

There is little research on the accuracy of self, peer, or parent nominations. It seems unlikely that severely disabled students would have enough self-confidence to nominate themselves or that they would be viewed as academically gifted by their peers or parents. It is possible, however, that such children might be identified by parents or peers in terms of having a good imagination or a large store of knowledge about a particular subject. Such nominations may not be taken very seriously if the child has a history of average or below-average performance in the classroom and/or on standardized tests of achievement.

For many years, Torrance (1977) has advocated the identification of intellectually able students on the basis of creative and productive thinking abilities (flexible, fluent, and elaborated thinking skills), especially with disadvantaged populations whose cleverness goes unrecognized because they have failed to master standard grammar and spelling. His arguments for the culturally different or economically disadvantaged would seem to apply to many learning-disabled children as well. Certainly it would be interesting to study the performance of learning-disabled children on measures of creativity that do not deduct points for language problems.

There is, however, considerable controversy surrounding the construct "creativity." It is alternately viewed as a personality trait, a specific cognitive ability, and a problem-solving skill that can be learned (Michael, 1977). To some it is an essential ingredient of the gifted person (Renzulli,

1978); to some it is a legitimate category of specific intellectual talent; and to others it is a process to be taught in much the same way as the model for the scientific method is taught. Perhaps because of this controversy most schools have focused on the identification of the intellectually and academically able in terms of achievement and aptitude tests and have ignored creative thinking despite its inclusion in the federal definition.

Little is known about the identification of leadership ability in children. Although some students who hold positions of leadership in high school also move into leadership positions in college, little is known about the relationship of these activities in the early years with adult leadership in the political arena, the professions, business, the community, or the church. For example, the president of a professional organization may have been elected in recognition of his or her outstanding contributions to research in the profession, whereas an executive in a large corporation may have assumed responsibilities because he or she had managerial skills. Both are leaders but the nature of their leadership roles is different, and both of these are probably different types of leadership from what may be involved in being popular in adolescence. Schools have generally ignored this category of giftedness when planning formal academic programs and let "leadership" activities be part of the extracurricular realm through self-nominations and peer selections. Perhaps some of these chosen students are indeed learning-disabled gifted leaders. It certainly would be interesting to study the patterns of abilities and achievements of different types of leaders in the school population and within the various domains of the adult world.

Most large secondary schools and some elementary and middle schools provide rather extensive programs in nonacademic areas such as music, visual art, and drama. In some cases selection into these programs is based on auditions or presentation of past products (such as art portfolios) independent of academic work. It is not uncommon, however, to require students to maintain certain academic standards in their regular school program. In some schools, relatively high achievement standards are set for gifted programs in the performing and visual arts. There appears to be no research on the extent of learning disabilities among students who are talented in the visual or performing arts. Presumably, people who have problems with auditory discrimination are not very musical, whereas those with visual discrimination problems may not be good at sketching, and people with various memory problems might find acting difficult. Yet people who cannot read are still able to conceive of clever stories or plays, and some musicians can compose music without being able to write or read the standard musical notation, so it seems reasonable that some aspects of creative production in the arts are independent of academic performance.

At present there is no systematic screening for the learning-disabled gifted so it is difficult to know how pervasive such a condition really is. Whitmore (1980) describes the case of a boy, named Robert, who at age 7 was judged to be doing unsatisfactory work in the second grade. Fortunately, he was carefully evaluated, and when he scored 163 on the Stanford-Binet he was placed in a special program for the underachieving gifted child. He was eventually able to overcome his perceptual and visual problems so well that he later participated in regular classes for gifted students. In high school he was active in student government and drama. Without early identification and intervention he might never have achieved so much and his self-esteem would have remained low. Do most schools find and nurture the students like Robert? The following suggests that they do not.

AN EMPIRICAL STUDY

When the Spencer Foundation awarded a three-year grant to a team of researchers at The John Hopkins University for the study of learning-disabled gifted children, one component of the study was the analysis of the problems and issues in identification. The Hopkins team hypothesized that there might be three sub-groups of students to be considered:

Subgroup 1. Students whose disabilities were acute and were identified as learning disabled and whose giftedness or special talents would be overlooked in the processes of prescribed treatment.

Subgroup 2. Students who were initially screened for programs for the gifted on the basis of a high intelligence test score or a teacher's nomination for a specific talent such as mathematical ability but who subsequently were eliminated for final consideration for a gifted program or were admitted to the program but later dropped for the reason of underachievement.

Subgroup 3. Children who perform near the mean on standardized achievement measures, who do adequate but not superior work in the classroom, and who for all intents and purposes appear to be "average" children but who in reality are very bright but learning-disabled.

Several clinicians interviewed by the Hopkins team felt sure that they had encountered children such as those described in subgroup 1. Schiffman and Daniels of the Hopkins team were certain that they had worked with children of the type described in both subgroups 2 and 3 in public schools as well as in special laboratory settings at the Temple Reading Clinic. Yet there seemed to be little in the research literature to document the existence of children in any of the three groups.

The Hopkins team studied the files of 17,000 cases contained in the records of the Reading Clinic of Temple University. Records for a sample of 321 boys and 111 girls who had scored 125 or higher on the verbal, performance, or full scale of the WISC or WISC-R were chosen for further analysis (Fox, 1983).

Only 10% of the boys and 6% of the girls in the gifted sample scored two or more years below grade placement on a standardized test of reading achievement. About a fourth of the students actually scored two or more years above grade level, which would qualify them for a gifted reading program in some school systems. On the subscales of the WISC-R, only a fourth showed a discrepancy favoring the verbal over the performance scale, while another fourth showed a discrepancy favoring the performance scales over the verbal ones. When the Myklebust formula (1968b) was applied to the test scores of the sample, only 35% of the boys and 30% of the girls were found to have a signficant discrepancy.

Although none of the above methods suggested that a sizable number of the sample were indeed disabled learners, a review of the records showed that 90% of the boys and 83% of the girls in the sample were considered by the clinician to have some reading problem. Clinical judgment is a complex process difficult to quantify and analyze. It appeared that a factor common to the vast majority of cases judged to have problems was a discrepancy between listening comprehension and instructional reading level by two or more years as measured by an informal reading inventory. About two-thirds of the students that clinicians viewed as disabled readers also showed a pattern of a high score on the Similarities and a low score on the Digit Span subtests of the WISC.

Thus, it appears there are students judged to have reading problems who score high enough on intelligence tests to be considered by some as intellectually gifted. The vast majority of these students would not be screened for learning disabilities in most school systems in which discrepancies between potential or grade placement and performance on standardized tests of reading achievement are used as the criterion. Even supposedly sophisticated formulas in which aptitude is supposed to be taken into account would have missed 62% of the students clinicans felt had problems in this gifted sample. Perhaps standardized reading tests are not valid measures of skills for this type of student. In this study, 10% or less of the gifted students with a reading problem were two or more years below grade level on the standardized measure, whereas on an informal reading inventory 50% of the cases were reading two or more years below grade level.

CLINICAL IMPRESSIONS

Rosner and Seymour (1983) note that on clinical measures used in assessing learning disabilities, the patterns of responses for gifted students are not significantly different from their average ability learning-disabled counterparts. They suggest that the differences are in the ways the students tend to try to mask their disabilities in the testing situation and in the classroom and school. For example, bright but disabled students may give long complex, unusual, or creative responses to the most elementary questions as if they are trying to impress the listener with their intellect through verbosity to cover up the real deficits in skills. Indeed, such children often become narrowly focused on one topic such as dinosaurs or mathematics to the exclusion of other interests in the basic school curriculum, pretending that it is their lack of interest in the mundane school work or their passion for their chosen topic that keeps them from completing school or home assignments.

The case study of George described by Rosner and Seymour (1983) is an example of how a very bright nonreader with poor handwriting can turn from a student who squeaks through elementary school by charming teachers with his wit and oral language into an adolescent who cannot handle the demands of secondary school. George is one of many students who, rather than admit their inability to perform, present the world with the image of being bright but naughty, perhaps smoking marijuana on the school ground, flaunting truancy, or using verbose logical arguments to confuse teachers and peers. At all costs they must not be found to be lacking in ability; they steadfastly maintain their air of rejection of the school and societal rules. Thus, attention is given to social maladjustment, and the learning disabilities go unnoticed.

Krippner (1968) noted that bright students may become painfully aware of the gaps in their abilities to the extend of developing more emotional adjustment problems than students of average ability who have learning problems. There is, then, a real danger that the children will mistakenly be viewed as doing poorly in school as a result of the emotional problems rather than being seen as having emotional or behavioral problems *as a result* of their inability to cope with the discrepancies in their intellectual functioning. Senf (1983) contends that in most schools today children with above average intelligence will not be carefully evaluated for learning disabilities and that they will never be referred for any type of evaluation unless they are extremely overactive, emotionally disturbed, completely lacking in social skills, or socially deviant. It is likely that some of this extreme behavior will not become manifest until adolescence, thus decreasing the probability of correct diagnosis and proper intervention.

Another case described by Rosner and Seymour (1983) illustrates the situation in which the child is not recognized as either gifted or learning disabled by the school but, instead, is seen as a child of average ability who is having trouble with reading. In this instance, it was the mother who quickly perceived that the phonics approach to reading was not the best one for her bright daughter. Clinical diagnosis confirmed an auditory discrimination problem, and the clinician agreed with the mother that a different approach to reading might be better for Wendy. Had the mother not had two older daughters who were identified as gifted, she might have been more willing to accept the school's judgment of Wendy's capabilities.

Tannenbaum and Baldwin (1983) point out that some typical characteristics of gifted students may take a few odd turns and twists among the learning-disabled gifted. For example, a good sense of humor is often said to be found among the gifted. Learning-disabled gifted students may find that they can use that sense of humor to divert attention away from their academic failure or shortcomings. If a child feels terribly thwarted and becomes hostile, he or she may turn the humor toward ridicule of peers or authority figures, perhaps as a defense against perceived rejection.

High levels of energy and quick thinking are also thought to be characteristic of most intellectually gifted children. If the children are also learning-disabled, these qualities may be interpreted somewhat differently. Tannenbaum and Baldwin (1983) suggest that such children are inaccurately described as hyperactive. Their impatience and fidgetiness are often the result of a specific type of activity in the classroom rather than chronic conditions. They may appear hyperactive when they are asked to read a textbook, or to write out long responses, or to use a workbook. When activities are centered on discussions of current events, they may behave quite differently.

GUIDELINES FOR IDENTIFICATION

Clinicians seem to feel that the correct diagnosis of a learning disability can be given only after detailed evaluation on a variety of measures. Giftedness in terms of potential is also best assessed by experts using a battery of measures. It is a rare school or school system that can afford the costs of giving every child a complete psychological examination to discover their gifts and their problems. What then can be done and by whom? There are two basic strategies: first, change the procedures for screening for gifted students to include more efforts to identify the learning-disabled students; and, second, change the identification procedures and program prototypes for the learning disabled to better identify and nurture the strengths of these children.

Perhaps the most sensible approach to identifying the gifted is to use a wide variety of psychometric and nonpsychometric measures to initially screen as many children as possible for consideration for the available programs or for individualized counseling and program adaptations. Perhaps for some programs self-nomination would be sufficient; if the student does not perform well in the program, he or she can then be further evaluated to determine the cause of the difficulties. Evidence of academic ability or potential might be assessed by a nonverbal measure of deductive reasoning such as the Raven's Progressive Matrices, and some measurement of creativity might be included to allow the child with problems in areas of reading, spelling, or handwriting to compete for recognition in other areas. While group tests of achievement and aptitude will continue to be useful in screening the vast majority of gifted students, some care and attention should be paid to looking closely at the child who scores well on these tests but does not do well in regular school placements according to the teacher. Also, evidence that suggests unevenness in abilities, such as very high scores in mathematics and much lower scores on the verbal subtests of group tests, should be viewed as a sign that clinical evaluation is needed.

Identification of the learning-disabled student should become a process in which the strengths of the child receive as much attention as the weaknesses. Children who are thought to have a problem need careful evaluation by experts and need to be tested on individual measures of intelligence to really determine the presence of real potential. In the initial screening procedure, however, a far less time-consuming and costly tool might be the individualized reading inventory administered by the classroom teacher who should be taught to look for gross differences between listening comprehension levels and instructional levels. Clearly, the regular classroom teacher as well as the specialist need to become more aware of the existence of the learning-disabled gifted child and the signs to look for in the classroom and on tests.

Any time decisions must be made in selection or classification of children, a value judgment must be made about false positives and false negatives. In the case of the learning-disabled gifted student, it is probably more important for society to provide extra services and opportunities to children who are identified as learning-disabled gifted and who later turn out not to be very gifted than to continue to withhold programs and services to those who are truly both learning disabled and gifted. In other words, we can afford more false positives than false negatives. Can society really get along without people like Albert Einstein, and do we dare leave educational experiences to the luck of the draw?

In time, diagnostic testing and prescriptive instruction may become the norm for all children. If so, it will not be necessary to have programs for special subpopulations because children will receive programs of instruction so uniquely matched to individual strengths and weaknesses that they will be challenged and remediated simultaneously. At present, we have much work to do to make this possible. In the interim, much can be done to watch for children whose profiles of abilities are a confusion of peaks and valleys. Parents and physicians may be very important sources of information. They are often likely to perceive changes in the student in the early elementary grades that the classroom teacher cannot appreciate. Confirmation of the condition must then come from thorough clinical assessment by psychologists who have some understanding of the nature and nurture of the learning-disabled gifted child.

PUTTING THE LEARNING-DISABLED IN GIFTED CLASSES

There is no universally accepted model or program prototype for students who are identified as intellectually or academically gifted (Baum, 1984). Although a wide variety of academic alternatives have been proposed through the years, most schools offer only one type of program. Some programs emphasize enrichment of the student's education by providing curricular content above and beyond the basic school program. Sometimes programs are developed to allow students to progress rapidly through existing curricular content. A few programs integrate acceleration and enrichment components; but, more often than not, a school or school system will decide to focus on enrichment activities rather than acceleration or allow acceleration but not provide special enrichment classes.

Acceleration

Educators who advocate acceleration may differ on how they think acceleration should be done. Despite any evidence as to the harmful effects of grade-skipping or double promotion, this practice is generally not favored for a variety of reasons. Some schools provide programs in which content is telescoped so that two or three years of academic work in a particular subject can be taught in one year. Sometimes gifted students can advance rapidly through the regular school offerings by taking extra courses in summer or after regular school hours. Indeed, many colleges now encourage bright high school students to begin taking college courses for credit on a part-time basis while still in high school.

Accelerative options for the academically gifted are probably not very viable for gifted students who have serious learning problems. Most such efforts require the student to learn a fair amount of material on his or her own in one way or another but probably primarily through reading textbooks. If a student skips a grade he or she must be able to learn the content of the skipped courses by some method — again, probably by reading a textbook. Gifted students who elect to enter college early often must double-up on high school courses or learn material outside of regular school classes in order to pass tests such as the Advanced Placement Program tests. Most gifted students who have reading problems are going to have difficulty keeping up with the pace of the class. Even in the area of mathematics, in which acceleration is often recommended, students may be required to read the textbook on their own to learn theorems or problem-solving paradigms. Steeves (1982) identified a group of students with severe reading problems who had high scores on the Raven's Progressive Matrices, an indication of good mathematical reasoning ability. When she compared these students with students in a gifted mathematics program in a normal private school, she found her students to do as well on both the Raven's test and a measure of computation. She felt, however, that her students would need to be taught differently from the other mathematically gifted students because they could not be expected to use workbooks on their own or read the algebra textbook in the way expected of nondisabled gifted students.

While it may be difficult for the learning-disabled gifted students to accelerate their progress in school the way nondisabled gifted students sometimes do, many programs recommended for the intellectually gifted are not radically accelerated in nature. Often these programs provide opportunities for creative expression, for career exploration, and for enriching experiences above and beyond the basic school curriculum. To deny these experiences to the bright but disabled in order that they may spend more hours trying to master other skills may be a poor decision. After all, the skills of accessing and communicating information are often the means to the end, not the end in and of themselves, for many bright people. It is wrong to neglect or overlook the talents and strengths of children in our diligent but perhaps misguided efforts to teach the cornerstones of education: reading, writing, spelling, and arithmetic.

For some students, even the very bright, no amount of remediation will allow them to totally overcome a spelling, reading, or handwriting problem. How can such students be given access to the advanced courses in high school that they need to prepare for college? And how will they survive in college? Clearly not all educators agree on the appropriateness of tools and "crutches" for the learning-disabled, and more and more educators are coming to accept the impact of technology and realize that handwriting may be a less important skill than typing for the college student, or that many students in college prefer to tape-record a lecture rather than try to take notes on it — and clearly those who have fought the use of the hand-held calculator in the schools have lost the battle. Bright adults who do not spell well now can use word processors with editing programs, use dictionaries, or hire secretaries who do spell well. Although reading will continue to be a valuable skill, some people can learn material as easily or more easily from listening to a tape-recorded lecture. Although reading is generally a faster way to access information, taped or televised programs have the advantage of allowing one to pursue other activities such as driving a car, knitting, or preparing meals while learning.

At present, many bright students who have reading or writing problems are excluded from enriched programs for the gifted when their lack of skill may be only tangentially related to the purpose of the course. For example, a student might do well in a creative writing class despite a disability if he or she could dictate his or her story or play into a tape recorder for someone else to type. Another student might be marvelous in a chemistry course once given a "talking book" version of the textbook. A potentially capable mathematician may have some problems with simple computation while being able to grasp far more complex theorems. A girl who appeared hopelessly confused in an advanced social studies class might appear to have become brilliant overnight if she were allowed to tape record lectures instead of trying to take notes (Fox, Tobin, & Schiffman, 1983).

Enrichment

Many different types of enrichment programs are recommended for the academically gifted. Some may be appropriate for the learning-disabled gifted student while others may not be very sensible or feasible.

Some courses are designed to offer more breadth and depth of coverage of topics from the basic curriculum. At the secondary school level these may take the form of an honors or advanced section of a course such as a fourth-year English. In the regular English class, much time and effort may be directed toward the study of grammar while only one play by Shakespeare is studied along with a collection of short stories by American writers. In the honors or advanced section, less time is spent on grammar, and the students might study three different Shakespearian plays in some comparison mode as well as read three or four novels along with the short story collection by American authors. Whether or not a learning-disabled student can or should participate in such a program will depend on many factors. If the disability is severe and the student reads below grade level, he or she may find the work load too demanding. If the student is scoring at or even somewhat above grade level on reading measures but still lower than measures of potential would predict, the student might handle the advanced courses but require some supplemental help or adaptations such as using talking books or watching the Shakespearian plays performed in addition to or in lieu of reading the plays. At some point, a decision must be reached in terms of the possible benefit to the student of being in the advanced class over spending more time reviewing or learning grammar and punctuation. The student's total program and special interests need to be taken into account.

Some schools offer enrichment classes on subjects not offered in the general curriculum. For example, classes in creative writing, or the history of art, or sociology might be created. In the areas of science and mathematics, special learning laboratories in which the students pursue independent study projects are sometimes created. These types of programs may be the most suitable for the learning-disabled gifted student. A skilled teacher can help the student develop research skills and study habits that will be useful in college and in later careers. Because these courses are often not offered for credit, there is less pressure for grades and less competition among students. Also, generally there is better teacher-pupil cooperation than in structured classes for large groups. Of course there is the possibility that a teacher will not know how to faciliate this type of self-directed study, in which case the experience may deteriorate into undirected playfulness or wasted energy.

At the elementary school level, programs are sometimes offered that are called *pull-out* programs because the students must leave their regular self-contained classes once or twice a week for periods ranging from one hour to half or whole days. Although these programs are sometimes organized around a specific topic (for example, archeology and oceanography have been fairly common offerings for children in grades 4 through 6), many times these programs offer a variety of activities and may cover a wide range of topics depending upon student interests. Recently there has been much interest in having children work on futuristic problem-solving tasks such as designing the first colony on Mars and solving all the physicial and social questions involved. Brain-storming and role-playing activities are stressed. This type of group may be combined with individual student projects on topics of interest that emerge in the process of group problem-solving activities. When the pull-out model is used, children may be expected to make up the work that they miss in their regular class — usually on their own time after school. In some cases the student may be excused from the regular work because the home teacher feels the child has already demonstrated mastery of the material. For the learning-disabled gifted child, participation in this type of program could become a burden unless the home teacher can adjust the work load. And yet, participating in such a program may be just what the child needs to bolster sagging morale and give the child an opportunity to experience success and the respect of peers and teachers in response to creative ideas.

Two relatively new program ideas for the gifted that might be very valuable for the learning-disabled gifted child are career symposiums and mentorships. Career symposiums are typically short-term projects lasting one day or, at most, one week. In the mentor programs the student is encouraged to form a close relationship with an adult who shares some common interests or who is in a career field of interest to the child. Occasionally, the model will involve the mentor in direct teaching activities but often the mentor is a friend outside the school setting with whom the child can correspond and perhaps visit periodically at his or her place of employment. The mentor is a role model for the child and can foster career awareness and communication skill development. Clearly the learning-disabled gifted child could benefit from interactions with sympathetic adults who have achieved career success — perhaps despite some learning difficulties, physical handicaps, or social handicaps of their own.

Of course, the underlying assumption behind most enrichment programs has been that gifted students need opportunities to deal with more advanced concepts or more challenging work than the basic program provided — usually because the students had already mastered the vast majority of the basic material of the in-grade curriculum. Thus, the programs were not intended to be rewards for good achievement but instead were intended to prevent boredom and stagnation of students who, without these programs, might be assigned busy work because their teachers were unable to provide the necessary individualization within the regular classroom. Therefore, the idea of putting learning-disabled students in some of these programs may not be viewed favorably by many teachers, both those in the home class and those who teach the enrichment classes.

How well a learning-disabled gifted child will function in a gifted class will depend on numerous factors. The nature and severity of the child's disability is certainly a major factor. The specific demands of the enrichment program should also be considered. For example, if an enrichment program is designed to foster creative problem-solving skills, a child's reading level or spelling and handwriting problems may not affect performance in the gifted class during group brainstorming sessions or role-playing. If, however, the program is trying to teach new content or utilizes critical reading skills, the child who has only average or poor reading skills may not be able to keep pace with the gifted class.

Perhaps the ideal program plan for the learning-disabled gifted child is one in which there are special self-contained classes for students in the early school years. These classes could be organized to provide enrichment activities and yet also deal directly with the areas of disability through a combination of remedial and adaptive training techiques in a clinical teaching mode. Eventually the child could move into a program of study that placed him or her in regular classes for some subjects and in gifted classes or programs for others (Moller, 1984). A few pilot efforts to create these programs are described in the following section.

CLINICAL TEACHING MODELS

If teachers are to foster children's giftedness and ameliorate learning disabilities, they had best be prepared to take a few professional risks; conventional remedial programs are not likely to prove satisfying, and standard in-grade curricular materials are apt to be of little help (Daniels, 1983). Teachers may need to use a multisensory approach to instruction following extensive diagnostic evaluation of each child; an eclectic approach to the curriculum may also be needed. Indeed, teachers must learn to use the children's own interests and natural curiosity as a springboard for curriculum development. For instance, the evening news programs on television can often stimulate thinking about a wide variety of issues in science and social studies. Simulation activities can also motivate children to seek out information from a variety of sources and practice basic skills in the process. For example, a simulation of weather-forecasting could lead to a serious study of meteorology. Daniels (1983) explains how this type of activity could be organized for subgroups of students, depending upon specific needs.

Daniels suggests that students who have trouble with comprehension but have good word recognition might be motivated to concentrate on the content of written materials by combining direct reading activities with independent research on such topics as the history of weather forecasting or folklore and the weather and so forth. Students who have poor organizational skills might combine directed reading activities with learning to read weather maps and teaching other students to read the maps.

In addition to teaching content, reading skills, and vocabulary, the above activities may foster self-confidence and positive self-esteem. Imagine how wise children will feel when they can explain or analyze the weather reports they see on television for their parents or friends. Such activities are challenging and will not become frustrating if the teacher is aware of the strengths and weaknesses of each child and adjusts the assignments accordingly.

A Model Program in the East

A self-contained classroom program for elementary-aged, learning-disabled gifted children in southern Westchester County, New York, is described in detail by Baldwin and Gargiulo (1983) as an example of the clinical approach in practice. The goal of the program is to prepare the children for eventual mainstreaming in the general school program or the gifted program, as appropriate for each child. The students begin in a total self-contained program in which both social and cognitive goals are emphasized. As each child gains confidence and acquires skills and coping strategies, he or she is gradually introduced to parts of the basic school program such as regular classes in art or music or physical education. After careful assessment in all aspects of the child's academic program, the child is mainstreamed into one or more specific academic classes and/or the gifted resource program. For example, if a child has strengths in science and mathematics, he or she would begin to work with regular classes or the resource teacher in these areas while remaining within the special classroom for part of the day to continue work in language arts and social studies. Eventually, each child will move to a program that is comprised totally of regular and gifted classes or resource room work.

One technique used in this program is the learning center approach to instruction. This is a creative alternative to the workbook or textbook with which the child has been unsuccessful in the past. Another aspect of the program that is atypical is the use of the classroom for group solving of problems that arise within the class. This type of activity promotes sharing of feelings and growth in social and communication skills. Many of the materials used in the program are those recommended for promoting higher-level thinking and creative problem-solving skills for gifted children.

A Model Program in the West

The pilot program developed by Udall and Maker (1983) in the Tucson Unified School District is more of a resource room model than a self-contained class. The children participate one day a week for an entire school day. The philosophy of the program emphasizes the need for special teaching techniques for these children in which the focus is on the children's giftedness rather than on their disability. Udall and Maker believe that the fostering of independence and self-directed learning is a central goal.

The program was comprised of three key components: a work-hour, a counseling activity, and enrichment. During the work hour the children worked on their assignments from their regular or learning-disabilities classes to prevent them from falling behind in their basic school programs as a result of missing one day of class a week. Although this sounded simple and straightforward, the teachers in the pilot class soon discovered how difficult it was to deal with such a diverse group of children who came from such a wide variety of classes.

The counseling component used a variety of activities such as class meetings, role playing, values clarification exercises, and games. The class meeting at the beginning of the day provided an opportunity for each child to help decide on the schedule of activities for the day.

The major focus of the content of the curriculum was science; art was a secondary focus. Neither subject required the children to read and write at the same levels of proficiency as each other or at the level of the content.

These topics were generally popular with the students. For example, a unit on electricity was developed using The Science Curriculum Improvement Study and Science-A Process Approach as a basis. Children could then develop their own project ideas, often using elaborate charts and pictures to illustrate the scientific principles.

Language arts activities are often more open-ended than traditional. Materials such as the *Choose Your Own Adventure Series* were utilized. The instructional techniques and philosophy were drawn from the work and writings of Taba, Parnes, and Taylor because they focused on the strengths of the child, they were adaptable for both high performance and high verbal groups, and they encouraged higher level thinking skills.

An Experiment With Computers

Although microcomputers may not be any more effective than worksheets for presenting new material or providing opportunities for drill of skills, they seem at the present to have a special appeal to some children and to have infinitely more patience with the slow learner's need for repetition than most teachers and parents do. Experimental summer classes for the learning-disabled gifted at the Johns Hopkins University have increasingly used computers in response to the children's obvious excitement about working with them (Tobin & Schiffman, 1983). The computer can function as a private tutor who never fails to praise with enthusiasm (a help sometimes to the child with poor self-esteem). Also, the computer is a tireless recorder of progress and this can be used to make detailed analyses of student needs; it can even be programmed to generate individualized practice assignments or to adjust the rate of presentation of material, based on each child's unique pattern of responses to diagnostic tests. The technology is now being developed to allow a multisensory approach to learning on the microcomputer (Schiffman, Tobin, & Buchanan, 1982; Tobin & Schiffman, 1983).

A microcomputer may be the ultimate tool for adaptive teaching techniques to circumvent disabilities. Word-processing and editing programs may help bright students communicate their ideas without becoming too bogged down by their spelling errors or word and letter reversal problems. Certainly, sophisticated logic games, simulations, and role-playing games, as well as the learning-by-discovery activities often recommended for the gifted, will be more easily understood and used by the learning-disabled gifted when they are presented in a combination of modes by the computer.

COUNSELING AND TRAINING FOR PARENTS

Sometimes parents realize that their child is learning-disabled but don't notice signs of giftedness while focusing on efforts to "rid the child of a terrible affliction." Sometimes parents are sure that their child is brilliant and interpret failures in school as lack of motivation or deliberate efforts by the child to displease the parents or persecution of the child by the school. Perhaps some parents never notice anything about their child and assume that he or she is average or normal. But many parents do notice both the giftedness and the disability and are terribly confused and frustrated. Perhaps they have other children in the family who have histories of great success in school and feel that this child is just as bright even though he or she seems to be progressing so much slower than the other siblings did. Such parents can find it difficult to decide how far to push their child and when to leave the child alone.

Sometimes families will have been struggling with problems for years and have become confused by receiving contradictory advice by the schools and experts. Sometimes the child will have a beautiful and happy life until about the second grade. All of sudden the teacher complains that the child is hyperactive, and the parent is perplexed or the cheerful cooperative child becomes sullen, depressed, and "naughty."

Because families are the most important element in the child's early life, they are critical factors in the way the child learns to feel about school, achievement in all types of activities, and self. Thus, programs for the learning-disabled really need to contain components of counseling for the parents. Whitmore (1980) suggested that teachers and parents must become partners in the education of the child. She even recommends formal contracts between parents and teachers to delineate what each will try to accomplish in and outside the classroom. If parents are to be effective, they will need some training in communication skills.

Bricklin (1983) has proposed three elements in the counseling and training of parents. First, parents need to know what to expect. They need to know about the characteristics of gifted children and the characteristics of learning-disabled children and how the two may become merged in the behaviors of one child. They need to understand the key elements of programs for gifted children as well as those recommended for the learning-disabled so that they can understand the types of experiences their child needs. Also, these parents need help dealing with their own feelings. Bricklin (1983) wrote that "the parents must first give up the child of their dreams, that fantasized child who was smart, well-behaved, and achieving with no complications . . . The process of 'mourning' the dream child often becomes the major task of counseling parents of learning-disabled gifted children" (p. 248). Bricklin then goes on to describe a process of "inner shouting" in which the parent finally learns to accept the real child and give up the dream child. The third component is the teaching of communication and coping skills. The parents need to express themselves clearly to the child, especially in the area of feelings. Parents need to develop their listening and observational skills. They will then be positive role models for the child.

CONCLUSIONS

Until very recently, the existence and plight of learning-disabled gifted children have been ignored in the research literature and in educational practice. Certainly, research is needed to determine how many such children there are, their characteristics in the early years, and how to best educate them.

Efforts to identify these children and to provide special programs or counseling for them and their parents are likely to encounter a few barriers. First, there is a question of who should be responsible for their educational programs. Should these children be considered a subset of learning-disabled children and identified and taught under the auspices of programs for the learning-disabled? Should they become the primary responsibility of educators and programs within the area of gifted and talented education? In many states these two programs are not under the same administrative structure with learning-disabilities classes being included in special education but gifted education often under curriculum and instruction rather than special education. While it seems likely that the best educational solutions for the children would involve enormous cooperation between educators in both fields, traditionally the two groups have not interacted very much. Teachers of the gifted are not typically trained in the clinical training methods recommended for the learning-disabled by Lewis and Daniels (1983). Nor have learning-disabilities teachers been required to take courses in gifted education. A second related issue will be money. If programs for the learning-disabled gifted require screening and special services for more children than are presently served in either area, where will the funding come from? Some school systems would really rather not hear about the existence of these students if it means that they must provide more testing and more special classes. A third possible barrier is the general lack of concern for gifted education. Some people view these programs as elitist. Parents whose children's reading levels are several years below their grade placement may be viewed sympathetically by the public, while parents whose children are doing grade level work or better may find less sympathetic reactions to their claim that their children are performing significantly below their potential.

The real hope for the learning-disabled gifted may lie in the gradual movement toward completely individualized educational planning for all children. Until then, some actions by parents, educators, researchers, and physicians will be necessary to create more awareness and acceptance of the needs of these children. Formal and informal networks of communication must be established among these groups to promote better methods of screening and classification of children for special programs and greater flexibility and creativity in the types of educational plans that are developed. Educators need to form closer partnerships with parents and physicians to promote early identification and to lobby for programs.

All children deserve an eduational environment that promotes the development of their talents. For the learning-disabled gifted child, this may require a carefully planned blending of activities designed to promote the development of their special talents with activities that provide the necessary remedial or adaptive training. Perhaps not every child who is considered learning-disabled gifted will become a famous scientist or a social leader but perhaps many will. Are a few special educational interventions really too costly when there may be so much to be gained? Can society really afford to ignore the needs of this group of potentially creative and productive adults?

CHAPTER 14

Dimensions of Learning Disabilities

with Chad Nye

T he field of learning disabilities (LD) has long been puzzled by a fundamental question: What is the basic nature of LD? Although LD has been viewed primarily as a problem of underachievement, historically concern has focused on problems associated with oral language, written language, and perceptual-motor processes (Weiderholt, 1974). Based on an hypothesis regarding the nature of LD, theories linking LD to perceptual, linguistic, attention, and memory deficits were conceptualized but generally failed to provide a broad perspective about LD (Kavale & Forness, 1985b; Wong, 1979b).

Research over the past 20 years, however, has revealed that the manifestations of LD are many and varied (Kirk & Elkins, 1975; Meier, 1971; Norman & Zigmond, 1980). The result has been an extensive catalog of deficits displayed by LD children (see Hallahan, Kauffman, & Lloyd, 1985; Kirk & Chalfant, 1984; Lerner, 1985; Myers & Hammill, 1982, for summaries) but no evaluation of their relative importance in contributing to LD. Although it is clear that single-syndrome theories cannot adequately explain the nature of LD, the form that multiple-syndrome theories should take is not clear (Doehring, 1978). Is it possible to identify deficit areas wherein LD and normal (N) samples exhibit differences of magnitude sufficient to warrant their inclusion in a multiple-syndrome theory?

Portions of this chapter originally appeared in an article by **Ken Kavale** and **Chad Nye**, which appeared in the *Journal of Special Education* (1985–1986, Volume 19, pp. 443–460).

This chapter provides a partial answer through a quantitative synthesis of research (Glass, 1977) in areas in which LD and N groups were found to differ. By statistically integrating data from studies in which LD and N groups have demonstrated differences, it is possible to quantify the level of group differentiation found across individual studies and to provide some insight into their relative contribution to the LD phenomenon. A comprehensive evaluation across several areas of investigation may generate a theoretical basis for understanding the nature and relationship of the characteristics associated with LD.

THE METHODS OF META-ANALYSIS

Meta-analysis is similar in scope to primary research and includes the following elements:

Problem Identification

Meta-analysis typically attempts to answer questions that are broad in scope in order to portray an entire domain. For example, in this study, the primary question was: *What is the basic nature of LD?* To provide an answer, it was decided that it would be necessary to define areas wherein it is assumed that differences between LD and N groups might exist. This was accomplished by surveying LD texts to obtain a list of variables in which LD versus N comparisons revealed group differences. After the individual variables were identified (e.g., semantics, word attack, mathematical reasoning , attention, memory, perceptual–motor, interpersonal behavior, intrapersonal perception, and like), they were then grouped into four primary dimensions: linguistic, achievement, neuropsychological, and social behavior. A total of 38 variables were identified, with 5 in the linguistic domain, 10 in the achievement domain, 20 in the neuropsychological domain, and 3 in the social/behavior domain.

Data Gathering

Meta-analysis typically attempts to be inclusive by capturing a majority of the studies in the area under consideration. Since the focus in this chapter was LD in general, study collection was aimed at obtaining as many studies as possible for each of the variables in the four primary dimensions. The only inclusion criterion was the presence of an experimental comparison between LD and N samples. Intervention studies were excluded. This search located 1,145 studies which, when overlapping, inappropriate, or insufficient studies were eliminated, yielded a final sample of 1,077 studies that served as the data base.

Data Coding

Once studies were located, attention was next directed toward identifying important characteristics assumed to be related to the problem under study. Study characteristics include both substantive features (e.g., sample attributes, outcome assessments) and methodologic features, which are more general aspects related to research design (e.g., test reliability, reactivity, internal validity). The goal was to determine whether findings vary with respect to the features identified in the studies surveyed.

Data Analysis

Meta-analysis is based upon the "effect size" statistic that represents the magnitude of group (LD vs. N) differences and is calculated from

$$ES = \frac{\bar{X}_N = \bar{X}_{LD}}{SD_N}$$

where X_N = average score for the normal comparison group
$\quad X_{LD}$ = average score for the learning-disabled group
$\quad SD_N$ = standard deviation for the normal group

In this comparison, a positive *ES* favors the N group (i.e., their mean score is larger than the mean for the LD group) while a negative *ES* favors the LD group. Although *ES* is simple in appearance, it may present problems in both conception and calculation. Glass, McGaw, and Smith (1981) showed how *ES* could be reconstructed from various other statistics when primary data (means and standard deviations) were not reported. Additionally, when necessary, procedures were applied to correct for either small sample size or violation of parametric assumptions (see Hedges, 1981; Kraemer & Andrews, 1982). Finally, it was necessary to distinguish between variance across studies due to artifacts (e.g., sampling error, measurement error, or range restriction) and variance attributable to real group differences. These corrections (see Hedges & Olkin, 1985; Hunter, Schmidt, & Jackson, 1982) were applied to *ES* estimates where appropriate and possible. In this way, the calculated *ES* value more closely represents the magnitude of the "true" differences among groups rather than differences due to artifact variance across studies.

Data Interpretation

An *ES* may be interpreted as a *z*–score and translated into notions of overlapping group distributions. For example, an *ES* of +1.00 indicates that the LD and N groups differ by one standard deviation. This difference suggests that 84% of the LD group could be differentiated from the N group whereas 16% could not. Thus, more than 8 of 19 LD subjects, on the average, score below the average level of the N group. Conversely, only 16% of the N group would reveal scores comparable to the average level of the LD group, suggesting limited overlap between groups. The obtained difference is approximately 34 percentile ranks on some measure. If the SD of some measure is known (standardized achievement tests), then *ES* can be translated into years and months. (For example, *ES* = +1.00 means that the LD group is depressed by one year.)

Data Aggregation

The 1,077 studies produced a total of 6,985 *ES* measurements for an average of 5.54 *ES* comparisons per study (range = 1 to 39). These data represented 106,000 subjects (LD = 67,000; N = 39,000) for an average of 109 per study, in which 66 were LD and 43 were N. For the LD sample, 80% of the subjects were male whose average age was 10.21 years and average IQ was 96.86. The N sample was 79% male, with an average age of 9.89 years and an average IQ of 101.13. These subjects were typically chosen from a school setting (74%) or clinical setting (22%), and were in grade 5.77. The nonsignificant comparisons between groups with respect to age (t_{964} = 1.12, $p < .30$), IQ (t_{937} = 1.74, $p < .10$), percent male (t_{931} = .583, p .50), and grade level (t_{943} = 1.02, $p < .40$) suggested that the LD and N groups did not differ along these dimensions. These factors also appeared to have a negligible influence on findings as evidenced by the small correlations between *ES* and age (r = .036), IQ (r = .071), percent male (r = .005), and grade level (r = -.059).

The LD subjects were most often selected from an intact group (43%), whereas 39% were chosen on the basis of some psychometric procedure (e.g., discrepancy index, test scores, rating scale) and 11% were chosen on the basis of their meeting some definitional criteria (federal, state, or local). A majority of the subjects (69%) were classified as LD, whereas 24% were categorized as reading disabled (RD); the remainder (7%) were classified under some other rubric subsuming LD (e.g., minimal brain dysfunction, neurologic impairment, hyperactivity, attention deficit syndrome). The average study was published in 1979; 39% (n = 409) were published between 1981 and 1985. There appeared to be no relationship between *ES* and either method of subject selection (r = .079), subject classification (r = .045), number of subjects in a study (r = .022), or date of publication (r = .082), suggesting that these factors had a minimal effect on outcome comparisons.

Because a single study may yield more than one comparison appropriate for *ES* calculation, it was necessary to decide how *ES* data should be aggregated for analysis. The *ES* data may be aggregated at either the individual level (i.e., *ES* comparisons are treated as independent units) or the study level (i.e., *ES* comparisons from a study are combined into a weighted average and the unit of analysis is that single *ES*). After an empirical test, it was decided that the data are best aggregated at the study level.

The next problem is whether the obtained sample of studies is large enough to answer the important questions about the dimensions of LD. Orwin (1983) proposed a method for calculating a fail-safe number (N_{fs}) based on *ES* rather than on probability levels. Assuming a "large" difference between LD and N groups approximately one SD (*ES* = 1.00), then N_{fs} = 560. Thus, the present sample of studies (*N* = 1,077) exceeds (by approximately 48%) the number of studies necessary to rule out the "file drawer problem" as a rival hypothesis.

THE DIMENSIONS OF LD

Overall Difference Between the LD and N Group

Across 1,077 studies, the mean effect size ($\overline{ES}$) was .660. The $\overline{ES}$ (.660) indicates that approximately 75% of the LD population differs from the N group across measures of achievement, neuropsychological, linguistic, and social/behavior characteristics. Thus, about three out of four LD subjects demonstrated deficits across domains that distinguished them clearly from their N counterparts by approximately 25 percentile ranks on the average. This level of differentiation is illustrated in Figure 14–1 in which two separate distributions are separated by .661 standard deviations at their means.

In order to further define the character of this differentiation, an index of effect magnitude called omega-squared (ω^2) (see Hays, 1981, p. 349) was calculated where possible (*n* = 752) and represents a measure of the strength of association between the variables considered and LD. The

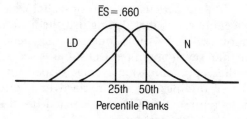

$\overline{ES} = .660$

LD   N

25th 50th
Percentile Ranks

Figure 14–1.
Level of differentiation across all
LD versus N comparisons.

calculated value of ω^2 (.408) can be interpreted directly as the percentage of variance accounted for by the variables. Thus, 41% of the variance in LD functioning can be accounted for by the four primary domains investigated.

Before further aggregation of data, it was necessary to determine whether the obtained differences are "real" (i.e., that they represent the true state of affairs) or are artifacts of research designs by assessing the quality of the research. This was accomplished by rating a study's design adequacy and testing whether well designed and poorly designed studies gave different results. Empirical tests revealed the "good" and "poor" studies provided different results, with the poorly designed studies possibly causing biased findings. To eliminate this bias, 183 studies rated "poor" on design were not included in subsequent findings leaving 894 studies as the data base.

Differences Between LD and N Groups by Dimension

By eliminating 183 studies, overall $\overline{ES}$ based on 894 studies was .646. The resulting $\overline{ES}$ reduction of .014 was not significant (t_{1969} = .625, $p < .50$), and reduced the level of group differentiation from 75% to 74%. Thus, the elimination of "poor" studies had minimal effect upon the overall findings. Although the single $\overline{ES}$ of .646 establishes group differences, no insight is provided into the source of those differences. This can be accomplished by further aggregation of the data into more discrete groupings. The fourfold division of LD dimensions provides a first level of aggregation to investigate the nature of LD versus N differences. The greatest differences ($\overline{ES}$ = .881) were found in the linguistic domain (n = 101), in which more than eight out of 10 LD subjects revealed language deficits that differentiated them clearly from N subjects by about 31 percentile ranks on a standardized language measure. The achievement domain (n = 268) revealed the next greatest group differentiation ($\overline{ES}$ = .683), in which 75% of LD subjects demonstrated levels of underachievement distinguishing them from N subjects. The differences amounted to 25 percentile ranks and suggests that the average LD child in this study (at fifth grade) showed an average grade level achievement score of 2.89, making the average discrepancy about 2.88 years. Only slightly smaller were the differences ($\overline{ES}$ = .635) found in the neuropsychological domain (n = 394). Almost three out of four LD subjects showed deficits in neuropsychological assessments amounting to 24 percentile ranks that distinguish them from N subjects. The least differentiation ($\overline{ES}$ = .584) was found in the social/behavior domain (n = 131). More than seven out of ten LD subjects scored about 22 percentile ranks below the expectations for average N performance on behavioral measures. These findings are summarized in Figure 14-2, in which the four dimensions representing LD are depicted in relation to the N group who are at the 50th percentile.

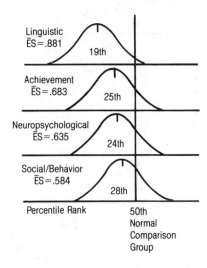

Linguistic
$\overline{ES}$ = .881
19th

Achievement
$\overline{ES}$ = .683
25th

Neuropsychological
$\overline{ES}$ = .635
24th

Social/Behavior
$\overline{ES}$ = .584
28th

Percentile Rank   50th
Normal
Comparison
Group

Figure 14–2.
Level of differentiation between LD
and N groups for the primary domains.

With respect to the omega-squared indices for the dimensions with ω^2 ranged from .271 (social/behavior) to .320 (linguistic), with the achievement (.302) and neuropsychological (.291) falling between these values. Among the dimensions that define LD, the following order for both $\overline{ES}$ and ω^2 emerged:

linguistic > achievement > neuropsychological > social/behavior.

When the $\overline{ES}$ and ω^2 values were compared, no differences emerged for either $\overline{ES}$ or ω^2. Thus, although the linguistic domain demonstrated both a greater level of group differentiation and explained a greater proportion of the variance, it was not significantly more than the other three domains. This suggests that linguistic problems cannot be singled out as a primary source of LD. Additionally, all six correlations between domains revealed significant associations ($p < .01$, at least), suggesting that the domains share a large proportion of common variance. In summation, these findings suggest that language problems are an important parameter of LD but probably no more important than the other domains in providing a complete description of LD.

Differences Between LD and N Groups Within Dimensions

With differences established among the four primary dimensions representing LD, attention was directed at examining differences within each dimension. This was accomplished by aggregating data for specific outcome categories within dimensions. These data are shown in Table 14–1.

TABLE 14-1.

Average Effect Sizes for Outcome Categories in Linguistic Achievement, Neuropsychological, and Social/Behavioral Dimensions.

Domain	n	M	SE	%
Linguistic				
Semantic	37	.790	.153	79
Syntactic	32	.879	.099	81
Phonologic	8	1.192	.481	88
Pragmatic	15	.824	.357	80
Achievement	9	1.143	.238	87
Achievement				
Reading achievement	46	.757	.096	78
Word attack	16	.597	.104	73
Reading comprehension	47	.714	.085	76
Word recognition	52	.736	.080	77
Reading rate	6	.332	.115	63
Math achievement	19	.607	.096	73
Computation	30	.503	.102	69
Reasoning	5	.280	.134	61
Spelling	38	.726	.202	77
Handwriting	9	.951	.186	83
Neuropsychological				
Intelligence (IQ)	71	.457	.055	68
Attention	37	.639	.111	74
Vigilance	10	.603	.120	73
Selective attention	4	.570	.215	72
Concentration	14	.718	.089	76
Cognitive style	9	.588	.087	72
Memory	60	.759	.092	78
Short-term	31	.759	.079	78
Long-term	18	.710	.101	76
Rehearsal strategies	11	.838	.128	80
Conceptual processes	44	.702	.129	76
Problem solving	17	.765	.169	76
Concept formation	24	.669	.099	75
Learning rate	3	.640	.178	74
Perceptual functioning	155	.677	.075	75
Visual perception	64	.675	.079	75
Auditory perception	40	.660	.081	75
Auditory-visual integration	19	.886	.147	81
Perceptual motor	32	.576	.017	72
Neurophysiologic	27	.530	.111	70
Social/Behavioral				
Interpersonal behavior	52	.653	.086	74
Interpersonal perception	41	.604	.071	73
Intrapersonal perception	38	.535	.069	70

Linguistic Dimension

The linguistic domain provided five outcome categories. The greatest differentiation was found in the phonologic category, in which 88% of LD subjects revealed deficits. Almost nine out of ten LD subjects demonstrated an inability to produce or discriminate the sounds of language; this tends to support Clements' (1966) suggestion that phonologic deficits are primary LD symptoms. Only slightly less prominent was the level of differentiation based on results from inferior performance on semantic, syntactic, and pragmatic areas. There were, however, no differences among any of the linguistic outcomes with respect to the level of differentiation. The pragmatic category (the social use of language) was divided into receptive aspects involving the comprehension of appropriate social uses of language, such as laughing at a joke, and expressive aspects focusing on subjects' ability to use socially appropriate language (saying "thank you" when appropriate). Analysis of these categories showed a receptive pragmatic language $\overline{ES}$ of 1.12 and an expressive pragmatic language $\overline{ES}$ of .531. The $\overline{ES}$ difference was significant, suggesting that the LD subject's understanding and use of language for the purpose of social interaction provided a greater degree of group differentiation.

Achievement Dimensions

Four major achievement outcomes were identified: reading, mathematics, spelling, and handwriting. Although reading achievement revealed somewhat greater group differentiation than mathematics achievement (.757 vs. .607), as evidenced on standardized test performance, the difference was not significant. This suggested approximately equal suppression on reading and mathematics outcomes by LD children, that is, an average of about 2.86 years.

With the exception of reading rate (where the limited number of cases suggests caution), the facets of reading achievement were approximately equal and revealed that about three out of four LD subjects could be clearly differentiated on the basis of their reading performance. With reading rate eliminated, no differences emerged among reading achievement categories, which suggests that LD students can be differentiated equally on the basis of their decoding and comprehension skills.

Within mathematics achievement, LD subjects appear to do more poorly on basic computation tasks (the small number of cases investigating problem-solving ability again suggests caution). In the area of spelling, 77% of LD subjects performed more poorly than their N counterparts. The greatest differentiation in the achievement domain was found for handwriting, which was assessed through some aspect of the writing process, such as neatness and speed. Thus, more than eight out of ten LD subjects performed at a level below the average performance of the N counterparts. Although handwriting achievement showed the greatest group differentiation, these data should be interpreted with caution because of (a) the small number of cases and (b) the lack of significance attributed to handwriting in the assessment of LD (at least as reported in the literature).

Thus, the $\overline{ES}$ values for each achievement outcome were relatively similar, suggesting that the various aspects of achievement performance were comparable among the LD group. This was substantiated by the finding of no differences among achievement outcomes. In terms of LD identification, the similarity among achievement outcomes suggests that LD children were likely to be identified with any achievement outcome.

Neuropsychological Dimension

The neurophysiologic domain was comprised of six major categories: intelligence, attention, memory, conceptual processes, perceptual functioning, and neurophysical functioning. Comparision of the $\overline{ES}$ for the six major categories revealed no differences, suggesting that no one facet of the neuropsychological domain provided a greater level of differentiation between LD and N groups.

Intelligence level was most often assessed with an individually administered IQ test (e.g., Stanford-Binet, Wechsler). The present findings showed that LD subjects were depressed by almost one-half standard deviation, and almost seven out of ten scored below the level of the N group. Using the average IQ (103) for the N group found in this study, it was possible to calculate the average IQ for the LD sample, which was found to be 96 (i.e., 103 − [15.5 × .457]). The IQ levels for both the LD and N groups were within the average range and did not differ as evidenced by the overlap in a 99% confidence interval.

Almost three-fourths of the LD subjects could be differentiated on the basis of attention deficits. Four facets of attention were identified:

- *vigilance* — usually assessed by some measure of distractibility such as a continuous performance test
- *selective attention* — usually measured by a central-incidental learning task
- *concentration* — usually assessed by time-on-task measures
- *cognitive style* — usually measured by impulsivity or field independence-dependence assessments

These facets of attention were approximately equal and revealed levels of group differentiation ranging 72% to 76%. No differences emerged among attention subsets, suggesting that LD subjects are about equally depressed on measures of attention deficits. Thus, three out of four LD subjects demonstrated attention problems that distinguished them from their N counterparts.

In the area of memory, almost eight out of ten LD subjects could be distinguished clearly from N subjects. Three subcategories were identified but comparison of these three dimensions revealed no differences. Whether the memory task is concerned with short-term recall, long-term recall, or rehearsal strategies to facilitate recall, LD subjects were about equally deficient. Thus, memory represents an area wherein LD and N comparisons revealed clearly that LD subjects perform more poorly.

Conceptual processes revealed that 76% of the LD subjects performed below the average level of the N comparison group. In general, conceptual processes reflect a person's ability to combine thoughts and ideas. Specifically, concept formation requires the person to select a specific way of categorizing stimuli from among several possibilities; the present findings indicate that three out of four LD subjects do not perform this task as well as N subjects. Problem solving usually refers to hypothesis testing tasks in which more than three out of four LD subjects perform poorly when compared with N counterparts, usually by solving fewer problems. This finding was confirmed in studies investigating learning rate, in which 74% of LD subjects were clearly slower than N subjects in their acquisition of information.

The category in the neuropsychological domain with the largest number of studies was perceptual functioning. On the average, three out of four LD subjects revealed deficits in perceptual functioning. Assessments measuring the ability to integrate auditory and visual stimuli showed the greatest group differentiation; more than eight out of ten LD subjects revealed inferior auditory–visual integration ability. Individually, visual and auditory perceptual skills, such as discrimination and memory, were about equally depressed in the LD group, and revealed that 75% of LD subjects demonstrated visual and auditory perceptual deficits that distinguished them from an N group. Slightly less prominent was the level of differentiation found on perceptual-motor assessments (e.g., Purdue Perceptual-Motor Survey, Bruininks-Oseretsky); nevertheless, seven out of ten LD subjects revealed deficits in perceptual-motor functioning that differentiate their performance from N counterparts. A comparison of the $\overline{\text{ES}}$s revealed no differences, suggesting approximately equal suppression in LD performance across assessments of perceptual functioning.

The final category in the neuropsychological domain was the assessment of neurophysiologic functioning, in which the differences between LD and N groups were slightly more than one-half SD. The measures focused on the identification of neurologic (e.g., EEG) or physiologic (e.g., biochemical imbalances) indices of LD which revealed $\overline{\text{ES}}$'s of .557 and .496, respectively. There was no difference between the neurologic and physiologic categories, suggesting that on the average seven out of ten LD subjects demonstrated differences in these neuropsychological indicators when compared with an N group.

Social/Behavioral Dimension

Three categories were identified in the social/behavior domain: interpersonal behavior, interpersonal perception, and intrapersonal perception. The greatest level of differentiation (.653) was found for interpersonal behavior that refers to the social interaction subjects engaged in with others (e.g., parents, teachers, peers). Almost three out of four LD subjects revealed interpersonal deficits marked by rejection by peers, being perceived as possessing more problems by parents and teachers, spending more time off-task, and the like. Only slightly less prominent were deficits in interpersonal perception manifested by LD subjects. The primary areas investigated include personality attribution and locus of control, in which more than seven out of ten LD subjects minimize effort as a source of their failure and manifest primarily an external or outer-directed locus of control. Just over one-half SD differentiation between LD and N groups emerged in assessments of intrapersonal perception reflected primarily in their view of self-worth (e.g., self-concept, self-esteem). The findings suggest that seven out of ten LD subjects experience reduced feelings of self-worth. No differences emerged among the three categories, suggesting that none of the three categories provided greater group differentiation.

CONCLUSION

The purpose of this chapter was to explore empirically the basic nature of LD. When compared along variables considered fundamental to LD, where would the greatest differences emerge between LD and N samples? If some areas revealed greater group differentiation than others, then it would be logical to assume that these areas represent basic dimensions of LD.

In general, LD and N subjects differed by about two-thirds SD across dimensions. This means that about 75% of LD subjects could be differentiated clearly from N subjects, and would demonstrate deficits that would interfere with their academic ability. The findings, however, failed to distinguish particular areas in which LD and N groups differed to the extent necessary to label that area *the* basic dimension of LD. It was found that LD and N groups revealed approximately the same level of differentiation across a wide assortment of variables. Thus, no one area of functioning could be said to be the basis of LD. Additionally, the level of differentiation indicated that although LD subjects revealed deficient performance in three out of four cases, a proportion of LD subjects (about 25%) did not exhibit deficits that distinguished them from N subjects. Consequently, no one pattern of deficits that could be said to delineate LD functioning was found, and no single problem area can be said to determine LD.

It is apparently true that LD is a complex and multivariate problem that is not easily defined by any one particular parameter. Furthermore, the Byzantine nature of LD was further substantiated by the fact that only 41% of the variance between LD and N groups was accounted for by the variables included in the investigation. Four primary dimensions, 18 general outcome categories, and 20 specific outcome categories were used to describe LD functioning; yet this comprehensive description of LD left about 60% of the variance between LD and N groups unexplained. Furthermore, the lack of any significant associations among demographic factors and these variables suggests that these factors had little relationship with LD functioning. Thus, it appears that much remains to be investigated if the nature of LD is to be more fully delineated and understood.

On the average, the greatest differentiation between LD and N groups was found in the linguistic domain. In terms of outcome assessments, LD subjects scored lowest on language measures when compared with outcome assessments in the other domains. However, neither the average level of group differentiation nor the proportion of variance explained by linguistic deficits was significantly different from the values found for the other three dimensions. When combined with the significant associations among the four dimensions, it appears that linguistic problems cannot stand alone as a primary LD deficit area. Thus, although the linguistic domain revealed the greatest group differentiation (i.e., the largest average score differences between LD and N subjects), further analysis failed to substantiate the primacy of linguistic deficits and, rather, revealed LD to be an amalgamation of deficits. When taken together, the findings by domains suggests that each dimension makes an important contribution to LD, and it is necessary to include each for a comprehensive description of LD.

Learning disability appears to involve a number of component deficits. Not all children with LD are deficient in the same areas; but, on the average, they can be distinguished from their N counterparts on the basis of these component deficits. Consequently, the single-syndrome conceptualizations common to LD (e.g., Birch & Belmont;s, 1964, intersensory integration; Clement's, 1966, minimal brain dysfunction; Frostig & Horne's, 1964, visual–perceptual problems; Kephart's, 1060, perceptual–motor mismatch; Kirk & Kirk's, 1971, psycholinguistic deficits; Myklebust's, 1964, psychoneurologic learning disability; and others) that emphasized primarily deficits in the neuropsychological dimension were too narrowly conceived to provide a comprehensive description of LD. The neuropsychological dimension showed no greater differences from those found between LD and N subjects in the other primary domains (linguistic, achievement, social/behavior). Thus, research has demonstrated a variety of differences spaning a wide variety of variables. This suggests that there is more than one form of LD and no uniform pattern of deficits. Consequently, unitary conceptions of LD that stress deficits in a single domain are inadequate for describing LD in general and can explain only a limited number of LD cases.

More comprehensive descriptions of LD require multiple-syndrome conceptualizations that take into account the multivariate nature of LD. Although it is true that deficits in any domain may be responsible for LD, a complete rendering of LD must include not only all the associated deficits but also the interactive nature among the domains and variables in producing LD. Any theoretical framework must make possible a unified organizational scheme for the entire pattern of deficits in LD. It appears that recent attempts to reduce heterogeneity through empirical classifications that produce subtypes of LD is a valuable first step in attempting to develop conceptualizations of LD that recognize it not as a singular problem but a complex amalgamation of an assortment of problems. The next step requires an organization of the many factors contributing to LD into a workable taxonomy. This would produce a less fragmented view of LD and allow for generalizations that are applicable across the LD phenomenon.

The task of describing LD would have been easier if, across the 894 studies reviewed comparing LD and N groups, a single area had emerged wherein almost all LD subjects clearly demonstrated a deficiency. This was not the case; in fact, across 38 variables investigated, the LD subjects showed about the same level of differentiation from N subjects across all 38 variables.

What is the basic nature of LD? The answer is complicated because there is no *one* area that reveals more about the nature of LD than any other area. Clearly, LD is not a unitary disorder because learning is not a unitary skill. Consequently, conceptualizations of LD that include all the necessary components will be complex and will probably require revolutionary changes to produce LD paradigms capable of explaining fully the LD phenomenon (Kuhn, 1970). The solutions are not easy and will continue to pose a challenge for some time.

CHAPTER 15

The Disassociated Learner

T he field of learning disabilities (LD) has attempted, since its inception, to provide conceptual insights that would describe its fundamental nature. Historically, conceptions of LD have focused on problems associated with oral language, written language, and perceptual-motor functioning (see Wiederholt, 1974). From these conceptualizations, theories linking LD to perceptual, linguistic, cognitive, attention, and memory deficits, for example, were proposed; but none were entirely satisfactory in providing a comprehensive perspective (Kavale & Forness, 1985a). These failures led to the conclusion that the nature of LD is not singular but rather possesses a complicated structure. The previous chapter affirmed LD as a complex and multivariate phenomenon. The difficulty then becomes one of describing the form of such a multiple-component conceptualization (Doehring, 1978). A comprehensive conceptualization must incorporate as many factors as possible but, at the same time, must not become unwieldy in the sense of becoming so complicated that its heuristic value is minimal. Therefore, the purpose of this chapter is to present a framework for viewing the nature of LD that integrates a variety of theoretical positions regarding both the nature of school learning and the nature of LD.

THEORIES OF SCHOOL LEARNING

Theories of learning, teaching, and instruction and their relationship to student achievement have produced a vast literature that serves only to document the complex nature of these relationships (Dunkin & Biddle, 1974; Gage, 1976; Stephens, 1967). This complexity has been partially harnessed in models of school learning that provide a framework for viewing the interrelationships among factors producing student learning. Although emphasizing different factors, these models derived from a common source found in Carroll's (1963) model of school learning, wherein the major constructs were defined in terms of time (i.e., time spent learning or time needed to learn). In a recent review, Carroll (1984) traced the development and progress of the model and emphasized how the model shifted the focus from a fixed time condition to a fixed achievement condition with time as a manipulable variable.

Carroll (1963) conceived the degree of learning to be a function of the ratio of the amount of time the learner actually spends on the learning task to the total amount of time needed as follows:

$$\frac{\text{Degree of}}{\text{Learning}} = \frac{\text{(time actually spent on task)}}{\text{(time needed to learn task)}}$$

Research evidence has emphasized the important role played by the allocation and use of school time in determining learning outcomes (Anderson, 1984; Borg, 1980; Caldwell, Hutt, & Graeber, 1982; Karweit, 1980). Although time is considered the critical variable, the elements representing time include a wide array of constructs. For example, time needed for learning is determined by (a) aptitude, (b) ability to understand instruction, and (c) quality of instruction while time actually spent on learning is determined by (a) opportunity (i.e., allocated time) and (b) perseverance (i.e., amount of time student is "willing" to spend on learning).

Models derived from Carroll's (1963) basic formulation attempted to expand and to amplify the determinants of both time variables. Bloom (1976), for example, included under the aptitude dimension two types of prerequisites: (a) cognitive entry behaviors and (b) affective entry behaviors. The quality of instruction factor has been expanded by Cooley and Leinhardt (1980) to include:

1. opportunity — which follows Carroll's (1963) notion of how time is spent
2. motivators
3. instructional events (e.g., the content, frequency, quality, and duration of instructional interactions)
4. structure (i.e., the level of organization)

This structure factor has been incorporated into a model that included the entire context of instruction and how school and teacher variables influence student achievement (Centra & Potter, 1980).

The quality of schooling is a primary contextual variable that focuses on the actual amount of schooling (i.e., days and hours) as well as the time allocated to curriculum activity (Borg, 1980; Hyman, Wright, & Reed, 1975; Wiley, 1976). Models emphasizing the quantity of schooling (Bennett, 1978; Harnischfeger & Wiley, 1976) also incorporated the idea of total active learning time (i.e., time engaged in learning). Within this framework, Berliner (1979) developed a model that suggests achievement to be a function of student aptitudes, teacher behavior, and classroom learning environment. The model developed from the large-scale Beginning Teacher Evaluation Study (Fisher, et al., 1980) where several key findings emerged:

1. different amounts of time were allocated to different subject matter areas (e.g., reading) by different teachers
2. students learned more in subject areas to which greater amounts of time were allocated
3. large differences in students' engaged time were observed both within and across classrooms
4. students who were engaged in learning for greater proportions of the allocated time learned more
5. student learning was maximized when more of the student's time was spent engaged in successful learning experiences
6. a variety of teaching practices were associated with higher degrees of engaged time

The classroom learning component was defined by Academic Learning Time (ALT) whose four elements included:

1. time allocated to instruction
2. time engaged in instruction
3. student success rate
4. task relevance

The ALT is, in turn, a function of classroom instructional processes and total classroom environment (Anderson, 1984; Fisher et al., 1980; Romberg, 1980). Thus, ALT is defined as the proportion of engaged time in which the student is experiencing a high degree of success.

THEORIES OF LEARNING DISABILITIES

Most proposed theories of LD have not satisfactorily brought closure to understanding LD's basic nature. Wong (1979a) suggested that theories of LD are weak because of their (a) unidimensional conceptualizations and (b) narrow and isolated context. For example, most early theoretical concepts proposed single-paradigm causes (e.g., Birch & Belmont's, 1964, intersensory integration; Clements', 1966, minimal brain dysfunction; Frostig & Horne's, 1964, visual perceptual problems; Kephart's, 1969, perceptual motor mismatch; Kirk & Kirk's, 1971, psycholinguistic deficits;

Myklebust's, 1964, psychoneurological learning disability, and the like) that were confined to specific areas of deficiency and could not explain a broad range of LD behavior. Later conceptualizations (e.g., Ross, 1976, selective attention deficits; Vellutino's, 1979, verbal deficits hypothesis; and so on), although broader in scope than earlier theories, remained basically singular notions that still provided a circumscribed focus that lacked the breadth to encompass the entire LD phenomenon.

With the realization that LD represented primarily a school-based problem, as opposed to either mental retardation or behavior disorders that can exist independently outside of school, there was increased attention paid to extrinsic variables (e.g., school) rather than intrinsic variables as possibly primary contributors to LD. These later conceptualizations, for example, Adelman's (1971) interactional model, Bateman's (1974) teaching disorders, Cohen's (1971) notion of dyspedagogia, viewed LD within the framework of schooling and the teacher–learning process. Yet, these conceptions were also, in a sense, unidimensional since they focused on deficient aspects of the teaching–learning process as the primary cause of LD and did not recognize the possibility of intrinsic variables as contributing factors.

Recent theoretical statements have provided a more comprehensive perspective than those found in single-paradigm conceptualizations that emphasized either process or educational factors. Torgesen's (1977) "inactive learner" notion, which suggests that the LD child lacks efficient learning strategies, in an example. By postulating a generalized performance deficit underlying LD, Torgesen's (1977) view can probably incorporate both intrinsic and extrinsic factors, but the nature of the interactions producing "passive learners" was not specified.

ANALYSIS OF MODELS OF SCHOOL LEARNING

Although school learning is the result of a complex amalgamation of factors, learning, at the most general level, can be conceived of as the product of three classes of variables: student attributes, environmental influences, and instructional features. Student attributes include general elements such as (a) cognitive abilities that include both aptitude (Hopkins & Bracht, 1975; McCall, Appelbaum, & Hogarty, 1973) and achievement (Bracht & Hopkins, 1972; Hilton, 1979), (b) psychomotor abilities (Cratty, 1981; Keogh, 1981), (c) affective characteristics (Hamachek, 1978; Kifer, 1975; Ringness, 1975), and (d) sex (Garai & Scheinfeld, 1968; Maccoby & Jacklin, 1974). Besides these general characteristics, individual differences in learning ability are also related to more specific variables like:

1. locus of control (Fanelli, 1977; Joe, 1971)
2. achievement motivation (Atkinson & Feather, 1966; McClelland, Atkinson, Clark, & Lowell, 1953)

3. cognitive style (Sigel & Coop, 1974)
4. conceptual tempo (Bentler & McClain, 1976; Kagan & Kagan, 1970)
5. psychological differentiation (Witkin, Moore, Goodenough, & Cox, 1977)
6. anxiety (Sarason, Lighthall, Davidson, Waite, & Ruebush, 1960; Speilberger, 1966)
7. attribution patterns (Weiner, 1977)
8. attitudes (Backman & Secord, 1968)
9. curiosity (Berlyne, 1965)

The environmental component contains elements related to general family characteristics (Freeburg & Payne, 1967; Hess, 1970; Hunt, 1961; Marjoribanks, 1972; Stevenson, Parker, Wilkenson, Bonneveaux, & Gonzalez, 1978; Werner & Smith, 1977) and educational environments (Anderson & Walberg, 1974; Marjoribanks, 1974; Walberg, 1969, 1976; Wang & Lindvall, 1984). The variables of instruction includes the elemenst of:

1. instructional design (Bruner, 1966; Gage, 1978; Gagne, 1977; Glaser, 1976)
2. teacher behavior (Good, Biddle, & Brophy, 1975; Rosenshine, 1971, 1979; Rosenshine & Furst, 1973; Ryan, 1960; Walberg & Anderson, 1968)
3. classroom processes (Brophy & Good, 1974; Jackson, 1968)
4. instructional processes (Berliner & Gage, 1976; Joyce & Weil, 1972; Rosenshine, 1976)
5. expectations (Braun, 1976; Good, 1979; Rosenthal & Jacobson, 1968)
6. psychological context, for example, school size, class size, grouping practices, classroom structure, and the like (see Glaser, 1977; Glass, Cahen, Smith & Filby, 1982; Gump, 1978; Krantz & Risley, 1977; Schweibel & Cherlin, 1972)
7. decision making practices (Brophy & Evertson, 1976; Shavelson, 1976)
8. classroom management (Brophy & Putnam, 1979; Kounin, 1970; Schmuck & Schmuck, 1971)
9. curriculum structure, for example, process, content (Rubin, 1977; Tanner & Tanner, 1980)
10. classroom interaction (Bennett, 1976; Cohen, 1972; Withall & Lewis, 1963)

RELATIONSHIP OF VARIABLES TO SCHOOL LEARNING

The models of school learning include the primary domains and their related elements and conceptualize learning (L) as a function (f) of student attributes (S_i), environmental influences (E_j), and instructional features (I_k), where the environmental component (E_j) can be conceptualized as consisting of two parts: one emphasizing the home environment (E_{jh}), and the other the school environment (E_{js}). In sum, $L = f(S_i)$, $f(E_{j[h+s]})$, $f(I_k)$. The domains, however, are not independent and, in fact, interact with one another to produce additional interactive terms that must be incorporated for a full description of the learning process. Thus, a simple additive model is not satisfactory. For example, there is evidence for:

1. an S_{ijh} interaction (Bloom, 1964; Fraser, 1959; Lightfoot 1979)
2. an $S_i E_{js}$ interaction (Keeves, 1972; Walberg & Anderson, 1968; Wang & Lindvall, 1984)
3. an $S_i I_k$ interaction, for example, aptitude by treatment interaction (Bracht, 1970; Cronbach & Snow, 1977; Messick, 1976), and
4. an $S_i E_j I_k$ interaction.

By including the interaction components, the resulting multiplicative model assumes that student abilities, environment, and instruction interact with one another to afford a better prediction of learning than that which can be achieved by the first three terms alone. The expanded model would look like the following:

$$L = f[(S_i) + (E_{j[h+s]}) + (I_k) + (S_i E_{jh}) + (S_i I_k) + (E_{js} I_k) + (S_i E_j I_k)]$$

Each term in the model can be viewed as a function of the interrelationships among the postulated elements that were included for each domain. Once the individual elements for each component are known, they can then be combined to attain a value for each term in the model through a matrix operation. In the most general form, values may be calculated by:

$$X = [^x ij] = [^x 11\, ^x 21\, ^x 31 \cdots ^x n]$$
$$
\begin{array}{llllll}
^x 1 & ^x 11 & ^x 12 & ^x 13 & \cdots & ^x 1n \\
^x 2 & = {}^x 21 & ^x 22 & ^x 23 & \cdots & ^x 2n \\
= {}^x 3 & ^x 31 & ^x 32 & ^x 33 & \cdots & ^x 3n \\
\cdot & \cdot & \cdot & \cdot & & \cdot \\
\cdot & \cdot & \cdot & \cdot & & \cdot \\
\cdot & \cdot & \cdot & \cdot & & \cdot \\
^x n & ^x m1 & ^x m2 & ^x m3 & \cdots & ^{xmn}
\end{array}
$$

where X = domain (e.g., S_i, E_j, or I_k) and x = factors contributing to the domain. In the case of an interaction (e.g., XY) that would be necessary for interactive components (e.g., $S_i E_j$, $S_i I_k$, $E_j I_k$), the matrix operation is the same except that values for both x and y are included in the calculation.

With the specification of a general equation that includes the primary domains, their interactions, and individual elements comprising the domains, it is possible to specify the major factors contributing to school learning. These conceptualizations must now be related to the critical variable of time (Fredrick & Walberg, 1980) as reflected in Carroll's (1963) model. Recall that:

$$L = \frac{f\,(\text{time actually spent on task})}{f\,(\text{time needed to learn task})}$$

$$= f\,\frac{Ta}{Tn}$$

If learning (L) is assumed comparable to Academic Learning Time (ALT) and Ta is assumed related to influences *on* learning (extrinsic) while Tn is assumed related to influences *in* learning, that is, intrinsic (Jensen, 1967), then the relationship between Ta and Tn can be conceptualized as defining the amount of time engaged on academic tasks (perseverance) and provide three possible outcomes:

$$
\begin{aligned}
& \quad\quad\; Ta < Tn \\
ALT = {}& Ta = Tn \\
& \quad\quad\; Ta > Tn
\end{aligned}
$$

When Ta = Tn (indicating that the student is willing to persevere to the extent needed for learning), an optimal learning situation is achieved but does not always occur because of changes in the value of either Ta or Tn or both. Because achievement is influenced by the amount of time engaged in academic pursuits (Anderson, 1984; Denham & Lieberman, 1980), Ta = Tn produces the desired degree of learning as does Ta > Tn since Millman, Bieger, Klag, and Pine (1983) found that increasing time on task will not alter degree of learning or learning rate, while Ta < Tn would be associated with a less than optimal degree of learning and, consequently, less achievement. Gettinger (1984) showed that there was a significant negative relationship between the Ta/Tn discrepancy and degree of learning. Approximately 30% to 65% of the variation in learning measures was explained by discrepancy scores.

Variations in Ta and Tn can be accounted for by distributing the components of the general, multiplicative model into the Carroll scheme. For Ta, the components dealing with instruction and environment (particularly school setting) are most prominent, while Tn is primarily affected by student ability and the interactions with environment (particularly home settings) and instruction. These relationships may be depicted as follows:

$$Ta = f[(E_{j[h+s]}) + I_k + (E_{js}I_k)] \text{ and}$$
$$Tn = f[S_i + (S_iE_{jh}) + (S_iI_k)]$$

If the $S_iE_jI_k$ interaction can be assumed to influence Ta and Tn equally, then its effects may be cancelled, and the remaining elements may be used to assign values to Ta and Tn. These values would provide an expected value of Ta and Tn in the form:

$$ALT = \frac{Ta}{Tn} = \frac{E(Ta)}{E(Tn)}$$

By providing hypothetical expected values, it is possible to see how variations in Ta and Tn can affect ALT. Recall that the optimal situation is represented by unity (i.e., 1) so assuming, for example, that $E(Ta) = 1$ and $E(Tn) = 1$ would result in:

$$ALT = \frac{Ta}{Tn} = \frac{1}{1} = 1$$

which is the desired situation. Now, if $E(Ta) = 2$ and $E(Tn)$ remains the same (i.e., 1), then $ALT = 2$ indicating increased time on task. This increased perseverance (perhaps as a result of rewards) will not, however, produce more learning (see Millman, et al., 1983). If however, $E(Tn) = 2$ while $E(Ta)$ remained the same, then:

$$ALT = \frac{1}{2} = .50$$

suggesting that academic learning time is decreased by one-half. Thus, the level of perserverance is reduced 50%.

A MODEL OF LEARNING DISABILITIES

Thus far the model outlined is descriptive of "normal" learning and can be used to account for individual variation that is within the boundaries that define "average" achievement levels (i.e., $\pm$ one standard deviation). Consequently, children in school would probably reveal restricted ranges for Tn, and any discrepancy between Ta and Tn would not vary over a wide range but rather fall within circumscribed boundaries (i.e., defining normal learning). The primary reason is the dynamic nature of schooling, which suggests that modifications in instruction (i.e., I_k) will be made periodically in an effort to reach a state of equilibrium (i.e., $ALT = 1$).

For "normal" children, $E(Tn)$ probably would not reveal wide variation since it is constrained by factors that operate within "normal" boundaries. Consequently, a child may be near the top or bottom of a distribution but, nevertheless, remains within "normal" limits as shown in Figure 15–1.

Thus, although variation may be found in individual factors contributing to learning ability, if most fall within the boundaries delineated

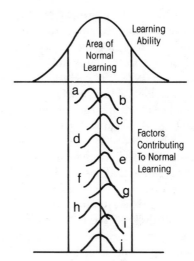

FIGURE 15–1
Factors contributing to
normal learning.

by normal learning (i.e., ± one standard deviation), then, on average, it will be nearly the case that Ta = Tn (or, at least, reasonably close to the optimal state).

With LD recognized as a school-based disorder wherein a child experiences difficulty on academic tasks and, ultimately, fails to achieve as expected, a major contributor is the failure to respond to instruction so that ALT is reduced significantly. Within the framework provided by Ta and Tn, LD can be conceived as an increasing disparity (i.e., discrepancy) between Ta and Tn by about third grade. For Tn, the disbributions of factors contributing to normal learning place the potential LD child at the lower end or below the area for normal learning as depicted in Figure 15–2.

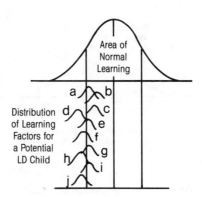

FIGURE 15–2
Distribution of factors
in an LD child.

When the distribution of abilities places the child at or near the low end of the normal learning area, the value of Ta needs to be increased. This will probably not occur, however, as shown in reports revealing that students spend little actual time reading during reading time (Allington, 1980; Durkin, 1978, 1979; Hall, Delquardi, Greenwood, & Thurston, 1982; Rosenshine, 1980; Thurlow, Graden, Ysseldyke, & Algozzine, 1984). Additionally, classroom instruction is typically targeted at the mean since, on average, this will insure that the greatest number of children will be in a situation where Ta = Tn (Kuethe, 1968). Thus, the value of Ta is not likely to reveal much variation in the average regular class, resulting in a mismatch between actual instruction and needed instructional level as shown in Figure 15–3.

The result is a situation where Ta < Tn within the "normal" learning situation. With Ta < Tn, the consequences are limited perseverance and a reduction in the degree of learning shown by approximately 16% of the students who represent those falling at or below one standard deviation below the mean. The time actually spent on learning is reduced significantly because the two primary criteria, opportunity (time allowed for task) and quality of instruction, are not met (Bloom, 1980). This situation represents the precursor of LD.

Walker (1980) proposed a theoretical formulation based upon complexity that can be used to explain why the situation (i.e., Ta < Tn) is not likely to improve on its own. This is shown in Figure 15–4.

The instructional mismatch shifts the optimal complexity level (where tasks are interesting and motivation is high) towards complexity overload in learning tasks (where they are viewed as confusing and difficult, thus reducing motivation) that results in a child who quits trying and becomes discouraged (Walker, 1980). Thus, a vicious cycle is formed and the consequences are found in reduced ALT when, in fact, the child requires an increase in Ta to allow for optimal learning based upon the increase in Tn. It is not likely that this situation will self-correct. Gettinger (1984) showed

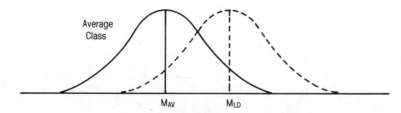

M_{AV} = Targeted Level of Instruction for Average Regular Class
M_{LD} = Level of Instruction Needed by a Potential LD Child

FIGURE 15–3
Discrepancy between classroom instruction and needs of an LD child.

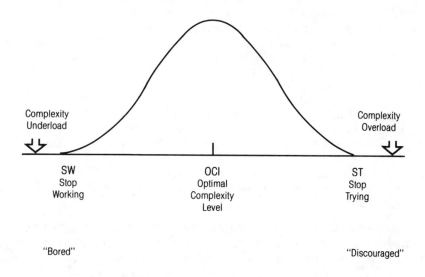

FIGURE 15–4
Depiction of psychological complexity theory.

that Tn accounted for about 90% of the variance in learning compared to 10% for Ta. Thus, the direct effect of Tn was greater than that of Ta.

LEARNING DISABILITIES AND THE DISASSOCIATED LEARNER

Although these notions account for the lowered achievement in about 16% of the population, how did the 5% or so (at least, theoretically) of that group come to be classified as LD? Besides the elements involved in producing differences in student abilities (S_i) for normal learning, about 5% of the low perseverance group will have additional factors operating that interfere with their learning ability. Among the factors assumed to be correlated with LD are:

1. maturational lag (Ames, 1968a; Bender, 1957; Kinsbourne, 1973a)
2. genetic variation (Owen, Adams, Forrest, Stolz, & Fisher, 1971; Silver, 1971)
3. minimal brain dysfunction (Kinsbourne, 1983; Rie & Rie, 1980)
4. biochemical irregularities (Mayron, 1979; Weiss, 1982; Wender, 1976)
5. physiological differences (deQuiros, 1976; Green & Perlman, 1971; Steg & Rapoport, 1975)
6. neuropsychological variables (Gaddes, 1980; Knights & Bakker, 1976)
7. nutritional factors (Conners, 1980; Cravioto & DeLicardie, 1975)
8. perinatal events (Balow, Rubin, & Rosen, 1975, 1976)

9. temperamental differences (Thomas & Chess, 1977)
10. ecological factors (Mayron, 1978)
11. cerebral specialization (Guyer & Freidman, 1975)
12. emotional/social differences (Bryan, 1981; Connolly, 1971; Kronnick, 1981)
13. linguistic deficits (Butler & Wallach, 1982; Vogel, 1975)
14. motor problems (Keogh, 1982)
15. visual perceptual problems (Frostig, 1975; Kavale, 1982)
16. auditory perceptual problems (Kavale, 1981b; Wepman, 1975a)
17. integrative deficits (Kavale, 1980a; Senf, 1972)
18. psycholinguistic deficits (Kass, 1966; McLeod, 1967)
19. cognitive disabilities (Keogh & Donlon, 1972; Myklebust, Bannochie, & Killen, 1971)
20. memory problems (Torgesen, 1978, 1982)
21. attention deficits (Keogh & Margolis, 1976; Kinsbourne & Caplan, 1979; Tarver & Hallahan, 1974)

These correlates of LD add another dimension to Tn that serve to increase the time needed to learn. Any of these correlates possesses the possibility of causing LD by itself. This possibility may be conceptualized in a manner similar to what physicists term "catastrophe theory" where a single event is of sufficient magnitude to create significant change in the state of equilibrium. The result is the addition of another factor(s) to the components found in the normal learning equation as follows:

$$Tn = f[(S_i + (S_iSE_{jh}) + (S_iI_k) + LD_c]$$

where LD_c = correlates of learning disability and may be obtained through the same matrix operation described earlier. Thus, for a child possessing LD correlates, another value would be added to the Tn equation that serves to increase the value of Tn.

For LD, the total model would look as follows:

$$ALT = \frac{Ta = f[(E_{j[h+s]}) + I_k + (E_{js}I_k)]}{Tn = f[S_i + (S_iE_{jh}) + (S_iI_k) + LD_c]}$$

where $E(Ta) = < 1$ and $E(Tn) = > 1$. To separate LD from low achievement, LD may be defined as the point where the discrepancy between Ta and Tn is of a magnitude that indicates little (if any) learning taking place. The problematic nature of discrepancy (see Reynolds, 1985; Schulte & Borich, 1984) is now put in a different perspective and many of the associated difficulties (e.g., regression) are eliminated.

It would be difficult to specifiy precise values for the Ta/Tn discrepancy defining LD, but if ALT is reduced to perhaps 10 to 20%, actual learning time would be so depressed in comparison to the optimal state (i.e., 100%) that the child is certain to experience difficulty with academic tasks and to reveal little achievement gain over time. For example, consider the following values for Ta and Tn:

1. if $E(Ta) = .75$ and $E(Tn) = 5$, then $ALT = \dfrac{.75}{5} = .15$

2. if $E(Ta) = .50$ and $E(Tn) = 4$, then $ALT = \dfrac{.50}{4} = .125$

3. if $E(Ta) = .25$ and $E(Tn) = 3$, then $ALT = \dfrac{.25}{3} = .08$

4. if $E(Ta) = 1$ and $E(Tn) = 6$, then $ALT = \dfrac{1}{6} = .17$

These examples all point to the fact that both factors (Ta and Tn) may make a contribution to the etiology of LD. For the child who will be classified LD, it is probably the case that Tn will always be > 1 and its value contingent upon how much normal variation is present as well as the number of LD correlates operating. But as illustration 4 suggests, even under optimum instruction, the negative influences may be great enough to disrupt the amount of time engaged in learning.

Regardless of the values for Ta and Tn found for any particular child, if the discrepancy limits learning time to perhaps 20% of normal, then the child becomes essentially disassociated from the formal learning process. Within the school setting, when instructional practices are not satisfactory for a particular child, thus reducing the time actually engaged in academic tasks, and normal variation plus correlative conditions increase the time required for academic learning, such a mismatch produces a discrepancy that reduces ALT significantly and results in a child disassociating from school learning. This disassociation represents the foundation of LD.

CONCLUSION

The basic nature of LD has proven to be an elusive problem for the field. The many proposed hypotheses regarding the essence of LD have generally failed to provide a comprehensive statement regarding the nature of LD. The many proposed hypotheses about LD provide only a singular viewpoint that usually emphasizes either intrinsic or extrinsic factors. Such models lack the explanatory power for the full range of LD behaviors and result in oversimplification or what Kaplan (1964) better terms "undercomplication" in the sense that something important is being overlooked. The result may be a false sense of closure.

Snow (1973) outlined the elements of theory construction and emphasized the role of metatheory, the description of theory itself. This chapter presented such a metatheoretical framework by incorporating elements of school learning theory and LD concepts to provide a structure for describing the nature of LD which, in this case, views the LD child as a disassociated learner. The resulting description is not a model (physical, semantic, mathematical, or theoretical) in the scientific sense but is closer to what Black (1962) terms an "archetype," that is, a systematic synthesis of ideas, by analogical extension, through which a domain to which those ideas do not literally apply is described. The resulting archetype may possess some practical value in providing a different perspective to the problems of definition, operational criteria, prevalence, and diagnosis found in LD.

By combining knowledge of the normal teaching–learning process with information about factors operating in LD, a description was offered that logically conceptualized how some children disassociate themselves from academic learning and come to be termed LD. It should not be viewed, however, as a metaphysical description of LD but rather as a heuristic device that possesses enough implicative power to be a useful speculative apparatus for explaining the basic nature of LD.

PART III

Evaluation and Assessment of LD

R egardless of what you believe a learning disability to be, at some point it is necessary to determine who might be learning disabled. While conceptualizing about learning disorders is of academic interest, the pragmatic demands of service delivery make it necessary to formulate rational means for identifying LD individuals. The purpose of this section is to provide perspective on the diagnostic process in learning disorders.

PL 94-142 formalized evaluation procedures in delineating the requirements for an individualized educational program (IEP). The law specified participants, parent participation, and procedural safeguards (i.e., due process). For example, the following participants are mandated: a representative of the public educational agency (other than the child's teacher), the child's teacher, one or both parents, the child (when appropriate) and other individuals (when appropriate). Because of the confusion and controversy surrounding LD, a separate set of supplemental regulations was issued for the evaluation of "specific learning disabilities" (*Federal Register,* 1977). Specific learning disabilities were defined as follows:

> "Specific learning disability" means a disorder in one or more of the basic psychological processes involved in understanding or in using language, spoken or written, which may manifest itself in an imperfect ability to listen, think, speak, read, write, spell, or to do mathematical calculations. The term includes such conditions as perceptual handicaps, brain injury, minimal brain dysfunction, dyslexia, and developmental aphasia. The term does not include children who have

learning problems which are primarily the result of visual, hearing, or motor handicaps, of mental retardation, or of environment, cultural, or economic disadvantage.

The special procedures for evaluating specific learning disabilities included:

I. Additional Team Members: In addition to the required team members previously listed, the evaluation team for children with specific disabilities must include:
1. the child's regular teacher
    a. if a child does not have a regular teacher, regular classroom teacher qualified to teach a child of his or her age
    b. for a child of less than school age, an individual qualified by the state educational agency to teach a child of his or her age
2. at least one person qualified to conduct individual diagnostic examinations of children, such as a school psychologist, a speech–language pathologist, or a remedial reading teacher (BEH, 1978)

II. The following criteria are used by the team to determine that a child has a specific learning disability:
1. The child does not achieve commensurate with his or her age and ability levels in one or more of seven areas when provided with learning experiences appropriate for the child's age and ability levels.
2. The child has a severe discrepancy between achievement and intellectual ability in one or more of the following areas:
    a. oral expression
    b. listening comprehension
    c. written expression
    d. basic reading skill
    e. reading comprehension
    f. mathematics calculation
    g. mathematics reasoning.

The team may not identify a child as having a specific learning disability if the severe discrepancy between ability and achievement is primarily the result of (1) a visual, hearing, or motor handicap; (2) mental retardation; (3) emotional disturbance; or (4) environmental, cultural, or economic disadvantage.

III. Observation: In the case of a suspected learning disability, at least one team member other than the child's regular teacher must observe the child's academic performance in the regular classroom setting. If the child is of less than school age or out of school, then a team member must observe the child in an environment appropriate for a child of that age.

IV. The regulations require that the multidisciplinary team prepare a written report of the evaluation which must include the following statements:
1. whether the child has a specific learning disability
2. the basis for making the determination
3. the relevant behavior noted during the observation of the child
4. the relationship of that behavior to the child's academic functioning
5. the educationally relevant medical findings, if any
6. whether there is a severe discrepancy between achievement and ability that is not correctable without special education and related services
7. the determination of the team concerning the effects of environmental, cultural, or economic disadvantage

Each team member must certify in writing whether the report reflects his or her conclusion. If a team member disagrees with the evaluation, then that individual must submit a separate statement presenting his or her own conclusions.

The first chapter in this section, Chapter 16, focuses on neurological assessment. Historically, the LD field has based much of its thinking upon the assumption that learning problems are a function of neurological dysfunction. Chapter 16 reviews basic information about neurological functioning and then focuses on the nature, significance, and limitations of neurological assessment.

The next two chapters examine and evaluate the responsibilities of members of the multidisciplinary team in diagnosing LD. The special procedures for evaluating LD mandate that the multidisciplinary team include "at least one person qualified to conduct individual diagnostic examinations." In a majority of instances, this person is the school psychologist, and the role of the school psychologist in assessing and identifying LD is outlined in Chapter 17. The responsibilities, practices, and directions for school psychologists in screening and assessment are reviewed. A variety of issues about tests and testing are then discussed in relation to LD identification and the role of the school psychologist. Given the strong association between learning disabilities and language disorders (see Chapters 5 and 6), the speech–language pathologist may be an important member of the evaluation team.

While there is controversy surrounding definitions of LD, there is also dispute about appropriate identification criteria. A variety of criteria have been operationalized, but the primary criterion has become underachievement. Underachievement is defined as a discrepancy between expected achievement (usually assessed with an aptitude measure, e.g., IQ) and actual achievement (usually obtained from a standardized achievement test). Although seemingly straightforward, a number of methods exist for determining a discrepancy, and each possesses both assets and liabilities. In Chapter 18 we examine the various procedures and discuss the advantages and disadvantages inherent in each. Although these psychometrically based methods appear scientific, they are fraught with difficulties that limit their usefulness in determining LD eligibility. Chapter 19 reviews the contribution of each multidisciplinary team member and suggests the speech–language pathologist may play a significant role in the team process. A general discussion that focuses on team assessment and team rememdiation design follows.

We have previously discussed the goal of effective assessment (i.e., a good remedial program) and why it is so difficult to achieve. In Chapter 20 we present guidelines for adequate assessment and describe the case-typing (i.e., student profile) approach as a framework for evaluating the LD individual. Case-typing involves qualitative and clinical analyses as well as quantitative methods and aims at providing understandable and directed information.

In Chapter 21 we discuss multicultural considerations in assessing LD. Although most definitions exclude children whose "learning problems are primarily the result of environmental, cultural, or economic disadvantage," the boundaries are so poorly defined that it is difficult to make a reliable differential diagnosis. A review of the issues associated with identification, assessment, and treatment that suggest the difficulties inherent in differentiating LD and cultural difference are presented. The role of the multicultural family is discussed and the findings of a survey of multicultural families' perceptions of school service are presented.

CHAPTER 16

Neurological Assessment

Robert B. Johnson

O ver the past years, there has been increasing interest in the possible role that the brain plays in a variety of behavior and learning disabilities. Strauss and Lehtinen (1947) were among the first investigators to ascribe a neuorological basis to behavioral features such as short attention span, distractibility, perseveration, and impulsiveness; and this conceptualization continues to influence the LD field (Cruickshank, 1983; Dykman, Ackerman, Holcomb, & Bondreau, 1983). Since that time, a number of basic and applied studies have been concerned with whether such academic and behavioral problems are a function of defective brain cell function or whether they are more related to extrinsic influences such as poor teaching techniques, psychosocial and cultural deprivation, and/or other emotional factors. Such a complex question has not been easy to resolve. The neurological exam is but one of many critical assessment tools attempting to provide information regarding the underlying factors contributing to behavioral and learning disabilities. This chapter will describe the neurological assessment from a multidisciplinary perspective. It will review basic neurological facts pertinent to learning disabilities and focus on the nature, significance, and limitations of the neurological assessment as it is presently utilized in clinical practice.

This chapter originally appeared as an article by **Robert Johnston** in *Learning Disabilities: An Interdisciplinary Journal* (Vol. I, 1982) and was adapted by permission of Grune & Stratton for inclusion in this *Handbook*.

BASIC NEUROLOGICAL CONSIDERATION

At the outset it is necessary to highlight a few basic facts concerning the nature of brain function, dysfunction, and clinical manifestations relevant to children with behavior and learning disabilities. Conceptually, such alleged brain involvement has traditionally been referred to as "damage." This term inaccurately implies that areas of the brain are scarred and /or absent. More recently, the term "dysfunction" has been utilized, which more appropriately reflects the underlying physiological or biochemical malfunctions that may be present. It may be helpful to picture the brain as a large, complex switchboard, which, in the case of the learning-disabled child, has a few wiring problems. Certain connections have been disrupted while most of the switchboard remains intact and functions in an appropriate fashion.

The exact nature of the underlying brain dysfunction is difficult to discern. It is known that brain involvement may be of a limited nature (focal) or affect a number of brain areas (diffuse). Clinical manifestations of focal involvement, then, would be limited to one or two isolated deficits, such as poor motor coordination and clumsiness, without any other evidence of neurological deficit, such as cognitive difficulties. The child with a diffuse distribution of brain dysfunction may exhibit a range of deficits including clumsiness, attentional peculiarities, left-right confusion, and reading disability — symptoms that are not necessary causally related to each other.

Actual location of such brain involvement in behavior and learning disorders has been studied by Nichols and Chen (1981), and areas of the brain such as the diencephalon, cerebellum, vestibular apparatus, and cerebral cortex have been implicated. The underlying cellular mechanisms contributing to neurological dysfunction involve complex anatomical, biochemical, and physiological mechanisms. Deficits in monoamine metabolism, underarousal of the reticular activating system (Wender, 1971), and general maturational lag (Kinsbourne, 1973b) have been suggested in learning and behavior disabilities.

Clinical manifestations of underlying brain dysfunction noted on neurological examination may be of two types. In one type, the aberration, such as paralysis or loss of vision, is abnormal regardless of age. The second type involves a maturational delay and is manifested by a level of functioning that is lower than expected for a given age; for example, a 6-year-old child with coordination abilities that are more consistent with that of a 3- or 4-year-old. However, it is possible that certain neurological deficits may be modified or omitted through a compensatory maturational process. Very simply, the brain may reroute pathways that underlie certain tasks from abnormal sites to other normal areas of the brain.

NORMAL NEURODEVELOPMENT

Gradual improvement in neurological function, such as is normally seen in infants who are rapidly gaining skills in walking, talking, and manipulating, comes about through the process of neurological maturation. Basically, maturation involves complex anatomical, biochemical, and physiological changes within the nervous system that improve cellular function and increase the number and complexity of interconnections among nerve cells. Impressive examples of developmental changes are seen in the motor (movement) system, where progress occurs in proximal-distal and head-to-foot (cephalocaudal) directions. Proximal-distal progression is noted in infancy by the gradual sophistication of the child's manipulative abilities, which begin with shoulder movement and extend over a period of time to increasingly sophisticated grasp capabilities, ultimately resulting in an adult level of fine motor coordination, such as that seen in handwriting and performance of intricate surgery. An example of the cephalocaudal progress is noted in the infant's initial ability to maintain head control, which is sequentially followed by improvement in trunk control, capacity to sit, integration of leg control, and the ultimate ability to walk by the end of the first year.

A neurodevelopmental assessment attempts to measure the improvement that gradually and sequentially occurs as the result of this ongoing process of maturation. Gesell (Knobloch & Pasamanick, 1975), among others, delineated developmental milestones during the first five years of life in motor, adaptive, language, and psychological spheres. Measurement of further maturational changes in the school-age child has traditionally fallen within the realm of the psychologist and educator in intellectual, cognitive, and perceptual spheres. Clinical neurology has focused its attention on other developmental manifestations, particularly in motor, sensory, and laterality spheres.

A developmental phenomenon exemplified well in the motor system is the inhibition of extraneous or overflow movements. From early stages of infancy, the nervous system strives to inhibit extraneous movements that occur in association with other voluntary movements. For instance, a 5-year-old concentrating on finger movement in one hand often will involuntarily mirror these movements in the resting hand. This overflow phenomenon is normal up until approximately age 9. In sensory spheres, a number of changes take place as the result of maturation. A child below the age of 5 who is touched simulatneously on the cheek and the hand may not perceive the stimulus on the hand. This phenomenon, known as rostral dominance (i.e., extinguishing the distal stimulus), disappears around 5 or 6 years of age as the result of continued neurological maturation.

In terms of laterality, a child usually develops a consistent preference for hand, eye, and leg use by age 5. In addition, the child's ability to identify left and right follows a sequential developmental pattern.

AN OVERVIEW OF NEUROLOGICAL ASSESSMENT

Typically, the traditional neurological examination detects gross abnormalities and delineates the extent of obvious neurological impairments. For the most part, however, this approach leaves undetected more subtle and developmental neurological deficits that may be associated with lesser degrees of brain dysfunction, such as is alleged to exist in learning disabilities. The traditional neurological exam results are usually normal in the learning disabled child, reflecting this inattention to the subtle and maturational aspects. While the traditional exam is well accepted and considered to be an authoritative guide to the general status of the nervous system, the developmental, nontraditional elements of the assessment are less well standardized and have not yet warranted the confidence that has been ascribed to the standard examination. For instance, if the traditional exam shows weakness and loss of feeling on one side of the body, this most likely indicates significant neurological involvement in the brain or spinal cord. Subtle findings, such as a deficient ability to touch the thumb to each of the four fingers in a smooth and sequential manner, are of less certain neurological significance.

MULTIDISCIPLINARY PERSPECTIVE

There has been considerable confusion and a lack of communication among professionals regarding the appropriate role of the neurodevelopmental assessment in psychoeducational interventions. It is quite common to expect the consultant physician to "do a good neurological examination to rule out brain damage." Unfortunately, no definitive battery of tests has proved a reliable resource for such an objective. It remains possible at this time to obtain a normal examination and not be able to categorically rule out certain types of subtle neurological dysfunction.

Some parents and counselors who have obtained complete psychoeducational assessments insist on holding off remediation recommendations until the "complete answer" can be obtained through the neurological examination. It may even be required that a neurological examination, performed by a neurologist, be completed prior to consideration of appropriate educational class placement. This requirement obviates the realistic need to incorporate results of neurological assessment with findings of other disciplines and claims for the examination a magical quality, portraying it as the definitive piece that will ultimately complete the puzzle. This is a portrayal that borders on fantasy.

It should be remembered that normal behavior and learning do not necessarily reflect a normal brain, just as disturbed learning and behavior do not necessarily imply a dysfunctioning brain. It is the role of the neurological assessment to identify the status of underlying neurological function, which may contribute to learning and/or behavorial difficulties. The magical qualities that are sometimes ascribed to the neurological assessment, with its capacity to "rule out brain damage," need to be dispelled. Its limitations prohibit it from being the final authoritative statement, and its findings need to be cautiously integrated with those of educational, psychological, and other investigtions.

CLINICAL ISSUES

Clinican Variability

In reality, a neurological examination is performed throughout the medical community by a variety of physicians with different backgrounds, interests, and levels of expertise. Consequently, a given child may obtain any one or a combination of the following "labels," depending on the examiner: "All boy who will outgrow it," "perfectly normal," "emotional disturbance," "late bloomer," "perceptual handicap," "neurotic inhibition of learning," "minimal brain damage," or "attentional deficit disorder."

Classification Difficulties

In addition to the lack of standardized approach to assessment, difficulties arise because of the heterogeneity of learning-disabled children. Often there appears to be a frantic quest for one label that would identify the nature of the entire group's disorders. This obsession, sometimes referred to as the "Rumplestiltskin fixation" (Ross, 1968), stems from the mistaken impression that if only these children could be appropriately labeled their difficulties would be more easily resolved. In part, this represents an attempt to apply the traditional medical model to complex neuropsychological and educational issues. The hope is that once a diagnosis is established, appropriate therapy can be prescribed and a "cure" is forthcoming. Needless to say, complex and chronic behavioral and learning disabilities do not fit into this traditional medical model approach. This is not to decry attempts to identify homogenous subgroups of individuals who share etiology, characteristic features, uniform response to intervention, and predictable outcomes; indeed, this syndrome analysis approach, when successful, may promote better understanding, more effective prevention efforts, and improved intervention strategies.

Generally, classification difficulties have been promoted and perpetuated by isolated discipline approaches and by failure to integrate efforts in an effective interdisciplinary way. Many of the classification attempts involve descriptive terms (hyperkinesis); others implicate etiology (minimal brain dysfunction, perpetual handicap); and each may reflect the particular bias or approach of the designator. Few of the many labels generated over the past 20 years have remained viable due to imprecise meaning, lack of significant remedial or therapeutic implication, and or limited prognostic capability. A brief review of some of the classification attempts will highlight the difficulties.

Hyperkinetic syndrome or *hyperactivity* is a term that has at least three meanings as a diagnostic entity: (a) motor restlessness (b) motor restlessness and attention peculiarities such as impulsivity and short attention span, or (c) learning disabilities in addition to the aforementioned motor and attentional difficulties. Thus, when a parent or teacher queries the physician as to whether a child is hyperactive, he or she may be asking far more than whether or not the child's motor activity is increased. The diagnostic entity *hyperkinesis* is also limited in scope since it excludes those children with academic and attentional problems who are normally active or hypoactive. The definition of "increased activity" is fraught with ambiguity. The term *perceptual handicap,* while applicable to some, oversimplifies the nature of the problems and disregards a large percentage of learning-disabled children who lack well-identified perceptual difficulties. As mentioned above, there are a number of other diagnostic labels that imply a neurological basis — for example, *minimal brain damage, minimal cerebral dysfunction —* without any clear, direct evidence of such brain abnormalties. Such terms inaccurately conjure up a mental image of a brain glutted with scars and/or holes. The term "damage" is quite stigmatizing, possibly implying a hopeless situation which may result in less-than-enthusiastic educational approaches. While a teacher may feel comfortable providing remedial help for a child with a learning difficulty, he or she may feel totally helpless in a situation where "damage" allegedly precludes successful remediation. While the term *minimal cerebral dysfunction* has gained wider acceptance because of its less stigmatizing nature, it also suffers from imprecision. *Minimal* is certainly relative only to the more severe forms of brain dysfunction, for example, mental retardation and cerebral palsy, and does not appropriately refer to the degree of potential handicap (which is by no means "minimal"). *Cerebral* refers to the cortical areas of the brain and not technically to the lower brain centers. This disregards that area of the brain comprising the reticular activating system, which has been implicated in attentional difficulties. The term *dysfunction* is certainly more acceptable than "damage" and encompasses a wide range of abnormalties that may involve biochemical, physiological, and/or maturational delay factors.

The term *psychoneurological learning disability* (Myklebust & Boshes, 1960) focused on learning disability as a common thread among a group of children. It also emphasized the educational role in addressing the problem. *Attentional deficit disorder* is of more recent vintage and reflects the attentional difficulties that are prominent and commonly present in some but not all learning-disabled children. Because of the variation in the degree of motor activity within the attentional deficit disorder category, it has been further subdivided into those with hyperkinesis and those without.

It is most likely that learning-disabled children make up several subgroups with a variety of etiologies, clinical features, and prognostic implications. Attempts to treat these groups as though they were homogeneous leads only to further frustration and misunderstanding.

Features of Behavior and Learning Disabilities

Confusion rests with the descriptive terms *hyperactivity* and *hyperkinesis,* which are used traditionally to describe a number of behaviors that may be stimulus-bound, lacking in consistent direction, and associated with frequent shifts in focus. The child shifts attention from one object to the other in a somewhat "driven" fashion. Because the degree of hyperactivity is difficult to quantify and may be relative to the observer, the hyperactive child in one classroom may be the child of average activity in another. The activity may not necessarily be increased but may be noticed because of its bothersome or inappropriate nature. Some children are temperamentally more active than others (Thomas, Chess, & Birch, 1968) and may fall at the far end of the spectrum of normal activity, which is not related to dysfunction at all. Finally, hyperactivity itself may not reflect an underlying neurological dysfunction but may be a response to such factors as anxiety, boredom, or hunger.

Other deficits that appear to be related to attention, interpersonal relations, and/or control of impulses and emotion include the following:

1. Short attention span — inability to focus on pertinent activities because of a low threshold to distracting extraneous stimuli
2. Perseveration — another attentional peculiarity, denoting a failure to shift attention appropriately from one activity to another
3. Impulsivity — evident in many actions initiated without prior thought and usually lacking in judgment.

Classic characteristics of a learning disability are found in an otherwise normally intelligent child who has specific deficits of learning in reading, mathematics, and/or spelling. There may also be other non-verbal learning deficiencies, such as social imperception (Wender, 1971), graphic learning deficiency, defective body image, and spatial orientation inadequacy.

The relationship between behavior and learning disabilities is complex and involves both academic and behavioral difficulties. A child may have a primary emotional problem that secondarily affects learning capacity or a primary learning disability that leads to secondary emotional problems brought on by such factors as low self-esteem, chronic frustration, and/or a feeling of inferiority.

Central Nervous System Measurement

Direct Measures

While behavioral and learning disorders may be influenced by such factors as anxiety, depression, boredom, temperament, hunger, and poor teaching, there is a strong effort to implicate the malfunctioning brain as the culprit.

If the technical capacity existed to gauge brain function directly through the measurement of specific anatomical, biochemical, and/or electrical parameters, it would be unnecessary to subject children to further clinical examination. For instance, if one could monitor the electrophysiological patterns that are generated by a visual stimulus as it travels from the optic nerve to the occipital cortex and to other association areas throughout the brain during the reading process, one could ostensibly identify and record deficits that would demonstrate directly an underlying processing malfunction. Likewise, if one could identify and measure directly the level of appropriate chemical activity at the site of certain brain functions such as attention, motivation, and cognition, one could ostensibly define such deficiencies and presumably prescribe appropriate replacement therapy. Such technical advances are not yet available.

One commonly held misconception is that the electroencephalogram (EEG) can measure brain function directly and subsequently indicate clearly whether dysfunction exists. In actuality, the EEG simply measures electrical activity on the outer surface of the brain and has little role in identifying cognitive or perceptual disorders, attentional peculiarties, and other aspects of brain dysfunction relevant to the learning-disabled child. While the EEG may be critical in identifying convulsive disorders it has little, if any, value in the assessment of behavior and learning dysfunctions. While there have been some reports of minor EEG abnormalities in the children with learning disorders or attentional difficulties, such findings offer little or no therapeutic advantage and merely add to the stigma of "brain damage" without providing clear evidence of it. Such EEG "abnormalities" can also be found in a small percentage of normal academic achievers.

Brain scan and skull x-rays have little use in identifying subtle neurological impairments (Denckla, LeMaya, & Chapman, 1985). Other specialized studies involve auditorily and visually evoked potentials and a variety of computer-assisted brain scans that have the potential for more clearly identifying directly types of neurological impairment, but at the present time these efforts have limited clinical relevance. Because of this obvious lack of capacity to directly measure brain function, the clinician must rely on indirect means of assessing the integrity of the central nervous system.

Indirect Clinical Measures

The clinical neurological assessment is the link that attempts to establish a relationship between aberrant learning and/or behavior with evidence of underlying brain dysfunction. Two types of deficits can be identified through this assessment. The first refers to subtle abnormalities on items included in the traditional neurological exam, which are abnormal at any age. The second type of deficit refers to those deviations from age-appropriate norms that are noted in the performance of tasks on the extended neurodevelopmental (nontraditioinal) examination. Those tasks characteristically involve motor, sensory, and/or laterality spheres. The two types of deficits are sometimes referred to as "soft signs."

Limitations inherent to such "soft sign" elicitation are many. The items involving motor, sensory, and laterality spheres identify only a small part of the vast repertoire of brain functions. Simple clinical tools to assess those areas of the brain that underlie learning and behavior unfortunately are not available. It is consequently unlikely that most of the items involved in the current nontraditional neurological exam (motor, sensory, laterality spheres) have much of a causal relationship with or bearing on overriding academic difficulties. For instance, a finding of specific motor incoordination on the neurological exam may translate directly to clumsiness on the baseball field but not to reading difficulty. The key to understanding the relevance of the clinical neurological exam is to acknowledge its indirect *associative* nature, in that evidence of dysfunction in areas of the brain underlying motor, sensory, or laterality function *may* be associated with deficits in those areas of the brain that more appropriately are involved in underlying learning and behavioral disabilities.

In practical terms, there is considerable misunderstanding among professionals regarding the nature of the neurological exam used in assessing children with learning and behavior disorders. The assessment usually consists of two distinct components: the standard neurological examination, based on adult standards, and the more developmentally oriented, nontraditional (extended) examination.

CLINICAL ASSESSMENT

Before detailing the exact nature of each aspect of the clinical assessment, it may be helpful to identify the state of the art in practice. The following anecdote highlights the practical problems facing those who seek an understanding of their learning-disabled child from an array of physicians of varying backgrounds and training. The child is initially seen by the family physician, who is a competent practitioner interested primarily in adult diseases. He or she has known this child since birth and realizes that there is no history of any severe central nervous system insult during pregnancy, labor, delivery, or thereafter. The physician has the general impression that the child is of at least average intelligence, and the brief traditional neurological exam finds no gross abnormalities. It is the physician's impression, then, that the child is neurologically intact and will probably outgrow this difficulty. However, the child is referred to the local pediatrician for a second opinion. This particular pediatrician conscientiously reviews the nature of the difficulties, repeats the traditional neurological exam, which is perfectly normal, and adds an EEG, which is also normal. The parents are again "reassured" that the nervous system is intact and that there are most likely other reasons for the child's difficulties (enter parental guilt). Next, a neurologist in the community is sought out, who happens to be an adult neurologist and is a respected leader in the field but who has little interest, training, or background in the developmental aspects of learning and behavior problems. Again, the general neurological examination is normal, the EEG is reviewed and found to be normal. At this stage the child and the family are referred for psychiatric assessment since "there is no evidence of neurological involvement."

The point is that these professionals have carried out perfectly competent assessments that reflect their levels of interest, training, and expertise but are lacking in the critical area of neurodevelopment. What is missing is an attempt to assess the level of maturation of the brain. The *total* neurological assessment requires the integration of findings from both the traditional approach and the neurodevelopmental, nontraditional approach.

Difference in Approaches

While similar test items may be utilized in both the traditional approach (TA) and the nontraditional approach (NTA), there are basic differences in emphasis regarding major areas of interest, degree of neurological involvement, nature and significance of findings, and availability of ancillary corroborative measures.

Areas of Emphasis

The TA primarily seeks out major disturbances that occur as the result of such entities as brain tumors, infections, malformations, degenerative diseases, or seizures. The NTA addresses more subtle disturbances and the lesser degrees and types of neurological involvement associated with behavior and learning disabilities. The degree of involvement identified by the TA usually covers obvious handicaps or deficits, whereas the NTA addresses minor deviations and developmental delays. For instance, the TA would depict paralysis, muscle wasting, and loss of sensation on one side of the body, the manifestations seen following a stroke; whereas less obvious deficits such as mild asymmetries in posture or function between opposite sides of the body are looked for in the NTA. Gross movement disorders such as chorea, characterized by involuntary movements of the extremities through rather wide excursions, are noted in the TA, whereas choreiform (chorea-like) movements — slight twitches noted in extended hands and arms — are more characteristically looked for in and emphasized by the NTA.

Nature and Significance of Findings

Differences between the two approaches arise in the consistency and reproducibility of findings, underlying clinical pathological correlation, establishment of norms, and standardization. Findings of the TA are, for the most part, consistent and reproducible under a variety of conditions. Findings of the NTA are subject to more variability, being relatively more influenced by individual cooperation and motivation. For the most part, good clinical-pathological correlation has been established for abnormalities noted on the TA. For instance, a characteristic finding of a one-sided facial weakness has a high correlation with an abnormality along the path of the facial nerve or its connections within the brain. No such clear-cut correlation has been established for minor deviations and delays noted in the NTA. This problem stems from the subtlety of the dysfunction, which may not be easily measured quantitatively through typical anatomical, biochemical, or physiological means. This is further compounded by the fact that such studies of clinical-pathological correlations are markedly limited in the NTA because of lack of autopsy material for direct investigation.

Norms

Standard of norms are well established in the TA. Deviation or deficit represents an abnormality regardless of chronological age; that is, deficits such as paralysis of the right side of the face and marked involuntary movements of the extremities are deviations from normal under any circumstances and at any age. However, functional items in the NTA have a wide spectrum of normal function, which has not been well identified. In addition, such deficits in function may very well be normal at a given age. It is quite normal for a 6-year-old child to perform inefficiently on a number of tasks but markedly abnormal for a 10-year-old to perform in a similar way. While years of experience have provided the benefits of standardized methods of elicitation, recording of findings, and establishment of norms in the traditional approach, these are presently lacking in the NTA.

Ancillary Measures

Abnormal findings on the TA may be corroborated through ancillary measures, which include computer-assisted tomography (CAT) scans, electroencephalograms, spinal taps, and nerve conduction studies. These studies, however, have little value in corroboration of subtle deficiencies or developmental lag. Diagnostic impressions derived from the NTA can be supported by a limited number of other measures, such as psychometric testing. The electroencephalogram, as noted previously, offers little help in supporting diagnostic impressions derived from the NTA. A normal EEG does not imply a normally functioning brain, nor does an abnormal EEG necessarily equate with dysfunction in learning and behavior spheres.

Components of the Traditional Neurological Exam

The traditional neurological exam assesses a number of neurological functions that involve cranial nerves, deep tendon reflexes, general sensation, motor abilities, and cerebellar coordination activities. The learning-disabled child's performance on this type of assessment is usually normal (Schain, 1977).

The cranial nerves innervate the face and neck. They serve both a sensory and motor function for the eyes, jaw, face, neck, tongue, and vocal cords. The senses of taste, vision, hearing, and smell are also served by the cranial nerves. Special emphasis is placed on vision, visual tracking, and hearing capabilities in the assessment of the learning-disabled child. The status of muscle tone and strength throughout the body is evaluated, along with such coordination abilities as walking, touching a finger to the nose, and rubbing the heel of the foot down the opposite shin. The general sensations of pain, touch, temperature, vibration, and position are included in the sensory examination. Deep tendon reflexes, particularly in the ankle, knee, and elbow, are tested for intensity and symmetry of response.

Components of the Nontraditional Exam

It is important to repeat the fact that the total neurological assessment has the capacity to demonstrate two types of so-called "soft signs." The first type, done primarily from measures in the traditional or standard examination, represents minor deviations from established standards. Their presence is never considered normal regardless of age. The second type includes components, primarily drawn from the nontraditional exam, that are essentially maturational in nature and derive their significance from deviation of observed performance from that expected for chronological age.

Neurodevelopmental measures and norms have been addressed in motor (Grant, Boelsche, & Zin, 1973; Kinsbourne, 1973), sensory (Benton, 1955; Kinsbourne & Warrington, 1962), and laterality relationships (Belmont & Birch, 1963; Berges & Lezine, 1965). Age-dependent minor neurological deficiencies are nearly universal in young children and become progressively more rare during later elementary school years. The persistence of these neuromaturational deficiencies beyond the age levels at which they generally disappear has been associated with learning disorders, behavior problems, language delay, and other manifestations of developmental dysfunction (Adams, Kocsis, & Estes, 1974; Hart, Rennick, Klinge, & Schwartz, 1974; Johnston, Stark, Mellits, & Tallal, 1981; Levine, Brooks, & Shonkoff, 1980; Stine, Saratsiotis, & Mosser, 1975).

The following description is intended to provide some insight into the nature of the test items, not to provide direction for the actual performance of the examination. The specific items of the examination are described, followed by comments regarding their developmental nature and potential usefulness in discriminating between normal and learning-disabled children. A number of neurological parameters are used in the assessment of children with behavioral and learning disabilities (Touwen, 1979), and those described below are only representative samples. Levine and colleagues (1980) included a number of other measures in their expanded neurodevelopmental exam, which screens for strengths and weaknesses often assessed by other disciplines and includes screening of gestalt and visual-spatial orientation, temporal sequential organization, memory, and language.

Motor Function Tests

Spooning (Touwen, 1979)

With eyes closed, arms extended in a horizontal plane, palms down, and fingers spread, flexion occurs at the wrist and extension of the fingers at the first metacarpal-phalangeal (MCP) joint. Spooning is recorded if flexion at the wrist and extension at the MCP joint exceeds 10 degrees from the horizontal. Although the appearance of spooning is not judged to be developmental in nature, it is unclear whether it is of any substanial clinical significance. Touwen (1979) cautioned against overinterpretation of this sign, since its presence may merely represent decreased tone, a normal difference in joint laxity, or a response to former training.

Involuntary Measurements (Touven, 1979)

With arms in the same position described above, involuntary movements in the face, shoulder, arm, forearm, and fingers are noted over a 20-second period. Choreiform movements are involuntary, brief rapid twitches, while athetotiform movements are mild writhing movements noted predominately in the fingers. There is no agreement as to whether there is a developmental pattern to these involuntary movements. Prechtl and Stemmer (1962) and Wolff and Hurwitz (1966) considered them abnormal at any age and felt they represented firm evidence of neurological involvement; however, such such a correlation has not been substantiated (Rutter, Graham, & Birch, 1966; Wikler, Dixon, & Parker, 1970). While Hertzig, Bortner, and Birch (1969), Peters, Romine, and Dykman (1975), and Rie, Rie, Stewart, and Rettemnier (1978) found a higher incidence of choreiform movements in learning-disabed children ranging in age from 7 to 12 years, Adams and coworkers (1974) found no difference in the incidence of choreiform movements between normals and learning-disabled children aged 9 to 11½ years.

Finger-to-Nose Touches (Touwen, 1979)

With eyes closed, five repetitions of touching the extended forefinger to the tip of the nose are completed by each hand. The number of inexact placements, based on failure to touch exactly a designated spot on the nose, is noted.

Finger Opposition (Touwen, 1979)

Repetitive finger-to-thumb touches that follow a designated sequence are observed over a 15-second period. The number of fingers touched and the number of errors (e.g., double finger touching, missed finger, etc.) are recorded. Mirror movements — extension of the wrist, finger movement at the metacarpal-phalangeal and interphalangeal joints — are recorded in the resting hand. During a second trial, the child is instructed to "keep the other (resting) hand still." Duration of obvious mirror movements is recorded for each hand.

Diadochokinesis (Touwen, 1979)

With the forearm at a 90-degree angle from the elbow, the palm and back of the hand alternately touch a designated spot on a table during a 15-second trial. The number of completed cycles and number of errors (missing the mark, double touching) are recorded during two trials. Mirror movements in the resting arm and hand, such as flexion at the elbow or alternating motions at the wrist, are noted. Onset and duration of mirror movements are recorded for each arm. During the second trial, the child is instructed to keep the "other (resting) arm still."

Diadochokinetic ability follows a maturational course, reaching completion by 8 years of age (Grant et al., 1973). The rate at which these movements are executed, particularly with regard to finger opposition and diadochokinesis, has distinguished normal controls from learning-disabled subjects (Adams et al., 1974; Denhoff, Siqueland, Komich, & Hainsworth, 1968) and from language-impaired children (Johnston et al., 1981). The inhibition of mirror movements in association with finger-to-thumb and alternating wrist movements is established by 9 years of age (Cohen, Taft, Mahadeviah, & Birch, 1967) Denckla (1974) noted that such overflow movements differentiated hyperactive boys from controls in all ages from 5 to 11 years. Persistence of overflow movements in neurologically involved children has been documented by studies of Hart and colleagues (1974) and Touwen (1979).

Bipedal Stand (Doll, 1946)

With the right foot placed directly in front of the left foot, arms at sides, and eyes closed, the duration that balance is maintained is recorded for a maximum of 15 seconds. The trial ends when foot positioning is upset.

Unipedal Stand (Touwen, 1979)

With eyes open and one leg flexed at the knee, the duration of unipedal stand is recorded for a maximum of 15 seconds. The ability to balance on one or both feet increases with age and has been noted to be a fairly good differentiator between normal and neurologically impaired children (Peters et al, 1975; Rie et al, 1978; Werry & Aman, 1976).

Sensory Function Tests

Evaluation of sensory skills is complicated by the potential influence of learning, motivation, and experience. Although parietal lobe sensory testing is sometimes an intrinsic part of the traditional neurological exam, it is included in this nontraditional extended assessment because of the need to apply developmental standards. Mature levels of performance are not expected until 6 or 7 years of age.

Simultactgnosia (Kraft, 1968)

Ten trials of double simultaneous touches are administered to the cheeks and/or backs of hands in a prescribed pattern. Errors of mislocation and extinction (failure to perceive a stimulus) are recorded. By the age of 7, the majority of children can identify simultaneous stimuli, whereas prior to this time many children will identify the proximal stimulus (face) and extinguish the distal stimulus (hand). It is unclear whether poor performance in this task reflects a neuromaturational delay or failure to interpret instructions appropriately (Nolan & Kagan, 1978).

Graphesthesia (Ayers, 1972)

Each of six standardized figures is drawn on the back of the hand out of sight of the child. The child reproduces the figure by redrawing it with his or her forefinger after each presentation. In a second trial the child selects the figure from an illustration of six figures.

Finger Identification (Satz & Friel, 1972)

A number of tests of finger identification may be used. The subject's vision is obstructed when a challenge touch is administered to the fingertip. The child is asked to:

1. Identify a single finger touched by examiner, pointing with forefinger of opposite hand.
2. Identify on a picture of two hands the finger touched by the examiner.
3. Designate the two simultaneously touched fingers by pointing with forefinger of opposite hand (Kinsbourne & Warrington, 1962).
4. Identify whether one or two matchboxes are touched to the side of the fingers.

The number of errors is recorded for each trial, which consists of five challenges.

The capacity to identify stimulated fingers progressively improves from 6 to 11 years of age (Benton, 1955). The ability to identify two simultaneously stimulated fingers matures around age 7, Kinsbourne and Warrington (1962) demonstrated a direct relationship between success on these tasks and chronological age and further noted that the delayed acquisition of finger sense was correlated with delayed acquisition of reading and writing skills in certain reading-impaired children. It may be that fine motor coordination difficulties are associated with poor sensory feedback from the fingers, as reflected in difficulties in finger identification.

Laterality Relationship Tests

The testing of laterality relationships is divided into two elements, dominance (preference) and left-right orientation.

Dominance (Preference) (Belmont & Birch, 1963)

HAND. Preference in the performance of 11 designated tasks, such as knocking on a door, combing hair, and so forth, is noted. The number of activities done with the right hand and the left hand is noted.

LEG. The leg chosen to do a total of eight activities, including hop, kick, or stand on one foot, is recorded.

EYE. The number of left or right choices in three visual tasks (e.g., looking through telescope pinhole, rifle sight) is recorded.

The main difficulty in assessing the significance of dominance is in the establishment of norms. It is generally accepted that a child begins to develop hand dominance by 18 months of age but remains somewhat ambidextrous until 5 years of age. Belmont and Birch (1963) indicated that hand perference, though established, is not well stabilized until 9 to 10 years of age. Eye preference may be established by age 2, but it may be more dependent upon which eye has the better vision than upon central brain organization factors.

Foot/leg performance is considerably more difficult to assess. One foot may be utilized for kicking and the other for standing on one leg. Children over the age of 8 often use either leg without any particular preference. Touwen (1979) notes that the development of performance in the legs appears to be different for balance than for voluntary motor movements. Children below the age of 7 use the preferred leg for balance and the non-preferred leg for kicking. Over the age of 7 years, balance is usually well established and children use the preferred leg for both kicking and hopping. The confusion of leg preference can only compound the confusion regarding overall unilateral preference implications.

It is an unproved assumption that establishment of unilateral dominance (i.e., preference to do everything on one side) reflects normal cerebral organization since a totally dominant hemisphere has been established. Incomplete dominance, therefore, would reflect cerberal disorganization. Although mixed dominance has been associated with reading difficulties in some studies (Corballis & Beale, 1976), other studies have shown no significant association with learning disabilities (Belmont & Birch, 1965; Vernon, 1960).

Left-Right Discrimination (Belmont & Birch, 1963)

SINGLE IDENTIFICATION. The child designates body parts according to right and left sides. The number of errors is recorded for four challenges.

DOUBLE IDENTIFICATION. The child identifies a designated body part utilizing a specific hand (touch left ear with right hand). The number of errors in four challenges is recorded.

CONFRONTATION. The child identifies a designated left or right body part of the confronting examiner. The number of errors on four trials is recorded.

There is a normal sequence for developing the ability to identify left and right. By the age of 6 or 7 a child is able to identify his or her own left and right. At the age of 9, the capacity to identify across the midline is established; and by age 10, identification of left and right on the opposing individual is established. There have been a number of studies supporting the association of left-right orientation difficulties with learning disabilities (Berges & Lezine, 1965; Croxen & Lytton, 1971).

Other Aspects Of Clinical Assessment

Medical History

The review of all potential factors that may relate to the child's academic performance and behavior is made through careful analysis of past history. Because of the question of possible central nervous system involvement, considerable attention is devoted to identifying potential insults to the nervous system, particularly during prenatal (pregnancy) and perinatal (labor and delivery) periods. While there is no guaranteed correlation between insults occuring during these times and subsequent neurological impairment, certainly the occurrence of such events places the child "at risk" for a range of neurological defects. Knoblach and Pasamanick (1959) introduced the concept of the continuum of reproductive causalty. The neurological dysfunction associated with learning and behavior disorders is at one end of this continuum, whereas mental retardation, severe cerebral palsy, blindness, and deafness are at the other end. Neonatal intensive care units and advanced technology in the care of newborns have been responsible for saving the lives of severely insulted babies. These advances may have incresed the number of children with subsequent minor neurological deficits as well as behavior and learning disabilities.

Factors such as medications during pregnancy, maternal nutrition, vaginal spotting, prolonged labor, and complicated labor and delivery should be sought in the maternal history. Abnormalities in the newborn baby such as prematurity, breathing difficulties, or chemical imbalances heighten the risk of subsequent neurological aberrations. An inquiry is made into insults occuring later in the child's life that may have affected the nervous system, such as meningitis, prolonged seizures, head trauma, lead poisoning, severe infections, and so on. It should be underscored that, although at higher risk, infants subjected to a variety of insults may not necessarily develop evidence of brain dysfunction. There certainly are a number of children with characteristic learning and behavior disorders who have no evidence of such insults in their history. In addition, the history includes other items that may affect academic performance, such as chronic illness, allergies, medication, prolonged hospitalization, and psychosocial factors. The history of developmental milestones is reviewed in detail, searching for clues as to possible time of onset and degree of developmental delay. There is a higher incidence of speech or language difficulties in children with reading disabilities. Family history is an important consideration, particularly familial patterns of learning disability and the level of academic performance of parents and siblings.

Physical Examination

A physical examination is performed to determine the status of general health. Effort is made to identify certain physical stigmata reflecting minor anomalies of physical development. They include items such as defects in external ear development, abnormalities in fingerprint patterns, tooth defects, and inturning or shortening of the fifth finger (Quinn & Rappaport, 1974). There may be a relationship between these signs and developmental disabilities; however, the presence of such minor elements, which are often present in normally functioning individuals, by themselves, ought not to be considered prime evidence of neurological involvement.

Laboratory Studies

Despite increasing pressure from a number of sources, the determination of blood glucose, calcium, zinc, and various enzymes very seldom adds to the diagnostic formulation (Levine et al., 1980).

Observation of Behaviors

The examining room is an artificial setting. Although behaviors there may not parallel those seen in the classroom, the opportunity exists to observe some of the child's behavioral repertoire. For instance, during the examination one may be able to gauge a child's capacity for social interaction, cooperation, response to reinforcement, cognitive strategies, emotional stability, and patterns of attention, particularly maintenance and shifting of attention.

SUMMARY AND CONCLUSIONS

The presence of minor deviations in the traditional neurological examination and/or evidence of inability to perform certain neurologically mediated tasks in an age-appropriate fashion on the nontraditional examination have been termed "soft signs." The presence of soft signs may provide indirect evidence of a link between dysfunction in behavioral and/or academic spheres and underlying central nervous system dysfunction. The presence of a single sign in isolation most likely has little or no significance. However, clusters of soft signs may indicate neurological involvement characterized by hemisyndromes, dyskinesias, associated movements, coordination difficulties, and sensory disturbances (Touwen, 1979). Although the presence of such clusters may provide better insight into the neurological influence on learning disabilities, at the present time they have little implication for specific psychoeducational intervention strategies.

The presence or absence of soft signs gives no clue to the potential response to medication. Behavioral and academic improvement in response to medication may be just as dramatic or just as minimal in children who demonstrate a variety of soft signs as in those who demonstrate none. However, the suggestion of neurological involvement should improve our understanding of the learning-disabled child. Awareness of a neurological component often goes a long way in relieving undue blame, scapegoating, or parental guilt. The consideration that the child does, in fact, have "invisible" handicaps that are interfering with performance in academic and behavioral spheres should focus attention on the child's specific needs.

Information from all sources should be utilized in developing a diagnostic and intervention strategy. The educational efforts addressing cognitive deficits and the psychological approaches directed toward psychosocial issues (self-concept, sibling and peer interactions, etc.) should not wait for nor should they be dependent upon the neurological assessment.

The role of the neurological assessment in prognosis needs to be clarified. Although certain soft signs suggest the presence of a maturational lag, there is no proof yet that the child will necessarily "outgrow" those difficulties. While attentional pecularities appear to be somewhat more responsive to the maturational process, other aspects of the symptom complex do not necessarily resolve with age.

The role that the neurological evaluation will play in diagnosis and intervention in the future will be dependent upon subsequent studies, which must take the following into consideration:

1. Items of the examination must be standardized, and responses must be quantified.
2. Studies of usefulness of soft signs must consider their developmental nature and refrain from comparing performance of children at widely discrepant age levels without regard for developmental changes.
3. Homogeneous subgroupings of children must be identified so that assessment measures and therapeutic modalities can be meaningfully evaluated and compared.

CHAPTER 17

School Psychology Assessment

Kevin P. Dwyer

The goal of this chapter is to explore the role of the school psychologist in the diagnosis of specific learning disability. The responsibilities of the school psychologist, the general practices in the field, some foundations for these practices, and suggested directions for modification of these practices are also explored. The problems of definition, misidentification, and overidentification will be discussed. A model for screening, assessment, and the team evaluation process will be explored, distinguishing each stage as it relates to the functions and responsibilities of the school psychologist.

A framework for using measurement techniques more cautiously will be presented. The value of clinical judgment in interdisciplinary assessment will also be explored. The thorny problems of bias in the testing of sociocultural minorities or of presenting the perfect test battery for the preschool child whom someone perceives as learning-disabled will not be addressed here. For a comprehensive discussion of these issues the reader is referred to the many state manuals on nonbiased assessment (Maryland, Mainzer, 1978; Iowa, Reschly, Grimes, & Ross-Reynolds, 1981) as well as

This chapter originally appeared as an article by **Kevin P. Dwyer** in *Learning Disabilities: An Interdisciplinary Journal* (Vol. I, 1982) and was adapted by permission of Grune & Stratton for inclusion in this *Handbook*.

to the specific studies on cognitive measures such as the WISC-R (Reynolds & Gutkin, 1980; Mercer & Lewis, 1979). For preschool assessment, Boehm and Sandberg (1982) have presented a well-organized, purposeful framework. Their cautions are most valuable and need to be read and reread before assessment decisions are made and diagnostic labels are given. It also is important for all school psychologists and educational evaluators to review the Standards for Educational and Psychological Tests (APA, 1986). These standards must be applied vigorously, recognizing the needs as well as the rights of the student.

Diagnosis should have a positive impact upon the student or should, at least provide useful information about the condition that needs remedying. As McDermott (1981) stated. "A diagnosis is valid only when it points to a potentially effective remedy for a child's problem, should no such remedy exist or presently be known, permits the psychologist to predict the course the child's problem will take in lieu of treatment" (p. 32).

Is our diagnostic system, theoretically sound, valid, and reliable? Is it theoretically sound to compare a student's cognitive ability measurements (IQ tests) with academic achievement measurements in search of a "severe discrepancy"? At a time when school psychologists are dealing with accountability systems in which effectiveness is measured by the number of completed assessments and in which quantity unfortunately seems more important than quality, the need for self-imposed standards of ethical practice in the assessment process is even greater and more demanding than it has been in the past (Perlmutter & Pecus, 1983).

TOWARD A DEFINITION

The National Joint Committee for Learning Disabilities (Hammill, Leigh, McNutt, & Larsen, 1981) offered the most recent definition of LD. This definition acknowledges that there is little validity in perceptual and psychological "process" testing (Salvia & Ysseldyke, 1981) and that the term "central nervous system dysfunction" is more appropriate than terms like "dyslexia" (Public Law 94-142, 1975). In this new definition, extrinsic influences and intrinsic conditions other than CNS dysfunction are excluded as primarily causal, but children with multiple intrinsic and extrinsic problems are not excluded provided there is presumed central nervous system dysfunction.

Definitions of learning disability use cognitive ability as the benchmark against which the child's achievement is compared. Achievement is limited to academic skills including oral expression, listening comprehension, written expression, basic reading skill, reading comprehension, mathematics calculation, and mathematics reasoning.

The assumption that intelligence and academic achievement measures are overlapping but unique factors of functioning has been disputed (Mercer & Lewis, 1979). Duffey, Salvia, Tucker, and Ysseldyke (1981) theorized that we are measuring "normal cultural diversity." Reynolds (1980) stressed that one should expect different achievement levels under different instructional and life experiences, making it extremely difficult to derive a single statement of expectation in school achievement.

It appears that more and more practitioners are going beyond the mechanics of testing and looking at the influences of experience on the samples of behavior gathered. A survey of over 200 Maryland school psychologists showed that there is general agreement among them in favor of placing greater emphasis upon observations and upon parent and teacher reports to validate any standardized assessment results (Dwyer, 1981).

OVERIDENTIFICATION, MISIDENTIFICATION

A statewide Colorado study (Shepard & Smith, 1981a) implied that school psychologists, like other team members that make the diagnosis of learning disability (LD), are swayed by something other than well-substantiated empirical data. Children in need of extra support, such as slow learners or those of borderline ability, are being classified as LD by school psychologists (Frame, Clarizio, & Porter, 1984). The Office of Special Education reported that from 1979 to 1980 45 of the 48 states that increased their LD special education population had a decrease in the number of mentally retarded served by special education programs (USDE, 1985). It may be presumptive to assume that children classified as mentally retarded in 1979 were labeled learning disabled in 1980. However, the Colorado study suggests those children with borderline or possibly less than borderline ability are entering the "handicapped" population as learning disabled.

By grouping slow learning children with learning-disabled children of average or better-than-average ability, it is implied to LD children that they too are intellectually below par. Special programs will only improve when LD students are clearly identified and not grouped with slow learners or other academically limited youngsters. Differential diagnosis — that is, making sure that children who are called learning disabled are truly handicapped by a central nervous system dysfunction — is vital to proper prescription. A learning disability is different from poor motivation or serious emotional handicap or limited ability.

There is evidence from the Colorado study (Shepard & Smith, 1981a) that as many as half of the children sampled may have been misdiagnosed. Glowa (1982), measuring similar diagnostic concerns, found that less than 30 percent of the first, second, and third grade students identified as LD and placed in special education classes had severe discrepancies between their aptitude and achievement measures. Glowa also found the sample to be significantly below average in ability: WISC-R mean IQ of 85.9, which is within the range of means reported by Kaufman (1979a) and Ysseldyke, Algozzine, Shinn, and McGue (1982). These means are close to a full standard deviation below the population mean of 100, suggesting that "slow learners" comprise a significant proportion of the identified LD population. Hobbs (1975) implied that school systems would label slow learners "learning disabled" in order to receive additional funds to teach those harder-to-teach youngsters: "Where school districts are able to obtain additional state or federal funds for each child enrolled in a special class, there has been some tendency to assign almost any child who was having difficulty in school to special classes for children with learning disabilities"(p. 303).

The negative impact of misdiagnosis on research was noted by Hobbs and others a decade ago, yet we continue to measure the effectiveness of our diagnostic instruments, techniques, and remedies using these poorly diagnosed samples. Overidentification and misidentification also reduce the cost-effectiveness of limited special educational resources and increase the chance that resources will be cut off because they have been misused and have not been allocated to help the truly handicapped. Should we not hypothesize, as did Hammill (1976), that only about 3 percent of the school-aged population have specific CNS learning disabilities and are in need of special education?

DO SPECIAL EDUCATION PROGRAMS WORK?

Cruickshank (1981) noted the frustration of many practitioners and parents over the lack of progress made by students in special education programs, particularly self-contained classes and residental centers. Judge Peckham's decision in the case of Larry P v. Wilson Riles (1979) was equally critical of these programs: "They are provided with instruction that deemphasizes academic skills...and naturally they will tend to fall farther and farther behind children in regular classes" (p. 18).

Even Lambert's (1981a) defense of special education programs was muted by her admission that there is little evidence that special education works: "In a careful analysis of the available research data, the evidence does not support the conclusion that there is a detrimental labeling effect but neither are there sufficient numbers of studies of the positive outcomes of special education placement. In the only controlled study the results showed that there were no differences in the achievement between regular and special class pupils (matched for ability and achievement problems)" (p. 939).

The development of resource room programs was seen as a solution to part of this problem. There is evidence that the rate of learning in resource programs is greater (particularly in language arts) than without resource programs. However, longitudinal studies suggest that this increased rate of progress is not maintained when the child is fully mainstreamed (Ito, 1981). Many studies report effectiveness in rate of academic learning measured over short periods of time, but there are few, if any, studies that suggest improved self-concept or personal-social functioning (Sindelar & Deno, 1978).

SCREENING

Special education screening should be preceded by regular education pre-referral problem solving. Team problem solving among regular educators appears to be an effective method for assisting the classroom teacher (s) in developing acceptable interventions (Chalfant & Pysh, 1981). The "teacher assistance team" (Chalfant & Pysh, 1979) or "educational management team" has as its goal, "To effectively help teachers establish successful classroom programs for children with learning and behavior problems..." (Chalfant and Pysh, 1984, p. 6). These problem-solving teams, composed of three or four regular education teachers and one or two specialists, generally meet once a week for an hour, discussing two students. This model reduces unnecessary referrals for special education screening and assessment and reenfranchises the classroom teacher. Graden, Casey, and Christenson (1985) provided a useful model for practical school implementation of a pre-referral system. A permanent, supportive problem-solving team has the advantage of communicating consistent teacher suppport as well as providing a mechanism for system and program analysis. Program, teacher, and curriculum modification are all potential outcomes of a well coordinated pre-referral team. The teacher assistance team frequently seeks the consultation support of the school psychologist to assist in developing the behavioral and instructional interventions to be carried out by the classroom teacher and other regular education staff.

Curtis and Zins (1981) reported that school psychological consultation is the preferred service requested by teachers and administrators. Consultation techniques that are clearly helpful to pre-referral problem solving are apparently not available at the requested rate. A national survey reported that, on the average, nearly 50% of school psychologist's time is spent in assessment and report writing whereas only 9% is spent in consultation with school staff (Lacayo, Sherwood, & Morris, 1981). Therefore, the professional school psychologist must recognize this dilemma and develop strategies to provide this needed consultative service, which in the long run can reduce unnecessary referrals for testing.

Screening begins with effective consultation techniques and cooperative in-service training, which can be preventive and reduce overidentification (Murray & Wallbrown, 1981). Preventive screening is geared to assisting the classroom teacher in understanding the range of normalcy and in developing practical methods to teach children without handicapping them for being different in their approach to learning.

Screening should take an organized look at the referral "problem." This problem should be discussed by a school-based team and followed by validating observations of the child's functioning in the "problem area" and by gathering information about the child's physical and developmental well-being. Screening using a validating school-based team exposes the referring teacher to an experiential in-service training process that can have a long-lasting effect in reducing unnecessary and inappropriate referrals and in improving the teacher's understanding of individual differences in students' learning styles. The State of Maryland Learning Disabilities Project (Mainzer, et al, 1982), a federally funded in-service and research project, has identified a series of screening devices that have this in-service impact. The series of screening forms used in the Maryland Project cover information from the referring teacher, the parent (s), and a trained special educator. The child's educational history is also used to help corroborate the referral concern. The parents' information and input enable the team to look at the physical, developmental, and environmental life of the child outside of school. The information is charted by the team, including the teacher, to determine if there is agreement that the problem may consititute a possible learning disability. This is a corroborative, validating screening process. Some of the information gathered in the screening may provide information as to the etiology of the problem. Information covering the socalled "exclusions" is also gathered in the screening. The process of information gathering and sharing when the school team meets also provides a complete feedback cycle for the classroom teacher and parents so that concerns can be clarified and appropriate modifications implemented. The school psychologist can act as a process coordinator, assisting the team in determining what, if any, action should be taken.

Referral Format

Teachers, like most professionals, do not like completing forms, and they see themselves as having progressively more forms and records to complete. They see little payoff for doing most of this paperwork. If a referral form is to be effective, it must produce some result, some direct response that has the potential of modifying or remedying the problem. A referral form should assist the referring teacher in thinking through the concern. The form should include:

- complete identifying data.
- complete statement of specific problem(s).
- detailed report of academic functioning: grade levels, books/materials of instruction.
- general instructional techniques and approaches used in the classroom.
- teacher/parent modifications, alternatives tried: specific modification, how long, and results.
- what methods or modifications work? How were the child's strengths enhanced by these methods?
- anticipated results from referral.
- specific academic behavior (multi-item checklist): i.e., "difficulty with letter sound discrimination;" "difficulty completing written sentences;" "problems retaining information over time."
- related behaviors (multi-item checklist): i.e., "poor self control": "overwhelmed by changes in routine " "self distracted"
- substantive work samples.

Presentation of Referral

The referral is reviewed by a school-based team composed of teacher peers, specialists, and the school psychologist. The school administrator may assist this support team as the technical/administrative coordinator. This team can determine if consultative services, administrative intervention (e.g., moving the child to another teaching team), or other modifications will remedy the problem. In the Maryland Project (Mainzer et al., 1982), the materials gathered by the team enable subjective corroborative validating. There is an opportunity to observe the instructional environment and the child's response patterns to that environment. There is an opportunity to determine if this pattern existed in any previous instructional environments. When the information is charted (Fig. 17-1), the profile enables the team to determine if there is significant suspicion that a learning disability may exist and what assessments are necessary to assist the team in the diagnostic evaluation of this suspicion. These materials are gathered prior to any assessment decision and stimulate problem-solving through consultation. Whereas in many states (e.g., Arkansas, Rogers, 1978) the screening process necessitates some testing, the Maryland Project process does not mandate any testing of the child other than what is carried out as part of the regular program. The classroom teacher who initiated

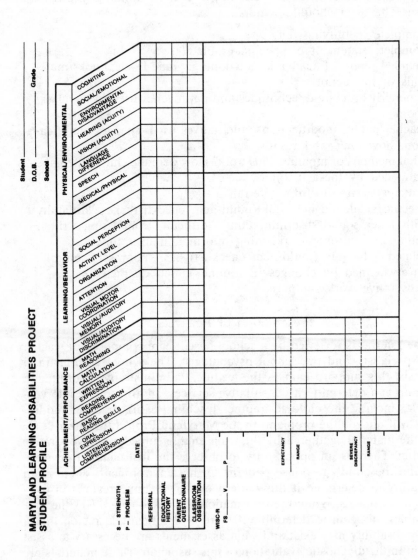

FIGURE 17-1
One example of assessment information.

the referral is involved throughout, which helps that teacher understand the value of accurately completing the referral form and the relationships between the referral information and decision-making about the student. If assessments are needed, the referring teacher has the opportunity to discuss what the assessments will entail and how they relate to classroom functioning.

ASSESSMENT

The assessment of a suspected learning disability by a school psychologist almost always involves a battery of tests including general intelligence, achievement, perceptual-motor coordination, and personality When reviewing the literature, it becomes evident that there are a handful of tests or techniques that are viewed as primary in this assessment process. For general intelligence or cognitive ability, the most frequently noted tests are the Wechsler Intelligence Scale for Children–Revised (WISC-R) (Wechsler, 1974); the Woodcock Johnston Tests of Cognitive Ability, part of the Psycho-educational Battery (Woodcock & Johnson, 1977); the Stanford-Binet Intelligence Scale-Revised (Terman & Merrill, 1986); and for younger children, the Wechsler Preschool and Primary Scale of Intelligence (WPPSI) (Wechsler, 1967) and the McCarthy Scales of Children's Abilities (McCarthy, 1972). The WISC-R is the general intelligence test most frequently used when a school psychologist suspects a learning disability.

The child's social adaptation, special skills, relevant knowledge of the environment, and nonverbal problem-solving skills are also considered ability factors. Validation of test measurements using special academic skills, conversational fluency, and demonstrations of abstract reasoning should also be considered. Information can be gathered from a variety of sources. It is not the *sole* responsibility of the school psychologist to gather this information.

Adaptive behavior rating scales, interviews, observations, and social developmental history information can provide supplementary information and validations for standardized intelligence tests. Sometimes the impressions of parents and persons working with a child can provide information about a child's ability. Diagnostic interview techniques are also valuable, as are testing-teaching approaches that can measure ability as well as learning style. Such ancillary techniques are extremely important in situations where an IQ test is felt to be inappropriate or where the IQ test results are questionable and there is reason to believe that the child does not fit the parameters of the standardization sample. Ability testing, assessment, and evaluation mean pulling together and analyzing all of the information available to secure a picture of the student's cognitive functioning.

There should be an emphasis upon the highest level of functioning that can be substantiated as the best measure of ability and cognition. It is common practice to use the highest IQ source on the WISC-R (either Verbal or Performance Scale). It is an attempt to focus on total cognitive functioning, not just on those behaviors measured by a standard intelligence test. Therefore, if there are unique indicators that suggest a higher ability or cognitive level than the standard IQ score, these should be noted.

Estimating a student's cognitive potential from one specific skill or trait is inappropriate. This is true of both subjective information and objective test data. As Wechsler noted, "the examiner should never estimate or infer a child's Full Scale IQ (or cognitive ability) from his scaled score on a single test" (1974, p. 26). Subjective information should be cross-validated and suggestive of generalized ability or global intelligence, which is the overall capacity of an individual to understand and cope with the world (and function in the learning environment).

The WISC-R is a normed and standardized individually administered intelligence test. Along with standardization, a test can only be viewed as a useful predictor if it is reliable, has a small error of measurement, and measures what it purports to measure and predict. The WISC-R and the other instruments noted meet these requirements (Buros, 1978). The WISC-R has the advantage of containing verbal and nonverbal (performance) components. The WISC-R also provides a rich sample of behavior, which can be crucial to diagnosis. The actual responses, the response pattern, the mannerisms, intonations, and style of approach are, in the hands of a qualified school psychologist, crucial to interpretation of the objective data.

Kaufman's (1979a) book, *Intelligence Testing with the WISC-R*, provides the school psychologist with an excellent guide to the strengths and weaknesses of the WISC-R and subtest analysis. As caution has been raised in relation to the validity of IQ as a measure of cognitive ability, even greater caution must be raised regarding "typical" subtest patterns for diagnosis of a learning disability (Kavale & Forness, 1984a).

Some research diagnosticians have focused upon the difference between verbal and performance IQ (V-P IQ) scores as indicative of cortical CNS dysfunction in combination with other frequently used assessment instruments (Hartlage, 1982). However, the use of such a difference has been questioned by Kaufman (1979a) and Gutkin (1979), among others. The problem with looking at V-P IQ difference has to do with the frequency of such differences in the normal population. There is evidence that the Verbal Scale provides an estimate of left hemisphere cortical functioning (in most persons) and that the Performance Scale provides a general estimate of right hemisphere cortical functioning. Rourke (1975) has shown the relationship of these scales to learning disabilities. Kaufman (1979a), however, urged school psychologist to be familiar with the frequency of a significant difference between these scores. There are many diagnostic reports that conclude that a child is learning disabled when the child's Verbal IQ is 95 and the Performance IQ is 110. This "significant difference" is found too frequently in the standardization sample of the WISC-R to be viewed as diagnostic of anything. A 25-point difference is infrequent enough in the normal population to warrant concern; if corroborated, this difference may enable the school psychologist to formulate diagnostic hunches, possibly with psychoneurological implications. The unusual and rare 35-point difference usually suggests a more serious problem.

The diagnostic significance of individual subtest differences depends upon the uniqueness of the subtest and its relationship to the scale with which it is compared. Kaufman (1982) reported that Information, Arithmetic, Digit Span, Picture Arrangement, Block Design, Coding, and Mazes are uniquely robust enought to enable specific interpretation when their scaled scores are ±3 from their Verbal or Performance Scale score averages. He suggested that ±4 scale score differences are needed for unique interpretation of the Vocabulary or Comprehension subtests and that Similarities and Object Assembly defy specific interpretation unless the difference is greater than 6 points. Discrepancies among subtests should not be given specific diagnostic meaning or coined "abnormal" unless they exceed these limits, and even then they should relate to other corroborative factors from other information and assessment data. Kaufman stated, "statistical significance is important, but it is not sufficient."

The tendency for a specific pattern of subtest scores (scatter pattern) to be found among learning-disabled children has been noted by Kaufman, Rugel (1974), and Smith (1978). The cluster of Arithmetic, Digit Span, and Coding referred to as the Sequential Factor (Bannatyne, 1974) or the Freedom from Distractability Factor (see Table 17-1) seems to be, along with Information, the subtests that give *some* learning-disabled youngsters the most trouble (Kaufman, 1979b)

The hypothetical basis for using scatter pattern analysis is that it demonstrates specific strengths and weaknesses in basic psychological processes or factors that are used in academic learning and may assist in instruction and diagnosis. It must be clearly understood by the qualified examiner that a specific pattern of subtest scores does not mean that a handicapping learning disability exists, since a significant percentage of able learners also show this pattern. Furthermore, other studies have shown that patterns and profiles like the so-called ACID profile (Arithmetic, Coding, Information, and Digit Span), which is significantly lower than other factor sets of subtests, are found among the emotionally disturbed, delinquents, and normal achievers (Clarizio & Bernard, 1981). Test anxiety also appears to depress Arithmetic and Digit Span subtest scores (Lutey, 1977).

TABLE 17-1.
WISC and WISC-R Subtest Regrouping.

Kaufman Factors	Bannatyne Factors
Verbal comprehensive	Acquired knowledge
Information	Information
Vocabulary	Vocabulary
Similarities	Arithmetic
Comprehension	Verbal conceptualization
Perceptual Organization	Vocabulary
Picture completion	Similarities
Picture arrangement	Comprehension
Block design	Spatial ability
Object Assembly	Picture completion
(Mazes)	Block design
Freedom from distractibility	Object assembly
Arithmetic	Sequencing ability
(Digit Span)	Arithmetic
Coding	(Digit span)
	Coding

Kauffman (1979b) clearly cautioned the practitioner not to use "group profiles" to make a diagnosis. He urged the individualized approach, seeing each assessment as a "special interpretive challenge" to be viewed in the context of the child's sociocultural and experiential background and response to the testing situation.

Clinical Judgment

Every qualified examiner recognizes that testing goes beyond standardized administration and scoring (Davis & Shepard, 1983). The subjective information gained during testing, observations, limit testing, and diagnostic teaching is frequently more informative of a child's cognitive functioning than the standard scores. Furthermore, the integration of this qualitative information into a holistic picture assists in determining diagnostic directions for the evaluation team. There is frequently as much diagnostic information in the errors the child makes as in correct responses and approaches. The child who gives the months of the year in response to a question requesting the names of the days of the week *may* have problems with recall of temporal categories, whereas the child who names three of the seven days *may* have retention recall problems. The child who can reproduce a design with blocks that is a mirror image of the model *may* have visual-perceptual integration problems; and if the child recognizes the error but can't correct it, it *may suggest* that something other than a perceptual problem prevents the child from making the correct motor movements. The child who makes correct responses to this spatial relations problem-solving task but takes more time than the standardization permits *may be* more reflective than others and different from the child who cannot reproduce the designs at all. The child who constantly asks if his or her responses are correct *may* have a strong need for approval or *may* have difficulty evaluating responses. The child who responds to questions quickly, blurting out answers sometimes before the question is finished, *may* be a classically impulsive responder who needs to learn to listen, reflect, and then respond.

There are thousands of possible responses to the hundreds of test interactions and questions that can result in the same scores but demonstrate significantly different patterns and styles. The reason that *may* is included in each statement is because these qualitative data are not easily analyzed or researched in any age-normed referenced way. Furthermore, it is the *pattern* of responses rather than any discrete atypical response that leads to clinical hunches, which then must be discarded or validated by other sources of information. Determining the child's mood, motivation, and level of tension and distractibility will assist in evaluating responses and determining the validity of normed results and interpretation of behavior.

It is these factors, clinically judged, in combination with test scores that enable the school psychologist to make suggestions to the teacher and parent(s) about techniques and approaches to academic problems. These recommendations should always be tempered by the examiner's self-questioning: How might this hunch or suggestion be misinterpreted as the *best* method of management or instruction? (Kavale & Andreassen, 1984). Preventing inappropriate interpretation does not end with report writing. We must continue to request feedback about our suggestions' effectiveness after the evaluation team conferences and the writing of an educational plan.

OTHER COGNITIVE MEASURES

The WISC-R is the most frequently used measure of intelligence, but other tests may be equally valid. The Stanford-Binet has a long history of reliable and valid use. The Woodcock-Johnson Psycho-educational Battery has a cognitive component as well as achievement components. It is seen by some school psychologists as an able addition to the test battery for assessing students with suspected learning disabilities. Ysseldyke, Shinn, and Epps (1981) reported, however, that the Woodcock-Johnson Battery may sometimes produce false-negatives. The report that "LD subjects" scored lower on the Woodcock-Johnson Test of Cognitive Ability than on the WISC-R. This may be a concern when any achievement measure and aptitude measure correlate too highly, producing two measures of the same problem. Caution must also be used with tests that purport to measure intelligence but actually measure a specific trait, such as tests that measure only vocabulary or only information.

One of the most potentially useful tools for looking at sequential and simultaneous thinking as significant constructs of cognition and as relevant factors associated with learning disabilities is the recently published Kaufman Assessment Battery for Children (K-ABC). This test has the advantage of being accurately normed, based upon psychoneurological hypotheses, and developed with a sensitivity toward possible item biases (racial, sexual, and ethic) as well as examiner bias. The test was standardized on a representative sample of children based upon the 1980 U.S. census. Handicapped children were included in the standardization ($N = 108$) as well as children categorized as gifted and talented ($N = 30$). Both aptitude and achievement components were nationally normed on the same children, thus improving the statistical comparison between these components. Statistically, there is a greater chance of error in comparing test results of instruments that do not have the same, or equivalent, norming samples (Berk, 1984b).

Another factor that may be of value in the complex diagnosis of learning disabilities is the Kaufman computation of "abnormal" amounts of scatter that occurred within the standardization sample ($N = 2000$). If there is an assumption that 10% is viewed as extreme, abnormal, and severe, the Interpretive Manual provides empirically derived discrepancy scores that conform to that percentage.

Studies are also reporting using the K-ABC with a variety of "exceptional children," including the learning disabled. These reports suggest that the diagnostic process will remain complex in the future. As Kaufman and Kaufman (1984) report:

> The apparent difficulty that some learning-disabled children have with integrated, as well as sequential, tasks makes the simple discrepancy between the Simultaneous and Sequential Standard Scores less sensitive than we had anticipated as a potential diagnostic indicator of learning disabilities. (p. 139)

BEYOND COGNITIVE INSTRUMENTS

School psychologists generally evaluate children suspected of a learning disability with a series of instruments that go beyond general intelligence testing. The Bender Gestalt (Bender, 1938) and achievement tests such as the Wide Range Achievement Test (Jastak & Jastak, 1976) and the Peabody Individual Achievement Test (Dunn & Markwardt, 1970) are almost always included. Criticisms of even these basic tests have been made (Berk, 1984b). Drawings of one or more humans are frequently requested of the child, as are other measures that evaluate emotional factors that may be influencing the child's academic progress.

The Bender Gestalt has been used for over 40 years. It, like the drawings, is easy to administer to school-aged children. Little language is needed to direct the child to carry out these pencil and paper tests. Hartlage (1982) reported that the Bender Gestalt has particular value in evaluating children in the primary grades, since copying geometric designs accurately is perceived to be associated with the nonverbal component of letter and number (symbol) perception and reproduction. The test was standardized by Koppitz (1964) for youngsters aged 6 through 11.5, and misdiagnosis occurs when the examiner relies solely upon age-equivalent sources. The overlap of such scores is so great that it is misleading to convert the scores to "age equivalents" without considering the standard deviation for each age group.

The number of Koppitz errors for children ages 5 through 11 is believed to discriminate normal from impaired, particularly if sufficient specific errors are noted. Perseveration and other problems are common and expected in young children but are frequently misread as significant of neurological dysfunction or delay (Koppitz, 1975). For example, the mean number of Koppitz errors on the Bender for an 8-year-old is 4.2 with a standard deviation of 2.5, meaning that 68 percent of children aged 8 years, 0 months through 8 years, 5 months will have as few as 2 errors to as many as 7 errors. Misinterpretation comes about when an 8-year-old child has seven Koppitz errors (about the average for 6-year-olds) and is then reported to be functioning two years below age expectancy on small-muscle, visual-motor integration processes and, therefore, is called learning disabled. The Koppitz norms were not developed to be used in this manner.

The Bender has been seen as a valid predictor of neurological as well as reading problems (Silver & Hagin, 1960; Lowell, 1964). However, the value of this instrument as a predictor of reading problems is strongly disputed by Vellutino (1979). Hartlage (1982) felt that the Bender is primarily a measure of right hemisphere motor functioning and is too specific a graphomotor task to draw conclusions about reading. Kaufman (1979b) suggested that the Bender be used to corroborate responses and standard scores on the Block Design and Coding subtests of the WISC-R, seeing the Bender as an "imitative" task involving similar psychoneurological processes needed for these WISC-R subtests.

Koppitz (1975) cautioned school psychologists against trying to prove a diagnostic hypothesis through overscoring: "They regard the Bender Test protocol as a final statement, when in fact it is only a child's response at a given moment" (p. 20). Salvia and Ysseldyke (1981) were critical of the low test–retest reliability of the Bender, and they questioned its diagnostic significance and validity. Correlations between the Bender, the Frostig Developmental Test of Visual Perception (Frostig, 1961), and the Developmental Test of Visual Motor Integration (Beery & Buktenica, 1967) suggest that they all may be measuring a relatively discrete factor of neurological functioning. Defining this factor or process and its effect on academic learning is clearly in dispute.

Achievement Testing

Achievement testing is frequently carried out by an educational specialist such as a special educator, reading specialist, or learning disability specialist. There are two concerns in achievement testing: (a) *diagnosis for eligibility,* helping to demonstrate a severe discrepancy between achievement and cognitive ability, and (b) the *diagnostic prescriptive* concerns, or assisting the team in developing a plan of action to remediate and/or circumvent the problem so that the child's academic functioning will be more commensurate with ability. Achievement testing may do one of these jobs better than the other. There are few tests that do both to the satisfaction of most educators, as noted in Chapter 18.

Standardized, normed reference tests of achievement such as the Wide Range Achievement Test or the Peabody Individual Achievement Test, provide standard scores that can be compared to IQ scores. However, these tests are seen as providing inadequate prescriptive information. Criterion reference tests are more appropriate for the latter task.

The Wide Range Achievement Test (WRAT) is the most commonly used achievement measure. It is standardized for ages 5 through adult in two forms. It involves reading recognition, spelling (writing words from dictation), and arithmetic (primarily written computation). Salvia and Ysseldyke (1981) suggested that the WRAT is weak in reliability and validity and inadequately standardized.

The Peabody Individual Achievement Test (PIAT), like the WRAT, tests a variety of academic skills including arithmetic, word recognition, reading comprehension, spelling, and general information. The PIAT provides a measure of passage comprehension, but the responses rely on visual discrimination skills. No oral reading subtest is provided to evaluate fluency.

The Woodcock Reading Mastery Tests consist of five subtests: letter identification, word identification, word attack (phonics), word comprehension, and passage comprehension. The test has norms and reported reliability and validity. The Woodcock is more diagnostic and prescriptive. It should be supplemented with an oral reading test to assist the clinican in the diagnosis of fluency problems. For young children, more than one measure should always be used.

Severe Discrepancy

Crucial to the diagnosis of a learning disability is a severe discrepancy between measures of ability and achievement (see Chapter 18, this volume). There have been many formulas for developing a number to quantify this discrepancy. The most frequently used numbers are based upon grade levels. Typically, two years below grade level has been viewed as a severe discrepancy. It is easy to recognize that two years below first grade is quite dramatic, but two years below eleventh grade has less meaning (a ninth grade reader in the eleventh grade is within the average range). Even when intelligence is taken into consideration, grade levels are not comparable to age-based standards such as IQ scores. Therefore, age-based standard scores should be used for calculating this diagnostic component.

Some formulas are founded upon the establishment of an "expectancy age," which is frequently based upon IQ, chronological age, and number of years in school. Bond and Tinker (1973) and Myklebust and Johnson (1967) have developed formulas that combine these elements. Many of the formulas tend to overidentify children from various IQ groups. None of these formulas takes into consideration the reliability of the instruments used in the comparison or the concept of regression toward the mean, which is expected in prediction when tests have a degree of error. Furthermore, developing a formula that mixes standard scores (IQ) with grade expectancies is statistically questionable. McLeod (1979) developed a statistical procedure that took regression into account in determining expectancy and severe discrepancy. Most of the commonly used achievement tests have adequate reported reliability coefficients and are correlated positively with the WISC-R, enabling the user to develop general ranges of educational expectancies and cutoff scores with minimal error. The McLeod construct was originally used by the Maryland Learning Disability Project to derive a table of severe discrepancy scores. However, some statistical assumptions and errors were noted in this process (Reynolds et al., 1984). A more refined formula for comparing a student's ability to achievement to determine if a statistically significant severe discrepancy exists has been applied by Cone and Wilson (1981). This model, adopted in the states of Iowa and Washington, among others, was was supported by the Reynolds work group (1984) on critical measurement issues in learning disabilities sponsored by the U.S. Department of Education.

Table 17-2 has been corrected from the one that will appear in the Maryland Learning Disabilities Diagnostic Handbook (Mainzer & Dwyer, in press). This revised guideline is based upon the concept that a

TABLE 17-2.
A Guideline for Numerical Comparisons of Expected and Actual Achievement.

IQ Range	Educational Expectancy Range*	Educational Discrepancy Range
130–139	118–123	95–100
120–129	112–117	89– 94
110–119	106–111	83– 88
100–109	100–105	77– 82
90–99	94–99	71– 76
80–89	88–93	65– 70
70–79	82–87	59– 64

* The numbers in this column are slightly different than those appearing in the LD Project, Diagnostic Guidelines.

student has a severe discrepancy between ability and achievement when the student's obtained score on the achievement measure is less than the estimated lower limit of a confidence interval (.05) around the student's expected achievement as predicted from the ability measure. It is also dependent upon the following assumptions:

1. The obtained scores are valid estimates
2. The scores are scaled in common metric where the means and standard deviations are equal (e.g. Deviation IQ, mean = 100, S.D. = 15)
3. The norming populations of each test are the same or, at least, equivalent and are representatives of the national population parameters
4. The scores are both derived from age-based norms
5. The reliability of each test is approximately .80
6. The correlation between the tests is approximately .60

As noted, in any prediction situation where the two scores are not perfectly correlated, there will be a phenomenon called regression to the mean. The equations for predicting achievement from ability taking this phenomeon into account are presented in Reynolds and colleagues (1984). Mainzer and Dwyer (in press) have derived the generic "severe discrepancy" scores found in Table 17-2.

Table 17-2 enables the user to estimate a discrepancy score taking regression into consideration. It uses age-based standard scores. The ranges of cutoff scores are based upon incidence of 3 to 5 percent. These discrepancy scores should only be used as a guide in the process of determining if a handicap exists. There are some statistical limitations to these measures; and, as Cone and Wilson (1981) stated, regression depends upon comparability of the norms used in the procedure as well as correlation between the achievement, aptitude instruments, and their reliabilities.

The determination of what scores to use when many achievement test scores are obtained is an interesting clinical dilemma. If the scores on achievement tests vary significantly, the team may wish to choose the more reliable instrument or to analyze the differences by looking for corrobative information (i.e., error analysis and classroom functioning). The difference may also have psychoneurological implications.

When there is a difference between the Verbal and Performance IQ on the WISC-R, Myklebust and Johnson (1967) supported the higher of the V-P IQs. Gore (1982) noted that, since the WISC-R Full Scale IQ is the most reliable of the three IQs (V-P-FS), the highest of the three should only be used when the difference is significant, that is, greater than 12 points.

Evaluation

The Maryland Learning Disabilities Project Student Profile Form (Fig. 17-1) provides a structured format for dealing with the cumulative information gathered in the screening and assessment. Problems, weaknesses, and concerns are noted in the boxes in the upper third of the form. There is an attempt to corroborate or reject the referral concerns through other information sources (educational history and parent interviews) and specialists' observations. The profile may end here if the referral concerns are found to be unwarranted and uncorroborated. Once the assessment data are gathered, the remainder of the profile can be completed as a diagnostic evaluation process. Objective data can be charted metrically on the achievement grid. Qualitative notes can be made to the right of the metric grid, and specific information of significance in relation to strengths, weaknesses, and hypothesized "causes" can also be noted on the right side for eventual use in instructional planning beyond the classification and eligibility decisions.

This profile reminds the evaluation team of the "exclusions" as well as listing some cognitive and behavorial factors, which are by intent neither comprehensive of nor exclusive of learning disabilities but which some feel will provide direction for educational planning. Blank spaces are provided for specific "behaviors" that the team may feel important.

The metric section can be completed using Table 17-2 to determine the expectancy level and range of discrepancy scores, recording test results scores below the achievement categories on the chart. For example, a child with an IQ of 87 would have an Educational Expectancy Range of 88 to 93 and a Cutoff Score Range of 65 to 70. Achievement test results would then be placed on the chart accordingly, for example, PIAT Mathematics SS = 70, and WRAT Math SS = 71. The math standard scores would be placed on the grid under math areas. The standard scores in mathematics would be seen as severe and significant, therefore meeting that component of federal and state guidelines. If the qualitative information from a variety of sources suggests that a child's problem is intrinsic (psychoneurological) rather than extrinsic and not primarily of emotional or physical (i.e., vision or hearing) origin, then the evaluation team would appropriately see this child as having a specific learning disability in mathematics.

Some Clinical Characteristics

Some learning-disabled children show a lack of feedback in the learning loop that may be conceptually analogous to some aphasics' inability to get the speech areas of the brain to work together. Some learning-disabled children seem to have a deficit in this "automatic" monitoring system. For example, a child may talk louder than necessary but be the only one who doesn't notice it. The awareness that words have multiple meanings seems to be missing; puns and jokes may be met with a blank stare. Some of these children may imitate the observed response of laughter, but, if asked what is funny, have no understanding in spite of good measured intelligence and appropriate age. Metalinguistic awareness may be absent or less functional in these children. Being aware of what is age-appropriate is important before one can determine the significance of redundancies, ambiguities, completeness of information, and relevance. In conversation, do you find yourself interpreting what the child is saying and finishing sentences and ideas? When ideas are tied together by illogical associations, does the child come back to the intended message or go further away from the original idea? Some emotionally disturbed children are unresponsive to being refocused, whereas some learning-disabled children can be refocused with minimal cues. Can the child monitor the discourse?

Some LD children fall into the impulsive category. There is a tendency for some impulsive, disinhibited LD students to ask socially inappropriate questions or to reveal intimate details about themselves or their family. These children may be able "word readers" who have no trouble with phonetic sound-symbol associations. However, inferences may seem beyond their grasp until they are focused. These youngsters may have difficulty with the sequential factor subtests of the WISC-R.

Walker (1981) showed that forced delay has a significant effect on improving some of the WISC-R verbal subtest scaled scores of 8-year-old impulsive boys. Rehearsal techniques, self-verbalization, and "chunking" were reported by Stevenson (1980) to be effective with children who are impulsive and disinhibited. Maier (1980) found similar results with LD youngsters who have problems in the listening-responding verbal loop; focused preorganized instruction positively affected cognitive functioning, generalization, and conceptual inferences in the sample studied.

The learning strategies approach of Alley and Deshler (1979) may be most effective with disinhibited LD students who have serious difficulties with appropriateness and organization as well as those who have difficulty discriminating between important and unimportant. As with any strategy, success with metacognitive approaches is highly correlated with ability (Deshler, Lowery, & Alley, 1979).

Youngsters called "dyslexic" or "dyscalculic" or "dysgraphic" may show similar difficulty with the sequencing subtests of the WISC-R. However, these LD youngsters are very different from their peers who have attentional disorders and those who have associative conceptual, language problems. Some youngsters who have basic skill problems in reading may be quite proficient in listening comprehension and verbal conceptual expression. Some dyslexic children may also be language disabled, with dysfunctions in the left hemisphere's language cortex. Others may have problems with integrated visual and language functioning of both hemispheres (Gaddes, 1983). In almost all cases of basic skill problems there appear to be problems with crossmodal functions of the cortex, with the greatest emphasis on left hemisphere "language" functions in relation to sensory inputs and motor outputs, particularly writing.

Neuropsychological Assessment

Gaddes (1980) is critical of educators for not looking at the information available through neuropsychological research and for frequently lumping different types of LD problems together in programs that are not focused to attack those specific problems. There is merit to neuropsychological assessment in the diagnostic evaluation of children suspected of having a learning disability. Selz and Reitan (1979) demonstrated the merit of such a process in differential diagnosis of normal, LD, and brain-damaged children aged 9 to 14 years. Using right side/left side differences in the Halstead-Reitan neuropsychological batteries, the authors concluded that these tests can differentiate and, furthermore, suggested that subjects suffering from well-defined learning disabilities have "a degree of cerebral dysfunction that is frequently undetected by neurological examinations" (p. 328). Gaddes also stated, "The neuropsychological approach to LD has a high level of validity and at present is the most promising method for understanding and treating the LD child" (p. 329).

The primary problem with using comprehensive neuropsychological assessment procedures is twofold: (a) the lack of school psychologists trained in the administration of neuropsychological tests and techniques and (b) the interpretation of the results in combination with other information that can produce prescriptive information that can be used by educators.

There seems to be general agreement that the school psychologist could easily incorporate some of these tests into an assessment that could be both diagnostic and cost-effective (Hartlage & Telznow, 1983). The batteries listed by Sely and Reitan seem appropriate, as well as a list of suggested procedures noted by Hynd and Obrzut (1981).

Other Concerns

The school psychologist and other members of the evaluation team should be prepared to answer questions put forth by knowledgeable parents who are generally concerned about their children. Hart-Johns and Johns (1982) listed questions parents should ask school psychologists and diagnosticians, such as:

- Why are you choosing to administer those particular tests to Johnny?
- How valid and useful are the tests which you gave Johnny?
- How much time did you spend talking with Johnny, and how did he respond to you?
- Did you tell Johnny why he was taking the tests and how he did on them?
- How is the label "learning disabled" useful to those working with my child? (pp. 170–173)

School psychologists also have a responsibility to convert their psychometric information into useful recommendations for teachers. Cruickshank, (1981) critically stated, "Psychologists in great numbers who function in schools, must also learn how to present to educators a psychological picture of these children which can be matched to educational methodology appropriate to the child's needs" (p. 27). It is this skill of making valid and useful statements about the child's functioning that discriminates the professional school psychologist from the psychological tester.

SUMMARY

The school psychologist has a significant role in and responsibility for improving the identification of learning-disabled students so that they can be differentiated from other "poor" academic achievers. Many students brought to the attention of the school psychologist and the diagnostic team are in need of assistance, usually involving modification of materials, techniques, attitudes, and/or programs. These children may be different from their classmates but they are not disabled or handicapped. The school psychologist has the responsibility to help teachers, parents, and educational agencies see that there is a wide range in learning styles, rate of learning, and expectancy. Curriculum expectations by grade level are dangerous rulers to use if the range of difference is not considered in formulating those measures. Children must have the right to be different and to develop differently. Difference can become disability when normal becomes a narrow range. Duffey, Salvia, Tucker, and Ysseldyke (1981) saw sociological implications to this problem and were critical of the "ill defined" norms for the handicapping LD category. They see "normal cultural diversity" as an equally valid explanation for the "symptoms" of the LD handicap. Racial or social bias may not be the problem. An average child may be seen as learning disabled in a school where 90% of the students are significantly above average. Difference being made a disability goes beyond sociocultural diversity, as we will see in Chapter 21.

CHAPTER 18

Discrepancy Methods

T hroughout this volume is ample evidence not only of the problematic
nature of learning disabilities but also of basic difficulties in their
definition and diagnosis. These issues involve not only problems in instrumentation but in methods of interpeting what our instruments tell us. Lack
of a systematic identification procedure for learning-disabled children has
therefore become a problem that will not go away and that continues to
defy consensual resolution (Adelman, 1979; Fuller & Davis, 1984; Harber,
1981; Kavale & Andreassen, 1984; Lerner, 1984; Tucker, Stevens & Ysseldyke, 1983; Ysseldyke, Algozzine & Epps, 1983).

One reason this issue has become particularly critical is that learning-
disabled children are now the largest-growing segment of the special
education population. Identification criteria have regrettably become tools
whereby at least some policy makers have sought to halt the increase in
services for LD children (Forness, 1985). This is currently being attempted
by the application of various psychometric formulas to the psychoeducational test results of potentially learning-disabled children in order to systematically weed out those children who are simply "underachievers" from
those who are truly "learning disabled."

In actual practice with individual children, the procedure is as follows.
Once a child's IQ and achievement test results become available, a school

psychologist or some other member of the IEP team has to make a decision, based on some mathematical approach, whether or not the obtained difference between the child's actual reading level and what should reasonably be expected (based on his or her age and/or IQ) is indeed a severe enough discrepancy to warrant an LD diagnosis. In the past, this has been done by what one might call the "Kentucky Windage" method. In such an approach, the school psychologist multiplies the child's age in years and months by the IQ expressed as a percentage (i.e., mental age) and "corrects" for month of the school year, age at kindergarten entrance, best guess on whether the child's test results were valid, cut of the teacher's jib, and who knows what else. More formal approaches are, of course, available and have been discussed by a wide variety of other authors (Algozzine, Ysseldyke, & Shinn, 1982; Berk, 1984a; Cone & Wilson, 1981; Danielson & Bauer, 1978; Hoffman, 1980; McLeod, 1979; Page, 1980; Salvia & Ysseldyke, 1978).

Exact methods and formulas for identifying such discrepancies in learning-disabled students come in a rather bewildering array of sizes and shapes. There is little consensus, however, concerning which approach is best; and as we shall show later in this chapter, the application of different formulas or methods often yields strikingly varied results in regard to prevalence rates for learning disabilities; and comparison of fomula-identified learning-disabled students with their actual classroom placements sometimes shows surprisingly little agreement. This chapter will thus address the major types of LD discrepancy formulas, review certain problems in their use, and comment on research developments in this area.

LD ABILITY–ACHIEVEMENT METHODS OR FORMULAS

The major defining characteristic of a child with learning disabilities is a discrepancy between his or her current academic achievement and intellectual ability. A review of approaches in this area reveals five major methods or types of formulas in general use in the determination of discrepancies between achievement and intellectual potential (Algozzine, Forgnone, Mercer, & Trifiletti, 1979; Berk, 1982, 1984b; Dore-Boyce, Misner, & McGuire, 1975; Hanna, Dyck, & Holen, 1979; Mellard, Cooley, Poggio, & Deshler, 1983; O'Donnell, 1980; Warner, 1981). These five types of methods or formulas are depicted in Table 18-1, along with an example of each. It should be pointed out that these are not formulas in the sense of $x - y = LD$. Most are, therefore, not sufficient in and of themselves to determine a discrepancy but rather serve to produce a score that can then be compared to an expected allowable minimum standard, which has been previously determined. Also note that there are at least 20 different formulas in exis-

TABLE 18.1
Examples of Commonly Used Discrepancy Methods.

Types of Approach	Formula	Source
1. Constant deviation	MA − 5	Harris (1961)
2. Graduated deviation	$\dfrac{\text{YIS} \times \text{IQ}}{100} + 1.0$	Bond and Tinker (1973)
3. Weighted formulas	$\dfrac{\text{CA (IQ} + .17)}{300} - 2.5$	Bureau of Education for the Handicapped (1976)
4. Standard score formulas	$z = \dfrac{\text{score R} - \text{GM}}{\text{SD of Scores}}$	Erikson (1975)
5. Regression formulas	(IQ − RS) − 1.5 (SD diff)	California State Department of Education (1983)

CA = Chronological Age; GM = Group Mean; IQ = Intelligence Quotient; MA = Mental Age; RS = Reading Standard Score (Mean = 100); Score R = Score in Reading; SD = Standard Deviation; SD diff = Standard Deviation of Distribution of Differences Between Ability and Achievement Tests; YIS = Years in School; z = z Score.

tence with some authors having produced multiple revisions of their formulas over the years.

Grade Equivalent Methods

The first two methods involve determination of grade-level expectancies and the degree to which a child's achievement score is or is not commensurate with his or her grade level. The first method involves a constant level of deviation, such as achievement of two years below expectations. Expected achievement is determined simply by subtracting the five preschool years from the child's mental age (MA) to arrive at the child's expected grade level, as shown in the formula. The MA is arrived at by conversion from IQ and chronological age. This method is easy to use but does not take into account the number of years a child has been in school or the fact that a one-year discrepancy in the ninth grade is not as significant as one-year discrepancy in the second grade. Note also that the determination of the number of years below grade placement that is considered a "significant" discrepancy is not specified. Such an approach is similar to that used in the psychiatric diagnostic and classification system found in hospital or clinics settings (Sinclair, Forness, & Alexson, 1985).

The second method involves a graduated deviation that increases as grade placement increases. This method uses a formula that is different from the first method only in the inclusion of the actual number of years of schooling the child has completed. As in the first method, it also leaves the standard for exact number of years of discrepancy unspecified. Thus a discrepancy of one year might be used for grades one and two, a discrepancy of one-and-one-half years might be used for grades three and four, and a discrepancy of two years might be used for grades five and six. This method is relatively easy to use and does take into account the gradually increasing range of variability of scores as children progress in school to the upper grades. In general, however, these grade-level discrepancy approaches tend to misidentify students who are close to the limits of the normal range of intelligence, that is, children who have IQs outside the 80 to 130 range (Cone & Wilson, 1981). These formulas depend on grade-level achievement scores that are misleading and have been the object of considerable criticism over the past decade (see Angoff, 1971; Horst, 1976; Linn, 1981; Reynolds, 1981); However, as Linn (1981) points out, "despite the criticisms the popularity of these scores has continued almost unabated" (p. 92). Seven serious deficiencies of grade-equivalent scores have been identified by Berk (1981). Grade-equivalent scores —

1. invite seemingly simple but misleading interpretation
2. assume that the rate of learning is constant throughout the school year and that either no growth occurs during the summer or that growth does occur equivalent to one month of growth during the school year
3. are derived primarily from interpolation and extrapolation rather than from real data
4. are virtually meaningless in the upper grade-levels for subjects that are not taught at those levels
5. do not comprise an equal-interval scale
6. exaggerate the significance of small differences in performance
7. vary markedly from test to test, from subtest to subtest within the same battery, from grade to grade, and from percentile to percentile.

These characteristics make it statistically possible to increase or decrease the incidence of learning disabilities at the local and state levels by selecting a standardized test based on its grade-equivalent distributions. This observation plus the distortion of a student's actual achievement level that results from deficiences 2, 3, 4, and 6 indicate that only one conclusion can be drawn about the usefulness of grade-equivalent scores (as well as age-equivalent scores and developmental quotients): *There is no technically sound reason to justify their use in the screening and diagnosis of learning disabilities.*

Weighted Formulas

A third general approach (see Table 18-1) uses a weighted formula to quantify achievement expectancy levels. Mathematically, this group of formulas may differ, but each emphasizes the variables of current reading achievement, IQ, and /or mental age (Algozzine, Forgnone, Mercer, & Trifiletti, 1979) with various weights assigned to these variables in an attempt to offset problems predicting expected versus observed grade scores at different age levels. These weights are sometimes based on some *fixed* estimate computed through ability–achievement correlations or estimates of deviation over increasing age. None of the above-mentioned formulas adeqately address the issues of measurement error, true regression toward the mean, or norm group comparability (McLeod, 1979). These limitations raise questions about the appropriateness of using this type of formula in difficult, questionable cases where eligibility is being challenged or disputed (Danielson & Bauer, 1978). Indeed, the formula that is depicted in Table 18-1 as an example of this type of approach was soundly criticized at the time it was proposed and was thus never adopted (U.S. Department of Education, 1977).

Standard Score Formulas

In contrast, the fourth type of approach involves the use of standard score discrepancies. Among the most frequently used procedures is Erikson's z-score model (Erikson, 1975), which is depicted in Table 18-1, that converts achievement and IQ scores into standard scores with the same mean and the same standard deviation. This conversion allows for the comparison of scores across tests, age, or grade levels and circumvents many of the statistical criticisms leveled at age and grade expectancy formulas (Reynolds et al., 1984).

Regression Formulas

The fifth type of approach utilizes regression models (Shepard, 1980; Wilson & Cone, 1984). Regression formulas attempt to correct for the effects of the regression of IQ on achievement, in which high-ability children are overidentified and low-ability children are underidentified. Utilization of regression approaches may thus better avoid the problems of overidentification of children with IQs well above 100. Unfortunately, the mathematical calculations used in these formulas are sometimes not only cumbersome and usually beyond the practical applicability of school personnel (Mellard et al., 1983) but are also not easily usable in smaller public school agencies without the support of sophisticated research facilities to carry out required statistical analyses on their populations.

For example, the California formula, depicted in Table 18-1, uses standard scores, as does Erikson's, but also contrasts the obtained difference with differences obtained in the distribution of all subjects taking the same ability and achievement tests. The manual containing specific IQ and achievement test tables (California State Department of Education, 1983) is over 40 pages long. Note that the formula in Table 18-1 depicts only an approximation of the actual calculations required, which have recently been modified to include a standard error of measurement of 4 points or less (CASP, 1985). This formula is also not without its problems in terms of its actual effects on prevalence of LD children (Boyan, 1985; Forness, 1985).

Finally, it should be pointed out that there is considerable overlap among the five types of formulas or methods described. For example, the second and third types can be seen as somewhat similar, with the exception that fixed or weighted estimates of age or regression effects are more prominent in the latter. The weighted method also includes some approaches that have also been termed *percentage formulas* in which a percentage that a student lags behind his peers is used as a cutoff (Mercer, Hughes, & Mercer, 1985). The standard score method is, in a sense, quite similar to the regression formulas with the possible exception of the specificity with which regression effects are controlled in terms of particular combinations of IQ and achievement measures. There is yet another developing approach, not discussed here, that has been termed the *true difference* method, which requires slightly more complex calculations, that extends some of the advantages of these regression formulas (Berk, 1984b).

PROBLEMS IN APPLICATION OF LD FORMULAS

As mentioned at the beginning of this chapter, learning disability discrepancy formulas have become somewhat of a focal point in a battle to keep the growing prevalence rate of LD children under control. Policy makers in various states have viewed tightening of discrepancy requirements (i.e., requiring a *larger* discrepancy between IQ and achievement as a criteria for LD eligibility) as a means to restrict numbers of LD children served and, hence, to keep special education cost increases under control. Parents and other advocacy groups, on the other hand, not only resist such efforts but also frequently seek to expand their state's LD discrepancy formula (i.e., require a *smaller* discrepancy in order for a child to qualify as LD). The difficulty with this tug-of-war is that what should be a *clinical* diagnosis of LD appears to have become a *political* diagnosis of LD. It can become so, at least partly as we have seen above, because there is so much confusion and controversy in regard to the discrepancy procedure itself.

In addition to the fact that there are at least five major approaches to establishing an ability-achievement discrepancy, other problems abound. These center on three areas:

1. validity of ability and achievement testing with LD children
2. uneven application of discrepancy formulas or variations in LD prevalence based on an arbitrary choice of formula
3. lack of evidence for the clinical significance of an obtained LD discrepancy

Each will be discussed briefly below.

Validity of IQ and Achievement Tests

The history of intelligence testing in the field of learning disabilities is a checkered one at best (Osgood, 1984). When one examines the current evolution of IQ testing, one generally encounters the WISC-R as its most highly evolved form. The reason for this is several fold. The WISC-R has several advantages that other commonly used IQ tests do not have. For example, it contains separate verbal and performance scales, as well as other potentially clinically relevant subscales that can be analyzed in relation to implications either for additional evaluation or for intervention. The practice of examining such variability among WISC-R IQs and subtest scores is so widespread and is so much a part of LD "lore" that it almost has to be considered a separate discrepancy procedure in itself (Berk, 1984b). Although discrepancies found in LD children's WISC-R profiles are frequently viewed by some professionals as definitive of an LD diagnosis, this practice has been shown to have very little empirical support. for example, Kavale and Forness (1984) in a meta-analysis of 94 studies in this area demonstrated that the mean verbal–performance IQ discrepancy of LD children amounts to the equivalent of only four IQ points, hardly a clinically significant difference. They also demonstrated that none of the WISC-R subtest-recategorization schemes clearly differentiated LD from non-LD subjects.

Another cited advantage of the WISC-R is that it appears to depend less on acquired learning or environmental advantage as a requisite for valid performance. This tends to be true at least in regard to certain identifiable subtests, for example, most items used to determine the performance IQ. Its only current serious rival in this area, other than certain cumbersome nonverbal tests, is the Kaufman Assessment Battery for Children (K-ABC) (see Klanderman, Perney, & Kroeschell, 1985). Items in the K-ABC mental processing section seem based on certain neuropsychological principles and generally appear to require less language skill or school experience. These items are, furthermore, identified as separate from achievement items, unlike the WISC-R that, for example, features "vocabulary" and "arithmetic" as so-called IQ measures. In a recent study on behaviorally disordered children, it was demonstrated that the ability-achievement discrepancy found on the K-ABC battery was much more likely to be significant than the discrepancy with the same group of children on the commonly used WISC-R and PIAT battery (Forness & Herman, 1984).

The WISC-R also seems more likely to have met currently acceptable standards for reliability, validity, and norms than two other quite commonly used IQ measures, the Stanford-Binet and the PPVT, which are both more highly dependent on language. For example, Berk (1984b) has provided evidence on technical adequacy for several different test instruments used in psychoeducational test batteries for LD children. Technical adequacy was judged in terms of recently revised joint standards for educational and psychological tests. Six commonly used measures, at least in regard to the discrepancy issue, are depicted (from Berk's analysis) in Table 18-2. In fact, only 7 of the 17 intelligence tests examined by Berk met criteria in all three areas.

It should be pointed out that achievement tests do not necessarily fare any better. Berk's analysis suggests that only 8 of the 19 achievement tests he reviewed met criteria in all three areas. As indicated in Table 18-2, the WRAT in particular did not fare well, even though it shows up in LD test batteries more frequently than any other individual achievement measure, sometimes by a ratio of 3 to 1 (Cone & Wilson, 1981). The implications for ability-achievement discrepancy are, unfortunately, clear. If a large number of intellectual and academic measures are technically limited, what confidence can one put in a discrepancy formula based solely on these

TABLE 18.2
Technical Adequacy of Selected Discrepancy Instruments.

Type of Test	Norms Met?	Validity Met	Reliability Met?
Ability:			
WISC-R	yes	yes	yes
Stanford-Binet	yes	no	no
PPVT	no	yes	yes
Achievement:			
PIAT	yes	yes	yes
Woodcock Reading	yes	yes	yes
WRAT	no	no	no

Adapted from tabular data appearing in Berk (1984b, pp. 58-59).

measures? Not only are the results of traditional psychoeducational assessments not likely to relate to actual classroom outcome (Sinclair, 1980; Ysseldyke, Algozzine, & Epps, 1983), but it appears that they may even be problematic in relation to basic eligibility criteria in LD. It has in fact been shown that remedial reading teachers, who often do not view themselves as within the "special educational–learning disability" professional baliwick and who usually serve poor readers directly without benefit of *formal* eligibility criteria, tend *not* to include discrepancy concepts or even intellectual measures in their diagnostic batteries. Instead, they tend to depend solely on formal or informal measures of reading achievement (German, Johnson, & Schneider, 1985). When it comes to actual classroom needs, even most professionals in special education see achievement as the main determinant for special education (Kavale & Andreasson, 1984).

Applicability of Discrepancy Formulas

As is obvious from Table 18-1, there are several methods of determining an ability–achievement discrepancy; and earlier discussion has indicated how each has certain offsetting disadvantages. Without a national standard for determining what constitutes a severe discrepancy between IQ and achievement, there is considerable variability in the prevalance rates of learning disabled children from state to state, in large measure because of methods of determining discrepancy and the exact cutoff points needed for a given child to qualify as LD (U.S. Department of Education, 1985). Morrison, MacMillan, and Kavale (1985) have suggested that these differences in LD determination are a significant contributor to the current confusion in learning disability research. They suggest that conflicting findings are often the result of differences in actual *populations* of LD subjects rather than true sampling differences or variations in research methodology.

Another major weakness in the application of discrepancy formulas is that none of them provides a mechanism for determining whether a discrepancy is due to chance or errors of measurement. A discrepancy score must be reliable before discriminative efficiency can be investigated. Interestingly, the method for assessing the reliability of a discrepancy between two scores of one student is not new (Payne & Jones, 1957). However, its application to the problem of learning disability identification is quite recent (Reynolds, 1981; Shepard, 1980). While the formulas involved are more complicated and time consuming to compute than those in Table 18-1, the dividends to accrue from the analysis can be justified. There are also some general guidelines one can follow to avoid the specific computations.

If the procedures for determining the reliability of a discrepancy score were followed, one important inference could be drawn from the results.

Suppose a discrepancy score was found to be statistically significant. One can then say that it is *real* since such a discrepancy would have occured by chance only five times (or less) in 100. This is one possible definition of a severe ability–achievement discrepancy, where the *criterion for a severe discrepancy* is the *magnitude of the discrepancy needed for statistical significance.* The risk of overinterpreting this finding, that is, committing a Type I (alpha) error, is minimized by the level of confidence that is set (see Feldt, 1967). Therefore, the probability of mislabeling a normal child as learning disabled (false positive) is quite small, if that interpretation of the discrepancy is valid. On the other hand, if the discrepancy score is not significant, a severe discrepancy between ability and achievement does not exist.

In a recent review of LD criteria in 50 states, Mercer, Hughes, and Mercer (1985) found that 22% of states included discrepancy in their LD *definition* and that 76% included it in their LD procedural *criteria.* The combined figure for states having a discrepancy component in their LD identification procedures (identification and/or criteria) was 84%. This represented an increase from the pre-PL 94–142 period (i.e., before 1976) of over 50%. Mercer and his colleagues further noted that, of all states that reported using a discrepancy criteria just over two-thirds used a graduated deviation, although there was overlap in that some states used more than one approach. Standard scores were used by fewer than one in five of the states using discrepancy procedures. Ten states gave IEP teams the option of "overriding" test scores, and hence the discrepancy formula, in determining the diagnosis of LD. This happened recently in California as a result of a possible legal suit brought by an advocacy group (CASP, 1985). A study of a relatively large sample of children in LD programs in Iowa, using a standard-score approach, revealed that nearly 75% of all children met the established criterion for LD (Wilson, 1985). Comparison, however, between these children and a comparable sample of referred children, who were not in LD programs, revealed that the LD children were more likely to have achievement that was also markedly below grade level, while the other group did not. Only about 60% of referred children were performing significantly below grade level, while the LD group was below grade level in over 90% of the cases. Thus, other determinants operate in actual LD diagnostic practice.

Relatively few studies have *directly* examined the question of effects of variability among formulas or methods used to establish discrepancy, although analysis of mathematic properties of the formulas themselves and the resulting implications have been extensive (Berk, 1984b; Cone & Wilson, 1981; Danielson & Bauer, 1978; McLeod, 1979; Mellard et al., 1983; Mercer, Hughes, & Mercer, 1985; Reynolds, 1985; Shepherd, 1980). In a study of effects of these formulas in actual practice, Forness, Sinclair, and Guthrie (1983) applied eight commonly used discrepancy formulas to a sample of 92 potentially learning-disabled youngsters and found that any-where from 11 to 37% of these children would have been identified as LD, the number depending solely on the choice of formula. Slightly less than half of the sample were not identified as LD by any formula, but only about 7% were identified by all eight of the formulas used. Sinclair and Alexson (1986) recently attempted to replicate this study with five carefully selected formulas roughly corresponding to the categories in Table 18-1. They found, interestingly, that a type of constant deviation formula iden-tified the *fewest* children (4%) while a standard score approach identified the most (28%). About three-fifths were not identified by any formula, and only 2% were identified by all five. From the above studies, it is clear that certain somewhat arbitrary choices of discrepancy method can have a significant effect on who gets identified as learning disabled.

Clinical Significance of Discrepancy

One of the questions that, in most cases, has *not* been addressed in much detail, if at all, is the issue of what LD discrepancy means for the classroom teacher. Although the above discussion shows quite clearly that choice of discrepancy method may well determine which children *enter* the system of LD services, what discrepancy means in regard to what happens *once they are there* has not been considered. Some questions that have *not* been asked are: What do various degrees of severe discrepancy imply? Are different degrees of severity actually found in children at various IQ levels? Does severity of discrepancy relate to other aspects of a learning disability such as so-called underlying psychological processes or LD subtypes? Do children at various levels of severe discrepancy require different teaching strategies or types of classroom placement? Are various degrees of severity related to prognosis or prospects for recovery? In other words, once it has determined that a child has exceeded the basic criterion for a significant discrepancy between ability and achievement, do degrees of severity beyond that minimum level mean anything?

These questions do not seem to be addressed in any systematic way in the LD literature. One reason for this may be that the concept of dis-crepancy, although it has been part of the basic diagnostic assumption in LD for at least two decades, has received attention only recently, largely because of controversial application of specific formulas in LD determina-tion. Attention has been focused on this question because of the promi-nence of the discrepancy concept in debates over the growing prevalence rate of learning disabled children and variability among LD samples. As is clear from what we have discussed so far, however, it is difficult to address the above questions when the field has almost as many conflicting views of how to measure discrepancy as it has over the precise definition of LD.

The question of clinical or practical usefulness of discrepancy, therefore, remains largely unexamined.

Related questions involve the fate of children who are significantly below grade level but who do not meet discrepancy criteria for special education eligibility and are thus not receiving services. Examination of California's LD discrepancy manual, for example, indicates that a child with an IQ in the low 80s may never meet the criterion for a "severe discrepancy" no matter how low his or her achievement score *in cases of certain combinations of IQ and achievement tests.* In fact, the minimum average IQ needed in California for discrepancy eligibility was 82.7 (Forness, 1985). How are such children different from children who also have not met the discrepancy index but whose IEP committee has overridden this consideration and determined that they are eligible for special education as learning disabled? As noted above, over 20% of the states now allow such overriding to happen.

It may thus be that the discrepancy issue will be examined not just in terms of methodological issues but in terms of its clinical or practical significance as well. An example of such a study is that by Sinclair, Guthrie, and Forness (1985) with a small sample of LD children in 16 special classrooms. Correlations were obtained between their ability–achievement discrepancies, as measured by a graduated deviation formula, and deviations in their attention levels, as observed over several days in their classroom settings. While correlations only barely reached significance, results suggested that this relationship may have been independent of absolute levels of IQ, achievement, and amount of teacher interaction with target LD subjects. If these results can be replicated more convincingly, they might either be interperted in terms of attention-deficit hypotheses (see Samuels & Edwall, 1981) or engaged-learning-time hypotheses (see Kavale & Forness, 1986). The important point here is that until recently relatively few attempts have been made to examine either the practical or the research implications of ability–achievement discrepancies.

CONCLUSION

Methods of determining an ability–achievement discrepancy in learning-disabled children have, perhaps rather unfortunately, become a focal point of the LD diagnostic and eligiblity process. Problems in determining an LD discrepancy include the multiplicity of available methods, lack of an agreed-upon standard for what constitutes a significant discrepancy, the technical adequacy of IQ and achievement test instruments, the uneven application of methods or formulas across populations, and the practical usefulness of an obtained discrepancy. Many of these problems derive from the adverse influence of certain psychological practices, which special education seems to have inherited, and suggestions have been made that involve removing many psychometrically based eligibility procedures from special education entry criteria (Forness & Kavale, 1986). In the meantime, however, discrepancy formulas seem to have become a fact of life in both LD practice and in LD research. Whether improvements in their use and application are also forthcoming remains to be seen.

CHAPTER 19

Multidisciplinary Team Assessment

Darlene G. Davies

A strong factor in multidisciplinary teams is the holistic approach to helping learning-disabled children. There are many disciplines that may play viable roles on teams, depending upon individual child needs. The potential for flexibility of team membership is another positive factor associated with a team approach. There is no substitute for professional stimulation within a multidisciplinary setting where the learning-disabled individual is the direct beneficiary of the multiple input to the team, but each team member also derives insight from review sessions. Assessment instrument selection and observation of children are influenced by communication between team members. As Shanks (1983) pointed out, "The team approach is absolutely necessary to thoroughly SEE a child and eliminate wasteful duplication. No one member can be solely responsible for deciding the most appropriate program to meet a child's needs."

The speech-language pathologist is an appropriate member of a learning-disabilities team, since the learning-disabled child is frequently an oral-language deficient child. Learning in the educational setting is dependent upon language competence and language performance. Listening, speaking, writing, and reading are all primary components of language processes. The American Speech–Language–Hearing Association (ASHA) pointed out as recently as 1982 that the problems identification of the learn-

This chapter originally appeared as an article by **Darlene G. Davies** in *Learning Disabilities: An Interdisciplinary Journal* (Vol. III, 1984) and was adapted by permission of Grune & Stratton for inclusion in this *Handbook*.

ing-disabled population and the definition of learning disabilities were still areas that lacked resolution. The federal government states that a learning disability may exist when there is a wide gap between intelligence and academic achievement. Those academic performance areas include verbal expression, auditory understanding, written expression, reading skills, and mathematical skills. The Office of Education reported in 1978 that more than 50% of handicapped children who participated in the national Head Start program were speech impaired. Additionally, almost 5% of the Head Start children were deaf or hearing impaired, according to statistics for 1977. It is valuable, therefore, to have the speech-language pathologist look at the language and speech comprehension, processing, and production of children.

The timeliness of the consideration of the speech–language pathologist as a member of the learning-disabilities team is underscored by the recent appearance in ASHA of two committee reports, Learning Disabilities: Issues on Definition (1982a) and the Position Statement on Language Learning Disorders (1982b). The educational and clinical training background of speech–language pathologists uniquely equips them to interface with other experts.

Note that the designation of *speech pathologist* of a few years ago is now modified to read *speech–language pathologist.* The official communicative disorder national organization and its monthly journal have been retitled the American Speech–Language–Hearing Association (ASHA), an altered form of the previously labeled American Speech–Hearing Association.

This chapter explores the roles and functions of members of the learning disabilities teams, as well as overall contributions of teams as total units. Particular emphasis is placed upon the special value of inclusion of a speech–language pathologist on a team. The assignment of team coordinator responsibility to the speech–language pathologist is also appropriate in specific circumstances.

The need for the presence of a speech–language pathologist on a team is pointed when the multidisciplinary team seeks information about "a child's inherent strategies and processing abilities" and is involved in ascertaining "how these inherent abilities interact with the environment, i.e., expectations of teachers, instructional language, and content of curricula" (ASHA, 1982a, 1982b). Piaget (1977) wrote about children's increasing development in cognitive sophistication. The processing and organizing of information, which is critical to academic success, becomes more complicated as the child matures at a normal rate. Piaget wrote that many of the metalinguistic skills are acquired in the early grades and that early school experiences can have a profound effect upon later development.

It is imperative that speech–language pathologists continue to provide language assessments and intervention programs for school-age language impaired children in view of (a) the important acquisitions and changes in both receptive and expressive language that occur beyond age 5, (b) the demands of the early school curricula, and (c) the profound effects that language may exert on students' academic achievements.

Recommendations published in *ASHA*) (1982) include:

1. the urging of inclusion of speech-language specialists on assessment and management multidisciplinary teams;
2. interface between state education departments, local education offices, colleges, universities, and spokesmen and policy formulating professional assocations;
3. heavy emphasis upon multidisciplinary team function as a component of student training;
4. participation of proven qualified administrators in coordination of multidisciplinary teams, rather than administrators with unproven abilities;
5. preparation of school and clinic personnel for research validation of designed and implemented programs for the learning-disabled child;
6. mandatory multidisciplinary training for individuals, so that those individuals in the classroom will be alert to language learning disorders; and
7. continuing education opportunities to gauge local needs and meet individual education needs. (*ASHA,* 1982)

The American Speech–Language–Hearing Association takes the official stand that the speech–language pathologist should assess children who manifest characteristics of disabilities to determine the functional levels of language, assess program planning development for children who are deemed to be learning disabled, and participate in design and implementation of programs to language-disordered children.

Therefore, the American Speech–Language–Hearing Association advocates that agencies having responsibility for providing programs and services to those individuals ensure that qualified speech–language pathologists are members of the multidisciplinary assessment and instructional team (*ASHA,* 1982a, 1982b).

POTENTIAL CONTRIBUTIONS OF TEAM MEMBERS

In order to speculate about the potential roles of team specialists, it is necessary to look at the areas of specialization of team members. Note that the makeup of multidisciplinary teams will vary according to the individual children being considered.

Potential contributory members of the learning-disabilities team include speech–language pathologists, learning-disabilities teachers, counselors, social workers, reading specialists, audiologists, classroom teachers, resource specialists, neurologists, opthalmologists, occupational therapists, physical therapists, psychologists, psychiatrists, school nurses, and adaptive physical education specialists. Each discipline has a distinct purpose. The learning-disabilities teacher and the resource specialist or the learning-disabilities teacher and the speech–language pathologist may have direct dialogue with each other in reporting observed behavior of children and in assessing appropriateness of curriculum materials. Because of the need for language-based approaches to the teaching of reading, the speech–language pathologist and the reading specialist aid, and illumine, one another's remediation efforts with children. Such crossover of information sharing is common but, unfortunately, is incident specific most of the time. Because of heavy professional workloads and responsibilities for many children, professional interdisciplinary sharing of information is not frequently regularized. Hopefully, the audiologist reports findings regarding a child's hearing acuity to the school nurse or speech–language pathologist; but, far too often, there is no school audiologist, and there is also no outside clinical audiological service routinely available for hearing screening and in-depth hearing testing of children.

Speech–Language Pathologist

Heward and Orlansky (1980) observed that "because acquiring language is so critical in the development of all children, a speech and language specialist is an important part of almost every intervention team." Since speech–language pathologists assess all children referred for special services at most schools, it is natural to routinely include them on multidisciplinary assessment teams. Heward and Orlansky (1980) point out that more than 50% of handicapped children who were included in Head Start programs in 1977 were communicatively handicapped and almost 5% were hearing impaired. The same authors conclude, therefore, that "for all these children, intervention must include a specialist in language acquisition and speech disorders."

Learning-Disabilities Teacher

This specialist will be a valuable member of the team. An instructor of a learning-disabled group of children will quickly sum and communicate critical observations of a child undergoing review. The learning-disabilities specialist describes the learning style of a child and relates possession of learning strategies or lack of strategies to the team. From the learning-disabilities teacher, a team gleans not only what a child does not do in the classroom but what he does with success.

Counselor

Counselors only occassionally serve on multidisciplinary teams, but when they do contribute information they are a fine source of information about a child's ability to relate emotionally to others and about students' reaction to school failure. A counselor's skills should be utilized when appropriate to team needs.

Social Worker

The social worker will visit the home environment of the child and will observe interaction between the child and peers, child and siblings, and child and parents.

This professional worker will interview parents and gain insight into the learning-disabled child and the effect of the learning disability upon significant others.

Reading Specialist

Reading specialists diagnose, assess, and plan remediation programs for students who test below grade levels and/or manifest reading difficulties in silent or verbal reading behaviors. They are knowledgeable and current on the subject of standardized reading tests and commerically available reading programs. In addition, the reading specialists has sufficient knowledge of instructional design and curriculum to be able to devise and supervise individualized reading development courses for individual pupils.

Goodman (1973) described three cueing systems used by readers: cues within words, cues related to relationships among words, and cues concerning pragmatic context and discourse structure. Goodman's definition of reading requires that reading processes be viewed as dynamic in nature. Many other researchers have examined the same notion that certain assumptions are made by individuals about textual meaning. Hypotheses are borne out or are refuted as the reader moves along the orthographic forms. If hypotheses are confirmed as readers read, then they continue along the progression of material. If the hypotheses are faulty, then it is necessary for readers to retrace their previous steps to formulate new hypotheses and make new assumptions. All of the skills of effective readers, as well as lack of skills of unsuccessful readers, can be understood and explained to other members of an interdisciplinary team. Hammermeister and Israelite (1983) commented:

> Language permeates all of school life, encompassing the entire curriculum, for both hearing and hearing-impaired children. Whether the school day includes science, mathematics, social studies, play activities, or physical education, language is the resource that each child encounters daily in the classroom and that must become a living part of communication and thinking. In particular, it is the resource that a child must bring to the act of reading, which is the key to school learning.

Children learn language through social interaction with other children. The rules of oral language are not didactically taught to children. Those rules are acquired through use, by *doing*. Trial and error, selection through sampling, shapes the language verbalized by children.

Reading is a language-based process. All communication skills are now viewed as being interrelated. Hall (1981) used an approach whereby children's oral language and experiences form the basis for the creation of personal reading materials. In this manner, four aspects of the language arts, listening, speaking, writing (expressive), and reading (receptive), are incorporated into the curriculum. Hall emphasized that reading has the most meaning for students when the materials are written in their own language and based on their own experiences.

Reading specialists consult with classroom teachers as resource specialists, and they provide additional insight into the reading and language skills of students. Advice regarding appropriate reading books and effective promotion of reading word attack skills, as well as suggestions regarding oral language work with the learning-disabled child, are all services available from the reading specialist who functions as a member of the team.

Audiologist

An audiologist is an expert in the measurement of hearing acuity in humans. Clinical audiologists administer pure-tone hearing tests and speech-reception threshold tests, as well as more specific tests that are designed to provide information about hearing and hearing loss to medical doctors to aid in diagnosis.

Classroom Teacher

If a child being reviewed is enrolled in a regular classroom at the time of team assignment, then the most important and fundamental information will be obtained from that classroom teacher. Observations about learning style and learning deficits will come firsthand from the on-site instructor who is most responsible for the child's learning experiences. Does the child attend to tasks. Can the child follow visual and auditory directions? Can the child produce in terms of the written, verbal, and action-involved task completion? What is the quality of written expression? What is the quality of verbal expression? Can the child physically perform mechanical tasks in meaningful ways (operation of computer, simple calculators, record cassette players, table games)?

Teacher observation about the general appearance of the children, including vitality and interest in what is happening around them, will play important parts in composition of the holistic picture of the student under consideraton.

It is the classroom teacher, by the way, who is the best referral source to the speech–language specialist. Classroom instructors may not know what is wrong with a child, but they will know that something about the communication system of a student is awry. Additionally, the teacher is an excellent potential implementer of remediation suggestions provided by the speech–language specialist.

Resource Specialist

This person is an innovator, coordinator, programmer, in short, an "ideas" staff professional. When the team considers potential commercially produced remediation programs, the resource specialist gives feedback concerning availability, suitability, flexibility, and limitations of the program. Information concerning possible local educational and clinical treatment sources should be supplied by the resource specialist as that information is needed by the team.

Neurologist

A neurologist specializes in the medical field of neurology, which is a branch of medicine that deals with the nervous system, the nervous structure, and associated diseases (see Chapter 16).

Ophthalomogist

An ophthalomogist is a doctor in the area of medicine that deals with the structure, functions, and diseases of the eye. Many vision defects go undetected unless examination by an ophthalmologist is undertaken. Children can exhibit poor learning behavior in the classroom because of faulty vision and eye diseases.

Occupational Therapist

The bulk of sensory-motor training carried out with children in educational settings and clinics is directed by occupational therapists (OTs). Motor and sensory development of children is facilitated through play activities specially designed to heighten sensory-motor awareness. The OT is frequently a specialist in augumentative communication devices, an area in which there is currently an explosion of information.

Physical Therapist

The physical therapist works with those learning-disabled students who have identifiable physical difficulties, which may range from mild to profound in severity. Intense one-to-one therapy programs are undertaken with physically disabled children, and useful carryover activities are shared by the physical therapist with all others on a team, as well as with caring family members. Usually, the physical therapist works rather closely with the occupational therapist in attempts to habilitate or rehabilitate physical and perceptual function in children. Sometimes the person in charge of what is, in some settings, referred to as the daily living classroom is a physical therapist. Within the daily living classroom, pupils learn skills of daily living, and the setting undertakes to simulate some of those environments. Usually, there is a modern kitchen, a bedroom, and a bathroom. These are rooms where students learn to dress themselves, feed themselves, prepare food, do household chores such as making beds, sweeping, mopping, wiping table tops, and taking care of personal toilet needs. Most of the activities offer positive opportunities for children to socialize and thus to gain experience with practical social language and to internalize many of the societal rules of behavior. The interpersonal exchanges are, of course, integral parts of human lives, and necessary to the emotional, social, and intellectual growth of children. Such opportunities present themselves in activities of daily living classrooms.

Psychologist

Dwyer (see Chapter 17) observes that the referral form to a school psychologist should take into account identifying information

- statement of presenting problem
- description of current academic performance (to include grade level and textbooks and curriculum materials used)
- teaching techniques used with the child who is being referred; alterations by the teacher or parents. What works? Why?

- what information is to be yielded as a result of the referral to the school psychologist
- other behaviors believed to be connected to the stated problem
- attached samples of student's academic work

The speech–language pathologist may ask the psychologist to administer a particular kind of psychometric test because of an identified student communicative disorder. A test such as the Leiter International Performance Scale may be requested for a hearing-impaired child, for instance, because the child will be less handicapped by his hearing deficit on that intelligence test.

The psychologist routinely administers psychometric tests, or directs the testing, of children. Interpretation of test performance is the responsibility of the psychologist, and this service is what is most needed by the assessment team. A psychometrist may administer but may not interpret them. The role of a psychometrist may be viewed as that of only a technician. The WISC-R is the most often administered measure of intelligence within the school setting. In a test battery, the psychologist may include the Bender Gestalt achievement test or the Peabody Individual Achievement Test or the Peabody Picture Vocabulary Test. ("Draw a person" or "Draw a family" measures may also be used.)

Psychiatrist

Psychiatrists treat the psyches of human beings according to differing schools of training. All psychiatrists hold medical degrees and spend post-M.D. years in residency training for advanced specialization.

Adaptive Physical Education Specialist

Adaptive physical education instructors can be valuable sources of information about children who are poorly coordinated, awkward in execution of physical movements, and who may not adequately perceive their own bodies or positioning in space. In addition to contributions regarding mobility of students, prescriptive suggestions concerning movement activities can frequently be incorporated into speech and language activities, classroom curriculum, and playground experiences. Children with apraxia or dyspraxia (motor planning difficulties) manifest speech problems through specific oral dyspraxia (oral motor planning for voluntary speech production). Since the purpose of the multidisciplinary approach to remediation is to develop means for treating the whole child, it becomes readily apparent that an adaptive physical education instructor's observations and comments, as well as ingenuity in modifying traditional physical education activities to make them uniquely appropriate for the special-education child, will be illuminating for the family and interdisciplinary team. One of the superb aspects of the team approach is the acquisition of, and increasing support for, the specific competencies of each professional within discrete disciplines. The adaptive physical education teacher can assess fine and gross motor coordination and can serve as ongoing observer of the child over periods of time and report on changes in physical status as remedial strategies are utilized with the child or as differing medical interventions are undertaken. Progress over time can be measured. Physical games for children with learning disabilities can be demonstrated. Physical equipment for those pupils who have specific visual, manual, and auditory needs will be described, demonstrated, and, in many cases, redesigned and utilized in ways not traditionally envisioned.

TEAM ASSESSMENT

As an example of one type of multidisciplinary team assessment, many hospitals hold regular monthly cleft palate board meetings. Such multidisciplinary team meetings are of high professional quality and are open to interested family, professional workers, paraprofessionals, and members of the general public. Usually, the board consists of permanently appointed members, such as a prominent plastic surgeon, dental surgeon, social worker, and communicologist, with rotating members who contribute to the team meetings as the needs of individual patients dictate. If a member from a local university communications program functions as a part of the team, graduate students in training may accompany faculty to the meetings. The same may be true of medical students. The high standards of professional deportment serve as excellent role models for students. A case is staffed thoroughly as medical, social, family, and developmental histories are reviewed by those present. If there has been surgery, pre- and postsurgery photographs and recorded speech samples are shared as management alternatives are considered. Cross-dissemination of information and opinions results in alteration and modification of various points of view. Decisions that are made without benefit of complete knowledge of the case are, in this way, avoided. Careful minutes of the board meeting proceedings are kept, and they are available for referral and consideration as the child is treated over time. The social worker may have gone into the home of the child and, therefore, be able give a firsthand account of environmental surroundings of the case being discussed. Many times, an educator who has directly observed or interacted with the child will be invited to participate in the meeting. Information regarding peer interaction, willingness to verbally communicate within formal and informal situations, academic and social readiness, and the child's self-image will be very helpful in gaining as complete a picture of the case as possible. The learning-disabilities specialist may be asked to participate because there is evidence in the literature that children with cleft palates may experience greater incidence of learning difficulty than most children in regular classrooms.

All of the pieces of a puzzle are needed in order to assemble a complete diagnostic picture. Too often, an intervention plan that is based on incomplete information is formulated. Team assessment prevents this. Generally a formal team meeting is scheduled and conducted. That meeting may be attended by interested family members, teachers, and other concerned professionals. Sometimes, the sessions are closed.

It is desirable for all professional team member diagnostic reports to be written, and then circulated to all participating team members prior to the formal meeting. This action allows sufficient lead time for reviewing of reports that represent differing aspects of student/patient/client function and, additionally, for reactions to be formulated by participants.

TEAM REMEDIATION DESIGN

Commercial programs may be modified to meet identified needs of learning-disabled children. For instance, a multisensory approach to learning may be adopted, if team conclusions indicate the wisdom of such input over a more traditional restricted modalities learning method. Conversely, learning-disabled children who are overstimulated by multiple sensory information input, or who cannot selectively attend to one or another input, may be candidates for unisensory teaching styles, that emphasize a particular element over another at any one time and thus select for the children until they can select and inhibit input for themselves at a future date. Teaching techniques such as repetition (partial or complete) open-ended time allowances for task completion, internal and external rehearsal techniques used by the child after instruction by a teacher, grouping or chunking of informational units, and direct verbal pretask organization, and visual and auditory cueing will be selected according to ascertained individual student needs. Resource and curriculum specialists can be actively involved in locating, combining, and recombining subject study materials, and creating appealing learning aids. What can be computerized for a certain child, and what must be individualized through personalized teaching-learning one-to-one contact? All of these questions are, or will be, addressed by the remediation team, which may be a smaller hybrid group drawn from the original group and modified to accommodate specific curriculum design talents.

The Maryland Student Profile (Manizer, et al, 1982) is recommended as a diagnostic team instructional aid for purposes of looking at assessment data in a nonsubjective manner (see Chapter 17). This profile attempts to reconcile information from team assessment members. This teaching guide should be watched as it is more frequently used as a prototype for other assessment and remediation tools.

Pragmatic intervention recommendations are the target of all thorough team assessments. Some course(s) of action should be stated and, hopefully, elaborated at the closing of the formal presentation of diagnostic information. Appropriate referrals are frequently made. The key word here is appropriate. Too often, referrals are made for want of anything else to recommend. A kind of "passing the buck" can take place when families don't qualify financially for certain services or a child does not meet the test score criteria for placement in certain classrooms. A student may exhibit certain physical disabilities in addition to critical learning disabilities and, therefore, not seem to be a candidate for settings that are not equipped to deal with physical limitations.

If curricula are designed specifically for a child and the evaluation team decides the nature of curricula creation, then who is firmly designated to implement and monitor that remediation program? When multiple programs are selected for the learning-disabled child, who is selected to act as coordinator of the programs in order to ensure maximum effectiveness of education for the student? These are critical questions that must be answered before the assessment team adjourns the formal meeting. Under no circumstances should that team constituency be disbanded until consensus is reached and responsibility for continued follow-up of the client is firmly placed.

A resource specialist may be the professional person most directly qualified to bring together many aspects of curricula and to design or modify present curricula for needs of a student that are defined by the multidisciplinary learning disabilities team. However, unique input from specialists will be needed, for example, those with expertise regarding management of the deaf, deaf-blind, nonambulatory or partially ambulatory, neurologically impaired, color blind, or learning-disabled child. Special techniques of teaching, availability of construction materials, computer hardware and software, other kinds of learning technology, modern equipment for physically handicapped, as well as nonvocal communication equipment are only some areas of expert knowledge that may be needed.

McCarthy (1982) outlined five steps in the teaching process, which are based upon theoretically identified weakness in children's learning strategies. The first step involves looking at where the child is currently operating. Ascertain whether the child has any problem-solving strategies available and usable to him as he is presently functioning in the classroom. Some of the strategies the assessor looks for are selective attention in all modalities, internal and external rehearsal, recoding from and between all sensory modalities, reauditorization and revisualization, chunking (grouping), mnemonic devices, and physical movement aids. How does the child set out to solve academic problems? Strategy use should be looked at in all children, of course, not just learning disabled children. What is the learning style of each child? But, since something has gone awry in the problem-solving system of the learning-disabled child, it is especially important to assess those deficit learning systems.

McCarthy (1982) correctly stated that "In production deficient children, instruction is given in the use of cognitive strategies." As a third step, McCarthy (1982) advises that "in knowledge deficient children, teaching is focused on when, where, and how to use the strategies."

By equipping the child with cognitive strategies, control of learning is shifted from the educator to the child being educated (or, to state it more directly, to children educating themselves).

Assessment of learning-disabled children should take into account compensatory behaviors for faulty areas of function, for example, talking abnormally loudly not only because of possible reduced hearing acuity but also a diminished self-monitoring system. The speech–language pathologist is trained to assess the abstract language facility of children. Many such children decode humor at only the most literal and concrete language levels. The fact that children may laugh and smile in imitation of observed behavior of others is no indication of understanding of intended humor. Information of this nature can be gathered by the language pathologist, but valuable observation can be contributed by learning-disabilities teachers as well as by regular classroom instructors. The child who cannot perceive the humor in verbal messages is notably handicapped in communication efforts. Verified brain damage to speech and language areas of the human brain has long been known to manifest itself in rigidity, concreteness, and lack of subtleness in language usage. It should be noted that, while emotionally disturbed children often fail to respond to refocusing teaching techniques, there are learning-disabled students who can be effectively refocused by the teacher. With judicious use of cues, these children can be switched to on-task behaviors and they can be returned to on-task features. The assessor-teacher must give direct pretask instructions to the student concerning performance focus, such as conversation monitoring. Concreteness of language comprehension will deprive learning-disabled children of the knack of drawing inferences, or multiple alternative interpretations of meanings from verbal messages, so direct verbal guides from teachers are necessary to shape strategy developing behaviors of learning-disabled children. Strategies of internal and external rehearsal and chunking of units, which were mentioned earlier, must be carefully and patiently explained. Learning-disabled children who do not respond to teacher refocusing techniques should be carefully described in team assessment reports, for this observation will have a bearing upon remediation recommendations and design. If the learning-disabled child functions at a higher level when he is verbally, formally preorganized by an examiner or teacher, this observation also must be carefully noted.

SUMMARY

The progress of the learning-disabled child must be monitored over time by professionals who are thoroughly familiar with diagnostic findings and remediation recommendations for the child. Ineffective teaching techniques must be quickly evaluated and either modified or replaced before learning fatigue or poor learning attitudes are firmly established in the child. Continual accountability methods will give immediate information about the success or failure of treatment of a student.

The assessment process should always be holistically oriented. That is, the *child,* not simply the symptoms, needs to be treated, and in such a way as to improve the child's chances of success in life, rather than simply trying to alleviate problems in the present.

To be effective, such an approach requires the cooperation of a number of professionals working together. Since so many learning-disabled children suffer from language or hearing impairment, the speech-language pathologist may be the most consistent member of a multidisciplinary team. Social skills of children are dependent upon verbal and nonverbal language, about which the speech-language pathologist possesses extensive knowledge and experience. Alternative methods of communication may also be needed, and the implementation of these methods will be accomplished by the speech-language pathologist. The field of communicative disorders (speech-language pathology) draws from other disciplines such as psychology, physiology, early childhood education, special education, linguistics, anthropology, medicine, and counseling. It is a field that blends many areas of knowledge regarding the human being and communication. Therefore, the speech-language pathologist (communicologist) is often qualified to function as a mediator, moderator, or coordinator between professional disciplines for purposes of completely defining the nature of a learning disability and the remediation strategies for enabling maximum learning by the learning-disabled child.

However, it should not be construed that the other members of the team are any less important to the child's welfare. For many learning-disabled children, the linchpin of the team may be the classroom teacher — often the professional who knows the child best and interacts with the child on the most consistent basis. In cases where the learning disability is coupled with a physical problem, the audiologist, ophthalmologist, neurologist, or physical therapist may be the critical team member. Indeed, each and every member, no matter how infrequently his or her services may be needed, is vital to the well-being of some learning-disabled children.

CHAPTER 20

Case-Typing Assessment

Stanley L. Rosner
Richard Selznick

O ver the past several years, the Maryland State Board of Education, has been carrying on a systematic program of formalizing and making more uniform the procedures utilized in the assessment and planning for youngsters who are judged to have a learning disability (Maryland Learning Disabilities Project, 1982). Participants in this project have wrestled with a number of critical issues including definition, the minimally acceptable procedures involved in assessment, and the nature of the decision-making process used in coming up with recommendations for learning-disabled youngsters. In part, this project was triggered by a marked variation by county in the number and percentage of youngsters being labeled learning disabled. As a part of this state-wide experience, project members met with the multidisciplinary teams that are charged with the diagnostic and prescriptive responsibility for learning-disabled youngsters. Even a brief acquaintance with this situation made it clear that time pressures, the demands of many cases, and the constant remedial education "paper chase" have led to the clinical process often being managed in a superficial fashion. We in no way intend to be critical of our colleagues who participated in this project but rather to suggest that the pressures of the real world require use of a system for approaching the assessment of learning-disabled and other youngsters that is comprehensive, clearly understandable, and communicable across professional lines. This last point is a critical one in light of the fact that, in many case conferences, it became obvious that people were listening to reports of quantitative data based upon measures that were either totally or largely

---

This chapter originally appeared as an article by **Stanley L. Rosner** and **Richard Selznick** in *Learning Disabilities: An Interdisciplinary Journal* (Vol. I, 1982) and was adapted by permission of Grune & Stratton for inclusion in this *Handbook*.

unknown to them. This fact certainly made the theoretical possibility of a true team decision highly unlikely.

A second experience that directly immersed us in the process of attempting to gather, coordinate, and integrate information was participation in a graduate seminar (Thurman, 1981–1982). Representatives of medicine, administration, social work, special education, school psychology, speech, and reading were gathered together to work out a system of evaluation and prescription that represented the spirit more than the letter of the requirements of various laws. This "ivory tower" experience was certainly quite the opposite from the real-world frustrations of time and work load present in the Maryland Project. Over the course of a full semester, the team of graduate students and professors had to work through only two cases and observe and evaluate a model Individualized Educational Program (IEP) conference. In light of the absence of practical pressure, it was interesting that many of the same kinds of problems that existed working in the schools existed in this more idealistic setting. Problems with communication, disagreement on definition, and lack of understanding of data continued to be central. However, this ivory-tower project was also faced with one reality. Our recommendations had to be followed in a real school district, which was experiencing significant economic and political pressure to reduce rather than increase special services.

In both experiences, it became apparent that the chronic difficulties were: dealing with definition, the standard of acheivement from which a child had to deviate in order to be seen as having a problem and the degree of discrepancy from normal that was necessary to suggest that a child had a significant problem, and the relative importance of various bits of information.

In the Maryland Project an attempt to arrive at a systematic approach led to returning to the case-typing method, which has been utilized in the Temple University Reading Clinic for over 30 years (Rosner & Cooper, 1982). This approach, which will be explained in detail later in this chapter, represented nothing startling or innovative, but it did push the process in the direction of attending to a variety of factors (Johnson, 1957; Robinson, 1946) rather than narrowing consideration to a single area or a limited number of preselected variables. By requiring attendance to a variety of qualitative and quantitative variables and human characteristics, case-typing de-emphasizes the dominance of any single bit of information, and demands the presence of patterns in order to perceive any area as having significance in assessment.

This chapter will attempt to look at a number of significant areas that came to light in these two experiences as well as in the daily clinical practice. The goal is to address assessment and prescription as simplifiers rather than complicators. Basically stated, the issue is, What should be done in assessment to enable the design of a pragmatic program based on a widely derived but coordinated data base?

CHARACTERISTICS OF GOOD REMEDIAL INSTRUCTION

It is important to attempt to delineate those dimensions of a child's learning program that can be and generally are altered through an effective remedial program. An attempt will be made to specify common denominators of change in remedial programs rather than the isolated factors that are built into an IEP and that lead to fragmented educational experience.

There is almost universal agreement that reduction of the teacher-pupil ratio is critical for an appropriate remedial program (Harris & Sipay, 1975). In many instances this has been translated into a legal requirement as to the maximum number of youngsters that may be placed in a special education classroom. As with many practices that have been around for a very long time, the specific reasons behind it often have become lost.

It is important to understand why a low teacher–pupil ratio would be desirable. There are some obvious answers. For one, a smaller number of students would allow the teacher to provide a more individualized program. For another, a youngster with a learning problem can be defined as one who produces less reinforceable behavior; therefore, the fewer the number of students, the greater the opportunity the teacher has for reinforcing desirable behavior. In a smaller group there is also the opportunity for more direct physical contact between teacher and child, indicating implicitly a value of the child as a human being worthy of personal attention. The "pat on the back" or the teacher's hand on a student during a word-learning lesson using the Fernald approach (1943) is an important but often neglected part of the gestalt of the learning situation. The teacher shares his or her ego strengths with the child in a way that is at once reaffirming and enhances control (Johnson, 1966). It must be stressed, however, that greater individual attention by someone who is either incompetent or ill-intentioned is not in any sense helpful or remedial (Gever, 1970).

A good remedial program provides a child with material that is at an appropriate level and provides sufficient challenge to keep the learner involved and interested. Interference with attention and concentration is another major reason for reduction of the teacher–pupil ratio (Dykman, Ackerman, Clements, & Peters, 1971; Estes, 1970). Such interference needs to be observed not only in tests specifically designed to measure attention and concentration, such as subtests of the Wechsler Intelligence Scale for Children-Revised (WISC-R) or Detroit Tests of Learning Aptitude, but also in actual learning situations (Bryan & Wheeler, 1972).

A major commonality of good remedial programs is the intensification of sensory input in the presentation of material. Approaches in the past have suggested that certain youngsters are much more efficient in learning when a single avenue of sensory input is utilized (Delacato, 1966;

Frostig & Horne, 1964; Kephart, 1960, 1964). This attempt to specify quite narrowly the most favored channel for learning does not, however, characterize those approaches that have remained in use over extended periods of time. The most valued and lasting approaches appear to be those in which there is a general increase in and involvement of as many sensory avenues as possible in specific learning areas (Fernald, 1943; Gillingham & Stillman, 1966). The increased sensory input appears to ameliorate the youngster's attention deficits as well as overcome inefficiencies in any particular sensory areas. The structure of the learning situation demands the youngster's total involvement. Note the contrast between structure imposed by the nature of the remedial techniques and that artificially created by systems that arrange the classroom environment to reduce attention deficits (Cruickshank, 1961).

Two related aspects of most good remedial programs are implicitly built into good assessment and the construction of individualized programs. The first is a rather major philosophical difference between remedial and regular classroom education. This can be labeled *judgmental shift*. The teacher, upon discovering that a youngster has not achieved mastery in the classroom, assigns the child a grade indicating the level of efficiency of the learning. While we have generally gone a significant distance from As, Bs, and Cs, there is still in virtually every grading system a message that the child has been adequate or less than adequate in mastering the material. In remedial programming and in assessment, there is an unspoken but strong assumption that if the youngster fails to learn or retain material there is something faulty about the methods being utilized.

The second aspect is *repetition to mastery*. A standard of adequacy of mastery is established, and then the youngster is provided with as many repetitions as necessary to attain that standard. This is in contrast to achieving whatever level of competence can be attained within a given set period of time for the lesson, an attitude that completely disregards individualized styles of learning. Obviously, one's sense of what is competence and who is responsible for learning taking place will strongly influence the way in which learning is structured.

A basic requirement of good remedial education is that the level of difficulty be tailored to the level of competence of the youngster. This requires an assessment battery in which the most inclusive measure available is used to assess each area to be evaluated. It is, for example, absolutely necessary that a general level of reading competence be established based on broadly defined evidence rather than very narrow data (Harris & Roswell, 1953). As an example of narrow data, the most commonly used numerical estimates of reading competence, for example, are derived from a combination of standardized test subscores, which reflect neither the subskills nor the total process. Yet this is what the schools and parents have been conditioned to think of in terms of a child's reading ability. Parents frequently come to the Temple Reading Clinic confident in the knowledge that their child is reading at a 3.3 level. Once the child's reading is assessed completely they are often surprised at how much more there is to reading competence. Where it is possible to define several levels of competence, such as through utilizing an Informal Reading Inventory (Johnson & Kress, 1965), this should be done, since single numerical values have an apparent importance beyond what they are capable of providing to a teacher.

In many instances where the assessment process is narrowly defined by classroom practice, remedial recommendations are nothing more than a suggestion that the youngster receive a further dose of what has already been provided in the classroom. Too often, "special education" instruction involves the same techniques being utilized in the regular classroom but with a greater emphasis on behavior management. Most good remedial techniques involve a degree of novelty for the child with the learning situation. This is not to suggest that novelty for its own sake is desirable. It is rather to indicate that the tendency to recommend a double dose of something which has already proved ineffective for the youngster is usually based on a narrow view of the learning process and of what needs to be assessed, as well as a preconceived idea about the possible remedial alternatives. Good remedial education is novel for the child because of the new feeling of success that he or she can achieve.

Good remedial programs are more dependent on the interest and desire for information that the youngster brings to the learning situation than on any present curriculum (Stauffer, Abrams, & Pikulski, 1978). Language has patterns, whether it deals with elephants, motorcycles, or going to the city. When the material used is based on the child's needs it is much more likely to be incorporated, since the gap between what the youngster is capable of learning and what is being learned is reduced. The standard argument against an experientially based approach is that the sequence of learning is accidental. The answer to this objection is that carefully planned lessons develop skills out of the content provided by the child (Stauffer, 1969). Further, as soon as the child closes the gap sufficiently, he or she can be moved into formal material.

Good remedial instruction is teacher-directed as opposed to teacher-assigned. The use of kits, programmed instruction, and work sheets is a distortion of the concept of individualization. A critical part of the teacher's role is to monitor and adjust the rate and content of instruction. The teacher-assigned, program-driven type of instruction relies very heavily on the intitial assessment, which should be seen only as a first formulation.

The utilization of sound psychological and educational practices with the child who has only known failure goes far to renew his or her damaged sense of self and faith in the education process (Purkey, 1970). We have frequently observed youngsters who had previously been described as hardened and embittered make seemingly astounding personality changes as a result of finally being taught by a method that matches their unique learning abilities (Johnson & Kress, 1970).

In summary, all good remedial instruction programs have basic philosophies: The child is treated as a complete human being. The learner is actively involved in the learning situation. Instruction focuses on a broad spectrum of behavior rather than on isolated deficits. Humanistic psychological and educational beliefs underlie all effective remedial programming. As educational technology and teaching procedures get more and more sophisticated, one could do worse than review Dewey's (1916) philosophy of education to understand the absurdity of many of the unidimensional special education programs.

OBSTACLES TO ADEQUATE ASSESSMENT

In his short story, "I Study the Soul," Hungarian writer Frigye Karinthy (1979) described a young man's conversation with someone he believes to be a patient in a mental hospital. The young man relentlessly presses his questioning until he "uncovers the delusions" characteristic of insanity. Upon questioning the hospital psychiatrist, he discovers he has been conversing with an unemployed carpenter who is making ends meet as a ward attendant.

The restrictive nature of prejudgment has plagued education as well as psychiatry. Unfortunately, a tendency to make a person fit *the* diagnostic pattern seems increasingly prevalent as the sources of funding become more tightly tied to a diagnostic label. One of the forces that has led to this tendency to prejudge youngsters is the sense that a precisely drafted definition is both possible and desirable. Any number of definitions and formulae have been used to define learning disabilities. Most of these definitions have in common a learning deficit and a developmental deficit or unevenness that caused the learning problem (Algozzine & Sutherland, 1977). However, a *universally acceptable* definition is impossible to achieve. The Task Force working on the Maryland Project arrived at the following definition, which incorporates the central themes of several other previous definitions:

Learning Disability is a generic term that refers to a heterogeneous group of learning disorders caused by varying forms of central nervous system (CNS) dysfunctions.

Central Nervous System Dysfunction can be the result of such factors as anatomical difference, genetic factors, neuromaturational delay, biochemical imbalance, metabolic imbalance, severe nutritional deficiency, or trauma. Many children with manifest CNS dysfunction do not necessarily have learning disabilities (e.g., cerebral palsied persons). At the present time evidence of CNS dysfunction is not necessarily elicited during medical examination and/or specific research procedures. However, such evidence can be elicited through psychological, educational, and/or language assessment. These learning disorders are manifested by *significant difficulties in the acquisition* and use of such language skills as listening, speaking, reading, writing abilities (skills), as well as mathematics. These disabilities are intrinsic to the individual. Even through they may occur concomitantly with other handicapping conditions (e.g., sensory impairment, mental retardation, social and emotional disturbance) or environmental influences (e.g., cultural differences, insufficient/inappropriate instruction, psychogenic factors), they are not the direct result of these conditions and influences. While it is recognized that there may be learning disabled children of less than average intelligence, *a marked discrepancy in achievement* areas should be documented by the evaluation team before labeling such a youngster learning disabled. It must also be recognized that a youngster who is near or at grade level with significantly above-average ability may also have a learning disability. (Maryland Learning Disabilities Project, 1982)

The definition above is not offered as a yardstick. Simply, it is hoped it contains the areas that seem generally acceptable to experienced practitioners. The individual words have been argued, can be argued, and in all likelihood will be argued. The italics in the definition attempt to spotlight the critical aspects. The emphasis is clearly on the youngster bringing something that causes the problem into school. The problem must be made manifest by failure to learn. However, in some cases we have seen children labeled learning disabled based on related symptoms, even in the absence of a significant problem in learning.

In the literature of learning problems there tend to be reoccurring discoveries of the "Holy Grail" — *the* solution. Those with long memories may recall the preeminence of *brain injury,* which was shortly followed by the more inclusive *minimal brain dysfunction,* which led to *perceptually impaired,* and *developmental lag.* Each of these diagnostic categories was adopted in turn by many professionals as encapsulating the explanation for a major percentage of those youngsters who were exhibiting learning impairments. In many cases, a label carried with it a specific test that was supposed to provide a definitive explanation for the etiology of the problem as well as a specific remedy to overcome the problem. Patterns based on group averages were dealt with as if they were templates that could fit neatly over any given set of data. In other instances, wide-ranging conclusions were drawn from very isolated physical measures (Delacato, 1966; Levinson, 1980). Elaborate schemes designed to illuminate the whole process of communication, such as the Illinois Test of Psycholinguistic Abilities (ITPA) (Kirk, McCarthy, & Kirk, 1968), held center stage for a time and then faded. Increasing concern has been expressed about the inability of many test or batteries to easily distinguish between groups (Coles, 1978; Venezky, 1974).

For a time, the educational approach mimicked the medical model, which suggested that specific symptom patterns or syndromes could be narrowly defined and matched with very specific treatment methods directly related to the etiology of the problem. Unfortunately, the exactness of the match between diagnostic label and treatment program was frequently more apparent in the literature than real in the day-to-day world of school (Ables, Aug, & Looff, 1971; Reger, 1979). For the most part, people working with actual diagnostic teams discovered that their decision-making was often most heavily influenced by the treatment available rather than by the treatment suggested by the individual diagnosis (Adelman, 1978). Programs were generally implemented by local option, which led to a wide variety of treatment methods being prescribed for similarly labeled groups. A particular group, therefore, could get one type of treatment in one state and a very different program in a neighboring state; or even more perplexing, a given youngster transferring from school to school within a district could receive a different program in spite of the basically similar labels and funding sources. The identification of the child's problem, then, has obviously not been tied to a single accepted treatment, thus eliminating the greatest value of a medical model.

The field of education has grown in recognition of a variety of different impediments to efficient and comfortable learning. However, the increased use of formal assessment measures seem to far outstrip the conditions known to have an impact on learning. Tests are essentially nothing more than a vehicle for structuring the observation of behavior. Increasing the numbers of tests used and increasing the number of youngsters for whom testing is a prerequisite for planning adequate instruction implies distrust in the ability of teachers to observe and systematically order their observations in a fashion that allows them to plan instructional strategies. What is it that has led to this distrust? Perhaps it is the need to explain all learning differences in terms of labels that imply rather complex causes for problems rather than accept a wide range in the normal curve (Bryan, 1974a; Reger, 1979). Teachers have been provided with very little training in *dealing* with individual differences, but they have been provided with the possibility of explaining all differences in learning rate as being based on a clinical problem. This may be referred to as the *clinicalization of classroom education*. It leads to a huge volume of referrals, which puts pressure on clinicans to increase the percentage of children with clinical problems.

The nature of clinical evaluation and assessment in education has been dramatically influenced not only by the state of the art but also by the nature of the legislation pushed by a variety of highly organized influence groups. Twenty-five to thirty years ago only a relatively small percentage of youngsters ever encountered the attention of a reading clinician, speech therapist, or school psychologist. Today a far larger band of the spectrum of the normal school population comes under the evaluative gaze of clinical personnel. The *Disability and Rehabilitation Handbook* (Edgar, 1978) indicates that the incidence of learning disability ranges anywhere between 1 and 20%.

For the mentally retarded, emotionally disturbed, or learning disabled youngster, or for the gifted or academically talented youngster, a complete assessment must be done leading toward the development of a program tailored to the specific strengths and needs of the individual child. Built into this current practice are a few assumptions that have not been rigorously examined in the research literature, although a few articles have surveyed the literature and commented on the typical effiacy of the evaluation (Algozzine & Sutherland, 1977; Campbell, 1979).

To provide adequate support for programming for learning-disabled children, the lobbying interests prevailed upon the government to fund and write laws relating to such youngsters. This situation should have led to concerned professionals being able to do their job without undue financial constraints. While it has certainly done this to some degree (up until recently), it seems also to be pushing practice in the direction of conforming to and being bound by the limits of the law. There are now two sets of definitions — a legislative and an educational-scientific definition, as well as two sets of paper. A look at the growing percentage of youngsters labeled learning-disabled makes it appear that the servant is taking control not only of the household but of the whole neighborhood. In addition, complying with legal requirements has led to the development of documents that are more useful to bureaucrats than to teachers (Schenck, 1980, 1981).

Legitimate parental concern that their children not be hidden away and ignored has been translated into a series of litigious forums that largely stifle communication between the home and school in a maze of forms and meetings. In summary, the roadblocks to adequate assessment and programming include:

1. a tendency to prejudge
2. an obsession with definitions
3. a series of fad solutions
4. an attempt to make youngsters fit classic patterns
5. the "clinicalization" of the education process
6. legislative pressure and paperwork

GUIDELINES FOR ADEQUATE ASSESSMENT

A major premise of this chapter is that the purpose of assessment can be defined by what we will call the *R* Formula: one does assessment or evaluation to *r*emove, *r*educe, or *r*eadjust requirements in reading, writing and arithmetic that would make a rational person react with *r*age, *r*etreat, or *r*owdiness; that is, the goal of diagnostic practice is to reduce discrepancy in expectancy in all directions in a learning situation. The teacher should not have expectations that are unrealistic or unreachable for the student. The student should not have unrealistic or unreachable expectations of him- or herself nor should the student have unrealistic expectations of what the teacher can do for him or her.

The process of sampling a child's behavior to determine his or her current level and requirements varies from the obligatory once-yearly standarized achievement testing to the complete assessment of the multidisciplinary team. The basic rules of evaluation do not appear very complex. At workshops and speeches all over this country general agreement seems easly to come by. In schools, however, one finds these guidelines more often being breached than followed.

One guideline for evaluation is that one never does assessment without having a clear-cut concept of the purpose and limitations of the instruments used. While there are a variety of reasons to test, and these reasons vary from level to level, the primary purpose ought to be to produce more appropriate programming. The administrator looks at the results of large-scale standardized testing and deals with teacher accountability and the appropriate expenditure of taxpayers' money. The clinican looks at the results of diagnostic testing and decides that Group A shall be in the Title I Program and Group B shall not. If this is the only purpose served, the act of assessment has been hollow. Ultimately, all assessment should be concerned with whether the program fits the needs and demands of the youngsters being served (Anderson, Barnes, & Larson, 1978). We reiterate that test results must provide qualitative as well as quantitative information, patterns of strengths as well as weakness, and indications of the learning situations that will be most and least effective for the child.

There are purposes that are valid at all levels of assessment, even the most superficial. As long as those purposes are clearly defined and understood and have a place in program planning, each type of assessment is worthwhile. To use standardized tests as if they were diagnostic is a distortion of purpose. At the other extreme, referring a youngster for clinical assessment prior to trying a variety of less intensive measures and adjustments in program is also a distortion.

In the assessment process, it is quite critical that the most adequate and representative sample of behavior be obtained for each area being assessed. In general, we should move from screening purposes to more diagnostic, individualized purposes. At each step the possibility of altering program and the impact that may have on a child can negate the need for going on to more in-depth assessment. The program must, therefore, contain a variety of options. Heavy emphasis must be put on samples of a youngster's behavior that provide a rich and complete picture of skills rather than simply an overview or numerical estimate. It would, for example, seem far more important to get a rich although unstandardized sample of behavior than a narrow statistically adequate but (in the real world) sterile sample designed to represent such a complex behavior as writing (Johnson & Kress, 1965; Vance, 1977). The best available sample of a youngster's learning is found in a good directed-learning activity that provides structure and a series of questions that delineate the child's funtioning far better than any highly standardized measure (Stauffer, 1975).

It seems counter-productive to move in the direction of more highly specific tests that assess rather limited, isolated skills. Reports on reading that reflect nothing more than the youngster's phonetic analysis abilities, for example, do not really make statements about the reading language process but rather abstract a narrow portion of this process and then produce results which by their quantitative and intensely limited nature appear to have greater significance than they actually do. Those tests that most closely approximate the steps of a good lesson provide the most useful information. An interesting example of this was the development of the predictive index (de Hirsch, Jansky, & Langford, 1972). In her initial research, de Hirsch looked at a variety of neurologically related and developmentally meaningful behavioral data. Ultimately, it became clear that those tests that most closely approximated what was required of the youngster in school were also the most highly predictive and, more importantly, provided evidence for tailoring a program to meet the needs of youngsters learning to read.

Clinicians often focus almost exclusively on describing what is wrong with the youngster. The unspoken message is that the purpose of evaluation is to delineate all of the deficits, faults, and problems. Having worked with youngsters in both remedial and developmental school settings, the authors believe that an evaluation that simply points out the deficits really does not have much value in terms of planning. While the areas in which the youngster is lacking must be understood, those skills the child has mastered also need to be identified. There is a very practical reason for understanding the pattern of strengths and weaknesses. A parent often says in essence "this kid can't read" or "he can't sound out words" or "he doesn't seem to retain what he reads." If the major focus of assessment is simply to see deficits, educators only mirror what the parent has stated as the presenting problem.

This is in no way a demand that people use more "technical" language in describing youngsters. All too frequently, people attempt to establish their level of competence and expertise by using a level of language designed to reflect the level of academic training the writer has completed. Extreme examples of this can be found in the reports of neurologists who are seeing youngsters for educationally based problems and who start their report with something like "this attractive, curly-headed, left-handed child" and finish the report by indicating that the youngster is suffering from "a mild defuse dysrythmia which frequently has concommitants in the learning area." If one accepts that the purpose of evaluation is to prescribe and reduce the expectancy gap, then such reports serve little purpose. An additional block to communication is that in education, to a far greater degree than virtually any other profession, the same words mean different things to different people. As has been suggested, diagnostic terminology varies from school district to school district and from geographical area to geographical area. Since the impact of an evaluation is only felt if its meaning can be conveyed to the people who have to deliver the program, it is important that the results of the evaluation be written in the clearest possible language. Experience with both the IEP Seminar at Temple and the project in Maryland suggests that this requires translating subtest names into the basic function being measured by the subtest and translating numerical values into the instructional ranges that can be indentified for classroom purposes. Wherever possible, the nature of weaknesses and strengths need to be spelled out with as little technical jargon as possible. In a number of instances, participating in large groups whose task it was to diagnose and plan a program for a youngster, we found that when people came to technical words outside of their field they simply moved over them, assuming that somebody else would take care of the problem. Communication needs to be as clear and straightforward as possible, interdisciplinary, and above all translatable into classroom practice.

To summarize, among the issues important in facilitating good assessment are:

1. clearly established purposes for assessment
2. a clear knowledge of the level and limitation of instruments
3. tests that are representative of the targeted behavior and approximate a good lesson
4. assessment that is active, not simply reactive to problems
5. a focus on strengths as well as weaknesses
6. clear, classroom-applicable communication.

THE CASE-TYPING APPROACH

The case-typing or student profile method involves a few major foundations. The first is a way of approaching data. Two areas that focus on the nature of this approach are the gathering of case history information and intelligence testing. Since it would be both tedious and repetitive to cover every area that should be evaluated thoroughly, these areas will be discussed as models of how other areas of assessment needed to be dealt with.

A major area of significant information is case history data (Abrams, 1969; Abrams & Kaslow, 1977), which should ideally be obtained from both parents and allow the opportunity for parents to answer widely drawn, open-ended questions. A case-typing approach demands that one look for mutually confirming data or information. Significant life issues are seldom demonstrable on the basis of a single incident or observation. Human development tends to run in threads. An important reason for seeking case history data in an open-ended fashion is that checklists or requests for specific events often force the individual to a greater precision of response than they genuinely have. If there has been a problem in the development of motor skills, a question such as "What do you remember about Charlie's ability to move himself around?" is much more likely to get at it than "When did he start to walk, or when did he sit up?" This is particularly true if there are many children in the family. Narrow questions may imply to the respondent that any good parent should know that information. The parent, thus challenged, provides information, whether it is factually based or not.

Case-typing also demands as much attention to qualitative as quantitative data. This is particularly important in obtaining case history information, since the attitude and tone of voice with which parents report information may well be more signficant than the data itself. The parent who reports with obvious concern that it was impossible to toilet train Susie prior to 1 year of age is suggesting something about Susie's development and, more importantly, something about her own attitude toward child development. In general, case history data should provide sensitizers or red flags to enable us to look thoroughly with test instruments for confirmation or negation of apparent patterns of strength or deficit. A look at some of the case studies that have been done on reading disability offer much in the way of illustrating the need to coordinate qualitative case history data with the quantitative test information (Harris, 1970; Spache, McIlroy, & Berg, 1981).

The principle of *dynamic interaction* (Rosner, Abrams, Daniels, & Schiffman, 1981a) demands that we focus on the milieu in which the child hits developmental checkpoints, the meaning of the child in the family, the meaning of the child's growing up, and so on. These broader issues are not illuminated by specific factual data so much as the tone, affect, and involvement with which the information is delivered. Parents are generally quite open, particularly if the clinician adopts the technique of listening in far greater proportion than talking.

An interesting aspect of final interviews with parents to feed back information after a complete assessment is that the parent's reaction is frequently one of, "Well, you didn't tell me anything I didn't already know."

Frequently, clinicians report that they feel that somehow this represents a failure of clinical insight. The opposite is true. This comment represents the most likely outcome of a good job of clinical evaluation, assuming a reasonably intact parent. If insight or findings are startling to the parent, they either may have been generated on the basis of narrow, factual information, or the parent has been largely out of touch with the child. A way to guard against isolated startling findings is attention to the need for multiple confirmation of the clinical hypothesis. The need for relatively "seamless" findings should not mean that one's clinical hypotheses are generated based on just case history information and then beefed up by selective use of test data. Insofar as possible, case history data should be put aside until after test information has been gathered and scored.

The thrust of a good deal of research into the causes of learning difficulty has been an attempt to narrowly define specific deficits or patterns indicating which individuals will have problems and which will not. Such studies have frequently been characterized by an attempt to look for average patterns, which by their very nature are not necessary true of any individual within the population (Lawson & Inglis, 1984).

Among the specific instruments that have been researched to come up with a characteristic profile, the Wechsler Intelligence Scale for Children-Revised (1974) may well be the most widely researched (Wechsler, 1974). Clinical observation going back to 1945 (Rapaport, Schaefer, & Gill, 1945) and followed by a line of other studies with more narrowly defined issues (Smith, 1978; Smith, Coleman, Dokecki, & Davis, 1977b) attempted to indicate patterns of high and low IQs or subtest scores on the Wechsler to provide insight into the nature and etiology of learning deficits. A close examination of the test, however, suggests that the quantitative nature of subtest scores frequently does not reflect the more significant and prescriptive qualitative nature of actual responses, which when carefully recorded provide data directly reflecting on the kinds of intervention required. For example, several wrong responses to the question, "What are the four seasons of the year?" illustrate the range of important differences between wrong responses:

1. Summer, Winter, Spring — I can't think of the other one
2. January, March, April, May
3. Duck, deer, crab, oyster (from a child on the Eastern shore of Maryland)
4. I don't know
5. January, Tuesday, Summer, Thanksgiving

Such wrong responses can indicate everything from blocking to impaired or uneven conceptual thinking.

While formal testing does not always permit a lot of in-depth questioning, "testing the limits" frequently allows us to know the style of the youngster's response as well as his or her level of functioning. Block design scores reflect the accuracy and speed of a youngster's performance but do not show the amount of planning or the degree of fiddling that leads to an "accidental" discovery or a solution. The importance of response style has been noted in other pursuits, such as the game of chess. Ernest Jones (Fine, 1967) wrote of "a rather quick player... choosing the best move almost at once and then in a state of self-doubting going on speculating and dreaming until in time-trouble they dash at a poorer move." Jones might have been reporting the observation of a youngster doing block design or mazes.

At times, the fullness of a response reflects not only a wealth of information but almost an embarrassment of riches. For example, consider this response to the question, Who discovered America? "Well, it was supposed to have been Columbus but many people say the Vikings or someone from Ireland in a leather boat...." This response said to the examiner "Just because I can't read doesn't mean I'm stupid and I'll prove it to you." A similar response in terms of conveying a sense of the youngster's overall response style or action tendency reportedly came from a group of "acting-out" children to the question, What should you do if someone smaller than yourself starts a fight with you? The classic answer was "Well... the thing to do is not hit him, but... I'd give him one good shot to let him know who is boss." This response implies, "I know the rules but I also have to let you know I am macho and impulsive."

In short, while there is information to be gained from quantitative data (level of expectation, relative strengths and weaknesses), the careful observer can give a good teacher far more help by conveying a sense of how much structure the child requires, what adjustment issues color his or her responses, whether the responses are full or limited. The works of Rappaport, Schaefer, and Gill (1945), Kaufman (1979a), and Glasser and Zimmerman (1967) embrace this philosophy and are excellent texts for the serious student of the WISC-R.

The procedures advocated for the gathering of case history information and testing with the WISC-R are models for the assessment of all other major areas of functioning in the case-typing approach. An adequate reading assessment requires a great deal of behavioral observation. It simply is not enough to respond that "Johnny has trouble with consonant digraphs and blends." The same is true of assessing such an area as visual perception, where the process yields a wealth of clinical data that usually takes the astute observer far beyond the scores derived.

The case-typing process itself requires of the clinican a series of hypotheses based on the information as it is added to the case-typing or student profile sheet. The sheets themselves are designed to provide a visual overview. The Temple Case-Typing Sheet (Fig. 20-1) has the areas

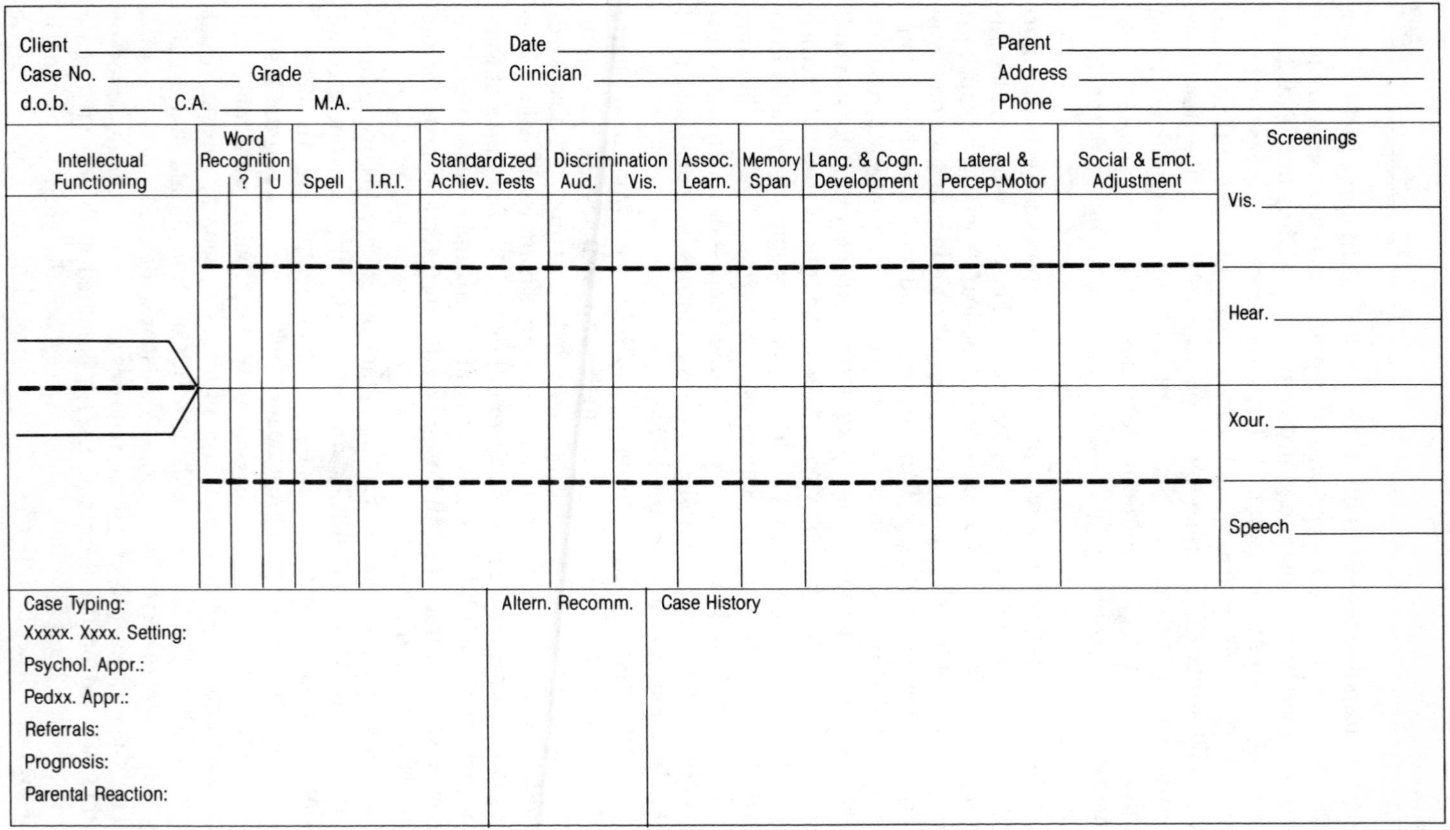

FIGURE 20–1. Case-typing profile sheet.

divided according to the tests that have traditionally been a part of that battery (Brown, 1965; Johnson, 1957; Rosner & Cooper, 1982).*

Areas are judged to represent strength and weakness either qualitatively or quantitatively. As with the area of definition, the quantitative standard to suggest an area is adequate or problematic can raise a discussion to the level of a duel. Clearly, single standards such as "two years below grade level" are unacceptable (Reynolds, 1981). The case-typing sheet at Temple used two basic standards, either a straight mental age-to-grade expectancy transformation or a formula such as that derived by Bond, Tinker, and Wasson (1979) that builds on in-school experience. The Maryland Project opted for more numerically grounded standards and the standard score format set forth by McLeod (1979). The critical difference is between grade-age standards and individual potential standards. Clearly, the case-typing format requires the latter.

Regardless of how broadly based a diagnosis is, it is necessary to include some areas and exclude others. In many situations the areas included were exclusively a function of the theoretical formulation as to what caused learning difficulty, dramatic examples being the formulations of Delacato (1966), Levinson (1980), and Feingold (1975). In proposing that learning problems be approached through the use of a case-typing method, there is no attempt to suggest that those areas included for assessment represent the complete and final definition of factors in reading and learning disability. Rather, it is hoped that any case-typing format be open to the addition or subtraction of areas of assessment based on their continued usefulness in program planning. The emphasis is clearly on usefulness in program planning rather than on simply the ability of the additional testing measure to differentiate between categories. In adopting a battery of tests one must be certain that all areas of significance are assessed. Adoption of the major suggestions for implementing a case-typing approach can lead to a variety of batteries that satisfy the need for a representative sample, qualitative patterns, and so forth.

The case-typing method requires a visual overview of a large body of data. This information is all organized around the central concept that the only meaningful profile is that which derives its shape from the individual's own capacity to learn, rather than from any arbitrary standard.

Upon completing a case-typing evaluation, one is faced with 40 or 50 bits of numerical data and hundreds of bits of qualitative data or information. The format of the case-typing sheet demands that the structure of the youngster's unique skills and abilities be viewed in a way that takes in a

---

* The Maryland Learning Disabilities Student Profile presented in Chapter 17 is also a case-typing sheet. It possesses the advantage of putting referral data, classroom observation, educational history, and case history information above the test data. It thus demands an evaluation of what happened to the child prior to testing.

broad range of information. The task would be simple if, after filling in a case-typing sheet, decisions could be based on a given set of patterns that will always be diagnostic. The essence of a case-typing approach is that in order to arrive at a conclusion we must ultimately be able to point to *multiply confirming data* that provide unique patterns rather than depending upon a single bit of information to direct our conclusion in any case. It would, for example, be contrary to a good case-typing approach to suggest, based on the results of a Bender-Gestalt alone, that a youngster was experiencing a developmental or neurological deficit. Additionally, it is important that the multiply confirming data be available from a variety of sources so that one would hope to see evidence of "hyperactivity" or "hyperdistractibility" in case history data, test scores, clinical observation, and teacher reports. It is not obligatory that all scores agree, but it is critical that, where there are markedly different perceptions from these areas of observation, the nature of the discrepancy of perception be clearly understood. For example, some youngsters might be extremely hyperactive in situations where they are frustrated by the demands of an impossible learning situation but quite attentive and controlled in situations where they feel confident and capable of achievement. The situational nature of such a problem would make the intensity and direction of our remedial effort different than if the hyperactivity was unrelated to specific educational dimensions.

A very important procedural issue in working through the case-typing process is the order of decision-making. In the real world, decision-making is often more heavily influenced by available programs, and an available program is often most prescribed on the basis of a room with a certain type of label, for example, a resource room or a self-contained Socially Emotionally Disturbed (SED) classroom. The IEP was supposed to keep each youngster from getting a prepackaged program, but since very often the setting was specified first, the range of recommendations that was made was clearly limited in the view of the IEP writers. The case-typing process demands that the requirements of the youngster for a more efficient learning program precede the choice of setting and that the nature of the program and the choice of setting precede the labeling of the youngster's overall condition or syndrome. This obviously presents some procedural problems in many settings where the label is necessary for funding. The point is not that labels are always bad, but that to label first or to choose a setting first can preclude a variety of solutions ever being made for a youngster.

In going beyond the legislative mandate to prepare an IEP for each youngster who has been identified as *special*, one encounters a series of levels for justifying the document. The first is to assure everyone involved that a systematic and carefully thought-out plan of action has been formulated. Secondly, such a document clearly has the intent of setting up a system of accountability in which special educators must demonstrate that they have formulated *and met* reasonable goals within reasonable time limits. The notion that a *speical* youngster requires such a plan to a greater degree than other children is an interesting one. Further, the concept that having established goals and desired levels of competence on a piece of paper assures that they will be followed by the classroom teacher is a kind of "as-if" thinking. The authors, having worked in a number of conferences that formulated IEPs and having spoken with special educators in a variety of roles over the years, have the impression that IEPs represent a tremendous investment of time and energy and that the results see the light of day infrequently after the details have been hammered out between the members of the team and parents. Practice suggests that parents very often view the IEP as a way to ensure that their ideas and concepts will be built into the program. It is difficult to understand why resistance to incorporating these ideas is lessened to any degree by putting them on paper.

Public Law 94-142 says that "The State Educational Agency shall insure that an IEP is developed and implemented." This IEP must include statements about present levels of performance, annual and short-term goals, objective evaluations, criteria, statement of specific services to be provided, and projected dates for meeting the goals. Once the IEP is completed, everyone signs on the dotted line, and the IEP is placed in the child's folder, only to re-emerge when more signatures are needed at the next annual IEP update. Even if the IEP were actually followed during the course of instruction, the typical learning-disabled child would be faced with dreary fragmented tasks that are neatly defined by short-term objectives.

While having objectives as goals for instruction is certainly commendable, the trivial mentality that is encouraged through the IEP process is abhorrent to the clinical case-typing process. The focus on neatly measurable aspects of instruction, as specified by many IEPs, creates a nightmare for the child and deprives him or her of the joy of learning. Were children taught to read in the manner that many IEPs prescribe, few would have any notion as to what the reading process is. Why should a child with learning problems be bombarded by a reading word list and the "grunt and groan" phonics approach. The current format of IEPs seems to demand such fragmentation.

Public Law 94-142 has been in existence since 1975 — time enough to assess its effectiveness in helping children with learning problems. As has already been indicated, the labeling of a child as learning disabled based on the definition provided in Public Law 94-142 has serious implications for the child and those who work and interact with the child. The process is often unwieldy and inefficient and does nothing more than give lip service to individual needs and parental involvement.

CONCLUSIONS

It appears that in some ways the attempts to meet the demands of law and economics have moved us away from some central concerns in the assessment of the learning disabled child. Assessment must be directed, broadly based, understandable, and multiply confirming to be useful. The neatness of IEPs does not provide any more assurance of an adequate program than pre-IEP plans. As educators move toward the utilization of computers in diagnostic work, they must keep their focus qualitative, patterned, and clinical.

CHAPTER 21

Multicultural Considerations

Eleanor W. Lynch
Rena B. Lewis

L earning and culture are inextricable. In learning new skills or information, individuals draw upon important cultural legacies: language
and linguistic competence, cognition and cognitive style, value systems and
beliefs, and self perceptions and esteem. This interrelationship between
culture and learning has critical implications for the professions that serve
persons characterized by learning difficulties. Cultural differences must
not be confused with deficiencies, yet services must not be denied to
individuals from minority cultures by dismissing true disabilities as expec-
table cultural variations.

With the handicap of learning disabilities, this dilemma becomes
more acute. Since variation in linguistic and cognitive functioning is one
of the hallmarks of learning disabilities, it becomes even more difficult to
separate out the effects of culture from the effects of the handicap itself
with this population. Because of this and other factors, efforts to address
the needs of the multicultural student with learning disabilities have been
few in number and modest in scope.

This chapter will explore some of the critical factors that have prevented
equitable treatment of the minority student with learning disabilities:
definitional issues, discriminatory practices in special education, issues in
identification and assessment, treatment considerations, and difficulties
inherent in the differentation of learning disability and cultural difference.

This chapter originally appeared as an article by **Eleanor W. Lynch** and **Rena B. Lewis** in
Learning Disabilities: An Interdisciplinary Journal (Vol. I, 1982) and was adapted by permission
of Grune & Stratton for inclusion in this *Handbook*.

While the home–school partnership is important for all handicapped students, it is particularly so for children and youth whose home culture is at variance with that of the school. To explore this important dimension of the problem, results of a study of parents' perceptions of and their satisfaction with their children's special education programs will be presented. In conclusion, methods for improving the quality of educational services for multicultural students with learning disabilities will be suggested.

DEFINITIONAL ISSUES

There have been many attempts to frame a clear, accurate, and understandable definition of the term *learning disabilities*. The definition that appears to have gained the most widespread acceptance, by both professionals and lawmakers, is that of the National Advisory Committee on Handicapped Children (1968). According to this definition, students with learning disabilities are those who have "a disorder in one or more of the basic psychological processes involved in understanding or in using language, spoken or written, which may manifest itself in imperfect ability to listen, think, speak, read, write, spell, or do mathematical calculations." Like many other definitions of learning disabilities, that of the National Advisory Committee contains exclusion clauses; not only does it describe which students are learning disabled, it also specifies which are not. One portion of the exclusionary language relates to the multicultural student: "The term does not include children who have learning problems which are primarily the result of . . . environmental, cultural, or economic disadvantage." While the definition does not forbid the inclusion of students with multicultural heritages, it forces a dichotomy between differences due to culture and differences due to deficits in psychological processes. Making this differentiation is extremely difficult not only because of the interrelationships among language, culture, and learning but also because of the problems inherent in the assumptions underlying the psychological processing deficit model (Arter & Jenkins, 1979).

In 1981, the National Joint Committee for Learning Disabilities (NJCLD) offered a new definitionn in an effort to correct some of the shortcomings of previous attempts. Specifically, the NJCLD definition modified the exclusion clause to read as follows:

> Even though a learning disability may occur concomitantly with other handicapping conditions (e.g., sensory impairment, mental retardation, social and emotional disturbance) or environmental influences (e.g., cultural differences, insufficient/inappropriate instruction, psychogenic factors), it is not the direct result of those conditions or influences.

While the exclusion clause of this new definition clarifies that learning disabilities and cultural differences can occur concomitantly, the problem of determining primary etiology remains (see Kavale, 1980b). For a culturally different individual to be considered learning disabled, there must be evidence both of a learning disorder and that this disorder is not due to cultural differences. Difficulties ensue when attempts are made to tease out which aspects of the student's performance (or failure to perform) are attributable to cultural variations and which are attributable to the intrinsic characteristics of the student.

Most definitional conceptualizations of learning disabilities present the same dilemma. Only if the relationship between culture and learning disorder is not causal in nature can the multicultural student be considered learning disabled. But how can this be established? One method is to compare culturally different students only to same-culture peers and identify those with the most severe disorders. This requires the assumption that the extent of culture's role in causation of the handicap is directly related to the severity of the handicap; however, it seems likely that the learning disabilities of multicultural students could be either mild or severe. If so, the problem remains: for a culturally different student to be learning disabled, the weakness of the causal link between culture and learning disorder must be established.

Even without cultural considerations, learning disabilities remain one of the handicapping conditions most difficult to conceptualize. Its manifestations in school failure are reasonably easy to identify; the cause of school failure is not. The handicap of learning disabilities is more subtle and elusive than other handicaps. The reasons for poor performance are not visible; they must be inferred. Whether these reasons are called psychological process deficits or inherent disorders presumed to be the result of central nervous system dysfunction, they lie within the individual. Because the individual also carries cognitive and linguistic characteristics attributable to culture, the separation of cultural differences from learning disorders becomes an exceedingly difficult task. Perhaps the solution is to frame a positive definition, one that includes but does not exclude. If the necessary and sufficient conditions for learning disability could be stated, then separation of learning, language, and culture would become less necessary.

DISCRIMINATORY PRACTICES IN SPECIAL EDUCATION

One of the major criticisms of the field of special education in the past was that its placement practices with multicultural students were discriminatory. The most common concern was overrepresentation of minority group students in special classes for the retarded (Dunn, 1968; Mercer,

1973). Related issues included the use of IQ tests for identification of handicaps in culturally or linguistically different students, the effects of misplacement in special education on students' self esteem, and the stigmatizing nature of the labeling process (*Diana,* 1970; Hobbs, 1975, 1976; Larry P. v. Riles, 1972).

One positive result of the furor over discriminatory treatment of the culturally different student has been the development of guidelines for exemplary practice (Lewis, 1982). One example is the Education for All Handicapped Children Act of 1975, which set standard procedures for the identification, assessment, and treatment of handicapped students. Included were safeguards against past abuses such as placement without parental notice or consent, use of culturally biased or linguistically inappropriate tests for evaluation, and reliance on IQ scores as the sole basis for placement in classes for the retarded. Although the establishment of a set of recommended practices is an appropriate first step, it must be recognized that legal guidelines do not necessarily translate into improved practice (Lynch & Lewis, 1981). In addition, legislated remedies such as PL 94-142 are subject to change over time as the political zeitgeist alters.

Another effect of the concerns about discrimination appears to be the reduction of numbers of minority group students served by special education, at least in some areas of handicap. Lambert (1981) examined data prepared by the California State Board of Education (1979) and concluded that, while the proportion of Black and Hispanic students in EMR classes remained the same, the total number of minority group students in such classes had dropped dramatically. This decrease could be attributed to a more cautious use of identification techniques or improvement in assessment tools. However, another likely factor is increased reluctance on the part of schools to label any minority student as mentally retarded.

While discriminatory practices in special education for the learning disabled have not been as great an issue as with the mentally retarded, there has been some concern. Instead of criticism for overrepresentation of minority group students, the charge has been underreprsentation (Hobbs, 1976). According to Kavale (1980b), programs for the learning disabled serve primarily white middle and upper socioeconomic status (SES) students, a fact related to the perception that learning disabilities is a more acceptable and positive handicap than mental retardation. If, as Brophy and Good (1974) note, teachers hold differential expectations regarding the academic skills of students who vary on dimensions such as gender, age, ethnicity, and race, it may be that the more attractive service is seen as most appropriate for majority group members while minority students are seen as candidates for classes for the mentally retarded. These types of biases contribute to the difficulties inherent in the identification of learning disabilities in culturally different students.

ISSUES IN IDENTIFICATION AND ASSESSMENT

One of the most controversial components of special education has been its identification and assessment practices. One major issue is the use of individual intelligence tests with culturally and linguistically different students. IQ tests are typically used in assessment to aid determining eligibility for special education services (McLoughlin & Lewis, 1981); some handicapping conditions such as mental retardation use poor test performance as an index of eligibility, while others such as learning disabilities require adequate performance. Intelligence tests are norm-referenced instruments that permit comparison of one student's performance to that of a norm group. Critics of IQ tests maintain that such norm groups reflect only the characteristics of the dominant culture, thereby penalizing individuals from nondominant cultures. One frequently used IQ test is the Weschesler Intelligence Scale for Children–Revised (Weschsler, 1974); while its norm group is a stratified sample reflecting the demographic characteristics of the United States as a whole, only 305 of the 2,200 in the sample represent Black individuals; and Hispanic, Oriental, and other non-Anglo groups are represented by 25 subjects spread over 11 age groups.

Many contend that multicultural students are at a decided disadvantage when their knowledge of and experience with the dominant culture is assessed as it is with individual intelligence tests. As Williams (1974), cited by Alley and Foster (1978), points out, the question "When is Washington's birthday?" may be answered either February 22 (for George) or April 5 (for Booker T.). The mountain boy who names the seasons of the year as "deer season, trout season, and bear season;" the desert child who responds "hot, rainy, and chilly;" the teenage Vietnamese refugee who answers "football, basketball, and baseball" — are these students less correct than their middle class American counterparts who reply "summer, fall, winter, and spring?"

Many strategies to reduce bias in the assessment of minority group students have been proposed (Alley & Foster, 1978; Bailey & Harbin, 1980; Duffey, Salvia, Tucker, & Ysseldyke, 1981; Lewis, 1982; Oakland, 1980). These include a moratorium on testing for minority group students; creation of culture-free, culture-fair, and culture-specific measures; the use of criterion-referenced tests in place of norm-referenced tests; and the development of pluralistic norms to compare minority students with same-culture peers rather than with dominant culture peers. The System of Multicultural Pluralistic Assessment or SOMPA (Mercer & Lewis, 1977) is one example of an evaluation system designed specifically to reduce assessment bias. In this collection of measures, students are compared with dominant culture peers by means of an individual intelligence test, to home and community expectations by means of a measure of adaptive behavior, and to same-culture peers by means of a rescored version of IQ test results. Students are considered at risk for mental retardation only if performance is poor on each of these three indices. Another example is the Learning Potential Assessment Device or LPAD of Feuerstein (1979). The purpose of this instrument is to evaluate the student's cognitive modifiability. The student is tested, instructed in deficient cognitive strategies, and then retested; the change produced by the instructional intervention is used as an index of the student's learning potential. Since the LPAD is made up of problem-solving tasks with little cultural interference, it is presumed to be culturally nondiscriminatory. While both the SOMPA and LPAD appear to be promising approaches, neither has yet gained widespread acceptance.

Problems of bias are complicated when students are not proficient in English (Ochoa, Pachero & Omark, 1983). For this group, determination of the student's dominant language is followed by assessment in that language. A major problem is the lack of appropriate measure in many of the languages spoken by students in school today; particular difficulties arise with the Pan-Asian group. One response has been the translation of existing English-language measures into the language of the student. While this approach may be preferable to assessment of a non-English speaker in English, it is less than a satisfactory solution. Even when measures are available in the student's language, problems may arise if the norm group differs in important characteristics; for example, Spanish-language tests prepared for use in Mexico may not be appropriate for Cuban refugees in urban areas of Florida or for Mexican-American students in the rural southwest.

Although it is generally acknowledged that assessment instruments should be nondiscriminatory in terms of ethnicity and culture, administered in the language of the child, and validated for the purpose for which they are used, the available technology does not always permit this. In many cases, appropriate instruments simply do not exist and, if they do, the absence of trained examiners with foreign language expertise may prevent their use. Despite this, professionals can work toward attainment of less biased assessment practices. As Oakland (1980) points out, bias may occur at any point in the process from referral to delivery of services. In addition to the obvious types of bias that are possible in test selection, administration, and interpretation, bias can also occur prior to and after assessment. Thus, it is necessary to consider not only the testing situation itself but also referral and screening procedures, placement decisions, actual delivery of services, and evaluation of program efficacy.

TREATMENT CONSIDERATIONS

If cultural differences affect learning, these differences should be taken into account in the design of instructional programs. In special education, however, more attention has been paid to the issues of identification and assessment of culturally different learners than to the educational treatment of this group (Argulewicz, 1983). This may be due to the belief that most culturally different students are inappropriately placed in special education and should instead receive services from regular or bilingual education. However, if handicapping conditions are distributed equitably among cultural groups, traditional prevalence estimates indicate that special education services may be appropriate for approximately 12% of all nondominant culture students. There is need to give thought to the provision of appropriate and nonbiased instructional programs to culturally different handicapped students, even if at present this group would represent a small minority of all handicapped individuals.

According to Almanza and Mosley (1980), several features of instruction should be considered when designing programs for the culturally diverse student with handicaps. First, it is important to ensure that instructional materials reflect the pluralistic nature of the American society. Another important factor is the value system of the students' culture, particularly if this is at variance with that of the teacher or school. As Pepper (1976) explains, students whose values are different from those of the educational system may be at a decided disadvantage; for example, in the Native American culture, persons seek to work cooperatively for the good of the community in contrast to the dominant culture where competition and striving for personal gain are valued.

Another important consideration in the design of instruction is optimal methods for teaching and learning. There is some evidence to suggest that cultural groups may differ in the manner in which they employ cognitive strategies in problem-solving tasks. Some groups may be more analytic than others, some more field dependent than others, and some less reflective and more impulsive (Almanza & Mosley, 1980; Chinn, 1979; Smith, 1979). Henderson (1980) adds that learned helplessness (i.e., self-attributions of inability) may characterize both culturally different students and those with learning disabilities.

If culture affects the ways in which students learn, it appears that this information should be incorporated into instructional programs for multicultural exceptional students. However, although there have been multicultural education programs developed to sensitize all students to cultural similarities and differences (Garcia, 1978) and extensive curriculum development in bilingual education for students not proficient in English, few attempts have been made to design programs for multicultural learners who are handicapped. According to Chinn (1979), "this absence of literature pertaining to specific curricula and instructional strategies for culturally diverse exceptional children suggests that either they do not exist or that the isolated curricula and strategies that do exist have not been published or disseminated" (p. 50).

DIFFICULTIES IN THE DIFFERENTIATION OF
LEARNING DISABILITY AND CULTURAL DIFFERENCE

One explanation for the scarcity of instructional programs for the multicultural handicapped learner is the difficulty inherent in separating out the effects of the disability from the effects of the student's cultural heritage. This differentiation is especially difficult with the subtle handicap of learning disabilities. The learning disabled are distinguished from normally developing students on the basis of cognitive, linguistic, and behavioral indices. These same indices characterize the differentiation between dominant and nondominant culture individuals. When the cultural differences overlay a learning disability, the distinctions between normal variations and indisputable disabilities begin to blur.

Another difficulty is the lack of accurate and nonbiased assessment tools with which to distinguish learning disability from cultural difference. Even if available measures were appropriate for the diversity of cultures found in many school systems, the majority of these instruments lack the precision for this type of differential diagnosis. Compounding this problem is the reluctance of many special education professionals to identify minority group members as handicapped. This attitude prevents early identification and intervention efforts that offer opportunities for minimization of the disability.

Another cluster of variables confounding attempts at identification are attributes of the culture that interact with the student's own individuality. Culture may affect the student's values and belief system, which may in turn influence his or her response to instruction in the traditional classroom setting. What may appear to be a difficulty in learning may, in fact, be an expression of a value held by the culture. For example, a Pan-Asian student may sit quietly in class in deference to the teacher who comes second in regard only to the king and father. Another factor is the child-rearing practices of the culture; these too may influence the student's classroom demeanor or even attendance. If the culture views older siblings as responsible for the care of younger children in the family, then the student may be expected to stay home even on school days if extra care is needed.

Linguistic differences also affect the issue of differentiation of learning disability and cultural difference. The most obvious problem is that of communication; students may be unable to understand what is required in school and also unable to express their beliefs, wishes, and desires. An important aspect of this problem is the relationship between language and cognition. Concepts in one language may not be present in another or a word specifying one concept in one language may refer to several concepts in another. Evans and Guevara (1974) present a case in point: "The preposition terms *in, on,* and *over* carry distinct concepts in English. However, in Spanish *en* is the equivalent of both *in* and *on; sobre* may mean *on* or *over*; and *encima* and *arriba de* can mean *on* or *on top of."* (p. 17).

Even if students are proficient in English, it is possible that some members of their families are not. This may present obstacles to the establishment of a strong home-school partnership, particularly if translators are not readily available. Even with English-speaking parents, it is often difficult to explain the condition of learning disabilities. With parents to whom the school represents an alien culture and for whom English is not a comfortable language, the task of describing the elusive characteristics of learning disabilities is formidable.

Poverty plays a part in the problem of differentiation of learning disability and cultural difference. Children of families subsisting on marginal economic resources are more likely to suffer from prematurity, poor nutrition, and inadequate medical care, factors that increase the likelihood of disabling conditions. The family characterized by cultural and linguistic differences is often also a low income family. According to Kavale (1980b), there exists a complex set of interrelationships among learning disabilities, brain dysfunction, and cultural-economic disadvantage. Culturally different children from economically deprived families are at particular risk for all types of school performance problems, learning disabilities included.

PARENTAL VIEWPOINT

The importance of parental involvement and the participation of parents in their child's special education program has been acknowledged for many years, but only with the passage of the Education for All Handicapped Children Act of 1975 did this acknowledgment gain the force of law. For the first time, parents of students receiving special education services were guaranteed the right to be involved in their child's assessment and in the development of his or her educational program. This legislated change of parental status formally recognized the importance of cooperation and collaboration between home and school in the delivery of special education programs and services.

When parents and teachers communicate, learning objectives can be more effectively selected, opportunities for practice can be increased, and evaluation of progress can be measured in both artificial (school) and natural (home and community) settings. Communication and collaboration between teachers and parents are particularly important when the family's culture is different from the dominant culture of the school. To minimize the differences between home and school, teachers and parents can work together to increase each other's awareness of and understanding of the other's values, customs, and priorities. When this is achieved, objectives that facilitate rather than inhibit functioning in both the home and school environments can be developed for the child. When this is not achieved, the student is often left with ambiguous standards and expectations that interfere with the acquisition of new behaviors. For example, in one classroom for students with learning disabilities, students were being taught to use checkbooks. A great deal of instructional time was spent on going to the bank, opening a checking account, writing checks, balancing checkbooks, and organizing records. Although this might be viewed as a set of skills that will aid independent functioning in the adult world, the skills being taught were foreign to the students in the class. They came from families who used only cash or money orders in their transactions; none of their parents went to the bank nor had any need to. Had the teacher been more aware of cultural mores of the students' families, she could have spent the instructional time teaching information that students could use in the community in which they lived and would probably continue to live.

The process and procedures used in the delivery of special education services can sometimes be as culturally inappropriate or irrelevant as the objectives selected for students. Delivering special education services is highly complex and requires the same kind of recordkeeping, efficiency, and monitoring that is required in the business world. Each step in the identification, assessment, and placement of a student into a special education program or service is now a bureaucratic procedure, leaving professionals less time and less flexibility for recognizing and attending to families' needs. Often, the process itself is in direct conflict with the family's cultural values and beliefs. For example, in many Latino communities, visiting the school is viewed as an embarassment. Parents do not enter the school unless there is trouble. Among these families, attending the IEP meeting is not a valued opportunity to provide input about their child's needs but a humiliating experience that they would prefer to avoid. In this instance and many others like it, what is viewed by the dominant culture as an advantage may be seen as a disadvantage to those with different cultural perspectives.

In addition to barriers created by differences in cultural values and beliefs, language differences also create barriers. For example, on special education forms, the word "parent" frequently appears. Flyers and announcements sent home to parents often describe activities for children and "parents," but in Spanish there is no word for parent. The word that is usually substituted, *padres,* meaning fathers, does not convey the same message. These problems of communication are increased when the language or dialect is oral rather than written or is understood by only a few people, making even a literal translation difficult to obtain.

RESEARCH REPORT ON PARENTAL PERCEPTIONS OF SCHOOL SERVICES

One way to initiate communication with families from diverse cultures is to elicit their perceptions of their child's special education program, the barriers that they confront when they attempt to participate in educational decision-making about their child, and what they think schools could do to help them overcome those barriers. One such study was conducted in a large, culturally diverse, metropolitan area in Southern California.

Method

Subjects

Parent subjects for the survey were randomly selected from the district special education rosters of two elementary, one junior high, one high school, and six special schools. The regular schools were selected because of the high number of low income families and the high percentage of Black, Hispanic, and Indochinese families who lived within their boundaries. The special schools were selected to represent opinions of parents whose children had more severely handicapping conditions such as severe mental retardation, physical handicaps, and autism. Although most of the families whose children attended special schools were low income, their socieonomic status was more variable since these schools include students from all areas of the city. A total of 106 families were interviewed; in most instances, the mother was the primary source of information.

Procedure

Each of the families was interviewed by a Special Education Parent Facilitator. All facilitators, who are parents of handicapped children, had received paraprofessional training in basic communication and counseling techniques. Eight Special Education Parent Facilitators were trained in the use of the 54-item structured interview. Included within this survey were questions about the parents' participation in their child's special education program and other school activities, their involvement in the IEP process, their satisfaction with school programs and personnel, and the barriers that they confront when interacting with the school system. One hundred of the interviews were conducted in the family's home in their preferred language; the other six were conducted over the telephone at the family's request. In several instances a family member served as an interpreter.

Results

For the purposes of this report, subjects were separated into two groups based on ethnicity. Both the Anglo group (N = 70) and the Other group, including Hispanic, Black, Asian/Pacific Island, and Filipino families (N=36), represented low SES families of students in all program categories.

Table 21-1 depicits the ethnicity, program category, and age of students represented in the study. Table 21-2 describes parents' perceptions of their participation in educational decision-making for their child. No significnt differences between Anglo and other-ethinicity families were found in their perceptions of their participation in the IEP process. However, a smaller percentage of non-Anglo families reported that they perceived themselves as active participants in the IEP meeting (57.6%); and an even smaller percentage reported that they had offered any suggestions about their child's placement at the IEP meeting (41.4%).

Responses of Anglo and other-ethnicity families were significantly different on one item related to communication between home and school

TABLE 21-1.
Family's Ethnicity and Child's Program Category and Age.

	Anglo Group		Other Group	
Subject Characteristics	**N**	**%**	**N**	**%**
Ethnicity of family				
Hispanic			12	33.3
White	70	100.0		
Black			22	61.1
Asian/Pacific Islander			1	2.8
Filipino			1	2.8
Total *N*	70		36	
Child's program category				
Mildly handicapped*	31	44.9	13	36.1
Speech and language	3	4.3	0	0.0
Physically handicapped	10	14.5	7	19.4
Emotionally disturbed**	7	10.1	7	19.4
Moderately and severely retarded	18	26.1	9	25.0
Total reported *N*	69		36	
Child's age				
C.A. 2–5	4	6.3	3	12.0
C.A. 6–11	14	21.9	3	12.0
C.A. 12–13	34	18.8	8	32.0
C.A. 14–20	34	53.1	11	44.0
Total reported *N*	64		25	

*Includes learning disabilities, mild mental retardation and behavior disorders.
**Includes autism.

TABLE 21-2.

Parents' Perceptions of Their Participation in Educational Decision-Making for Their Child.

Item	Percent of Parents Expressing Agreement	
	Anglo Group	Other Group
Contacted by district before child was assessed for special education	63.2	65.6
Rights explained in a clear, understandable manner	72.5	63.6
Viewed self as an active participant at IEP meeting	72.3	57.6
Offered suggestions about placement at IEP meeting	58.3	41.4
Signed and received a copy of the IEP	98.5	93.9

(Table 21-3). Non-Anglo families stated that IEP goals and objectives were less clear and understandable ($X2 = 6.24$, df = 1, $p = .05$). Although the difference was not statistically significant, a smaller percentage of other-ethnicity families reported that they had been invited to observe classroom teaching in their child's school; however, an almost equal percentage of Anglo and non-Anglo families had visited their child's classroom. A larger percentage of Anglo families reported having difficulty with school personnel although this finding was not statistically significant.

Items depicted in Table 21-4 relate to parents' perceptions of the congruence between goals, values, and priorities at home and at school. No significant differences were found between the Anglo and other-ethnicity groups on these items although a smaller percentage of non-Anglo families felt that parents of all cultural groups were equally welcome at their child's school and its activities.

In addition to the items that clustered around participation in educational decision-making, communication, and congruence between home and school, parents were asked about their satisfaction with special education services and personnel, their child's acceptance by members of the regular education teaching staff, and their child's satisfaction with the school as a place to learn. From 84% to 100% of the families reported satisfaction with their child's classroom teacher, teacher aide, principal, psy-

TABLE 21–3.
Parent Perceptions of and Satisfaction with Communication Between Home and School.

	Percent of Parents Expressing Disagreement	
Item	Anglo Group	Other Group
Heard personally from child's teacher during current academic year	82.6	80.6
Have talked to or written to child's teacher during current academic year	85.5	83.3
Have been invited to observe teaching in child's school	54.4	44.1
Have observed in child's classroom	56.1	51.6
IEP goals written in clear understandable manner	91.0	84.4
Work with teacher to accomplish IEP goals	68.7	61.3
Have had problems dealing with school personnel	28.8	17.1
Would feel comfortable contacting school about child	85.1	81.5

chologist, resource specialist, and school office staff; no significant differences emerged between Anglo families and other-ethnicity families. Seventy-seven to 86% of the families in both groups were satisfied with their child's current special education program; and 82% to 86% rated district professionals who make decisions about their child as effective to very effective. Over 70% of Anglo families and over 72% of non-Anglo families felt that their child receiving special education services was satisfied to very satisfied with school as a place to learn, and between 61% and 75% of the families felt that their child had been well accepted by the regular teaching staff. In both the child's perception of school as a place to learn and acceptance by regular teaching staff, non-Anglo parents reported the higher percentages of perceived acceptance. Although there was a high degree of satisfaction with special education programs, services, and personnel, only 54% of other-ethnicity families and 71% of Anglo families felt that their child's special education program was successful in preparing the child to be a responsible member of society.

TABLE 21-4.
Parent Perceptions of Congruence Between Home and School

	Percent of Parents Expressing Agreement	
Item	Anglo Group	Other Group
Agreement with rules or policy of child's school for handling discipline	77.3	80.0
Child being taught knowledge or behavior in school which conflicts with that being taught at home	10.8	8.3
Each cultural group represented at child's school is equally welcome	98.0	88.9

Discussion

In the study reported, few significant differences between low income parents of Anglo and other-ethnicity parents emerged when parents were asked about their participation in, perceptions of, and satisfaction with their child's special education program and services. In general, however, lower percentages of participation were reported by non-Anglo parents in activities that require self-initiation such as speaking out in the IEP meeting and working with teachers to accomplish IEP goals and objectives. This may be attributable to the perception by other-ethnicity parents that not all cultural groups are equally welcome at their child's school or to the finding that families from the nondominant culture do not perceive IEP goals and objectives to be as clear or as understandable as do parents from the dominant culture.

These and other issues need further exploration. The limitations of this study — small numbers, unequal ethnic distributions, sampling from a limited geographic area, and sampling of primarily low income families — may have masked differences between the two groups. Until other research that increases our understanding of the most effective and sensitive ways in which to work with families from diverse cultures is conducted, the following suggestions should be considered by those who provide special education services to students from diverse cultures.

SUGGESTIONS FOR CHANGE

Continue efforts to improve assessment instruments and strategies so that the tests and their administration do not handicap children with different cultural experiences. Although several significant contributions have been made in this area (Feuerstein, 1979; Mercer, 1979), a great deal remains to be done to improve assessment techniques. Perhaps of greatest promise is the system of assessment being used with many severely handicapped students which relies on inventorying the skills that they currently have, inventorying the skills that are necessary for successful performance in their current and predicted future environments, determining the discrepancies, and writing objectives that fill in the gaps (Holvoet, Guess, Mulligan, & Brown, 1980). This emphasis on testing and teaching functional skills that improve one's ability to be a productive member of society may prove far more important to effective, pluralistic education than the emphasis on pure measurement and categorization, which has driven the fields of psychology and special education since early in this century.

Train assessment teams in cultural issues, special education issues, and their interaction. Until each member of the team is aware of his or her own biases, cultural myths, and limitations, he or she cannot be an effective assessor. Likewise, not until all team members understand the complexity of special education issues and their interaction with cultural issues can assessments be considered adequate or even valid. Recognizing that competition is negatively valued by some cultures, that sharing answers on written examinations is the norm for others, and that never acknowledging that you don't understand what is expected of you is an important value of still other cultures is critical information for an assessor making educational decisions about a student. Knowing the different cognitive styles that are preferred by different cultural groups and the relationship of these learning styles to special education "symptoms" is another necessity for assessment team members.

Shift to more balanced assessments, which do not rely totally on the student's performance or on cultural expectations. Currently, there is so much concern about the interaction of assessment and culture that in some areas of the country nearly all formal assessment has been abandoned. In other regions, traditional kinds of assessments are conducted without regard for the differences that culture may make. It is time to develop a perspective that acknowledges and accounts for cultural diversity without abandoning the collection of information that will lead to more effective programming.

Move from pure measurement, which results in categorization, to an investigation of what each student can do and needs to be able to do to fit into society. Looking at discrepancies between current skills and needed skills may assist schools in developing a wider range of curricular options. This need for more program options, especially evident with learning disabled students, could provide a model for programming that is truly noncategorical.

Moving from placement of students on the basis of diagnosed handicap to provision of service in terms of needed skills — reading, writing, arithmetic, problem solving — obviates the need to differentiate cultural characteristics from other attributes of the student.

Develop curricular materials for culturally diverse students who have special education needs. These materials should incorporate what is known about differences in cognitive styles across cultures so that content is presented to students in ways that facilitate acquisition of skills and information. Instructional materials should also be designed to train functional rather than peripheral skills; and decisions about which skills are most functional must take culture and societal mores into account.

Increase parental input through studies such as the one reported in this chapter as well as through regular home–school contacts. These strategies can assist in breaking down cultural barriers within the school system. Increased and improved communication may allow parents and teachers to understand one another better, to develop more appropriate goals and objectives, and to acknowledge that home and school play two different and sometimes incongruent roles in the socialization process.

Work toward attitude changes around the concept of difference. In no area are attitudes about difference of greater concern than in the education of culturally different students with disabilities. All of the myths and fears of ethnicity and disability are combined into the attitudes that influence behavior. What has been done or believed in the past is of little consequence or concern, but what is done tomorrow is under our control. As individuals and systems, it is imperative to work to eliminate prejudices and to be open to changing beliefs and behaviors as they relate to services for handicapped students from diverse cultures. When special education personnel are willing to engage in this most difficult process, children from all cultures will be assured a more appropriate education.

SUMMARY

This chapter has explored the relationship of cultural diversity to learning disabilities in terms of issues of definition, identification, assessment, curriculum, and parental perspectives. Because of the interrelationship between culture and learning and the past inequities experienced by minority students in special education classes, professionals often hesitate to identify culturally or linguistically different students as needing special education services. This reluctance to identify and place has created a new inequity; many students who are learning disabled and also members of the nondominant culture are not provided the special education services they need in order to progress academically. Until this inequity is addressed through the review and modification of definitions, through assessment procedures that focus on skills present and skills needed, through the development of curricular materials that teach necessary information in culturally relevant and preferred ways, and through a process of continual communication with families, learning disabled students from culturally and linguistically diverse backgrounds will not be assured an equitable and appropriate education.

References

Abikov, H. (1979). Cognitive training interventions in children: Review of a new approach. *Journal of Learning Disabilities, 12,* 123–125.

Ables, B. S., Aug, R. G., & Looff, D. H. (1971). Problems in the diagnosis of dyslexia: A case study. *Journal of Learning Disabilities, 4,* 409–417.

Abrams, J. C. (1969). An interdisciplinary approach to learning disabilities. *Journal of Learning Disabilities, 2,* 575–578.

Abrams, J. C. (1973). *Learning disabilities: Behavioral pathology of childhood and adolescence.* New York: Basic Books.

Abrams, J. C., & Kaslow, F. (1977). Family systems and the learning disabled child: Intervention and treatment. *Journal of Learning Disabilities, 10,* 86–90.

Adams, R. M., Kocsis, J. J., & Estes, R. E. (1974). Soft neurological signs in learning-disabled children and controls. *American Journal of Diseases of Children, 128,* 614–618.

Adamson, W. C., & Adamson, K. K. (1979). *A handbook for specific learning disabilities.* New York: Gardner Press.

Adelman, H. S. (1971). The not so specific learning disability population. *Exceptional Children, 37,* 528–533.

Adelman, H. S. (1972). Teacher education and youngsters with learning problems: Part III:' The problem pupil and the specialist teachers. *Journal of Learning Disabilities, 5,* 593–604.

Adelman, H. S. (1978). Diagnostic classification of learning problems: Some data. *American Journal of Orthopsychiatry, 48,* 717–726.

Adelman, H. S. (1979). Diagnostic classification of LD: Research and ethical perspectives as related to practice. *Learning Disabilities Quarterly, 2*(3), 5–15

Ad Hoc Committee on Genetic Couseling. American Society of Human Genetics. (1975). *American Journal of Human Genetics, 27,* 240–242.

Aiken, L. R., Jr. (1970). Nonintellective variables and mathematics achievement: Directions for research. *Journal of School Psychology, 8,* 28–36.

Aiken, L. R., Jr. (1972). Language factors in learning mathematics. *Review of Educational Research, 42,* 359–385.

Algozzine, B. (1979). *The disturbing child: A validation report* (Research Report No. 8). Minnesota University, Institute for Research in Learning Disabilities. Washington, DC: Bureau of Education for the handicapped (DHE-WIOE).

Algozzine, B., Forgonne, C., Mercer, C., & Trifiletti, J. (1979). Toward defining discrepancies for specific learning disabilities: A analysis and alternatives. *Learning Disability Quarterly, 2,* 25-31.

Algozzine, B., & Korinek, L. (1985). Where is special education for students with high prevalence handicaps going? *Exceptional Children, 51*(5), 388-394.

Algozzine, B. F., & Sutherland, J. (1977). Non-psychoeducational foundations of learning disabilities. *Journal of Special Education, 11,* 91-98.

Algozzine, B., & Ysseldyke, J. (1983). Learning disabilities as a subset of school failure: The oversophistication of a concept. *Exceptional Children, 50*(3), 242-246.

Allardice, B. S., & Ginsburg, H. P. (1983). Children's psychological difficulties in mathematics. In H. P. Ginsburg (Ed.), *The development of mathematical thinking.* New York: Academic Press.

Alley, G., & Deshler, D. (1979). *Teaching the learning disabled adolescent: Strategies and methods.* Denver: Lowe Publishing.

Alley, G., & Foster, C. (1978). Nondiscriminatory testing of minority and exceptional children. *Focus on Exceptional Children, 9,* 1-14.

Allington, R. L. (1980). Teacher interruption behaviors during primary-grade oral reading. *Journal of Educational Psychology, 72,* 371-377.

Allington, R. L. (1982). The persistence of teacher beliefs in facets of the visual perceptual deficit hypothesis. *Elementary Education, 82,* 351-359.

Almanza, H. P., & Mosley, W. J. (1980). Curriculum adaptations and modifications for culturally diverse handicapped children. *Exceptional Children, 46,* 608-614.

American National Standards Institute. (1970). *Specifications for audiometers. ANSI S3.6-1969.* New York: American National Standards Institute, Inc.

American Psychiatric Association. (1987). *Diagnostic and statistical manual-Revised. DSM-III-R.* Washington, DC: American Psychiatric Association.

American Psychological Association, American Educational Research Association, & National Council on Measurement in Education. (1986). *Standards for educational and psychological tests.* Washington, DC: American Psychological Association.

American Speech-Language-Hearing Association. (1982a). Learning disabilities: Issues on definition. *ASHA, 24*(11), 945-947.

American Speech-Language-Hearing Association. (1982b). Position statement on language learning disorders. *ASHA, 24*(11), 9-94.

Ames, L. B. (1968a). Learning disabilities: The developmental point of view. In H. Myklebust (Ed.), *Progress in learning disabilities* (Vol. 1). New York: Grune & Stratton.

Ames, L. B. (1968b). A low intelligence quotient often not recognized as the chief cause of many learning disabilities. *Journal of Learning Disabilities, 1,* 735-739.

Ames, L. B. (1983). Learning disability: Truth or trap? *Journal of Learning Disabilities, 16*(1), 19-20.

Anderson, G., & Walberg, H. (1974). Learning environments. In H. Walberg (Ed.), *Evaluating educational performance: A sourcebook of methods, instruments, and examples.* Berkeley, CA: McCuthan.

Anderson, L. H., Barnes, S. L., & Larson, H. J. (1978). Evaluation of written individualized educational programs. *Exceptional Children, 45,* 207-208.

Anderson, L. W. (Ed.). (1984). *Time and school learning.* New York: St. Martin's Press.

Anderson, M. R. (1980). Is there a tyrant in the house? *Journal of Learning Disabilities, 13,* 361-363.

Andreski, S. (1972). *Social sciences as sorcery.* London: Andre Deutsch.

Angoff, W. H. (1971). Scales, norms, and equivalent scores. In R. L. Thorndike (Ed.),

Educational measurement (2nd ed., pp. 508–600). Washington, DC: American Council on Education.

Ansara, A. (1973). The language therapist as a basic mathematics tutor for adolescents. *Bulletin of the Orton Society, 23* (Reprint No. 57).

Applebee, A. N. (1978). *The child's concept of story: Ages two to seventeen.* Chicago: University of Chicago Press.

Apter, S. J. (1982). *Troubled children/troubled systems.* New York: Pergamon Press.

Ayres, A. J. (1973). *Sensory integration and learning disorders.* Los Angeles: Western Psychological Services.

Argulewicz, E. N. (1983). Effects of ethnic membership, SES, and home language on LD, EMR, and EH placements. *Learning Disability Quarterly, 6,* 195–200.

Argyle, M., Graham, J. A., Campbell, A., & White, P. (1979). The rules of different situations. *New Zealand Psychologist, 8,* 13–22.

Arter, J. A., & Jenkins, J. R. (1977). Examining the benefits and prevalence of modality considerations in special education. *Journal of Special Education, 11,* 281–298.

Arter, J. A., & Jenkins, J. R. (1979). Differential diagnosis-prescriptive teaching: A critical appraisal. *Review of Educational Research, 49,* 517–555.

Artley, A., & Hardin, V. (1976). A current dilemma: Reading disability or learning disability. *The Reading Teacher, 29,* 361–366.

Atkinson, J. W., & Feather, N. T. (1966). *A theory of achievement motivation.* New York: John Wiley & Sons.

Austin, J. L. (1962). *How to do things with words.* Oxford: Oxford University Press.

Ayres, A. J. (1972). *Southern California Sensory Integration Tests.* Los Angeles: Western Psychological Services.

Backman, C. W., & Secord, P. F. (1968). *A social psychological view of education.* New York: Harcourt, Brace & World.

Badian, N. A. (1983). Dyscalculia and nonverbal disorders of learning. In H. R. Myklebust (Ed.), *Progress in learning disabilities* (Vol. 5). New York: Grune & Stratton.

Badian, N. A., & Ghublikian, M. (1983). The personal-social characteristics of children with poor mathematical computation skills. *Journal of Learning Disabilities, 16,* 154–157.

Bailey, D. B., & Harbin, G. L. (1980). Nondiscriminatory evaluation. *Exceptional Children, 46,* 590–596.

Bakker, D. J. (1970). Temporal order perception and reading retardation. In D. Bakker & P. Satz (Eds.), *Specific reading disability — advances in theory and method.* Potterdam: Potterdam University Press.

Bakker, D. J. (1972). *Temporal order in disturbed reading — developmental and neuropsychological aspects in normal and reading-retarded children.* Rotterdam, the Netherlands: Rotterdam University Press.

Bakker, D. J., & Schroots, H. J. (1981). Temporal order in normal and disturbed reading. In G. Pavlidis & T. Miles (Eds.), *Dyslexia research and its application to education.* New York: John Wiley & Sons.

Baldwin, L. J., & Garguilo, D. A. (1983). A model program for elementary-age learning-disabled/gifted students. In L. H. Fox, L. Brody, & D. Tobin (Eds.), *Learning-disabled/gifted children: Identification and programming* (pp. 207–221). Baltimore, MD: University Park Press.

Balow, B., Rubin, R., & Rosen, M. (1975–1976). Perinatal events as precursors of reading disabilities. *Reading Research Quarterly, 11,* 36–71.

Bandura, A. (1969). *Principles of behavior modification.* New York: Holt, Rinehart & Winston.

Bandura, A. (1977). *Social learning theory.* Englewood Cliffs, NJ: Prentice-Hall.

Bannatyne, A. (1971). *Language, reading, and learning disabilities: Psychology, neuropsychology, diagnosis, and remediation.* Springfield, IL: Charles C. Thomas.

Bannatyne, A. (1974). Diagnosis: A note on recategorization of the WISC scaled scores.

Journal of Learning Disabilities, 7, 272–274.

Barakat, M. K. (1951). A factorial study of mathematical ability. *The British Journal of Psychology,* Statistical Section, *4,* 137–156.

Barnes, T., & Forness, S. (1982). Learning characteristics of children and adolescents with various psychiatric diagnoses. In R. Rutherford (Ed.), *Severe behavior disorders of children and youth* (Vol. 5, pp. 32–41). Reston, VA: Council for Children with Behavioral Disorders.

Baron, J. (1972). Orthrographic and word specific mechanisms in children's reading of words. *Child Development, 50,* 60–72.

Barr, K., & McDowell, R. (1974). Comparison of learning disabled and emotionally disturbed children on three deviant classroom behaviors. *Exceptional Children, 39,* 60–162.

Barsch, R. H. (1965). *A movigenic curriculum* (Publ. No. 25). Madison: Wisconsin State Department of Instruction.

Barsch, R. H. (1967). *Achieving perceptual-motor deficiency: A space-oriented approach to learning* (Vol. 1 of a perceptual-motor curriculum). Seattle: Special Child Publications.

Bateman, B. D. (1965a). An educator's view of a diagnostic approach to learning disorders. In J. Hellmuth (Ed.), *Learning disorders 1.* Seattle: Special Child Publications.

Bateman, B. (1965b). *The Illinois Test of Psycholinguistic Abilities in current research.* Urbana: University of Illinois, Institute for Research on Exceptional Children.

Bateman, B. (1967). The efficacy of an auditory and a visual method of first-grade reading instruction with auditory and visual learners. In H. Smith (Ed.), Perception and reading. *Proceedings of the International Reading Association Convention, 12*(4), 105–112.

Bateman, B. (1969). Reading: A controverisal view — research and rationale. In L. Tarnapol (Ed.), *Learning disabilities: Introduction to educational and medical management.* Springfield, IL: Charles C. Thomas.

Bateman, B. (1974). Educational implications of minimal brain dysfuction. *Reading Teacher, 27,* 622–668.

Bates, E. (1976a). *Language and context: The acquisition of pragmatics.* New York: Academic Press.

Bates, E. (1976b). Pragmatics and sociolinguistics in child language. In D. M. Morehead & A. E. Morehead (Eds.), *Normal and deficient child language.* Baltimore: University Park Press.

Bates, E. (1979). A functionalist approach to the acquisition of grammar. In B. Ochs & B. Schiefflin (Eds.), *Developmental pragmatics.* New York: Academic Press.

Battista, M. (1980). Interrelationships between problem solving ability, right-left hemisphere processing facility, and mathematics learning. *Focus on Learning Problems in Mathematics, 2,* 53–60.

Battle, J., & Blowers, T. A. (1982). A longitudinal comparative study of the self-esteem of students in regular and special education classes. *Journal of Learning Disabilities, 15,* 100–102.

Baum, S. (1984). Meeting the needs of learning disabled students. *Roeper Review, 7*(1), 16–19.

Bax, M., & MacKeith, R. (Eds.). (1963). *Minimal cerebral dysfunction.* (Little Club Clinics in Developmental Medicine, No. 10). London: Heinemann.

Becker, J. M. (1977). A learning analysis of the development of peer-oriented behavior in nine month old infants. *Developmental Psychology, 13,* 481–489.

Beery, K., & Buktenica, N. (1967). *Developmental test of visual-motor integration.* Chicago: Follett.

Belmont, I., & Belmont, L. (1980). Is the slow learner in the classroom learning disabled? *Journal of Learning Disabilities, 13,* 496–499.

Belmont, L., & Birch, H. G. (1963). Lateral dominance and right-left awareness in children. *Child Development, 34,* 257–270.

Belmont, L., & Birch, H. G. (1965). Lateral dominance, lateral awareness and reading disability. *Child Development, 36,* 57–71.

Belmont, L., & Birch, H. (1966). The intellectual profile of retarded learners. *Perceptual and Motor Skills, 22,* 787–816.

Bender, L. A. (1938). Visual motor Gestalt test and its clinical use. *Research Monographs of the American Orthopsychiatric Association, 3.*

Bender, L. A. (1957). Specific reading disability as a maturational lag. *Bulletin of the Orton Society, 7,* 9–18.

Bender, M., & Valletutti, P. J. (1982). *Teaching functional academics: A curriculum guide for adolescents and adults with learning problems.* Baltimore: University Park Press.

Bennett, S. N. (1976). *Teaching styles and pupil progress.* London: Open Books.

Bennett, S. N. (1978). Recent research on teaching: A dream, a belief, and a model. *British Journal of Educational Psychology, 48,* 127–147.

Benson, D. F. (1976). Alexia. In J. Guthrie (Ed.), *Aspects of reading acquisition.* Baltimore, MD: Johns Hopkins University Press.

Benson, D. F., & Denckla, M. B. (1969). Verbal paraphasia as a source of calculation disturbance. *Archives of Neurology, 21,* 96–102.

Bentler, P., & McClain, J. (1976). A multitrait-multimethod analysis of reflection-impulsivity. *Child Development, 47,* 218–226.

Benton, A. (1955). Development of finger localization capacity in school children. *Child Development, 26,* 225.

Benton, A. L. (1961). The fiction of the Gerstmann syndrome. *Journal of Neurology, Neurosurgery and Psychiatry, 24,* 176–181.

Benton, A. L. (1962). Dyslexia in relation to form perception and directional sense. In J. Money (Ed.), *Reading disability: Progress and research needs in dyslexia.* Baltimore, MD: Johns Hopkins University Press.

Benton, A. L. (1973). Minimal brain dysfunction from a neuropsychological point of view. *Annals of the New York Academy of Science, 205,* 29–37.

Benton, A. L. (1975). Developmental dyslexia: Neurological aspects. In W. J. Friedlander (Ed.), *Advances in neurology* (Vol. 7). New York: Raven Press.

Benton, A. L. (1978). Some conclusions about dyslexia. In A. L. Benton & D. Pearl (Eds.), *Dyslexia: An appraisal of current knowledge.* New York: Oxford University Press.

Benton, A. L., & Pearl, D. (Eds.) (1978). *Dyslexia: An appraisal of current knowledge.* New York: Oxford University Press.

Berges, J., & Lezine, T. (1965). The imitation of gestures. Clinics in Developmental Medicine. *Developmental Medicine and Child Neurology, 18* (Suppl.). London: Heinnemann.

Berk, R. A. (1981). What's wrong with using grade-equivalent scores to identify LD children? *Academic Therapy, 17*(2), 133–140.

Berk, R. (1982). Effectiveness of discrepancy score methods for screening children with learning disabilities. *Learning Disabilities, 1*(2), 11–24.

Berk, R. A. (1984a). An evaluation of procedures for computing an ability-achievement discrepancy score. *Journal of Learning Disabilities, 17,* 262–266.

Berk, R. (1984b). *Screening and diagnosis of children with learning disabilities.* Springfield, IL: Charles C. Thomas.

Berliner, D. C. (1979). Tempus educare. In P. Peterson & H. Walberg (Eds.), *Research on teaching: Concepts, findings, and implications.* Berkeley, CA: McCuthan.

Berliner, D. C., & Gage, N. L. (1976). The psychology of teaching methods. In N. Gage (Ed.), *The psychology of teaching methods: The 75th yearbook of the National Society for the Study of Education, Part I.* Chicago: University of Chicago Press.

Berlyne, D. E. (1965). Curiosity and education. In J. Krumholtz (Ed.), *Learning and the educational process.* Chicago: Rand-McNally.

Berry, J. W. (1967). Matching of auditory and visual stimuli by average and retarded readers.

Child Development, 38, 827–833.

Bettleheim, B., & Zelan, K. *On learning to read.* New York: Knopf.

Bibace, R., & Hancock, K. (1969). Relationships between perceptual and conceptual cognitive processes. *Journal of Learning Disabilities, 2,* 17–29.

Bingham, G. (1980). Self-esteem among boys with and without specific learning disabilities. *Child Study Journal, 10,* 41–47.

Birch, H. (1962). Dyslexia and maturation of visual function. In J. Money (Ed.), *Reading disability: Progress and research needs in dyslexia.* Baltimore, MD: Johns Hopkins University Press.

Birch, H. G. (1964). The problem of "brain damage" in children. In H. Birch (Ed.), *Brain damage in children: The biological and social aspects* (pp. 3–12). Baltimore, MD: Williams & Wilkins.

Birch, H. G., & Belmont, L. (1964). Auditory-visual integration in normal and retarded readers. *American Journal of Orthopsychiatry, 34,* 852–861.

Birch, H., & Belmont, L. (1965). Auditory-visual integration, intelligence and reading ability in school children. *Perceptual and Motor Skills, 20,* 295–305.

Birch, H. G., & Bortner, M. (1968). Brain damage: An educational category? In M. Bortner (Ed.), *Evaluation and education of children with brain damage* (pp. 3–11). Springfield, IL: Charles C. Thomas.

Black, F. W. (1974). Achievement test performance of high and low perceiving learning-disabled children. *Journal of Learning Disabilities, 2,* 178–182.

Black, M. (1962). *Models and metaphors.* Ithaca, NY: Cornell University Press.

Black, W. F. (1974). Achievement test performance of high and low perceiving learning disabled children. *Journal of Learning Disabilities, 7,* 178–182.

Blackman, S., & Goldstein, K. (1982). Cognitive styles and learning disabilities. *Journal of Learning Disabilities, 15,* 106–115.

Blalock, J. W. (1982). Persistent auditory language deficits in adults with learning disabilities. *Journal of Learning Disabilities, 15,* 604–609.

Blank, M., Gessner, M., & Esposito, A. (1979). Language without communication: A case study. *Journal of Child Language, 6,* 329–352.

Bocca, E., & Calearo, C. (1963). Central hearing processes. In J. Jerger (Ed.), *Modern developments in audiology.* New York: Academic Press.

Bloom, B. S. (1976). *Human characteristics and school learning.* New York: McGraw-Hill.

Bloom, B. S. (1980). *All our children learn.* New York: McGraw-Hill.

Bloom, L. (1970). *Language development: Form and function in emerging grammar.* Cambridge, MA: The MIT Press.

Bloom, L., & Lahey, M. (1978). *Language development and language disorders.* New York: John Wiley & Sons.

Bloomfield, L. (1933). *Language.* New York: Henry Holt and Company.

Bock, R. D., & Kolakowski, D. (1973). Further evidence of sex-linked major gene influence on human spatial visualizing ability. *American Journal of Human Genetics, 25,* 1–14.

Boder, E. (1973). Developmental dyslexia: A diagnostic approach based on three atypical reading parameters. *Developmental Medicine and Child Neurology, 15,* 663–687.

Boehm, A. E., & Sandberg, B. R. (1982). Assessment of the preschool child. In C. R. Reynolds & T. B. Gutkin (Eds.), *The handbook of school psychology.* New York: John Wiley & Sons.

Bohman, M., & Sigvardsson, S. (1980). An 18 year prospective, longitudinal study of adopted boys. In J. Anthony & C. Koupernik (Eds.), *The child and his family — vulnerable children.* London: John Wiley & Sons.

Bond, G. L., & Tinker, M. A. (1973). *Reading difficulties, their diagnosis and correction* (3rd ed.). New York: Appleton-Century-Crofts.

Bookman, M. O. (1984). Spelling as a cognitive-developmental linguistic process. *Academic Therapy, 20*(1), 21–32.

Borg, W. R. (1980). Time and school learning. In C. Denham & A. Lieberman (Eds.), *Time to learn*. Washington, DC: National Institute of Education.

Boring, E. G. (1923, June 6). Intelligence as the tests test it. *The New Republic,* 35–37.

Bower, E. M., & Lambert, N. M. (1965). In-school screening of children with emotional handicaps. In N. Long, W. Morse, & R. Newman (Eds.), *Conflicts in the classroom* (pp. 84–96). Belmont, CA: Wadsworth.

Bower, G. H. (1978). Experiments on story comprehension and recall. *Discourse Processes, 1,* 211–231.

Boyan, C. (1985). California's new eligibility criteria: Legal and program implications. *Exceptional Children, 52,* 131–143.

Boyce, N., & Larsen, V. (1983). *Adolescents' communication*. Eau Claire, WI: Thinking Ink Publication.

Bracht, G. H. (1970). Experimental factors related to aptitude — treatment interactions. *Review of Educational Research, 40,* 627–645.

Bracht, G. H., & Hopkins, K. D. (1972). Stability of general academic achievement. In G. Bracht, K. Hopkins, & J. Stanley (Eds.), *Perspectives in educational and psychological measurement*. Englewood Cliffs, NJ: Prentice-Hall.

Bransford, J. D., Stein, B. S., & Vye, N. J. (1982). Helping students learn how to learn from written texts. In M. Singer (Ed.), *Competent reader, disabled reader: Research and application*. (pp. 141–150). Hillsdale, NJ: Lawrence Erlbaum.

Braun, C. (1976). Teacher expectations: Socio-psychological dynamics. *Review of Educational Research, 46,* 185–213.

Brenner, A. Nutrition. In P. J. Valletutti & F. Christoplos (Eds.), *Preventing physical and mental disabilities: Multidisciplinary approaches*. Baltimore, MD: University Park Press.

Brewer, W. F. (1963). *Specific language disability: Review of the literature and family study*. P.B. honors thesis, Harvard College.

Bricklin, P. M. (1983). Working with parents of learning-disabled/gifted students. In L. H. Fox, L. Brody, & D. Tobin (Eds.), *Learning-disabled/gifted children: Identification and programming* (pp. 243–260). Baltimore, MD: University Park Press.

Bronfenbrenner, U. (1970). *Two worlds of childhood: U.S. and U.S.S.R.* New York: Russell Sage Foundation.

Brophy, J., & Everston, C. (1976). *Learning from teaching: A developmental perspective*. Boston: Allyn & Bacon.

Brophy, J., & Good, T. (1974). *Teacher–student relationships: Causes and consequences*. New York: Holt, Rinehart & Winston.

Brophy, J., & Putnam, J. (1979). Classroom management in the elementary grades. In D. Duke (Ed.), *Classroom management: The 78th yearbook of the National Society for the Study of Education, Part II*. Chicago: University of Chicago Press.

Brown, C. G. (1965). *A longitudinal study of the psychological test results of severely retarded readers*. Unpublished doctoral dissertation, Temple University.

Brown, R. (1973). *A first language: The early stages*. Cambridge: Harvard University Press.

Brown, R. T. (1980). Impulsivity and psychoeducational interventions in hyperactive children. *Journal of Learning Disabilities, 13,* 249–254.

Brown, R. T., & Sleator, E. K. (1979). Methylphenidate in hyperactive children: Differences in dose effects on impulsive behavior. *Pediatrics, 64,* 2936–2942.

Brownell, W. A. (1935). Psychological considerations in the learning and teaching of arithmetic. *Teaching of arithmetic: Tenth yearbook of the National Council of Teachers of Mathematics*. New York: Columbia University, Bureau of Publications.

Bruininks, V. L. (1978). Peer status and personality characteristics of learning disabled and non-disabled students. *Journal of Learning Disabilities, 11,* 484–489.

Bruininks, R. H., Glaman, G. M., & Clark, C. R. (1973). Issues in determining prevalence of reading retardation. *The Reading Teacher, 27,* 177–185.

Bruner, J. S. (1966). *Toward a theory of instruction.* New York: Norton.

Bryan, J. H. (1981). Social behaviors of learning disabled children. In J. Gottlieb & S. Strichart (Eds.), *Developmental theory and research in learning disabilities.* Baltimore, MD: University Park Press.

Bryan, J. H., & Permutter, B. (1979). Female adults' immediate impressions of learning disabled children. *Learning Disability Quarterly, 2,* 80–88.

Bryan, J. H., & Sherman, R. (1980). Immediate impressions of nonverbal ingratiation attempts by learning disabled boys. *Learning Disability Quarterly, 3,* 19–28.

Bryan, J. H., & Sonnefeld, L. J. (1981). Children's social desirability ratings of ingratiation tactics. *Learning Disability Quarterly, 4,* 287–293.

Bryan, J. H., Sonnefeld, L. J., & Greenberg, F. Z. (1981). Ingratiation preferences of learning-disabled children. *Learning Disability Quarterly, 4,* 170–179.

Bryan, T. H. (1974a). Learning disabilities: A new stereotype. *Journal of Learning Disabilities, 7,* 304–309.

Bryan, T. (1974b). Peer popularity of learning disabled children. *Journal of Learning Disabilities, 7,* 621–625.

Bryan, T. H. (1976). Peer popularity of learning disabled children: A replication. *Journal of Learning Disabilities, 9,* 307–311.

Bryan, T. H. (1978). Social relationships and verbal interactions of learning disabled children. *Journal of Learning Disabilities, 11,* 107–115.

Bryant, T. H. (1979). Communicative competence in reading and learning disabilities. *Bulletin of the Orton Society, 29,* 172–188.

Bryan, T. (1982). Social skills of learning disabled children and youth: An overview. *Learning Disability Quarterly, 5*(4), 332–333.

Bryan, T., & Bryan, J. H. (1977). The socio-emotional side of learning disabilities. *Behavioral Disorders, 2,* 141–145.

Bryan, T., & Bryan, J. (1978a). Social interactions of learning disabled children. *Learning Disability Quarterly, 1,* 33–38.

Bryan, T. H., & Bryan, J. H. (1978b). *Understanding learning disabilities* (2nd ed.). Sherman Oaks, CA: Alfred Publishing.

Bryan, T., Donahue, M., & Pearl, R. (1981). Learning disabled children's peer interactions during a small-group problem-solving task. *Learning Disability Quarterly, 4,* 13–22.

Bryan, T., Donahue, M., Pearl, R., & Herzog, A. (1984). Conversational interactions between mothers and learning-disabled or nondisabled children during a problem-solving task. *Journal of Speech and Hearing Disorders, 49,* 64–71.

Bryan, T., Donahue, M., Pearl, R., & Sturm, C. (1981). Learning disabled children's conversational skills: The "TV talk show," *Learning Disability Quarterly, 4,* 250–259.

Bryan, T. H., & Pearl, R. (1979). Self-concepts and locus of control of learning-disabled children. *Journal of Clinical Child Psychology, 8,* 1223–1226.

Bryan, T., & Pflaum, S. (1978). Social indications of learning disabled children: A linguistic, social, and cognitive analysis. *Learning Disability Quarterly, 6,* 70–79.

Bryan, T., Werner, M., & Pearl, R. (1982). Learning disabled students' conformity responses to prosocial and antisocial situations. *Learning Disability Quarterly, 5*(4), 344–353.

Bryan, T. H., & Wheeler, R. (1972). Perception of learning disabled children: The eye of the observer. *Journal of Learning Disabilities, 5,* 484–488.

Bryan, T. H., Wheeler, R., Felcan, J., & Henek, T. (1976). "Come on dummy": An observational study of children's communications. *Journal of Learning Disabilities, 9,* 661–669.

Bryant, P. E. (1975). *Perception and understanding in young children.* New York: Basic Books.

Bryden, M. P. (1972). Auditory-visual and sequential-spatial matching in relation to reading ability. *Child Development, 43,* 824–832.

Bureau of Education for the Handicapped. (1976). *Federal Register, 41*(230), 52407.

Bureau of Education for the Handicapped. (1978, April 19). *Informal letter to the chief state school officers, state directors of special education, state coordinators of Part B of EHA and state coordinators of the ESEA Title 1 Handicapped Program (PL 89-313): Clarification of evaluation team requirements for learning disabled children* (DAS Bulletin No. 9). Washington, DC: U.S. Government Printing Office.

Burns, H. P. (1976, August). *Emotional problems of the learning disabled.* Paper presented at the Third International Scientific Conference of IFLD, Montreal, Canada.

Buros, O. K. (Ed.). (1978). *The eighth mental measurements yearbook.* Highland Park, NJ: Gryphon Press.

Butler, K. G., & Wallach, G. P. (Eds.). (1982). Language disorders and learning disabilities. *Topics in Language Disorders.* Rockville, MD: Aspen.

Cadoret, R. J., & Gath, A. (1978). Inheritance of alcoholism in adoptees. *British Journal of Psychiatry, 132,* 252–258.

Caldwell, J. H., Hutt, W. G., & Graeber, A. D. (1982). Time spent in learning: Implications from research. *Elementary School Journal, 82,* 471–480.

Calhoun, G., Jr., & Elliott, R. N., Jr. (1977). Self-concepts and academic achievement of educable mentally retarded and emotionally disturbed pupils. *Exceptional Children, 43,* 379–380.

California Association of School Psychologists. (1985). New eligibility criteria proposed. *CASP Today, 35,* 1–2.

California State Board of Education. (1979, May). *Ethnic survey of pupils assigned to special education classes for the educable mentally retarded (EMR), school year 1977–1978.* Sacramento, CA.

California Department of Education. (1983). *A manual for the determination of a severe discrepancy as defined by Title 5, CAC, Section 3030(J).* Sacramento, CA.

Cambourne, B. L., & Rousch, P. (1982). How do learning disabled children read? *Topics in Learning and Learning Disability, 15,* 59–60.

Camp, B. W. (1973). Psychometric tests and learning in severely disabled readers. *Journal of Learning Disabilities, 6,* 512–517.

Camp, B. W., & Bash, M. A. S. (1981). *Think aloud: Increasing social and cognitive skills — A problem-solving program for children, primary level.* Champaign, IL: Research Press.

Campbell, S. B. (1974). Cognitive styles and behavior problems of clinic boys: A comparison of epileptic, hyperactive, learning disabled and normal groups. *Journal of Abnormal Child Psychology, 2,* 307–312.

Campbell, S. (1979). Problems for clinical diagnosis. *Learning Disabilities, 12,* 511–513.

Cantwell, D. P. (1975). Genetic studies of hyperactive children. In R. R. Fieve, D. Rosenthal, & H. Brill (Eds.), *Genetic research in psychiatry.* Baltimore, MD: Johns Hopkins University Press.

Carbo, M. Teaching reading with talking books. *The Reading Teacher, 32,* 267–273.

Caro, D., & Schneider, P. (1982). Creating referents in text: A comparison of learning-disabled and normal adolescents' texts. *Proceedings of the University of Wisconsin Symposium for Research in Child Language Disorders 3.*

Carroll, J. B. (1963). *A model of school learning. Teachers College Record, 64,* 723–733.

Carroll, J. B. (1984). The model of school learning: Progress of an idea. In L. Anderson (Ed.), *Time and school learning.* New York: St. Martin's Press.

Carrow-Woolfolk, E. C., & Lynch, J. (1982). *An integrative approach to language disorders in children.* New York: Grune & Stratton.

Carter, C. O. Genetics of common disorders. *British Medical Bulletin, 25,* 52–57.

Cartledge, G., & Milburn, J. F. (1978). The case for teaching social skills in the classroom: A review. *Review of Educational Research, 48,* 133–156.

Case, R. (1982). General developmental influences on the acquisition of elementary concepts and algorithms in arithmetic. In T. P. Carpenter, J. M. Moser, & T. A. Romberg (Eds.), *Addition and subtraction: A cognitive perspective.* Hillsdale, NJ: Lawrence Erlbaum.

Cawley, J. F. (1978). An instructional design for children with learning disabilities: Emphasis on secondary school mathematics. In L. Mann & L. Goodman (Eds.), *Teaching the learning disabled adolescent.* Boston: Houghton-Mifflin.

Cawley, J. F. (1981a). Commentary. *Topics in Learning and Learning Disabilities, 1,* 83–94.

Cawley, J. F. (Ed.). (1981b). *Topics in Learning and Learning Disabilities, 1,* 3.

Cawley, J. F., & Goodman, J. O. (1968). Interrelationships among mental abilities, reading, language arts and arithmetic in the mentally handicapped. *Arithmetic Teacher, 15,* 631–636.

Cazden, C. B., Michaels, S., & Tabors, P. (in press). Spontaneous repairs in sharing time narratives: The intersection of metalinguistic awareness, speech event, and narrative style. In S. W. Freeman (Ed.), *The acquisition of written language: Revision and response.* Norwood, NJ: Ablex.

Centra, J. A., & Potter, D. A. (1980). School and teacher effects: An interrelational model. *Review of Educational Research, 50,* 273–291.

Cermak, L., Goldberg, J., Cermak, S., & Drake, C. (1980). The short-term memory ability of children with learning disabilities. *Journal of Learning Disabilities, 13,* 25–29.

Chalfant, J. C. (1984). *Identifying learning disabled students: Guidelines for decision making.* Burlington, VT: Regional Resource Center.

Chalfant, J. C., & Pysh, M. V. (1979). Teacher assistance teams: A model for within-building problem solving. *Learning Disability Quarterly, 2*(3), 85–96.

Chalfant, J. C., & Pysh, M. V. (1981, November). Teacher assistance teams: A model for within-building problem solving. *Counterpoint, 1,* 21–24.

Chalfant, J. C., & Pysh, M. V. (1984). *Educational management teams: Recommended practices and procedures* (field test ed.). Baltimore: Maryland State Department of Education.

Chalfant, J. C., & Scheffelin, M. A. (1969). *Central processing dysfunctions in children: A review of research* (NINDS Monograph No. 9). Washington, DC: U.S. Department of Health, Education, and Welfare.

Chandler, H. N., & Jones, K. (1983a). Learning disabled or emotionally disturbed: Part I. Does it make any difference? *Journal of Learning Disabilities, 160*(7), 432–434.

Chandler, H. N., & Jones, K. (1983b). Learning disabled or emotionally disturbed: Part II. Does it make any difference? *Journal of Learning Disabilities, 16*(9), 561–564.

Chandler, M. J. (1973). Egocentrism and antisocial behavior: The assessment and training of social perceptive-taking skills. *Developmental Psychology, 9,* 326–332.

Chapman, R., Larsen, S., & Parker, R. (1979). Interaction of first-grade teachers with learning disordered children. *Journal of Learning Disabilities, 12,* 225–230.

Childs, B. (1972). Genetic analysis of human behavior. *Annual Review of Medicine, 23,* 373–406.

Childs, B., & Finucci, M. (1979). The genetics of learning disabilities. *Ciba Foundation Symposium, 66,* 359–376.

Childs, B., Finucci, J., & Preston, M. A. (1978). A medical genetics approach to the study of reading disability. In A. Benton & D. Pearl (Eds.), *Dyslexia: An appraisal of current knowledge.* New York: Oxford University Press.

Chinn, P. (1979). Curriculum development for culturally different exceptional children. *Teacher Education and Special Education, 2*(4), 49–58.

Chomsky, C. (1976). After decoding: What? *Language Arts, 53,* 288–296.

Christianson, S., Ysseldyke, J., & Algozzine, B. (1982). Institutional constraints and external pressures influencing referral decisions. *Psychology in the Schools, 19,* 341–345.

Cicourel, A. V. (1981). Cognitive and linguistic aspects of socialization. *Annual Review of Sociology, 7,* 87–106.

Clarizio, H., & Bernard, R. (1981). Recategorizing WISC-R scores of learning disabled children and differential diagnosis. *Psychology in the Schools, 18,* 5–12.

Clark, E. V., & Andersen, E. S. (1979). Spontaneous repairs: Awareness in the process of acquiring language. *Papers and Reports on Child Language Development, 16,* 1–12.

Clay, M. M., & Imlach, R. H. (1971). Juncture, pitch, and stress as reading behavior variables. *Journal of Verbal Learning and Verbal Behavior, 10,* 133–139.

Clements, S. D. (1966). *Minimal brain dysfunction in children: Terminology and identification* (NINDS Monograph No. 3, U.S. Public Health Service Publication No. 1415). Washington, DC: U.S. Department of Health, Education and Welfare.

Cohen, E. (1972). Sociology and the classroom: Setting the condition for teacher–student interaction. *Review of Educational Research, 42,* 441–452.

Cohen, H. J., Birch, H. G., & Taft, L. T. (1970). Some considerations for evaluating the Doman-Delacato patterning method. *Pediatrics, 45,* 302–314.

Cohen, H., Taft, L., Mahadeviah, M., & Birch, H. (1967). Developmental changes in overflow in normal and aberrantly functioning children. *Journal of Pediatrics, 71,* 39–47.

Cohen, S. A. (1969). Studies in visual perception and reading in disadvantaged children. *Journal of Learning Disabilities, 2,* 498–507.

Cohen, S. A. (1971). Dyspedagogia as a cause of reading retardation: Definition and treatment. In B. Bateman (Ed.), *Learning disorders* (Vol. 4). Seattle: Special Child Publications.

Cohen, S. A. (1973). Minimal brain dysfunction and practical matters such as teaching kids to read. *Annals of the New York Academy of Sciences, 205,* 251–261.

Cohn, R. (1961). Dyscalculia. *Archives of Neurology, 4,* 301–307.

Cohn, R. (1964). The neurological study of children with learning disabilities. *Exceptional Children, 31,* 179–185.

Cohn, R. (1968). Developmental dyscalculia. *Pediatric Clinics of North America, 15,* 651–658.

Cohn, R. (1971). Arithmetic and learning disabilities. In H. R. Myklebust (Ed.), *Progress in learning disabilities.* New York: Grune & Stratton.

Colbert, P., Newman, B., Ney, P., & Young, J. (1982). Learning disabilities as a symptom of depression in children. *Journal of Learning Disabilities, 15,* 333–336.

Coleman, J. M. (1983a). Handicapped labels and instructional segregation: Influences on children's self-concepts versus the perceptions of others. *Learning Disability Quarterly, 6,* 3–11.

Coleman, J. M. (1983b). Self-concept and the mildly handicapped: The role of social comparisons. *Journal of Special Education, 17,* 37–45.

Coleman, J., & Sandhu, M. (1967). A descriptive relational study of 364 children referred to a university clinic for learning disorders. *Psychological Reports, 20,* 1091–1105.

Coleman, W., & Cureton, E. E. (1954). Intelligence and achievement: The jangle fallacy again. *Educational and Psychological Measurement, 14,* 347–351.

Coles, G. S. (1978). The learning disability test battery: Empirical and social issues. *Harvard Educational Review, 48,* 313–340.

Coltheart, M., Patterson, K., & Marshall, J. (Eds.). (1980). *Deep dyslexia.* London: Routledge & Keegan Paul.

Cone, T. E., & Wilson, L. R. (1981). Quantifying a severe discrepancy: A critical analysis. *Learning Disability Quarterly, 4,* 359–371.

Conners, C. K. (1980). *Food additives and hyperactive children.* New York: Plenum Press.

Connolly, C. (1971). Social and emotional factors in learning disabilities. In H. Myklebust

(Ed.), *Progress in learning disabilities* (Vol. II). New York: Grune & Stratton.

Connor, F. P. (1983). Improving school instruction for learning disabled children: The Teachers College Institute. *Exceptional Education Quarterly, 4,* 1.

Conti, G., & Friel-Patti, S. (1982, November). *Normal and language impaired children's comprehension of indirect requests.* Paper presented at the annual meeting of the American Speech–Language–Hearing Association, Toronto, Canada.

Cook, P. S., & Woodhill, J. M. (1976). The Feingold dietary treatment of the hyperkinetic syndrome. *The Medical Journal of Australia, 2,* 85–90.

Cooke, T. P., & Apolloni, T. (1976). Developing positive social-emotional behaviors: A study of training and generalization effects. *Journal of Applied Behavioral Analysis, 9,* 65–78.

Cooley, W. W., & Leinhardt, G. (1980). The instructional dimensions study. *Educational Evaluation and Policy Analysis, 2,* 7–25.

Copple, P. J., & Isom, J. B. (1968). Soft signs and scholastic sucess. *Neurology, 18,* 304–308.

Corballis, M. C., & Beale, I. L. (1976). *The psychology of left and right.* New York: John Wiley & Sons.

Corkin, S. (1974). Serial-ordering deficits in inferior readers. *Neuropsychologia, 12,* 347–354.

Craig, H. (1983). Applications of pragmatic language models for intervention. In T. Gallagher & C. Prutting (Eds.), *Pragmatic assessment and intervention issues in language.* San Diego: College-Hill Press.

Crane, A. R. (1959). An historical and critical account of the accomplishment quotient idea. *British Journal of Educational Psychology, 29,* 252–259.

Cratty, B. J. (1981). Sensory-motor and perceptual-motor theories and practices: An overview and evaluation. In R. Walk & H. Pick (Eds.), *Intersensory perception and sensory interaction.* New York: Plenum Press.

Cravioto, J., & DeLicardie, E. R. (1975). Environmental and nutritional deprivation in children with learning disabilities. In W. Cruickshank & D. Hallahan (Eds.), *Perceptual and learning disabilities in children, Vol. 2: Research and theory.* Syracuse, NY: Syracuse University Press.

Crinella, F. M. (1973). Identification of brain dysfunction syndromes in children through profile analysis: Patterns associated with so-called "minimal brain dysfunction." *Journal of Abnormal Psychology, 82,* 33–45.

Cromer, W., & Weiner, M. (1966). Idiosyncratic response patterns among good and poor readers. *Journal of Consulting Psychology, 30,* 1–10.

Cronbach, L., Gleser, G., Nanda, H., & Rajoratnam, N. (1972). *The dependability of behavioral measurements: Theory of generalizability for scores and profiles.* New York: John Wiley & Sons.

Cronbach, L. J., & Meehl, P. E. (1955). Construct validity in psychological tests. *Psychological Bulletin, 52,* 281–301.

Cronbach, L. J., & Snow, R. E. (1977). *Aptitudes and instructional methods: A handbook for research on interactions.* New York: Irvington.

Crook, W. C. (1980). Can what a child eats make him dull, stupid, or hyperactive? *Journal of Learning Disabilities, 13,* 281–286.

Croxen, M. E., & Lytton, H. (1971). Reading disabilities and difficulties in finger localization and left-right discrimination. *Developmental Psychology, 5,* 256–262.

Cruickshank, W. M. (1967). *The brain-injured child in home, school and community.* Syracuse, NY: Syracuse University Press.

Cruickshank, W. M. (1977). Myths and realities in learning disabilities. *Journal of Learning Disabilities, 10,* 51–58.

Cruickshank, W. M. (1981). *Concepts in learning disabilities: Selected writings* (Vol. 2). Syracuse, NY: Syracuse University Press.

Cruickshank, W. M. (1981). Learning disabilities: A definitional statement. In W. M. Cruickshank (Ed.), *Concepts in learning disabilities* (Vol. 2, pp. 80–110). Syracuse, NY: Syracuse University Press.

Cruickshank, W. M. (1983). Learning disabilities: A neurophysiological dysfunction. *Journal of Learning Disabilities, 16,* 27–29.

Cruickshank, W. M., Bentzen, S. A., Ratzeburg, F. H., & Tannhauser, M. T. (1961). *A teaching method for brain-injured and hyperactive children.* Syracuse: Syracuse University Press.

Crum, M. A. (1974). Effects of reverberation, noise and distance upon speech intelligibility in small, classroom size acoustic enclosures (Doctoral dissertation, Northwestern University, 1974). *Dissertation Abstracts International, 35,* 2555B–2556B. (University Microfilms No. 74-28, 604)

Crystal, D., Fletcher, P., & Garman, M. (1976). *The grammatical analysis of language disability.* London: Edward Arnold.

Cuisinaire, G. (1972). *Opening doors in mathematics.* New York: Cuisinaire Company of America.

Cullen, J. L., Boersma, F., & Chapman, J. (1981). Characteristics of third-grade learning disabled children. *Learning Disability Quarterly, 4,* 224–230.

Cullinan, D., Epstein, M., & McLinden, D. (in press). *Status and change in state administrative definitions in behavior disorders* (Grant No. G00 8307145, O.S.E). DeKalb, IL: Northern Illinois University.

Curry, F. (1966). *A comparison of left-handed and right-handed subjects on verbal and nonverbal dichotic listening tasks.* Unpublished doctoral dissertation, Northwestern University, Evanston, IL.

Curtis, M. J., & Zins, J. E. (Eds.). *The theory and practice of school consultation.* Springfield, IL: Charles C. Thomas.

Dahl, P. R. (1979). An experimental program for teaching high speed word recognition and comprehension skills. In J. Button, T. Lovitt, & T. Rowland (Eds.), *Communication research in learning disabilities and mental retardation.* Baltimore, MD: University Park Press.

Dalby, J. T. (1979). Deficit or delay: Neuropsychological models of developmental dyslexia. *Journal of Special Education, 13,* 239–264.

Daneman, M., & Carpenter, P. (1980). Individual differences in working memory and reading. *Journal of Verbal Learning and Verbal Behavior, 119,* 450–456.

Daniels, P. R. (1983). Teaching the learning-disabled/gifted child. In L. H. Fox, L. Brody, & D. Tobin (Eds.), *Learning disabled/gifted children: Identification and programming* (pp. 153–169). Baltimore, MD: University Park Press.

Danielson, L. C., & Bauer, N. J. (1978). A formula based classification of learning disabled children: An examination of the issues. *Journal of Learning Disabilities, 11,* 163–176.

Darden, L., & Maull, N. (1977). Interfield theories. *Philosophy of Science, 44,* 43–64.

Das, J. P., Leong, C. K., & Williams, N. H. (1978). The relationships between learning disability and simultaneous-successive processing. *Journal of Learning Disabilities, 11,* 618–625.

Davis, S. M., & Bray, N. W. (1975). Bisensory memory in normal and reading disability children. *Bulletin of the Psychonomic Society, 6,* 572–574.

Davis, W. A., & Shepherd, L. A. (1983). Specialists' use of tests and clinical judgment in the diagnosis of learning disabilities. *Learning Disability Quarterly, 6,* 128–138.

Decker, S. N., & DeFries, J. C. (1980). Cognitive abilities in families with reading disabled children. *Journal of Learning Disabilities, 13,* 517–522.

Decker, S. N., & DeFries, J. C. (1981). Cognitive ability profiles in families of reading-disabled children. *Developmental Medicine and Child Neurology, 23,* 217–227.

DeFries, J. C. & Plomin, R. (1978). Behavioral genetics. *American Review in Psychology. 29,* 473–515.

DeFries, J. C., Johnson, R. C., Kuse, A. R., McClearn, G. E., Polovina, J., Vanderberg, S. G., & Wilson, J. R. (1979). Familial resemblance for specific cognitive abilities. *Genetics, 9,* 23–43.

de Hirsch, K. (1963). Two categories of learning disabilities in adolescents. *American Journal of Orthopsychiatry, 33,* 87–91.

de Hirsch, K., Jansky, J., & Langford, W. (1966). *Predicting reading failure.* New York: Harper & Row.

de Hirsch, K., Jansky, J. J., & Langford, W. S. (1972). *Preventing reading failure.* New York: Harper & Row.

Delacato, C. H. (1966). *Neurological organization and reading.* Springfield, IL: Charles C. Thomas.

Dell, G. S., & Reich, P. (1980). Toward a unified model of slips of the tongue. In V. Fromkin (Ed.), *Errors in linguistic performance.* New York: Academic Press.

Denckla, M. B. (1972). Clinical syndromes in learning disabilities: The case for "splitting vs. lumping." *Journal of Learning Disabilities, 5,* 401–406.

Denckla, M. B. (1974). Development of motor coordination in normal children. *Developmental Medicine and Child Neurology. 16,* 729–741.

Denckla, M. B. (1975). *Visual perception and the third R: The role of spatial orientation in learning arithmetic.* Paper presented at the Community School Symposium, Englewood, NJ.

Denckla, M. B., LeMay, M., & Chapman, C. A. (1985). Few CT scan abnormalities found even in neurologically impaired learning disabled children. *Journal of Learning Disabilities, 18,* 132–135.

Denckla, M. B., & Rudel, R. (1976). Rapid "automatized" naming (R.A.N.): Dyslexia differentiated from other learning disabilities. *Neuropsychologia, 14,* 471–479.

Denham, C., & Lieberman, A. (Eds.). (1980). *Time to learn.* Washington, DC: National Institute of Education.

Denhoff, H. E., Siqueland, M. L., Komich, M. P., & Hainsworth, P. K. (1968). Developmental and predictive characteristics of items from the Meeting Street School Screening Test. *Developmental Medicine and Child Neurology, 10,* 220–234.

deQuiros, J. B. (1976). Diagnosis of vestibular disorders in the learning disabled. *Journal of Learning Disabilities, 9,* 39–47.

Deshler, D., Lowery, N., & Alley, G. (1979). Programming alternatives for learning disabled adolescents: A nationwide survey. *Academic Therapy, 14*(4), 389–398.

Dever, R. B. (1978). *TALK: Teaching the American language to kids.* Columbus, OH: Charles E. Merrill.

Devito, J. A. (1978). *Communicology: An introduction to the study of communication.* New York: Harper & Row.

DeVries, H. (1966). In C. Stern & E. R. Sherwood (Trans.), *The origin of genetics: A Mendel source book.* San Francisco: Freeman.

Dewey, J. (1916). *Democracy and education: An introduction to the philosophy of education.* New York: MacMillan Company.

Diana v. California State Board of Education. (1970). United States District Court, Northern District of California, C-70 37 RFP.

Dickie, R. F. (1982). Still crazy after all these years: Another look at the questions of labeling and non-categorical conceptions of exceptional children. *Education and Treatment of Children, 5,* 355–363.

Dickstein, E. B., & Warren, D. R. (1980). Role-taking deficits in LD children. *Journal of Learning Disabilities, 13,* 378–382.

Doehring, D. G. (1968). *Patterns of impairment in specific reading disability.* Bloomington: Indiana University Press.

Doehring, D. G. (1978). The tangled web of behavioral research on developmental dyslexia. In A. L. Benton & D. Pearl (Eds.), *Dyslexia: An appraisal of current knowledge* (pp. 123–135). New York: Oxford University Press.

Doehring, D. G., Hoshko, I. M., & Bryans, B. N. (1979). Statistical classification of children with reading problems. *Journal of Clinical Neuropsychology, 1,* 5–16.

Doll, E. (1946). *Oseretsky tests.* Circle Pines, MN: American Guidance Service.

Donahue, M. (1981a). *Learning disabled children's comprehension and production of syntactic devices for marking given vs. new information.* Paper presented at the Boston University Conference on Language Development, Boston.

Donahue, M. (1981b). Requesting strategies of learning disabled children. *Applied Psycholinguistics, 2,* 213–234.

Donahue, M., & Bryan, T. (1983). Conversational skills and modeling in learning disabled boys. *Applied Psycholinguistics, 4,* 251–278.

Donahue, M., Pearl, R., & Bryan, T. (1980). Learning disabled children's conversational competence: Responses to inadequate messages. *Applied Psycholinguistics, 1,* 387–403.

Donnellan, A. M. (1984). The criterion of the least dangerous assumption. *Behavior Disorders, 9*(2), 141–149.

Dore, J. (1977). "Oh them sheriff": A pragmatic analysis of children's responses to questions. In S. Ervin-Tripp & C. Mitchell-Kernan (Eds.), *Child discourse.* New York: Academic Press.

Dore-Boyce, K., Misner, M., & McGuire, L. D. (1975). Comparing reading expectancy formulas. *The Reading Teacher, 29,* 8–14.

Douglas, V. I. (1972). Stop, look and listen: The problems of sustained attention and impulse control in hyperactive and normal children. *Canadian Journal of Behavioral Science, 4,* 259–281.

Douglas, V. I. (1974). Differences between normal and hyperkinetic children. In C. K. Conners (Ed.), *Clinical use of stimulant drugs in children.* Princeton: Excerpta Medica.

Douglas, V. I., Parry, P., Marton, P., & Garson, C. (1976). Assessment of a cognitive training program for hyperactive children. *Journal of Abnormal Child Psychology, 4,* 389–410.

Drabman, R. S., & Patterson, J. N. (1981). Disruptive behavior and the social standing of exceptional children. *Exceptional Education Quarterly, 1,* 45–55.

Dribben, E., & Brabender, V. (1979). The effect of mood inducement upon audience receptiveness. *Journal of Social Psychology, 107,* 135–136.

Duffey, J. B., Salvia, J., Tucker, T., & Ysseldyke, J. (1981). Non-biased assessment: A need for operationalism. *Exceptional Children, 47,* 427–434.

Dunkin, M. J., & Biddle, B. J. (1974). *The study of teaching.* New York: Holt, Rinehart & Winston.

Dunn, L. M. (1968). Special education for the mildly retarded — Is much of it justifiable? *Exceptional Children, 35,* 5–22.

Dunn, L. M., & Markwardt, F. C. (1970). *Peabody Individual Achievement Test.* Circle Pines, MN: American Guidance Service.

Durkin, D. (1978–1979). What classroom observations reveal about reading comprehension instruction. *Reading Research Quarterly, 14,* 481–533.

Durrant, J. D., & Lovrinic, J. H. (1977). *Bases of hearing science.* Baltimore, MD: Williams & Wilkins.

Dwyer, K. P. (1981, January). Maryland school psychologists' role in the identification of learning disabilities: Results of fall workshop. *Maryland School Psychologists Association, Inc., Newsletter,* 1–3.

Dykman, R. A., Ackerman, P. T., Clements, S. D., & Peters, J. E. (1971). Specific learning disabilities: An attentional deficit syndrome. In H. R. Myklebust (Ed.), *Progress in learning disabilities* (Vol. 2). New York: Grune & Stratton.

Dykman, R. A., Ackerman, P. T., Holcomb, P. J., & Bondreau, A. Y. (1983). Physiological manifestations of learning disabilities. *Journal of Learning Disabilities, 16,* 46–53.

Dykstra, R. (1966). Auditory discrimination abilities and beginning reading achievement. *Reading Research Quarterly, 1,* 5–33.

Edgar, E. B. (1978). Learning disabilities. In R. M. Goldenson, J. R. Dunham, & C. S. Dunham (Eds.), *Disability and rehabilitation handbook.* New York: McGraw-Hill.

Edgar, E., & Hayden, A. H. (1984–1985). Who are the children special education should serve and how many children are there? *The Journal of Special Education, 18*(4), 523–539.

Egolf, D., & Chester, S. (1973). Nonverbal communication and the disorders of speech and language. *ASHA, 15,* 511–518.

Eisenberg, L. (1966). Reading retardation: I. Psychiatric and sociologic aspects. *Pediatrics, 37*(2), 21–28.

Ekman, P., & Friesen, W. V. (1969). The repertoire of nonverbal behavior: Categories, origin, usage, and coding. *Semiotica, 1,* 49–98.

Elkind, J. (1973). The gifted child with learning disabilities. *Gifted Child Quarterly, 17,* 96–97, 115.

Ellis, A. W. (1979). Developmental and acquired dyslexia: Some observations on Jorm. *Cognition, 7,* 421–428.

Epps, S., Ysseldyke, J. E., & Algozzine, B. (1984). "I know one when I see one" — Differentiating LD and non-LD students. *Learning Disability Quarterly, 7,* 89–101.

Epstein, M. H., Cullinan, D., & Lloyd, J. W. (1986). Behavior problem patterns among the learning disabled: III. A replication across age and sex. *Learning Disability Quarterly, 9,* 43–44.

Epstein, M., Cullinan, D., & Rosemier, R. (1983). Behavior problem patterns among the learning disabled: Boys aged 6-11. *Learning Disability Quarterly, 6,* 305–311.

Erikson, M. T. (1975). The Z-score discrepancy method for identifying reading disabled children. *Journal of Learning Disabilities, 8,* 308–312.

Estes, W. H. (1970). *Learning theory and mental development.* New York: Academic Press.

Evans, J. & Guevara, A. E. (1974). Classroom instruction for young Spanish speakers. *Exceptional Children, 41,* 16–19.

Fain, P. R. (1976). *Major gene analysis: An alternative approach to the study of the genetics of human behavior.* Unpublished doctoral dissertation, University of Colorado.

Falconer, D. S. (1960). *Introduction to quantitative genetics.* New York: Ronald Press.

Fanelli, G. (1977). Locus of control. In S. Ball (Ed.), *Motivation in education.* New York: Academic Press.

Feagans, L., Fisher, L., & Short, S. (1982, October). *Effect of context and structure on the comprehension and recall of stories in LD and non-LD children.* Paper presented at the Boston University Conference on Language Development, Boston.

Federal Register. (1977, August 23). Washington, DC: Government Printing Office.

Federal Register. (1977, December 29). Washington, DC: U.S. Government Printing Office.

Feingold, B. F. (1975). *Why your child is hyperactive.* New York: Random House.

Feldt, L. A. (1967). Reliability of differences between scores. *American Educational Research Journal, 4,* 139–145.

Fernald, G. (1943). *Remedial techniques in basic school objectives.* New York: McGraw-Hill.

Feschbach, S., Adelman, H., & Fuller, W. (1977). Prediction of reading and related academic problems. *Journal of Educational Psychology, 69,* 299–308.

Feuerstein, R. (1979). *The dynamic assessment of retarded performers.* Baltimore, MD: University Park Press.

Fey, M. E., & Leonard, L. B. (1983). Pragmatic skills of children with specific language impairment. In T. M. Gallagher & C. A. Prutting (Eds.), *Pragmatic assessment and intervention issues in language.* San Diego, CA: College-Hill Press.

Fey, M. E., Leonard, L., Fey, S., & O'Connor, K. (1978, October). *The intent to communicate in language-impaired children.* Paper presented at the Boston University Conference on Language Development, Boston.

Fey, M. E., Leonard, L. B., & Wilcox, K. A. (1981). Speech style modifications of language impaired children. *Journal of Speech and Hearing Disorders, 46,* 91–96.

Feyerabend, P. K. (1975). *Against method: An outline of an anarchistic theory of knowledge.* London: NLB.

Fillmore, C. (1975). *Santa Cruz lectures on diexis.* MS. summer program in linguistics (1971), University of California at Santa Cruz. Bloomington, IN: Indiana University Linguistics Club.

Filmer, H. T., & Kohn, H. S. (1967). Race, socio-economic level, housing and reading readiness. *The Reading Teacher, 21*(2), 81–86.

Finch, A. J., & Spirito, A. (1980). Use of cognitive training to change cognitive processes. *Exceptional Education Quarterly, 1,* 31–39.

Fincham, F. (1979). Conservation and cognitive role-taking ability in learning disabled boys. *Journal of Learning Disabilities, 12,* 25–31.

Fine, R. (1967). *The psychology of a chess player.* New York: Dover.

Finitzo-Hieber, T., & Tillman, T. W. (1978). Room acoustic effects on monosyllabic word discrimination ability for normal and hearing impaired children. *Journal of Speech and Hearing Research, 21,* 440–448.

Finucci, J. M. (1978). Genetic considerations in dyslexia. In H. Myklebust (Ed.), *Progress in learning disabilities* (Vol. 4). New York: Grune & Stratton.

Fisher, C. W., Berliner, D. C., Filby, N. N., Marhave, R., Cahen, L. S., & Dishaw, M. M. (1980). Teacher behaviors, academic learning time, and student achievement: An overview. In C. Denham & A. Lieberman (Eds.), *Time to learn.* Washington, DC: National Institute of Education.

Fisher, D. F. (1979). Dysfunctions in reading ability: There's more than meets the eye. In L. Resnick & P. Weaver (Eds.), *Theory and practice of early reading* (Vol. 1). Hillsdale, NJ: Lawrence Erlbaum.

Fisher, D. F., & Frankfurter, A. (1977). Normal and disabled readers can locate and identify letters: Where's the perceptual deficit? *Journal of Reading Behavior, 9,* 31–43.

Fleischner, J. E., & Frank, B. (1979). Visual-spatial ability and mathematics achievement in learning disabled and normal boys. *Focus on Learning Mathematics, 1,* 7–22.

Fleischner, J. E., Garnett, K., & Preddy, D. (1982). *Mastery of basic number facts by learning disabled students: An intervention study* (Tech. Report No. 17). New York: Teachers College, Columbia University, Research Institute for the Study of Learning Disabilities.

Fleischner, J. E., Garnett, K., & Shepherd, M. J. (1982). Proficiency in arithmetic basic fact computation of learning disabled and nondisabled children. *Focus on Learning Problems in Mathematics, 4,* 47–55.

Fletcher, J. M. (1981). Linguistic factors in reading acquistion: Evidence for developmental changes. In F. Pirozzolo & M. Wittrock (Eds.), *Neuropsychological and cognitive processes in reading.* New York: Academic Press.

Fletcher, J. M., & Satz, P. (1979). Unitary deficit hypotheses of reading disabilities: Has Vellutino led us astray? *Journal of Learning Disabilities, 12,* 155–159.

Fletcher, S. G. (1970). Acoustic phonetics. In F. S. Berg & S. G. Fletcher (Eds.), *The hard of hearing child.* New York: Grune & Stratton.

Foch, T., DeFries, J., McLearn, G., & Singer, S. (1977). Familial patterns of impairment in reading disability. *Journal of Educational Psychology, 69,* 316–319.

Forman, G. E., & Sigel, I. E. (1979). *Cognitive development: A life span view.* Monterey, CA: Brooks/Cole.

Forness, S. (1982). Diagnosing dyslexia: A note on the need for ecologic assessment. *American Journal of Diseases of Children, 136,* 794–799.

Forness, S. R. (1985). Effects of public policy at the state level: California's impact on MR, LD and ED categories. *Remedial and Special Education, 6,* 36–43.

Forness, S., Bennett, L., & Tose, J. (1983). Academic deficits in emotionally disturbed children revisited. *Journal of Child Psychiatry, 22,* 140–144.

Forness, S., & Cantwell, D. (1982). DSM III psychiatric diagnosis and special education categories. *Journal of Special Education, 16,* 49–63.

Forness, S. R., & Herman, M. (1984). Sequential and simultaneous processing in children with behavioral or psychiatric disorders: Validity of the K-ABC. *Monographs in Behavioral Disorders, 7,* 60–66.

Forness, S. R., & Kavale, K. (1986). De-psychologizing special education. *Monographs in Behavioral Disorders, 9,* 2–14.

Forness, S., Sinclair, E., & Guthrie, D. (1983). Learning disability discrepancy formulas: Their use in actual practice. *Learning Disablity Quarterly, 6,* 107–114.

Foster, G. G., Schmidt, C. R., & Sabatino, D. (1976). Teacher expectancies and the label "learning disabilities." *Journal of Learning Disabilities, 9,* 111–114.

Fox, F., & Routh, D. (1980). Phonemic analysis and severe reading disability in children. *Journal of Psycholinguistic Research, 9,* 115–119.

Fox, L. H. (1981). Identification of the academically gifted. *American Psychologist, 36,* 1103–1111.

Fox, L. H. (1983). Gifted students with reading problems: An empirical study. In L. H. Fox, L. Brody, & D. Tobin (Eds.), *Learning-disabled/gifted children: Identification and programming* (pp. 117–130). Baltimore, MD: University Park Press.

Fox, L. H., & Brody, L. (1983). Models for identifying giftedness: Issues related to the learning-disabled child. In L. H. Fox, L. Brody, & D. Tobin (Eds.), *Learning-disabled/gifted children: Identification and programming* (pp. 101–116). Baltimore, MD: University Park Press.

Fox, L. H., Tobin, D., & Schiffman, G. B. (1983). Adaptive methods and techniques for learning-disabled/gifted children. In L. H. Fox, L. Brody, & D. Tobin (Eds.), *Learning-disabled/gifted children: Identification and programming.* Baltimore, MD: University Park Press.

Frame, R. E., Clarizio, H. F., & Porter, A. (1984). Diagnostic and prescriptive bias in school psychologists' reports of a learning-disabled child. *Journal of Learning Disabilities, 17,* 12–15.

Frank, B. (1982). *Whole number computational processes in learning disabled and non-handicapped students* (Progress Report, September 30, 1982). New York: Teachers College, Columbia University, Research Institute for the Study of Learning Disabilities.

Frankenberger, W. (1984). A survey of state guidelines for identification of mental retardation. *Mental Retardation, 22*(1), 17–20.

Frazer, J. G. (1963). *The golden bough.* New York: Macmillan.

Frederick, W. C., & Walberg, H. J. (1980). Learning as a function of time. *Journal of Educational Research, 73,* 183–194.

Freeburg, N., & Payne, D. (1967). Parental influence on cognitive development in early childhood: A review. *Child Development, 38,* 65–87.

Freeman, R. D. (1967). Special education and the electroencephalogram: Marriage of convenience. *Journal of Special Education, 2,* 61–73.

Freides, D. (1974). Human information processing and sensory modality: Cross-modal functions, information complexity, memory, and deficit. *Psychological Bulletin, 81,* 284–310.

Freud, S. (1966). *Psychology of everyday life.* (A. Tyson, Trans.). London: Bern. (Original work published in 1901)

Friedrich, D., Fuller, G., & Davis, D. (1984). Learning disability: Fact or fiction. *Journal of Learning Disability, 17*(4), 205–209.

Friedrich, V., Dalby, M., Stachelin-Jensen, T., & Bruun-Peterson, G. (1982). Chromosomal studies of children with developmental language retardation. *Developmental Medicine and Child Neurology, 24,* 645–652.

Fromkin, V. A. (Ed.). (1973). *Speech errors as linguistic evidence.* The Hague: Mouton.

Fromkin, V. A. (Ed.). (1980). *Errors in linguistic performance.* New York: Academic Press.

Frostig, M. (1961). *Frostig developmental test of visual perception* (3rd ed.). Palo Alto, CA: Consulting Psychologists Press.

Frostig, M. (1975). The role of perception in the integration of psychological functions. In W. Cruickshank & D. Hallahan (Eds.), *Perceptual and learning disabilities in children: I. Psychoeducational practices.* Syracuse, NY: Syracuse University Press.

Frostig, M., & Horne, D. (1964). *The Frostig program for the development of visual-perception.* Chicago: Follett.

Frostig, M., & Horne, D. (1964). *The Frostig program for the development of visual-perception. Teacher's guide.* Chicago: Follett.

Frostig, M., Maslow, P., Lefever, D. W., & Whittlesey, J. R. B. (1964). *The Marianne Frostig Development Test of Visual Perception* (1963 standardization). Palo Alto, CA: Consulting Psychologist.

Fuller, J. L., & Thompson, W. R. (1978). *Foundation of behavioral genetics.* St. Louis: C. V. Mosby & Company.

Gable, R. A., Strain, P. S., & Hendrickson, J. M. (1979). Strategies for improving the status and social behavior of learning disabled children. *Learning Disability Quarterly, 2,* 33–39.

Gaddes, W. H. (1980). *Learning disabilities and brain function.* New York: Springer Verlag.

Gaddes, W. H. (1981). Neuropsychology, fact or mythology, educational help or hinderance? *School Psychology, 10,* 322–330.

Gage, N. J. (Ed.). (1976). *The psychology of teaching methods: The 75th yearbook of the National Society for the Study of Education. Part I.* Chicago: University of Chicago Press.

Gage, N. J. (1978). *The scientific basis of the art of teaching.* New York: Teachers College Press.

Gagne, R. M. (1977). *The conditions of learning* (3rd ed.). New York: Holt, Rinehart & Winston.

Gajar, A. (1979). Educable mentally retarded, learning disabled, emotionally disturbed: Similarities and differences. *Exceptional Children,* 470–472.

Gajar, A. H. (1980). Characteristics across exceptional categories: EMR, LD, and ED. *Journal of Special Education, 14,* 165–173.

Galaburda, A. M. (1980). Language representation in the brain and findings in dyslexia. *Perspectives on Dyslexia, 5,* 7.

Galaburda, A. M., & Kemper, T. L. (1979). Cytoarchetectonic abnormalities in developmental dyslexia: A case study. *Annals of Neurology, 6,* 94–100.

Gallagher, J. J. (1966). Children with developmental imbalances: A psychoeducational definition. In W. Cruickshank (Ed.), *The teacher of brain-injured children* (pp. 23–43). (Syracuse University Special Education and Rehabilitation Monograph Series 7). Syracuse, NY: Syracuse University.

Gallagher, J., & Moss, J. (1963). New concepts of intelligence and their effect on exceptional children. *Exceptional Children, 30,* 1–5.

Garai, J. E., & Scheinfeld, A. (1968). Sex differences in mental and behavioral traits. *Genetic Psychology Monographs, 77,* 189–299.

Garcia, R. L. (1978). *Fostering a pluralistic society through multi-ethnic education.* Bloomington, IN: Phi Delta Kappa Educational Foundation.

Garrett, M. D., & Crump, W. D. (1980). Peer acceptance, teacher preference, and self-appraisal of social status among learning disabled students. *Learning Disability Quarterly, 3,* 42–48.

Garrett, M. D., & Crump, W. D. (1980). Peer acceptance, teacher preference, & self-appraisal of social status among learning disabled students. *Learning Disability Quarterly, 1,* 40–48.

Garvey, C. (1975). Requests and responses in children's speech. *Journal of Child Language, 2,* 41–64.

Garvey, C. (1977a). The contingent query: A dependent act in conversation. In M. Lewis & L. Rosenblum (Eds.), *Interaction, conversation, and the development of language: The origins of behavior* (Vol. 5). New York: John Wiley & Sons.

Garvey, C. (1977b). *Play.* Cambridge, MA: Harvard University Press.

Gaskins, I. W. (1982). Let's end the reading disabilities/learning disabilities debate. *Journal of Learning Disabilities, 15,* 81–83.

Gear, G. H. (1976). Accuracy of teacher judgment in identifying intellectually gifted children: A review of the literature. *Gifted Child Quarterly, 22,* 478–490.

Gear, G. H. (1978). Effects of training on teachers' accuracy in the identification of gifted children. *Gifted Child Quarterly, 22,* 90–97.

Gearhart, B. R. (1973). *Learning disabilities.* St. Louis: C. V. Mosby.

Gelfand, D. M., Jenson, W. R., & Drew, C. J. (1982). *Understanding child behavior disorders.* New York: Holt, Rinehart & Winston.

Gelfand, S. A., & Hochberg, I. (1976). Binaural and monaural speech discrimination under reverberation. *Audiology, 15,* 72–84.

Geller, E. F., & Wollner, S. G. (1976). *A preliminary investigation of the communicative competence of three linguistically impaired children.* Paper presented at the New York Speech and Hearing Association, New York.

Gentry, S. R. (1984). Developmental aspects of learning to spell. *Academic Therapy, 20*(1), 11–19.

Gerber, A., & Bryen, D. (1981). *Language and learning disabilities.* Baltimore, MD: University Park Press.

Gerber, M. M. (1984). The department of education's sixth annual report to Congress on P.L. 94-142: Is Congress getting the full story? *Exceptional Children, 51*(3), 209–244.

German, D., Johnson, B., & Schneider, M. (1985). Learning disability vs. reading disability: A survey of pracitioners diagnostic populations and test instruments. *Learning Disability Quarterly, 8,* 141–158.

Gerstmann, J. (1940). Syndrome of finger agnosia: Disorientation for right and left, agraphia and acalculia. *Archives of Neurology and Psychiatry, 44,* 398–408.

Geschwind, N., & Behan, P. (1982). Left-handedness: Association with immune disease, migraine, and developmental learning disorder. *Proceedings of the National Academy of Sciences, 79,* 5097–5100.

Getman, G. N. (1965). The visuomotor complex in the acquisition of learning skills. In J. Helmuth (Ed.), *Learning disorders* (Vol. 1, pp. 49–76). Seattle: Special Child Publications.

Gettinger, M. (1984). Achievement as a function of time spent on learning and time needed for learning. *American Educational Research Journal, 21,* 617–628.

Gever, B. E. (1970). Failure and learning disability. *The Reading Teacher, 23,* 311–317.

Gibbs, R. W., & Tenney, Y. L. (1980). The concept of scripts in understanding stories. *Journal of Psycholinguistic Research, 9,* 275–284.

Gillingham, A., & Stillman, B. W. (1966). *Remedial training for children with specific disability in reading, spelling, and penmanship* (7th ed.). Cambridge, MA: Educators Publishing Service.

Ginsburg, H. (1977). *Children's arithmetic: The learning process.* New York: D. VanNostrand Company.

Glaser, R. (1976). Components of a psychology of instruction: Toward a science of design. *Review of Educational Research, 46,* 1–24.

Glaser, R. (1977). *Adaptive education: Individualized diversity and learning.* New York: Holt, Rinehart & Winston.

Glaser, R., Pellegrino, J., & Lesgold, A. (1978). Some directions for a cognitive psychology of instruction. In A. Lesgold, J. Pellegrino, S. Fokkema, & R. Glaser (Eds.), *Cognitive psychology and instruction.* New York: Plenum Press.

Glass, G. V. (1977). Integrating findings: The meta-analysis of research. In L. Shulman (Ed.), *Review of research in education, 5,* 351–379.

Glass, G. V., Cahen, L. S., Smith, M. L., & Filby, N. N. (1982). *School class size: Research and policy.* Beverly Hills, CA: SAGE.

Glass, G. V., McGaw, B., & Smith, M. L. (1981). *Meta-analysis in social research.* Beverly Hills, CA: SAGE.

Glasser, A. J., & Zimmerman, I. L. (1967). *Clinical interpretation of the Wechsler Intelligence Scale for Children.* New York: Grune & Stratton.

Glavin, J. P., Quay, H. C., & Werry, J. S. (1971). Behavioral and academic gains of conduct problem children in different classroom settings. *Exceptional Children, 37,* 441–446.

Glowa, A. (1982). Bannatyne's recategorization of the WISC-R subtest scores: Indicative of learning disabilities? Unpublished doctoral dissertation, American University, Washington, DC.

Goertzel, V., & Goertzel, M. (1962). *Cradles of eminence.* Boston: Little, Brown and Company.

Golinkoff, R. M., & Rosinski, R. R. (1976). Decoding, semantic processing and reading comprehension skill. *Child Development, 42,* 252–258.

Good, C. V. (Ed.). (1973). *Dictionary of education.* New York: McGraw-Hill.

Good, T. (1979). Classroom expectations: Teacher–pupil interactions. In J. McMillan (Ed.), *The social psychology of school learning.* New York: Academic Press.

Good, T., Biddle, B., & Brophy, J. (1975). *Teachers make a difference.* New York: Holt, Rinehart & Winston.

Goodfellow, P. N., Jones, E. A., Van Heyningen, V., Solomon, E., & Bobrow, M. (1975). The beta 2-microglobulin gene is on chromosome 15 and not in the HL-A region. *Nature, 254,* 267–269.

Goodman, K. (Ed.). (1973). *The psycholinguistic nature of the reading process.* Detroit: Wayne State University Press.

Goodman, L., & Hammill, D. (1973). The effectiveness of the Kephart-Getman activities in developing perceptual-motor and cognitive skills. *Exceptional Children, 4,* 1–10.

Goodstein, H. A., & Kahn, H. (1974). Pattern of achievement among children with learning difficulties. *Exceptional Children, 5,* 47–49.

Goolsby, T. M. (1971). Appropriateness of subtests in achievement test selection. *Educational and Psychological Measurement, 31,* 967–972.

Gordon, H. W. (1980). Cognitive asymmetry in dyslexic families. *Neuropsychologia, 18,* 645–656.

Gore, W. (1982). *Guidelines for the assessment and evaluation of children referred for a suspected learning disability.* Worchester County, MD: Worchester County Public Schools.

Gottesman, R. L., Croen, L., & Rotkin, L. (1982). Urban second grade children: A profile of good and poor readers. *Journal of Learning Disabilities, 15,* 268–272.

Government Accounting Office. (1981). *Report to the Chairman, Subcommittee on Select Educational Costs, House of Representatitves: Disparities still exist in who gets special education.* Washington, DC.

Graden, J. L., Casey, A., & Christenson, S. L. (1985). Implementing a pre-referral intervention system: Part I. The model. *Exceptional Children, 51*(5), 377–384.

Grant, W. W., Boelsche, A., & Zin, D. (1973). Developmental patterns of two motor functions. *Developmental Medicine and Child Neurology, 15,* 171–177.

Graybeal, C. M. (1981). Memory for stories in language-impaired children. *Applied Psycholinguistics, 2,* 269–283.

Green, O. C., & Perlman, S. M. (1971). Endocrinology and disorders of learning. In H. Myklebust (Ed.), *Progress in learning disabilities* (Vol. 2). New York: Grune & Stratton.

Gresham, F. M. (1982). Misguided mainstreaming: The case for social skills training with handicapped children. *Exceptional Children, 48,* 422–433.

Grice, H. P. (1975). Logic and conversation. In P. Cole & J. L. Morgan (Eds.), *Syntax and semantics: Speech Acts* (Vol. 3). New York: Academic Press.

Grimes, L. (1981). Learned helplessness and attribution theory: Redefining children's learning problems. *Learning Disabilities, 4,* 91–100.

Groen, G., & Parkman, L. A. (1972). A chronometric analysis of simple addition. *Psychological Review, 79,* 329–343.

Groen, G. J., & Resnick, L. B. (1977). Can preschool children invent addition algorithms? *Journal of Educational Psychology, 69,* 645–652.

Gross, K., & Rothenberg, S. (1979). An examination of methods used to test the visual perceptual deficit hypothesis of dyslexia. *Journal of Learning Disabilities, 12,* 670–677.

Gross, K., Rothenberg, S., & Schottenfeld, S. (1978). Duration thresholds for letter identification in left and right visual fields for normal and reading disabled children. *Neuropsychologia, 16,* 709–715.

Gump, P. (1978). School environments. In I. Altman & J. Wohlwill (Eds.), *Children and the environment.* New York: Plenum Press.

Gupta, R., Ceci, S. J., & Slater, A. M. (1978). Visual discrimination in good and poor readers. *Journal of Special Education, 12,* 409–416.

Guralnick, M. I. (1978). *Early intervention and the integration of handicapped and nonhandicapped children.* Baltimore, MD: University Park Press.

Gutkin, T. B. (1979). WISC-R scatter indices: Useful information for differential diagnosis? *Journal of School Psychology, 17,* 368–371.

Guyer, B. L., & Freidman, M. P. (1975). Hemispheric processing and cognitive styles in learning disabled and normal children. *Child Development, 46,* 658–668.

Hacaen, J. (1962). Clinical symptomatology in right and left hemisphere lesions. In V. B. Mountcastle (Ed.), *Interhemispheric relations and cerebral dominance.* Baltimore, MD: Johns Hopkins University Press.

Hagen, J. W., Barclay, C. R., & Newman, R. S. (1982). Metacognition, self-knowledge, and learning disabilities: Some thoughts on knowing and doing. *Topics in Learning and Learning Disabilities, 2,* 19–26.

Haight, S. L. (1977). Learning disabilities perspectives. *Academic Therapy, 15,* 191–199.

Hall, M. A. (1981). *Teaching reading as a language experience.* Columbus, OH: Charles E. Merrill.

Hall, R. V., Delquadri, J., Greenwood, C. R., & Thurston, I. (1982). The importance of opportunity to respond to children's academic success. In E. Edgar, N. Haring, J. Jenkins, & C. Pious (Eds.), *Mentally handicapped children: Education and training.* Baltimore, MD: University Park Press.

Hallahan, D. P., & Cruickshank, W. M. (1973). *Psychoeducational foundations of learning disabilities.* Englewood Cliffs, NJ: Prentice-Hall.

Hallahan, D. P., & Kauffman, J. M. (1976). *Introduction to learning disabilities: A psychobehavioral approach.* Englewood Cliffs, NJ: Prentice-Hall.

Hallahan, D. P., & Kauffman, J. M. (1977). Labels, categories, behaviors: ED, LD, and EMR reconsidered. *Journal of Special Education, 11,* 139–149.

Hallahan, D. P., Kauffman, J. M., & Lloyd, J. W. (1985). *Introduction to learning disabilities* (2nd ed.). Englewood Cliffs, NJ: Prentice-Hall.

Hallgren, B. (1950). Specific dyslexia: A clinical and genetic study. *Acta Psychiatrica et Neurologica* (Suppl. 65).

Halliday, M. A. K., & Hasan, R. (1976). *Cohesion in English.* London: Longman.

Hamachek, D. E. (1978). *Encounters with the self* (2nd ed.). New York: Holt, Rinehart & Winston.

Hammermeister, F. K., & Israelite, N. K. (1983). Reading instruction for the hearing impaired: An integrated language arts approach. *The Volta Review, 85*(3), 136–148.

Hammill, D. D. (1972). Training visual perceptual processes. *Journal of Learning Disabilities, 5,* 552–560.

Hammill, D. D. (1976). Defining "LD" for programmatic purposes. *Academic Therapy, 12*(1), 29–37.

Hammill, D. D. (1980). The field of learning disabilities: A futuristic perspective. *Learning Disability Quarterly, 3,* 2–9.

Hammill, D. D., & Larsen, S. C. (1974a). The effectiveness of psycholinguistic training. *Exceptional Children, 41,* 5–14.

Hammill, D. D., & Larsen, S. C. (1974b). Relationship of selected auditory perceptual skills and reading disability. *Journal of Learning Disabilities, 7,* 429–435.

Hammill, D. D., & Larsen, S. C. (1978). The effectiveness of psycholinguistic training: A reaffirmation of position. *Exceptional Children, 44,* 402–414.

Hammill, D. D., Leight, J. E., McNutt, G., & Larsen, S. C. (1981). A new definition of learning disabilities. *Learning Disability Quarterly, 4,* 336–342.

Hammond, W. D. (1972). Teaching reading in the elementary school. *Projections for reading: Preschool through adulthood* (HEW Publication No. (OE) 77-00110). Washington, DC: U.S. Government Printing Office.

Hanna, P. R., Hanna, I. S., Hodges, R. E., & Rudorf, E. H. (1966). *Phoneme-grapheme correspondance as cues to spelling improvement.* Washington, DC: U.S. Government Printing Office.

Harber, J. R. (1981). Learning disability research: How far have we progressed? *Learning Disability Quarterly, 4,* 372–381.

Hare, B. (1977). Perceptual deficits are not a cue to reading problems in second grade. *The Reading Teacher, 30,* 624–627.

Harnischfeger, A., & Wiley, D. E. (1976). The teaching learning process in elementary schools: A synoptic view. *Curriculum, 4,* 226–232.

Harris, A. J. (1961). *How to increase reading ability* (4th ed.). New York: David McKay.

Harris, A. J. (Ed.). (1970). *Casebook on reading disability.* New York: David McKay.

Harris, A. J. (1982). How many kinds of reading disability are there? *Journal of Learning Disabilities, 15,* 456–460.

Harris, A., & Roswell, F. (1953). Clinical diagnosis of reading disability. *Journal of Psychology, 53,* 323–340.

Harris, A., & Sipay, E. R. (1975). *How to increase reading ability* (6th ed.). New York: David McKay.

Harris, J. C., King, S. L., Reifler, J. P., & Rosenberg, L. A. (in press). Emotional and learning disorders in 6-12 year old boys attending special schools. *Journal of the American Academy of Child Psychiatry.*

Harris-Schmidt, G. (1983). In C. T. Wren (Ed.), *Language learning disabilities*. Rockville, MD: Aspen Systems.

Hart, Z., Rennick, P. M., Klinge, V., & Schwartz, M. L. (1974). A pediatric neurologist's contributions to evaluations of school underachievers. *American Journal of Diseases of Children, 128,* 319–323.

Hart-Johns, M., & Johns, B. (1982). *Give your child a chance*. Reston, VA: Reston Publishing Company.

Hartlage, L. (1970). Differential diagnosis of dyslexia, minimal brain damage, and emotional disturbances in children. *Psychology in the Schools, 7,* 403–406.

Hartlage, L. C. (1982). Neuropsychological assessment techniques. In C. R. Reynolds & T. B. Gutkin (Eds.). *The handbook of school psychology*. New York: John Wiley & Sons.

Hartlage, L. C., & Telznow, C. F. (1983). The neuropsychological basis of educational intervention. *Journal of Learning Disabilities, 16,* 521–528.

Hartman, N., & Hartman, R. (1973). Perceptual handicap or reading disability? *The Reading Teacher, 26,* 684–695.

Haseman, J. K., & Elston, R. C. (1972). The investigation of linkage between a quantitative trait and a marker locus. *Behavioral Genetics, 2,* 3–19.

Havard, J. (1973). School problems and allergies. *Journal of Learning Disabilities, 6,* 492–494.

Hawke, W. A., & Lesser, S. R. (1977). The child with a learning disability. In P. D. Steinhauer & Q. Rae-Grant (Eds.), *Psychological problems of the child and his family*. Toronto: Macmillan of Canada.

Hays, W. L. (1981). *Statistics* (3rd ed.). New York: Holt, Rinehart & Winston.

Heath, D. H. (1971). *Humanizing schools: New directions, new decisions*. New York: Hayden Book Company.

Hecaen, H., & Kremin H. (1976). Neurolinguistic research on reading disorders resulting from left hemisphere lesions: Aphasic and "pure" alexias. In H. Whitaker & H. Whitaker (Eds.), *Studies in neurolinguistics* (Vol. 2). New York: Academic Press.

Heckelman, R. A. (1969). A neurological impress method of remedial reading instruction. *Academic Therapy, 4,* 272–282.

Hedges, L. V. (1981). Distribution theory for Glass's estimator of effect size and related estimators. *Journal of Educational Statistics, 6,* 107–128.

Hedges, L. V., & Olkin, I. (1985). *Statistical methods for meta-analysis*. New York: Academic Press.

Helgott, J. (1976). Phonemic segmentation and blending skills of kindergarten children: Implications for beginning reading acquisition. *Contemporary Educational Psychology, 2,* 157–169.

Henderson, R. W. (1980). Social and emotional needs of culturally diverse children. *Exceptional Children, 46,* 598–605.

Henschen, S. (1925). Clinical and anatomical contributions on brain pathology. *Archives of Neurology and Psychiatry, 13,* 226–249.

Herbert, M. (1964). The concept and testing of brain-damage in children: A review. *Journal of Child Psychology and Psychiatry, 5,* 197–216.

Herrmann, K. (1959). *Reading disability*. Copenhagen: Munksgaard.

Herrick, M. J. (1973). Disabled or disadvantaged: What's the difference? *Journal of Special Education, 7,* 381–386.

Herschel, M. (1978). Dyslexia revisited: A review. *Human Genetics, 40,* 115–134.

Hertzig, M. E., Bortner, M., & Birch, H. G. (1969). Neurologic findings in children educationally designated as "brain-damaged." *American Journal of Orthopsychiatry, 39,* 473–446.

Hess, R. (1970). Class and ethnic influences upon socialization. In P. Mussen (Ed.), *Carmichael's manual of child psychology* (3rd ed., Vol. 2). New York: John Wiley & Sons.

Hessler, G. L., & Kitchen, D. W. (1980). Language characteristics of a purposive sample of early elementary learning disabled students. *Learning Disability Quarterly, 3,* 36–41.

Heward, W. L., & Orlansky, M. O. (1980). Exceptional children: An introductory survey of special education. Columbus, OH: Charles Merrill.

Hewett, F. M., & Forness, S. R. (1974). *Education of exceptional learners.* Boston: Allyn & Bacon.

Hewett, F. M., & Forness, S. R. (1983). *Education of exceptional learners* (3rd ed.). Boston: Allyn & Bacon.

Hewett, F., & Taylor, F. D. (1980). *The emotionally disturbed child in the classroom: The orchestration of success* (2nd ed.). Boston: Allyn & Bacon.

Hildum, D. C., & Brown, R. W. (1956). Expectancy and the identification of syllables. *Language, 32,* 411–419.

Hilton, T. L. (1979). ETS study of academic prediction and growth. In J. Mulholland (Ed.), *New directions for testing and measurement.* San Francisco: Jossey-Bass.

Hinshelwood, J. (1900). Congenital word-blindness. *Lancet, 1,* 1506–1508.

Hinshelwood, J. (1917). *Congenital word-blindness.* London: H. K. Lewis.

Hobbs, N. (1975). *The futures of children: Categories, labels and their consequences* (Report of the Project on Classification of Exceptional Children). San Francisco: Jossey-Bass.

Hobbs, N. (1976). *Issues in the classification of children* (Vols. 1 & 2). San Francisco: Jossey-Bass.

Hodges, R. E., & Rudorf, E. H. (1965). Searching linguistics for cues for the teaching of spelling. *Elementary English, 42,* 527–533.

Hoffman, J. V. (1980). The disabled reader: Forgive us our regressions and lead us not into expectations. *Journal of Learning Disabilities, 13,* 7–11.

Holland, R. P. (1982). Learner characteristics and learner performance: Implications for instructional placement decisions. *Journal of Special Education, 16,* 7–20.

Hollingsworth, P. M. (1970). An experiment with the impress method of teaching reading. *The Reading Teacher, 24,* 112–114.

Hollingsworth, P. M. (1978). An experimental approach to the impress method of teaching reading. *The Reading Teacher, 31,* 624–626.

Holm, V. A., & Kunze, L. H. (1969). Effect of chronic otitis media on language and speech development. *Pediatrics, 43,* 833–839.

Holmes, D. L., & Peper, R. J. (1977). An evaluation of the use of spelling error analysis in the diagnosis of reading disabilities. *Child Development, 48,* 1708–1711.

Holvoet, J., Guess, D., Mulligan, M., & Brown, F. (1980). The individualized curriculum sequencing model (II): A teaching strategy for severely handicapped students. *Journal of the Association for the Severely Handicapped, 5,* 337–367.

Hopkins, K. D., & Bracht, G. H. (1975). Ten-year stability of verbal and nonverbal IQ scores. *American Educational Research Journal, 12,* 469–477.

Hornstein, H. A. *Cruelty and kindness: A new look at aggression and altruism.* Englewood Cliffs, NJ: Prentice-Hall.

Horowitz, E. C. (1981). Popularity, decentering ability, and role-taking skills in learning disabled and normal children. *Learning Disability Quarterly, 4,* 23–30.

Horst, D. P. (1976). *What's bad about grade-equivalent scores. ESEA Title I evaluation and reporting system* (Technical Report No. 1). Mountain View, CA: RMC Research Corporation.

Hoskins, B. (1983). Semantics. In C. T. Wren (Ed.), *Language learning disabilities.* Rockville, MD: Aspen Systems.

Hoskisson, K., & Krohn, B. (1974). Reading by immersion: Assisted reading. *Elementary English, 51,* 832–836.

Hresko, W. P., & Reid, D. (1981). Five faces of cognition: Theoretical influences on approaches to learning disabilities. *Learning Disability Quarterly, 4,* 238–243.

Hughes, J. R. (1978). Electroencephalographic and neurophysiological studies in dyslexia. In A. L. Benton & D. Pearl (Eds.), *Dyslexia: An appraisal of current knowledge* (pp. 205–249). New York: Oxford University Press.

Hunt, J. McV. (1961). *Intelligence and experience.* New York: John Wiley & Sons.

Hunter, J. E., Schmidt, F. L., & Jackson, G. B. (1982). *Meta-analysis: Cumulating research findings across studies.* Beverly Hills, CA: SAGE.

Hyman, H. H., Wright, C. R., & Reed, J. S. (1975). *The enduring effects of education.* Chicago: University of Chicago Press.

Hymes, D. (1971). Competence and performance in linguistic theory. In R. Huxley & E. Ingram (Eds.), *Language acquisition: Models and methods.* New York: Academic Press.

Hynd, G. W., & Obrut, J. E. (Eds.). (1951). *Neuropsychological assessment and the school-age child: Issues and procedures.* New York: Grune & Stratton.

Ingram, T. T. S. (1973) Soft signs. *Developmental Medicine and Child Neurology, 15,* 527–529.

Ingram, T. T. S., Mason, A. W., & Blackburn, I. A. (1970). A retrospective study of 82 children with reading disability. *Developmental Medicine and Child Neurology, 12,* 271–281.

Isakson, R., & Miller, J. (1976). Sensitivity to syntactic and semantic cues in good and poor comprehenders. *Journal of Educational Psychology, 68,* 787–792.

Ito, H. R. (1981). After the resource room — Then what? *Academic Therapy 16*(3), 283–287.

Jackson, P. W. (1968). *Life in classrooms.* New York: Holt, Rinehart & Winston.

Jakupcak, M. (1975). Areas of congruence in remedial reading and learning disabilities. *Journal of Special Education, 9,* 155–157.

Jastak, J. E., & Jastak, S. R. (1976). *Wide range achievement test.* Wilmington, DE: Guidance Associates.

Jenkins, J., & Pany, D. (1978). Standardized achievement tests: How useful for special education? *Exceptional Children, 44,* 448–453.

Jensen, A. R. (1967). Varieties in individual differences in learning. In R. Gagne (Ed.), *Learning and individual differences.* Columbus, OH: Charles E. Merrill.

Joe, V. (1971). Review of the internal-external control construct as a personality variable. *Psychological Reports, 28,* 619–640.

Johnson, D. J. (1981). Factors to consider in programming for children with language disorders. *Topics in Language and Learning Disabilities, 1,* 13–28.

Johnson, D. J. (1982). Programming for dyslexia: The need for interaction analyses. *Annals of Dyslexia, 32,* 61–70.

Johnson, D. J., & Myklebust, H. R. (1967). *Learning disabilities: Educational principles and practices.* New York: Grune & Stratton.

Johnson, M. S. (1957). Factors related to disability in reading. *Journal of Experimental Education, 26,* 1–26.

Johnson, M. S. (1966). Tracing and kinesthetic techniques. In J. Money (Ed.), *The disabled reader.* Baltimore, MD: Johns Hopkins Press.

Johnson, M. S., & Kress, R. A. (1965). *Informal reading inventories.* Newark, DE: International Reading Association.

Johnson, M. S., & Kress, R. A. (1966). *Eliminating word learning problems in reading disability cases.* Philadelphia, PA: Temple University.

Johnson, M. S., & Kress, R. A. In A. J. Harris (Ed.), *Casebook on reading disability.* New York: David McKay.

Johnston, J. R. (1982). Narratives: A new look at communication problems in older language-disordered children. *Language, Speech, and Hearing Services in Schools, 13,* 144–155.

Johnston, R. B., Stark, R. E., Mellits, E. D., & Tallal, P. (1981). Neurological status of language-impaired and normal children. *Annals of Neurology, 10,* 159–163.

Jorm, A. F. (1979). The nature of reading deficit in developmental dyslexia. *Cognition, 7,* 429–433.

Joyce, B., & Weil, M. (1972). *Models of teaching.* Englewood Cliffs, NJ: Prentice-Hall.

Just, M. A., & Carpenter, P. A. (1980). A theory of reading from eye fixation to comprehension. *Psychological Review, 87,* 329–354.

Kagan, J., & Kagan, N. (1970). Individual variation in cognitive processes. In P. Mussen (Ed.), *Carmichael's manual of child psychology* (3rd ed., Vol. 1). New York: John Wiley & Sons.

Kagan, J., & Moore, M. J. (1981). Retrieval and evaluation of symbolic information on dyslexia. *Bulletin of the Orton Society, 31,* 65–73.

Kahn, D., & Birch, H. (1968). Development of auditory-visual integration and reading achievement. *Perceptual and Motor Skills, 67,* 459–468.

Kalinski, L. (1962). Arithmetic and the brain-injured child. *The Arithmetic Teacher, 9,* 245–251.

Kamin, L. J. (1974). *The science and politics of IQ.* New York: John Wiley & Sons.

Kann, R. (1983). The method of repeated readings: Expanding the neurological impress method for use with disabled readers. *Journal of Learning Disabilities, 16,* 90–92.

Kaplan, A. (1964). *The conduct of inquiry: Methods for behavioral science.* San Francisco: Chandler.

Kaplan, G. K., Fleshman, J. K., Bender, T. R., Baum, C., & Clark, P. S. (1973). Long-term effects of otitis media: A 10-year cohort study of Alaska Eskimo children. *Pediatrics, 52,* 577–585.

Karinthy, F. (1979). The sick and the mad. In T. Szass (Ed.), *The age of madness.* New York: Aronson.

Karnes, F. A., & Collins, E. C. (1978). State definitions on the gifted and talented: A report and analysis. *Journal of Education of the Gifted, 1,* 44–62.

Karweit, N. L. (1980). Time in school. In *Research in sociology of education and socialization: An annual compilation of research.* Greenwich, CT: JAI Press.

Kass, C. (1966). Psycholinguistic disabilities of children with reading problems. *Exceptional Children, 32,* 533–539.

Kauffman, J. M. (1980). Where special education for disturbed children is going: A personal view. *Exceptional Children, 46,* 522–526.

Kauffman, J. (1982). Social policy issues in special education and related services for emotionally disturbed children and youth. In M. Noel & N. Haring (Eds.), *Progress of change: Issues in educating the emotionally disturbed: Vol. I. Identification and program planning.* Spokane: University of Washington, Program Development Assistance System.

Kaufman, A. S. (1979a). *Intelligence testing with the WISC-R.* New York: John Wiley & Sons.

Kaufman, A. S. (1979b). WISC-R research: Implications for interpretation: *School Psychology Digest, 8,* 5–27.

Kaufman, A. S. (1982). The impact of WISC-R research for school psychologists. In C. R. Reynolds & T. B. Gutkin (Eds.), *The handbook of school psychology.* New York: John Wiley & Sons.

Kaufman, A. S., & Kaufman, N. L. (1984). *Kaufman Assessment Battery for Children: Interpretive manual.* Circle Pines, MN: American Guidance Service.

Kavale, K. A. (1980a). Auditory-visual integration and its relationship to reading achievement: A meta-analysis. *Perceptual and Motor Skills, 51,* 947–955.

Kavale, K. A. (1980b). Learning disability and cultural-economic disadvantage: The case for a relationship. *Learning Disability Quarterly, 3,* 97–112.

Kavale, K. A. (1980c). The reasoning abilities of normal and learning disabled readers on measures of reading comprehension. *Learning Disability Quarterly, 3,* 34–45.

Kavale, K. A. (1981a). Functions of the Illinois Test of Psycholinguistic Abilities (ITPA): Are they trainable? *Exceptional Children, 47,* 496–510.

Kavale, K. A. (1981b). The relationship between auditory perceptual skills and reading ability: A meta-analysis. *Journal of Learning Disabilities, 14,* 539–546.

Kavale, K. A. (1982). Meta-analysis of the relationship between visual perceptual skills and reading achievement. *Journal of Learning Disabilities, 15,* 42–51.

Kavale, K. A. (1987). Theoretical quandries in learning disabilities. In S. Vaughn & C. Boss (Eds.), *Issues and directions for research in learning disabilities.* San Diego. College-Hill Press.

Kavale, K. A., Alper, A. E., & Purcell, L. L. (1981). Behavior disorders, reading disorders, and teacher perceptions. *The Exceptional Child, 28,* 114–118.

Kavale, K., & Andreassen, E. (1984). Factors in diagnosing the learning disabled: Analysis of judgmental policies. *Journal of Learning Disabilities, 17,* 273–278.

Kavale, K., & Forness, S. R. (1984a). A meta-analysis assessing the validity of Wechsler Scale profiles and recategorization: Patterns or parodies? *Learning Disability Quarterly, 7,* 136–156.

Kavale, K., & Forness, S. (1984b). The historical foundation of learning disabilities: A quantitative synthesis assessing the validity of Strauss and Werner's exogenous versus endogenous distinction of mental retardation. *Remedial and Special Education, 6*(4), 18–24.

Kavale, K. A., & Forness, S. R. (1985a). Learning disability and the history of science: Paradigm or paradox? *Remedial and Special Education, 6,* 12–23.

Kavale, K. A., & Forness, S. R. (1985b). *The science of learning disabilities.* San Diego: College-Hill Press.

Kavale, K. A., & Forness, S. R. (1986). School learning time and learning disabilities: The disassociated learner. *Journal of Learning Disabilities, 19,* 130–138.

Kavale, K. A., & Forness, S. R. (in press). A matter of substance over style: A quantitative synthesis assessing the efficacy of modality testing and teaching. *Exceptional Children.*

Kavale, K. A., Forness, S. R., & Alper, A. E. (1986). Research in behavioral disorders/emotional disturbance: A survey of subject identification criteria. *Behavioral Disorders, 11*(3), 159–167.

Kavale, K. A., & Mattson, P. (1983). "One jumped off the balance beam." Meta-analysis of perceptual motor training. *Journal of Learning Disabilities, 16,* 165–173.

Kavale, K., & Nye, C. (1981). Identification criteria for learning disabilities: A survey of the research literature. *Learning Disability Quarterly, 4*(4), 383–388.

Keeves, J. P. (1972). *Educational environment and student achievement.* Stockholm: Almquist & Wiksell.

Keller-Cohen, D. (1978). Context in child language. *Annual Review of Anthropology, 7,* 453–482.

Kelley, T. L. (1927). *Interpretation of educational measurements.* New York: World Book.

Kenny, T. J., & Clemens, R. C. (1971). Medical and psychological correlates in children with learning disabilities. *Journal of Pediatrics, 78,* 273–277.

Keogh, B. K. (1974). Optometric vision training programs for children with learning disabilities: Review of issues and research. *Journal of Learning Disabilities, 7,* 219–231.

Keogh, B. K. (1978). Marker variables: A search for comparability and generalizability in the field of learning disabilities. *Learning Disability Quarterly, 3,* 5–11.

Keogh, B. K. (1983). Clarification, compliance and confusion. *Journal of Learning Disabilities, 16*(1), 25–26.

Keogh, B. K., & Donlon, G. (1972). Field dependence, impulsivity, and learning disabilities. *Journal of Learning Disabilities, 5,* 331–336.

Keogh, B. K., & MacMillan, D. L. (1983). The logic of sample selection: Who represents what? *Exceptional Education Quarterly, 4*(3), 84–96.

Keogh, B. K., Major, S. M., Reid, H. P., Gandara, P., & Omori, H. (1978). Marker variables: A search for comparability and generalizability in the field of learning disabilities. *Learning Disability Quarterly, 1,* 5–11.

Keogh, B., Major-Kingsley, S., Omori-Gordon, & Reid, H. P. (1982). *A system of marker variables for the field of learning disabilities.* Syracuse, NY: Syracuse University Press.

Keogh, B. K., & Margolis, J. (1976). Learn to labor and wait: Attention problems of children with learning disabilities. *Journal of Learning Disabilities, 9,* 276–286.

Keogh, B. K., Tehir, C., & Windeguth-Behn, A. (1974). Teachers' perceptions of educationally high risk children. *Journal of Learning Disabilities, 7,* 367–374.

Keogh, J. F. (1981). A movement development framework and a perceptual-cognitive perspective. In G. Brooks (Ed.), *Perspectives on the academic discipline of physical education.* Champaign, IL: Human Kinetics.

Keogh, J. (1982). The study of movement learning disabilities. In J. Das, R. Mulcahy, & A. Wall (Eds.), *Theory and research in learning disabilities.* New York: Plenum Press.

Kephart, N. C. (1960). *The slow learner in the classroom.* Columbus, OH: Charles E. Merrill.

Kephart, N. C. (1964). Perceptual-motor aspects of learning disabilities. *Exceptional Children, 31,* 201–206.

Kifer, E. Relationships between academic achievement and personality characteristics: A quasi-longitudinal study. *American Educational Research Journal, 12,* 191–210.

Kinsbourne, M. (1973a). Minimal brain dysfunction as a neurodevelopmental lag. *Annals of the New York Academy of Sciences, 205,* 268–273.

Kinsbourne, M. (1973b). School problems. *Pediatrics, 52,* 697–710.

Kinsbourne, M. (Ed.). (1983). *Brain basis of learning disabilities. Topics in Learning and Learning Disabilities.* Rockville, MD: Aspen Systems.

Kinsbourne, M., & Caplan, P. J. (1979). *Children's learning and attention problems.* Boston: Little, Brown and Company.

Kinsbourne, M., & Warrington, E. K. (1962). A study of finger agnosia. *Brain, 85,* 47–66.

Kirk, S. A. (1962). *Educating exceptional children.* Boston: Houghton Mifflin.

Kirk, S. A. (1966). *The diagnosis and remediation of psycholinguistic disabilities.* Urbana: University of Illinois Press.

Kirk, S. A. (1968). Illinois Test of Psycholinguistic Abilities: Its origin and implications. In J. Hellmuth (Ed.), *Learning disorders* (Vol. 3). Seattle, WA: Special Child Publications.

Kirk, S. A., & Chalfant, J. C. (1984). *Academic and developmental learning disabilities.* Denver: Love.

Kirk, S. A., & Elkins, J. (1975a). Characteristics of children enrolled in the Child Service Demonstration Centers. *Journal of Learning Disabilities, 4,* 6–21.

Kirk, S. A., & Elkins, J. (1975b). Characteristics of children enrolled in the Child Service Demonstration Centers. *Journal of Learning Disabilities, 8,* 630–637.

Kirk, S. A., & Kirk, W. D. (1971). *Psycholinguistic learning disabilities: Diagnosis and remediation.* Urbana, IL: University of Illinois Press.

Kirk, S. A., McCarthy, J. J., & Kirk, W. D. (1968). *Illinois Test of Psycholinguistic Abilities* (Rev. ed.). Urbana, IL: University of Illinois Press.

Kirk, W. D. (1975). The relationship of reading disabilities to learning disabilities. *Journal of Special Education, 9,* 132–137.

Klanderman, J. W., Perney, J., & Kroeschell, Z. (1985). Comparisons of the K-ABC and WISC-R for LD children. *Journal of Learning Disabilities, 18,* 524–527.

Klein, R. S., Altman, S. D., Dreizen, K., Friedman, R., & Powers, L. (1981). Structuring dysfunctional parental attitudes toward children's learning and behaving in school: Family-oriented psychoeducational therapy. Part I. *Journal of Learning Disabilities, 14,* 15–19.

Knight, F. B., & Behrens, M. S. (1928). *The learning of the 100 addition combinations and the 100 subtraction combinations.* New York: Longmans, Green.

Knights, R. M., & Bakker, D. J. (Eds.). (1976). *The neuropsychology of learning disorders: Theoretical approaches.* Baltimore, MD: University Park Press.

Knobloch, H., & Pasamanick, B. (1959). Syndrome of minimal cerebral damage in infancy. *Journal of the American Medical Association, 170,* 1384–1387.

Knobloch, H., & Pasamanick, B. *Gesell and the Amatruda's developmental diagnosis.* Hagerstown, MD: Harper & Row.

Koppell, S. (1979). Testing the attentional deficit notion. *Journal of Learning Disabilities, 12,* 43–48.

Koppitz, E. M. (1964). *The Bender Gestalt test for young children.* New York: Grune & Stratton.

Koppitz, E. M. (1971). *Children with learning disabilities: A five year follow-up study.* New York: Grune & Stratton.

Koppitz, E. M. (1975). *The Bender Gestalt test for young children: Research and application, 1963–1973.* New York: Grune & Stratton.

Kosc, L. (1974). Developmental dyscalculia. *Journal of Learning Disabilities, 7,* 165–178.

Kosc, L. (1981). Neuropsychological implications of diagnosis and treatment of mathematical learning disabilities. *Topics in Learning and Learning Disabilities, 1,* 19–30.

Kounin, J. S. (1970). *Discipline and group management in classroom.* New York: Holt, Rinehart & Winston.

Koupernik, C., MacKeith, R., & Francis-Williams, J. (1975). Neurological correlates of motor and perceptual development. In W. Cruickshank & D. Hallahan (Eds.), *Perceptual and learning disabilities in children: Vol. 2. Research and Theory* (pp. 105–135). Syracuse, NY: Syracuse University Press.

Kraemer, H. C., & Andrews, G. (1982). A nonparametric technique for meta-analysis effect size calculation. *Psychological Bulletin, 91,* 404–412.

Kraft, M. B. (1968). The face-hand test. *Developmental Medicine and Child Neurology, 10,* 214–219.

Krantz, P., & Risley, T. (1977). Behavioral ecology in the classroom. In K. O'Leary & S. O'Leary (Eds.), *Classroom management: The successful use of behavior modification* (2nd ed.). New York: Pergamon Press.

Krauss, R. M., Apple, W., Morency, N., Wenzel, C., & Winston, W. (1981). Verbal, vocal, and visible factors in judgments of another's affect. *Journal of Personality and Social Psychology, 40,* 312–320.

Kripke, B., Lynn, R., Madsen, J. A., & Gay, P. E. (1982). Familial learning disablity, easy fatigue, and maladroitness: Preliminary trial of monosodium glutamate in adults. *Developmental Medicine and Child Neurology, 24,* 745–751.

Krippner, S. (1968). Etiological factors in reading disabilities of the academically talented, in comaprison with pupils of average and slow learning ability. *Journal of Educational Research, 61,* 275–279.

Krippner, S. (1972). Illicit drug usage: Hazards for learning disability students. *Orthomolecular Psychiatry, 1,* 67–78.

Kronick, D. (1975). *What about me? The LD adolescent.* Novato, CA: Academic Therapy Publications.

Kronick, D. (1976). The importance of a sociological perspective towards learning disabilities. *Journal of Learning Disablities, 9,* 115–119.

Kronick, D. (1978). An examination of psychosocial aspects of learning disabled adolescents. *Learning Disablity Quarterly, 6,* 86–93.

Kronick, D. (1981). *Social development of learning disabled persons.* San Francisco: Jossey-Bass.

Krupski, A. (1981). An interactional approach to the study of attention problems in children with learning handicaps. *Exceptional Education Quarterly, 2,* 1–11.

Kuethe, J. L. (1968). *The teaching-learning process.* Glenview, IL: Scott, Foresman & Company.

Kuhn, T. S. (1970). *The structure of scientific revolutions* (rev. ed.). Chicago: University of Chicago Press.

Lacayo, N., Sherwood, G., & Morris, J. (1981). Daily activities of school psychologistis: A national survey. *Psychology in the Schools, 18,* 184–190.

Ladd, G. W. (1981). Effectiveness of a social learning method for enhancing children's social interaction and peer acceptance. *Child Development, 52,* 171–178.

LaGreca, A. M., & Mesibov, G. (1979). Social skills intervention with learning-disabled children. *Clinical Child Psychiatry, 8,* 234–241.

LaGreca, A. M., & Mesibov, G. B. (1982). Facilitating interpersonal interaction with peers in learning-disabled children. *Journal of Learning Disabilities, 13,* 197–199, 238.

Lambert, N. M. (1981). Psychological evidence in *Larry P. v. Wilson Riles:* An evaluation by a witness for the defense. *American Psychologist, 36,* 937–952.

Langford, K., Slade, K., & Barnett, A. (1974). An examination of impress techniques in remedial reading. *Academic Therapy, 6,* 293–323.

Larivee, B. (1981). Modality preference as a model for differentiating beginning reading instruction: A review of the issues. *Learning Disability Curriculum, 4,* 181–188.

Larry P., et al., Plaintiffs, v. Riles, Superintendent of Public Instruction for the State of California et al. (1972, July, 1974, 1979). United States District Court for the Northern District of California. Before: The Honorable Robert F. Peckham, Chief Judge. No. C-71-2270-RFP.

Larsen, S., & Hammill, D. (1975). The relationship of selected visual perceptual skills to academic abilities. *Journal of Special Education, 9,* 281–291.

Laver, J. D. M. (1969). The detection and correction of slips of the tongue. *Work in progress 3.* Edinburgh: University of Edinburgh, Department of Phonetics and Linguistics.

Laver, J. D. M. (1980). Monitoring systems in the neurolinguistic control of speech production. In V. Fromkin (Ed.), *Errors in linguistic performance.* New York: Academic Press.

Lavin, D. E. (1965). *The prediction of academic performance.* New York: Russell Sage Foundation.

Lawson, J. S., & Inglis, J. (1984). The psychometric assessment of children with learning disabilities: An index derived from a principal components analysis of the WISC-R. *Journal of Learning Disabilities, 17,* 517–522.

LeBerge, D., & Samuels, S. J. (1974). Toward a theory of automatic information processing in reading. *Cognitive Psychology, 6,* 293–323.

Ledebur, G. W. (1977). The elementary learning disability process group and the school psychologist. *Psychology in the Schools, 14,* 62–66.

Lee, L. *Developmental sentence analysis.* Evanston, IL: Northwestern University Press.

Leisman, G. (Ed.). (1975). *Basic visual processes and learning disability.* Springfield, IL: Charles C Thomas.

Lennon, R. T. (1951). The stability of achievement test results from grade to grade. *Educational and Psychological Measurement, 11,* 121–127.

Leonard, L. B., Camarata, S., Rowan, L. E., & Chapman, K. (1982). The communicative functions of lexical usage by language impaired children. *Applied Psycholinguistics, 3,* 109–126.

Lerner, J. W. (1975). Remedial reading and learning disabilities: Are they the same or different? *Journal of Special Education, 9,* 119–131.

Lerner, J. W. (1981). *Learning disabilities* (3rd ed). Boston: Houghton Mifflin.

Lerner, J. W. (1985). *Learning disabilities: Theories, diagnosis, and teaching strategies* (4th ed.). Boston: Houghton Mifflin.

Levine, M. D., Brooks, R., & Shonkoff, J. P. (1980). *A pediatric approach to learning disorders.* New York: John Wiley & Sons.

Levinson, H. (1980). *A solution to the riddle dyslexia.* New York: Springer-Verlag.

Lewis, M. E. B. (1982). Use of the thematic approach for learning-disabled students. *Learning Disability Quarterly, 1*(3).

Lewis, M. E. B., & Daniels, P. R. (1983). Teacher training in the clinical method for learning-disabled/gifted children. In L. H. Fox, L. Brody, & D. Tobin (Eds.), *Learning-disabled/gifted children: Identification and programming* (pp. 261–273). Baltimore, MD: University Park Press.

Lewis, R. B. (1982). Assessing retarded development. In P. T. Cegelka & H. J. Prehm (Eds.), *Mental retardation: From categories to people.* Columbus, OH: Charles E. Merrill.

Lewitter, F. I., DeFries, J. C., & Elston, R. C. (1980). Genetic models of reading disablity. *Behavioral Genetics, 10,* 9–30.

Lezak, M. (1976). *Neuropsychological assessment.* London: Oxford University Press.

Liberman, I. Y. (1971). Basic research in speech and literalization of language: Some implications for reading disability. *Bulletin of the Orton Society, 21,* 71–87.

Liberman, I., & Shankweiler, D. (1979). Speech, the alphabet, and teaching to read. In L. Resnick & P. Weaver (Eds.), *Theory and practice of early reading* (Vol. 1). Hillsdale, NJ: Lawerence Erlbaum.

Liberman, I. Y., Shankweiler, D., Fischer, F. W., & Carter, B. (1974). Explicit syllable and phoneme segmentation in the young child. *Journal of Experimental Child Psychology, 18,* 201–212.

Liberman, I. Y., Shankweiler, D., Orlando, C., Harris, K. S., & Berti, F. B. (1971). Letter confusion and reversals of sequence in the beginning reader: Implications for Orton's theory of developmental dyslexia. *Cortex, 7,* 127–142.

Lieberman, L. M. (1982, May/June). Learning disablities: The solution — or how I became disabled without being handicapped. Presentation at the ACLD International Conference, Chicago. *ACLD Newsbriefs, 144,* 3–5.

Liles, B. Z. (1982, November). *Use of cohesion in verbal narratives by normal and language disordered children.* Paper presented at the annual convention of the American Speech–Language–Hearing Association, Toronto, Canada.

Lilly, M. S. (1977). The merger of categories: Are we finally ready? *Journal of Learning Disabilities, 10,* 115–121.

Lindsay, G. A., & Wedell, K. (1982). The early identification of educationally "at risk" children revisited. *Journal of Learning Disabilities, 15,* 211–217.

Linn, R. L. (1981). Measuring pretest-posttest performance changes. In R. A. Berk (Ed.), *Educational evaluation methodology: The state of the art* (pp. 84–109). Baltimore, MD: Johns Hopkins University Press.

Lochner, J. P. A., & Burger, J. F. (1964). The intelligibility of speech under reverberant conditions. *Acustica, 4,* 426–454.

Loehlin, J. C. (1980). Recent adoption studies of IQ. *Human Genetics, 55,* 297–302.

Loehlin, J. C., Sharan, S., & Jacoby, R. (1978). In pursuit of the "spatial gene": A family study. *Behavioral Genetics, 8,* 27–41.

Lovinger, S. L. (1974). Learning disabilities and games. *Academic Therapy, 9,* 183–185.

Lowell, K. (1964). A study of some cognitive and other disabilities in backward readers of average non-verbal reasoning scores. *British Journal of Educational Psychology, 34,* 275–279.

Lund, N., & Duchan, J. (1983). *Assessing children's language in naturalistic contexts.* Englewood Cliffs, NJ: Prentice-Hall.

Lund, K. A., Foster, G. E., & McCall-Perez, F. C. (1978). The effectiveness of psycholinguistic training: A re-evaluation. *Exceptional Children, 44,* 310–319.

Luria, A. R. (1961). *The role of speech in the regulation of normal and abnormal behavior.* New York: Liveright.

Lutey, C. L. (1977). *Individual intelligence testing: A manual and sourcebook* (2nd ed.). Greeley, CO: Carol L. Lutey Publishing.

Lyle, J. G. (1970). Certain antenatal, perinatal, and developmental variables and reading retardation in middle-class boys. *Child Development, 41,* 481–491.

Lynch, E., & Lewis, R. (1981). *Nonbiased assessment of severely handicapped individuals.* Sacramento: California State Department of Education.

Lyon, R., & Watson, B. (1981). Empirically derived subgroups of learning disabled readers: Diagnostic characteristics. *Journal of Learning Disabilities, 14,* 256–261.

Macoby, E. E., & Jacklin, C. N. (1974). The psychology of sex differences. Palo Alto, CA: Stanford University Press.

MacKay, D. G. (1970). Spoonerisms: The structure of errors in the serial order of speech. *Neuropsychologia, 8,* 323–350.

MacMillan, D. L. (1973). *Behavior modification in education.* New York: Macmillan.

MacMillan, D. L., Meyers, C., & Morrison, G. (1980). System identifications of mildly mentally retarded children: Implications for interpreting and conducting research. *American Journal of Mental Deficiency, 85,* 108–115.

Macy, D. J., Baker, J. A., & Kosinski, S. C. (1979). An empirical study of the Myklebust learning quotient. *Journal of Learning Disabilities, 12,* 93–96.

Madden, N. A., & Slavin, R. E. (1982). *Count me in: Academic achievement and social outcomes of mainstreaming students with mild academic handicaps* (Report No. 329). Baltimore, MD: The Johns Hopkins University, Center for Socal Organization of Schools.

Maier, A. S. (1980). The effect of focusing on the cognition processes of learning disabled children. *Journal of Learning Disabilities, 13*(3), 34–38.

Mainzer, R. (1978). Protection in evaluation: Guidelines for assessing students with special education needs. Baltimore: Maryland State Department of Education.

Mainzer, R. W. & Dwyer, K. P. (in press). *The Maryland Learning Disabilities Project: A practical guideline for assessing severe discrepancy.*

Mainzer, R., Dwyer, K. P., Mitchell, D., Mowery, F., Rofel, M., & Simon, K. (1982). *Learning disabilities handbook.* Baltimore: Maryland State Department of Education.

Majoribanks, K. (1972). Environment, social class, and mental abilities. *Journal of Educational Psychology, 63,* 103–109.

Majoribanks, K. (Ed.). (1974). Environments for learning. London: National Foundation for Educational Research.

Mandler, J. M., & Goodman, M. S. (1982). On the psychological validity of story structure. *Journal of Verbal Learning and Verbal Behavior, 21,* 507–523.

Mandler, J. M., & Johnson, N. S. (1977). Remembrance of things parsed: Story structure and recall. *Cognitive Psychology, 9,* 111–151.

Mann, L. (1971). Psychometric phrenology and the new faculty psychology: The case against ability assessment and training. *Journal of Special Education, 5,* 3–14.

Mann, L. (1979). *On the trail of process: A historical perspective on cognitive processes and their training.* New York: Grune & Stratton.

Mann, L., & Phillips, W. A. (1967). Fractional practices in special education: A critique. *Exceptional Children, 33,* 311–317.

Markosi, B. D. (1983). Conversational interactions of the learning disabled and non-disabled child. *Journal of Learning Disabilities, 16,* 606–609.

Marland, S. P. (1972). *Education of the gifted and talented: Report to the Congress of the United States by the U.S. Commissioner of Education.* Washington, DC: Government Printing Office.

Marshall, J., & Newcombe, F. (1977). Variability and constraint in acquired dyslexia. In H. Whitaker & H. Whitaker (Eds.), *Studies in neurolinguistics* (Vol. 3). New York: Academic Press.

Marshall, W., & Ferguson, J. (1939). Hereditary word-blindness as a defect of selective association. *Journal of Nervous and Mental Disease, 89,* 164–173.

Martin, F. N., & Clark, J. G. (1977). Audiologic detection of auditory processing disorders in children. *Journal of American Audiology Society, 3,* 140–146.

Maryland Learning Disabilities Project, 1982 (unpublished). Maryland State Board of Education. Johns Hopkins University.

Mason, M. (1975). Reading ability and letter search time: Effects of orthographic structure defined by single-letter positional frequency. *Journal of Experimental Psychology: General, 104,* 146–166.

Massaro, D. W. (1977). Capacity limitations in auditory information processing. In S. Dornic (Ed.), *Attention and performance* (Vol. 6). New York: John Wiley & Sons.

Mattingly, I. G. (1972). Reading, the linguistic process, and linguistic awareness. In J. I. Kavanaugh & I. G. Mattingly (Eds.), *Language by ear and by eye.* Cambridge, MA: The MIT Press.

Mattis, S. (1978). Dyslexia syndromes: A working hypothesis that works. In A. I. Benton & D. Pearl (Eds.), *Dyslexia: An appraisal of current knowledge* (pp. 43–58). New York: Oxford University Press.

Matzker, J. (1962). The binaural test. *Journal of International Audiology, 1,* 209–211.

Mayron, L. W. (1978). Ecological factors in learning disabilities. *Journal of Learning Disabilities, 11,* 40–50.

Mayron, L. W. (1979). Allergy, learning and behavior problems. *Journal of Learning Disabilities, 12,* 41–49.

McCall, R., Appelbaum, M., & Hogarty, P. (1973). Developmental changes in mental performance. *Monographs of the Society for Research in Child Development, 38*(3), 1–84.

McCarthy, D. (1972). *The McCarthy Scales of Children's Abilities.* New York: Psychological Corporation.

McCarthy, J. M. (1982). Cross currents and prevailing winds. *Learning Disabilities: An Interdisciplinary Journal, 1,* 3–10.

McCarthy, J. M., & Paraskevopoulos, J. (1969). Behavior patterns of learning disabled, emotionally disturbed, and average children. *Exceptional Children, 35,* 69–74.

McCarthy, J. M., & Paraskevopoulos, J. (1970). Behavior patterns of children with special learning disabilities. *Journal of School Psychology, 8,* 112–118.

McCauley, R., & Swisher, L. (1984). Psychometric review of language and articulation tests for preschool children. *Journal of Speech and Hearing Disorders, 49,* 34–42.

McClelland, D. C., Atkinson, J. W., Clark, R. A., & Lowell, E. L. (1953). *The achievement motive.* New York: Appleton-Century-Crofts.

McConaughy, S. H., & Ritter, D. R. (1986). Social competence and behavioral problems of learning disabled boys, aged 6–11. *Journal of Learning Disabilities, 19,* 39–45.

McConkie, G. W. (1979). What the study of eye movement reveals about reading. In L. Resnick & P. Weaver (Eds.), *Theory and practice of early reading* (Vol. 3, pp. 71–87). Hillsdale, NJ: Lawrence Erlbaum.

McDermott, P. A. (1981). Sources of error in the psychoeducational diagnosis of children. *The Journal of School Psychology, 19,* 31–44.

McGrady, H. (1980). Communication disorders and specific learning disabilities. In R. J. Van Hatum (Ed.), *Communication disorders: An introduction.* New York: Macmillan.

McKinney, J. D., & Forman, S. G. (1982). Classroom behavior patterns of EMH, LD, and

EH students. *Journal of School Psychology, 20*(4), 271–279.

McKinney, J. D., Short, E. J., & Feagans, L. (1985). Academic consequences of perceptual-linguistic subtypes of learning disabled children. *Learning Disabilities Research, 1*(1), 6–17.

McLeod, J. (1967). Some psycholinguistic correlates of reading disability in young children. *Reading Research Quarterly, 2,* 5–32.

McLeod, J. (1979). Educational underachievement: Toward a defensible psychometric definition. *Journal of Learning Disabilities, 12,* 322–330.

McLeod, J. (1983). Learning disability is for educators. *Journal of Learning Disabilities, 16,* 23–24.

McLoughlin, J. A., & Lewis, R. B. (1981). *Assessing special students.* Columbus, OH: Charles E. Merrill.

McNamee, G. D. (1985). The social origins of narrative skills. In M. Hickman (Ed.), *Social and functional approaches to language and thought.* New York: Macmillian.

McNamee, G. D., & Harris-Schmidt, G. (1984). *Enhancement of literacy development in learning disabled children 5 to 9 years of age.* Austin, TX: Foundation for Children with Learning Disabilities.

McNemar, Q. (1964). Lost: Our intelligence? Why? *American Psychologist, 19,* 871–882.

Mehan, H., Meihls, J. L., Hertweck, A., & Crowdes, M. (1981). Identifying handicapped students. In S. B. Bacharach (Ed.), *Organizational behavior in school & school districts.* New York: Praeger Publications.

Meichenbaum, D. (1977). *Cognitive-behavior modification: An integrative approach.* New York: Plenum Press.

Meichenbaum, D., & Goodman, J. (1971). Training impulsive children to talk to themselves: A means of developing self-control. *Journal of Abnormal Psychology, 77,* 115–126.

Meier, J. (1971). Prevalence and character of learning disabilities found in second grade children. *Journal of Learning Disabilities, 4,* 6–21.

Meisgeier, C. A. (1981). A social behavioral program for the adolescent student with serious learning problems. *Focus on Exceptional Children, 13,* 1–13.

Mellard, D., Cooley, S., Poggio, J., & Deshler, D. (1983). *A comprehensive analysis of four discrepancy methods* (Research Monographs No. 15). Lawrence: University of Kansas Institute for Research in Learning Disabilities.

Mendel, G. (1866). Versuch uber pflanzen-hybriden. *Proceeding of the Brunn Natural History Society.*

Mercer, C. D. (1983). *Students with learning disabilities* (2nd ed.). Columbus, OH: Charles E. Merrill.

Mercer, C. D., Forgonne, C., & Wolking, W. D. (1976). Definitions of learning disabilities used in the United States. *Journal of Learning Disabilities, 9,* 376–386.

Mercer, C. D., Hughes, C., & Mercer, A. (1985). Learning disabilities definitions used by state education departments. *Learning Disability Quarterly, 8,* 45–56.

Mercer, J. R. (1973). *Labeling the mentally retarded.* Berkeley, CA: University of California Press.

Mercer, J. R. (1979). *System of multicultural pluralistic assessment: Technical manual.* New York: Psychological Corporation.

Mercer, J. R., & Lewis, J. F. (1977). *System of multicultural pluralistic assessment.* New York: Psychological Corporation.

Mercer, J. R., & Lewis, J. F. (1979). *Technical manual: SOMPA system of multicultural pluralistic assessment.* New York: Psychological Corporation.

Messick, S. (Ed.). (1976). *Individuality in learning: Implications of cognitive styles and creativity for human development.* San Francisco: Jossey-Bass.

Meyen, E. L., & Hieronymous, A. N. (1970). The age placement of academic skills in curriculum for EMR. *Exceptional Children, 36,* 333–390.

Meyers, A. C., & Thornton, C. A. (1977). The learning disabled child: Learning the basic facts. *Arithmetic Teacher, 24,* 46–50.

Michael, W. B. (1977). Cognitive and affective components of creativity in mathematics and the physical sciences. In J. C. Stanley, W. G. George, & C. H. Solano (Eds.), *The gifted and creative: A fifty year perspective* (pp. 141–172). Baltimore, MD: The Johns Hopkins University Press.

Morrison, F. J., Giordani, B., & Nagy, I. (1977). Reading disability: An information processing analysis. *Science, 196,* 77–79.

Michaels, S. (1981). "Sharing time": Children's narrative styles and differential access to literacy. *Language in Society, 10,* 423–442.

Miller, J. (1981). *Assessing language production in children: Experimental procedures.* Baltimore, MD: University Park Press.

Miller, M. (1984). Social acceptability characteristics of learning disabled students. *Journal of Learning Disabilities, 17,* 619–621.

Millman, J., Bieger, G. R., Klag, P. A., & Pine, C. K. (1983). Relation between perseverance and rate of learning: A test of Carroll's model of school learning. *American Educational Research Journal, 20,* 425–434.

Minskoff, E. (1975). Research on psycholinguistic training: Critique and guidelines. *Exceptional Children, 42,* 136–144.

Minskoff, E. H. (1980a). Teaching approach for developing nonverbal communication skills in students with social perception deficits. Part I. *Journal of Learning Disabilities, 13,* 118–124.

Minskoff, E. H. (1980b). Teaching approach for developing nonverbal communication skills in students with social perception deficits. Part II. *Journal of Learning Disabilities, 13,* 203–208.

Minskoff, E. H. (1982). Training LD students to cope with the everyday world. *Academic Therapy, 17,* 311–316.

Moats, L. C. (1983). A comparison of the spelling errors of older dyslexic and second-grade normal children. In R. L. Cicci et al. (Eds.), *Annals of Dyslexia* (Vol. 33). Orton Dyslexia Society.

Moller, B. W. (1984). Special techniques for the gifted LD student. *Academic Therapy, 20*(2), 67–71.

Moncur, J. P., & Dirks, D. (1967). Binaural and monaural speech intelligibility in reverberation. *Journal of Speech and Hearing Research, 10,* 186–195.

Money, J. (1973). Turner's syndrome and parietal lobe function. *Cortex, 9,* 387–393.

Monroe, M. (1932). *Children who cannot read.* Chicago: University of Chicago Press.

Morgan, W. P. (1896). A case of congenital word-blindness. *British Medical Journal, 11,* 378.

Morrison, F. J., Giordani, B., & Nagy, J. (1977). Reading disability: An information-processing system. *Science, 196,* 77–79.

Morrison, G., MacMillan, D., & Kavale, K. (1985). System identification of learning disabled children: Implications for research sampling. *Learning Disability Quarterly, 8,* 2–10.

Morrison, J. R., & Stewart, M. A. (1973). The psychiatric status of the legal family of adopted hyperactive children. *Archives of General Psychiatry, 28,* 888–891.

Morrison, R. L., & Bellack, A. S. (1981). The role of social perception in social skill. *Behavior Therapy, 12,* 69–79.

Morse, W. C., Cutler, R. L., & Fink, A. H. (1964). *Public school classes for the emotionally handicapped: A research analysis.* Washington, DC: Council for Exceptional Children.

Morton, R. L. (1927). *Teaching arithmetic in the primary grades.* Newark, NJ: Silver Burdett Company.

Moyer. S. (1982). Repeated reading. *Journal of Learning Disabilities, 15.* 619–623.

Moyer. S. B.. & Newcomer. P. L. (1977). Reversals in reading: Diagnosis and remediation. *Exceptional Children. 43.* 424–429.

Muehl. S.. & Kremenak. S. (1966). Ability to match information within and between auditory and visual sense modalities and subsequent reading achievement. *Journal of Educational Psychology. 57.* 230–239.

Mueller. E. (1972). The maintenance of verbal exchange between young children. *Child Development. 43.* 930–938.

Muma. J. (1978). *Language handbook: Concepts. assessment. intervention.* Englewood Cliffs, NJ: Prentice-Hall.

Muma. J. (1981). *Language primer.* Lubbock. TX: Natural Child Publications.

Muma. J. (1983). Speech–language pathology: Emerging clinical expertise in language. In T. Gallagher. & C. Prutting (Eds.). *Pragmatic assessment and intervention issues in language.* San Diego: College-Hill Press.

Murray. J. N.. & Wallbrown. F. H. (1981). School psychological services for learning disabled students. *Journal of Learning Disabilities. 14.* 385–387.

Myers. P. I.. & Hammill. D. D. (1982). *Learning disabilities: Basic concepts. assessment practices. and instructional strategies.* Austin. TX: ProEd.

Myklebust. H. R. (1964). Learning disorders: Psychoneurological disturbances in childhood. *Rehabilitation Literature. 25.* 354–359.

Myklebust. H. R. (1968a). Learning disabilities: Definition and overview. In H. R. Myklebust (Ed.). *Progress in learning disabilities.* New York: Grune & Stratton.

Myklebust. H. R. (Ed.). (1968b). *Progress in learning disabilities* (Vol. 1). New York: Grune & Stratton.

Myklebust. H. R.. Bannochie. M. N.. & Killen. J. R. (1971). Learning disabilities and cognitive processes. In H. Myklebust (Ed.). *Progress in learning disabilities* (Vol. 2). New York: Grune & Stratton.

Myklebust. H. R.. & Boshes. B. (1960). Psychoneurological learning disorders in children. *Pediatrics. 77.* 247–256.

Myklebust. H.. & Johnson. O. (1967). *Learning disabilities: Educational principles and practices.* New York: Grune & Stratton.

Nabelek. A. K.. & Pickett. J. M. (1974). Reception of consonants in a classroom as affected by monaural and binaural listening. noise. reverberation and hearing aids. *Journal of the Acoustical Society of America. 56.* 628–639.

Nabelek. A. K.. & Robinette. L. (1978). Influence of the precedence effect on word identification by normally hearing and hearing impaired subjects. *Journal of the Acoustical Society of America. 63.* 187–194.

Nagle. R. J.. & Thwaite. B. C. (1979). Are learning disabled children more impulsive? A comparison of learning disabled and normally-achieving children on Kagan's Matching Familiar Figures Test. *Psychology in the Schools. 16.* 351–355.

Natchez. G. (1968). *Children with reading problems.* New York: Basic Books.

National Advisory Committee on Handicapped Children. (1968). *First annual report. special education for the handicapped.* Washington. DC: U.S. Office of Education. Department of Health. Education. and Welfare.

National Joint Committee for Learning Disabilities. (1981). Learning disabilities: Issues on definition. Unpublished manuscript. (Available from Drake Duane. NJCLS chairperson. 8415 Bellona Lane. Towson. MD 21204.)

Needleman. H. (1977). Effects of hearing loss from early recurrent otitis media on speech and language development. In B. F. Jaffe (Ed.). *Hearing loss in children.* Baltimore, MD: University Park Press.

Neisworth, J., & Greer, W. (1975). Functional similarities of LD and mild mental retardation. *Exceptional Children, 42,* 17–21.

Nelson, H. E., & Warrington, E. K. (1974). Developmental spelling retardation and its relation to other cognitive abilities. *British Journal of Psychology, 2,* 265–274.

Nesher, P. (1982). Levels of description in the analysis of addition and subtraction word problems. In T. P. Carpenter, J. M. Moser, & T. A. Romberg (Eds.), *Addition and subtraction: A cognitive perspective.* Hillsdale, NJ: Lawrence Erlbaum.

Newcomer, P., Larsen, S., & Hammill, D. (1975). A response. *Exceptional Children, 42,* 144–148.

Nichol, H. (1974). Children with LD referred to psychiatrists: A follow-up study. *Journal of Learning Disabilities, 7,* 118–122.

Nichols, P. L., & Chen, T. C. (1981). *Minimal brain dysfunction: A prospective study.* Hillsdale, NJ: Lawrence Erlbaum.

Noel, M. M. (1980). Referential communication abilities of learning disabled children. *Learning Disability Quarterly, 3,* 70–75.

Nolan, E., & Kagan, J. (1978). Psychological factors in the face-hand test. *Archives of Neurology, 35,* 41–42.

Noland, E. C., & Schuldt, W. J. (1971). Sustained attention and reading retardation. *Journal of Experimental Education, 40,* 73–76.

Norman, C. A., & Zigmond, N. (1980). Characteristics of children labeled and served as learning disabled in school systems affiliated with Child Service Demonstration Centers. *Journal of Learning Disabilities, 13,* 542–547.

Nuffield Mathematics Project. (1967). New York: John Wiley & Sons.

Nuzum, M. (1982). *The effects of a curriculum based on the information processing paradigm on the arithmetic problem solving performance of four learning disabled students.* Unpublished doctoral dissertation, Teachers College, Columbia University, New York.

Oakland, T. (1980). Nonbiased assessment of minority group children. *Exceptional Education Quarterly, 1*(3), 31–46.

Obrzut, J. E., & Hynd, G. W. (1983). The neurological and neuropsychological foundation of learning disabilities. *Journal of Learning Disabilities, 16,* 515–520.

Ochoa, A. M. Pacheco, R., & Omark, D. R. (1983). Addressing the needs of limited English proficient learning disabled students: Beyond language and race issues. *Learning Disability Quarterly, 6,* 416–423.

O'Donnell, L. E. (1980). Intra-individual discrepancy in diagnosing specific learning disabilities. *Learning Disability Quarterly, 3,* 10–18.

Olsen, W. O. (1981). The effects of noise and reverberation on speech intelligibility. In F. H. Bess, B. A. Freeman, & J. S. Sinclair (Eds.), *Amplification in education.* Washington, DC: Alexander Graham Bell Association.

Omenn, G. S., & Weber, B. A. (1978). Dyslexia: Search for phenotypic and genetic heterogeneity. *American Journal of Medical Genetics, 1,* 333–342.

O'Neill, G., & Stanley, G. (1976). Visual processing of straight lines in dyslexic and normal children. *British Journal of Educational Psychology, 46,* 323–327.

Opie, N., & Lemasters, G. (1975). Do boys with a low-average I.Q. actually have a low self-esteem? *Journal of School Health, 45,* 381–385.

O'Quinn, K., & Aronoff, J. (1981). Humor as a technique of social influence. *Social Psychology Quarterly, 44,* 349–357.

Orton, S. T. (1925). "Word-blindness" in school children. *Archives of Neurology and Psychiatry, 14,* 581–615.

Orwin, R. G. (1983). A fail-safe N for effect size in meta-analysis. *Journal of Educational Statistics, 8,* 157–159.

Osgood, R. L. (1984). Intelligence testing and the field of learning disabilities: An historical and critical perspective. *Learning Disablity Quarterly, 7,* 343–348.

Osgood, C. E. (1957). Motivational dynamics of language behavior. In M. Jones (Ed.), *Nebraska symposium on motivation.* Lincoln: University of Nebraska Press.

Owen, F. W., Adams, P. A., Forrest, T., Stolz, L. M., & Fisher, S. (1971). Learning disorders in children: Sibling studies. *Monographs of the Society for Research in Child Development, 36*(Serial No. 144).

Page, E. B. (1980). Tests and decisions for the handicapped: A guide to evaluation under the new laws. *Journal of Special Education, 14,* 423–483.

Paine, R. S., Werry, J. S., & Quay, H. C. (1968). A study of "minimal brain dysfunction." *Developmental Medicine and Child Neurology, 10,* 505–529.

Park, J., Johnson, R. C., DeFries, J. C., McClearn, G. E., Mi, M. P., Rashad, M. N., Vandenberg, S. G., & Wilson, J. R. (1978). Parent-offspring resemblance for specific cognitive abilities in Korea. *Behavioral Genetics, 8,* 43–52.

Patten, B. (1972). Visually mediated thinking: A report on the case of Albert Einstein. *Journal of Learning Disabilities, 6,* 415–420.

Patterson, K. E. (1979). What is right with "deep" dyslexic patients? *Brain and Language, 8,* 111–129.

Pavlidis, G. T. (1982). *Erratic eye movement and dyslexia: The search for linkage.* Presentation at the National Reading Conference. Clearwater Beach, FL.

Payne, R. W., & Jones, H. G. (1957). Statistics for the investigation of individual cases. *Journal of Clinical Psychology, 13,* 115–121.

Pearl, R., Donahue, M., & Bryan, T. (1981a, October). *Learning disabled children's tactfulness.* Paper presented at the Council for Learning Disabilities, Houston, TX.

Pearl, R., Donahue, M., & Bryan, T. (1981b). Learning disabled and normal children's responses to non-explicit requests for clarification. *Perceptual and Motor Skills, 53,* 919–925.

Pearson, G. (1972). *Psychoanalysis and the education of the child.* Greenwood, CT: Greenwood Press.

Pelham, W. E. (1979). Selective attention deficits in poor readers? Dichotic listening, speeded classification, and auditory and visual central and incidental learning tasks. *Child Development, 50,* 1050–1061.

Pelham, W. E., & Milich, R. (1984). Peer relations in children with hyperactivity/attention deficit disorder. *Journal of Learning Disabilities, 17,* 609–611.

Pepper, F. C. (1976). Teaching the American Indian Child in mainstream settings. In R. L. Jones (Ed.), *Mainstreaming and the minority child.* Reston, VA: Council for Exceptional Children.

Perfetti, C. A., Finger, E., & Hogaboam, T. W. (1978). Sources of vocalization latency differences between skilled and less-skilled readers. *Journal of Educational Psychology, 70,* 730–739.

Perfetti, C., & Goldman, S. (1976). Discourse memory and reading comprehension skill. *Journal of Verbal Learning and Verbal Behavior, 14,* 33–42.

Perfetti, C., & Hogaboam, T. (1975). Relationship between single word decoding and reading comprehension skill. *Journal of Educational Psychology, 67,* 461–469.

Perfetti, C. A., & Lesgold, A. M. (1977). Discourse comprehension and sources of individual differences. In M. Just & P. Carpenter (Eds.), *Cognitive processes in comprehension.* Hillsdale, NJ: Lawrence Erlbaum.

Perfetti, C. A., & Lesgold, A. M. (1979). Coding and comprehension in skilled reading and implications for reading instruction. In L. Resnick & P. Weaver (Eds.), *Theory and practice of early reading* (Vol. 1). Hillsdale, NJ: Lawrence Erlbaum.

Perlmutter, B. F., & Bryan, J. H. (1984). First impressions, ingratiation, and the learning disabled child. *Journal of Learning Disabilities, 17,* 157–161.

Perlmutter, B. F., & Parus, M. V. (1983). Identifying children with learning disabilities: A comparison of diagnostic procedures across school districts. *Learning Disability Quarterly, 6,* 321–328.

Peters, J. E., Romine, J. S., & Dykman, R. A. (1975). A special neurological examination of children with learning disabilities. *Developmental Medicine and Child Neurology. 17,* 63–78.

Pflaum, S. W., & Bryan, T. H. (1982). Oral reading research and learning disabled children. *Topics in Learning and Learning Disabilities, 1,* 33–42.

Piaget, J. (1962). *Play dreams and imitation in childhood.* New York: W. W. Norton.

Piaget, J. (1965). *The moral judgment of the child.* New York: Free Press.

Piaget, J. (1977). Judgment and reasoning in the child. In H. E. Gruber & J. J. Voneche (Eds.), *The essential Piaget.* New York: Basic Books.

Pirozzolo, F., & Rayner, K. (1978). The neural control of eye movements in acquired and developmental reading disorders. In H. Whitaker & H. Whitaker (Eds.), *Studies in neurolinguistics* (Vol. 4). New York: Academic Press.

Plessas, G. P. (1963). Children's error in spelling homonyms. *Elementary School Journal, 64,* 163–168.

Polyani, M. (1958). *Personal knowledge.* London: Routledge & Kegan Paul.

Poling, D. L. (1953). Auditory deficiencies of poor readers. *Clinical Studies in Reading II, Supplementary Education Monographs, 77,* 107–111.

Polloway, E. A., & Smith, J. D. (1983). Changes in mild mental retardation: Population, programs, and perspectives. *Exceptional Children, 50*(2), 149–159.

Postman, N. (1982). *The disappearance of childhood.* New York: Delacorte Press.

Prechtl, H., & Stemmer, C. J. (1962). The choreiform syndrome in children. *Developmental Medicine and Child Neurology, 4,* 119–127.

Prinz, P. M., & Ferrier, L. J. (1983). "Can you give me that one?" The comprehension, production, and judgments of directives in language-impaired children. *Journal of Speech and Hearing Disorders, 48,* 44–54.

Prutting, C. A. (1979). Process: The action of moving forward progressively from one point to another on the way to completion. *Journal of Speech and Hearing Disorders, 44,* 3–30.

Public Law 94-142. (1975). Education for All Handicapped Children Act. Washington, DC: U.S. Department of Health, Education and Welfare.

Purkey, W. (1970). *Self-concept and school achievement.* Englewood Cliffs, NJ: Prentice-Hall.

Quay, H. C., & Peterson, D. R. (1967). *Manual for the Behavior Problem Checklist.* Urbana: University of Illinois Press.

Quinn, P., & Rappaport, L. (1974). Minor physical anomalies and neurological status in hyperactive boys. *Pediatrics, 53,* 742–474.

Rabinovich, R. D. (1962). Dyslexia: Psychiatric considerations. In J. Money (Ed.), *Reading disability: Progress and research needs in dyslexia.* Baltimore, MD: Johns Hopkins Press.

Rabinovitch, R. D. (1972). A research approach to reading retardation. In S. Harrison & J. D. McDermott (Eds.), *Childhood psychopathology.* New York: International Universities Press, Inc.

Raiser, L., & Van Nagel, C. (1980). The loophole in PL 94-142. *Exceptional Children, 46,* 516–520.

Rao, D. C., & Morton, N. E. (1978). IQ as a paradigm in genetic epidemiology. In N. E. Morton & C. S. Chung (Eds.), *Genetic Epidemiology.* New York: Academic Press.

Rao, D. C., Morton, N. E., Elston, R. C., & Yee, S. (1977). Causal analysis of academic performance. *Behavioral Genetics, 7,* 147–159.

Rapaport, D., Schaefer, R., & Gill, M. M. (1945). *Diagnostic psychological testing: The theory, statistical evaluation, and diagnostic application of a battery of tests.* Chicago: Year Book Publishers.

Rapaport, D., Gill, M., & Schofer, R. (1968). *Diagnostic psychological testing* (pp. 188–189, 191). New York: International University Press.

Rapp, D. (1978). *Hyperactivity, allergy and foods.* New York: Simon & Schuster.

Rathmell, E. C. (1978). Using thinking strategies to learn the basic facts. In M. Suydam (Ed.), *1978 yearbook of the National Council of Teachers of Mathematics.* Reston, VA: NCTM.

Rees, N. S. (1973). Auditory procesing factors in language disorders: The view from Procrustes' bed. *Journal of Speech and Hearing Disorders, 38,* 304–315.

Reger, R. (1979). Learning disabilities: Futile attempts at simplistic definition. *Journal of Learning Disabilities, 12,* 529–532.

Renzulli, J. S. (1978). What makes giftedness? Reexamining a definition. *Phi Delta Kappan, 60,* 180–184, 261.

Reschly, D., Grimes, J., & Ross-Reynolds, J. (1981). *State norms for IQ, adaptive behavior, and sociocultural status: Implications of nonbiased assessment.* Des Moines: State of Iowa Department of Public Instruction.

Resnick, L. B. (1983). Mathematics and science learning: A new conception. *Science, 220,* 477–478.

Resnick, L. B., & Ford, W. W. (1981). *The psychology of mathematics for instruction.* Hillsdale, NJ: Lawrence Erlbaum.

Reynolds, C. R. (1981). The fallacy of "two-years below grade level for age" as a diagnostic criterion for reading disorders. *Journal of School Psychology, 19,* 350–358.

Reynolds, C. R. (1985). Critical measurement issues in learning disabilities. *Journal of Special Education, 19,* 451–476.

Reynolds, C. R., Berk, R. A., Boodoo, G. M., Cox, J., Gutkin, T. B., Mann, L., Page, E. B., & Wilson, V. L. (1984). *Critical measurement issues in learning disabilities.* Report to the U.S. Department of Education.

Reynolds, C. R., Berk, R. A., Gwyneth, M. B., Cox, J., Gutkin, T. B., Mann, L., Page, E. B., & Wilson, V. L. (1984). *Critical measurement issues in the assessment of learning disabilities.* Report to the U.S. Department of Education.

Reynolds, C. R., & Gutkin, T. B. (1980). A regression analysis of test bias on the WISC-R for Anglos and Chicanos referred to psychological services. *Journal of Abnormal Child Psychology, 8,* 237–243.

Reynolds, M. C. (1980, May). Education of handicapped students: Some areas of confusion. *Phi Delta Kappan,* 603, 604.

Rice, M. (1980). *Cognition and language: Categories, word meanings, and training.* Baltimore, MD: University Park Press.

Riddle, K. D., & Rapaport, J. L. (1976). A 2-year follow-up of 72 hyperactive boys. *Journal of Nervous and Mental Diseases, 162,* 126–134.

Rie, E. D., Rie, H. E., Stewart, S., & Rettemnier, S. C. (1978). An analysis of neurological soft signs in children with learning problems. *Brain and Language, 6,* 32–46.

Rie, H. E., & Rie, E. D. (Eds.). (1980). *Handbook of minimal brain dysfunctions.* New York: John Wiley & Sons.

Ringness, T. (1975). *The affective domain in education.* Boston: Little, Brown and Company.

Rist, R. C., & Herrell, J. E. (1982). Labeling the learning disabled child: The social ecology of educational practice. *American Journal of Orthopsychiatry, 52,* 146–160.

Robbins, C. R., Mercer, J. R., & Meyers, C. E. (1967). The school as a selecting-labeling system. *Journal of School Psychology, 5,* 270–279.

Robbins, M. P., & Glass, G. V. (1968). The Doman-Delacato rationale: A critical analysis. In J. Hellmuth (Ed.), *Educational therapy* (Vol. 2). Seattle: Special Child Publications.

Robinson, H. M. (1946). *Why pupils fail in reading.* Chicago: University of Chicago Press.

Robinson, H. M. (1972). Visual and auditory modalities related to methods for beginning reading. *Reading Research Quarterly, 8,* 7–39.

Rogers, L. L. (1978). *Program standards and eligibility criteria for special education.* Little Rock: Arkansas Department of Education, Division of Instructional Services, Special Education Section.

Rom, A., & Bliss, L. (1981). A comparison of verbal communication skills of language impaired and normal speaking children. *Journal of Communication Disorders, 14,* 133–140.

Romberg, T. A. (1980). Salient features of the BTES framework of teacher behaviors. In C. Denham & A. Lieberman (Eds.), *Time to learn.* Washington, DC: National Institute of Education.

Rose, R. J., Miller, J. Z., & Fulker, D. W. (1981). Twin family studies of perceptual speed ability: II. Parameter estimation. *Behavioral Genetics, 6,* 565–575.

Rosenshine, B. (1971). *Teaching behaviors and student achievement.* London: National Foundation for Educational Research.

Rosenshine, B. V. (1976). Classroom instruction. In N. Gage (Ed.), *The psychology of teaching methods: The 75th yearbook of the National Society for the Study of Education, Part I.* Chicago: University of Chicago Press.

Rosenshine, B. W. (1979). The third cycle of research on teacher effects: Content covered, academic engaged time, and direct instruction. In P. Peterson & H. Walberg (Eds.), *Research on teaching: Concepts, findings, and implications.* Berkeley, CA: McCuthan.

Rosenshine, B. V. (1980). How time is spent in elementary classrooms. In C. Denham & A. Lieberman (Eds.), *Time to learn.* Washington, DC: National Institute of Education.

Rosenshine, B., & Furst, N. (1973). The use of direct observation to study teaching. In R. Travers (Ed.), *Second handbook on research on teaching.* Chicago: Rand McNally.

Rosenthal, R., & Jacobson, L. (1968). *Pygmalion in the classroom.* New York: Holt, Rinehart and Winston.

Rosner, S. L., Abrams, J. C., Daniels, P. R., & Schiffman, G. B. (1981a). Dealing with the reading needs of the learning disabled child. *Journal of Learning Disabilities, 8,* 436–448.

Rosner, S., Abrams, J., Daniels, P., & Schiffman, G. (1981b). Focus on reading. *Journal of Learning Disabilities, 14*(8), 436–448.

Rosner, S. L., & Cooper, F. H. (1982). The Temple University Reading Clinic. *Journal of Learning Disabilities, 15,* 294–298.

Rosner, S. L., & Seymour, J. (1983). The gifted child with a learning disability: Clinical evidence. In L. H. Fox, L. Brody, & D. Tobin (Eds.), *Learning-disabled/gifted children: Identification and programming* (pp. 77–97). Baltimore, MD: University Park Press.

Ross, A. O. (1968). Conceptual issues in the evaluation of brain damage. In H. Khanna (Ed.), *Brain damage and mental retardation* (pp. 20–43). Springfield, IL: Charles C Thomas.

Ross, A. O. (1976). *Psychological aspects of learning disabilities and reading disorders.* New York: McGraw-Hill.

Roth, F. P., & Spekman, N. J. (1984a). Assessing the pragmatic abilities of children: Part 1. Organizational framework and assessment parameters. *Journal of Speech and Hearing Disorders, 49,* 2–11.

Roth, F. P., & Spekman, N. J. (1984b). Assessing the pragmatic abilities of children: Part 2. Guidelines, considerations, and specific evaluation procedures. *Journal of Speech and Hearing Disorders, 49,* 12–17.

Rourke, B. (1975). Brain behavior relationships in children with learning disabilities: A research program. *American Psychologist, 30,* 911–920.

Rourke, B. P. (Ed.). (1985). *Neuropsychology of learning disabilities: Essentials of subtype analysis.* New York: Guilford Press.

Rourke, B., & Finlayson, M. (1978). Neuropsychological significance of variations in patterns of academic performance: Verbal and visual-spatial abilities. *Journal of Abnormal Child Psychology, 6,* 121-133.

Rourke, B., & Strang, J. (1978). Neuropsychological significance of variations in patterns of academic performance: Motor, psychomotor, and tactile-perceptual abilities. *Journal of Pediatric Psychology, 3,* 62-66.

Routh, D. K., & Roberts, R. D. (1972). Minimal brain dysfunction in children: Failure to find evidence for a behavioral syndrome. *Psychological Reports, 31,* 307-314.

Rowan, L., & Leonard, L. (1981, November). *Performative and presuppositional skills in language disorders and normal children.* Paper presented at the annual meeting of the American Speech-Language-Hearing Association, Los Angeles.

Rudel, R., Denckla, M., & Broman, H. (1981). The effect of varying stimulus contact or word finding ability: Dyslexia further differentiated from other learning disabilities. *Brain and Language, 13,* 130-144.

Rubin, K. H., & Schneider, F. W. (1973). The relationship between moral judgment, egocentrism, and altruistic behavior. *Child Development, 44,* 661-665.

Rubin, L. (Ed.). (1977). *Curriculum handbook: The disciplines, current movements, and instructional methodology.* Boston: Allyn & Bacon.

Rugel, R. (1974). WISC subtest scores of disabled readers: A review with respect to Bannatyne recategorization. *Journal of Learning Disabilities, 7,* 48-55.

Ruit, M. L., & McKenzie, R. G. (1985). Disorders of written communication: An instructional priority for LD students. *Journal of Learning Disabilities, 18*(5), 258-260.

Russell, R. L., & Ginsburg, H. P. (1982). *Cognitive analysis of children's mathematical difficulties.* Rochester, NY: University of Rochester.

Rutter, M., Graham, P., & Birch, H. G. (1966). Interrelations between choreiform syndrome, reading disability and psychiatric disorders in children 8-11 years old. *Developmental Medicine and Child Neurology, 8,* 149-159.

Ryan, D. G. (1960). *Characteristics of teachers.* Washington, DC: American Council on Education.

Sadler, R. 91982). *Variations in language impaired preschool children's participation in the maintenance of conversations with language impaired and language normal children.* Unpublished master's thesis, University of Maryland.

Saffran, E. M. (1980). Reading in deep dyslexia is not ideographic. *Neuropsychologia, 18,* 219-223.

Salvia, J., & Ysseldyke, J. E. (1978). *Assessment in special and remedial education.* Boston: Houghton Mifflin.

Salvia, J., & Ysseldyke, J. E. (1981). *Assessment of special and remedial education* (2nd ed.). Boston: Houghton Mifflin.

Salvia, J., & Ysseldyke, J. (1985). *Assessment in special and remedial education* (3rd ed.). Boston: Houghton Mifflin.

Salzano, F. M., & Rao, D. C. (1976). Path analysis of aptitude, personality and achievement scores in Brazilian twins. *Behavioral Genetics, 6,* 461-466.

Samuels, S. C. (1981). *Disturbed exceptional children.* New York: Human Sciences Press.

Samuels, S. J. (1979). The method of repeated readings. *The Reading Teacher, 32,* 403-408.

Samuels, S., & Edwall, G. (1981). The role of attention in reading with implications for the learning disabled student. *Journal of Learning Disabilities, 14,* 353-361.

Sanders, D. (1965). Noise conditions in normal classrooms. *Exceptional Children, 31,* 344-353.

Sarason, S. B. (1949). *Psychological problems in mental deficiency.* New York: Harper & Row.

Sarason, S. B., Lighthall, F. F., Davidson, K. S., Waite, R. R., & Ruebush, B. K. (1960). *Anxiety in elementary school children*. New York: John Wiley & Sons.

Satterfield, J. H. (1973). EEG issues in children wi th minimal brain dysfunction. In S. Walzer & P. Wolff (Eds.), *Minimal cerebral dysfunction in children* (pp. 35–46). New York: Grune & Stratton.

Sattler, J. S. (1974). *Assessment of children's intelligence*. Philadelphia: W. B. Saunders.

Satz, P., & Fletcher, J. (1980). Minimal brain dysfunction: An appraisal of research concepts and methods. In H. Rie & E. Rie (Eds.), *Handbook of minimal brain dysfunctions: A critical view* (pp. 667–714). New York: Wiley Intersciences Press.

Satz, P., & Friel, J. (1972). Some predictive antecedents of specific learning disability. In P. Satz & J. Ross (Eds.), *The disabled reader*. Rotterdam: Rotterdam University Press.

Satz, P., & Friel, J. (1978). The predictive validity of an abbreviated screening battery: A three-year cross validation follow-up. *Journal of Learning Disabilities, 11*, 347–351.

Satz, P., & Morris, R. (1980). The search for subtype classification in learning disabled children. In R. E. Tarter (Ed.), *The child at risk*. New York: Oxford University Press.

Satz, P., & Morris, R. (1981). Learning disability subtypes: A review. In M. Pirozzolo & M. Wittrock (Eds.), *Neuropsychological and cognitive processes in reading* (pp. 109–141). New York: Academic Press.

Satz, P., & Sparrow, S. S. (1970). Specific developmental dyslexia. In D. Bakker & P. Satz (Eds.), *Specific reading disability*. Rotterdam: Rotterdam University Press.

Satz, P., Taylor, H. G., Friel, J., & Fletcher, J. (1978). Some developmental and predictive precursors of reading disabilities: A six-year follow-up. In A. L. Benton & D. Pearl (Eds.), *Dyslexia: An appraisal of current knowledge*. New York: Oxford University Press.

Satz, P., & Van Nostrand, G. K. (1973). Developmental dyslexia: An evaluation of a theory. In P. Satz & J. Ross (Eds.), *The disabled learner: Early detection and intervention* (pp. 121–148). Rotterdam: The Rotterdam University Press.

Schain, R. (1970). Neurological examination of 40 children with learning disorders. *Neuropaediatric, 3*, 307–317.

Schain, R. J. (1977). *Neurology of childhood learning disorders* (2nd ed.). Baltimore, MD: Williams & Wilkins.

Schank, R., & Abelson, R. (1977). *Scripts, plans, goals, and understanding: An inquiry into human knowledge structures*. Hillsdale, NJ: Lawrence Erlbaum.

Schantz, C. W. (1975). The development of social cognition. In E. M. Hetherington (Ed.), *Review of child development research* (Vol. 5). Chicago: University of Chicago Press.

Schegloff, E. (1972). Sequencing in conversational openings. In J. Gumperz & D. Hymes (Eds.), *Directions in sociolinguistics: The ethnography of communication*. New York: Holt, Rinehart & Winston.

Schenck, S. J. (1980). The diagnostic/instructional link in individualized education programs. *Journal of Special Education, 14*, 337–345.

Schenck, S. J. (1981). An analysis of individualized educational programs for learning disabled youngsters. *Journal of Learning Disabilities, 14*, 221–223.

Schiffman, G., Tobin, D., & Buchanan, B. (1982). Microcomputer instruction for the learning disabled. *Journal of Learning Disabilities, 15*, 557–559.

Schmuck, R. A., & Schmuck, P. A. (1971). *Group processes in the classroom*. Dubuque, IA: William C. Brown.

Schulman, J. L., Kaspar, J. C., & Throne, F. M. (1965). *Brain damage and behavior: A clinical-experimental study*. Springfield, IL: Charles C Thomas.

Schulte, A., & Borich, G. D. (1984). Considerations in the use of difference scores to identify learning-disabled children. *Journal of School Psychology, 22*, 381–390.

Schumaker, J. B., Deshler, D. D., Alley, G. R., & Warner, M. M. (1980). *An epidemiological study of learning disabled adolescents in secondary schools: Details of the methodology* (Research Report No. 12). Lawrence: The University of Kansas Institute for Research in Learning Disabilities.

Schumaker, J. B., & Hazel, J. S. (1984a). Social skills assessment and training for the learning disabled: Who's on first and what's on second? Part I. *Journal of Learning Disabilities, 17,* 422–430.

Schumaker, J. B., & Hazel, J. S. (1984b). Social skills assessment and training for the learning disabled: Who's on first and what's on second. Part II. *Journal of Learning Disabilities, 17,* 492–499.

Schumaker, J. B., Hazel, J. S., Sherman, J. A., Sheldon, A. (1982). Social skill performances of learning disabled, non-learning disabled, and delinquent adolescents. *Learning Disability Quarterly, 5,* 388–397.

Schumaker, J. B., Wildgen, J. S., & Sherman, J. A. (1982). Social interaction of LD junior high students in the regular classrooms: An observational analysis. *Journal of Learning Disabilities, 15,* 355–358.

Schwartz, R. H. (1969). Mental age as it relates to school achievement among educable mentally retarded adolescents. *Education and Training of the Mentally Retarded, 4,* 53–56.

Schwartz, R. H., & Cook, J. J. (1971). Mental age as a predictor of academic achievement. *Education and Training of the Mentally Retarded, 6,* 12–15.

Schweibel, A., & Cherlin, D. (1972). Physical and social distancing in teacher–pupil relationships. *Journal of Educational Psychology, 63,* 543–550.

Scott, W. O., & Edelstein, B. A. (1981). The social competence of two interaction strategies: An analog evaluation. *Behavior Therapy, 12,* 482–492.

Scranton, T. R., & Ryckman, D. B. (1979). Sociometric status of learning disabled children in an integrative program. *Journal of Learning Disabilities, 12,* 402–407.

Searle, J. R. (1969). *Speech acts: An essay on the philosophy of language.* Cambridge: Cambridge University Press.

Selz, M., & Reitan, R. M. (1979). Rules for neuropsychological diagnosis: Classification of brain function in older children. *Journal of Consulting and Clinical Psychology, 47,* 258–264.

Senf, G. M. (1972). An information-integration theory and its application to normal reading acquisition and reading disability. In N. D. Bryant & C. E. Kass (Eds.), *Leadership training institute in learning disabilities: Final report* (Vol. 2, pp. 305–391). Tucson, AZ: University of Arizona.

Senf, G. M. (1976). Future research needs in learning disabilities. In R. P. Anderson & C. G. Halcomb (Eds.), *Learning disabilities/minimal brain dysfunction syndrome: Research perspectives and applications.* Springfield: Charles C. Thomas.

Senf, G. M. (1983). The nature and identification of learning disabilities and their relationship to the gifted child. In L. H. Fox, L. Brody, & D. Tobin (Eds.), *Learning-disabled/gifted children: Identification and programming* (pp. 37–49). Baltimore, MD: University Park Press.

Senf, G. M., & Freundl, P. C. (1971). Memory and attention factors in specific learning disabilities. *Journal of Learning Disabilities, 4,* 94–106.

Shanks, S. J. (Ed.). (1983). *Nursing and the management of pediatric communication disorders.* San Diego: College-Hill Press.

Shankweiler, D., & Liberman, Y. (1972). In J. F. Kavanaugh & I. G. Mattingly (Eds.), *Language by ear and by eye.* Cambridge, MA: MIT Press.

Shankweiler, D., Liberman, I., Mark, L., Fowler, C., & Fisher, W. (1979). The speech code and learning to read. *Journal of Experimental Psychology: Human Learning and Memory, 5,* 531–545.

Shavelson, R. J. (1976). Teachers' decision-making. In N. Gage (Ed.), *The psychology of teaching methods: The 75th yearbook of the National Society for the Study of Education. Part I.* Chicago, University of Chicago Press.

Sheare, J. B. (1978). The impact of resource programs upon the self-concept and peer acceptance of learning disabled children. *Psychology in the School, 15,* 406–412.

Shepard, L. A. (1980). An evaluation of the regression discrepancy method for identifying children with learning disabilities. *Journal of Special Education, 14,* 80–91.

Shepard, L., & Smith, M. L. (1981a). *Evaluation of the identification of perceptual-communicative disorders in Colorado: Final Report.* Boulder: University of Colorado, Laboratory of Educational Research.

Shepard, L. A., & Smith, M. L. (1981b). *The identification, assessment, placement, and remediation of perceptual communication disordered children in Colorado.* Boulder: University of Colorado, Laboratory of Educational Research.

Shepard, L. A., & Smith, M. L. (1983). An evaluation of the identification of learning disabled students in Colorado. *Learning Disability Quarterly, 6,* 115–127.

Siegel, E., & Gold, R. (1982). *Educating the learning disabled.* New York: Macmillan.

Siegel, E., Siegel, R., & Siegel, P. (1978). *Help for the lonely child.* New York: E. P. Dutton.

Siegel, I., & Coop, R. (1974). Cognitive style and classroom practice. In R. Coop & K. White (Eds.), *Psychological concepts in the classroom.* New York: Harper & Row.

Silva, P. A., Chalmers, D., & Stewart, I. (1986). Some audiological, psychological, educational, and behavioral characteristics of children with bilateral otitis media with effusion: A longitudinal study. *Journal of Learning Disabilities, 19,* 165–169.

Silver, A., & Hagin, R. (1960). Specific reading disability: Delineation of the syndrome and relationship to cerebral dominance. *Comparative Psychiatry, 1,* 126–134.

Silver, L. (1971). Familial patterns in children with neurologically-based learning disabilities. *Journal of Learning Disabilities, 4,* 349–358.

Silverman, R., & Zigmond, N. (1983). Self-concept in learning-disabled adolescents. *Journal of Learning Disabilities, 16,* 478–482.

Simmons, G. A., & Shapiro, B. J. (1968). Reading expectancy formulas: A warning note. *Journal of Reading, 2,* 625–629.

Simon, C. (1979). *Communicative competence: A functional pragmatic approach to language therapy.* Tucson, AZ: Communication Skill Builders.

Simon, D. P., & Simon, H. A. (1973). Alternative use of phonemic information in spelling. *Review of Educational Research, 43,* 115–136.

Sinclair, E. (1980). Relationship of psychoeducational diagnosis to educational placement. *Journal of School Psychology, 18,* 349–353.

Sinclair, E., & Alexson, J. (1986). Learning disability discrepancy formulas: Similarities and differences among them. *Learning Disability Research.*

Sinclair, E., Forness, S., & Alexson, J. (1985). Psychiatric diagnosis: A study of its relationship to school needs. *Journal of Special Education, 19,* 333–334.

Sinclair, E., Guthrie, D., & Forness, S. (1985). Establishing a connection between severity of learning disabilities and classroom attention problems. *Journal of Educational Research, 78,* 18–21.

Sindelar, P. T., & Deno, S. L. (1978). The effectiveness of resource programming. *Journal of Special Education, 12*(1), 17–28.

Singer, S. M., Stewart, M. A., & Pulaski, L. (1981). Minimal brain dysfunction: Differences in cognitive organization in two groups of index cases and their relatives. *Journal of Learning Disabilities, 14,* 170–173.

Siperstein, G. N., Bopp, M. J., & Bak, J. J. (1978). Social status of learning disabled children. *Journal of Learning Disabilities, 11,* 98–102.

Eighth Annual Report to Congress on the Implementation of Public Law 94–142; The Education for All Handicapped Children Act. (1986). Office of Special Education, U.S. Department of Education.

Smith, J. (1979). The education of Mexican-Americans: Bilingual, bicognitive, or biased? *Teacher Education and Special Education 2*(2), 37–48.

Smith, M. D. (1978). Stability of WISC-R subtest profiles for learning disabled children. *Psychology in the Schools, 15,* 4–7.

Smith, M. D., Coleman, J. M., Dobecki, P. R., & Davis, E. E. (1977a). Recategorized WISC-R scores of learning disabled children. *Exceptional Children, 43,* 352–357.

Smith, M. D., Coleman, J. M., Dobecki, P. R., & Davis, E. (1977b). Recategorized WISC-R subtest scores of school verified learning disabled children. *Journal of Learning Disabilities, 10,* 437–443, 444–449.

Smith, M. L. (1982). *How educators decide who is learning disabled: Challenge to psychology of public policy in the schools.* Springfield, IL: Charles C. Thomas.

Smith, S. D., Kimberling, W. J., Pennington, B. F., & Lubs, H. A. (1983). Specific reading disability: Identification of an inherited form through linkage analysis. *Science, 221,* 184–187.

Snow, R. E. (1973). Theory construction for research on teaching. In R. Travers (Ed.), *Second handbook of research on teaching.* Chicago: Rand-McNally.

Snyder, L. S. (1978). Communicative and cognitive abilities and disabilities in the sensorimotor period. *Merrill-Palmer Quarterly, 24,* 161–180.

Snyder, L. S., & Downey, D. C. (1983). Pragmatics and information processing. *Topics in Language Disorders, 3,* 75–86.

Spache, G. D. (1969). Review: Myklebust, H. R. (Ed.), *Progress in learning disabilities* (Vol. 1). *Journal of Reading Behavior, 1,* 93–97.

Spache, G. D., McIlroy, K., & Berg, P. (1981). *Case studies in reading disability.* Boston: Allyn & Bacon.

Speer, S. K., & Douglas, D. R. (1981). Helping LD students improve social skills: Ten tips. *Academic Therapy, 17,* 221–224.

Speilberger, C. D. (Ed.). (1966). *Anxiety and behavior.* New York: Academic Press.

Spekman, N. J. (1978). *An investigation of the dyadic, verbal problem-solving communication abilities of learning disabled and normal children.* Unpublished doctoral dissertation, Northwestern University.

Spekman, N. J. (1981). Dyadic verbal communication abilities of learning disabled and normally achieving 4th and 5th grade boys. *Learning Disability Quarterly, 4,* 139–151.

Spekman, N. J. (1983). Discourse and pragmatics. In C. Wren (Ed.), *Language learning disabilities: Diagnosis and remediation.* Rockville, MD: Aspen Systems.

Spekman, N. J., & Roth, F. P. (1982). An intervention framework for learning disabled students with communication disorders. *Learning Disability Quarterly, 5,* 429–437.

Spekman, N. J., & Roth, F. P. (1984). Intervention strategies for learning disabled children with oral communication disorders. *Learning Disability Quarterly, 7,* 7–18.

Spellacy, S., & Peter, B. (1978). Dyscalculia and elements of developmental Gerstmann syndrome in school children. *Cortex, 14,* 197–206.

Spignesi, A., & Shor, R. E. (1981). The judgment of facial expression, contexts, and their combinations. *Journal of General Psychology, 104,* 41–58.

Spivack, G., Platt, J. J., & Shure, M. B. (1976). *The problem-solving approach to adjustment.* San Francisco: Jossey-Bass.

Spring, C. (1976). Encoding speed and memory span in dyslexic children. *Journal of Special Education, 10,* 35–40.

Spring, C., & Capps, C. (1974). Encoding speed, rehearsal, and probed recall of dyslexic boys. *Journal of Educational Psychology, 66,* 780–786.

Stafford, R. E. (1961). Sex differences in spatial visualization as evidence of sex-linked inheritance. *Perceptual Motor Skills, 13,* 428.

Stanley, G., Kaplan, I., & Poole, C. (1975). Cognitive and nonverbal perceptual processing in dyslexia. *Journal of General Psychology, 43,* 67–72.

Stanley, J. C., & Hopkins, K. D. (1981). *Educational and psychological measurement and evaluation* (2nd ed.). Englewood Cliffs, NJ: Prentice-Hall.

Stanovich, K. E. (1982). Individual differences in the cognitive processes of reading: II. Text-level processes. *Journal of Learning Disabilities, 15*(9), 549–554.

Stark, J. H. (1982). Tragic choices in special education: The effects of scarce resources on the implementation of Pub. L. No. 94-142. *Connecticut Law Review, 14*(47), 477–493.

Stauffer, R. G. (1969). *Directing reading maturity as a cognitive process.* New York: Harper & Row.

Stauffer, R. G. (1975). *Directing the reading-thinking process.* New York: Harper & Row.

Stauffer, R. G., Abrams, J. C., & Pikulski, J. J. (1978). *Diagnosis and prevention of reading disabilities.* New York: Harper & Row.

Steeves, K. J. (1982). *Memory as a factor in the computational efficiency of dyslexic children with high abstract reasoning ability.* Unpublished doctoral dissertation, The Johns Hopkins University, Baltimore, MD.

Steg, J. P., & Rapaport, J. L. (1975). Minor physical anomalies in normal, neurotic, learning disabled, and severely disturbed children. *Journal of Autism and Childhood Schizophrenia, 5,* 299–307.

Stein, N., & Glenn, C. (1979). An analysis of story comprehension in elementary school children. In R. O. Freedle (Ed.), *New directions in discourse processing* (Vol. 2). Norwood, NJ: Ablex.

Stephens, J. M. (1967). *The process of schooling: A psychological examination.* New York: Holt, Rinehart & Winston.

Stern, C., & Stern, M. B. (1971). *Children discover arithmetic: An introduction to structural arithmetic.* New York: Harper & Row.

Stevenson, H., Parker, T., Wilkenson, A., Bonneveaux, B., & Gonazalez, M. (1978). Schooling, environment, and cognitive development: A cross-cultural study. *Monographs of the Society for Research in Child Development, 43* (Serial No. 175).

Stevenson, L. P. (1980). WISC-R analysis: Implications for diagnosis and intervention. *Journal of Learning Disabilities, 13,* 346–349.

Stewart, M. A., deBlois, C. S., & Cummings, C. (1980). Psychiatric disorder in the parents of hyperactive boys and those with conduct disorders. *Journal of Child Psychology and Psychiatry, 21,* 283–292.

Stine, O. C., Sarasiotis, J. B., & Mosser, R. S. (1975). Relationships between neurological findings and classroom behavior. *American Journal of Diseases of Children, 129,* 1036–1040.

Stone, F., & Rowley, V. N. (1964). Educational disability in emotionally disturbed children. *Exceptional Children, 30,* 422–426.

Strain, P. S., & Shores, R. E. (1977). Social reciprocity: A review of research and educational implications. *Exceptional Children, 43,* 526–530.

Strauss, A. A., & Kephart, W. C. (1955). *Psychopathology and education of the brain-injured child: Vol. II. Progress in theory and clinic.* New York: Grune & Stratton.

Strauss, A. A., & Lehtinen, L. E. (1947). *Psychopathology and education of the brain-injured child.* New York: Grune & Stratton.

Strauss, A. A., & Werner, H. (1943). Comparative psychopathology of the brain-injured child and the traumatic brain-injured adult. *American Journal of Psychiatry, 19,* 835–838.

Stubblefield, J. H., & Young, C. E. (1975). Central auditory dysfunction in learning disabled children. *Journal of Learning Disabilities, 8,* 89–94.

Suppes, P. (1965). *Sets and numbers.* New York: Random House.

Suydam, M. N., & Weaver, J. F. (1975). Research on mathematics learning. In *Mathematics learning in childhood.* Thirty-seventh yearbook. National Council of Teachers of Mathematics. Reston, VA: NCTM.

Swanson, L. (1982). Verbal short-term memory encoding of learning disabled, deaf, and normal readers. *Learning Disability Quarterly, 5,* 21–28.

Tallal, P. (1976). Auditory perceptual factors in language and learning disabilities. In R. Knights & D. Bakker (Eds.), *The neuropsychology of learning disorders: Theoretical approaches* (pp. 315–323). Baltimore, MD: University Park Press.

Tallal, P. (1980). Auditory temporal perception, phonics, and reading disabilities in children. *Brain and Language, 9,* 182–198.

Tamkin, A. S. (1960). A survey of educational disability in emotionally disturbed children. *Journal of Educational Research, 54,* 67–69.

Tannenbaum, A. J., & Baldwin, L. J. (1983). Giftedness and learning disability: A paradoxical combination. In L. H. Fox, L. Brody, & D. Tobin (Eds.), *Learning-disabled/gifted children: Identification and programming* (pp. 11–36). Baltimore, MD: University Park Press.

Tanner, D., & Tanner, L. N. (1980). *Curriculum development: Theory into practice* (2nd ed.). New York: Macmillan.

Tarver, S. G., & Dawson, M. M. (1978). Modality preference and the teaching of reading: A review. *Journal of Learning Disabilities, 11,* 5–17.

Tarver, S. G., & Hallahan, D. P. (1974). Attention deficits in children with learning disabilities: A review. *Journal of Learning Disabilities, 7,* 560–569.

Terman, L. M., & Merrill, M. A. (1986). *Stanford-Binet intelligence scale — revised. Form LM.* Boston: Houghton Mifflin.

Thiele, C. L. (1938). *The contribution of generalization to the learning of addition facts: Contributions to education.* New York: Teachers College, Columbia University.

Thomas, A. (1979). Learned helplessness and expectancy factors: Implications for research in learning disabilities. *Review of Educational Research, 49,* 208–211.

Thomas, A., & Chess, S. (1977). *Temperament and development.* New York: Brunner/Mazel Publishers.

Thomas, A., Chess, S., & Birch, H. (1968). *Temperament and behavior disorders in children.* New York: New York University Press.

Thompson, L. (1971). Language disabilities in men of eminence. *Journal of Learning Disabilities, 4,* 34–45.

Thorndike, E. L. (1917). Reading as reasoning: A study of mistakes in paragraph reading. *Journal of Educational Psychology, 8,* 323–332.

Thorndike, E. L. (1922). *The psychology of arithmetic.* New York: MacMillan Company.

Thorndike, R. L. (1963). *The concepts of over- and under-achievement.* New York: Teachers College Press, Columbia University.

Thornton, C. A. (1978). Emphasizing thinking strategies in basic fact instruction. *Journal for Research in Mathematics Education, 9,* 214–227.

Thurlow, M., Graden, J., Ysseldyke, J. E., & Algozzine, R. (1984). Student reading during reading class: The lost activity in reading instruction. *Journal of Educational Research, 77,* 267–272.

Thurman, K. (1981–1982). Interdisciplinary IEP training seminar. Temple University.

Tobin, D., & Schiffman, G. B. (1983). Computer technology for learning-disabled/gifted students. In L. H. Fox, L. Brody, & D. Tobin (Eds.), *Learning-disabled/gifted children: Identification and programming* (pp. 195–206). Baltimore, MD: University Park Press.

Torgesen, J. K. (1977). The role of nonspecific factors in the task performance of learning disabled children: A theoretical assessment. *Journal of Learning Disabilities, 10,* 33–40.

Torgeson, J. K. (1978). Performance of reading disabled children on serial memory tasks. *Reading Research Quarterly, 14,* 57-87.

Torgeson, J. K. (1979). Factors related to poor performance on memory tasks in reading disabled children. *Learning Disability Quarterly, 2,* 17-23.

Torgeson, J. K. (1982). The study of short-term memory in learning disabled children: Goals, methods, and conclusions. In K. Gadow & I. Bialer (Eds.), *Advances in learning and behavioral disabilities* (Vol. 1). Greenwich, CT: JAI Press.

Torgeson, J., & Dice, C. (1980). Characteristics of research on learning disabilities. *Journal of Learning Disabilities, 13,* 531-535.

Torgeson, J. K., Murphy, L. A., & Ivey, C. I. (1979). The influence of an orienting task on the memory performance of children with reading problems. *Journal of Learning Disabilities, 12,* 396-401.

Torrance, E. P. (1977). Creatively gifted and disadvantaged gifted students. In J. C. Stanley, W. C. George, & C. H. Solano (Eds.), *The gifted and the creative: A fifty year perspective* (pp. 173-196). Baltimore, MD: The Johns Hopkins University Press.

Touwen, B. C. L. (1979). Examination of the child with minor neurological dysfunction. *Clinics in Developmental Medicine, 71*(2), 1-59.

Touwen, B. C. L., & Sporrel, T. (1979). Soft signs and MBD. *Developmental Medicine and Child Neurology, 21,* 528-538.

Tucker, J., Stevens, L. J., & Ysseldyke, J. E. (1983). Journal of Learning Disabilities, 16(1), 6-13.

Turner, K., & Wade, G. C. (1982). Learning disabled, birth to three: Fact or artifact? *Journal of the Division for Early Childhood, 5,* 79-85.

Udall, A. J., & Maker, C. J. (1983). A pilot program for elementary-age learning-disabled/gifted students. In L. H. Fox, L. Brody, & D. Tobin (Eds.), *Learning-disabled/gifted children: Identification and programming* (pp. 223-242). Baltimore, MD: University Park Press.

Ullman, C. A. (1969). Prevalence of reading disabilities as a function of the measure used. *Journal of Reading Disabilities, 2,* 556-558.

Ullman, L. P., & Krasner, L. (1965). *Case studies in behavior modification.* New York: Holt, Rinehart & Winston.

U.S. Department of Education. (1977). Assistance to states for education for handicapped children: Procedures for evaluating specific learning disabilities. *Federal Register, 42*(250), 62082-62085.

U.S. Department of Education. (1976). Education of handicapped children: Assistance to states. *Federal Register, 41,* 52404-52407.

U.S. Department of Education. (1985). *Seventh annual report to Congress on the implementation of the Education of the Handicapped Act.* Washington, DC: Government Printing Office.

Vandenburg, S. G., & Wilson, K. (1979). Failure of the twin situation to influence twin-differences in cognition. *Behavioral Genetics, 9,* 55-60.

Valletutti, P. J., & Bender, M. (1982). *Teaching interpersonal and community living skills: A curriculum model for handicapped adolescents and adults.* Baltimore, MD: University Park Press.

Vance, B., Singer, M. G., Kitson, D. L., & Brenner, O. C. (1983). WISC-R profile analysis differentiating LD from ED children. *Journal of Clinical Psychology, 39*(1), 125-132.

Vance, H. B. (1977). Informal assessment techniques with learning disabled children. *Academic Therapy, 12,* 291-303.

Vandenberg, S. (1967). Heredity and dyslexia. *Bulletin of the Orton Society, 17,* 54-56.

Vandervoort, L. V., & Senf, G. M. (1973). Audiovisual integration in retarded readers. *Journal of Reading Disabilities, 6,* 170-179.

Vaughn, S. R. (1985). Why teach social skills to learning disabled students? *Journal of Learning Disabilities, 18,* 588–591.

Vellutino, F. R. (1977). Alternative conceptualization of dyslexia: Evidence in support of a verbal deficit hypothesis. *Harvard Educational Review, 47,* 334–354.

Vellutino, F. R. (1978). Toward an understanding of dyslexia: Psychological factors in specific reading disability. In A. L. Benton & D. Pearl (Eds.), *Dyslexia: An appraisal of current knowledge.* New York: Oxford University Press.

Vellutino, F. R. (1979). *Dyslexia: Theory and research.* Cambridge, MA: MIT Press.

Vellutino, F. R., Harding, C. J., Phillips, F., & Steger, J. A. (1975). Differential transfer in poor and normal readers. *Journal of Genetic Psychology, 126,* 3–18.

Vellutino, F. R., Smith, H., Steger, J. A., & Kaman, M. (1975). Reading disability: Age differences and the perceptual deficit hypothesis. *Child Development, 46,* 487–493.

Vellutino, F. R., Smith, H., Steger, J. A., & Kaman, M. (1975). Reading disability: Age differences and the perceptual deficit hypothesis. *Child Development, 46,* 487–493.

Vellutino, R. R., Steger, J. A., Kaman, M., & DeSetto, L. (1975). Visual form perception in deficient and normal readers as a function of age and orthographic linguistic familiarity. *Cortex, 11,* 22–30.

Vellutino, F. R., Steger, B. M., Moyer, S. C., Harding, C. J., & Niles, J. A. (1977). Has the perceptual deficit hypothesis led us astray? *Journal of Learning Disabilities, 10,* 375–385.

Venezky, R. L. (1974). *Testing in reading: Assessment and instructional decision-making.* Urbana, IL: National Council of Teachers of English.

Vernon, M. D. (1960). *Backwardness in reading* (2nd ed.). Cambridge: Cambridge University Press.

Visonhaler, J. S., Weinshank, A. B., Wagner, C. C., & Polin, R. M. (1983). Diagnosing children with educational problems: Characteristics of reading and learning disabilities specialists and classroom teachers. *Reading Research Quarterly, 18,* 134–164.

Vogel, S. A. (1974). Syntactic abilities in normal and dyslexic children. *Journal of Learning Disabilities, 7,* 103–109.

Vogel, S. A. (1975). *Syntactic abilities in normal and dyslexic children.* Baltimore, MD: University Park Press.

Wacker, J. A. (1982, May/June). How long do we wait? Presentation at the ACLD International Conference, Chicago. *ACLD Newsbriefs, 144,* 10.

Wagonseller, B. R. (1973). Learning disability and emotional disturbance: Factors relating to differential diagnosis. *Exceptional Children, 40,* 205–206.

Walberg, H. J. (1969). Predicting class learning: A multivariate approach to the class as a social system. *American Educational Research Journal, 4,* 529–542.

Walberg, H. J. (1971). Models for optimizing and individualizing school learning. *Interchange, 3,* 15–27.

Walberg, H. J., & Anderson, G. J. (1968). Classroom climate and individual learning. *Journal of Educational Psychology, 59,* 414–419.

Walberg, H. J., & Anderson, G. J. (1972). Properties of the achieving urban classes. *Journal of Educational Psychology, 63,* 381–385.

Walberg, J. J. (1976). Psychology of the learning environment: Behavioral, structural, or perceptual? In L. Shulman (Ed.), *Review of research in education* (Vol. 4). Itasca, IL: F. E. Peacock.

Walker, E. L. (1980). *Psychological complexity and preference: A hedge-hog theory of behavior.* Monterey, CA: Brooks/Cole.

Walker, W. N. (1981). Modifying impulsive responding to four WISC-R subtests. *Journal of School Psychology, 19,* 335–339.

Wallace, G., & Larsen, S. C. (1978). *Educational assessment of learning problems: Testing for teaching.* Boston: Allyn & Bacon.

Wallbrown, F. H., Fremont, T. S., & Wilson, J., & Fischer, J. (1979). Emotional disturbance or social misperception? An important classroom management question. *Journal of Learning Disabilities, 12,* 645-648.

Waller, T. G. (1976). Children's recognition memory for written sentences: A comparison of good and poor readers. *Child Development, 47,* 90-95.

Wanant, T. E. (1983). Social skills: An awareness program with learning disabled adolescents. *Journal of Learning Disabilities, 16,* 35-38.

Wang, M. C., & Lindvall, C. M. (1984). Individual differences and school learning environments. In E. Gordon (Ed.), *Review of Research in Education, 11,* 161-225.

Warner, M. M. (1981). *A comparison of five discrepancy criteria for determining learning disabilities in secondary school populations* (Research Report No. 50). Lawrence: University of Kansas Institute for Research in Learning Disabilities.

Warner, M. M., Schumaker, J. B., Alley, G. B., & Deshler, D. D. (1980). Learning disabled adolescents in the public schools: Are they different from other low achievers? *Exceptional Education Quarterly, 1,* 27-36.

Washburne, C. (1930). The graded placement of arithmetic topics. *Report of the Society's Committee on Arithmetic.* Twenty-ninth year of the National Society for the Study of Education. Bloomington, IL: Public School Publishing Company.

Wasson, A. S. (1980).. Stimulus-seeking, perceived school environment and school misbehavior. *Adolescence, 15,* 603-608.

Watson, J. D., & Crick, F. C. (1953). Molecular structure of nucleic acids. A structure for deoxyribose nucleic acids. *Nature, 171,* 737-738.

Watson, L. R. (1977). Conversational participation by language deficient and normal children. In J. Andrews & M. Burns (Eds.), *Selected papers in language and phonology II: Remediation of language disorders* (pp. 104-105). Evanston, IL: Institute for Continuing Professional Education.

Weaver, P. A., & Dickinson, D. K. (1979). Story comprehension and recall in dyslexic students. *Bulletin of the Orton Society, 28,* 157-171.

Webster, R. E., & Schenck, S. J. (1978). Diagnostic test pattern differences among LD, ED, EMH, and multi-handicapped students. *Journal of Educational Research, 72,* 75-80.

Webster, R. E., & Schenck, S. J. (1982). Diagnostic test pattern differences among LD, ED, EMH, and multi-handicapped students. *Journal of Educational Research,* 75-80.

Wechsler, D. (1967). *Wechsler Preschool and Primary Scale of Intelligence.* New York: Psychology Corporation.

Wechsler, D. (1974). *Manual for the Wechsler Intelligence Scale for Children—Revised.* New York: Psychological Corporation.

Weiderholt, J. L. (1974). Historical perspectives on the education of the learning disabled. In L. Mann & D. Sabatino (Eds.), *The second review of special education* (pp. 103-152). Philadelphia: JSE Press.

Weiner, B. (1977). An attributional approach for educational psychology. In L. Shulman (Ed.), *Review of research in education* (Vol. 4). Itasca, IL: Peacock.

Weiner, P., & Hoock, W. (1973). The standardization of tests: Criteria and criticisms. *Journal of Speech and Hearing Research, 16,* 616-626.

Weinstein, M. A. (1980). A neuropsychological approach to math disability. *New York University Education Quarterly, 11,* 22-28.

Weiss, B. (1982). Food additives and environmental chemicals as sources of childhood behavior disorders. *Journal of American Academy of Child Psychiatry, 21,* 144-152.

Weiss, C. E., & Lillywhite, H. S. (1981). *Communicative disorders* (2nd ed.). St. Louis: C. V. Mosby.

Weiss, E. (1984). Learning disabled children understanding social interactions by peers. *Journal of Learning Disabilities, 17,* 612-615.

Wender, P. H. (1971). *Minimal brain dysfunction in children.* New York: John Wiley & Sons.

Wender, P. H. (1976). Hypothesis for possible biochemical basis of minimal brain dysfunction. In R. Knights & D. Bakker (Eds.), *The neuropsychology of learning disorders: Theoretical approaches.* Baltimore, MD: University Park Press.

Wepman, J. M. (1961). The interrelationships of hearing, speech, and reading. *The Reading Teacher, 14,* 245–247.

Wepman, J. M. (1964). The perceptual basis for learning. In H. A. Robinson (Ed.), *Meeting individual differences in reading.* Chicago: University of Chicago Press.

Wepman, J. M. (1975a). Auditory perception and imperception. In W. Cruickshank & D. Hallahan (Eds.), *Perceptual and learning disabilities in children, Vol. 2: Research and Theory.* Syracuse, Syracuse University Press.

Wepman, J. (1975b). New and wider horizons for speech and hearing specialists. *ASHA, 17,* 9–10.

Wepman, J. M., Cruickshank, W. M., Deutsch, C. P., Morency, A., & Strother, C. R. (1975). Learning disabilities. In N. Hobbs (Ed.), *Issues in the classification of children* (Vol. 1, pp. 300–317). San Francisco: Jossey-Bass.

Werner, E. E., & Smith, R. (1977). *Kauai's children come of age.* Honolulu: University of Hawaii Press.

Werner, H. (1948). *Comparative psychology of mental development.* New York: International Universities Press.

Werry, J. S., & Aman, M. G. (1976). The reliability and diagnostic validity of the physical and neurological examination for soft signs (PANESS). *Journal of Autism and Childhood Schizophrenia, 6,* 253–262.

Wheatley, G., Franklin, R., Mitchell, R., & Kraft, R. (1978). Hemispheric specialization and cognitive development: Implications for mathematics education. *Journal for Research in Mathematics Education, 9,* 20–32.

Whitmore, J. (1980). *Giftedness, conflict, and underachievement.* Boston: Allyn & Bacon.

Wiig, E. H., & Harris, S. P. (1974). Perception and interpretation of nonverbally expressed emotions by adolescents with learning disabilities. *Perceptual and Motor Skills, 38,* 239–245.

Wiig, E. H., & Semel, E. M. (1976). *Language disabilities in children and adolescents.* Columbus, OH: Charles E. Merrill.

Wigg, E. H., & Semel, E. M. (1980). *Language assessment and intervention for the learning disabled.* Columbus, OH: Charles E. Merrill.

Wikler, A., Dixon, J. F., & Parker, J. B. (1970). Brain function in problem children and controls. *American Journal of Psychiatry, 127,* 94–105.

Wiley, D. E. (1976). Another hour, another day: Quantity of schooling, a potent path for policy. In W. Sewell, R. Hauser, & D. Featherman (Eds.), *Schooling and achievement in American Society.* New York: Academic Press.

Willeford, J. A. (1976). Central auditory function in children with learning disabilities. *Audiology and Hearing Education, 2,* 12–20.

Willeford, J. A., & Billger, J. M. (1978). Auditory perception in children with learning disabilities. In J. Katz (Ed.), *Handbook of clinical audiology* (2nd ed.). Baltimore, MD: Williams & Wilkins.

Williams, B. W. (Ed.). (1980). *Diagnostic and statistical manual of mental disorders* (3rd ed.). Washington, DC: American Psychiatric Association.

Williams, R. L. (1974). Black pride, academic relevance, and individual achievement. In R. W. Tyler & R. M. Wolf (Eds.), *Crucial issues in testing.* Berkeley, CA: McCutchan.

Willows, D. M. (1974). Reading between the lines: Selective attention in good and poor readers. *Child Development, 45,* 408–415.

Wilson, L. (1985). Large scale learning disability: The reprieve of a concept. *Exceptional Children, 52,* 44–51.

Wilson, L., & Cone, T. (1984). The regression equation method of determining academic discrepancy. *Journal of School Psychology, 22,* 95–110.

Wilson, S. P., Harris, C., & Harris, M. L. (1976). Effects of an auditory perceptual remediation program on reading performance. *Journal of Learning Disabilities, 9,* 670–675.

Wimmer, H. (1979). Processing of script deviations by young children. *Discourse Processes, 2,* 301–310.

Winer, D., Bonner, T. O., Blancy, P. H., & Murray, E J. (1981). Depression and social attraction. *Motivation and Emotion, 5,* 153–166.

Winn, M. (1977). *The plug-in drug.* New York: Viking Press.

Witelson, S. F. (1976). Abnormal right hemisphere specialization in developmental dyslexia. In R. M. Knights & D. J. Bakker (Eds.), *The neuropsychology of learning disorders.* Baltimore, MD: University Park Press.

Witelson, S. F. (1977). Developmental dyslexia: Two right hemispheres and none left. *Science, 195,* 309–311.

Withall, J., & Lewis, W. W. (1963). Social interaction in the classroom. In N. Gage (Ed.), *Handbook of research on teaching.* Chicago: Rand-McNally.

Witkin, H., Moore, C., Goodenough, D., & Cox, P. (1977). Field-dependent and field-independent cognitive styles and their educational implications. *Review of Educational Research, 47,* 1–64.

Wolff, P., & Hurwitz, I. (1966). The choreiform syndrome. *Developmental Medicine and Child Neurology, 8,* 160–165.

Wong, B. (1979a). The role of theory in learning disabilities research: Part I. An analysis of problems. *Journal of Learning Disabilities, 12,* 585–595.

Wong, B. (1979b). The role of theory in learning disabilities research: Part II. A selective review of current theories of learning and reading disabilities, 12, 649–658.

Woodcock, R., & Johnson, B. (1977). *Woodcock-Johnson psychoeducational battery.* Boston: Teaching Resources Corporation.

Worden, P. E., Malmgren, I., & Gaborie, P. (1982). Memory for stories in learning disabled children. *Journal of Learning Disabilities, 15,* 145–152.

Wormack, L. (1980). Sex differences in factorial dimension of verbal, logical, mathematical and visuospatial ability. *Perceptual and Motor Skills, 50,* 445–446.

Wren, C. T. (1983). *Language learning disabilities.* Rockville, MD: Aspen Systems.

Wright, L. S. (1974). Conduct problem or learning disability? *Journal of Special Education, 8,* 331–336.

Wrigley, J. (1958). The factorial nature of ability in elementary mathematics. *British Journal of Educational Psychology, 28,* 61–78.

Yates, A. J. (1954). The validity of some psychological tests of brain damage. *Psychological Bulletin, 51,* 359–379.

Ysseldyke, J. E. (1983). Current practices in making psychoeducational decisions about learning disabled students. *Journal of Learning Disabilities, 16,* 226–233.

Ysseldyke, J. E., & Algozzine, B. (1979). Perspectives on assessment of learning disabled students. *Learning Disability Quarterly, 2,* 3–13.

Ysseldyke, J. E., & Algozzine, B. (1983). LD or not LD: That's not the question! *Journal of Learning Disabilities, 16*(1), 29–32.

Ysseldyke, J., Algozzine, B., & Epps, S. (1983). A logical and empirical analysis of current practice in clarifying students as handicapped. *Exceptional Children, 50*(2), 160–166.

Ysseldyke, J. E., Algozzine, B., Richey, L., & Graden, J. (1982). Declaring students eligible for learning disability services: Why bother with the data? *Learning Disability Quarterly, 5,* 37–43.

Ysseldyke, J., Algozzine, B., Shinn, M. R., & McGue, M. (1982). Similarities and differences between low achievers and students classified as learning disabled. *Journal of Special Education, 16,* 73–85.

Ysseldyke, J., Shinn, M., & Epps, S. (1981). A comparison of WISC-R and the Woodcock-Johnson tests of cognitive ability. *Psychology in the Schools, 18*(1), 15–19.

Yule, W., Rutter, M., Berger, M., & Thompson, J. (1974). Over- and under-achievement in reading: Distribution in the general population. *British Journal of Educational Psychology, 44*, 1–12.

Zach, L., & Kaufman, J. (1972). How adequate is the concept of perceptual deficit for education? *Journal of Learning Disabilities, 5*, 351–356.

Zahalkova, M., Vrzal, V., & Kloboukova, E. (1972). Genetical investigation in dyslexia. *Journal of Medical Genetics, 9*, 48–52.

Zemlin, W. R. (1968). *Speech and hearing science: Anatomy and physiology.* Englewood Cliffs, NJ: Prentice-Hall.

Zigler, E., & Seitz, V. (1975). An evaluation of sensorimotor patterning: A critique. *American Journal of Mental Deficiency, 79*, 483–492.

Zigmond, N. (1983). *Toward a new definition of learning disabilities.* Paper presented at the annual meeting of the American Educational Research Association, Montreal, Canada.

Zigmond, N., & Brownlee, J. (1980). Social skills training for adolescents with learning disabilities. *Exceptional Education Quarterly, 1*, 77–83.

Zurif, E. B., & Carson, G. (1970). Dyslexia in re ation to cerebral dominance and temporal analysis. *Neuropsychologia, 8*, 351–361.

Index

A

Academic deficiency
  association between emotional/
    behavioral problems and, 243
  extent of in ED/behaviorally
    disordered students, 243–244
Academic deficits of ED students, 238–239
  assumptions regarding, 238
Academic failure and definitions of LD
  actual achievement, 10
  expected achievement, 10
  procedures for determining
    discrepancy, 10–11
  underachievement, 10
Academic Learning Time (ALT), 287,
  291–292, 293, 294, 296–297
Acalculia
  in adults, 193–194
  developmental, 195–198
  Gerstmann syndrome, 194–195
  right and left hemispheres, 194
Accelerative options for LD
  academically gifted, 260–262
Achievement dimensions of LD, 279–280
Achievement, low, and prevalence of
  LD children, 15–17
Achievement methods or formulas in
  defining LD child, 350–351

grade equivalent methods, 351–352
regression formulas, 353–354
weighted formulas, 353
Achievement testing of LD
  concerns for, 340
  tests used in, 340–341
  validity of, 355–357
ACID profile (Arithmetic, Coding,
  Information, Digit-Span), 335
ACLD. *See* Association of Children
  with Learning Disabilities
Adaptive physical education specialist,
  as part of multidisciplinary team,
  366, 371–372
Adoption studies and genetic
  influences, 59–61, 62, 67
Adult rejection of LD children, 217–
  218
Aggression, unsocialized, as ED
  behavior dimension, 240
Alleles, as codes for genetic traits
  autosomal dominant genes, 52
  autosomal recessive genes, 52
  chromosomal disorders, 55–56
  dominant, 51
  multifactoral, 54
  recessive, 51
  sex-linked, 53
ALT. *See* Academic Learning Time

Key: (*t*) indicates *table*, (*f*) indicates *figure*, and (*App*) indicates *Appendix*.

XYZ